As You Like It

Texts and Contexts

——————————————————— ❈ ———————————————————

OTHER BEDFORD/ST. MARTIN'S TITLES OF INTEREST

The First Part of King Henry the Fourth: Texts and Contexts
EDITED BY BARBARA HODGDON, UNIVERSITY OF MICHIGAN, ANN ARBOR

Hamlet
(Case Studies in Contemporary Criticism)
EDITED BY SUSANNE L. WOFFORD, NEW YORK UNIVERSITY

Macbeth: Texts and Contexts
EDITED BY WILLIAM C. CARROLL, BOSTON UNIVERSITY

Measure for Measure: Texts and Contexts
EDITED BY IVO KAMPS AND KAREN RABER, UNIVERSITY OF MISSISSIPPI

The Merchant of Venice: Texts and Contexts
EDITED BY M. LINDSAY KAPLAN, GEORGETOWN UNIVERSITY

A Midsummer Night's Dream: Texts and Contexts
EDITED BY GAIL KERN PASTER, THE FOLGER SHAKESPEARE LIBRARY
AND SKILES HOWARD, RUTGERS UNIVERSITY AT NEW BRUNSWICK

Othello: Texts and Contexts
EDITED BY KIM F. HALL, BARNARD COLLEGE

Romeo and Juliet: Texts and Contexts
EDITED BY DYMPNA CALLAGHAN, SYRACUSE UNIVERSITY

The Taming of the Shrew: Texts and Contexts
EDITED BY FRANCES E. DOLAN, UNIVERSITY OF CALIFORNIA, DAVIS

The Tempest
(Case Studies in Critical Controversy)
EDITED BY GERALD GRAFF, UNIVERSITY OF ILLINOIS AT CHICAGO
AND JAMES PHELAN, OHIO STATE UNIVERSITY

Twelfth Night, or What You Will: Texts and Contexts
EDITED BY BRUCE R. SMITH, UNIVERSITY OF SOUTHERN CALIFORNIA

The Winter's Tale: Texts and Contexts
EDITED BY MARIO DIGANGI, CITY UNIVERSITY OF NEW YORK

———

The Bedford Shakespeare
A COLLECTED WORKS EDITED BY RUSS MCDONALD,
GOLDSMITHS COLLEGE, UNIVERSITY OF LONDON
AND LENA COWEN ORLIN, GEORGETOWN UNIVERSITY

The Bedford Companion to Shakespeare:
An Introduction with Documents, Second Edition
BY RUSS MCDONALD, GOLDSMITHS COLLEGE, UNIVERSITY OF LONDON

WILLIAM SHAKESPEARE

As You Like It

Texts and Contexts

>‹

Edited by

PAMELA ALLEN BROWN

University of Connecticut

and

JEAN E. HOWARD

Columbia University

Bedford/St. Martin's   BOSTON ◆ NEW YORK

For Bedford/St. Martin's

Developmental Editor: Sherry Mooney
Publishing Services Manager: Andrea Cava
Production Supervisor: Victoria Anzalone
Marketing Manager: Stacey Propps
Project Management: DeMasi Design and Publishing Services
Senior Art Director: Anna Palchik
Text Design: Claire Seng-Niemoeller
Cover Design: Donna Lee Dennison
Cover Art: (top) *Portrait of a Young Man* (oil on panel), Parmigianino (Francesco Mazzola)
(1503/40) / Louvre, Paris, France / Peter Willi / The Bridgeman Art Library; (bottom)
[Poly-Olbion. Part 1] *Poly-Olbion* by Michaell Drayton Esqr: between pp. 226 and 227,
Morris dancers in map of Gloucestershire. By permission of the Folger Shakespeare
Library.
Composition: Jeff Miller Book Design
Printing and Binding: RR Donnelley and Sons

President, Bedford/St. Martin's: Denise B. Wydra
Editorial Director, English and Music: Karen S. Henry
Director of Marketing: Karen R. Soeltz
Production Director: Susan W. Brown
Director of Rights and Permissions: Hilary Newman

Manufactured in the United States of America.

8   7   6   5   4   3
f   e   d   c   b   a

For information, write: Bedford/St. Martin's, 75 Arlington Street, Boston, MA 02116
(617-399-4000)

ISBN 978-0-312-39932-0

Acknowledgments

*Acknowledgments and copyrights are continued at the back of the book on pages 429–30, which
constitute an extension of the copyright page. It is a violation of the law to reproduce these selections
by any means whatsoever without the written permission of the copyright holder.*

Distributed outside North America by
PALGRAVE MACMILLAN
Houndmills, Basingstoke, Hampshire RG21 6XS
Companies and representatives throughout the world.

ISBN 978-1-4039-4634-8

A catalogue record for this book is available from the British Library.

About the Series

———————————————— >< ————————————————

Shakespeare wrote his plays in a culture unlike, though related to, the culture of the emerging twenty-first century. The Bedford Shakespeare Series resituates Shakespeare within the sometimes alien context of the sixteenth and seventeenth centuries while inviting students to explore ways in which Shakespeare, as text and as cultural icon, continues to be part of contemporary life. Each volume frames a Shakespearean play with a wide range of written and visual material from the early modern period, such as homilies, polemical literature, emblem books, facsimiles of early modern documents, maps, woodcut prints, court records, other plays, medical tracts, ballads, chronicle histories, and travel narratives. Selected to reveal the many ways in which Shakespeare's plays were connected to the events, discourses, and social structures of his time, these documents and illustrations also show the contradictions and the social divisions in Shakespeare's culture and in the plays he wrote. Engaging critical introductions and headnotes to the primary materials help students identify some of the issues they can explore by reading these texts with and against one another, setting up a two-way traffic between the Shakespearean text and the social world these documents help to construct.

Jean E. Howard
Columbia University
Series Editor

About This Volume

⋙⋘

As *You Like It* is a high-spirited play, and this edition aims to enhance students' pleasure when reading or watching it. This, of course, in part means unfolding some of the complex traditions of jesting and fooling that the comedy offers up in such profusion. But pleasure doesn't just come from hearing jokes whiz by or watching foolish lovers display their folly in extravagant ways. It also comes from understanding some of the larger cultural conversations that shape *As You Like It*, including the pastoral debates (which still go on today) about whether it is better to live in the country or the city and how one acts when faced with unrequited love or the prompting of unfamiliar desires for someone new. *As You Like It* shows that wittiness is not the enemy of serious thought, but its vehicle, and it shows that the dialogic form of drama lets debates unfold in many keys. If Corin the shepherd has his views on what makes for a good life, so too does Jaques the disaffected courtier. In Arden voices and ideas proliferate, as does make-believe, and the play enables us to take part in a polyphonic exploration of important questions about love, gentility, civil behavior, good government, gender, and power. It unfolds these questions in a way that is accessible to students today, but that also bears traces of the particular historical moment in which the play was produced. This edition situates *As You Like It* in historical context, including in the context of the history of literary forms such as pastoral and comedy, the jest book and the conduct manual; but its aim is not to fetishize historical knowledge. Such knowledge is a gateway to the pleasure of understanding a complex play better, rather than an end in itself. The Introduction to this volume explains our rationale for the book's four-part structure. As co-editors, we have found it pleasurable, and very much in the spirit of *As You Like It*, to work on this book in dialogue with one another. We see different potentials within the play text and different cultural conversations in which it plays a part, and we hope that something intriguing, fresh, and distinctively feminist has emerged from our collaboration.

The text of *As You Like It* used for this volume was edited by David Bevington for *The Complete Works of Shakespeare*, Sixth Edition (Upper Saddle River: Pearson, 2009). We are extremely grateful to Professor Bevington for allowing us to use this edition, including his notes and glosses, as the basis for our text. Nearly all of the contextual material that follows the play has been newly edited by Pamela Brown and Jean Howard from early modern editions of the works in question. We have lightly modernized punctuation and spelling and have provided a level of glossing that we hope will let students read these texts easily without being swamped by the apparatus. We have collected images from many sources, and we are grateful to the numerous libraries and collections that have granted us permission to use them, a full list of which is provided at the end of this book.

We have worked on this edition for rather a long time, and have been helped by many people along the way. Collectively, we wish to express our gratitude to a series of Columbia graduate students who have gathered materials, modernized texts, and double-checked our facts with good cheer and amazing professionalism. These include Musa Gurnis, John Kuhn, Bryan Lowrance, Fred Bengtsson, and especially Emily Shortslef. Karen Henry, Martha Friedman, and Sherry Mooney of Bedford/St. Martins along with Linda DeMasi of DeMasi Design and Publishing Service have been valiant allies in the complicated process of bringing the book into being.

Jean wishes, as well, to express her gratitude to her reading group (you know who you are!) and to the Huntington Library, which offered her a short-term fellowship crucial in the finalizing of the manuscript. As ever, she is indebted to the rich network of friends that make life, including intellectual life, such fun, and to her all-important and sustaining family, which has now expanded its capacious embrace to include Karel, Darius, Morgan, Rosie, Josie, and Noah.

Pam wants to express her loving thanks to friends who encouraged, criticized, and inspired her, including Jean (of course!), Richard Andrews, Bianca Calabresi, Julie Crawford, Mario DiGangi, Lisa Freedman, Natasha Korda, Ian Moulton, Bella Mirabella, Peter Parolin, Tanya Pollard, Susan

O'Malley, and the late Sasha Roberts. She gives special thanks to Nancy Selleck, whose insights on the play as a director-scholar were enormously helpful. Her labors were enlivened and assisted by her Shakespeare students, especially those who performed in the spoof *As We Like It*; by her colleagues in Theater Without Borders; and by Jonathan Soffer, who urged her to take on the project. She is grateful to the University of Connecticut for support in the form of grants and reduced course loads, and to the staff of the Huntington and Folger libraries and Sally-Beth MacLean of the Records of Early English Drama for their kindness and help with documents. Sherry Mooney, Martha Friedman, and Karen Sikola each deserve a medal for helping her survive months of toil obtaining images and permissions from archives. Pam and Jean dedicate their work on the volume to the memory of their mothers, Carmele Spadafora Brown (1928–2013) and Eleanor Ross Howard (1917–2012).

Pamela Allen Brown
University of Connecticut

Jean E. Howard
Columbia University

Contents

><+

Illustrations

><‹

Introduction

→‹←

As You Like It is Shakespeare's most inviting comedy. Its stated goal, from the title to the epilogue, is to please us. Yet the title is more a provocation than a promise since no two people desire the same thing, or just one thing. The play entices us to explore the possibilities of pleasure without limiting us to any one object. As Rosalind says, teasing Orlando, "Can one desire too much of a good thing?" (4.1.92).

Probably written sometime between 1598 and 1600, *As You Like It* rounded out a decade in which Shakespeare experimented over and over with the possibilities of the comic form. In each of his comedies, young lovers overcome obstacles to achieve the social norm of marriage, but that bland generalization hides a world of difference. *The Taming of the Shrew* draws heavily on the knockabout energies of farce; *A Midsummer Night's Dream*, richly lyrical, uses a contrast between court and forest to structure the lovers' confusing journey into adulthood; *The Merchant of Venice* verges on tragicomedy as the lovers' plot threatens to be dwarfed by a life-threatening confrontation between Christian merchant and Jewish money-lender; and *Twelfth Night*, the play most often paired with *As You Like It*, uses the comic device of long-separated twins to explore the malleability of erotic desire in a seaside town where disguises and mistaken identities abound.

As You Like It and Renaissance Pastoral

As You Like It represents another kind of experiment: the refashioning of sophisticated pastoral conventions into a play of witty and socially inclusive conversation and debate. Typically pastoral works place shepherds, or courtly figures posing as shepherds, in rural settings where they reflect on elemental experiences such as love, the pain of rejection, or the evils of the town or the court from which they have fled. In classical pastoral the poet-lovers are men, and the nymphs stay offstage or speak standard speeches of disdain, existing mainly as objects of male poetic address. Under the influence of contemporary Italian pastorals, *As You Like It* gives extraordinary prominence to women and their desires. Not only does the witty Rosalind direct the central love plot, but she also has more lines than any other female role in Shakespeare. Celia, Phoebe, and Audrey are also outspoken about what they want and do not want, which creates an unusually *female* pastoral comedy: in fact, the number of lines spoken by women in this play surpasses that spoken by female characters in any other play in the adult repertory from 1500–1614.[1]

Partly because of its pastoral heritage, critics often say that not much happens in *As You Like It*. That is not strictly true. In act 1, an evil Duke, Frederick, who has stolen his brother's kingdom and driven him into exile in the Forest of Arden likewise drives out the good Duke's daughter, Rosalind, who also takes flight to the same forest, accompanied by Celia, the daughter of the bad Duke, and the court clown, Touchstone. Simultaneously, Orlando, a young gentleman deprived of a good education by his older brother, beats Duke Frederick's wrestler in a fair fight but also draws down the wrath of this tyrannical sovereign and flees the court after his brother plans to burn his house and kill him. There is plenty of action in these scenes, and it motivates a general escape plot: everyone into the forest! Once all the exiles arrive in Arden, however, the audience witnesses another kind of action: the witty back and forth banter of its diverse inhabitants — real shepherds, court exiles, melancholy travelers, cross-dressed women, unlettered priests. The forest becomes a space of liberty and play in which the characters argue about everything from how a lover should behave to the ethics of killing deer for food. As a result of this time in the forest, things change for some characters. Some marry and others decide they will not; some return to the court and some don't. The beating heart of the play lies

---

[1] David Mann, "Female characters in the adult repertory, 1500–1614," appendix, *Shakespeare's Women: Performance and Conception* (Cambridge: Cambridge UP, 2008), 241–45.

not in these outcomes, however, but in the debates and conversations that unfold within the forest walls.

Formally, the play's last four acts depend on a dense structure of juxtapositions between court clown and rural shepherd, between urbane and rustic lovers, between the well-educated and the unschooled. These juxtapositions keep the audience busy sorting out the divergent perspectives held by various actors in these woodland encounters. There are, for example, at least four potential pairs of lovers in the forest: Rosalind and Orlando; Celia and Oliver, Orlando's older brother who eventually repents his former evil; Touchstone and Audrey, an uneducated country lass; and Silvius and Phoebe, a stereotypical lovelorn shepherd and his hard-hearted shepherdess mistress. But these lovers are not always "properly" paired up. Rosalind is disguised in the forest as the boy, Ganymede, and does not reveal herself to Orlando but instead promises to teach him how to fall *out* of love with Rosalind. Phoebe scorns Silvius and pines after Ganymede. Celia, for a long time, seems more attached to her cousin Rosalind than to any man, and Touchstone and Audrey are separated by education and background. He is a clever man from the court; she has basic vocabulary trouble.

In setting these characters talking and interacting, the play also sets the audience thinking. Certainly, love is a confusing business that makes people mad and melancholy and euphoric by turns. That we quickly discern. But, more profoundly, what really makes for a "good" pairing? Must there be anything more than physical attraction? As Touchstone says: "man hath his desires" (3.3.60). But is a meeting of minds also important? Equality of education, of rank? And are the truest unions or deepest affections shared between men and women? What makes Celia's love for Rosalind different from her love for Oliver? Could Phoebe really love the Rosalind lurking beneath the disguise of Ganymede and not the "boy" she pursues? Why does Orlando spend so much time playing games with Ganymede when he is pining for Rosalind? Do people always know what their true desires are? *As You Like It* is both the play's title and its guiding principle. In the space of the forest, characters can experiment with what they "like" (and who is "like" them) without sharp penalty or bars to their desires, and the action invites the audience to the same liberty of thought.

Though the play is full of lively conversations that enlarge thought, everything in the Forest of Arden unfolds at a leisurely pace. As Orlando famously says: "There's no clock in the forest" (3.2.253–54). This sense of pastoral *otium*, or leisure, forms a necessary part of the recreative process. Before they return to the flawed worlds they have left, characters have the luxury of living in "slow time." They fill their hours with debate, conversation, song, lament, game, and jest—activities that invite mental gymnastics, upend convention, suspend the law, and allow for fresh perspectives on love, desire, and justice.

But though *As You Like It* slows time down within its fiction, it nonetheless is surprisingly timely in the sense of participating in contemporary fashions and social debates. For example, its embrace of popular culture puts the play delicately but firmly against those forces, loosely labeled "Puritan," that were attempting to reform or suppress popular festivity, including Maygames and popular theater.[2] While *As You Like It* draws on pastoral conventions that in some cases go back to the Greeks, it also refers to the popular outlaw-hero Robin Hood to whom the banished Duke is explicitly compared. The play also highlights popular clowning and cross-dressing, longtime staples of English plays, festive rites, and theatrical entertainments, and delights in jokes and japes, many of them about cuckolds and men who "wear the horns," drawn from popular jest books and village shaming rituals. Some of Shakespeare's contemporaries, such as Philip Stubbes or Stephen Gosson, viewed theater (with its cross-dressed actors) and other popular pastimes as satanic inventions that disrupted pious thoughts, Sabbath solemnity, and virtuous marriage and encouraged disorder, sexual experimentation, and a concern with newfangled fashions. Self-consciously celebrating role-playing, disguise, horn jokes, transvestism, and many varieties of love play, *As You Like It* thus embraces what more straitlaced Elizabethans would suppress.

Setting the play in the Forest of Arden summoned other associations for Shakespeare's audience. The English forest of that name was located in Warwickshire, near where Shakespeare was born. The reputed home of "outlaws" and vagrants who poached deer and cut down the ancient trees, the forest is a special place where the truly gentle and noble find refuge, even if they have been banished as "traitors" by an unjust Duke. In stressing the wind and rough weather that trouble the exiled Duke and the hunger that overtakes Orlando and Adam as they enter the forest, the play throws a sympathetic light on the suffering of those who might otherwise be regarded as vagrants or villains. Furthermore, in embracing the famished travelers, Duke Senior both embodies Christian charity and evokes the popular hero Robin Hood, who traditionally protected the poor against tyrants. When Orlando enters, sword in hand, crying out: "I almost die for food, and let me have it!" (2.7.103), he is met with the unfeigned hospitality of the Duke and invited to his communal feast.

---

[2] See Christopher Fitter, "Betrayed to Every Modern Censure": *As You Like It* and Vestry Values," *Radical Shakespeare: Politics and Stagecraft in the Early Career* (New York: Routledge, 2012), 191–228, and Ronald Hutton, *The Rise and Fall of Merry England: The Ritual Year, 1400–1700* (Oxford: Oxford UP, 1994).

Continental Influences

At the same time that the play evokes the English Forest of Arden, the action supposedly occurs in France, where another forest, the forest of Ardennes, is located, and where Shakespeare's source tale, Thomas Lodge's *Rosalynde*, is set. This doubleness of location is interesting in that it connects the play both to celebrations of English country and forest life and simultaneously to Continental romances and to the pan-European interest in new versions of pastoral and female performance. As much recent scholarship has shown, the English were not innocent of theatrical developments on the Continent, especially the striking roles played by professional actresses in Italian commedia dell'arte companies, and by aristocrats and women players in salons and court entertainments in France.[3] Actresses first appeared in Italian companies in the 1560s and gained international fame in the 1570s, when commedia dell'arte companies first ventured across the Alps and played for the French royalty. English diplomats and travelers brought home the news of the actresses to England. Soon Elizabeth was importing Italian companies to play for her; in 1574 one troupe played the first Italian pastoral seen in England before the queen, and a troupe with actresses played in London in 1578.[4] The leading Italian actresses changed the male-centered humanist and popular drama in which they appeared, and writers quickly created newly expanded and complex roles for them.

By the 1580s, English playwrights were creating a new kind of leading woman on the Italian model in both pastoral and romantic comedy: an articulate, volatile, adventurous, and resourceful young woman in love (the inamorata) whose choices and actions widened the scope of drama. The advent of the actress and the change it wrought in playwriting across the board influenced the creation of outspoken leading female characters, such as Rosalind of *As You Like It*, Viola of *Twelfth Night*, Beatrice of *Much Ado about Nothing*, and Portia of *The Merchant of Venice*. All these heroines of Shakespeare's 1590s comedies are linked through their sources and theatrical modes to Continental plays and players, both professional and courtly. When Rosalind decides to play "a busy actor," improvising in the "pageant truly played" between Silvius and Phoebe (3.4.49, 42), she resembles the actresses who made pastoral comedies and crossdressing their specialty, and

[3] Julie D. Campbell, "'Merry, nimble, stirring spirit[s]': Academic, Salon and Commedia dell'arte Influence on the *Innamorate* of *Love's Labour's Lost*," *Women Players in England, 1500–1600: Beyond the All-Male Stage*, eds. Pamela Allen Brown and Peter Parolin (Aldershot, UK: Ashgate, 2005), 145–70.
[4] E. K. Chambers, *The Elizabethan Stage*, 4 vols. (Oxford: Clarendon, 1923), II, 261–62, and Robert Henke, "Back to the Future: A Review of Twentieth-Century Commedia-Shakespeare Studies," *Early Theatre* 11.2. (2008): 227–40.

whose roles expanded as demand to see them grew. As an aristocratic performer, Rosalind also resembles the witty princesses and their ladies who played so often in pastorals produced by and for the theater-loving dowager queen Catherine de'Medici, the first and most important patron of Italian actors and actresses in France.

While the English stage managed to remain all-male, Elizabeth showed a determination to keep up with her glittering European counterparts in other ways. Courtly theater and spectacle blended Italian and French fashion with more homely English traditions, a hybrid that forms an important context for *As You Like It*. When Queen Elizabeth visited the country estates of her noblemen, she was often greeted by pastoral entertainments in which men dressed as shepherds would step from the forest of the estate to address poems of love and praise to her as a goddess; if she was pleased, she would make witty rejoinders. In the 1580s, the court playwright John Lyly staged pastoral plays for the queen and her court, including *Gallatea* (pub. 1592) a graceful exploration of disguise and same-sex love that undoubtedly influenced Shakespeare's creation of his cross-dressed Rosalind. Recently, Juliet Dusinberre has tentatively suggested that *As You Like It* may even have been performed before the court at Richmond Palace in 1599.[5] Whether or not this last speculation is true, *As You Like It* is as much linked to courtly as to popular festivity, and to Continental as to native traditions.

As You Like It and the Arts of Civility

The play's interest in courtly manners and gentle behavior is rooted firmly in Continental writings on courtiership and grace, the most important of which was Baldassare Castiglione's famous conduct book *Il libro del Cortegiano* (1528), translated into English by Thomas Hoby in 1561 as *The Courtyer*. Castiglione praised the virtues of grace and *sprezzatura*, that is, the ability to behave elegantly without apparent effort, hiding the labor through which this pose of nonchalance is forged. *Sprezzatura* is the essence of the true courtier, the man or woman who has mastered the arts of civility and knows how to conduct him- or herself on every occasion with effortless decorum. Gentlemen and gentlewomen might learn their manners at court or in the country great houses of the nobility. Those further down the social ladder might learn from courtesy books that followed in the wake of Castiglione's, more than one thousand of which were written in English over the course of the sixteenth and seventeenth centuries.

[5] Juliet Dusinberre, ed., introduction, *As You Like It* (London: Arden Shakespeare of Thompson Learning, 2006), 6–7.

Many characters in *As You Like It* undergo lessons in the civilizing process. Orlando, deprived of a proper education by a cruel brother, quickly learns from the Duke that his attempt to command food by means of a sword lacks "civility" (2.7.93). Rather, "Your gentleness shall force / More than your force move us to gentleness" (2.7.101–02). Almost imperceptibly, the Duke is modeling civility and teaching manners, a task that Rosalind takes up later when she schools Orlando in punctuality and tells him, half jokingly, half seriously, when to kiss his beloved and when to desist. Touchstone has a more daunting job. His beloved, Audrey, has to be enjoined to "bear your body more seeming" (5.4.61–62), and she is not "poetical" (3.3.12). Her induction into the arts of civility may be a rocky one.

Nonetheless, the space of the forest allows time to practice the arts of civility, one of which is conversation, and to meditate on what it means to be truly "civil," truly "gentle." Certainly it is not simply a matter of rank and education, since both Frederick, the usurping Duke, and Oliver, Orlando's cruel brother, lack these qualities, at least until they undergo miraculous conversions in the Forest of Arden. And in the quiet manners of Corin, Arden's one true shepherd, one can discern a "natural" civility that derives neither from gentle birth nor education.

It is perhaps useful, too, to think of Shakespeare's stagecraft in *As You Like It* as itself demonstrating a kind of *sprezzatura*, a seemingly effortless weaving together of native and Continental, high and low, themes and characters. Shakespeare's control of his material is so complete that he can touch on many serious matters (many of which we will elaborate in the selections that follow) without becoming crabbed and didactic, just as he can make fun of many of the conventions of pastoral comedy while still employing them. Silvius, for example, is an exaggerated version of a pastoral lover. He runs through the forest crying "Phoebe, Phoebe, Phoebe!" (2.4.37), failing to attend to his sheep, and insisting that he will die for love and that no one has ever loved as he loves—and all for a woman who makes no bones about her indifference to him. Shakespeare is making fun of clichéd behavior, of people so in love with the role of lover that they are blind to what is in front of them. Both Silvius and Phoebe have to get a surprising jolt of reality before they finally are allowed to wend their way to the altar, just as Rosalind has to teach Orlando that "Men have died from time to time, and worms have eaten them, but not for love" (4.1.78–79). In the sanely comic world of *As You Like It*, Rosalind speaks a truth that temporarily holds in check emotional self-indulgence, even as she admits that she herself is "many fathom deep . . . in love" (4.1.159). She too succumbs to folly at times, raging in despair at Orlando's lateness, mocking and toying with Phoebe, and falling in a swoon at the sight of blood.

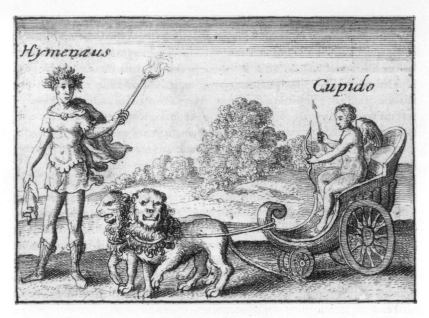

FIGURE 1 *Hymen, god of marriage with torch in hand, goes in procession with Cupid, god of love, in "Hymenaeus and Cupido," a drawing by Wenceslas Hollar (ca. 1650).*

The play's ending displays the same mixture of pleasure in convention and arch awareness of its silly and artificial dimensions. It lays on marriage with a trowel. Four couples put themselves forward, and to the cynical Jaques, they are no better than the beasts trooping into Noah's ark: "There is, sure, another flood toward, and these couples are coming to the ark. Here comes a pair of very strange beasts [Audrey and Touchstone], which in all tongues are called fools" (5.4.35–37). Yes, lovers are fools and marriage is a cliché, and yet the world must be peopled and love will have its way. When Hymen, god of marriage, comes on stage to bless these couples, he hints at a cosmic harmony that is expressed through these earthly unions (Figure 1).

> Then is there mirth in heaven,
> When earthly things made even
>   Atone together. (5.4.90–92)

Nothing could be more artificial than the idea of a god walking on the stage of the Globe Playhouse, and yet the illusion that he does is part of what the space of play makes possible. In some productions, like the one staged by the Public Theater in Central Park in summer of 2012, Hymen was cut out entirely and closure was achieved by the communal dance that heralds the wedding feast to come.[6] Yet in many pastoral fictions, the gods walk among men and converse with them. *As You Like It* stages that encounter, taking liberties with common sense to open a space where the everyday can be transcended.

The best productions of *As You Like It* take risks with realism. They ask the audience to suspend disbelief and play at "what if." What if a poor man should have more gentility than a nobleman? In a society in which social rank was imagined to determine worth, that is a radical thought. What if daughters could live free of fathers and woo at will without ruining their reputations? What if the law of human kindness trumps the king's law? What if conversion is so complete that men can slough off their evil habits like a snake sloughs off last year's skin? The list goes on. As Touchstone says, "much virtue in If" (5.4.85). *As You Like It* emerges as a challenging and daring play when, beneath its assured exterior, we take the full measure of what it means to create a space of liberty and play where one can think the unthinkable.

As You Like It and Renaissance Satirical Traditions

In the late 1590s when *As You Like It* was first staged, liberty of thought and expression would have been a politically charged topic. In June of 1599 the ecclesiastical authorities in London prohibited the publication of certain books and even had some offending books publicly burned. Informally known as the Bishops' Ban, this crackdown was aimed at some books considered pornographic, but primarily at works of satire, a craze which had developed in the prior decade.[7] The authorities had first become worried in 1588 when pamphlets attacking the ecclesiastical hierarchy, and especially the role of bishops, began appearing in bookstalls under the pseudonym Martin Marprelate. There ensued an all-out pamphlet war deploying harsh satire and insults between those who wanted to reform the established church and demote its bishops (the Marprelates) and those who defended them (the anti-Marprelates). The church considered these clandestinely published attacks so serious that one printer was hunted down and executed.[8]

---

[6] William Shakespeare, *As You Like It*, dir. Daniel Sullivan, Delacorte Theater in Central Park, New York, June 2012.
[7] Richard A. McCabe, "Elizabethan Satire and the Bishops' Ban of 1599," *The Yearbook of English Studies* 11 (1981): 188–93.
[8] Joseph Black, "Introduction," *The Martin Marprelate Tracts: A Modernized and Annotated Edition* (Cambridge, UK: Cambridge UP, 2008).

Among other accusations, each side taunted the other for breeding foolish priests who lacked learning. *As You Like It* obliquely refers to this debate through the figure of Sir Oliver Mar-text, a hedge-priest who is about to "mar" the traditional marriage ceremony by conducting it in the forest without proper witnesses. When Jaques interrupts and urges Touchstone to find "a good priest that can tell you what marriage is" (3.3.63–64), he insults Mar-text as ignorant of church doctrine and its primary texts. Mar-text returns insult with insult: "Ne'er a fantastical knave of them all shall flout me out of my calling" (3.4.81–82).

In 1599 the bishops again took aim at satirists even though the Marprelate scandal was over. Edward Guilpin, John Marston, and Thomas Nashe were among those whose books were marked for destruction along with Christopher Marlowe's elegies and John Davies' epigrams. In addition, plays dealing with English history were not to be printed unless they had been allowed by a member of the Privy Council, and all plays were to be subject to renewed scrutiny by those in authority before publication could occur. What particularly seemed to have worried the authorities was the kind of social criticism the satires and epigrams slyly encouraged and the way that under cover of pseudonyms and allegorical personae, specific individuals could be criticized or slandered. In addition, officials were rankled by ferociously critical satirists such as Marston, who adopted a mask of savage indignation in the mode of the Roman poet Juvenal and a "railing" style that seemed dangerously destabilizing because it painted a world so corrupt and fallen that no power of church or state could redeem or control it.[9]

As You Like It is not a satire, though it contains satirical elements. Touchstone, for example, parodies and makes fun of fashionable gentlemen who trade insults by the book but draw back from the actual duels that their insults would seem to provoke; and Jaques, envious of Touchstone, longs for a fool's motley coat so that he can deliver satiric medicine and "through and through / Cleanse the foul body of th'infected world" (2.7.59–60). In a way reminiscent of the "snarling" satirists whose works were banned by the bishops, Jaques is checked by the good Duke Senior, who sharply reminds Jaques that he is himself a libertine and a sinner, so that his railing would be at best a form of hypocrisy. The play thus attempts the almost impossible task of drawing a line between "license"—permission to skewer and defame others without fear of reprisal, as Jaques craves to do—and "liberty"—the freedom to think and to speak freely, which could also be a dangerous endeavor in the period. Though its approach to formal satire is cautious,

---

[9] William R. Jones, "The Bishops' Ban of 1599 and the Ideology of English Satire," *Literature Compass* 7.5 (May 2010): 322–76. Web. <http://onlinelibrary.wiley.com/doi/10.1111/j.1741-4113.2010.00701.x/abstract>.

As You Like It embraces in the forest a freedom of thought and speech that enacts a quiet rejoinder to the forces that would curb both. It even incorporates an unmistakable reference to Christopher Marlowe, one of those poets whose works were posthumously banned by the bishops. When Phoebe falls head over heels with Rosalind disguised as Ganymede, she says: "Dead shepherd, now I find thy saw of might, / 'Who ever loved that loved not at first sight?'" (3.5.80–81), a line taken from Marlowe's highly erotic poem, *Hero and Leander*.

The Organization of This Book

This edition of *As You Like It* aims to take the measure both of the playfulness and the seriousness of this comedy. The texts that follow fall into four categories. First is a section on pastoral and rural life. Of all Shakespeare's plays, *As You Like It* is the one most steeped in the pastoral tradition. In order to see how the playwright uses, alters, and comments on pastoral conventions, we offer selections from a number of pastoral works from the Greeks to Shakespeare's contemporaries. The cruelty of hard-hearted mistresses, the pains of unrequited love, the evils of the court, the town, or the clergy, the simplicity and integrity of the shepherd's existence, the solace of song and art—these are some of the motifs that occur again and again in pastoral works and are echoed in Shakespeare's play. As a pre-text to that play we have chosen an extended excerpt from Thomas Lodge's *Rosalynde* (1590), the lengthy prose romance Shakespeare used as his primary source for *As You Like It*, but which he altered in significant ways.

PASTORAL

The key to pastoral is critique: a dissection of the evils of the times. In Shakespeare's play that critique takes many forms, a few of which seem to us to bear special examination. These include the play's allusions to the hardships caused by enclosures and the decay of rural hospitality, the evils of court life, and the suffering caused by the English custom of primogeniture. This was the practice by which a family's land and property usually passed to the first-born son, often leaving younger sons to live by their wits and pushing daughters into sometimes unwanted marriages with wealthier husbands who could provide for their support. Key to the play's social critique is its engagement with the Robin Hood tradition. Strictly speaking, the stories of Robin Hood are not pastorals. They do not involve shepherds, and they are really adventure tales, dealing more with action against fat churchmen and corrupt rulers than with meditations on love and life. Nonetheless, the Robin

Hood canon shares with pastoral a basic opposition of court to country or forest and a deep investment in remaking the world so that justice, and not greed, will prevail. Selections from the long evolution of this body of material show some of the many points at which it intersects with *As You Like It*. This section ends by turning from the artificial world of pastoral literature to the actual rural life of Shakespeare's England where sheep were not just inert symbols of country life but for a long time were the driving element in the nation's economy and the catalyst for huge changes in how land was used and owned. In the sixteenth century, in particular, large-scale sheep farming encouraged the enclosure, or fencing in, of what had once been common lands to which laborers had access for growing subsistence crops or pasturing their family's animals. Protests against enclosures periodically erupted in the sixteenth and seventeenth centuries as enclosures came to symbolize the destruction of traditional ways of life and the decay of traditions of mutual care and dependence between landowners and the laborers who were their tenants. Forests, too, were contested sites. Many were royal domains, and the timber and deer within them considered property of the king. But these same forests were also places of refuge for vagrants and outlaws, and those who lived on the skirts or purlieus of the forest had traditional rights, for example, to trees and branches that had fallen down and could be used for firewood. By setting *As You Like It* in a forest, and one inhabited by political exiles who kill deer, Shakespeare was dabbling in provocative subject matter, just as he was by having the shepherd Corin complain about the churlish master who has let his sheepcote decay. Documents on the law of the forest, on enclosures, and on sheep farming will give some idea of how the seemingly timeless pastoral world of *As You Like It* intersects with the real world in which Shakespeare lived.

LOVE, MARRIAGE, AND DESIRE

The second section of documents deals with love, marriage, and the unpredictable and shifting nature of erotic desire. *As You Like It* is a love comedy ending in marriage, and marriage was one of the central institutions of early modern life. The church developed a normative picture of marriage, and we include that here; but not all marriages operated as church doctrine decreed. Sometimes people entered into bigamous or adulterous relationships; sometimes they were married by hedge-priests (irregular or itinerant clergy who would not inquire too strictly into the appropriateness of the union); sometimes they wed in irregular ways in order to be able to slip out of marriages later; sometimes they did not want to marry at all or formed their deepest attachments with people of the same sex. *As You Like It* touches on all these possibilities, and by having its heroine cross-dressed for much of the play, it multiplies the possible trajectories that love could take. Rosalind's assumed name, Ganymede, is laden with homoerotic overtones. Ganymede was a beautiful boyish cupbearer to the gods and beloved by Jove. In adopting that name, Rosalind makes herself a magnet to men and women alike. On the way to the quadruple marriages with which this comedy closes, the drama plays with multiple forms of desire, and in doing so it expands the ways we think about how and whom we might like to love and the adequacy of the institutional form into which desire is channeled.

In this section we also deal with some of the literary languages through which love and desire were expressed in the sixteenth century, including the conventions inaugurated by the fourteenth century Italian poet Petrarch, whose sonnets to Laura gave rich expression to the idealization of the distant beloved and the pains of unrequited love; and the more earthy love poetry of the Roman poet Ovid, to whom Touchstone, the play's earthiest lover, makes reference. Shakespeare both uses and makes fun of these conventional languages, just as he uses and makes fun of the convention by which a lover carves verses to his beloved on the bark of trees, an action familiar from many medieval and early modern romances. Orlando has caught the tree-writing disease. Not only does he carve poems on trees, but he writes poems on paper and pins them everywhere in the forest, opening himself to a world of mockery from Touchstone and others. As the play makes clear, love is madness and rapture, and it is a miracle when two, any two, finally "atone together" (5.4.92).

FOLLY

Love-madness was folly by another name, something that the pastoral world seems to nurture and magnify. Even Touchstone feels it: "now am I in Arden; the more fool I" (2.4.12). The third section takes stock of the multifold kinds of folly and its practitioners in the early modern period. While folly had many meanings, including tragic insanity and doltish stupidity, the chief forms in the play are those attending love and its excesses, including self-love. Counterintuitively, Renaissance folly was not always bad: it could be proof of innocence and humanity. Fools might be better and wiser than the noble and learned, as many jokes and stories showed. At carnival time "Mother Folly" helped unleash sexual and political energy and creativity that was repressed at other times. Shakespeare draws on many levels of this discourse about fools, from the most learned humanist writing to the simplest jestbook, ballad, and jig. Humanists Sir Thomas More and his friend Desiderius Erasmus played the fool and exploited the contradictions of folly to address such weighty issues as Christian doctrine, political corruption, and the ideal state, while less sophisticated readers smiled at the silly capers of fools in moral tracts such as Sebastian Brant's *The Ship of Fools*, translated by Alexander Barclay (1570). Fools were useful teaching aids: parents warned children to behave themselves and pointed to the fool as a warning, citing the Bible and its many proverbs about fools. *As You Like It* teems with fools and clowns of all stripes. Even those who consider themselves quite serious, sane, and intelligent, such as Rosalind's father, Duke Senior, sometimes go to extremes, fool themselves, or get fooled by others. Of the play's many passionate lovers, earthy clowns, and gamesome courtiers, Rosalind, Touchstone, and Jaques do the most to entertain others by talking about and performing deeds that others might denounce as pure folly. All three take on the persona of the wise sage who instructs others in the civil art of avoiding folly, but none escapes its overwhelming influence.

EDUCATION AND MANNERS

Fittingly, the fourth and final section of documents takes on the play's preoccupation with education and manners, which are bound up with an even more basic issue: What makes a person a gentleman or a gentlewoman? What makes one civil and another uncivil, and does gentle status ensure civility and gentility? Orlando was born into a gentry family, but he feels bereft of the education that would make him truly gentle. His burning desire triggers the first conflict in the play: he accuses Oliver of neglect, Oliver insults him, and the two fall to blows. Neither brother acts civilly, and their hatred leads Oliver to plot murder and Orlando to flee. Lack of parental discipline and training in the "exercises as may become a gentleman" (1.1.53) have made even Orlando incline toward rudeness and violence, despite his countervailing inborn virtues and graces (as Oliver says, "he's gentle, never schooled and yet learned" 1.1.120–21). Orlando's time in Arden serving Duke Senior and wooing Rosalind goes a long way toward redressing that imbalance. Some of the documents in this section concern the types of training that a boy from a family of means might have received, including years studying Latin and other subjects at grammar school, informal training in manners in service at the tables of the great, tutoring in special skills such as riding and languages, and possibly advanced training at university or the Inns of Court. Many young men who did not receive these years of education and wanted to achieve polish would read books on conduct and special skills associated with, but not limited to, the gentry. Such books of instruction intended to help young people with little schooling acquire the requisite social skills to rise in society.

Orlando doesn't study on his own. Instead Shakespeare has him take a crash course in gentility from Rosalind, a much higher-ranked aristocrat who shows a clear interest in him but realizes his shortcomings. She invites him to court her, but he answers her compliments with dumb silence and later commits the gaffe of writing bad love poems to her. Luckily, she is so in love already that she overlooks all this and devises her plan to flirt and play with him in the guise of Ganymede. The side effect of her masked seduction is to teach Orlando how to woo properly. But how did Rosalind acquire her own considerable literary, theatrical, and rhetorical skills? As the documents show, education for girls was far more limited than education for boys and young men. When girls were given any training at all, they generally learned only reading, not writing, and they were never sent to grammar school or university. Some writers opposed the idea of training girls for anything more than Bible reading, sewing, and keeping house. Rosalind and Celia, by contrast, have been raised together at court, and have studied together, probably with tutors. Their sophisticated conversation and allusions show that their level of education is extraordinarily high, signaling their lofty social status. High female literacy confers an unlikely sort of glamour on Phoebe, who composes her "chiding" love letter to Ganymede in verse; her literacy shows she is a pastoral artifice and nothing like a real shepherdess, most of whom were illiterate.

Early modern educational theory was predicated on the imitation of the best models. These could be found in the literary and moralizing texts one read, or in the persons of the masters who provided both formal instruction and informal training to children, protégés, and students. Socializing with those who could speak and act gently and wittily assisted the civilizing process, as did travel and the observation of foreign customs and manners. In *As You Like It*, all the main characters end up on the road, traveling to the Forest of Arden, and all are changed in one way or another because of this experience. Leaving home broadens cramped perspectives and makes some characters (such as Oliver and Duke Frederick) more civil and accepting. Orlando learns how to return the rhetorical balls that Rosalind/Ganymede lobs at him, and she, in learning what he thinks and feels, falls ever more deeply in love.

While folly can never be entirely banished from any walk of life, it can be recognized and tempered through the civil arts of the tongue. Characters act as both teachers and students, as spectators and players, as they orate and philosophize, banter and joke. Language is the chief means of showing one's qualities and social place, and each character plays with language in his or her own way, with variations ranging from Corin's engaging candor and good humor, to Rosalind's witty audacity, to Jaques's flamboyant attitudinizing and his "Greek invocation, to call fools into a circle" (2.5.51). All these performances succeed or fail according to the judgment of others. This is a truth that liveried fools, saucy lackeys, and stage clowns know best of all. Aptly, in this pastoral comedy set in an ambiguous space called Arden, packed with fond-foolish lovers, conceited melancholics, and exiles playing Robin Hood, Touchstone gestures toward the forest of eyes and ears at his feet, the spectators in the theater, and makes them the final arbiters of wit: "You have said; but whether wisely or no, let the forest judge" (3.2.103–04).

Pre-Text

→ THOMAS LODGE

From *Rosalynde* 1592

Like many of his contemporaries, Shakespeare found inspiration and source material for many of his plays in the genre of romance. Romances, written in prose and verse, were long episodic narratives popular from the twelfth century onward. They typically featured the adventures of knights, including the quest for love; lost and then reunited family members; magical objects; and feats of heroism. In the sixteenth century, new translations of Greek romances spurred the production of homegrown romances, including Sir Philip Sidney's *Arcadia* (1593). Some romances were pastoral in character in that they involved sojourns in a pastoral landscape, presented encounters with shepherds, and sometimes featured aristocratic characters disguised as shepherds.

In writing *As You Like It*, Shakespeare drew heavily on the popular pastoral prose romance *Rosalynde, Euphues Golden Legacie* by Thomas Lodge (1558–1625), which was published in 1590. The reference to *Euphues* points back to John Lyly's *Euphues, The Anatomy of Wit* (1578) and *Euphues and His England* (1580), prose works notable for their elaborately ornate and sophisticated style, which Lodge imitates. Shakespeare's play does not adopt a Euphuistic style, but it does repeat the basics of Lodge's story about a younger brother, Rosader, who is basely kept by his older brother, Saladin. Rosader escapes to a forest that also shelters a king, Gerismond, banished by his usurping brother, Torismond. Eventually, the daughters of the former king and of the usurping king also arrive in the forest, and in this pastoral landscape, surrounded by shepherds, Rosader woos the banished king's daughter, Rosalind, disguised in the person of Ganymede.

Shakespeare made many changes to Lodge's tale, starting with the names of many of the characters. Rosader, for example, becomes Orlando, and

Saladin becomes Oliver; Gerismond becomes Duke Senior; Torismond becomes Duke Frederick; the shepherd Montanus becomes Silvius; and Rosalind's cousin, Alinda, becomes Celia. Moreover, Shakespeare's play mitigates the violence of the original. In Lodge, for example, Rosader is a real fighter who several times attacks his older brother and his brother's retainers and fights off a group of rascals who attempt to abduct Alinda. At the end of Lodge's romance, the evil Torismond is killed in battle rather than undergoing a conversion as happens in Shakespeare. In addition, there is a sharp reduction in Shakespeare's play of Alinda/Celia's role. In Lodge's romance she appears in nearly every scene with Rosalind. Why do you think Shakespeare reduced the violence of his source tale, and what are the consequences of reducing Alinda/Celia's part? Besides these cuts and changes, Shakespeare also added some characters to his story, including Touchstone, Audrey, William, Jaques, and Oliver Mar-text. A key question is why? Why make these additions? How do these characters color an audience's reception of the actions of Duke Senior, Orlando, Ganymede/Rosalind, and the shepherd lovers, Phoebe and Silvius?

To give you a feel for Lodge's romance, below are several sections of it. These include the parts of *Rosalynde* that would become, in *As You Like It*, Rosalind and Celia's flight into the forest, Orlando's indirect courtship of the disguised Rosalind, and the love triangle between Phoebe, Silvius, and Rosalind-as-Ganymede. As you read these selections, consider how they differ from Shakespeare's reworking of them. For example, in *As You Like It*, Orlando carves or pins poems on trees; in *Rosalynde* Montanus does so. Is this change of any significance? Do Lodge's characters speak in the same way as Shakespeare's? Is the language of Shakespeare's play more stylized, or less? What other changes do you notice in how Shakespeare adapted Lodge's work as represented in the following selections?

From *Rosalynde*

[In what follows, Rosalind and Alinda decide to flee from the court of Torismond and come upon the shepherds Montanus and Corydon.]

At this Rosalind began to comfort her,[1] and after she had wept a few kind tears in the bosom of her Alinda, she gave her hearty thanks, and then they sat them down to consult how they should travel. Alinda grieved at nothing

[1] comfort her: comfort herself.

Thomas Lodge, *Rosalynde, Euphues Golden Legacie* (London, 1592); STC 16665; D3v–F1r, J2r–J4v, N2v–O1r.

but that they might have no man in their company, saying it would be their greatest prejudice[2] in that two women went wandering without either guide or attendant. "Tush," (quoth Rosalind), "art thou a woman, and has not a sudden shift[3] to prevent a misfortune? I, (thou seest), am of a tall stature, and would very well become the person and apparel of a page. Thou shalt be my mistress, and I will play the man so properly, that (trust me) in what company so ever I come I will not be discovered. I will buy me a suit, and have my rapier very handsomely at my side, and if any knave offer wrong, your page will show him the point of his weapon."

At this Alinda smiled, and upon this they agreed, and presently gathered up all their jewels, which they trussed up in a casket,[4] and Rosalind in all haste provided her of robes, and Alinda being called Aliena,[5] and Rosalind Ganymede,[6] they travelled along the vineyards, and by many by-ways. At last they got to the forest side, where they travelled by the space of two or three days without seeing any creature, being often in danger of wild beasts, and pained with many passionate sorrows. Now the black ox began to tread on their feet,[7] and Alinda thought of her wonted[8] royalty, but when she cast her eyes on her Rosalind, she thought every danger a step to honor. Passing thus on along, about midday they came to a fountain, compassed with a grove of cypress trees, so cunningly and curiously planted, as if some goddess had entreated nature in that place to make her an arbor. By this fountain sat Aliena and her Ganymede, and forth they pulled such victuals as they had, and fed as merrily as if they had been in Paris with all the King's delicates, Aliena only grieving that they could not so much as meet with a shepherd to discourse[9] them the way to some place where they might make their abode. At last Ganymede casting up his eye espied where on a tree was engraven certain verses, which as soon as he espied, he cried out, "Be of good cheer, mistress, I spy the figures of men, for here in these trees be engraven certain verses of shepherds, or some other swains that inhabit here about."

With that Aliena started up, joyful to hear these news, and looked, where they found carved in the bark of a pine tree this passion:

Montanus' Passion

Hadst thou been born whereas perpetual cold
Makes Tanais[10] hard, and mountains silver old,
Had I complained unto a marble stone,

<hr>

[2] **prejudice:** danger. [3] **sudden shift:** resourcefulness and cunning. [4] **trussed ... casket:** wrapped up in a box. [5] **Aliena:** one who is estranged. [6] **Ganymede:** in classical mythology, the beautiful Trojan boy whom Zeus kidnaps and makes his cupbearer. [7] **black ox ... feet:** melancholy came over them. [8] **wonted:** accustomed. [9] **discourse:** tell. [10] **Tanais:** the ancient name for the river Don, in Russia.

Or to the floods bewrayed[11] my bitter moan,
   I then could bear the burden of my grief:
But even the pride of countries[12] at thy birth,
Whilst heavens did smile did new array the earth with flowers chief.
Yet thou the flower of beauty blessed born,
Hast pretty looks, but all attired in scorn.

. . . .

"No doubt," (quoth Aliena), "this poesy is the passion of some perplexed shepherd, that being enamored of some fair and beautiful shepherdess, suffered some sharp repulse, and therefore complained of the cruelty of his mistress."

"You may see," (quoth Ganymede), "what mad cattle you women be, whose hearts sometimes are made of adamant[13] that will touch with no impression, and sometime of wax that is fit for every form: they delight to be courted, and then they glory to seem coy, and when they are most desired then they freeze with disdain. And this fault is so common to the sex, that you see it painted out in the shepherd's passions, who found his mistress as froward[14] as he was enamored."

"And I pray you," (quoth Aliena), "if your robes were off, what metal are you made of that you are so satirical against women? Is it not a foul bird defiles its own nest? Beware, Ganymede, that Rosader hear you not: if he do, perchance you will make him leap so far from love, that he will anger every vein in your heart."

"Thus," (quoth Ganymede), "I keep decorum: I speak now as I am Aliena's page, not as I am Gerismond's daughter, for put me but into a petticoat, and I will stand in defiance to the uttermost, that women are courteous, constant, virtuous, and whatnot."

"Stay there," (quoth Aliena), "and no more words, for yonder be characters graven upon the bark of the tall beech tree."

"Let us see," (quoth Ganymede), and with that they read a fancy written to this effect:

First shall the heavens want[15] starry light,
The seas be robbed of their waves,
The day want sun, and sun want bright,
The night want shade, the dead men graves,
   The April, flowers and leaf and tree,
   Before I false my faith to thee.

---

[11]bewrayed: exposed.   [12]pride of countries: best of countries (as opposed to the cold regions). [13]adamant: used poetically to denote unyielding hardness. [14]froward: hard to please. [15]want: lack.

First shall the tops of highest hills
By humble plains be overpried,[16]
And poets scorn the Muses' quills,[17]
And fish forsake the water glide,
    And Iris lose her colored weed,[18]
    Before I fail thee at thy need.

. . . .

First direful hate shall turn to peace,
And love relent in deep disdain,
And death his fatal stroke shall cease,
And envy pity every pain,
    And pleasure mourn, and sorrow smile,
    Before I talk of any guile.
First time shall stay his stayless race,
And winter bless his brows with corn,
And snow bemoisten July's face,
And winter spring, and summer mourn,
    Before my pen by help of fame,
    Cease to recite thy sacred name.
                Montanus.

"No doubt," (quoth Ganymede), "this protestation grew from one full of passions."

"I am of that mind too," (quoth Aliena), "but see, I pray, when poor women seek to keep themselves chaste, how men woo them with many feigned promises, alluring with sweet words as the Sirens,[19] and after proving as trothless as Aeneas.[20] Thus promised Demophon to his Phyllis,[21] but who at last grew more false?"

"The reason was," (quoth Ganymede), "that they were women's sons, and took that fault of their mother, for if man had grown from man, as Adam did from the earth, men had never been troubled with inconstancy."

"Leave off," (quoth Aliena), "to taunt thus bitterly, or else I'll pull off your page's apparel and whip you as Venus[22] doth her wantons, with nettles."

"So you will," (quoth Ganymede), "persuade me to flattery, and that needs not. But come, seeing we have found here by his fount the trace of

---

[16]**overpried:** overlooked (i.e., the plains will be higher than the hills).   [17]**Muses' quills:** pens. (In classical mythology, the Muses are the goddesses that inspire literary creation.)   [18]**Iris . . . weed:** Iris is the goddess of the rainbow.   [19]**Sirens:** mythical creatures, half-bird and half-woman, who lured sailors to their deaths with their enchanting songs.   [20]**Aeneas:** in Virgil's *Aeneid* (late first century B.C.E.) Aeneas deserts his lover Dido, who then commits suicide.   [21]**Demophon . . . Phyllis:** in Greek mythology Demophon is the King of Athens and son of Theseus who falls in love with Phyllis of Thrace but leaves her behind when he returns to Athens to help his father. Phyllis gives up hope of Demophon's return and kills herself.   [22]**Venus:** the goddess of love.

shepherds by their madrigals and roundelays,[23] let us forward, for either we shall find some folds, sheepcotes,[24] or else some cottages wherein for a day or two to rest."

[In the following passage, Rosalind, disguised as Ganymede, momentarily takes pity on Rosader and agrees to let him court her.]

Ganymede pitying her Rosader, thinking to drive him out of his amorous melancholy, said that now the sun was in his meridional heat,[25] and that it was high noon, "Therefore we shepherds say 'tis time to go to dinner, for the sun and our stomachs, are shepherds' dials. Therefore, forester, if thou wilt take such fare as comes out of our homely scrips,[26] welcome shall answer whatsoever thou wantest in delicates."[27]

Aliena took the entertainment by the end,[28] and told Rosader he should be her guest. He thanked them heartily, and sat with them down to dinner, where they had such cates[29] as country state did allow them, sauced[30] with such content, and such sweet prattle, as it seemed far more sweet, than all their courtly junkets.[31]

As soon as they had taken their repast,[32] Rosader giving them thanks for his good cheer, would have been gone, but Ganymede, that was loath to let him pass out of her presence, began thus: "Nay, forester, quoth he, if thy business be not the greater, seeing thou sayest thou art so deeply in love, let me see how thou canst woo: I will represent Rosalind, and thou shalt be as thou art Rosader. See in some amorous eclogue, how if Rosalind were present, how thou couldst court her, and while we sing of love, Aliena shall tune her pipe, and play us melody."

"Content," quoth Rosader.

And Aliena, she to show her willingness, drew forth a recorder, and began to wind it.[33] Then the loving forester began thus:

The wooing Eclogue betwixt Rosalind and Rosader.

ROSADER:

I pray thee nymph by all the working words,
By all the tears and sighs that lovers know,
Or what or[34] thoughts or faltering tongue affords,
I crave for mine in ripping up my woe.
Sweet Rosalind my love (would God my love)

---

[23] **madrigals and roundelays:** pastoral songs.   [24] **sheepcotes:** shelters for sheep.   [25] **meridional heat.** the position of the sun at noon.   [26] **scrips:** satchels.   [27] **delicates:** dainty or luxurious foods.   [28] **took . . . end:** took charge.   [29] **cates:** delicates.   [30] **sauced:** seasoned.   [31] **junkets:** feasts.   [32] **repast:** refreshment.   [33] **recorder . . . wind it:** a reedless wind instrument, played by blowing into (or "winding") it.   [34] **or:** either.

My life (would God my life) ay pity me:
Thy lips are kind, and humble like the dove,
And but with beauty pity will not be.
Look on mine eyes made red with rueful tears,
From whence the rain of true remorse descendeth,
All pale in looks, and I though young in years,
And nought but love or death my days befriendeth.
Oh let no stormy rigor knit thy brows,
Which love appointed for his mercy seat:
The tallest tree by Boreas' breath[35] it bows,
The iron yields with hammer, and to heat.
> Oh Rosalind then be thou pitiful,
> For Rosalind is only beautiful.

ROSALIND:

Love's wantons[36] arm their traitorous suits with tears,
With vows, with oaths, with looks, with showers of gold:
But when the fruit of their affects[37] appears,
The simple heart by subtle sleights[38] is sold.
Thus sucks the yielding ear the poisoned bait,
Thus feeds the heart upon his endless harms,
Thus glut the thoughts themselves on self-deceit,
Thus blind the eyes their sight by subtle charms.
The lovely looks, the sighs that storm so sore,
The dew of deep dissembled doubleness:[39]
These may attempt, but are of power no more,
Where beauty leans to wit and soothfastness.[40]
> Oh Rosader then be thou witiful,
> For Rosalind scorns foolish pitiful.

ROSADER:

I pray thee Rosalind by those sweet eyes
That stain[41] the sun in shine, the morn in clear,
By those sweet cheeks where love encamped lies
To kiss the roses of the springing year.
I tempt thee Rosalind by ruthful plaints,
Not seasoned with deceit or fraudful guile,
But firm in pain, far more than tongue depaints,[42]

---

[35] **Boreas' breath:** the North wind.   [36] **Love's wantons:** lovers.   [37] **affects:** passions.   [38] **sleights:** tricks.   [39] **deep dissembled doubleness:** carefully disguised deceit.   [40] **soothfastness:** truthfulness.   [41] **stain:** surpass.   [42] **depaints:** depicts.

Sweet nymph be kind, and grace me with a smile.
So may the heavens preserve from hurtful food
Thy harmless flocks, so may the summer yield
The pride of all her riches and her good,
To fat thy sheep (the citizens of field).
Oh leave[43] to arm thy lovely brows with scorn:
The birds their beak, the lion hath his tail,
And lovers nought but sighs and bitter mourn,
The spotless fort of fancy[44] to assail.
    Oh Rosalind then be thou pitiful:
    For Rosalind is only beautiful.

ROSALIND:

The hardened steele by fire is brought in frame.

ROSADER:

And Rosalind my love than any wool more softer:
And shall not sighs her tender heart enflame?

ROSALIND:

Were lovers true, maids would believe them ofter.

ROSADER:

Truth and regard, and honor guide my love.

ROSALIND:

Fain would I trust, but yet I dare not try.

ROSADER:

Oh pity me sweet nymph, and do but prove.[45]

ROSALIND:

I would resist, but yet I know not why.

ROSADER:

Oh Rosalind be kind, for times will change,
Thy looks ay nill[46] be fair as now they be,
Thine age from beauty may thy looks estrange:
Ah yield in time sweet nymph and pity me.

ROSALIND:

Oh Rosalind, thou must be pitiful:
For Rosader is young and beautiful.

ROSADER:

Oh gain more great than kingdoms or a crown.

ROSALIND:

Oh trust betrayed if Rosader abuse me.

---

[43] leave: cease. [44] spotless . . . fancy: the innocent mind. [45] prove: try me. [46] ay nill: will not always.

ROSADER:

> First let the heavens conspire to pull me down,
> And heaven and earth as abject quite refuse me,
> Let sorrows stream about my hateful bower,
> And restless horror hatch within my breast,
> Let beauty's eye afflict me with a lour,[47]
> Let deep despair pursue me without rest:
> Ere Rosalind my loyalty disprove,
> Ere Rosalind accuse me for unkind.

ROSALIND:

> Then Rosalind will grace thee with her love,
> Then Rosalind will have thee still in mind.

ROSADER:

> Then let me triumph more than Tithon's dear,[48]
> Since Rosalind will Rosader respect:
> Then let my face exile his sorry cheer,
> And frolic in the comfort of affect:[49]
> > And say that Rosalind is only pitiful,
> > Since Rosalind is only beautiful.

When thus they had finished their courting eclogue in such a familiar clause, Ganymede as augur[50] of some good fortunes to light upon their affections, began to be thus pleasant: "How now, forester, have I not fitted your turn? Have I not played the woman handsomely, and showed myself as coy in grants, as courteous in desires, and been as full of suspicion, as men of flattery? And yet to salve[51] all, jump I not all up with the sweet union of love? Did not Rosalind content her Rosader?"

The forester at this smiling, shook his head, and folding his arms made this merry reply: "Truth, gentle swain, Rosader hath his Rosalind, but as Ixion had Juno, who thinking to possess a goddess, only embraced a cloud:[52] in these imaginary fruitions of fancy, I resemble the birds that fed themselves with Zeuxis' painted grapes,[53] but they grew so lean with pecking at shadows, that they were glad with Aesop's cock to scrape for a barley kernel.[54] So fareth it with me, who to feed myself with the hope of my mistress'

---

[47]lour: frown.   [48]Tithon's dear: Aurora, the goddess of the dawn.   [49]affect: affection.
[50]augur: prophet.   [51]salve: reconcile.   [52]Ixion . . . cloud: in classical mythology, when Ixion grew lustful for Jove's wife Juno, Jove deceived Ixion by making a cloud in her shape.   [53]Zeuxis' painted grapes: Zeuxis, a Greek painter of the fifth century B.C.E., was said to have been such a skilled artist that when he unveiled a painting of grapes, birds began pecking at it.   [54]Aesop's cock . . . barley kernel: in Aesop's fable "Of the Cock and Precious Stone," the cock says he prefers something useful — the barley corn — to the vain learning represented by something he cannot eat, like a precious stone.

favors, soothe myself in thy suits, and only in conceit reap a wished-for content, but if my food be no better than such amorous dreams, Venus at the year's end, shall find me but a lean lover. Yet do I take these follies for high fortunes, and hope these feigned affections do divine some unfeigned end of ensuing fancies."

"And thereupon," (quoth Aliena), "I'll play the priest, from this day forth Ganymede shall call thee husband, and thou shalt call Ganymede wife, and so we'll have a marriage."

"Content," quoth Rosader, and laughed.

"Content," quoth Ganymede, and changed as red as a rose, and so with a smile and a blush, they made up this jesting match, that after proved to a marriage in earnest; Rosader full little thinking he had wooed and won his Rosalind.

[In the following section, Phoebe, having met Ganymede in the forest, expresses her love for him.]

Phoebe, fired with the uncouth[55] flame of love, returned to her father's house, so galled with restless passions, as now she began to acknowledge, that as there was no flower so fresh but might be parched with the sun, no tree so strong but might be shaken with a storm, so there was no thought so chaste, but time armed with love could make amorous, for she that held *Diana*[56] for the goddess of her devotion, was now fain to fly to the altar of *Venus*, as suppliant now with prayers, as she was froward afore with disdain. As she lay in her bed, she called to mind the several beauties of young *Ganymede*: first his locks, which being amber-hued, passeth the wreath that *Phoebus* puts on to make his front glorious; his brow of ivory was like the seat where love and majesty sit enthroned to enchain fancy; his eyes as bright as the burnishing[57] of the heavens, darting forth frowns with disdain and smiles with favor, lightning such looks as would enflame desire, were she wrapped in the circle of the frozen zone; in his cheeks the vermillion teinture[58] of the rose flourished upon natural alabaster, the blush of the morn and *Luna's* silver show[59] were so lively portrayed that the *Trojan* that fills out wine to *Jupiter*[60] was not half so beautiful; his face was full of pleasance,[61] and all the rest of his lineaments proportioned with such excellence, as *Phoebe* was fettered in the sweetness of his feature. The *idea* of these perfections tumbling in her mind made the poor shepherdess so perplexed, as feeling a pleasure tempered with intolerable pains, and yet a

---

[55] uncouth: unfamiliar. [56] *Diana*: goddess of chastity. [57] burnishing: brightness. [58] vermillion teinture: red dye. [59] *Luna's* silver show: the light of the moon. [60] *Trojan . . . Jupiter*: Ganymede. [61] pleasance: delight.

disquiet mixed with a content: she rather wished to die, than to live in this amorous anguish.

[Phoebe is in such distress that she ceases to eat and grows sick.]

   The news of her sickness was bruited abroad[62] through all the forest, which no sooner came to *Montanus'* ear, but he like a madman came to visit *Phoebe.* Where, sitting by her bedside, he began his exordium[63] with so many tears and sighs that she, perceiving the extremity of his sorrows, began now as a lover to pity them, although *Ganymede* held her from redressing them. *Montanus* craved to know the cause of her sickness, tempered with secret plaints, but she answered him (as the rest) with silence, having still the form of *Ganymede* in her mind, and conjecturing how she might reveal her loves. To utter it in words she found herself too bashful; to discourse by any friend she would not trust any in her amours; to remain thus perplexed still and conceal all; it was a double death. Whereupon for her last refuge she resolved to write unto *Ganymede,* and therefore desired *Montanus* to absent himself a while, but not to depart, for she would see if she could steal a nap. He was no sooner gone out of the chamber, but reaching to her standish,[64] she took pen and paper, and wrote a letter to this effect:

Phoebe to Ganymede wisheth what she wants herself.

Fair Shepherd, (and therefore is *Phoebe* infortunate, because thou art so fair), although hitherto mine eyes were adamants to resist love, yet I no sooner saw thy face, but they became amorous to entertain love, more devoted to fancy, than before they were repugnant to affection, addicted to the one by nature, and drawn to the other by beauty, which being rare, and made the more excellent by many virtues, hath so snared the freedom of *Phoebe,* as she rests at thy mercy, either to be made the most fortunate of all maidens, or the most miserable of all women. Measure not, *Ganymede,* my loves by my wealth, nor my desires by my degrees, but think my thoughts as full of faith, as thy face of amiable favors. Then as thou knowest thyself most beautiful, suppose me most constant. If thou deemest me hardhearted because I hated *Montanus,* think I was forced to it by fate: if thou sayest I am kindhearted, because so lightly[65] I loved thee at the first look, think I was driven to it by destiny, whose influence as it is mighty, so is it not to be resisted. If my fortunes were anything but infortunate love, I would strive with fortune, but he that wrests against the will of *Venus,* seeks to quench fire with oil, and to thrust out one thorn by putting in another. If then, *Ganymede,* love enters at the eye, harbors in the heart,

[62] **bruited abroad:** made known.   [63] **exordium:** the beginning of his speech.   [64] **standish:** ink-stand.   [65] **lightly:** easily.

and will neither be driven out with physic nor reason, pity me, as one whose malady hath no salve but from thy sweet self, whose grief hath no ease but through thy grant, and think I am a virgin, who is deeply wronged, when I am forced to woo, and conjecture love to be strong, that is more forcible than nature. Thus distressed, unless by thee eased, I expect either to live fortunate by thy favor, or die miserable by thy denial. Living in hope. Farewell.

She that must be thine, or not be at all.

Phoebe.

[Phoebe also writes a poem to Ganymede and persuades Montanus to deliver both texts to Ganymede.]

When she had read and over-read them, *Ganymede* began to smile, and looking on *Montanus*, fell into a great laughter, and with that called *Aliena*, to whom she showed the writings. Who, having perused them, conceited[66] them very pleasantly, and smiled to see how love had yoked her, who before would not stoop to the lure, *Aliena*, whispering *Ganymede* in the ear, and saying: "Knew *Phoebe* what want there were in thee to perform her will, and how unfit thy kind is to be kind to her, she would be more wise, and less enamored: but leaving that, I pray thee let us sport with this swain."

At that word, *Ganymede*, turning to *Montanus*, began to glance at him thus. "I pray thee tell me, shepherd, by those sweet thoughts and pleasing sighs that grow from my mistress' favors, art thou in love with *Phoebe*?"

"Oh, my youth," quoth *Montanus*, "were *Phoebe* so far in love with me, my flocks would be more fat and their master more quiet, for through the sorrows of my discontent grows the leanness of my sheep."

"Alas, poore swain," quoth *Ganymede*, "are thy passions so extreme, or thy fancy so resolute, that no reason will blemish the pride of thy affection, and rase out[67] that which thou strivest for without hope?"

"Nothing can make me forget *Phoebe*, while[68] *Montanus* forget himself, for those characters which true love hath stamped, neither the envy of time nor fortune can wipe away."

[Ganymede then gives the letters to Montanus to read.]

With that *Montanus* took them and perused them, but with such sorrow in his looks, as they bewrayed a source of confused passions in his heart, at every line his color changed, and every sentence was ended with a period of sighs. At last, noting *Phoebe's* extreme desire toward *Ganymede*, and her

---

[66] **conceited:** considered.   [67] **rase out:** obliterate.   [68] **while:** unless.

disdain towards him, giving *Ganymede* the letter, the shepherd stood as though he had neither won nor lost. Which *Ganymede* perceiving, wakened him out of his dream thus:

"Now *Montanus*, dost thou see thou vowest great service, and obtainest but little reward, but in lieu of thy loyalty, she maketh thee as *Bellephoron* carry thine own bane.[69] Then drink not willingly of that potion wherein thou knowest is poison, creep not to her that cares not for thee. What, *Montanus*, there are many as fair as *Phoebe*, but most of all more courteous than *Phoebe*. I tell thee, shepherd, favor is love's fuel: then since thou canst not get that, let the flame vanish into smoke, and rather sorrow for a while, then repent thee forever."

"I tell thee, *Ganymede*," (quoth *Montanus*), "as they which are stung with the scorpion cannot be recovered but by the scorpion, nor he that was wounded with *Achilles'* lance be cured but with the same truncheon,[70] so *Apollo* was fain to cry out, that love was only eased with love, and fancy healed by no medicine but favor. *Phoebus* had herbs to heal all hurts but this passion, *Circe*[71] had charms for all chances but for affection, and *Mercury*[72] subtle reasons to refel[73] all griefs but love. Persuasions are bootless, reason lends no remedy, counsel no comfort, to such whom fancy hath made resolute, and therefore though *Phoebe* loves *Ganymede*, yet *Montanus* must honor none but *Phoebe*."

---

[69] *Bellephoron* . . . **bane:** hero in Greek mythology who delivered a message that, when opened, asked its recipient to put him to death (a fate that Bellephoron avoided).   [70] **wounded . . . same truncheon:** in some of the many stories about the Greek hero Achilles, his spear is also able to heal the wounds it inflicts.   [71] *Circe:* goddess-enchantress who could turn humans into animals.   [72] *Mercury:* Roman god known for his skills at rhetoric and trickery.   [73] **refel:** reject.

PART ONE

>—<

WILLIAM SHAKESPEARE
As You Like It

Edited by David Bevington

As You Like It

>‹

[DRAMATIS PERSONAE

DUKE SENIOR, *a banished duke*
DUKE FREDERICK, *his usurping brother*
ROSALIND, *daughter of Duke Senior, later disguised as* GANYMEDE
CELIA, *daughter of Duke Frederick, later disguised as* ALIENA

OLIVER,
JAQUES,   } *sons of Sir Rowland de Boys*
ORLANDO,

AMIENS,   } *lords attending Duke Senior*
JAQUES,

LE BEAU, *a courtier attending Duke Frederick*
CHARLES, *a wrestler in the court of Duke Frederick*
ADAM, *an aged servant of Oliver and then Orlando*
DENNIS, *a servant of Oliver*

TOUCHSTONE, *the* CLOWN *or* FOOL

CORIN, *an old shepherd*
SILVIUS, *a young shepherd, in love with Phoebe*
PHOEBE, *a shepherdess*
WILLIAM, *a country youth, in love with Audrey*
AUDREY, *a country wench*
SIR OLIVER MAR-TEXT, *a country vicar*

HYMEN, *god of marriage*

Lords and Attendants waiting on Duke Frederick and Duke Senior

SCENE: *Oliver's house; Duke Frederick's court; and the Forest of Arden*]

ACT 1, SCENE 1°

Enter Orlando and Adam.

ORLANDO: As I remember, Adam, it was upon this fashion bequeathed me by will but poor a thousand crowns,° and, as thou say'st, charged my brother on his blessing to breed me well;° and there begins my sadness. My brother Jaques he keeps at school,° and report speaks goldenly of his profit.° For my part, he keeps me rustically at home — or, to speak more ⁵ properly, stays° me here at home unkept;° for call you that "keeping" for a gentleman of my birth that differs not from the stalling of an ox? His horses are bred better, for besides that they are fair with their feeding,° they are taught their manage,° and to that end riders° dearly° hired; but I, his brother, gain nothing under him but growth, for the which his ani- ¹⁰ mals on his dunghills are as much bound to him as I. Besides this nothing that he so plentifully gives me, the something that nature gave me his countenance° seems to take from me. He lets me feed with his hinds,° bars me° the place of a brother, and as much as in him lies, mines my gentility with my education.° This is it, Adam, that grieves me; and the ¹⁵ spirit of my father, which I think is within me, begins to mutiny against

ACT 1, SCENE 1. **Location:** The garden of Oliver's house.   **1–2. it was . . . crowns:** it was in this way that I was left, by the terms of my father's will, a mere thousand crowns or £250. **2. crowns:** coins worth five shillings.   **2–3. charged . . . well:** my brother was instructed as a condition of my father's blessing to educate me well.   **4. My . . . school:** my oldest brother Oliver maintains my other brother, Jaques, at university.   **5. profit:** progress.   **6. stays:** detains.   **unkept:** poorly supported.   **8. fair . . . feeding:** kept well groomed with good diet. **9. manage:** manège, paces and maneuvers in the art of horsemanship.   **riders:** trainers. **dearly:** expensively.   **13. countenance:** behavior, (neglectful) patronage.   **hinds:** farm hands. **14. bars me:** excludes me from.   **14–15. as much . . . education:** with all the power at his disposal, undermines my right to be educated as a gentleman.

this servitude. I will no longer endure it, though yet I know no wise remedy how to avoid it.

Enter Oliver.

ADAM: Yonder comes my master, your brother.

ORLANDO: Go apart,° Adam, and thou shalt hear how he will shake me up.°   20

[*Adam stands aside.*]

OLIVER: Now, sir, what make° you here?

ORLANDO: Nothing. I am not taught to make anything.

OLIVER: What mar° you then, sir?

ORLANDO: Marry,° sir, I am helping you to mar that which God made, a poor unworthy brother of yours, with idleness.   25

OLIVER: Marry, sir, be better employed, and be naught awhile.°

ORLANDO: Shall I keep your hogs and eat husks with them? What prodigal portion have I spent, that I should come to such penury?°

OLIVER: Know you where° you are, sir?

ORLANDO: Oh, sir, very well: here in your orchard.°   30

OLIVER: Know you before whom, sir?

ORLANDO: Ay, better than him I am before knows me. I know you are my eldest brother, and in the gentle condition of blood° you should so know me. The courtesy of nations° allows you my better in that you are the firstborn, but the same tradition takes not away my blood,° were there   35 twenty brothers betwixt us. I have as much of my father in me as you, albeit I confess your coming before me is nearer to his reverence.°

OLIVER: What, boy!   [*He strikes Orlando.*]

ORLANDO: Come, come, elder brother, you are too young° in this.

[*He seizes Oliver by the throat.*]

OLIVER: Wilt thou lay hands on me, villain?°   40

ORLANDO: I am no villain. I am the youngest son of Sir Rowland de Boys. He was my father, and he° is thrice a villain that says such a father begot

---

20. **Go apart:** Stand aside. **shake me up:** abuse me.   21. **make:** do. (But Orlando takes it in the more usual sense.)   23. **mar:** ("To make or mar" is a commonplace antithesis.)   24. **Marry:** i.e., indeed. (Originally an oath by the Virgin Mary.)   26. **be naught awhile:** i.e., stay in your place, don't grumble.   27–28. **Shall . . . penury?:** (Alluding to the story of the Prodigal Son, in Luke 15:11–32, who, having wasted his "portion" or inheritance, had to tend swine and eat with them.)   29. **where:** in whose presence. (But Orlando sarcastically takes the more literal meaning.)   30. **orchard:** garden.   33. **in . . . blood:** acknowledging the bond of our being of gentle birth.   34. **courtesy of nations:** recognized custom (or primogeniture, whereby the eldest son inherits all the land).   35. **blood:** (1) gentlemanly lineage (2) spirit.   37. **is nearer . . . reverence:** is closer to his position of authority (as head of family).   39. **young:** inexperienced (at fighting).   40. **villain:** i.e., wicked fellow. (But Orlando plays on the literal meaning of "bondman" or "serf," as well as Oliver's meaning.)   42. **he:** anyone.

villains. Wert thou not my brother, I would not take this hand from thy throat till this other had pulled out thy tongue for saying so. Thou hast railed on thyself.°   45

ADAM: Sweet masters, be patient! For your father's remembrance,° be at accord.

OLIVER: Let me go, I say.

ORLANDO: I will not, till I please. You shall hear me. My father charged you in his will to give me good education. You have trained me like a   50 peasant, obscuring and hiding from me all gentlemanlike qualities.° The spirit of my father grows strong in me, and I will no longer endure it; therefore allow me such exercises° as may become a gentleman, or give me the poor allottery° my father left me by testament. With that I will go buy my fortunes.   [He releases Oliver.]   55

OLIVER: And what wilt thou do? Beg when that is spent? Well, sir, get you in. I will not long be troubled with you; you shall have some part of your will.° I pray you leave me.

ORLANDO: I will no further offend you than becomes me for my good.

OLIVER: [To Adam]   Get you with him, you old dog.   60

ADAM: Is "old dog" my reward? Most true, I have lost my teeth in your service. God be with my old master! He would not have spoke such a word.

                                        Exeunt Orlando [and] Adam.

OLIVER: Is it even so? Begin you to grow upon me?° I will physic your rankness, and yet give no thousand crowns neither.° — Holla, Dennis!

Enter Dennis.

DENNIS: Calls Your Worship?   65

OLIVER: Was not Charles, the Duke's wrestler, here to speak with me?

DENNIS: So please you,° he is here at the door and importunes access to you.

OLIVER: Call him in.   [Exit Dennis.]
        'Twill be a good way; and tomorrow the wrestling is.

Enter Charles.

CHARLES: Good morrow° to Your Worship.   70

OLIVER: Good Monsieur Charles, what's the new news at the new court?

---

45. **railed on thyself:** insulted your own blood.   46. **your father's remembrance:** the sake of your father's memory.   51. **qualities:** (1) characteristics (2) accomplishments.   53. **exercises:** employments.   54. **allottery:** portion.   58. **will:** (1) desire (2) portion from your father's will (3) willfulness (i.e., you'll get what is coming to you).   63. **grow upon me:** take liberties with me; grow too big for your breeches.   63–64. **physic your rankness:** apply medicine to your overweening.   64. **neither:** either.   67. **So please you:** if you please.   70. **Good morrow:** good morning.

CHARLES: There's no news at the court, sir, but the old news: that is, the
old Duke is banished by his younger brother the new Duke, and three or
four loving lords have put themselves into voluntary exile with him,
whose° lands and revenues enrich the new Duke; therefore he gives them   75
good leave° to wander.

OLIVER: Can you tell if Rosalind, the Duke's daughter, be banished with
her father?

CHARLES: Oh, no; for the Duke's daughter, her cousin, so loves her, being°
ever from their cradles bred together, that she would have followed her   80
exile or have died to stay° behind her. She is at the court, and no less
beloved of her uncle than his own daughter, and never two ladies loved as
they do.

OLIVER: Where will the old Duke live?

CHARLES: They say he is already in the Forest of Arden, and a many merry   85
men with him; and there they live like the old Robin Hood of England.
They say many young gentlemen flock to him every day, and fleet° the
time carelessly,° as they did in the golden world.°

OLIVER: What, you wrestle tomorrow before the new Duke?

CHARLES: Marry, do I, sir; and I came to acquaint you with a matter. I am   90
given, sir, secretly to understand that your younger brother Orlando hath
a disposition to come in disguised against me to try a fall.° Tomorrow,
sir, I wrestle for my credit;° and he that escapes me without some broken
limb shall acquit him well.° Your brother is but young and tender, and
for your love I would be loath to foil° him, as I must for my own honor if   95
he come in. Therefore, out of my love to you, I came hither to acquaint
you withal,° that either you might stay him from his intendment° or
brook° such disgrace well as he shall run into, in that it is a thing of his
own search° and altogether against my will.

OLIVER: Charles, I thank thee for thy love to me, which thou shalt find I   100
will most kindly requite. I had myself notice of my brother's purpose
herein and have by underhand° means labored to dissuade him from it;
but he is resolute. I'll tell thee, Charles, it is the stubbornest young fellow
of France, full of ambition, an envious emulator° of every man's good

---

75. **whose:** all of whose.   76. **good leave:** full permission.   79. **being:** they being.   81. **died
to stay:** died from being forced to stay.   87. **fleet:** pass.   88. **carelessly:** free from care.
golden world: the primal age of innocence and ease from which humankind was thought to
have degenerated. (See Ovid, *Metamorphoses* 1.)   92. **a fall:** a bout of wrestling.   93. **credit:**
reputation.   94. **shall . . . well:** (1) must exert himself very skillfully (2) will be lucky indeed.
95. **foil:** defeat.   97. **withal:** with this.   **stay . . . intendment:** restrain him from his intent.
98. **brook:** endure.   99. **search:** seeking.   102. **underhand:** unobtrusive.   104. **envious
emulator:** malicious disparager.

parts,° a secret and villainous contriver° against me his natural° brother.   105
Therefore use thy discretion. I had as lief° thou didst break his neck as
his finger. And thou wert best look to't;° for if thou dost him any slight
disgrace, or if he do not mightily grace himself on thee,° he will practice°
against thee by poison, entrap thee by some treacherous device, and
never leave thee till he hath ta'en thy life by some indirect means or   110
other; for I assure thee, and almost with tears I speak it, there is not one
so young and so villainous this day living. I speak but brotherly° of him,
but should I anatomize° him to thee as he is, I must blush and weep, and
thou must look pale and wonder.

CHARLES: I am heartily glad I came hither to you. If he come tomorrow,   115
I'll give him his payment. If ever he go alone° again, I'll never wrestle for
prize more. And so, God keep Your Worship!

OLIVER: Farewell, good Charles.   *Exit [Charles].*
Now will I stir this gamester.° I hope I shall see an end of him; for my
soul, yet I know not why, hates nothing more than he. Yet he's gentle,°   120
never schooled and yet learned, full of noble device,° of all sorts° enchant-
ingly° beloved, and indeed so much in the heart of the world, and especially of my own people,° who best know him, that I am altogether
misprized.° But it shall not be so long; this wrestler shall clear all.° Nothing remains but that I kindle the boy thither,° which now I'll go about.   125
                                                                Exit.

ACT 1, SCENE 2°

Enter Rosalind and Celia.

CELIA: I pray thee, Rosalind, sweet my coz,° be merry.

ROSALIND: Dear Celia, I show more mirth than I am mistress of, and
would you yet I were merrier? Unless you could teach me to forget a banished father, you must not learn° me how to remember any extraordinary
pleasure.   5

---

105. **parts:** qualities. **contriver:** plotter. **natural:** blood. 106. **lief:** willingly. 106–
07. **thou . . . to't:** you'd better beware. 108. **if he . . . on thee:** if he fails to distinguish himself at your expense. **practice:** plot. 112. **brotherly:** as a brother should. 113. **anatomize:**
analyze. 116. **go alone:** walk unassisted. 119. **gamester:** sportsman. (Said sardonically.)
120. **gentle:** gentlemanly. 121. **noble device:** lofty aspiration. **sorts:** classes of people. 121–
22. **enchantingly:** as if they were under his spell. 123. **people:** servants. 124. **misprized:**
undervalued, scorned. **clear all:** solve everything. 125. **kindle . . . thither:** inflame Orlando
with desire to go to the wrestling match. ACT 1, SCENE 2. **Location:** Duke Frederick's court.
A place suitable for wrestling. 1. **sweet my coz:** my sweet cousin. 4. **learn:** teach.

CELIA: Herein I see thou lov'st me not with the full weight that° I love thee. If my uncle, thy banished father, had banished thy uncle, the Duke my father, so° thou hadst been still with me, I could have taught my love to take thy father for mine; so wouldst thou, if the truth of thy love to me were so righteously tempered° as mine is to thee.   10

ROSALIND: Well, I will forget the condition of my estate° to rejoice in yours.

CELIA: You know my father hath no child but I, nor none is like° to have. And truly, when he dies thou shalt be his heir, for what he hath taken away from thy father perforce° I will render thee again in affection. By   15 mine honor, I will, and when I break that oath, let me turn monster. Therefore, my sweet Rose, my dear Rose, be merry.

ROSALIND: From henceforth I will, coz, and devise sports. Let me see, what think you of falling in love?

CELIA: Marry, I prithee, do, to make sport° withal. But love no man in   20 good earnest, nor no further in sport neither than with safety of a pure° blush thou mayst in honor come off° again.

ROSALIND: What shall be our sport, then?

CELIA: Let us sit and mock the good huswife° Fortune from her wheel, that her gifts may henceforth be bestowed equally.   25

ROSALIND: I would we could do so, for her benefits are mightily misplaced, and the bountiful blind woman° doth most mistake in her gifts to women.

CELIA: 'Tis true, for those that she makes fair she scarce° makes honest,° and those that she makes honest she makes very ill-favoredly.°   30

ROSALIND: Nay, now thou goest from Fortune's office to Nature's. Fortune reigns in gifts of the world,° not in the lineaments of Nature.°

Enter [Touchstone° the] Clown.

CELIA: No; when Nature hath made a fair creature, may she° not by Fortune fall into the fire? Though Nature hath given us wit to flout° at Fortune, hath not Fortune sent in this fool to cut off the argument?   35

---

6. **that:** with which.   8. **so:** provided that.   10. **righteously tempered:** harmoniously composed.   11. **condition of my estate:** state of my fortunes.   13. **like:** likely.   15. **perforce:** by force.   20. **sport:** pastimes.   21. **pure:** (1) mere (2) innocent.   22. **come off:** retire, leave.   24. **huswife:** one who manages household affairs and operates the spinning wheel. (Shakespeare conflates this wheel with the commonplace wheel of Fortune.) *Huswife* is used derogatorily here, with a suggestion of "hussy."   27. **bountiful blind woman:** i.e., Fortune.   29. **scarce:** rarely.   **honest:** chaste.   30. **ill-favoredly:** ugly.   32. **gifts of the world:** e.g., riches and power.   **the lineaments of Nature:** the features that Nature provides (like beauty or ugliness).   32. s.d. *Touchstone:* a stone used to test for gold and silver.   33. **she:** the woman whom Nature has made beautiful.   34. **flout:** scoff.

ROSALIND: Indeed, there° is Fortune too hard for Nature, when Fortune makes Nature's natural the cutter-off of Nature's wit.°

CELIA: Peradventure° this is not Fortune's work neither but Nature's, who perceiveth our natural wits too dull to reason of such goddesses° and hath sent this natural for our whetstone;° for always the dullness of the fool is the whetstone of the wits.° — How now, wit, whither wander you?°   40

TOUCHSTONE: Mistress, you must come away to your father.

CELIA: Were you made the messenger?

TOUCHSTONE: No, by mine honor, but I was bid to come for you.

ROSALIND: Where learned you that oath, fool?   45

TOUCHSTONE: Of a certain knight that swore by his honor they were good pancakes,° and swore by his honor the mustard was naught.° Now I'll stand to it° the pancakes were naught and the mustard was good, and yet was not the knight forsworn.°

CELIA: How prove you that in the great heap of your knowledge?   50

ROSALIND: Ay, marry, now unmuzzle your wisdom.

TOUCHSTONE: Stand you both forth now. Stroke your chins, and swear by your beards that I am a knave.

CELIA: By our beards, if we had them, thou art.

TOUCHSTONE: By my knavery, if I had it, then I were; but if you swear by that that is not, you are not forsworn. No more was this knight, swearing by his honor, for he never had any; or if he had, he had sworn it away before ever he saw those pancakes or that mustard.   55

CELIA: Prithee, who is't that thou mean'st?

TOUCHSTONE: One that old Frederick, your father, loves.   60

CELIA: My father's love is enough to honor him enough. Speak no more of him; you'll be whipped for taxation° one of these days.

TOUCHSTONE: The more pity that fools may not speak wisely what wise men do foolishly.

CELIA: By my troth, thou sayest true; for since the little wit that fools have was silenced,° the little foolery that wise men have makes a great show. Here comes Monsieur Le Beau.   65

36. there: in that instance.   36–37. when . . . wit: i.e., when Fortune makes this natural half-wit (Touchstone) the cutter-off of witty dialogue that our natural gifts enable us to engage in. A *natural* here means a born idiot; also in line 40.)   38. Peradventure: perhaps.   39. to reason . . . goddesses: to engage in debate about Reason and Nature.   40. whetstone: grinding stone against which to sharpen things (in this case, wit).   40–41. the dullness . . . wits: i.e., the mindless things said by an idiot serve as material on which to sharpen our wits.   41. whither wander you: (An allusion to the expression "wandering wits.")   47. pancakes: fritters (which might be made of meat and so require mustard).   naught: worthless.   48. stand to it: maintain, argue.   49. forsworn: perjured.   62. taxation: censure, slander.   65–66. since . . . silenced: (Perhaps refers specifically to the bishops' order of June 1599 banning satirical books.)

Enter Le Beau.

ROSALIND: With his mouth full of news.

CELIA: Which he will put on° us as pigeons feed their young.

ROSALIND: Then shall we be news-crammed. 70

CELIA: All the better; we shall be the more marketable.° — *Bonjour*, Monsieur Le Beau. What's the news?

LE BEAU: Fair princess, you have lost much good sport.

CELIA: Sport? Of what color?°

LE BEAU: What color, madam? How shall I answer you? 75

ROSALIND: As wit and fortune will.

TOUCHSTONE: Or as the Destinies decrees.

CELIA: Well said. That was laid on with a trowel.°

TOUCHSTONE: Nay, if I keep not my rank° —

ROSALIND: Thou loosest thy old smell. 80

LE BEAU: You amaze° me, ladies. I would have told you of good wrestling, which you have lost the sight of.

ROSALIND: Yet tell us the manner of the wrestling.

LE BEAU: I will tell you the beginning, and if it please Your Ladyships you may see the end, for the best is yet to do,° and here, where you are, they 85 are coming to perform it.

CELIA: Well, the beginning,° that is dead and buried.

LE BEAU: There comes an old man and his three sons —

CELIA: I could match this beginning with an old tale.

LE BEAU: Three proper° young men, of excellent growth and presence — 90

ROSALIND: With bills° on their necks, "Be it known unto all men by these presents."°

LE BEAU: The eldest of the three wrestled with Charles, the Duke's wrestler, which Charles in a moment threw him and broke three of his ribs, that there is little hope of life in him. So° he served the second, and so the 95 third. Yonder they lie, the poor old man their father making such pitiful dole° over them that all the beholders take his part with weeping.

ROSALIND: Alas!

TOUCHSTONE: But what is the sport, monsieur, that the ladies have lost?

LE BEAU: Why, this that I speak of. 100

---

69. **put on:** force upon. 71. **marketable:** i.e., like animals that have been crammed with food before being sent to market. 74. **color:** kind. 78. **with a trowel:** i.e., thick. 79. **rank:** i.e., status as a wit. (But Rosalind plays on the sense of "stench.") 81. **amaze:** bewilder. 85. **yet to do:** still to come. 87. **the beginning:** tells us what has already occurred. 90. **proper:** handsome. 91. **bills:** proclamations. 91–92. **these presents:** the present document. (Rosalind uses this legal phrase to pun on *presence* in line 90.) 95. **So:** similarly. 97. **dole:** lamentation.

TOUCHSTONE: Thus men may grow wiser every day. It is the first time that ever I heard breaking of ribs was sport for ladies.

CELIA: Or I, I promise° thee.

ROSALIND: But is there any else° longs to see this broken music° in his sides? Is there yet another° dotes upon rib breaking? — Shall we see this 105 wrestling, cousin?

LE BEAU: You must if you stay here, for here is the place appointed for the wrestling, and they are ready to perform it.

CELIA: Yonder, sure, they are coming. Let us now stay and see it.

Flourish. Enter Duke [Frederick], Lords, Orlando, Charles, and attendants.

DUKE FREDERICK: Come on. Since the youth will not be entreated, his 110 own peril on his forwardness.°

ROSALIND: [*to Le Beau*] Is yonder the man?

LE BEAU: Even he, madam.

CELIA: Alas, he is too young! Yet he looks successfully.°

DUKE FREDERICK: How now, daughter and cousin?° Are you crept hither 115 to see the wrestling?

ROSALIND: Ay, my liege, so please you give us leave.°

DUKE FREDERICK: You will take little delight in it, I can tell you, there is such odds in the man.° In pity of the challenger's youth I would fain° dissuade him, but he will not be entreated. Speak to him, ladies; see if you 120 can move him.

CELIA: Call him hither, good Monsieur Le Beau.

DUKE FREDERICK: Do so. I'll not be by.   [*He steps aside.*]

LE BEAU: [*to Orlando*] Monsieur the challenger, the princess calls for you.

ORLANDO: [*approaching the ladies*] I attend them with all respect and duty. 125

ROSALIND: Young man, have you challenged Charles the wrestler?

ORLANDO: No, fair princess, he is the general challenger.° I come but in, as others do, to try with him the strength of my youth.

CELIA: Young gentleman, your spirits are too bold for your years. You have seen cruel proof of this man's strength. If you saw yourself with your 130 eyes, or knew yourself with your judgment,° the fear of your adventure

---

103. **promise:** assure. 104. **any else:** anyone else who. **broken music:** literally, music arranged in parts for different instruments; here applied to the breaking of ribs. 105. **another:** another who. 110–11. **entreated . . . forwardness:** i.e., entreated to desist, let the risk be blamed upon his own rashness. 114. **successfully:** i.e., as if he would be successful. 115. **cousin:** i.e., niece. 117. **so . . . leave:** if you will permit us. 118–19. **there . . . man:** Charles is such an odds-on favorite to win. 119. **fain:** willingly. 127. **the general challenger:** the one who is ready to take on all comers. (Orlando is the challenger in a more limited sense.) 130–31. **If . . . judgment:** if you saw yourself objectively.

would counsel you to a more equal° enterprise. We pray you, for your own sake, to embrace your own safety and give over this attempt.

ROSALIND: Do, young sir. Your reputation shall not therefore be misprized.° We will make it our suit to the Duke that the wrestling might not go 135
forward.

ORLANDO: I beseech you, punish me not with your hard thoughts, wherein° I confess me much guilty to deny° so fair and excellent ladies anything. But let your fair eyes and gentle wishes go with me to my trial, wherein if I be foiled, there is but one shamed that was never gracious,° if killed, but 140 one dead that is willing to be so. I shall do my friends no wrong, for I have none to lament me; the world no injury, for in it I have nothing. Only in the world I° fill up a place which may be better supplied when I have made it empty.

ROSALIND: The little strength that I have, I would it were with you. 145

CELIA: And mine, to eke out hers.

ROSALIND: Fare you well. Pray heaven I be deceived in you!°

CELIA: Your heart's desires be with you!

CHARLES: Come, where is this young gallant that is so desirous to lie with his mother earth? 150

ORLANDO: Ready, sir, but his will hath in it a more modest working.°

DUKE FREDERICK: You shall try but one fall.

CHARLES: No, I warrant Your Grace, you shall not entreat him to a second, that have so mightily persuaded him from a first.

ORLANDO: You mean to mock me after; you should not have mocked me 155 before. But come your ways.°

ROSALIND: Now Hercules be thy speed,° young man!

CELIA: I would I were invisible, to catch the strong fellow by the leg.

[Orlando and Charles] wrestle.

ROSALIND: Oh, excellent young man!

CELIA: If I had a thunderbolt in mine eye,° I can tell who should down.° 160

Shout. [Charles is thrown.]

DUKE FREDERICK: No more, no more.

ORLANDO: Yes, I beseech Your Grace. I am not yet well breathed.°

DUKE FREDERICK:
How dost thou, Charles?

---

132. **equal:** i.e., where the odds are more equal.   134. **misprized:** despised, undervalued.
137. **wherein:** though.   138. **to deny:** in denying.   140. **gracious:** looked upon with favor.
143. **Only . . . I:** in the world I merely.   147. **deceived in you:** i.e., mistaken in fearing you will lose.   151. **modest working:** decorous endeavor (than to lie with one's mother earth. For a man to lie with his mother is to commit incest.)   156. **come your ways:** come on.   157. **Hercules be thy speed:** may Hercules help you.   160. **If . . . eye:** i.e., if I were Zeus or Jupiter.   **down:** fall.   162. **well breathed:** warmed up.

LE BEAU: He cannot speak, my lord.

DUKE FREDERICK:
   Bear him away.—What is thy name, young man?   [*Charles is borne out.*]

ORLANDO: Orlando, my liege, the youngest son of Sir Rowland de Boys.   165

DUKE FREDERICK:
   I would thou hadst been son to some man else.
   The world esteemed thy father honorable,
   But I did find him still mine enemy.
   Thou shouldst have better pleased me with this deed
   Hadst thou descended from another house.   170
   But fare thee well; thou art a gallant youth.
   I would thou hadst told me of another father.
                       Exit Duke [with train, and others. Rosalind and Celia remain;
                                      Orlando stands apart from them].

CELIA: [*to Rosalind*]
   Were I my father, coz, would I do this?

ORLANDO: [*to no one in particular*]
   I am more proud to be Sir Rowland's son,
   His youngest son, and would not change that calling°   175
   To be adopted heir to Frederick.

ROSALIND: [*to Celia*]
   My father loved Sir Rowland as his soul,
   And all the world was of my father's mind.
   Had I before known this young man his son,
   I should have given him tears unto° entreaties   180
   Ere he should thus have ventured.

CELIA: [*to Rosalind*]   Gentle cousin,
   Let us go thank him, and encourage him.
   My father's rough and envious disposition
   Sticks° me at heart.—Sir, you have well deserved.
   If you do keep your promises in love   185
   But justly° as you have exceeded all promise,
   Your mistress shall be happy.

ROSALIND: [*giving him a chain° from her neck*]   Gentleman,
   Wear this for me, one out of suits with fortune,°
   That could° give more, but that her hand lacks means.
   [*To Celia*] Shall we go, coz?

---

175. **change that calling**: exchange that name and vocation.   180. **unto**: in addition to.
184. **Sticks**: stabs.   186. **But justly**: exactly.   187. **s.d. chain**: (See 3.2.157, where Celia speaks of a chain given to Orlando by Rosalind.)   188. **out . . . fortune**: (1) whose petitions to Fortune are rejected (2) not wearing the livery of Fortune, not in her service.   189. **could**: would.

CELIA: Ay.—Fare you well, fair gentleman.   190

[*Rosalind and Celia start to leave.*]

ORLANDO: [*aside*]

Can I not say, "I thank you"? My better parts
Are all thrown down, and that which here stands up
Is but a quintain,° a mere lifeless block.

ROSALIND: [*to Celia*]

He calls us back. My pride fell with my fortunes;
I'll ask him what he would.°—Did you call, sir?   195
Sir, you have wrestled well and overthrown
More than your enemies.

CELIA: Will you go, coz?

ROSALIND: Have with you.°—Fare you well.   *Exit* [*with Celia*].

ORLANDO:

What passion hangs these weights upon my tongue?   200
I cannot speak to her, yet she urged conference.°
O poor Orlando, thou art overthrown!
Or° Charles or something weaker masters thee.

Enter Le Beau.

LE BEAU:

Good sir, I do in friendship counsel you
To leave this place. Albeit you have deserved   205
High commendation, true applause, and love,
Yet such is now the Duke's condition°
That he misconsters° all that you have done.
The Duke is humorous.° What he is indeed
More suits you to conceive° than I to speak of.   210

ORLANDO:

I thank you, sir. And, pray you, tell me this:
Which of the two was daughter of the Duke
That here was at the wrestling?

LE BEAU:

Neither his daughter, if we judge by manners,
But yet indeed the taller° is his daughter.   215
The other is daughter to the banished Duke,

---

193. **quintain:** wooden figure used as a target in tilting.   195. **would:** wants.   199. **Have with you:** I'll go with you.   201. **urged conference:** invited conversation.   203. **Or:** either.   207. **condition:** disposition.   208. **misconsters:** misconstrues.   209. **humorous:** capricious.   210. **conceive:** imagine, understand.   215. **taller:** (Perhaps a textual error for *smaller* or *lesser*, or else an inconsistency on Shakespeare's part; at 1.3.104, Rosalind is shown to be the taller.)

And here detained by her usurping uncle
To keep his daughter company, whose loves
Are dearer than the natural bond of sisters.
But I can tell you that of late this Duke   220
Hath ta'en displeasure gainst his gentle niece,
Grounded upon no other argument°
But that the people praise her for her virtues
And pity her for her good father's sake;
And, on my life, his malice gainst the lady   225
Will suddenly° break forth. Sir, fare you well.
Hereafter, in a better world° than this,
I shall desire more love and knowledge of you.

ORLANDO:
I rest much bounden° to you. Fare you well.   [*Exit Le Beau.*]
Thus must I from the smoke into the smother,°   230
From tyrant Duke unto a tyrant brother.
But heavenly Rosalind!

                                                            Exit.

ACT 1, SCENE 3°

Enter Celia and Rosalind.

CELIA: Why, cousin, why, Rosalind! Cupid have mercy! Not a word?
ROSALIND: Not one to throw at a dog.
CELIA: No, thy words are too precious to be cast away upon curs. Throw
some of them at me. Come, lame me with reasons.°
ROSALIND: Then there were two cousins laid up, when the one should be   5
lamed with reasons and the other mad without any.
CELIA: But is all this for your father?
ROSALIND: No, some of it is for my child's father.° Oh, how full of briers is
this working-day world!
CELIA: They are but burrs, cousin, thrown upon thee in holiday foolery. If   10
we walk not in the trodden paths, our very petticoats will catch them.°

---

222. **argument:** reason.   226. **suddenly:** very soon.   227. **in . . . world:** in better times.
229. **bounden:** indebted.   230. **from . . . smother:** i.e., out of the frying pan into the fire.
(*Smother* means "a dense suffocating smoke.")   **ACT 1, SCENE 3. Location:** Duke Frederick's
court.   4. **lame . . . reasons:** throw some explanations (for your silence) at me.   8. **my child's
father:** one who might father my children, i.e., Orlando.   10–11. **They . . . them:** i.e., you
are making too much of minor difficulties; one catches such burrs on one's clothes constantly if
one strays from the path of propriety (by falling into the folly of love). (*Holiday* and *working-
day*, lines 10 and 9, form a crucial comic binary in this play.)

ROSALIND: I could shake them off my coat. These burrs are in my heart.

CELIA: Hem° them away.

ROSALIND: I would try, if I could cry "hem"° and have him.

CELIA: Come, come, wrestle with thy affections.   15

ROSALIND: Oh, they take the part of a better wrestler than myself.

CELIA: Oh, a good wish upon you! You will try in time, in despite of a
fall.° But, turning these jests out of service,° let us talk in good earnest. Is
it possible, on such a sudden, you should fall into so strong a liking with
old Sir Rowland's youngest son?   20

ROSALIND: The Duke my father loved his father dearly.

CELIA: Doth it therefore ensue that you should love his son dearly? By this
kind of chase,° I should hate him, for my father hated his father dearly;°
yet I hate not Orlando.

ROSALIND: No, faith,° hate him not, for my sake.   25

CELIA: Why should I not?° Doth he not deserve well?

Enter Duke [Frederick], with Lords.

ROSALIND: Let me love him for that, and do you love him because I do. —
Look, here comes the Duke.

CELIA: With his eyes full of anger.

DUKE FREDERICK: *[to Rosalind]*
Mistress, dispatch you with your safest haste   30
And get you from our court.

ROSALIND: Me, uncle?

DUKE FREDERICK: You, cousin.°
Within these ten days if that thou be'st found
So near our public court as twenty miles,
Thou diest for it.

ROSALIND: I do beseech Your Grace,
Let me the knowledge of my fault bear with me.   35
If with myself I hold intelligence°
Or have acquaintance with mine own desires,

---

13. **Hem:** (1) tuck (2) cough (since you say they are in the chest.) A *burr* can be something that
sticks in the throat.   14. **cry "hem":** attract Orlando's attention by coughing. (But with the
suggestion too of a bawd's warning cry to the lovers whose secrecy is being guarded. With a
pun on "*hem*" and *him*.)   17–18. **Oh . . . fall:** i.e., good luck to you; you'll undertake to wrestle
with Orlando sooner or later, despite the danger of your being thrown down. (With sexual
suggestion.)   18. **turning . . . service:** i.e., dismissing this banter.   22–23. **By . . . chase:** to
pursue this line of reasoning.   23. **dearly:** intensely.   25. **faith:** in truth.   26. **Why . . . not?:**
why shouldn't I hate him, i.e., love him? (Celia has just argued by chop-logic, in lines 22–24,
that to love is to hate and vice versa.)   31. **cousin:** i.e., niece.   36. **If . . . intelligence:** if I
understand my own feelings.

If that° I do not dream or be not frantic° —
As I do trust I am not—then, dear uncle,
Never so much as in a thought unborn   40
Did I offend Your Highness.

DUKE FREDERICK: Thus do all traitors.
If their purgation° did consist in words,
They are as innocent as grace itself.
Let it suffice thee that I trust thee not.

ROSALIND:
Yet your mistrust cannot make me a traitor.   45
Tell me whereon the likelihood depends.

DUKE FREDERICK:
Thou art thy father's daughter. There's enough.°

ROSALIND:
So was I when Your Highness took his dukedom;
So was I when Your Highness banished him.
Treason is not inherited, my lord;   50
Or, if we did derive it from our friends,°
What's that to me? My father was no traitor.
Then, good my liege, mistake me not so much
To think° my poverty is treacherous.

CELIA: Dear sovereign, hear me speak.   55

DUKE FREDERICK:
Ay, Celia, we stayed° her for your sake,
Else had she with her father ranged° along.

CELIA:
I did not then entreat to have her stay;
It was your pleasure, and your own remorse.°
I was too young that time° to value her,   60
But now I know her. If she be a traitor,
Why, so am I. We still° have slept together,
Rose at an instant,° learned, played, eat° together,
And wheresoe'er we went, like Juno's swans°
Still we went coupled and inseparable.   65

---

38. If that: if. frantic: insane. 42. purgation: clearing of guilt. (A medical, legal, and theo-
logical metaphor.) 47. There's enough: that's reason enough. 51. friends: relatives. 54. To
think: as to think. 56. stayed: kept. 57. ranged: roamed. 59. remorse: compassion.
60. that time: at that time. 62. still: continually. 63. at an instant: at the same time. eat:
ate. 64. Juno's swans: i.e., yoked together. (Though according to Ovid it was Venus, not
Juno, who used swans to draw her chariot.)

DUKE FREDERICK:
    She is too subtle for thee; and her smoothness,
    Her very silence and her patience
    Speak to the people, and they pity her.
    Thou art a fool. She robs thee of thy name,°
    And thou wilt show more bright and seem more virtuous   70
    When she is gone. Then open not thy lips.
    Firm and irrevocable is my doom°
    Which I have passed upon her; she is banished.

CELIA:
    Pronounce that sentence, then, on me, my liege!
    I cannot live out of her company.   75

DUKE FREDERICK:
    You are a fool. — You, niece, provide yourself.°
    If you outstay the time, upon mine honor,
    And in the greatness of my word,° you die.   *Exit Duke [with Lords].*

CELIA:
    O my poor Rosalind, whither wilt thou go?
    Wilt thou change° fathers? I will give thee mine.   80
    I charge thee, be not thou more grieved than I am.

ROSALIND:
    I have more cause.

CELIA: Thou hast not, cousin.
    Prithee be cheerful. Know'st thou not the Duke
    Hath banished me, his daughter?

ROSALIND: That he hath not.

CELIA:
    No, hath not? Rosalind lacks, then, the love   85
    Which teacheth thee that thou and I am one.
    Shall we be sundered? Shall we part, sweet girl?
    No, let my father seek another heir.
    Therefore devise with me how we may fly,
    Whither to go, and what to bear with us.   90
    And do not seek to take your change° upon you,
    To bear your griefs yourself and leave me out;
    For, by this heaven, now at our sorrows pale,°
    Say what thou canst, I'll go along with thee.

---

69. **name:** reputation.   72. **doom:** sentence.   76. **provide yourself:** get ready.   78. **in . . .
word:** upon my authority as Duke.   80. **change:** exchange.   91. **change:** change of fortune.
93. **pale:** (Heaven is pale in sympathy with their plight.)

ROSALIND: Why, whither shall we go?   95
CELIA:
   To seek my uncle in the Forest of Arden.
ROSALIND:
   Alas, what danger will it be to us,
   Maids as we are, to travel forth so far!
   Beauty provoketh thieves sooner than gold.
CELIA:
   I'll put myself in poor and mean° attire,   100
   And with a kind of umber° smirch my face;
   The like do you. So shall we pass along
   And never stir assailants.
ROSALIND: Were it not better,
   Because that I am more than common tall,
   That I did suit me all points° like a man?   105
   A gallant curtal ax° upon my thigh,
   A boar spear in my hand, and—in my heart
   Lie there what hidden woman's fear there will—
   We'll have a swashing° and a martial outside,
   As many other mannish cowards have   110
   That do outface it with their semblances.°
CELIA:
   What shall I call thee when thou art a man?
ROSALIND:
   I'll have no worse a name than Jove's own page,
   And therefore look you call me Ganymede.° ˙
   But what will you be called?   115
CELIA:
   Something that hath a reference to my state:
   No longer Celia, but Aliena.°
ROSALIND:
   But, cousin, what if we assayed° to steal
   The clownish fool out of your father's court?
   Would he not be a comfort to our travel?°   120

---

100. **mean:** lowly.   101. **umber:** yellow-brown pigment (to give a tanned appearance appropriate to countrywomen).   105. **suit me all points:** outfit myself in all ways.   106. **curtal ax:** broad cutting sword.   109. **swashing:** swaggering.   111. **outface . . . semblances:** bluff their way through with mere appearances.   114. **Ganymede:** Jupiter's cupbearer. (The name used for disguise also in Lodge's *Rosalynde*.)   117. **Aliena:** the estranged one.   118. **assayed:** undertook.   120. **travel:** (1) movement from place to place (2) labor, hardship (*travail*).

CELIA:

He'll go along o'er the wide world with me.
Leave me alone to woo him.° Let's away,
And get our jewels and our wealth together,
Devise the fittest time and safest way
To hide us from pursuit that will be made   125
After my flight. Now go we in content°
To liberty, and not to banishment.   *Exeunt.*

ACT 2, SCENE 1°

Enter Duke Senior, Amiens, and two or three Lords, [dressed] like foresters.

DUKE SENIOR:

Now, my co-mates and brothers in exile,
Hath not old custom° made this life more sweet
Than that of painted pomp? Are not these woods
More free from peril than the envious court?
Here feel we not the penalty of Adam,   5
The seasons' difference,° as° the icy fang
And churlish chiding of the winter's wind,
Which when it bites and blows upon my body
Even till I shrink with cold, I smile and say
"This is no flattery; these are counselors   10
That feelingly persuade me what I am."
Sweet are the uses of adversity,
Which, like the toad, ugly and venomous,
Wears yet a precious jewel in his head;°
And this our life, exempt° from public haunt,°   15
Finds tongues in trees, books in the running brooks,
Sermons in stones, and good in everything.

AMIENS:

I would not change it. Happy is Your Grace
That can translate the stubbornness of fortune
Into so quiet and so sweet a style.   20

---

122. **Leave . . . him:** Leave it to me to persuade him. 126. **content:** contentment. ACT 2,
SCENE 1. **Location:** The Forest of Arden. 2. **old custom:** long experience. 5–6. **feel . . .
difference:** we don't mind the consequences of Adam's original sin — the hardship of the seasons. (*Not* is often emended to *but*.) 6. **as:** such as. 13–14. **like . . . head:** (Alludes to the
widespread belief that the toad was a poisonous creature but with a jewel embedded in its head
that worked as an antidote.) 15. **exempt:** cut off. **haunt:** society.

DUKE SENIOR:

 Come, shall we go and kill us venison?
 And yet it irks me the poor dappled fools,°
 Being native burghers° of this desert city,°
 Should in their own confines with forkèd heads°
 Have their round haunches gored.

FIRST LORD: Indeed, my lord,   25

 The melancholy Jaques grieves at that,
 And in that kind° swears you do more usurp
 Than doth your brother that hath banished you.
 Today my Lord of Amiens and myself
 Did steal behind him as he lay along°   30
 Under an oak whose antique° root peeps out
 Upon the brook that brawls° along this wood,
 To the which place a poor sequestered° stag
 That from the hunter's aim had ta'en a hurt
 Did come to languish. And indeed, my lord,   35
 The wretched animal heaved forth such groans
 That their discharge did stretch his leathern coat
 Almost to bursting, and the big round tears
 Coursed° one another down his innocent nose
 In piteous chase. And thus the hairy fool,   40
 Much markèd of° the melancholy Jaques,
 Stood on th'extremest verge° of the swift brook,
 Augmenting it with tears.

DUKE SENIOR: But what said Jaques?

 Did he not moralize° this spectacle?

FIRST LORD:

 Oh, yes, into a thousand similes.   45
 First, for his weeping into the needless° stream:
 "Poor deer," quoth he, "thou mak'st a testament°
 As worldlings° do, giving thy sum of more
 To that which had too much."° Then, being° there alone,

---

22. **fools:** innocents. 23. **burghers:** citizens. **desert city:** uninhabited place. 24. **forkèd heads:** barbed hunting arrows, but also suggesting antlers. 27. **kind:** regard. 30. **along:** stretched out. 31. **antique:** (1) ancient or (2) *antic*, "gnarled." 32. **brawls:** noisily flows. 33. **sequestered:** separated (from the herd). 39. **Coursed:** chased. 41. **markèd of:** observed by. 42. **th'extremest verge:** the very edge. 44. **moralize:** draw out the hidden meaning of. 46. **needless:** having no need of more water. (Weeping deer are common in literature.) 47. **testament:** will. 48. **worldlings:** worldly men. 48–49. **giving . . . much:** bequeathing your superabundance of wealth to heirs who are already too wealthy. 49. **being:** the deer being.

Left and abandoned of° his velvet° friends: 50
"'Tis right,"° quoth he, "thus misery doth part
The flux of company."° Anon, a careless° herd,
Full of the pasture,° jumps along by him
And never stays to greet him. "Ay," quoth Jaques,
"Sweep on, you fat and greasy° citizens;   55
'Tis just the fashion. Wherefore do you look
Upon that poor and broken bankrupt there?"°
Thus most invectively° he pierceth through
The body of the country, city, court,
Yea, and of this our life, swearing that we   60
Are mere usurpers, tyrants, and what's worse,°
To fright the animals and to kill them up°
In their assigned and native dwelling place.

DUKE SENIOR:
And did you leave him in this contemplation?

SECOND LORD:
We did, my lord, weeping and commenting   65
Upon the sobbing deer.

DUKE SENIOR: Show me the place.
I love to cope° him in these sullen fits,
For then he's full of matter.°

FIRST LORD: I'll bring you to him straight.°   *Exeunt.*

Act 2, Scene 2°

Enter Duke [Frederick], with Lords.

DUKE FREDERICK:
Can it be possible that no man saw them?
It cannot be. Some villains of my court
Are of consent and sufferance in this.°

---

50. of: by. velvet: i.e., prosperous. (Velvet was an appropriately rich dress for a courtier; the term also alludes here to the deers' velvety coat or to the covering of their antlers during rapid growth.) 51. 'Tis right: i.e., that's how it goes. 51–52. thus . . . company: thus the miserable are separated from and forgotten by the herd. 52. careless: (1) carefree (2) uncaring. 53. the pasture: i.e., good food. 55. greasy: fat and unctuously prosperous, like rich burghers or *citizens.* 56–57. Wherefore . . . there?: why do you even bother to glance at that poor physically shattered deer there? (*Broken* also hints at a financial ruin appropriate to *citizens* in line 55.) 58. invectively: in the most bitter terms. 61. what's worse: whatever is worse than these. 62. up: off, utterly. 67. cope: encounter. 68. matter: substance. 69. straight: at once. ACT 2, SCENE 2. Location: Duke Frederick's court. 3. Are . . . this: have conspired in and permitted this.

FIRST LORD:
I cannot hear of any that did see her.°
The ladies, her attendants of her chamber,   5
Saw her abed, and in the morning early
They found the bed untreasured of their mistress.

SECOND LORD:
My lord, the roinish° clown, at whom so oft
Your Grace was wont to laugh, is also missing.
Hisperia, the princess' gentlewoman,   10
Confesses that she secretly o'erheard
Your daughter and her cousin much commend
The parts° and graces of the wrestler
That did but lately foil the sinewy Charles,
And she believes wherever they are gone   15
That youth is surely in their company.

DUKE FREDERICK:
Send to his brother. Fetch that gallant hither.°
If he° be absent, bring his brother° to me;
I'll make him find him. Do this suddenly,°
And let not search and inquisition quail°   20
To bring again° these foolish runaways.   *Exeunt.*

ACT 2, SCENE 3°

Enter Orlando and Adam, [meeting].

ORLANDO: Who's there?

ADAM:
What, my young master? Oh, my gentle master,
Oh, my sweet master, oh, you memory°
Of old Sir Rowland! Why, what make you° here?
Why are you virtuous? Why do people love you?   5
And wherefore are you gentle, strong, and valiant?
Why would you be so fond to° overcome

---

4. **her:** Celia.   8. **roynish:** scurvy, rascally. (Literally, covered with scale or scurf.)   13. **parts:** good qualities.   17. **Send . . . hither:** i.e., send word to Oliver to bring Orlando here.   18. **he:** i.e., Orlando.   **his brother:** i.e., Oliver. (Or possibly referring to Jaques de Boys, the other brother.)   19. **suddenly:** speedily.   20. **inquisition quail:** investigation fail.   21. **again:** back.   ACT 2, SCENE 3. Location: Before Oliver's house.   3. **memory:** likeness, reminder.   4. **what make you:** what are you doing.   7. **fond to:** foolish as to.

The bonny prizer° of the humorous° Duke?
Your praise is come too swiftly home before you.
Know you not, master, to some kind of men   10
Their graces serve them but as enemies?
No more do yours.° Your virtues, gentle master,
Are sanctified and holy traitors to you.
Oh, what a world is this, when what is comely
Envenoms him that bears it!   15

ORLANDO:
Why, what's the matter?

ADAM: O unhappy youth,
Come not within these doors! Within this roof
The enemy of all your graces lives.
Your brother—no, no brother; yet the son—
Yet not the son; I will not call him son   20
Of him I was about to call his father—
Hath heard your praises,° and this night he means
To burn the lodging where you use° to lie,
And you within it. If he fail of that,
He will have other means to cut you off.   25
I overheard him and his practices.°
This is no place,° this house is but a butchery.
Abhor it, fear it, do not enter it.

ORLANDO:
Why, whither, Adam, wouldst thou have me go?

ADAM:
No matter whither, so° you come not here.   30

ORLANDO:
What, wouldst thou have me go and beg my food?
Or with a base and boist'rous° sword enforce
A thievish living on the common road?
This I must do or know not what to do;
Yet this I will not do, do how I can.   35
I rather will subject me to the malice
Of a diverted blood° and bloody brother.

---

8. **bonny prizer:** sturdy prizefighter.   **humorous:** temperamental.   12. **No . . . yours:** your
fine qualities serve you no better than that.   22. **your praises:** people's praise of you.   23. **use:**
are accustomed.   26. **practices:** plots.   27. **place:** place for you.   30. **so:** provided that.
32. **boist'rous:** rough.   37. **diverted blood:** kinship diverted from the natural source.

ADAM:
> But do not so. I have five hundred crowns,
> The thrifty hire I saved° under your father,
> Which I did store to be my foster nurse   40
> When service should in my old limbs lie lame°
> And unregarded age in corners thrown.°
> Take that, and He that doth the ravens feed,
> Yea, providently caters for the sparrow,°
> Be comfort to my age! Here is the gold;   [*offering gold*]   45
> All this I give you. Let me be your servant.
> Though I look old, yet I am strong and lusty,°
> For in my youth I never did apply
> Hot and rebellious liquors in my blood,
> Nor did not with unbashful forehead woo   50
> The means of weakness and debility;°
> Therefore my age is as a lusty winter,
> Frosty,° but kindly. Let me go with you.
> I'll do the service of a younger man
> In all your business and necessities.   55

ORLANDO:
> Oh, good old man, how well in thee appears
> The constant° service of the antique° world,
> When service sweat° for duty, not for meed!°
> Thou art not for the fashion of these times,
> Where none will sweat but for promotion,   60
> And having that do choke their service up
> Even with the having.° It is not so with thee.
> But, poor old man, thou prun'st a rotten tree,
> That cannot so much as a blossom yield
> In lieu of° all thy pains and husbandry.   65
> But come thy ways. We'll go along together,
> And ere we have thy youthful wages spent,
> We'll light upon some settled low content.°

---

39. thrifty . . . saved: wages I thriftily saved.   **41. lie lame:** i.e., be performed only lamely.
42. And . . . thrown: and when I will be neglected and thrown aside because of my old age.
43–44. and He . . . sparrow: i.e., and may God, who guards over all His creatures (see Luke 12:6, 22–4, Psalms 147:9, etc.).   **47. lusty:** vigorous.   **50–51. Nor . . . debility:** nor did I with shameless countenance chase after pleasures that would have weakened and disabled me.
53. Frosty: i.e., white-haired.   **57. constant:** faithful.   **antique:** ancient (as in the Golden Age).
58. sweat: sweated.   **meed:** reward.   **61–62. do choke . . . having:** i.e., cease serving once they have gained promotion.   **65. lieu of:** return for.   **68. low content:** lowly contented state.

ADAM:

Master, go on, and I will follow thee
To the last gasp, with truth and loyalty.   70
From seventeen years till now almost fourscore
Here livèd I, but now live here no more.
At seventeen years many their fortunes seek,
But at fourscore it is too late a week;°
Yet fortune cannot recompense me better   75
Than to die well and not my master's debtor.   *Exeunt.*

Act 2, Scene 4°

Enter Rosalind for° Ganymede, Celia for Aliena, and Clown, alias Touchstone.

ROSALIND: Oh, Jupiter, how weary are my spirits!

TOUCHSTONE: I care not for my spirits, if my legs were not weary.

ROSALIND: I could find in my heart to disgrace my man's apparel and to
cry like a woman; but I must comfort the weaker vessel,° as doublet and
hose° ought to show itself courageous to petticoat. Therefore courage,   5
good Aliena!

CELIA: I pray you, bear with me; I cannot go no further.

TOUCHSTONE: For my part, I had rather bear with you than bear you; yet I
should bear no cross° if I did bear you, for I think you have no money in
your purse.   10

ROSALIND: Well, this is the Forest of Arden.

TOUCHSTONE: Ay, now am I in Arden; the more fool I. When I was at
home I was in a better place, but travelers must be content.

Enter Corin and Silvius.

ROSALIND: Ay, be so, good Touchstone. —Look you who comes here, a
young man and an old in solemn talk.   [*They stand aside and listen.*] 15

CORIN:

That is the way to make her scorn you still.

SILVIUS:

Oh, Corin, that thou knew'st how I do love her!

CORIN:

I partly guess; for I have loved ere now.

74. **too . . . week:** i.e., too late in life. **ACT 2, SCENE 4. Location:** The Forest of Arden.
s.d. *for:* i.e., disguised as. **4. comfort the weaker vessel:** (The First Epistle of Peter 3:7, bids
husbands give honor to their wives "as unto the weaker vessel.") **4–5. doublet and hose:**
close-fitting jacket and breeches; typical male attire. **9. cross:** (1) burden (2) coin having on it
a figure of a cross.

SILVIUS:

No, Corin, being old, thou canst not guess,
Though in thy youth thou wast as true a lover   20
As ever sighed upon a midnight pillow.
But if thy love were ever like to mine —
As sure I think did never man love so —
How many actions most ridiculous
Hast thou been drawn to by thy fantasy?°   25

CORIN:

Into a thousand that I have forgotten.

SILVIUS:

Oh, thou didst then never love so heartily!
If thou rememb'rest not the slightest folly
That ever love did make thee run into,
Thou hast not loved.   30
Or if thou hast not sat as I do now,
Wearing° thy hearer in thy mistress' praise,
Thou hast not loved.
Or if thou hast not broke from company
Abruptly, as my passion now makes me,   35
Thou hast not loved.
O Phoebe, Phoebe, Phoebe!   *Exit.*

ROSALIND:

Alas, poor shepherd! Searching of° thy wound,
I have by hard adventure° found mine own.

TOUCHSTONE: And I mine. I remember, when I was in love I broke my   40
sword upon a stone and bid him take that for coming a-night to Jane
Smile;° and I remember the kissing of her batler,° and the cow's dugs°
that her pretty chapped hands had milked; and I remember the wooing
of a peascod instead of her, from whom I took two cods and, giving her
them again, said with weeping tears, "Wear these for my sake."° We that   45
are true lovers run into strange capers; but as all is mortal° in nature, so is
all nature in love mortal° in folly.

ROSALIND: Thou speak'st wiser than thou art ware° of.

---

25. **fantasy:** love imaginings.   32. **Wearing:** wearing out.   38. **Searching of:** probing.
39. **hard adventure:** painful experience.   40–42: **I broke . . . Smile:** (In his parody of a dis-
traught lover, Touchstone imagines himself attacking a stone as if it were his rival for a country
maiden named Jane Smile. *A-night* means "by night.")   42. **batler:** club for beating clothes in
process of washing.   **dugs:** udder.   43–45. **and I . . . sake:** (Touchstone absurdly imagines
himself courting a pea plant as though it were Jane Smile and exchanging pea pods with her
by way of love tokens.)   46. **mortal:** subject to death.   47. **mortal:** typically human, frail.
48. **ware:** aware.

TOUCHSTONE: Nay, I shall ne'er be ware of mine own wit till I break my
    shins against° it.   50

ROSALIND:
    Jove, Jove! This shepherd's passion
    Is much upon° my fashion.

TOUCHSTONE:
    And mine, but it grows something° stale with me.

CELIA:
    I pray you, one of you question yond man
    If he for gold will give us any food.   55
    I faint almost to death.

TOUCHSTONE: [to Corin]   Holla: you clown!°

ROSALIND:
    Peace, fool! He's not thy kinsman.

CORIN: Who calls?

TOUCHSTONE:
    Your betters, sir.

CORIN: Else are they very wretched.

ROSALIND:
    Peace, I say. — Good even° to you, friend.

CORIN:
    And to you, gentle sir, and to you all.   60

ROSALIND:
    I prithee, shepherd, if that° love or gold
    Can in this desert° place buy entertainment,°
    Bring us where we may rest ourselves and feed.
    Here's a young maid with travel much oppressed,
    And faints for succor.°

CORIN: Fair sir, I pity her   65
    And wish, for her sake more than for mine own,
    My fortunes were more able to relieve her;
    But I am shepherd to another man
    And do not shear the fleeces° that I graze.
    My master is of churlish° disposition,   70
    And little recks° to find the way to heaven

49–50. Nay . . . against it: (Touchstone, as a professional fool, laughs at the idea of stum-
bling on or discovering his own capacity for saying something wise. His use of ware plays on
[1] aware [2] wary.)   52. upon: after, according to.   53. something: somewhat.   56. clown:
yokel. (But Rosalind then alludes to the word as it applies to Touchstone as a court fool or
clown.)   59. even: evening, i.e., afternoon.   61. if that: if.   62. desert: uninhabited.   entertainment: hospitality, provision.   65. for succor: for lack of food.   69. do . . . fleeces: i.e., do
not obtain the profits from the flock.   70. churlish: miserly.   71. recks: reckons.

By doing deeds of hospitality.
Besides, his cote,° his flocks, and bounds of feed°
Are now on sale, and at our sheepcote now,
By reason of his absence, there is nothing   75
That you will feed on.° But what is, come see,
And in my voice° most welcome shall you be.

ROSALIND:
What° is he that shall buy his flock and pasture?

CORIN:
That young swain that you saw here but erewhile,°
That little cares for buying anything.   80

ROSALIND:
I pray thee, if it stand° with honesty,
Buy thou the cottage, pasture, and the flock,
And thou shalt have to pay° for it of us.

CELIA:
And we will mend° thy wages. I like this place
And willingly could waste° my time in it.   85

CORIN:
Assuredly the thing is to be sold.
Go with me. If you like upon report
The soil, the profit, and this kind of life,
I will your very faithful feeder° be
And buy it with your gold right suddenly.°   *Exeunt.*   90

ACT 2, SCENE 5°

Enter Amiens, Jaques, and others. [A table is set out.]

Song

AMIENS: [*Sings*]
        Under the greenwood tree
        Who° loves to lie° with me,
        And turn his merry note
        Unto the sweet bird's throat,°

---

73. **cote:** cottage.   **bounds of feed:** range of pasture.   76. **That . . . feed on:** suitable for your
refined tastes.   77. **in my voice:** insofar as I have authority to speak.   78. **What:** who.
79. **but erewhile:** just now.   81. **stand:** be consistent.   83. **have to pay:** have the money.
84. **mend:** improve.   85. **waste:** spend.   89. **feeder:** dependent, servant.   90. **right suddenly:**
without delay.   ACT 2, SCENE 5. **Location:** The forest.   2. **Who:** anyone who.   **lie:** dwell.
3–4. **And . . . throat:** and tune his song to the bird's voice.

Come hither, come hither, come hither. 5
Here shall he see
No enemy
But winter and rough weather.

JAQUES: More, more, I prithee, more.
AMIENS: It will make you melancholy, Monsieur Jaques. 10
JAQUES: I thank it. More, I prithee, more. I can suck melancholy out of a
song as a weasel sucks eggs. More, I prithee, more.
AMIENS: My voice is ragged.° I know I cannot please you.
JAQUES: I do not desire you to please me, I do desire you to sing. Come,
more, another stanzo.° Call you 'em "stanzos"? 15
AMIENS: What you will, Monsieur Jaques.
JAQUES: Nay, I care not for their names; they owe me nothing.° Will you
sing?
AMIENS: More at your request than to please myself.
JAQUES: Well then, if ever I thank any man, I'll thank you; but that° they 20
call "compliment"° is like th'encounter of two dog-apes,° and when a
man thanks me heartily, methinks I have given him a penny and he renders me the beggarly° thanks. Come, sing; and you that will not, hold
your tongues.
AMIENS: Well, I'll end the song. — Sirs, cover the while;° the Duke will 25
drink under this tree. — He hath been all this day to look° you.
[Food and drink are set out.]
JAQUES: And I have been all this day to avoid him. He is too disputable°
for my company. I think of as many matters as he, but I give heaven
thanks and make no boast of them. Come, warble, come.

Song

AMIENS: [*Sings*]
Who doth ambition shun 30
And loves to live i'th' sun,°
Seeking° the food he eats
And pleased with what he gets,
All together here.

---

13. **ragged:** hoarse. 15. **stanzo:** (The word *stanza*, variously spelled, was newfangled and
therefore of ironic interest to Jaques.) 17. **they owe me nothing:** (Jaques speaks of names as of
something valuable only when written as signatures to a bond of indebtedness.) 20. **that:**
what. 21. **"compliment":** courtesy. **dog-apes:** dog-faced baboons. 23. **beggarly:** effusive,
like the thanks of a beggar. 25. **cover the while:** set the table for a meal meanwhile. 26. **to
look:** looking for. 27. **disputable:** inclined to dispute. 31. **live i'th' sun:** dwell in the open
air, without the cares of the court. 32. **Seeking:** hunting for.

Come hither, come hither, come hither.
    Here shall he see
    No enemy
But winter and rough weather.   35

JAQUES: I'll give you a verse to this note° that I made yesterday in despite
of my invention.°
AMIENS: And I'll sing it.   40
JAQUES: Thus it goes:

    If it do come to pass
    That any man turn ass,
    Leaving his wealth and ease,
    A stubborn will to please,   45
Ducdame,° ducdame, ducdame.
    Here shall he see
    Gross fools as he,
An if he will come to me.

AMIENS: What's that "ducdame"?   50
JAQUES: 'Tis a Greek invocation, to call fools into a circle. I'll go sleep, if I
can; if I cannot, I'll rail against all the firstborn of Egypt.°
AMIENS: And I'll go seek the Duke. His banquet° is prepared.
                            Exeunt [*separately*].

ACT 2, SCENE 6°

Enter Orlando and Adam.

ADAM: Dear master, I can go no further. Oh, I die for food! Here lie I
down, and measure out my grave. Farewell, kind master.   [*He lies down.*]

---

38. **note:** tune. 38–39. **in . . . invention:** i.e., without needing to make use of my powerful
rhetorical skills. (The nonsense that follows will make a mockery of true invention.) 46. **Ducdame:** (Probably a nonsense term devised to puzzle Jaques's hearers, although with the
intriguing resemblances to phrases in Romany, *dukrà me,* "I foretell," or Welsh *Dewch da mi,*
"Come with [or to] me," or dog-Latin *Duc ad me,* "Lead him to me," or simply "Duke damn
me.") 52. **firstborn of Egypt:** (In Exodus 12:28–33, the firstborn of Egypt are slain by the
Lord as the enemies of Moses and the Israelites, who, like the Duke and his followers, are in
exile.) 53. **banquet:** wine and dessert after dinner. (This repast, now prepared on stage,
seemingly is to remain there during the short following scene.) ACT 2, SCENE 6. **Location:**
The forest. The scene is continuous. By convention we understand that Adam and Orlando are
in a different part of the forest and do not "see" the table remaining onstage.

ORLANDO: Why, how now, Adam? No greater heart in thee? Live a little,
comfort° a little, cheer thyself a little. If this uncouth° forest yield anything savage, I will either be food for it or bring it for food to thee. Thy   5
conceit is nearer death than thy powers.° For my sake be comfortable;°
hold death awhile at the arm's end. I will here be with thee presently, and
if I bring thee not something to eat, I will give thee leave to die; but if
thou diest before I come, thou art a mocker of my labor. Well said!°
Thou look'st cheerly, and I'll be with thee quickly. Yet thou liest in the   10
bleak air. Come, I will bear thee to some shelter; and thou shalt not die
for lack of a dinner, if there live anything in this desert. [*He picks up Adam.*]
Cheerly, good Adam!   *Exeunt.*

ACT 2, SCENE 7°

Enter Duke Senior and Lords, like outlaws

DUKE SENIOR:
I think he be transformed into a beast,
For I can nowhere find him like a man.

FIRST LORD:
My lord, he is but even now gone hence.
Here was he merry, hearing of a song.

DUKE SENIOR:
If he, compact of jars,° grow musical,   5
We shall have shortly discord in the spheres.°
Go seek him. Tell him I would speak with him.

Enter Jaques

FIRST LORD:
He saves my labor by his own approach.

DUKE SENIOR:
Why, how now, monsieur, what a life is this,
That your poor friends must woo your company!   10
What, you look merrily.

JAQUES:
A fool, a fool! I met a fool i'th' forest,

---

4. **comfort:** comfort yourself.   **uncouth:** strange, wild.   5–6. **Thy conceit . . . powers:** you
imagine you are nearer death than you really are.   6. **comfortable:** comforted.   9. **Well said!:**
well done!   ACT 2, SCENE 7. **Location:** The forest; the scene is continuous. (A repast, set out
for the Duke in 2.5, has remained onstage during 2.6.)   5. **compact of jars:** composed of dis-
cords.   6. **the spheres:** the concentric spheres of the old Ptolemaic solar system (which, by
their movement, were thought to produce harmonious music).

A motley° fool. A miserable world!
As I do live by food, I met a fool,
Who laid him down and basked him in the sun,   15
And railed on Lady Fortune in good terms,
In good set° terms, and yet a motley fool.
"Good morrow, Fool," quoth I. "No, sir," quoth he,
"Call me not fool till heaven hath sent me fortune."°
And then he drew a dial° from his poke°   20
And, looking on it with lackluster eye,
Says very wisely, "It is ten o'clock.
Thus we may see," quoth he, "how the world wags.°
'Tis but an hour ago since it was nine,
And after one hour more 'twill be eleven;   25
And so from hour to hour we ripe and ripe,
And then from hour to hour we rot and rot,
And thereby hangs a tale." When I did hear
The motley fool thus moral° on the time,
My lungs began to crow° like Chanticleer,°   30
That fools should be so deep-contemplative,
And I did laugh sans° intermission
An hour by his dial. Oh, noble fool!
A worthy fool! Motley's the only wear.°
DUKE SENIOR: What fool is this?   35
JAQUES:
Oh, worthy fool! One that hath been a courtier,
And says, if ladies be but young and fair,
They have the gift to know it.° And in his brain,
Which is as dry° as the remainder° biscuit
After a voyage, he hath strange places° crammed   40
With observation, the which he vents°
In mangled forms. Oh, that I were a fool!
I am ambitious for a motley coat.
DUKE SENIOR:
Thou shalt have one.

---

13. motley: wearing motley, the parti-colored dress of the professional jester.   17. set: carefully composed.   19. Call . . . fortune: (An allusion to the proverb "Fortune favors fools.")
20. dial: pocket sundial or watch.   poke: pouch or pocket.   23. wags: goes.   29. moral:
moralize.   30. crow: i.e., laugh merrily.   Chanticleer: a rooster.   32. sans: without.
34. only wear: only thing worth wearing.   38. know it: i.e., put their beauty to advantage.
39. dry: (According to Elizabethan physiology, a dry brain was marked by a strong memory
but a slowness of apprehension.)   remainder: left over.   40. places: (1) nooks and corners
(2) rhetorical topics.   41. vents: utters.

JAQUES: It is my only suit,°
    Provided that you weed your better judgments 45
    Of all opinion that grows rank° in them
    That I am wise. I must have liberty
    Withal,° as large a charter° as the wind,
    To blow on whom I please, for so fools have.
    And they that are most gallèd° with my folly, 50
    They most must laugh. And why, sir, must they so?
    The "why" is plain as way to parish church:
    He that a fool doth very wisely hit
    Doth very foolishly, although he smart,
    Not to seem senseless of the bob.° If not, 55
    The wise man's folly is anatomized
    Even by the squand'ring glances of the fool.°
    Invest° me in my motley; give me leave
    To speak my mind, and I will through and through
    Cleanse° the foul body of th'infected world, 60
    If they will patiently receive my medicine.

DUKE SENIOR:
    Fie on thee! I can tell what thou wouldst do.

JAQUES:
    What, for a counter,° would I do but good?

DUKE SENIOR:
    Most mischievous foul sin, in chiding sin.
    For thou thyself hast been a libertine, 65
    As sensual as the brutish sting° itself;
    And all th'embossèd° sores and headed evils°
    That thou with license of free foot° hast caught
    Wouldst thou disgorge° into the general world.

JAQUES: Why, who cries out on pride 70
    That can therein tax any private party?°
    Doth it not flow as hugely as the sea,

---

44. **suit:** (1) request (2) suit of clothes. 46. **rank:** wildly, coarsely. 48. **Withal:** in addition. **charter:** license, privilege. 50. **gallèd:** rubbed sore. 53–55: **He . . . bob:** he whom a fool wittily attacks behaves very foolishly, no matter how much he feels the sting, unless he pretends to be unaware of the taunt. 55–57. **If not . . . fool:** otherwise, the folly of even a wise person is dissected and laid open even by the variously directed shots of wit made by the fool. 58. **Invest:** array. 60. **Cleanse:** purge. (A medical metaphor.) 63. **counter:** (1) thing of no intrinsic value, a metal disk used in counting (2) parry. 66. **brutish sting:** carnal impulse. 67. **th'embossèd:** the swollen. **headed evils:** sores that have come to a head. 68. **license . . . foot:** the licentious freedom of a libertine. 69. **disgorge:** vomit. 70–71. **who . . . party?:** what true satirist inveighs against extravagance in dress with only some private individual in mind?

Till that the weary very means do ebb?°
What woman in the city do I name,
When that I say the city woman bears   75
The cost of princes on unworthy shoulders?°
Who can come in° and say that I mean her,
When such a one as she, such is her neighbor?
Or what is he of basest function
That says his bravery is not on my cost,   80
Thinking that I mean him, but therein suits
His folly to the mettle of my speech?°
There then, how then? What then? Let me see wherein
My tongue hath wronged him: if it do him right,
Then he hath wronged himself. If he be free,   85
Why then my taxing like a wild goose flies,
Unclaimed of any man.°—But who comes here?

Enter Orlando [with his sword drawn].

ORLANDO:
Forbear, and eat no more!
JAQUES: Why, I have eat° none yet.
ORLANDO:
Nor shalt not, till necessity be served.
JAQUES:
Of what kind should this cock come of?°   90
DUKE SENIOR:
Art thou thus boldened, man, by thy distress?
Or else a rude despiser of good manners,
That in civility thou seem'st so empty?
ORLANDO:
You touched my vein at first.° The thorny point
Of bare distress hath ta'en from me the show   95
Of smooth civility; yet am I inland bred,°

72–73. **Doth . . . ebb?:** is not pride as universal as the sea, overflowing everywhere until it
finally ebbs like the tide, having exhausted what it fed upon?   75–76. **When . . . shoulders?:**
when I characterize the typical citizen's wife as dressing herself in finery that is costly enough to
adorn a prince?   77. **come in:** i.e., come into court as a complainant.   79–82. **Or . . . speech?:**
or who is he of even the lowest social standing that does not object to my saying that sartorial
finery is a fit subject for my satirical spleen, thinking I am satirizing him when his own folly
shows how well he fits the contents of my speech?   85–87. **If . . . man:** if my satirical sketch
fits him, then he condemns himself by resembling my portrait of folly. If he does not resemble
my sketch, my criticism does him no harm.   88. **have eat:** have eaten. (Pronounced "et.")
90. **Of . . . of?:** what sort of fighting cock is this?   94. **You . . . first:** your first supposition is
correct.   96. **inland bred:** i.e., raised in the center of civilization rather than on the outskirts.

And know some nurture.° But forbear, I say.
He dies that touches any of this fruit
Till I and my affairs are answerèd.°

JAQUES:
An° you will not be answered with reason,° I must die.   100

DUKE SENIOR:
What would you have? Your gentleness shall force
More than your force move us to gentleness.

ORLANDO:
I almost die for food, and let me have it!

DUKE SENIOR:
Sit down and feed, and welcome to our table.

ORLANDO:
Speak you so gently? Pardon me, I pray you.   105
I thought that all things had been savage here,
And therefore put I on the countenance
Of stern commandment. But whate'er you are
That in this desert inaccessible,
Under the shade of melancholy° boughs,   110
Lose and neglect the creeping hours of time;
If ever you have looked on better days,
If ever been where bells have knolled° to church,
If ever sat at any good man's feast,
If ever from your eyelids wiped a tear   115
And know what 'tis to pity and be pitied,
Let gentleness my strong enforcement be;
In the which hope I blush, and hide my sword.   [*He sheathes his sword.*]

DUKE SENIOR:
True is it that we have seen better days,
And have with holy bell been knolled to church,   120
And sat at good men's feasts, and wiped our eyes
Of drops that sacred pity hath engendered.
And therefore sit you down in gentleness,
And take upon command° what help we have
That to your wanting° may be ministered.   125

ORLANDO:
Then but forbear your food a little while,
Whiles, like a doe, I go to find my fawn

---

97. **nurture:** education, training.   99. **answerèd:** satisfied.   100. **An:** if.   **reason:** (A pun on "raisin" plays upon *fruit* in line 98.)   110. **melancholy:** dark, shadowy.   113. **knolled:** knelled, rung.   124. **upon command:** for the asking.   125. **wanting:** need.

And give it food. There is an old poor man
Who after me hath many a weary step
Limped in pure love. Till he be first sufficed,   130
Oppressed with two weak evils,° age and hunger,
I will not touch a bit.

DUKE SENIOR: Go find him out,
And we will nothing waste° till you return.

ORLANDO:
I thank ye; and be blest for your good comfort!   [*Exit.*]

DUKE SENIOR:
Thou see'st we are not all alone unhappy.   135
This wide and universal theater
Presents more woeful pageants than the scene
Wherein we play in.

JAQUES: All the world's a stage,
And all the men and women merely players.
They have their exits and their entrances,   140
And one man in his time plays many parts,
His acts being seven ages. At first the infant,
Mewling° and puking in the nurse's arms.
Then the whining schoolboy, with his satchel
And shining morning face, creeping like snail   145
Unwillingly to school. And then the lover,
Sighing like furnace, with a woeful ballad
Made to his mistress' eyebrow. Then a soldier,
Full of strange oaths, and bearded like the pard,°
Jealous in honor,° sudden, and quick in quarrel,   150
Seeking the bubble reputation
Even in the cannon's mouth. And then the justice,
In fair round belly with good capon° lined,
With eyes severe and beard of formal cut,
Full of wise saws° and modern instances;°   155
And so he plays his part. The sixth age shifts
Into the lean and slippered pantaloon,°
With spectacles on nose and pouch on side,

131. **weak evils:** disabilities causing weakness. 133. **waste:** consume. 143. **Mewling:** crying
with a catlike noise. 149. **bearded . . . pard:** having bristling mustaches like the leopard's.
150. **Jealous in honor:** quick to anger in matters of honor. 153. **capon:** rooster castrated to
make the flesh more tender for eating (and often presented to judges as a bribe). 155. **saws:**
sayings. **modern instances:** commonplace illustrations. 157. **pantaloon:** ridiculous, enfee-
bled old man. (A stock type in Italian commedia dell'arte.)

His youthful hose, well saved, a world too wide
For his shrunk shank;° and his big manly voice,   160
Turning again toward childish treble, pipes
And whistles in his° sound. Last scene of all,
That ends this strange eventful history,
Is second childishness and mere oblivion,°
Sans° teeth, sans eyes, sans taste, sans everything.   165

Enter Orlando, with Adam.

DUKE SENIOR:
Welcome. Set down your venerable burden
And let him feed.
ORLANDO: I thank you most for him.   [*He sets down Adam.*]
ADAM: So had you need.
I scarce can speak to thank you for myself.   170
DUKE SENIOR:
Welcome. Fall to. I will not trouble you
As yet to question you about your fortunes. —
Give us some music; and, good cousin,° sing.
                    [*They eat, while Orlando and Duke Senior converse apart.*]

Song

AMIENS: ⌊*Sings*⌋
Blow, blow, thou winter wind.
Thou art not so unkind   175
    As man's ingratitude.
Thy tooth is not so keen,
Because thou art not seen,
    Although thy breath be rude.°
Heigh-ho, sing heigh-ho, unto the green holly.°   180
Most friendship is feigning, most loving mere folly.
    Then heigh-ho, the holly!
        This life is most jolly.
Freeze, freeze, thou bitter sky,
That dost not bite so nigh°   185
    As benefits forgot.

160. **shank:** calf. 162. **his:** its. 164. **mere oblivion:** total forgetfulness. 165. **Sans:** without. 173. **cousin:** (A term used by sovereigns to address their nobility.) 179. **rude:** rough. 180. **holly:** (An emblem of Christmastime and holiday cheer, as in "the holly and the ivy.") 185. **nigh:** deeply, near (to the heart).

    Though thou the waters warp,°
    Thy sting is not so sharp
      As friend remembered not.
Heigh-ho, sing heigh-ho, unto the green holly.   190
Most friendship is feigning, most loving mere folly.
    Then heigh-ho, the holly!
      This life is most jolly.

DUKE SENIOR: [*to Orlando*]
  If that° you were the good Sir Rowland's son,
  As you have whispered faithfully° you were   195
  And as mine eye doth his effigies witness°
  Most truly limned° and living in your face,
  Be truly welcome hither. I am the Duke
  That loved your father. The residue of your fortune,°
  Go to my cave and tell me. — Good old man,   200
  Thou art right welcome as thy master is. —
  Support him by the arm. Give me your hand,
  And let me all your fortunes understand.   *Exeunt.*°

ACT 3, SCENE 1°

Enter Duke [Frederick], Lords, and Oliver.

DUKE FREDERICK:
  Not see him since?° Sir, sir, that cannot be.
  But were I not the better part made mercy,°
  I should not seek an absent argument
  Of my revenge, thou present.° But look to it:
  Find out thy brother, wheresoe'er he is.   5
  Seek him with candle.° Bring him dead or living
  Within this twelvemonth, or turn° thou no more
  To seek a living in our territory.

---

187. **warp:** freeze so that the surface of the ice cracks and forces up ridges.   **194. If that:** if. **195. faithfully:** persuasively and honestly.   **196. doth . . . witness:** witnesses the likeness of the dead Sir Rowland.   **197. limned:** painted.   **199. The . . . fortune:** the rest of your adventure.   **203. s.d. *Exeunt*:** (The table must be removed at this point.)   **ACT 3, SCENE 1.** **Location:** Duke Frederick's court.   **1. Not . . . since?:** i.e., you mean to tell me you claim not to have seen Orlando since the disappearance of Celia and Rosalind?   **2. were . . . mercy:** i.e., if I were not a merciful man. (Literally, if I were not composed mostly of mercy.)   **3–4. I . . . present:** i.e., I would seek revenge not on the absent Orlando, but on you, who are right here. **6. Seek . . . candle:** i.e., look for him everywhere, even in the darkest corners. (See Luke 15:8.) **7. turn:** return.

Thy lands and all things that thou dost call thine
Worth seizure do we seize into our° hands, 10
Till thou canst quit thee by thy brother's mouth°
Of what we think against thee.

OLIVER:
Oh, that Your Highness knew my heart in this!
I never loved my brother in my life.

DUKE FREDERICK:
More villain thou. — Well, push him out of doors, 15
And let my officers of such a nature°
Make an extent° upon his house and lands.
Do this expediently,° and turn him going.° *Exeunt.*

ACT 3, SCENE 2°

Enter Orlando [with a paper].

ORLANDO:
Hang there, my verse, in witness of my love;
   And thou, thrice-crownèd queen of night,° survey
With thy chaste eye, from thy pale sphere above,
   Thy huntress'° name that my full life doth sway.°
O Rosalind! These trees shall be my books, 5
   And in their barks my thoughts I'll character,°
That every eye which in this forest looks
   Shall see thy virtue witnessed everywhere.
Run, run, Orlando, carve on every tree
The fair, the chaste, and unexpressive° she. *Exit* 10

Enter Corin and [Touchstone the] Clown.

CORIN: And how like you this shepherd's life, Master Touchstone?
TOUCHSTONE: Truly, shepherd, in respect of itself,° it is a good life; but in respect that it is a shepherd's life, it is naught.° In respect that it is

10. **we . . . our:** (The royal plural.) 11. **quit . . . mouth:** acquit yourself by the direct testimony of Orlando. (The Duke suspects that Oliver has murdered Orlando.) 16. **of such a nature:** who attend to such duties. 17. **extent:** writ of seizure. 18. **expediently:** expeditiously. **turn him going:** send him packing. ACT 3, SCENE 2. Location: The forest. 2. **thrice-crownèd . . . night:** i.e., Diana in the three aspects of her divinity: as Luna or Cynthia, goddess of the moon; as Diana, goddess on earth; and as Hecate or Proserpina, goddess in the lower world. 4. **Thy huntress':** i.e., Rosalind's, who is here thought of as accompanying Diana, patroness of the hunt and of chastity. **sway:** control. 6. **character:** inscribe. 10. **unexpressive:** inexpressible. 12. **in respect of itself:** considered in and for itself. 13. **naught:** vile, of no social consequence.

solitary, I like it very well; but in respect that it is private, it is a very vile
life. Now in respect it is in the fields, it pleaseth me well; but in respect it   15
is not in the court, it is tedious. As it is a spare° life, look you, it fits my
humor° well; but as there is no more plenty in it, it goes much against my
stomach. Hast any philosophy in thee, shepherd?

CORIN: No more but that I know the more one sickens the worse at ease
he is; and that he that wants° money, means, and content is without   20
three good friends; that the property of rain is to wet, and fire to burn;
that good pasture makes fat sheep and that a great cause of the night is
lack of the sun; that he that hath learned no wit° by nature nor art° may
complain of° good breeding or comes of a very dull kindred.

TOUCHSTONE: Such a one is a natural philosopher. Wast ever in court,   25
shepherd?

CORIN: No, truly.

TOUCHSTONE: Then thou art damned.

CORIN: Nay, I hope.°

TOUCHSTONE: Truly, thou art damned, like an ill-roasted egg, all on one   30
side.

CORIN: For not being at court? Your reason.

TOUCHSTONE: Why, if thou never wast at court, thou never saw'st good
manners;° if thou never saw'st good manners,° then thy manners must
be wicked; and wickedness is sin, and sin is damnation. Thou art in a   35
parlous° state, shepherd.

CORIN: Not a whit, Touchstone. Those that are good manners at the court
are as ridiculous in the country as the behavior of the country is most
mockable at the court. You told me you salute° not at the court but
you kiss your hands;° that courtesy would be uncleanly if courtiers were   40
shepherds.

TOUCHSTONE: Instance,° briefly; come, instance.

CORIN: Why, we are still° handling our ewes, and their fells° you know are
greasy.

TOUCHSTONE: Why, do not your courtier's° hands sweat? And is not the   45
grease of a mutton as wholesome as the sweat of a man?° Shallow, shallow.° A better instance, I say. Come.

CORIN: Besides, our hands are hard.

---

16. spare: frugal.   17. humor: temperament.   20. wants: lacks.   23. wit: wisdom.   art: study.
24. complain of: lament the lack of.   29. hope: i.e., hope not.   34. manners: etiquette.   manners: etiquette, morals.   36. parlous: perilous.   39. salute: greet.   39–40. but . . . hands:
without kissing the other person's hands.   42. Instance: proof.   43. still: constantly.   fells:
skins with the wool, or fleeces.   45. your courtier's: your typical courtier's.   45–46. And . . .
man?: (Human sweat was thought to be fat oozing from the pores.)   46–47. Shallow, shallow:
weak or faulty (referring to Corin's reasoning).

TOUCHSTONE: Your lips will feel them the sooner. Shallow again. A more
sounder instance. Come. 50
CORIN: And they are often tarred over° with the surgery of our sheep; and
would you have us kiss tar? The courtier's hands are perfumed with civet.°
TOUCHSTONE: Most shallow man! Thou worm'smeat, in respect of a good
piece of flesh indeed!° Learn of the wise, and perpend°: civet is of a
baser birth than tar, the very uncleanly flux° of a cat. Mend° the instance, 55
shepherd.
CORIN: You have too courtly a wit for me. I'll rest.
TOUCHSTONE: Wilt thou rest damned? God help thee, shallow man! God
make incision° in thee! Thou art raw.°
CORIN: Sir, I am a true laborer: I earn that I eat,° get that I wear, owe no 60
man hate, envy no man's happiness, glad of other men's good, content
with my harm,° and the greatest of my pride is to see my ewes graze and
my lambs suck.
TOUCHSTONE: That is another simple sin° in you, to bring the ewes and
the rams together and to offer° to get your living by the copulation of 65
cattle;° to be bawd to a bellwether,° and to betray a she-lamb of a twelvemonth to crooked-pated° old cuckoldly° ram, out of° all reasonable
match. If thou be'st not damned for this, the devil himself will have no
shepherds;° I cannot see else how thou shouldst scape.°
CORIN: Here comes young Master Ganymede, my new mistress's brother. 70

Enter Rosalind [with a paper, reading].

ROSALIND:
"From the east to western Ind,°
No jewel is like Rosalind.
Her worth, being mounted on the wind,
Through all the world bears Rosalind.

---

51. **tarred over:** anointed with tar on their cuts and sores.   52. **civet:** a musky perfume derived
from glands in the anal pouch of the civet cat. (As Touchstone points out.)   53–54. **Thou . . .
indeed!:** you miserable creature (literally, you food for worms, subject to the decay of death), if
we compare you with any worthy sample of humankind!   54. **perpend:** consider.   55. **flux:**
secretion.   **Mend:** improve.   59. **incision:** a cut, perhaps for the purpose of letting blood
(here, to let out folly); or for seasoning as raw meat is scored and salted before cooking.   **raw:**
(1) wet behind the ears (2) uncooked (3) afflicted with a raw wound.   60. **earn . . . eat:** earn
my living.   61–62. **content . . . harm:** patient with my ill fortune.   64. **simple sin:** sin arising
from simplicity.   65. **offer:** undertake.   66. **cattle:** livestock.   **bellwether:** the leading male
sheep of a flock, wearing a bell.   67. **crooked-pated:** with crooked horns.   **cuckoldly:** i.e.,
horned like a cuckold (husband of an unfaithful wife).   **out of:** contrary to.   68–69. **If . . .
shepherds:** i.e., your only possible escape from damnation would be if the devil should find
shepherds too objectionable to have in hell under any circumstances.   69. **scape:** escape.
71. **Ind:** Indies.

All the pictures fairest lined°   75
Are but black to° Rosalind.
Let no face be kept in mind
But the fair° of Rosalind."

TOUCHSTONE: I'll rhyme you so eight years together,° dinners, and sup-
pers, and sleeping hours excepted. It is the right butter-women's rank to   80
market.°

ROSALIND: Out,° fool!

TOUCHSTONE: For a taste:
If a hart do lack a hind,°
Let him seek out Rosalind.   85
If the cat will after kind,°
So, be sure, will Rosalind.
Wintered° garments must be lined,°
So must slender Rosalind.
They that reap must sheaf and bind;°   90
Then to cart° with Rosalind.
Sweetest nut hath sourest rind;
Such a nut is Rosalind.
He that sweetest rose will find
Must find love's prick° and Rosalind.   95

This is the very false gallop° of verses. Why do you infect yourself with
them?

ROSALIND: Peace, you dull fool! I found them on a tree.

TOUCHSTONE: Truly, the tree yields bad fruit.

ROSALIND: I'll graft it with you,° and then I shall graft it with a medlar.°   100
Then it will be the earliest fruit i'th' country; for you'll be rotten ere you
be half ripe, and that's the right virtue° of the medlar.

TOUCHSTONE: You have said; but whether wisely or no, let the forest
judge.

75. **lined:** drawn.   76. **black to:** dark-complexioned and hence ugly compared to.   78. **fair:**
beauty.   79. **together:** without stop.   80–81. **It is . . . market:** i.e., the rhymes, all alike, follow each other precisely like a line of butter women or dairy women jogging along to market.
82. **Out:** (An exclamation here denoting comic indignation.)   84. **If . . . hind:** if a male deer
longs for a female deer. (Touchstone wryly suggests in his verses that Rosalind is the responsive
object of male desire.)   86. **after kind:** follow its natural instinct.   88. **Wintered:** old, worn;
used in winter.   **lined:** (1) given a winter lining (2) stuffed. (The term was sometimes used for
the copulating of dogs.)   90. **sheaf and bind:** tie in a bundle.   91. **to cart:** (1) onto the harvest cart (2) onto the cart used to carry prostitutes through the streets, exposing them to public
ridicule.   95. **prick:** thorn. (With bawdy suggestion.)   96. **false gallop:** canter.   100. **you:**
(With a pun on "yew.")   **medlar:** a fruit like a small brown-skinned apple that is eaten when it
starts to decay. (With a pun on "meddler.")   102. **right virtue:** true quality.

Enter Celia, with a writing.

ROSALIND: Peace! Here comes my sister, reading. Stand aside.   105
CELIA: [*reads*]
  "Why should this a desert be?
    For° it is unpeopled? No.
  Tongues I'll hang on every tree
    That shall civil sayings° show:
  Some, how brief the life of man   110
    Runs his erring° pilgrimage,
  That the stretching of a span
    Buckles in his sum of age;°
  Some, of violated vows
    Twixt the souls of friend and friend;   115
  But upon the fairest boughs,
    Or at every sentence end,
  Will I 'Rosalinda' write,
    Teaching all that read to know
  The quintessence° of every sprite°   120
    Heaven would in little show.°
  Therefore heaven Nature charged°
    That one body should be filled
  With all graces wide-enlarged.°
    Nature presently distilled   125
  Helen's cheek, but not her heart,°
    Cleopatra's majesty,
  Atalanta's better part,°
    Sad Lucretia's° modesty.
  Thus Rosalind of many parts   130
    By heavenly synod° was devised

---

107. **For:** because.   109. **civil sayings:** maxims of civilized life.   111. **his erring:** its wandering.   112–13. **That . . . age:** i.e., so that a very brief span encompasses his whole life. (A *span* is a handbreadth. See Psalm 39:5.)   120. **quintessence:** highest perfection. (Literally, the fifth essence or element of the medieval alchemists, purer even than fire.)   **sprite:** spirit.   121. **Heaven . . . show:** that heaven wishes to show in one small person, Rosalind (who, in microcosm, embodies the supreme essence of the heavens, or macrocosm).   122. **heaven . . . charged:** heaven commanded Nature.   124. **wide-enlarged:** all-encompassing.   126. **Helen's . . . heart:** i.e., the beauty of Helen of Troy but not her false heart.   128. **Atalanta's better part:** i.e., her beauty or her fleetness of foot, not her scornfulness and greed. (She refused to marry any man who was unable to defeat her in a foot race and, when challenged by Hippomenes, lost to him because Hippomenes dropped in her way three golden apples of the Hesperides.)   129. **Lucretia's:** Lucretia was an honorable Roman lady raped by Tarquin (whose story Shakespeare tells in *The Rape of Lucrece*).   131. **synod:** assembly.

Of many faces, eyes, and hearts
    To have the touches° dearest prized.
Heaven would° that she these gifts should have,
And I to° live and die her slave."   135

ROSALIND: O most gentle Jupiter,° what tedious homily of love have you wearied your parishioners withal, and never cried, "Have patience, good people!"

CELIA: How now? Back,° friends. Shepherd, go off a little. [*To Touchstone*] Go with him, sirrah.°   140

TOUCHSTONE: Come, shepherd, let us make an honorable retreat, though not with bag and baggage,° yet with scrip and scrippage.°

                                      Exit [with Corin].

CELIA: Didst thou hear these verses?

ROSALIND: Oh, yes, I heard them all, and more too, for some of them had in them more feet than the verses would bear.   145

CELIA: That's no matter. The feet might bear the verses.

ROSALIND: Ay, but the feet were lame and could not bear themselves without° the verse and therefore stood lamely in the verse.

CELIA: But didst thou hear without wondering how thy name should be hanged and carved upon these trees?   150

ROSALIND: I was seven of the nine days out of the wonder° before you came; for look here what I found on a palm tree. I was never so berhymed since Pythagoras'° time, that° I was an Irish rat,° which° I can hardly remember.

CELIA: Trow you° who hath done this?   155

ROSALIND: Is it a man?

CELIA: And a chain° that you once wore about his neck. Change you color?

ROSALIND: I prithee, who?

CELIA: Oh, Lord, Lord, it is a hard matter for friends to meet; but mountains may be removed with° earthquakes, and so encounter.°   160

---

133. **touches:** traits.   134. **would:** decreed.   135. **And I to:** and that I should.   136. **Jupiter:** (Often emended to "pulpiter.")   139. **Back:** i.e., move back, away. (Addressed to Corin and Touchstone.)   140. **sirrah:** a form of address to inferiors (here, Touchstone.)   142. **bag and baggage:** i.e., equipment appropriate to a retreating army.   **scrip and scrippage:** shepherd's pouch and its contents.   148. **without:** (1) without the help of (2) outside.   151. **seven . . . wonder:** (A reference to the common phrase "a nine days' wonder.")   153. **Pythagoras:** Greek philosopher credited with the doctrine of the transmigration of souls.   **that:** when.   **Irish rat:** (Refers to a current belief that Irish enchanters could rhyme rats and other animals to death.)   **which:** a thing which.   155. **Trow you:** have you any idea.   157. **And a chain:** and with a chain.   159–60. **it is . . . encounter:** (A playful inversion of the proverb, "Friends may meet, but mountains never greet." Celia appears to be teasing Rosalind's eagerness to meet Orlando.)   160. **removed with:** moved by.

ROSALIND: Nay, but who is it?

CELIA: Is it possible?°

ROSALIND: Nay, I prithee now with most petitionary vehemence, tell me who it is.

CELIA: Oh, wonderful, wonderful, and most wonderful-wonderful! And   165
yet again wonderful, and after that, out of all whooping!°

ROSALIND: Good my complexion!° Dost thou think, though I am capari-soned° like a man, I have a doublet and hose in my disposition?° One inch of delay more is a South Sea of discovery.° I prithee, tell me who is it quickly, and speak apace. I would thou couldst stammer, that thou   170
mightst pour this concealed man out of thy mouth as wine comes out of narrow-mouthed bottle, either too much at once or none at all. I prithee, take the cork out of thy mouth that I may drink thy tidings.

CELIA: So you may put a man in your belly.°

ROSALIND: Is he of God's making?° What manner of man? Is his head   175
worth a hat, or his chin worth a beard?

CELIA: Nay, he hath but a little beard.

ROSALIND: Why, God will send more, if the man will be thankful. Let me stay° the growth of his beard, if thou delay me not the knowledge of his chin.   180

CELIA: It is young Orlando, that tripped up the wrestler's heels and your heart both in an instant.

ROSALIND: Nay, but the devil take mocking. Speak sad brow and true maid.°

CELIA: I' faith, coz, 'tis he.   185

ROSALIND: Orlando?

CELIA: Orlando.

ROSALIND: Alas the day, what shall I do with my doublet and hose? What did he when thou saw'st him? What said he? How looked he? Wherein went he?° What makes° he here? Did he ask for me? Where remains° he?   190
How parted he with thee? And when shalt thou see him again? Answer me in one word.

CELIA: You must borrow me Gargantua's mouth° first; 'tis a word too great

---

162. **possible:** i.e., possible you don't know.   166. **out . . . whooping:** beyond all power to utter.   167. **Good my complexion!:** oh, my (feminine) temperament, my woman's curiosity!   167–68. **caparisoned:** bedecked. (Usually said of a horse.)   168. **I have . . . disposition?:** i.e., that I have a man's patience?   169. **a South Sea of discovery:** i.e., as tedious as a long explor-atory voyage to the South Pacific Ocean.   174. **belly:** (1) stomach (2) womb.   175. **of God's making:** i.e., a real man, not of a tailor's making.   179. **stay:** wait for.   183–84. **sad . . . maid:** i.e., seriously and truthfully.   189–90. **Wherein went he?:** in what clothes was he dressed?   190. **makes:** docs.   **remains:** dwells.   193. **Gargantua's mouth:** (Gargantua is the giant of popular literature who, in Rabelais' novel, swallowed five pilgrims in a salad.)

for any mouth of this age's size. To say ay and no to these particulars is more than to answer in a catechism.° 195

ROSALIND: But doth he know that I am in this forest and in man's apparel? Looks he as freshly as he did the day he wrestled?

CELIA: It is as easy to count atomies° as to resolve the propositions° of a lover. But take a taste of my finding him, and relish it° with good observance.° I found him under a tree, like a dropped acorn. 200

ROSALIND: It may well be called Jove's tree,° when it drops forth such fruit.

CELIA: Give me audience,° good madam.

ROSALIND: Proceed.

CELIA: There lay he, stretched along like a wounded knight.

ROSALIND: Though it be pity to see such a sight, it well becomes° the ground. 205

CELIA: Cry "holla"° to thy tongue, I prithee; it curvets° unseasonably. He was furnished° like a hunter.

ROSALIND: Oh, ominous! He comes to kill my heart.°

CELIA: I would sing my song without a burden.° Thou bring'st° me out of tune. 210

ROSALIND: Do you not know I am a woman? When I think, I must speak. Sweet, say on.

Enter Orlando and Jaques.

CELIA: You bring me out. — Soft,° comes he not here?

ROSALIND: 'Tis he. Slink by, and note him. [*They stand aside and listen.*]

JAQUES: [*To Orlando*] I thank you for your company, but, good faith, I had 215 as lief have been myself alone.

ORLANDO: And so had I; but yet, for fashion° sake, I thank you too for your society.

JAQUES: God b'wi'you.° Let's meet as little as we can.

ORLANDO: I do desire we may be better strangers. 220

JAQUES: I pray you, mar no more trees with writing love songs in their barks.

ORLANDO: I pray you, mar no more of my verses with reading them ill-favoredly.°

194–95. To . . . catechism: to give even yes and no answers to these questions would take longer than to go through the catechism (i.e., the formal questioning used in the Church to teach the principles of faith). 198. atomies: motes, specks of dirt. propositions: questions. 199. relish it: heighten its pleasant taste. 199–200. observance: attention. 201. Jove's tree: the oak. 202. Give me audience: listen to me. 205. becomes: adorns. 206. holla: stop. curvets: prances. 207. furnished: equipped, dressed. 208. heart: (With pun on "hart.") 209. burden: refrain, or bass part. Thou bring'st: you put. 213. Soft: i.e., wait a minute, or, stop talking. 217. fashion: fashion's. 219. God b'wi'you: God be with you, good-bye. 223–24. ill-favoredly: unsympathetically.

JAQUES: Rosalind is your love's name?   225
ORLANDO: Yes, just.°
JAQUES: I do not like her name.
ORLANDO: There was no thought of pleasing you when she was christened.
JAQUES: What stature is she of?
ORLANDO: Just as high as my heart.   230
JAQUES: You are full of pretty answers. Have you not been acquainted
   with goldsmiths' wives, and conned° them out of rings?°
ORLANDO: Not so; but I answer you right painted cloth,° from whence you
   have studied your questions.
JAQUES: You have a nimble wit; I think 'twas made of Atalanta's heels.°   235
   Will you sit down with me? And we two will rail against our mistress the
   world and all our misery.
ORLANDO: I will chide no breather° in the world but myself, against whom
   I know most faults.
JAQUES: The worst fault you have is to be in love.   240
ORLANDO: 'Tis a fault I will not change for your best virtue. I am weary
   of you.
JAQUES: By my troth, I was seeking for a fool when I found you.
ORLANDO: He is drowned in the brook. Look but in, and you shall see him.
JAQUES: There I shall see mine own figure.°   245
ORLANDO: Which I take to be either a fool or a cipher.°
JAQUES: I'll tarry no longer with you. Farewell, good Seigneur Love.
ORLANDO: I am glad of your departure. Adieu, good Monsieur Melancholy.
                                                               [Exit Jaques.]
ROSALIND: [aside to Celia]   I will speak to him like a saucy lackey and under
   that habit play the knave° with him. — Do you hear, forester?   250
ORLANDO: Very well. What would you?
ROSALIND: I pray you, what is't o'clock?
ORLANDO: You should ask me what time o' day. There's no clock in the
   forest.
ROSALIND: Then there is no true lover in the forest, else sighing every   255
   minute and groaning every hour would detect° the lazy foot of Time as
   well as a clock.

---

226. **just:** just so.   232. **conned:** memorized.   **rings:** (Verses or "posies" were often inscribed
in rings.)   233. **right painted cloth:** in the true spirit of a painted cloth decorated with commonplace pictures and cliché mottoes (frequently mythological or scriptural).   235. **Atalanta's
heels:** (See above, the note for line 128.)   238. **breather:** living being.   245. **figure:** reflection. (Narcissus fell in love with his own reflection in a pool.)   246. **cipher:** nonentity, zero.
249–50. **and under . . . knave:** and in that disguise (1) pose as a boy (2) deal mischievously.
256. **detect:** reveal.

ORLANDO: And why not the swift foot of Time? Had not that been as proper?

ROSALIND: By no means, sir. Time travels in divers paces with divers persons. I'll tell you who Time ambles withal,° who Time trots withal, who Time gallops withal, and who he stands still withal.   260

ORLANDO: I prithee, who doth he trot withal?

ROSALIND: Marry, he trots hard with a young maid between the contract of her marriage and the day it is solemnized. If the interim be but a se'nnight,° Time's pace is so hard that it seems the length of seven year.   265

ORLANDO: Who ambles Time withal?

ROSALIND: With a priest that lacks Latin and a rich man that hath not the gout, for the one sleeps easily because he cannot study, and the other lives merrily because he feels no pain, the one lacking the burden of lean° and wasteful° learning, the other knowing no burden of heavy tedious penury. These Time ambles withal.   270

ORLANDO: Who doth he gallop withal?

ROSALIND: With a thief to the gallows, for though he go as softly as foot can fall, he thinks himself too soon there.   275

ORLANDO: Who stays it still withal?

ROSALIND: With lawyers in the vacation; for they sleep between term° and term, and then they perceive not how Time moves.

ORLANDO: Where dwell you, pretty youth?

ROSALIND: With this shepherdess, my sister, here in the skirts of the forest, like fringe upon a petticoat.   280

ORLANDO: Are you native of this place?

ROSALIND: As the coney° that you see dwell where she is kindled.°

ORLANDO: Your accent is something° finer than you could purchase° in so removed° a dwelling.   285

ROSALIND: I have been told so of many. But indeed an old religious° uncle of mine taught me to speak, who was in his youth an inland° man, one that knew courtship° too well, for there he fell in love. I have heard him read many lectures° against it; and I thank God I am not a woman, to be touched° with so many giddy offences as he hath generally taxed their whole sex withal.   290

---

261. withal: with.   266. se'nnight: week.   270. lean: unremunerative.   271. wasteful: making one waste away.   277. term: court session.   283. coney: rabbit.   kindled: littered, born.   284. something: somewhat.   purchase: acquire.   285. removed: remote.   286. religious: i.e., belonging to a religious order.   287. inland: from a center of civilization.   288. courtship: (1) wooing (2) knowledge of courtly manners.   289. read many lectures: deliver many admonitory speeches.   290. touched: tainted.

ORLANDO: Can you remember any of the principal evils that he laid to the charge of women?

ROSALIND: There were none principal; they were all like one another as halfpence are, every one fault seeming monstrous till his° fellow fault   295 came to match it.

ORLANDO: I prithee, recount some of them.

ROSALIND: No, I will not cast away my physic° but on those that are sick. There is a man haunts the forest that abuses our young plants with carving "Rosalind" on their barks, hangs odes upon hawthorns and elegies on   300 brambles, all, forsooth, deifying the name of Rosalind. If I could meet that fancy-monger,° I would give him some good counsel, for he seems to have the quotidian° of love upon him.

ORLANDO: I am he that is so love-shaked. I pray you, tell me your remedy.

ROSALIND: There is none of my uncle's marks upon you. He taught me   305 how to know a man in love, in which cage of rushes° I am sure you are not prisoner.

ORLANDO: What were his marks?

ROSALIND: A lean cheek, which you have not; a blue eye° and sunken, which you have not; an unquestionable° spirit, which you have not; a   310 beard neglected, which you have not—but I pardon you for that, for simply your having in beard is a younger brother's revenue.° Then your hose should be ungartered, your bonnet unbanded,° your sleeve unbuttoned, your shoe untied, and everything about you demonstrating a careless desolation. But you are no such man. You are rather point-device°   315 in your accoutrements, as loving yourself, than seeming the lover of any other.

ORLANDO: Fair youth, I would I could make thee believe I love.

ROSALIND: Me believe it? You may as soon make her that you love believe it, which I warrant she is apter to do than to confess she does. That is one   320 of the points in the which women still° give the lie to their consciences. But, in good sooth,° are you he that hangs the verses on the trees, wherein Rosalind is so admired?

ORLANDO: I swear to thee, youth, by the white hand of Rosalind, I am that he, that unfortunate he.   325

ROSALIND: But are you so much in love as your rhymes speak?

---

295. his: its.   298. physic: medicine.   302. fancy-monger: love peddler.   303. quotidian: fever recurring daily. (See *love-shaked*, line 304.)   306. cage of rushes: i.e., flimsy prison. 309. blue eye: i.e., having dark circles.   310. unquestionable: unwilling to be conversed with. 312. simply . . . revenue: what beard you have is like a younger brother's inheritance (i.e., small).   313. bonnet unbanded: hat lacking a band around the crown.   315. point-device: faultless.   321. still: continually.   322. good sooth: honest truth.

ORLANDO: Neither rhyme nor reason can express how much.

ROSALIND: Love is merely° a madness and, I tell you, deserves as well a
dark house and a whip° as madmen do; and the reason why they are not
so punished and cured is that the lunacy is so ordinary that the whippers   330
are in love too. Yet I profess° curing it by counsel.

ORLANDO: Did you ever cure any so?

ROSALIND: Yes, one, and in this manner. He was to imagine me his love,
his mistress; and I set him every day to woo me. At which time would I,
being but a moonish° youth, grieve, be effeminate, changeable, longing   335
and liking, proud, fantastical, apish, shallow, inconstant, full of tears, full
of smiles; for every passion something and for no passion truly anything,
as boys and women are for the most part cattle of this color; would now
like him, now loathe him; then entertain° him, then forswear him; now
weep for him, then spit at him; that° I drave° my suitor from his mad   340
humor of love to a living humor of madness,° which was to forswear the
full stream of the world and to live in a nook, merely monastic. And thus
I cured him; and this way will I take upon me to wash your liver° as clean
as a sound sheep's heart, that there shall not be one spot of love in't.

ORLANDO: I would not be cured, youth.   345

ROSALIND: I would cure you, if you would but call me Rosalind and come
every day to my cote° and woo me.

ORLANDO: Now by the faith of my love, I will. Tell me where it is.

ROSALIND: Go with me to it, and I'll show it you; and by° the way you
shall tell me where in the forest you live. Will you go?   350

ORLANDO: With all my heart, good youth.

ROSALIND: Nay, you must call me Rosalind. —Come, sister, will you go?

Exeunt.

Act 3, Scene 3°

Enter [Touchstone the] Clown, Audrey, and Jaques [apart].

TOUCHSTONE: Come apace,° good Audrey. I will fetch up your goats,
Audrey. And how,° Audrey, am I the man yet? Doth my simple feature°
content you?

---

328. **merely:** utterly.   329. **dark . . . whip:** (The common treatment of lunatics.)   331. **profess:** am expert in.   335. **moonish:** changeable.   339. **entertain:** receive cordially.   340. **that:**
with the result that.   **drave:** drove.   340–41. **mad . . . madness:** mad fancy of love to a real
madness.   343. **liver:** (Supposed seat of the emotions, especially love.)   347. **cote:** cottage.
349. **by:** on.   **Act 3, Scene 3. Location:** The forest.   1. **apace:** quickly.   2. **And how:** i.e.,
what do you say.   **simple feature:** plain appearance. (But Audrey, in her answer, may have her
mind on *features* as "parts of the body.")

AUDREY: Your features! Lord warrant° us! What features?

TOUCHSTONE: I am here with thee and thy goats, as the most capricious°   5
poet, honest Ovid, was among the Goths.°

JAQUES: [*aside*]   Oh, knowledge ill-inhabited,° worse than Jove in a thatched
house!°

TOUCHSTONE: When a man's verses cannot be understood,° nor a man's
good wit seconded with the forward child, understanding,° it strikes a   10
man more dead than a great reckoning in a little room.° Truly, I would
the gods had made thee poetical.

AUDREY: I do not know what "poetical" is. Is it honest in deed and word?
Is it a true thing?

TOUCHSTONE: No, truly; for the truest poetry is the most feigning,° and   15
lovers are given to poetry, and what they swear in poetry may be said° as
lovers they do feign.°

AUDREY: Do you wish, then, that the gods had made me poetical?

TOUCHSTONE: I do, truly; for thou swear'st to me thou art honest.° Now, if
thou wert a poet, I might have some hope thou didst feign.°   20

AUDREY: Would you not have me honest?

TOUCHSTONE: No, truly, unless thou wert hard-favored;° for honesty°
coupled to beauty is to have honey a sauce to sugar.

JAQUES: [*aside*]   A material° fool!

AUDREY: Well, I am not fair, and therefore I pray the gods make me   25
honest.

TOUCHSTONE: Truly, and to cast away honesty upon a foul° slut were to
put good meat into an unclean dish.

AUDREY: I am not a slut, though I thank the gods I am foul.°

---

4. **warrant:** protect.   5. **capricious:** witty, fanciful. (Derived from the Latin *caper*, "male
goat"; hence, "goatish, lascivious.")   6. **Goths:** (With pun on "goats"; the two words were
pronounced alike.) The line refers to the Roman poet's exile among the Goths.   7. **ill-
inhabited:** ill-lodged.   7–8. **Jove . . . house!:** (An allusion to Ovid's *Metamorphoses* 8, containing the story of Jupiter and Mercury lodging disguised in the humble cottage of Baucis and
Philemon.)   9. **verses . . . understood:** (Ovid's verses were misunderstood by the barbaric
Goths, among whom he lived in exile, just as Touchstone's wit is misunderstood by Audrey.)
9–10. **nor . . . understanding:** (Wisdom, understanding, and memory were thought to occupy
three main ventricles in the brain, and to be interconnected in the process of thought. *Forward*
means "precocious.")   11. **great . . . room:** exorbitant charge for refreshment or lodging in a
cramped tavern room. (Some scholars see in this passage an allusion to the death of Christo
pher Marlowe, who was stabbed by Ingram Frysar at an inn in Deptford in a quarrel over
a tavern reckoning, May 30, 1593.)   15. **feigning:** inventive, imaginative. (But Touchstone
plays on the sense of "false, lying.")   16. **may be said:** i.e., it may be said.   17. **feign:** (With a
further play on "desire.")   19. **honest:** chaste.   20. **feign:** (1) pretend (2) desire.   22. **hard-
favored:** ugly.   **honesty:** chastity.   24. **material:** full of pithy matter.   27. **foul:** ugly.   29. **I
thank . . . foul:** i.e., my unattractive looks are what destiny has allotted to me.

TOUCHSTONE: Well, praised be the gods for thy foulness! Sluttishness 30
may come hereafter. But be it as it may be, I will marry thee, and to
that end I have been with Sir° Oliver Mar-text, the vicar of the next
village, who hath promised to meet me in this place of the forest and to
couple us.

JAQUES: [aside] I would fain° see this meeting. 35

AUDREY: Well, the gods give us joy!

TOUCHSTONE: Amen. A man may, if he were of a fearful heart, stagger° in
this attempt; for here we have no temple but the wood, no assembly but
horn-beasts.° But what though?° Courage! As° horns are odious, they are
necessary.° It is said, "Many a man knows no end of his goods."° Right! 40
Many a man has good horns and knows no end of them.° Well, that is the
dowry° of his wife; 'tis none of his own getting.° Horns? Even so.° Poor
men alone? No, no, the noblest deer° hath them as huge as the rascal.° Is
the single° man therefore blessed? No. As a walled town is more worthier
than a village, so is the forehead of a married man more honorable than 45
the bare brow of a bachelor; and by how much defense° is better than no
skill, by so much is a horn more precious than to want.°

Enter Sir Oliver Mar-text.

Here comes Sir Oliver. — Sir Oliver Mar-text, you are well met. Will you
dispatch us° here under this tree, or shall we go with you to your chapel?

SIR OLIVER: Is there none here to give the woman?° 50

TOUCHSTONE: I will not take her on gift of any man.

SIR OLIVER: Truly, she must be given, or the marriage is not lawful.

JAQUES: [advancing] Proceed, proceed. I'll give her.

TOUCHSTONE: Good even, good Master What-ye-call-'t.° How do you,
sir? You are very well met. God 'ild you° for your last° company. I am 55

---

32. **Sir:** (Courtesy title for a clergyman.)   35. **fain:** gladly.   37. **stagger:** hesitate.   39. **horn-beasts:** antlered animals like deer and cattle, and therefore resembling cuckolded men with their cuckolds' horns.   **what though:** what though it be so.   **As:** though.   40. **necessary:** (1) useful to horned animals (2) unavoidable to cuckolds.   **knows . . . goods:** is endlessly well provided.   41. **knows . . . them:** i.e., is endlessly supplied with cuckold's horns. (A sardonic interpretation of the proverb in line 40.)   42. **dowry:** marriage gift.   **getting:** (1) obtaining (2) begetting (in the sense that his wife's children will not be his).   **Even so:** that's just how it is.   43. **deer:** (1) horned animal (2) dear husband.   **rascal:** (1) young deer that are lean and out of season (2) poor ordinary husband.   44. **single:** unmarried.   46. **defense:** (1) fortifications (including a type known as "hornwork") (2) the art of self-defense.   47. **than to want:** i.e., than to be without a horn. (Recalling the "horn of plenty," which is indeed precious.)   49. **dispatch us:** finish off our business.   50. **give the woman:** give away the bride; conventionally, the bride's father answered the question, "Who giveth this woman to be married to this man?"   54. **What-ye-call-'t:** (Probably joking on *Jakes* as "outhouse.")   55. **'ild you:** yield you, reward you.   **last:** most recent.

very glad to see you. Even a toy in hand° here, sir.—Nay, pray be covered.°

JAQUES: Will you be married, motley?

TOUCHSTONE: As the ox hath his bow,° sir, the horse his curb,° and the falcon her bells,° so man hath his desires; and as pigeons bill,° so wedlock   60
would be nibbling.

JAQUES: And will you, being a man of your breeding, be married under a bush° like a beggar? Get you to church, and have a good priest that can tell you what marriage is.° This fellow will but join you together as they join wainscot; then one of you will prove a shrunk panel, and, like green   65
timber warp,° warp.

TOUCHSTONE: I am not in the mind but I were better° to be married of° him than of another, for he is not like° to marry me well;° and not being well married, it will be a good excuse for me hereafter to leave my wife.

JAQUES: Go thou with me, and let me counsel thee.   70

TOUCHSTONE:

Come, sweet Audrey.
We must be married,° or we must live in bawdry.
Farewell, good Master Oliver; not
   "O sweet Oliver,
   O brave° Oliver,   75
  Leave me not behind thee";
but
   "Wind° away,
   Begone, I say,
I will not to wedding with thee."°   80

                     [*Exeunt Jaques, Touchstone, and Audrey.*]

SIR OLIVER: 'Tis no matter. Ne'er a fantastical° knave of them all shall flout me out of my calling.   *Exit.*

---

56. **a toy in hand:** a trifle to be attended to, or literally by the hand.   56–57. **be covered:** put on your hat, i.e., no need to show respect; or, cover up your bosom. (Said to Audrey, or perhaps to Jaques, who may have removed his hat in sardonic deference to the ceremony.)   59. **bow:** yoke.   **curb:** chain or strap attached to the horse's bit and used to control it.   60. **bells:** (Attached to a falcon's leg during training.)   **bill:** stroke bill with bill.   62–63. **under a bush:** i.e., by a "hedge-priest," an uneducated clergyman.   64. **tell . . . is:** expound the obligations of marriage.   66. **warp:** (1) shrivel and fit badly together (2) stray from the true path.   67. **I am . . . better:** I do not know but that it would be better for me. (Touchstone may be speaking aside here to Jaques.)   **of:** by.   68. **like:** likely.   **well:** (1) suitably (2) legally.   72. **married:** i.e., properly married, as Jaques suggests, not by a hedge-priest. (Having been found out, Touchstone wryly defers matters for the present.)   73–80. **"O . . . thee.":** (Phrases from a current ballad.)   75. **brave:** worthy.   78. **Wind:** wend, go.   81. **fantastical:** affected.

ACT 3, SCENE 4°

Enter Rosalind and Celia.

ROSALIND: Never talk to me. I will weep.

CELIA: Do, I prithee, but yet have the grace to consider that tears do not become a man.

ROSALIND: But have I not cause to weep?

CELIA: As good cause as one would desire; therefore weep.   5

ROSALIND: His very hair is of the dissembling° color.

CELIA: Something° browner than Judas's. Marry, his kisses are Judas's own children.°

ROSALIND: I'faith, his hair is of a good color.

CELIA: An excellent color. Your chestnut° was ever the only° color.   10

ROSALIND: And his kissing is as full of sanctity as the touch of holy bread.°

CELIA: He hath bought a pair of cast° lips of Diana.° A nun of winter's sisterhood° kisses not more religiously; the very ice of chastity is in them.

ROSALIND: But why did he swear he would come this morning, and comes   15
not?

CELIA: Nay, certainly, there is no truth in him.

ROSALIND: Do you think so?

CELIA: Yes. I think he is not a pickpurse nor a horse-stealer, but for his verity in love, I do think him as concave° as a covered goblet or a worm-   20
eaten nut.

ROSALIND: Not true in love?

CELIA: Yes, when he is in, but I think he is not in.

ROSALIND: You have heard him swear downright he was.

CELIA: "Was" is not "is." Besides, the oath of a lover is no stronger than   25
the word of a tapster; they are both the confirmer of false reckonings.°
He attends here in the forest on the Duke your father.

ROSALIND: I met the Duke yesterday, and had much question° with him.
He asked me of what parentage I was. I told him, of as good as he; so he

---

ACT 3, SCENE 4. **Location:** The forest.   **6. the dissembling color:** i.e., reddish, traditionally the color of Judas's hair.   **7. Something:** somewhat.   **7-8. Judas's own children:** i.e., as false and betraying as the kiss given by Judas to Jesus when he betrayed him to the high priests.
10. Your chestnut: i.e., this chestnut color that people talk about.   **only:** only fashionable.
11. holy bread: either the unleavened bread of the Eucharist or ordinary leavened bread that was blessed after the Eucharist and distributed to those who had not received communion.
12. cast: (1) chaste, cold (2) molded (3) cast off.   **Diana:** goddess of chastity.   **12-13. of winter's sisterhood:** i.e., devoted to barrenness and cold.   **20. concave:** hollow, i.e., insincere.
26. false reckonings: (Tapsters, or barkeeps, were notorious for inflating bills.)   **28. question:** conversation.

laughed and let me go. But what° talk we of fathers, when there is such a   30
man as Orlando?

CELIA: Oh, that's a brave° man! He writes brave verses, speaks brave words,
swears brave oaths, and breaks them bravely, quite traverse,° athwart the
heart of his lover, as a puny° tilter, that spurs his horse but° on one side,
breaks his staff like a noble goose.° But all's brave that youth mounts and   35
folly guides.° Who comes here?

Enter Corin.

CORIN:
Mistress and master, you have oft inquired
After the shepherd that complained of° love,
Who you saw sitting by me on the turf,
Praising the proud disdainful shepherdess   40
That was his mistress.

CELIA: Well, and what of him?

CORIN:
If you will see a pageant truly played
Between the pale complexion° of true love
And the red glow of scorn and proud disdain,
Go hence a little, and I shall conduct you,   45
If you will mark° it.

ROSALIND: Oh, come, let us remove!°
The sight of lovers feedeth those in love.
Bring us to this sight, and you shall say
I'll prove a busy actor in their play.   *Exeunt.*

Act 3, Scene 5°

Enter Silvius and Phoebe.

SILVIUS:
Sweet Phoebe, do not scorn me, do not, Phoebe!
Say that you love me not, but say not so
In bitterness. The common executioner,

---

30. **what:** why.   32. **brave:** fine, excellent.   33. **traverse:** across, awry. (A term from medieval jousting or tilting; hence *tilter*, line 34.)   34. **puny:** inexperienced. (Literally, junior.) **but:** only.   35. **a noble goose:** i.e., a goose-headed young gallant.   35–36. **But . . . guides:** but everything is admirable that youth undertakes under the influence of folly. (Said sardonically.)   38. **complained of:** uttered a lament against.   43. **pale complexion:** (Sighing was believed to draw the blood from the heart.)   46. **will mark:** wish to observe.   **remove:** leave here and go. **Act 3, Scene 5. Location:** The forest.

Whose heart th'accustomed sight of death makes hard,
Falls° not the ax upon the humbled neck   5
But first begs pardon.° Will you sterner be
Than he that dies and lives by bloody drops?°

Enter Rosalind, Celia, and Corin [behind].

PHOEBE:
    I would not be thy executioner;
    I fly thee, for I would not injure thee.
    Thou tell'st me there is murder in mine eye.   10
    'Tis pretty, sure,° and very probable,
    That eyes, that are the frail'st and softest things,
    Who shut their coward gates on atomies,°
    Should be called tyrants, butchers, murderers!
    Now I do frown on thee with all my heart,   15
    And if mine eyes can wound, now let them kill thee.
    Now counterfeit to swoon; why, now fall down,
    Or if thou canst not, oh, for shame, for shame,
    Lie not, to say° mine eyes are murderers!
    Now show the wound mine eye hath made in thee.   20
    Scratch thee but with a pin, and there remains
    Some scar of it; lean upon a rush,°
    The cicatrice and capable impressure
    Thy palm some moment keeps;° but now mine eyes,
    Which I have darted at thee, hurt thee not   25
    Nor, I am sure, there is no force in eyes
    That can do hurt.
SILVIUS: O dear Phoebe,
    If ever—as that "ever" may be near—
    You meet in some fresh cheek the power of fancy,°
    Then shall you know the wounds invisible   30
    That love's keen arrows make.
PHOEBE: But till that time
    Come not thou near me; and when that time comes,

---

5. Falls: lets fall.   **6. But first begs pardon:** without first begging pardon (as executioners did in Elizabethan times).   **7. dies . . . drops:** makes his living by the deaths of others. (Stated as an oxymoron.)   **11. sure:** to be sure.   **13. coward gates on atomies:** i.e., sensitive eyelids to protect against specks of dirt.   **19. to say:** by saying.   **22. a rush:** a reed.   **23–24. The cicatrice . . . keeps:** the scarlike and perceptible impression is retained by one's palm for a moment.   **29. You . . . fancy:** you yourself feel the powerful spell of love for some new face.

Afflict me with thy mocks; pity me not,
As° till that time I shall not pity thee.

ROSALIND: [*advancing*]

And why, I pray you? Who might be your mother,°   35
That you insult,° exult, and all at once,°
Over the wretched? What though you have no beauty°—
As, by my faith, I see no more in you
Than without candle may go dark to bed°—
Must you be therefore proud and pitiless?   40
Why, what means this? Why do you look on me?
I see no more in you than in the ordinary°
Of nature's sale-work.° 'Od's° my little life,
I think she means to tangle° my eyes too!
No faith, proud mistress, hope not after it.   45
'Tis not your inky brows, your black silk hair,
Your bugle° eyeballs, nor your cheek of cream
That can entame my spirits to your worship.°
[*To Silvius*] You foolish shepherd, wherefore do you follow her,
Like foggy south,° puffing with wind and rain?   50
You are a thousand times a properer° man
Than she a woman. 'Tis such fools as you
That makes the world full of ill-favored° children.
'Tis not her glass,° but you, that flatters her,
And out of you° she sees herself more proper   55
Than any of her lineaments° can show her.—
But, mistress, know yourself. Down on your knees,
And thank heaven, fasting, for a good man's love!
For I must tell you friendly in your ear,
Sell when you can. You are not for all markets.   60
Cry the man mercy,° love him, take his offer;

---

34. **As:** since. 35. **Who . . . mother:** (1) what human mother could have produced so inhuman a daughter (2) from what sort of a mother did you learn such scorn. 36. **insult:** exult scornfully. **all at once:** all at the same time. 37. **have no beauty:** are not particularly beautiful. 38–39. **I see . . . bed:** i.e., I see nothing in your beauty that might not go entirely unnoticed, nothing to distinguish you from other young women. 42. **ordinary:** common run. 43. **sale-work:** ready-made products, not of the best quality, not distinctive. **'Od's:** may God save. 44. **tangle:** ensnare. 47. **bugle:** beadlike, black and glassy. 48. **to your worship:** (1) to the worship of you (2) to adore Your Worship (as such beauty deserved an honorific title). 50. **south:** south wind (from which came fog and rain; hence, Silvius's sighs and tears). 51. **properer:** better-looking (since handsome is as handsome does). 53. **ill-favored:** ugly. 54. **glass:** mirror. 55. **out of you:** i.e., with you as her mirror. 56. **lineaments:** features. 61. **Cry . . . mercy:** beg the man's pardon.

Foul is most foul, being foul to be a scoffer.° —
So take her to thee, shepherd. Fare you well.

PHOEBE:
Sweet youth, I pray you chide a year together.°
I had rather hear you chide than this man woo.   65

ROSALIND: [*to Phoebe*]   He's fallen in love with your foulness, [*to Silvius*] and
she'll fall in love with my anger. If it be so, as fast as she answers thee
with frowning looks, I'll sauce° her with bitter words. [*To Phoebe*] Why
look you so upon me?

PHOEBE: For no ill will I bear you.   70

ROSALIND:
I pray you, do not fall in love with me,
For I am falser than vows made in wine.°
Besides, I like you not. [*To Silvius*] If you will know my house,
'Tis at the tuft of olives here hard by. —
Will you go, sister? — Shepherd, ply her hard.° —   75
Come, sister. — Shepherdess, look on him better,
And be not proud. Though all the world could see,°
None could be so abused in sight° as he. —
Come, to our flock.   *Exit* [*with Celia and Corin*].

PHOEBE:
Dead shepherd,° now I find thy saw° of might,°   80
"Who ever loved that loved not at first sight?"°

SILVIUS:
Sweet Phoebe —

PHOEBE: Ha! What say'st thou, Silvius?

SILVIUS: Sweet Phoebe, pity me.

PHOEBE:
Why, I am sorry for thee, gentle Silvius.

SILVIUS:
Wherever sorrow is, relief would be.°   85
If you do sorrow at my grief in love,
By giving love, your sorrow and my grief
Were both extermined.°

---

62. Foul . . . scoffer: i.e., unattractive behavior like yours is at its most foul when it consists of
scoffing. (Plays on two meanings of *foul*.)   **64. together:** without intermission.   **68. sauce:**
rebuke.   **72. in wine:** while drunk.   **75. ply her hard:** woo her energetically.   **77. could see:**
could look at you.   **78. abused in sight:** deceived through the eyes.   **80. Dead shepherd:**
i.e., Christopher Marlowe, who died in 1593.   **saw:** saying.   **of might:** forceful, convincing.
81. Who . . . sight?: (From Marlowe's *Hero and Leander*, Sestiad 1, 176, first published in 1598.)
85. Wherever . . . be: sorrow cries out for relief.   **88. Were both extermined:** would both be
exterminated, ended.

PHOEBE:
 Thou hast my love. Is not that neighborly?°
SILVIUS:
 I would have you.
PHOEBE: Why, that were covetousness.°   90
 Silvius, the time was that I hated thee,
 And yet it is not° that I bear thee love;
 But since that° thou canst talk of love so well,
 Thy company, which erst° was irksome to me,
 I will endure, and I'll employ thee too.   95
 But do not look for further recompense
 Than thine own gladness that thou art employed.
SILVIUS:
 So holy and so perfect is my love,
 And I in such a poverty of grace,°
 That I shall think it a most plenteous crop   100
 To glean the broken ears after the man
 That the main harvest reaps. Loose now and then
 A scattered° smile, and that I'll live upon.
PHOEBE:
 Know'st thou the youth that spoke to me erewhile?°
SILVIUS:
 Not very well, but I have met him oft,   105
 And he hath bought the cottage and the bounds°
 That the old carlot° once was master of.
PHOEBE:
 Think not I love him, though I ask for him.
 'Tis but a peevish boy—yet he talks well—
 But what care I for words? Yet words do well   110
 When he that speaks them pleases those that hear.
 It is a pretty youth—not very pretty—
 But sure he's proud—and yet his pride becomes him.
 He'll make a proper° man. The best thing in him
 Is his complexion; and faster than his tongue   115
 Did make offense, his eye did heal it up.

---

89. **Is . . . neighborly?:** i.e., may not I love you in the sense of loving one's neighbor as oneself?
90. **covetousness:** (The tenth commandment forbids coveting anything that is one's neighbor's.)   92. **yet it is not:** the time has not yet come.   93. **since that:** since.   94. **erst:** formerly.
99. **poverty of grace:** lack of reciprocated affection.   103. **scattered:** thrown negligently, as in the gleanings of the harvest.   104. **erewhile:** just now.   106. **bounds:** pastures.   107. **carlot:** churl, countryman. (Perhaps a proper name.)   114. **proper:** handsome.

He is not very tall—yet for his years he's tall.
His leg is but so-so—and yet 'tis well.
There was a pretty redness in his lip,
A little riper and more lusty red   120
Than that mixed in his cheek; 'twas just the difference
Betwixt the constant red and mingled damask.°
There be some women, Silvius, had they marked him
In parcels° as I did, would have gone near
To fall° in love with him; but for my part,   125
I love him not nor hate him not; and yet
I have more cause to hate him than to love him.
For what had he to do° to chide at me?
He said mine eyes were black, and my hair black,
And, now I am remembered,° scorned at me.   130
I marvel why I answered not again.°
But that's all one; omittance is no quittance.°
I'll write to him a very taunting letter,
And thou shalt bear it. Wilt thou, Silvius?

SILVIUS:
Phoebe, with all my heart.

PHOEBE: I'll write it straight;°   135
The matter's in my head and in my heart.
I will be bitter with him and passing short.°
Go with me, Silvius.   *Exeunt.*

ACT 4, SCENE 1°

Enter Rosalind and Celia, and Jaques.

JAQUES: I prithee, pretty youth, let me be better acquainted with thee.
ROSALIND: They say you are a melancholy fellow.
JAQUES: I am so. I do love it better than laughing.
ROSALIND: Those that are in extremity of° either are abominable fellows
     and betray themselves to every modern censure° worse than drunkards.   5
JAQUES: Why, 'tis good to be sad and say nothing.

---

122. **mingled damask:** mingled red and white, the color of the damask rose.   124. **In parcels:**
bit by bit.   124–25: **gone . . . fall:** been on the point of falling.   128. **what . . . do:** what business had he.   130. **am remembered:** remember.   131. **again:** back.   132. **But . . . quittance:**
i.e., but just the same, my failure to answer him doesn't mean I won't do so later.   135. **straight:**
immediately.   137. **passing short:** exceedingly curt.   ACT 4, SCENE 1. **Location:** The forest.
4. **are . . . of:** go to extremes in.   5. **modern censure:** common judgment.

ROSALIND: Why then, 'tis good to be a post.

JAQUES: I have neither the scholar's melancholy, which is emulation,° nor the musician's, which is fantastical,° nor the courtier's, which is proud, nor the soldier's, which is ambitious, nor the lawyer's, which is politic,° nor the lady's, which is nice,° nor the lover's, which is all these; but it is a melancholy of mine own, compounded of many simples, extracted from many objects, and indeed the sundry contemplation of my travels, in which my often rumination wraps me in a most humorous sadness.°

ROSALIND: A traveler! By my faith, you have great reason to be sad. I fear you have sold your own lands to see other men's. Then to have seen much and to have nothing is to have rich eyes and poor hands.

JAQUES: Yes, I have gained my experience.

Enter Orlando.

ROSALIND: And your experience makes you sad. I had rather have a fool to make me merry than experience to make me sad—and to travel° for it too!

ORLANDO: Good day and happiness, dear Rosalind!

JAQUES: Nay, then, God b'wi' you, an° you talk in blank verse.

ROSALIND: Farewell, Monsieur Traveler. Look° you lisp° and wear strange suits, disable° all the benefits of your own country, be out of love with your nativity,° and almost chide God for making you that countenance you are,° or I will scarce think you have swam in a gondola.° [*Exit Jaques.*] Why, how now, Orlando, where have you been all this while? You a lover? An you serve me such another trick, never come in my sight more.

ORLANDO: My fair Rosalind, I come within an hour of my promise.

ROSALIND: Break an hour's promise in love? He that will divide a minute into a thousand parts and break but a part of the thousandth part of a minute in the affairs of love, it may be said of him that Cupid hath clapped him o'th' shoulder, but I'll warrant him heart-whole.°

ORLANDO: Pardon me, dear Rosalind.

8. **emulation:** envy (of the fellow scholar). 9. **fantastical:** extravagantly fanciful. 10. **politic:** grave and diplomatic, calculated. 11. **nice:** fastidious. 12–14. **compounded . . . sadness:** made up of many ingredients, extracted from the many objects of my observation and, indeed, from the diversified considerations of my travels, my frequent rumination upon which wraps me in a most whimsical and moody sadness. 20. **travel:** (Meaning also "travail," labor.) 23. **an:** if. 24. **Look:** be sure. (Said ironically.) **lisp:** i.e., affect a foreign accent. 25. **disable:** disparage. 26. **nativity:** country of birth. 27. **are:** i.e., have. **swam . . . gondola:** floated in a gondola, i.e., been in Venice, where almost all travelers go. 33–34. **Cupid . . . heart-whole:** Cupid may have tried to arrest him, but I'm sure his heart remains unengaged. (Arresting officers customarily grasped the culprit by the shoulder.)

ROSALIND: Nay, an you be so tardy, come no more in my sight. I had as
lief° be wooed of° a snail.

ORLANDO: Of a snail?

ROSALIND: Ay, of a snail; for though he comes slowly, he carries his house
on his head—a better jointure,° I think, than you make a woman.°   40
Besides, he brings his destiny with him.

ORLANDO: What's that?

ROSALIND: Why, horns,° which such as you are fain° to be beholding° to
your wives for. But he comes armed in his fortune,° and prevents the
slander of his wife.   45

ORLANDO: Virtue is no horn-maker; and my Rosalind is virtuous.

ROSALIND: And I am your Rosalind.

CELIA: It pleases him to call you so; but he hath a Rosalind of a better leer°
than you.

ROSALIND: Come, woo me, woo me, for now I am in a holiday humor,   50
and like enough to consent. What would you say to me now, an I were
your very very Rosalind?

ORLANDO: I would kiss before I spoke.

ROSALIND: Nay, you were better speak first, and when you were graveled°
for lack of matter, you might take occasion to kiss. Very good orators,   55
when they are out,° they will spit; and for lovers lacking—God warrant°
us!—matter, the cleanliest shift° is to kiss.

ORLANDO: How if the kiss be denied?

ROSALIND: Then she puts you to entreaty, and there begins new matter.

ORLANDO: Who could be out, being before his beloved mistress?   60

ROSALIND: Marry, that should you, if I were your mistress, or I should
think my honesty ranker° than my wit.

ORLANDO: What, of my suit?°

ROSALIND: Not out of your apparel, and yet out of your suit. Am not I
your Rosalind?   65

---

37. lief: willingly.   **of:** by.   **40. jointure:** marriage settlement.   **than . . . woman:** than you,
Orlando, are able to settle on your prospective wife.   **43. horns:** (1) snails' horns (2) cuckold's horns, signs of an unfaithful wife.   **fain:** obliged.   **beholding:** beholden, indebted.
44. But . . . fortune: the snail comes already provided with the horns that are his nature and
his destiny, thereby forestalling the scandal that would otherwise attach to his wife. (Since a
snail is naturally horned, no scandal can be adduced from them.)   **48. leer:** appearance, color.
54. graveled: stuck. (Literally, run aground on a shoal.)   **56. out:** at a loss through forgetfulness or confusion.   **warrant:** defend.   **57. shift:** tactic.   **62. honesty ranker:** chastity more
corrupt. (Rosalind would rely on her wit to keep her lover off balance and thus defend her
chastity. She may use Orlando's *out*, line 60, in a sexual sense of not being admitted.)   **63. of
my suit:** (Orlando means "out of my suit," at a loss for words in my wooing; but Rosalind puns
on the meaning "suit of clothes"; to be out of apparel would be to be undressed.)

ORLANDO: I take some joy to say you are, because I would be talking of her.

ROSALIND: Well, in her person, I say I will not have you.

ORLANDO: Then, in mine own person, I die.

ROSALIND: No, faith, die by attorney.° The poor world is almost six thousand years old,° and in all this time there was not any man died° in his   70
own person, videlicet,° in a love cause. Troilus° had his brains dashed out
with a Grecian club,° yet he did what he could to die before, and he is
one of the patterns of love. Leander,° he would have lived many a fair
year though Hero had turned nun, if it had not been for a hot midsummer night; for, good youth, he went but forth to wash him in the Helles-   75
pont and being taken with the cramp was drowned; and the foolish
chroniclers of that age found it was°—Hero of Sestos. But these are all
lies. Men have died from time to time, and worms have eaten them, but
not for love.

ORLANDO: I would not have my right° Rosalind of this mind, for I protest°   80
her frown might kill me.

ROSALIND: By this hand, it will not kill a fly. But come, now I will be your
Rosalind in a more coming-on° disposition; and ask me what you will,
I will grant it.

ORLANDO: Then love me, Rosalind.   85

ROSALIND: Yes, faith, will I, Fridays and Saturdays and all.

ORLANDO: And wilt thou have me?

ROSALIND: Ay, and twenty such.

ORLANDO: What sayest thou?

ROSALIND: Are you not good?   90

ORLANDO: I hope so.

ROSALIND: Why then, can one desire too much of a good thing? Come,
sister, you shall be the priest and marry us.—Give me your hand,
Orlando.—What do you say, sister?

ORLANDO: Pray thee, marry us.   95

CELIA: I cannot say the words.

ROSALIND: You must begin, "Will you, Orlando—"

CELIA: Go to.° Will you, Orlando, have to wife this Rosalind?

---

69. **attorney:** proxy. **69–70. six . . . old:** (A common figure in biblical calculation.) **70. died:**
who died. **71. videlicet:** namely. **Troilus:** hero of the story of Troilus and Cressida, in
which he remains faithful to her, but she is faithless to him. **71–72. had . . . club:** (Troilus
was slain by Achilles with sword or spear in more traditional accounts. Rosalind's version
is calculatedly unromantic.) **73. Leander:** the male protagonist of the story of Hero and
Leander, who lost his life swimming the Hellespont to visit his sweetheart. (Rosalind's account
of the cramp again undercuts romantic idealism.) **77. found it was:** arrived at the verdict that
the cause (of his death) was. **80. right:** real. **protest:** insist, proclaim. **83. coming-on:** com-
pliant. **98. Go to:** (An exclamation of mild impatience.)

ORLANDO: I will.

ROSALIND: Ay, but when?   100

ORLANDO: Why now, as fast as she can marry us.

ROSALIND: Then you must say, "I take thee, Rosalind, for wife."

ORLANDO: I take thee, Rosalind, for wife.

ROSALIND: I might ask you for your commission;° but I do take thee, Orlando, for my husband. There's a girl goes before the priest,° and cer-   105
tainly a woman's thought runs before her actions.°

ORLANDO: So do all thoughts; they are winged.

ROSALIND: Now tell me how long you would have her after you have possessed her.

ORLANDO: For ever and a day.   110

ROSALIND: Say "a day," without the "ever." No, no, Orlando, men are April when they woo, December when they wed. Maids are May when they are maids, but the sky changes when they are wives. I will be more jealous of thee than a Barbary cock-pigeon° over his hen, more clamor-
ous than a parrot against° rain, more newfangled° than an ape, more giddy   115
in my desires than a monkey. I will weep for nothing,° like Diana in the fountain,° and I will do that when you are disposed to be merry; I will laugh like a hyena, and that when thou art inclined to sleep.

ORLANDO: But will my Rosalind do so?

ROSALIND: By my life, she will do as I do.   120

ORLANDO: Oh, but she is wise.

ROSALIND: Or else she could not have the wit to do this. The wiser, the waywarder.° Make° the doors upon a woman's wit, and it will out at the casement;° shut that, and 'twill out at the keyhole; stop that, 'twill fly with the smoke out at the chimney.   125

ORLANDO: A man that had a wife with such a wit, he might say, "Wit, whither wilt?"°

---

104. ask . . . commission: ask you what authority you have for taking her (since no one is here to give the bride away and since she herself has not yet consented).   105. goes . . . priest: who anticipates before the "priest" has even asked the question.   106. runs . . . actions: i.e., goes flightily on, outstripping sane conduct.   114. Barbary cock-pigeon: an ornamental pigeon actually from the Orient, not the Barbary (north) coast of Africa. (Following Pliny, the cock-pigeon's jealousy was often contrasted with the mildness of the hen.)   115. against: in expectation of.   newfangled: infatuated with novelty.   116. for nothing: for no apparent reason.   116–17. Diana in the fountain: (Diana frequently appeared as the centerpiece of fountains. Stow's *Survey of London* describes the setting up of a fountain with a Diana in green marble in the year 1596.)   122–23. The wiser, the waywarder: i.e., the more experience in the war of the sexes, the more insisting on her own way.   123. Make: make fast, shut.   124. casement: hinged window.   126–27. Wit, whither wilt?: wit, where are you going? (A common Elizabethan expression implying that one is talking fantastically, with a wildly wandering wit.)

ROSALIND: Nay, you might keep that check° for it till you met your wife's wit going to your neighbor's bed.

ORLANDO: And what wit could wit have to excuse that? 130

ROSALIND: Marry, to say she came to seek you there. You shall never take her without her answer unless you take her without her tongue. Oh, that woman that cannot make her fault her husband's occasion,° let her never nurse her child herself, for she will breed it° like a fool!

ORLANDO: For these two hours, Rosalind, I will leave thee. 135

ROSALIND: Alas, dear love, I cannot lack thee two hours!

ORLANDO: I must attend the Duke at dinner. By two o'clock I will be with thee again.

ROSALIND: Ay, go your ways, go your ways. I knew what you would prove. My friends told me as much, and I thought no less. That flattering tongue 140 of yours won me. 'Tis but one cast away,° and so, come death! Two o'clock is your hour?

ORLANDO: Ay, sweet Rosalind.

ROSALIND: By my troth, and in good earnest, and so God mend me, and by all pretty oaths that are not dangerous,° if you break one jot of your 145 promise or come one minute behind your hour, I will think you the most pathetical° break-promise, and the most hollow lover, and the most unworthy of her you call Rosalind, that may be chosen out of the gross band° of the unfaithful. Therefore beware my censure, and keep your promise. 150

ORLANDO: With no less religion° than if thou wert indeed my Rosalind. So, adieu.

ROSALIND: Well, Time is the old justice that examines all such offenders, and let Time try.° Adieu. *Exit* [*Orlando*].

CELIA: You have simply misused° our sex in your love prate. We must have 155 your doublet and hose plucked over your head and show the world what the bird hath done to her own nest.°

ROSALIND: Oh, coz, coz, coz, my pretty little coz, that thou didst know how many fathom deep I am in love! But it cannot be sounded;° my affection hath an unknown bottom, like the Bay of Portugal. 160

---

128. **check:** retort.   133. **make . . . occasion:** i.e., turn a defense of her own conduct into an accusation against her husband.   134. **breed it:** bring it up.   141. **but one cast away:** only one woman jilted.   145. **dangerous:** i.e., blasphemous. (Rosalind's oaths are decorous.) 147. **pathetical:** awful, miserable.   148–49. **gross band:** whole troop.   151. **religion:** strict fidelity.   154. **try:** determine, judge.   155. **simply misused:** absolutely slandered.   155–57. **We . . . nest:** i.e., we must expose you for what you are, a woman, and show everyone how a woman has defamed her own kind just as a foul bird proverbially fouls its own nest.   159. **sounded:** measured for depth.

CELIA: Or rather, bottomless, that° as fast as you pour affection in, it
runs out.

ROSALIND: No, that same wicked bastard of Venus,° that was begot of
thought,° conceived of spleen,° and born of madness, that blind rascally
boy that abuses° everyone's eyes because his own are out,° let him be judge   165
how deep I am in love. I'll tell thee, Aliena, I cannot be out of the sight of
Orlando. I'll go find a shadow,° and sigh till he come.

CELIA: And I'll sleep.   *Exeunt.*

ACT 4, SCENE 2°

Enter Jaques and Lords [dressed as] foresters.

JAQUES: Which is he that killed the deer?

FIRST LORD: Sir, it was I.

JAQUES: Let's present him to the Duke, like a Roman conqueror, and it
would do well to set the deer's horns upon his head for a branch° of victory. Have you no song, Forester, for this purpose?   5

SECOND LORD: Yes, sir.

JAQUES: Sing it. 'Tis no matter how it be in tune, so° it make noise enough.
                                                                    Music.

                              Song.

SECOND LORD: [*sings*]
        What shall he have that killed the deer?
        His leather skin and horns to wear.
        Then sing him home; the rest shall bear   10
            This burden.°
        Take thou no scorn° to wear the horn;
        It was a crest ere thou wast born.
            Thy father's father wore it,
            And thy father bore it.   15
        The horn, the horn, the lusty horn,
        Is not a thing to laugh to scorn.   *Exeunt.*

---

161. **that:** so that.   163. **bastard of Venus:** i.e., Cupid, son of Venus and Mercury (or
Zeus) rather than Vulcan, Venus's husband.   164. **thought:** fancy. **spleen:** i.e., impulse.
165. **abuses:** deceives. **out:** blinded.   167. **shadow:** shady spot. ACT 4, SCENE 2. Location: The forest.   4. **branch:** wreath.   7. **so:** provided that.   10–11. **bear This burden:**
(1) sing this refrain (2) wear the horns that all cuckolds must wear.   12. **Take . . . scorn:** be not
ashamed. (Alludes to joke about cuckold's horns.)

ACT 4, SCENE 3°

Enter Rosalind and Celia.

ROSALIND: How say you now? Is it not past two o'clock? And here much°
Orlando!

CELIA: I warrant° you, with pure love and troubled brain he hath ta'en his
bow and arrows and is gone forth—to sleep.

Enter Silvius [with a letter].

Look who comes here.   5

SILVIUS: [*to Rosalind*]
My errand is to you, fair youth.
My gentle Phoebe did bid me give you this.   [*He gives the letter.*]
I know not the contents, but as I guess,
By the stern brow and waspish action
Which she did use as she was writing of it,   10
It bears an angry tenor. Pardon me;
I am but as a guiltless messenger.

ROSALIND: [*examining the letter*]
Patience herself would startle at this letter
And play the swaggerer. Bear this, bear all!°
She says I am not fair, that I lack manners;   15
She calls me proud, and that she could not love me
Were man as rare as phoenix.° 'Od's my will!°
Her love is not the hare that I do hunt.
Why writes she so to me? Well, shepherd, well,
This is a letter of your own device.   20

SILVIUS:
No, I protest, I know not the contents.
Phoebe did write it.

ROSALIND: Come, come, you are a fool,
And turned° into the extremity of love.
I saw her hand; she has a leathern° hand,
A freestone-colored° hand. I verily did think   25

ACT 4, SCENE 3. Location: The forest.   1. much: (Said ironically: A fat lot we see of
Orlando!)   3. warrant: assure.   13–14. Patience . . . all!: Patience herself would be startled
into a violent display by this letter. If one were to put up with such a missive, one would have
to accept any insult!   17. phoenix: a fabulous bird of Arabia, the only one of its kind, which
lived five hundred years, died in flames, and was reborn of its own ashes.   'Od's my will!:
(An oath: "May God's will be done!")   23. turned: transformed.   24. leathern: leathery.
25. freestone-colored: sandstone-colored, brownish-yellow.

That her old gloves were on, but 'twas her hands;
She has a huswife's hand°—but that's no matter.
I say she never did invent this letter;
This is a man's invention, and his hand.

SILVIUS: Sure it is hers. 30

ROSALIND:
Why, 'tis a boisterous and a cruel style,
A style for challengers. Why, she defies me,
Like Turk to Christian. Women's gentle brain
Could not drop forth such giant-rude invention,
Such Ethiop° words, blacker in their effect 35
Than in their countenance.° Will you hear the letter?

SILVIUS:
So please you, for I never heard it yet;
Yet heard too much of Phoebe's cruelty.

ROSALIND:
She Phoebes me.° Mark how the tyrant writes.
    (Read) "Art thou god to shepherd turned, 40
    That a maiden's heart hath burned?"
Can a woman rail thus?

SILVIUS: Call you this railing?

ROSALIND:
    (Read) "Why, thy godhead laid apart,°
    War'st thou with a woman's heart?" 45
Did you ever hear such railing?
    "Whiles the eye of man did woo me,
    That could do no vengeance° to me."—
Meaning me° a beast.
    "If the scorn of your bright eyne° 50
    Have power to raise such love in mine,
    Alack, in me what strange effect
    Would they work in mild aspect!°
    Whiles you chid° me, I did love;
    How then might your prayers move! 55
    He that brings this love to thee

27. hand: handwriting. (With play on "dishpan hands.") 35. Ethiop: i.e., black.
35–36. blacker . . . countenance: even blacker in what they say than in their black appearance
on the page. 39. Phoebes me: i.e., addresses me in her cruel style. 44. thy . . . apart: having laid aside your godhead (for human shape). 48. vengeance: mischief, harm. 49. Meaning me: i.e., implying that I am. 50. eyne: eyes. 53. in mild aspect: i.e., if they looked on
me mildly. (Suggests also astrological influence.) 54. chid: chided.

Little knows this love in me;
And by him seal up thy mind,°
Whether that thy youth and kind°
Will the faithful offer take   60
Of me and all that I can make,°
Or else by him my love deny,
And then I'll study how to die."

SILVIUS: Call you this chiding?

CELIA: Alas, poor shepherd!   65

ROSALIND: Do you pity him? No, he deserves no pity. —Wilt thou love
such a woman? What, to make thee an instrument° and play false strains°
upon thee! Not to be endured! Well, go your way to her, for I see love
hath made thee a tame snake,° and say this to her: that if she love me, I
charge her to love thee; if she will not, I will never have her unless thou   70
entreat for her. If you be a true lover, hence, and not a word; for here
comes more company.   *Exit Silvius.*

Enter Oliver.

OLIVER:
Good morrow, fair ones. Pray you, if you know,
Where in the purlieus° of this forest stands
A sheepcote fenced about with olive trees?   75

CELIA:
West of this place, down in the neighbor bottom;°
The rank of osiers° by the murmuring stream
Left° on your right hand brings you to the place.
But at this hour the house doth keep itself;
There's none within.   80

OLIVER:
If that an eye may profit by a tongue,
Then should I know you by description,
Such garments and such years: "The boy is fair,
Of female favor,° and bestows° himself
Like a ripe° sister; the woman, low   85

---

58. by . . . mind: i.e., send your thoughts in a letter via Silvius.   59. Whether . . . kind:
if your youthful nature.   61. make: make offer of.   67. to make . . . instrument: to make
an instrument (i.e., messenger) of you. (With a suggestion of making a person into a musical instrument; cf. *Hamlet*, 3.2.363, "You would play upon me," etc.)   strains: parts of a piece
of music.   69. tame snake: i.e., pathetic wretch.   74. purlieus: borders, boundaries.
76. neighbor bottom: neighboring dell.   77. rank of osiers: row of willows.   78. Left: left
behind, passed.   84. favor: features.   bestows: comports.   85. ripe: mature or elder.

And browner than her brother." Are not you
The owner of the house I did inquire for?

CELIA:
It is no boast, being asked, to say we are.

OLIVER:
Orlando doth commend him° to you both,
And to that youth he calls his Rosalind   90
He sends this bloody napkin.° Are you he?

[*He produces a bloody handkerchief.*]

ROSALIND:
I am. What must we understand by this?

OLIVER:
Some of my shame, if you will know of me
What man I am, and how, and why, and where
This handkerchief was stained.

CELIA: I pray you, tell it.   95

OLIVER:
When last the young Orlando parted from you,
He left a promise to return again
Within an hour; and, pacing through the forest,
Chewing the food of sweet and bitter fancy,°
Lo, what befell! He threw his eye aside,   100
And mark what object did present itself:
Under an old oak, whose boughs were mossed with age
And high top bald with dry antiquity,
A wretched, ragged man, o'ergrown with hair,
Lay sleeping on his back. About his neck   105
A green and gilded snake had wreathed itself,
Who with her head, nimble in threats, approached
The opening of his mouth; but suddenly,
Seeing Orlando, it unlinked° itself
And with indented° glides did slip away   110
Into a bush, under which bush's shade
A lioness, with udders all drawn dry,°
Lay couching, head on ground, with catlike watch,
When° that the sleeping man should stir; for 'tis
The royal disposition of that beast   115

---

89. **doth commend him**: sends his greetings.   91. **napkin**: handkerchief.   99. **Chewing . . . fancy**: ruminating on the bittersweet nature of love.   109. **unlinked**: uncoiled.   110. **indented**: zigzag.   112. **with . . . dry**: (It would therefore be fierce with hunger.)   114. **When**: for the moment.

To prey on nothing that doth seem as dead.
This seen, Orlando did approach the man,
And found it was his brother, his elder brother.

CELIA:
Oh, I have heard him speak of that same brother,
And he did render him° the most unnatural   120
That lived amongst men.

OLIVER: And well he might so do,
For well I know he was unnatural.

ROSALIND:
But to Orlando: did he leave him there,
Food to the sucked and hungry lioness?

OLIVER:
Twice did he turn his back, and purposed so;   125
But kindness, nobler ever than revenge,
And nature, stronger than his just occasion,°
Made him give battle to the lioness,
Who quickly fell before him; in which hurtling°
From miserable slumber I awaked.   130

CELIA:
Are you his brother?

ROSALIND: Was't you he rescued?

CELIA:
Was't you that did so oft contrive to kill him?

OLIVER:
'Twas I, but 'tis not I. I do not shame°
To tell you what I was, since my conversion
So sweetly tastes, being the thing I am.   135

ROSALIND:
But for° the bloody napkin?

OLIVER: By and by.
When from the first to last, betwixt us two
Tears our recountments° had most kindly bathed,
As how I came into that desert place,
In brief, he led me to the gentle Duke,   140
Who gave me fresh array° and entertainment,°
Committing me unto my brother's love;

120. **render him:** describe him as.   127. **just occasion:** just opportunity and motive (for revenge).   129. **hurtling:** conflict, tumult.   133. **do not shame:** am not ashamed.   136. **for:** as regards.   138. **recountments:** relating of events (to one another).   141. **array:** attire.   **entertainment:** hospitality, provision.

Who led me instantly unto his cave,
There stripped himself, and here upon his arm
The lioness had torn some flesh away,   145
Which all this while had bled; and now he fainted,
And cried, in fainting, upon Rosalind.
Brief,° I recovered° him, bound up his wound,
And after some small space, being strong at heart,
He sent me hither, stranger as I am,   150
To tell this story, that you might excuse
His broken promise, and to give this napkin,
Dyed in his blood, unto the shepherd youth
That he in sport doth call his Rosalind.   [*Rosalind swoons.*]

CELIA:
Why, how now, Ganymede, sweet Ganymede!   155
OLIVER:
Many will swoon when they do look on blood.
CELIA:
There is more in it.—Cousin Ganymede!
OLIVER: Look, he recovers.
ROSALIND: I would I were at home.
CELIA: We'll lead you thither.—   160
I pray you, will you take him by the arm?   [*They help Rosalind up.*]
OLIVER: Be of good cheer, youth. You a man? You lack a man's heart.
ROSALIND: I do so, I confess it. Ah, sirrah, a body° would think this was
well counterfeited. I pray you, tell your brother how well I counterfeited.
Heigh-ho!   165
OLIVER: This was not counterfeit. There is too great testimony in your
complexion that it was a passion of earnest.°
ROSALIND: Counterfeit, I assure you.
OLIVER: Well then, take a good heart and counterfeit to be a man.
ROSALIND: So I do; but, i'faith, I should have been a woman by right.   170
CELIA: Come, you look paler and paler. Pray you, draw homewards.—
Good sir, go with us.
OLIVER:
That will I, for I must bear answer back
How you excuse my brother, Rosalind.
ROSALIND: I shall devise something. But, I pray you, commend my coun-   175
terfeiting to him. Will you go?
                                                Exeunt.

148. **Brief:** in brief.   **recovered:** revived.   163. **a body:** anybody.   167. **a passion of earnest:** a
genuine swoon.

ACT 5, SCENE 1°

Enter [Touchstone the] Clown and Audrey.

TOUCHSTONE: We shall find a time, Audrey. Patience, gentle Audrey.

AUDREY: Faith, the priest was good enough, for all the old gentleman's° saying.

TOUCHSTONE: A most wicked Sir Oliver, Audrey, a most vile Mar-text. But Audrey, there is a youth here in the forest lays claim to you. 5

AUDREY: Ay, I know who 'tis. He hath no interest in° me in the world. Here comes the man you mean.

Enter William.

TOUCHSTONE: It is meat and drink to me to see a clown.° By my troth, we that have good wits have much to answer for. We shall be flouting; we cannot hold.° 10

WILLIAM: Good even, Audrey.

AUDREY: God gi' good even,° William.

WILLIAM: And good even to you, sir. *[He removes his hat.]*

TOUCHSTONE: Good even, gentle friend. Cover thy head, cover thy head. Nay, prithee be covered. How old are you, friend? 15

WILLIAM: Five-and-twenty, sir.

TOUCHSTONE: A ripe age. Is thy name William?

WILLIAM: William, sir.

TOUCHSTONE: A fair name. Wast born i'th' forest here?

WILLIAM: Ay, sir, I thank God. 20

TOUCHSTONE: "Thank God"—a good answer. Art rich?

WILLIAM: Faith, sir, so so.

TOUCHSTONE: "So-so" is good, very good, very excellent good; and yet it is not; it is but so-so. Art thou wise?

WILLIAM: Ay, sir, I have a pretty wit. 25

TOUCHSTONE: Why, thou say'st well. I do now remember a saying, "The fool doth think he is wise, but the wise man knows himself to be a fool." The heathen philosopher, when he had a desire to eat a grape, would open his lips when he put it into his mouth, meaning thereby that grapes were made to eat and lips to open.° You do love this maid? 30

ACT 5, SCENE 1. Location: The forest. 2. **the old gentleman's:** i.e., Jaques's. 6. **interest in:** claim to. 8. **clown:** i.e., country yokel. 10. **we . . . hold:** i.e., we professional fools have much to answer for in providing a model of folly that yokels like William are too apt to imitate. We fools are always scoffing; we can't restrain ourselves. 12. **God gi' good even:** God give you good evening. (Here, afternoon.) 28–30. **The heathen . . . open:** (This bit of fatuously self-evident wisdom parodies the logical proofs of the ancient philosophers. William, whose mouth is no doubt gaping like a rustic's, is invited to consider the consequences of his desire.)

WILLIAM: I do, sir.

TOUCHSTONE: Give me your hand. Art thou learned?

WILLIAM: No, sir.

TOUCHSTONE: Then learn this of me: to have is to have. For it is a figure° in rhetoric that drink, being poured out of a cup into a glass, by filling the 35 one doth empty the other.° For all your writers do consent that *ipse* is he. Now, you are not *ipse*, for I am he.°

WILLIAM: Which he, sir?

TOUCHSTONE: He, sir, that must marry this woman. Therefore, you clown, abandon—which is in the vulgar "leave"—the society—which 40 in the boorish is "company"—of this female—which in the common is "woman"; which together is, abandon the society of this female, or, clown, thou perishest; or, to thy better understanding, diest; or, to wit, I kill thee, make thee away, translate thy life into death, thy liberty into bondage. I will deal in poison with thee, or in bastinado,° or in steel; I 45 will bandy° with thee in faction,° I will o'er-run thee with policy;° I will kill thee a hundred and fifty ways. Therefore tremble and depart.

AUDREY: Do, good William.

WILLIAM: God rest you merry,° sir.   *Exit.*

Enter Corin.

CORIN: Our master and mistress seeks you. Come, away, away!   50

TOUCHSTONE: Trip,° Audrey, trip, Audrey!—I attend, I attend.   *Exeunt.*

ACT 5, SCENE 2°

Enter Orlando [with his wounded arm in a sling] and Oliver.

ORLANDO: Is't possible that on so little acquaintance you should like her? That but seeing, you should love her? And loving, woo? And, wooing, she should grant? And will you persevere to enjoy her?

OLIVER: Neither call the giddiness° of it in question, the poverty of her, the small acquaintance, my sudden wooing, nor her sudden consenting; 5 but say with me, "I love Aliena"; say with her that she loves me; consent with both that we may enjoy each other. It shall be to your good; for my

---

34. **figure:** figure of speech, trope.   35–36. **drink . . . other:** i.e., both Touchstone and William cannot possess Audrey.   36–37. **For . . . am he:** for all the ancient authorities concur that the word *ipse* in Latin means "he." But you are not *ipse*, i.e., the man of the hour, the one destined to win Audrey, for I am that man.   45. **bastinado:** beating with a cudgel. 46. **bandy:** contend.   **in faction:** factiously.   **o'errun . . . policy:** overwhelm you with craft, cunning.   49. **God . . . merry:** (A common salutation at parting.)   51. **Trip:** Go nimbly. **ACT 5, SCENE 2. Location:** The forest.   4. **giddiness:** sudden speed.

father's house and all the revenue that was old Sir Rowland's will I estate°
upon you, and here live and die a shepherd.

Enter Rosalind.

ORLANDO: You have my consent. Let your wedding be tomorrow. Thither   10
will I invite the Duke and all 's° contented followers. Go you and prepare
Aliena; for, look you, here comes my Rosalind.

ROSALIND: God save you, brother.°

OLIVER: And you, fair sister.°   [*Exit.*]

ROSALIND: O my dear Orlando, how it grieves me to see thee wear thy   15
heart in a scarf!°

ORLANDO: It is my arm.

ROSALIND: I thought thy heart had been wounded with the claws of a lion.

ORLANDO: Wounded it is, but with the eyes of a lady.

ROSALIND: Did your brother tell you how I counterfeited to swoon when   20
he showed me your handkerchief?

ORLANDO: Ay, and greater wonders than that.

ROSALIND: Oh, I know where you are.° Nay, 'tis true. There was never
anything so sudden but the fight of two rams and Caesar's thrasonical°
brag of "I came, saw, and overcame."° For your brother and my sister no   25
sooner met but they looked; no sooner looked but they loved; no sooner
loved but they sighed; no sooner sighed but they asked one another the
reason, no sooner knew the reason but they sought the remedy; and in
these degrees° have they made a pair° of stairs to marriage, which they will
climb incontinent,° or else be incontinent before marriage. They are in   30
the very wrath° of love, and they will together. Clubs° cannot part them.

ORLANDO: They shall be married tomorrow; and I will bid the Duke to the
nuptial. But oh, how bitter a thing it is to look into happiness through
another man's eyes! By so much the more shall I tomorrow be at the
height of heart-heaviness, by how much I shall think my brother happy   35
in having what he wishes for.

---

8. **estate:** settle as an estate, bestow.   11. **all 's:** all his.   13. **brother:** i.e., brother-in-law to be.
14. **sister:** (Rosalind is still dressed as a man, but Oliver evidently adopts the fiction that
"Ganymede" is Orlando's Rosalind. See 4.3.81 ff.)   16. **scarf:** sling.   23. **where you are:** i.e.,
what you mean.   24. **thrasonical:** boastful. (From Thraso, the boaster in Terence's *Eunuchus.*)
25. **"I came . . . overcame":** (Julius Caesar's famous pronouncement, *Veni, vidi, vici,* on the
occasion of his victory over Pharnaces at Zela in 47 B.C.E.)   29. **degrees:** (Plays on the original
meaning, "steps," and also on the rhetorical figure of climax illustrated by Rosalind's sentence
as it moves from one step to the next by linked words, *looked, loved, sighed,* etc.)   **pair:** flight.
30. **incontinent:** immediately. (Followed by a pun on the meaning "unchaste or sexually unrestrained.")   31. **wrath:** impetuosity, ardor.   **Clubs:** i.e., physical force, such as that employed
by nightwatchmen armed with clubs.

ROSALIND: Why, then, tomorrow I cannot serve your turn for Rosalind?

ORLANDO: I can live no longer by thinking.

ROSALIND: I will weary you then no longer with idle talking. Know of me then — for now I speak to some purpose — that I know you are a gentle-   40 man of good conceit.° I speak not this that° you should bear a good opinion of my knowledge, insomuch I say I know you are;° neither do I labor for a greater esteem than may in some little measure draw a belief from you to do yourself good, and not to grace me.° Believe then, if you please, that I can do strange things. I have, since I was three year old, conversed°   45 with a magician, most profound in his art and yet not damnable.° If you do love Rosalind so near the heart as your gesture° cries it out,° when your brother marries Aliena shall you marry her. I know into what straits of fortune she° is driven; and it is not impossible to me, if it appear not inconvenient° to you, to set her before your eyes tomorrow, human° as   50 she is, and without any danger.°

ORLANDO: Speak'st thou in sober meanings?°

ROSALIND: By my life, I do, which I tender dearly,° though I say I am a magician.° Therefore, put you in your best array; bid° your friends;° for if you will be married tomorrow, you shall, and to Rosalind, if you will.   55

Enter Silvius and Phoebe.

Look, here comes a lover of mine, and a lover of hers.

PHOEBE: [*to Rosalind*]
Youth, you have done me much ungentleness,°
To show the letter that I writ to you.

ROSALIND:
I care not if I have. It is my study°
To seem despiteful and ungentle to you.   60
You are there followed by a faithful shepherd.
Look upon him; love him. He worships you.

---

41. **conceit:** intelligence, understanding. **that:** in order that. 42. **insomuch . . . are:** from my saying I know you to be intelligent. 42–44. **neither . . . grace me:** nor am I interested in winning approval except insofar as it may, by inspiring your confidence in my ability, prompt you to do something for your own benefit; it is not intended to bring favor on myself. 45. **conversed:** associated. 46. **not damnable:** not a practicer of forbidden or black magic, worthy of execution and damnation. 47. **gesture:** bearing. **cries it out:** proclaims. 49. **she:** Rosalind. 50. **inconvenient:** inappropriate. **human:** i.e., the real Rosalind, not a phantom. 51. **danger:** i.e., the danger to the soul from one's involvement in magic or witchcraft. 52. **in sober meanings:** seriously. 53. **tender dearly:** value highly. 53–54. **though . . . magician:** (According to Elizabethan antiwitchcraft statutes, some forms of witchcraft were punishable by death; Rosalind thus endangers her life by what she has said.) 54. **bid:** invite. **friends:** family and friends. 57. **ungentleness:** discourtesy. 59. **study:** conscious endeavor.

PHOEBE: [*to Silvius*]
  Good shepherd, tell this youth what 'tis to love.
SILVIUS:
  It is to be all made of sighs and tears;
  And so am I for Phoebe. 65
PHOEBE: And I for Ganymede.
ORLANDO: And I for Rosalind.
ROSALIND: And I for no woman.
SILVIUS:
  It is to be all made of faith and service;
  And so am I for Phoebe. 70
PHOEBE: And I for Ganymede.
ORLANDO: And I for Rosalind.
ROSALIND: And I for no woman.
SILVIUS:
  It is to be all made of fantasy,°
  All made of passion, and all made of wishes, 75
  All adoration, duty, and observance,°
  All humbleness, all patience and impatience,
  All purity, all trial, all observance;°
  And so am I for Phoebe.
PHOEBE: And so am I for Ganymede. 80
ORLANDO: And so am I for Rosalind.
ROSALIND: And so am I for no woman.
PHOEBE: [*to Rosalind*]
  If this be so, why blame you me to love you?°
SILVIUS: [*to Phoebe*]
  If this be so, why blame you me to love you?
ORLANDO:
  If this be so, why blame you me to love you? 85
ROSALIND: Why do you speak too, "Why blame you me to love you?"
ORLANDO: To her that is not here, nor doth not hear.
ROSALIND: Pray you, no more of this; 'tis like the howling of Irish wolves
  against the moon. [*To Silvius*] I will help you, if I can. [*To Phoebe*] I would
  love you, if I could. — Tomorrow meet me all together. [*To Phoebe*] I will 90
  marry you, if ever I marry woman, and I'll be married tomorrow. [*To
  Orlando*] I will satisfy you, if ever I satisfied man, and you shall be married

---

74. **fantasy:** fancy, imagination.   76. **observance:** devotion, respect.   78. **observance:** (Perhaps a compositor's error, repeated from two lines previous; many editors emend it to *obedience*.)   83. **to love you:** for loving you.

tomorrow. [*To Silvius*] I will content you, if what pleases you contents you, and you shall be married tomorrow. [*To Orlando*] As you love Rosalind, meet. [*To Silvius*] As you love Phoebe, meet. And as I love no woman, 95 I'll meet. So, fare you well. I have left you commands.

SILVIUS: I'll not fail, if I live.

PHOEBE: Nor I.

ORLANDO: Nor I. *Exeunt [separately].*

ACT 5, SCENE 3°

Enter [Touchstone the] Clown and Audrey.

TOUCHSTONE: Tomorrow is the joyful day, Audrey; tomorrow will we be married.

AUDREY: I do desire it with all my heart; and I hope it is no dishonest° desire to desire to be a woman of the world.° Here come two of the banished Duke's pages. 5

Enter two Pages.

FIRST PAGE: Well met, honest° gentleman.

TOUCHSTONE: By my troth, well met. Come sit, sit, and a song. [*They sit.*]

SECOND PAGE: We are for you.° Sit i'th' middle.

FIRST PAGE: Shall we clap into't roundly,° without hawking° or spitting or saying we are hoarse, which are the only° prologues to a bad voice? 10

SECOND PAGE: I'faith, i'faith, and both in a tune,° like two gypsies on a° horse.

Song.

BOTH PAGES:
> It was a lover and his lass,
>   With a hey, and a ho, and a hey-nonny-no,
> That o'er the green cornfield° did pass 15
>   In springtime, the only pretty ring time,°
> When birds do sing, hey ding a ding, ding,
> Sweet lovers love the spring.

ACT 5, SCENE 3. Location: The forest. **3. dishonest:** immodest. **4. woman of the world:** married woman; also, one who advances herself socially. **6. honest:** worthy. **8. We are for you:** i.e., fine, we're ready. **9. clap . . . roundly:** begin briskly and with spirit. **hawking:** clearing the throat. **10. only:** customary. **11. in a tune:** (1) in unison (2) keeping time. **on a:** on one. **15. cornfield:** field of grain. **16. ring time:** time most apt for marriage.

Between the acres° of the rye,
    With a hey, and a ho, and a hey-nonny-no,   20
These pretty country folks would lie
    In springtime, the only pretty ring time,
When birds do sing, hey ding a ding, ding,
Sweet lovers love the spring.

This carol they began that hour,   25
    With a hey, and a ho, and a hey-nonny-no,
How that a life was but a flower
    In springtime, the only pretty ring time,
When birds do sing, hey ding a ding, ding,
Sweet lovers love the spring.   30

And therefore take the present time,
    With a hey, and a ho, and a hey-nonny-no,
For love is crownèd with the prime°
    In springtime, the only pretty ring time,
When birds do sing, hey ding a ding, ding,   35
Sweet lovers love the spring.

TOUCHSTONE: Truly, young gentlemen, though there was no great matter°
in the ditty, yet the note° was very untunable.°
FIRST PAGE: You are deceived,° sir; we kept time, we lost not our time.
TOUCHSTONE: By my troth, yes; I count it but time lost to hear such a   40
foolish song. God b'wi'you, and God mend your voices! Come, Audrey.
                                        Exeunt [separately].

ACT 5, SCENE 4°

Enter Duke Senior, Amiens, Jaques, Orlando, Oliver, [and] Celia.

DUKE SENIOR:
    Dost thou believe, Orlando, that the boy
    Can do all this that he hath promisèd?
ORLANDO:
    I sometimes do believe, and sometimes do not,
    As those that fear they hope,° and know they fear.

19. **Between the acres:** on unplowed strips between the fields.   33. **prime:** (1) height of perfection (2) spring.   37. **matter:** sense, meaning.   38. **note:** music.   **untunable:** discordant.
39. **deceived:** mistaken.   ACT 5, SCENE 4. Location: The forest.   4. **they hope:** i.e., that they merely hope.

Enter Rosalind, Silvius, and Phoebe.

ROSALIND:

Patience once more, whiles our compact is urged.°   5
[*To the Duke*] You say, if I bring in your Rosalind,
You will bestow her on Orlando here?

DUKE SENIOR:

That would I, had I kingdoms to give with her.

ROSALIND: [*to Orlando*]

And you say you will have her when I bring her?

ORLANDO:

That would I, were I of all kingdoms king.   10

ROSALIND: [*to Phoebe*]

You say you'll marry me, if I be willing?

PHOEBE:

That will I, should I die the hour after.

ROSALIND:

But if you do refuse to marry me
You'll give yourself to this most faithful shepherd?

PHOEBE: So is the bargain.   15

ROSALIND: [*to Silvius*]

You say that you'll have Phoebe if she will?

SILVIUS:

Though to have her and death were both one thing.

ROSALIND:

I have promised to make all this matter even.°
Keep you your word, O Duke, to give your daughter;
You yours, Orlando, to receive his daughter;   20
Keep you your word, Phoebe, that you'll marry me,
Or else, refusing me, to wed this shepherd;
Keep your word, Silvius, that you'll marry her
If she refuse me; and from hence I go,
To make these doubts all even.   *Exeunt Rosalind and Celia.*   25

DUKE SENIOR:

I do remember in this shepherd boy
Some lively° touches of my daughter's favor.°

ORLANDO:

My lord, the first time that I ever saw him

---

5. **urged:** put forward.   18. **make . . . even:** set all this to rights, square accounts.   27. **lively:**
lifelike.   **favor:** appearance.

Methought he was a brother to your daughter.
But, my good lord, this boy is forest-born   30
And hath been tutored in the rudiments
Of many desperate° studies by his uncle,
Whom he reports to be a great magician,
Obscurèd° in the circle° of this forest.

Enter [Touchstone the] Clown and Audrey.

JAQUES: There is, sure, another flood toward,° and these couples are com-   35
ing to the ark. Here comes a pair° of very strange beasts, which in all
tongues are called fools.

TOUCHSTONE: Salutation and greeting to you all!

JAQUES: [*To the Duke*]   Good my lord, bid him welcome. This is the motley-
minded gentleman that I have so often met in the forest. He hath been a   40
courtier, he swears.

TOUCHSTONE: If any man doubt that, let him put me to my purgation.° I
have trod a measure;° I have flattered a lady; I have been politic° with my
friend, smooth° with mine enemy; I have undone° three tailors; I have
had four quarrels and like° to have fought one.   45

JAQUES: And how was that ta'en up?°

TOUCHSTONE: Faith, we met, and found the quarrel was upon the seventh
cause.

JAQUES: How seventh cause?—Good my lord, like this fellow.

DUKE SENIOR: I like him very well.   50

TOUCHSTONE: God 'ild° you, sir, I desire you of the like.° I press in here,
sir, amongst the rest of the country copulatives,° to swear and to forswear,
according as marriage binds and blood breaks.° A poor virgin, sir, an ill-
favored thing, sir, but mine own; a poor humor° of mine, sir, to take that
that no man else will. Rich honesty° dwells like a miser, sir, in a poor   55
house, as your pearl° in your foul oyster.

DUKE SENIOR: By my faith, he is very swift and sententious.°

---

32. **desperate:** dangerous.   34. **Obscurèd:** hidden.   **circle:** compass, boundaries. (With a
possible allusion to the magic circle that protected the magician from the devil during incan-
tation.)   35. **toward:** coming on.   36. **a pair:** (In Genesis 7:2, God commands Noah to take
on board every "clean" beast by sevens but those that are not clean, by twos.)   42. **purgation:**
proof, trial.   43. **measure:** slow, stately dance.   **politic:** cunning, Machiavellian.   44. **smooth:**
insinuating.   **undone:** bankrupted (by refusing to pay debts owed them).   45. **like:** came
close.   46. **ta'en up:** settled, made up.   51. **'ild:** yield, reward.   **I . . . like:** I wish the same
to you. (A polite phrase used to reply to a compliment.)   52. **country copulatives:** country
couples about to marry and with sex on their minds.   53. **blood breaks:** as desire bursts forth.
54. **humor:** whim.   55. **honesty:** chastity.   56. **your pearl:** i.e., the pearl that one hears about.
57: **swift and sententious:** quick-witted and good at aphorisms.

TOUCHSTONE: According to the fool's bolt,° sir, and such dulcet diseases.°
JAQUES: But for the seventh cause. How did you find the quarrel on the
seventh cause?   60
TOUCHSTONE: Upon a lie seven times removed—bear your body more
seeming,° Audrey—as thus, sir. I did dislike° the cut of a certain courtier's beard. He sent me word if I said his beard was not cut well, he was
in the mind it was: this is called the Retort Courteous. If I sent him
word again it was not well cut, he would send me word he cut it to please   65
himself: this is called the Quip Modest. If again it was not well cut, he
disabled° my judgment: this is called the Reply Churlish. If again it was
not well cut, he would answer I spake not true: this is called the Reproof
Valiant. If again it was not well cut, he would say I lie: this is called the
Countercheck° Quarrelsome. And so to the Lie Circumstantial and the   70
Lie Direct.
JAQUES: And how oft did you say his beard was not well cut?
TOUCHSTONE: I durst go no further than the Lie Circumstantial, nor he
durst not give me the Lie Direct; and so we measured swords° and parted.
JAQUES: Can you nominate in order now the degrees of the lie?   75
TOUCHSTONE: Oh, sir, we quarrel in print, by the book,° as you have books
for good manners. I will name you the degrees. The first, the Retort
Courteous; the second, the Quip Modest; the third, the Reply Churlish;
the fourth, the Reproof Valiant; the fifth, the Countercheck Quarrelsome; the sixth, the Lie with Circumstance; the seventh, the Lie Direct.   80
All these you may avoid but the Lie Direct; and you may avoid that too,
with an If. I knew when seven justices could not take up° a quarrel, but
when the parties were met themselves, one of them thought but of an
If, as, "If you said so, then I said so"; and they shook hands and swore
brothers.° Your If is the only peacemaker; much virtue in If.   85
JAQUES: Is not this a rare fellow, my lord? He's as good at anything, and
yet a fool.
DUKE SENIOR: He uses his folly like a stalking-horse,° and under the pre-
sentation° of that he shoots his wit.

---

58. fool's bolt: (Alluding to the proverb "A fool's bolt [arrow] is soon shot.")   **dulcet diseases:**
pleasant afflictions, entertaining yet sharp. (Touchstone wryly agrees with the Duke's assess-
ment of the Fool as swift and sententious.)   **62. seeming:** seemly.   **dislike:** express dislike of.
67. disabled: disparaged.   **70. Countercheck:** rebuff.   **74. measured swords:** i.e., as in the
mere preliminary to a duel.   **76. in . . . book:** in a precise way. (Touchstone is travestying
books on the general subject of honor and arms, which dealt with occasions and circumstances of the duel.)   **82. take up:** settle.   **84–85. swore brothers:** became sworn brothers.
88. stalking-horse: a real or artificial horse under cover of which the hunter approached his
game.   **88–89. presentation:** semblance.

Enter Hymen,° Rosalind, and Celia. Still° music. [Rosalind and Celia are no longer disguised.]

HYMEN:
Then is there mirth° in heaven,   90
When earthly things made even°
    Atone° together.
Good Duke, receive thy daughter;
Hymen from heaven brought her,
    Yea, brought her hither,   95
That thou mightst join her hand with his
Whose° heart within his bosom is.

ROSALIND: [*to the Duke*]
To you I give myself, for I am yours.
[*To Orlando*] To you I give myself, for I am yours.
DUKE SENIOR:
If there be truth in sight, you are my daughter.   100
ORLANDO:
If there be truth in sight, you are my Rosalind.
PHOEBE:
If sight and shape be true,
Why then, my love adieu!
ROSALIND: [*to the Duke*]
I'll have no father, if you be not he;
[*To Orlando*] I'll have no husband, if you be not he;   105
[*To Phoebe*] Nor ne'er wed woman, if you be not she.
HYMEN:
Peace, ho! I bar confusion.
'Tis I must make conclusion
    Of these most strange events.
Here's eight that must take hands   110
To join in Hymen's bands,
    If truth holds true contents.°
[*To Orlando and Rosalind*]
You and you no cross° shall part.
[*To Oliver and Celia*]
You and you are heart in heart.

89. s.d. *Hymen*: Roman god of faithful marriage. *Still*: soft. 90. mirth: joy. 91. made even: set straight. 92. Atone: are at one. 97. Whose: (Refers to Rosalind.) 112. If . . . contents: if the newly revealed truths are indeed true and bring true contentment. 113. cross: vexation, mischance.

[*To Phoebe*]
    You to his° love must accord° 115
    Or have a woman to your lord.°
[*To Touchstone and Audrey*]
    You and you are sure° together,
    As the winter to foul weather.
[*To All*]
    Whiles a wedlock hymn we sing,
    Feed° yourselves with questioning, 120
    That reason wonder may diminish,°
    How thus we met, and these things finish.

          Song.

    Wedding is great Juno's° crown,
      O blessèd bond of board and bed!°
    'Tis Hymen peoples every town; 125
      High° wedlock then be honorèd.
    Honor, high honor and renown
      To Hymen, god of every town!

DUKE SENIOR: [*to Celia*]
    O my dear niece, welcome thou art to me!
    Even daughter, welcome, in no less degree.° 130
PHOEBE: [*to Silvius*]
    I will not eat my word, now thou art mine;
    Thy faith my fancy to thee doth combine.°

Enter Second Brother [*Jaques de Boys*].

JAQUES DE BOYS:
    Let me have audience for a word or two.
    I am the second son of old Sir Rowland,
    That bring these tidings to this fair assembly. 135
    Duke Frederick, hearing how that every day
    Men of great worth resorted to this forest,
    Addressed° a mighty power,° which were on foot

---

115. **his:** i.e., Silvius's. **accord:** agree. 116. **to your lord:** for your husband. 117. **sure:** closely united. 120. **Feed:** satisfy. 121. **That ... diminish:** that understanding may lessen your wonder. 123. **Juno's:** (Juno was the Roman queen of the gods, presiding, in the Renaissance view, over faithful wedlock.) 124. **board and bed:** sustenance and lodging; the household. 126. **High:** solemn. 130. **Even ... degree:** You are as welcome as a daughter. 132. **Thy faith ... combine:** your faithful love for me ties my love to you. 138. **Addressed:** prepared. **power:** army.

In his own conduct,° purposely to take
His brother here, and put him to the sword;   140
And to the skirts of this wild wood he came,
Where, meeting with an old religious man,
After some question° with him, was converted
Both from his enterprise and from the world,
His crown bequeathing to his banished brother,   145
And all their lands restored to them again
That were with him exiled. This to be true
I do engage° my life.

DUKE SENIOR: Welcome, young man.
Thou offer'st fairly° to thy brothers' wedding:
To one° his lands withheld and to the other   150
A land itself at large,° a potent dukedom.
First, in this forest let us do those ends°
That here were well begun and well begot;°
And after, every° of this happy number
That have endured shrewd° days and nights with us   155
Shall share the good of our returnèd fortune,
According to the measure of their states.°
Meantime, forget this new-fall'n° dignity,
And fall into our rustic revelry.
Play, music! And you brides and bridegrooms all,   160
With measure heaped in joy, to th' measures fall.°

JAQUES:
Sir, by your patience.° — If I heard you rightly,
The Duke hath put on a religious life,
And thrown into neglect the pompous° court.

JAQUES DE BOYS: He hath.   165

JAQUES:
To him will I. Out of these convertites°
There is much matter° to be heard and learned.
[*To the Duke*] You to your former honor I bequeath;

Your patience and your virtue well deserves it.
[*To Orlando*] You to a love that your true faith doth merit;   170
[*To Oliver*] You to your land and love and great allies;°
[*To Silvius*] You to a long and well-deservèd bed;
[*To Touchstone*] And you to wrangling, for thy loving voyage
Is but for two months victualed.° So, to your pleasures.
I am for other than for dancing measures.   175

DUKE SENIOR: Stay, Jaques, stay.

JAQUES:
To see no pastime I. What you would have
I'll stay to know at your abandoned cave.   *Exit.*

DUKE SENIOR:
Proceed, proceed. We'll begin these rites,
As we do trust they'll end, in true delights.   180
                              [*They dance.*] *Exeunt* [*all but Rosalind*].

EPILOGUE

ROSALIND: It is not the fashion to see the lady the epilogue; but it is no
more unhandsome° than to see the lord the prologue. If it be true that
good wine needs no bush,° 'tis true that a good play needs no epilogue.
Yet to good wine they do use good bushes, and good plays prove the better by the help of good epilogues. What a case am I in then, that am   5
neither a good epilogue nor cannot insinuate° with you in the behalf of a
good play! I am not furnished° like a beggar; therefore to beg will not
become me. My way is to conjure° you, and I'll begin with the women. I
charge you, O women, for the love you bear to men, to like as much of
this play as please you; and I charge you, O men, for the love you bear to   10
women—as I perceive by your simpering, none of you hates them—
that between you and the women the play may please. If I were a woman,°
I would kiss as many of you as had beards that pleased me, complexions
that liked° me, and breaths that I defied° not; and, I am sure as many as
have good beards or good faces or sweet breaths will, for my kind offer,   15
when I make curtsy, bid me farewell.°   *Exit.*

FINIS

171. **allies:** kinfolk.   174. **victualed:** provisioned.   EPILOGUE   2. **unhandsome:** in bad taste.
3. **good . . . bush:** (A proverb derived from the custom of displaying a piece of ivy or holly at
the tavern door to denote that wine was for sale there.)   6. **insinuate:** ingratiate myself.
7. **furnished:** equipped, decked out.   8. **conjure:** adjure, earnestly charge.   12. **If . . . woman:**
(Women's parts on the Elizabethan stage were played by boys in feminine costume.)
114. **liked:** pleased.   **defied:** rejected, disdained.   16. **bid me farewell:** i.e., applaud me.

As You Like It

Copy text: the First Folio. Act and scene divisions follow the Folio text throughout.
ACT 1, SCENE 1. 80. she: hee. 118. OLIVER: [not in F]. 118. s.d. *Exit*: [at line 117 in F].
ACT 1, SCENE 2. 3. I were: were. 39. goddesses and: goddesses. 41. [and elsewhere]
whither: whether. 42. [and elsewhere] TOUCHSTONE: *Clow*. 42. father: farher.
61. CELIA: *Ros*. 67. Le: the. 185. love: loue: 203. s.d. [at line 201 in F]. 232. [and
occasionally elsewhere] Rosalind: *Rosaline*.
ACT 1, SCENE 3. 46. likelihood: likelihoods. 67. her: per. 78. *with Lords*: &c. 115. be:
by. 120. travel: trauaile. 122. [and elsewhere] woo: woe. 126. we in: in we.
ACT 2, SCENE 1. 31. antique: anticke. 49. much: must. 50. friends: friend. 59. of the: of.
ACT 2, SCENE 3. 10. some: seeme. 16. ORLANDO: [not in F]. 29. ORLANDO: *Ad*.
71. seventeen: seauentie.
ACT 2, SCENE 4. 1. weary: merry. 38. thy wound: they would. 59. you: your.
ACT 2, SCENE 5. 1. AMIENS: [not in F; also at line 30]. 33. *All together here* [before line 30
in F]. 36–37. No . . . weather: &c. 41. JAQUES: *Amy*.
ACT 2, SCENE 7. s.d. *Lords*: *Lord*. 38. brain: braiue. 55. Not to seem: Seeme. 87. comes:
come. 161. treble, pipes: trebble pipes. 174. AMIENS: [not in F]. 182. Then: *The*.
190–03. heigh-ho . . . jolly: &c. 201. master: masters.
ACT 3, SCENE 2. 22. good: pood. 100. graft: grafe [twice]. 106. a desert: *Desert*.
126. her: *his*. 166. whooping: hooping. 201. such fruit: fruite. 206. thy: the.
219. [and elsewhere] b'wi'you: buy you. 289. lectures: Lectors. 301. deifying: defying.
306. are: art.
ACT 3, SCENE 3. 42–43. so. Poor men alone? No: so poore men alone: No. 71. TOUCH-
STONE: *Ol*. 82. s.d. *Exit*: *Exeunt*.
ACT 3, SCENE 4. 25. a lover: Louer. 34. puny: puisny.
ACT 3, SCENE 5. 11. pretty, sure: pretty sure. 65. hear: here. 104. erewhile: yere-while.
127. I have: Haue.
ACT 4, SCENE 1. 1. me be: me. 14. my: by. 20. travel: trauaile. 27. gondola: Gundello.
32. thousandth: thousand. 56. warrant: warne. 118. hyena: Hyen. 161. it: in.
ACT 4, SCENE 2. 2. FIRST LORD: *Lord*. 6. SECOND LORD: *Lord*. 8. SECOND LORD: [not
in F].
ACT 4, SCENE 3. 4. s.d. [after line 3 in F]. 7. bid: did bid. 11. tenor: tenure. 76. bottom:
bottom. 101. itself: it selfe. 140. In: I. 153. his: this.
ACT 5, SCENE 1. 12. gi': ye. 31. sir: sit. 46. policy: police.
ACT 5, SCENE 2. 5. nor her: nor. 25. overcame: ouercome.
ACT 5, SCENE 3. 13. BOTH PAGES: [not in F]. 16. In: In the. ring: rang. 22–24. In . . .
spring: *In spring time*, &c [also at lines 28–30 and 34–36]. 31–36. [this stanza comes after
line 30 in F].
ACT 5, SCENE 4. 25. *Exeunt*: *Exit*. 34. s.d. [after line 33 in F]. 70. so to the: so ro. 96. her:
his. 133. JAQUES DE BOYS: *2 Bro*. [also at line 165]. 146. them: him. 153. were: vvete.
179. rites: rights. 180. trust they'll end, in: trust, they'l end in. 180. s.d. *Exeunt*: *Exit*.

PART TWO

Cultural Contexts

CHAPTER I

Pastoral and Rural Life

Court and Country

※

Strikingly, four-fifths of *As You Like It* takes place in the Forest of Arden, wherever that may be! Thomas Lodge's prose romance *Rosalynde* (1590), Shakespeare's source for many of the play's events, takes place in France. There are at least two French forests bearing the name Ardennes: one lies in the southwest near Bordeaux, the city where Lodge begins his story; the other is in the northeast on the Belgian border.[1] Shakespeare is partly faithful to his source in that many of his characters are given French names such as Jaques and Sir Rowland du Bois, and there are general references to a French context for the action. On the other hand, the play has seemed to many to be quintessentially English. It refers to the English outlaw hero Robin Hood, for example, and its Arden could well be the famous forest in Shakespeare's own Warwickshire, not far from where he was born. That forest was sufficiently famous that in 1612 Michael Drayton included it, both in word and image, within his very long poem, *Poly-Olbion*, which describes the history and landscape of each of the counties of Britain and Wales. In Drayton's poem, some of which will be included in the selections that follow, the Forest of Arden is made to speak directly to the reader, describing

---

[1] See Juliet Dusinberre's discussion of the play's possible settings in the introduction to her recent edition of the play. Juliet Dusinberre, ed., *As You Like It* (London: Arden Shakespeare of Thompson Learning, 2006), 48–52.

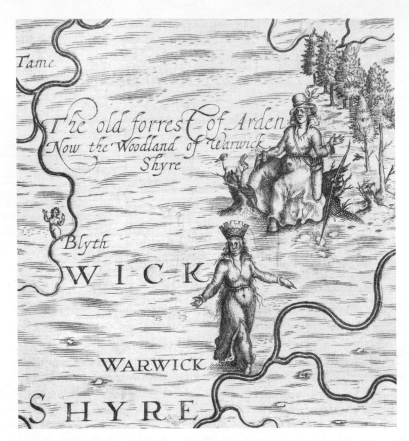

FIGURE 2 *A seated woman with a hunter's bow and quiver of arrows personifies the Forest of Arden in this map of Warwickshire from* Poly-Olbion, *by Michael Drayton (1612).*

her woodlands and its history, and is also named on the map that precedes the Warwickshire section of the text (see Figure 2). The Forest of Arden, also called the Woodland of Warwickshire, appears as a slightly disheveled woman archer sitting on what looks like a tree stump with a quiver on her shoulder and a bow beside her. She is clearly a huntress, suggesting one of the chief activities, hunting, with which the forest was associated in Shakespeare's play as well as in Warwickshire history.

The play, however, is never really explicit as to the precise situation of the forest in which so much of the action occurs. The Forest of Arden is a nowhere land, a woodland of the imagination as much as it is a specific geographical location in either France or England. Arden puns with Eden, and there is something Edenic about the forest retreat toward which so many beleaguered souls converge, though one must quickly add that the forest is less than Edenic in its wind and rough weather, its dangerous lions and snakes, and the flawed natures and discontents of many of its inhabitants. In the end, the Forest of Arden is probably most fruitfully connected to the rich symbolic landscapes of pastoral literature than to the biblical Eden. It is the themes and conventions of pastoral that provide Shakespeare with the generative mix of materials from which much of his play derives.

So, what is pastoral literature? It is a mode of writing that uses bucolic settings to consider basic questions of human life, including the pleasures and sorrows of love; the relative virtues of living in the country or at court or in the city; and the injustices that mar human communities, whether those injustices are the result of tyrannical rulers, covetous landlords, arbitrary and unfair social conventions, or corrupt churchmen.[2] The simplicity of the rural setting allows pastoral figures to focus on elemental questions, undisturbed by the hubbub of the town or the complexities of court life, and to think about what constitutes the good life and the social arrangements that would support it. The speakers of pastoral are often shepherds, like Corin and Silvius in Shakespeare's play, or sophisticated people pretending to be shepherds, like Celia and Rosalind, who buy a sheepcote from a departing landlord on the skirts of the Forest of Arden and play at tending sheep in their disguises as Aliena and Ganymede. Sometimes, figures sojourn in the pastoral landscape only for a time, refreshing themselves or getting a new perspective on life before returning to more complicated existences elsewhere. At the end of *As You Like It*, a number of characters are poised to leave Arden, but some will stay. Some important questions are: Why do some stay and some go? Are those who have been to Arden somehow changed by their time in the forest? Has the larger social world been righted by what has taken place there?

Typically, while in the pastoral landscape people do some conventional things: they take part in singing contests, for example, in which they extol the beauty of their beloveds or lament their cruelty; they engage in dialogues and debates with their companions in the fields and forests; and they complain about hard-hearted lovers, cruel landlords, and evil churchmen. *As You Like It* shows its kinship with pastoral in that it is unusually full of songs; it

---

[2] For a rich but economical introduction to Shakespeare's use of pastoral paradigms in his plays, and in *As You Like It* in particular, see Rosalie Colie, "Perspectives on Pastoral: Romance, Comic, and Tragic," *Shakespeare's Living Art* (Princeton: Princeton UP, 1974), 243–83. See also Renato Poggiolo, *The Oaten Flute* (Cambridge: Harvard UP, 1975), and Paul Alpers, *What Is Pastoral?* (Chicago: Chicago UP, 1996).

is also an unusually "talky" play. Corin talks with Touchstone about the relative merits of living in the country or at court; Silvius complains to anyone who will listen about the cruelty and beauty of his mistress, Phoebe; Jaques uses the death of a deer to remark on the injustices of the world and moralizes on the seven ages through which every man or woman lives; and Rosalind in her guise as Ganymede talks endlessly with Orlando about the nature of love. Pastoral is a genre of talk and reflection, of meditation on the essential matters of life, death, love, and the proper way to behave toward one's fellow creatures, be they sheep, deer, lovers, masters, or friends. Since many of the figures of pastoral are common men and women — shepherds, mowers, plowmen — their virtues call in question the social priority that the world typically gives to nobles or those of higher social class, many of whom are shown to be corrupt or vicious. In act 1 of *As You Like It*, for example, we learn that Duke Frederick has driven his older brother, Duke Senior, from his throne and that a nobleman, Oliver, has mistreated his young brother, Orlando, keeping him from the education suited to his rank. These acts of cruelty and violence are done by people of high rank. In what sense are Duke Frederick and Oliver *gentlemen*? Is true gentility a matter of social standing or of good behavior, no matter what a person's rank? Pastoral invites these questions, asking the reader to think about what makes one worthy of admiration and whether people who display bad behavior, perhaps corrupted by the privileges that come with rank, can be reformed. Do our natures determine who we are, or can nurture and good education change us?

In the 1590s, Shakespeare was heir to a long pastoral tradition that had been taken up and vigorously used and modified by his contemporaries. Pastoral had its origins in the third century B.C.E. in the *Idylls* of Theocritus, whose short poems, typically dialogues, focused on the rural life of shepherds and their romantic woes. The form was picked up by the Latin author Virgil, whose use of it in his *Eclogues* served as the primary source and inspiration for later writers. Virgil's pastorals preserve the bucolic setting, to which he gave the name Arcadia, and love themes, but added a dimension of political critique that would endure in later iterations of the form. Virgil's work was printed in Rome in 1469 and was subsequently widely taught, reprinted, translated, and imitated throughout Europe. The pastoral's popularity in England in the sixteenth and seventeenth centuries was fueled in part by the importation of Continental editions of Virgil, which were quickly followed by domestically produced translations. Of particular importance was the 1579 publication of Edmund Spenser's *The Shepheardes Calender*, a work in twelve books, each dedicated to one of the months of the year, that modeled itself self-consciously on Virgil's *Eclogues*. The first book of *The*

Shepheardes Calender introduces the reader to Colin Clout, a shepherd (who to some extent represents the poet Spenser) who laments the cruelty of his beloved, Rosalind. That name, of course, is also given to the protagonist of Shakespeare's play.

Many other Elizabethan works share pastoral elements. These include some of the period's lengthy prose romances — long episodic tales of adventure and love set at least in part in rural fields and forests — such as Sir Philip Sidney's popular work *Arcadia* (1593), and Thomas Lodge's *Rosalynde*, Shakespeare's primary source for *As You Like It*.[3] Pastoral was not, of course, just an English passion. It was popular throughout the period in Italian and French court entertainments, and a number of Elizabethan pastoral dramas, such as John Lyly's *Gallatea* (published 1592), were written for performance at court. *Gallatea*'s plot features two women who fall in love, one of whom must be turned by the gods into a man at the play's conclusion so that the two of them can marry. Pastoral often highlights love's variety, the fiercely passionate relationships that can spring up between man and man, man and boy, woman and woman, as well as man and woman. These attachments raise the question: What is natural? And who decides which of the many forms of erotic attachment will be granted social sanction? Lyly's play was performed before Queen Elizabeth, famously known as the Virgin Queen, and many of the pastoral plays and entertainments performed before her at court or at the country estates of her nobles in some way refer to the advantages or disadvantages of marriage or of the single life. After the great flourishing of pastoral writing in the last decades of Elizabeth's reign, when *As You Like It* was composed, the mode was given new life in the seventeenth century in the form of Italianate pastoral tragicomedies such as Shakespeare's *The Winter's Tale* (1609), in which act 4 is set in the pastoral landscape of Bohemia and includes a famous sheep-shearing festival. What happens in this rural place allows the corrupt court world of the tyrant Leontes to be redeemed and his family restored.

By the time Shakespeare wrote *As You Like It*, pastoral, as we have seen, could take many forms, but it provided a horizon of expectations about what themes one would encounter in a pastoral work, and the elements of critique and celebration that it embraced. *As You Like It* is concerned with some very specific social problems, many of which will be explored in the pages that follow. It is centrally concerned with political tyranny, with the act of usurpation that sent Duke Senior into exile in the Forest of Arden, and with the abuses of primogeniture, the social arrangement by which in

---

[3] For an introduction to the romance genre, see Patricia Parker, *Inescapable Romance: Studies in the Poetics of a Mode* (Princeton: Princeton UP, 1979) and Barbara Fuchs, *Romance* (New York: Routledge, 2004).

most parts of England oldest brothers inherited all their fathers' lands, leaving younger brothers like Orlando at the mercy of their older siblings. Central, too, are issues having to do with love and marriage. Is marriage a burden or a blessing? Should people marry outside their social class? What forms of nonheteroerotic love are at play in Arden? But other more subtly insinuated social issues are also part of the play's fabric. The shepherd Corin, for example, complains about the inhospitable and grasping landowner by whom he is hired, pointing to the controversial practice of enclosing or fencing in lands for large-scale sheep farming and pushing small tenants from their customary use of common pastures and fields.[4] The plight of Adam, treated cruelly by Oliver after decades in service to Rowland de Boys's family, suggests not only the thoughtless cruelty of his young master, but also the decay of traditional forms of service and of the mutual obligations master-servant relations were assumed to entail.[5] In short, in ways large and small, from Jaques's railing against the ills of the world to the play's more general critique of bad rulers, *As You Like It* uses the pastoral setting of the Forest of Arden, and the contrast between the forest and the court, to comment on social ills that invite redress.

The play gives a particularly English twist to its pastoral setting, moreover, by using the forest to evoke the figure of Robin Hood, that most English of folk heroes.[6] Good Duke Senior in exile is described as living "in the Forest of Arden, and a many merry men with him; and there they live like the old Robin Hood of England" (1.1.85–86). Robin Hood, of course, fled to Sherwood Forest to escape the tyranny of the Sheriff of Nottingham and of evil King John, the bad brother of Richard the Lionheart. Ubiquitous in ballads, folk dramas, Maygames, and stories throughout the late medieval and early modern period, Robin Hood was lionized as a champion of the poor against the rich and as a defender of women. Lawlessly, but in the service of a higher morality, he hunted the king's deer and robbed fat abbots and other gluttonous clergy, redistributing wealth down the social ladder. In a wonderfully inventive way, Shakespeare grafts this folktale material onto the classical pastoral paradigm, deepening and complicating the

[4] Joan Thirsk, *Tudor Enclosures* (London: Routledge and Paul, 1959); Richard Burt and John Archer, eds., *Enclosure Acts: Sexuality, Property, and Culture in Early Modern England* (Ithaca: Cornell UP, 1994).

[5] For a discussion of early modern hospitality, see Felicity Heal, *Hospitality in Early Modern England* (Oxford: Clarendon, 1990). For service, see Mark Thorton Burnett, *Masters and Servants in Early Modern Drama and Culture: Authority and Obedience* (New York: St. Martin's, 1997); David Evett, *Discourses of Service in Shakespeare's England* (New York: Macmillan, 2005); and David Schalkwyk, *Shakespeare, Love, and Service* (Cambridge: Cambridge UP, 2008).

[6] For a good introduction to the evolution of the Robin Hood story, see Jeffrey Singman, *Robin Hood: The Shaping of the Legend* (Westport: Greenwood, 1998).

play's exploration of justice and of the social uses of the games and playful inversions that mark both the world of pastoral and the world of Sherwood Forest.

Pastoral also has Christian overtones. In the New Testament, Christ is described as the shepherd of his flock, and Psalm 23 is one of many biblical texts to envision Christ's pastoral care of believers. "The LORD is my shepherd; I shall not want. He maketh me to lie down in green pastures; he leadeth me beside the still waters" (Psalm 23:1–2). This connection between the rural life of shepherds and a life of Christian virtue and simplicity has powerful resonances for a play in which many have fled to the forest away from the vices and bad behavior of the court.

And yet, behind the allegorical sheep of the Old and New Testaments, and behind the notional sheep ubiquitous in most pastoral literature, stand the real four-footed creatures of early modern England. Corin nods to the world of actual farm labor when he describes to Touchstone how hard his hands have become from tending to his sheep and the messy reality of their greasy fleeces and the sticky tar with which their wounds and scabs have to be treated (3.2.43–52). Part of the fun and of the play of perspectives in Shakespeare's pastoral world comes from his occasional hint of what it would be like to deal with actual sheep and actual deer rather than their stylized or symbolic representations. People in Shakespeare's England were never far removed from rural life. They understood its seasonal rhythms of planting and harvest and the many kinds of labor that went into shearing sheep, birthing lambs, hunting for game, and gathering firewood (Figure 3). Increasingly, books of husbandry—texts that dealt with every aspect of farming, fishing, hunting, and foresting—poured from early modern presses. They drew both from classical manuals and from everyday experience to prescribe and describe the routines of rural life, including an awareness of the cyclical temporalities that governed the rural calendar and the laws that governed the use of forests and common lands. As You Like It sometimes gives the illusion of bringing the reader into touch with "the real" by juxtaposing to the conventional pastoral lover, Silvius, the stolid William or the phlegmatic Corin with his tar-covered hands, just as it represents the horned stags of Arden as, variously, emblems of the king's authority or emblems of cuckoldry—or simply as food. And if to some of Arden's characters there is a timelessness to pastoral existence, there being "no clock in the forest" (3.2.253–54), the play also insistently points to the cycling round of the seasons, to the work that accompanies each, and to men and women's relentless progress through the temporal stages of human life. The ideal and the real, the timeless and the temporal: the pastoral world of Arden holds them in carefully calibrated juxtaposition, inviting recognition

This hurtlesse beast with meeke moode yelds his woll
And skin, to cloth our naked clotte of claye
He giues his flesh to feede our bellies full
Nought for him selfe he bringe but for our staye

June
Cancer

mayd milke cleane

FIGURE 3 *Rural workers washing sheep in the sun, in "June," a drawing from a manuscript book by Thomas Fella (c. 1585–1622).*

of the partiality of all perspectives and the need to think critically about where true value lies.

The selections that follow invite readers to consider one overarching question from various angles: How did Shakespeare use and modify the resources of pastoral, of the Robin Hood legend, and of more pragmatic writings about rural life in the creation of his play? How does its structured movement from court to forest allow for the ills and pleasures of both to be exposed? What, exactly, are the sources of discontent that need redress, and is such redress achieved? The first selections come from works in the classical pastoral tradition, including poems by Theocritus and Virgil, followed by pastorals written by Shakespeare's near contemporaries, such as works by Edmund Spenser, Christopher Marlowe, and Mary Wroth. These are followed by texts that take up some of the social ills, such as enclosures or the craze for ducling, with which Shakespeare's pastoral play engages. Robin Hood materials follow, including some of the ballads and historical accounts from which this hugely popular legend was created. Finally come selections from other genres of writing that touch on aspects of rural life such as the laws governing the use of forest and manuals dealing with the tending of sheep and the hunting of deer. The intent is to open the play to new interpretations and questions by putting it into conversation with many of the texts and contexts related to the play's concerns that were well known in Shakespeare's day, but are perhaps less so today.

Pastoral Conventions

→ THEOCRITUS

From The XXI Idyllion   *English translation 1588*

Below are samples from the two most widely known classical pastorals in Renaissance England. The first is from the *Idyllia* of Theocritus, a Sicilian poet who lived in the third century B.C.E. (310–250 B.C.E.). Little is known of his life, and some of the works attributed to him are of doubtful origin. The poem included below comes from an anonymous late-sixteenth-century English text printed at Oxford: the first translation of the poet into English. The *Idyllia*— the primary source for love-related pastoral conventions, including those in *As You Like It*—often took the form of songs from lovesick shepherds. In Theocritus's poem, why does Eunica reject the neteherd (which can mean either a

---

Theocritus, *Six Idyllia, That Is, Six Small, or Petty Poems, or Eglogues, Chosen out of the Right Famous Sicilian Poet Theocritus, and Translated into English Verse* (Oxford, 1588); STC 23937.

cowherd or a shepherd)? What is she seeking in a beloved? Is he lacking in beauty? What precedent in mythology does the netetherd find for his union with a socially exalted woman, or a woman who thinks herself better than he? Compare this to the relationship between Silvius and Phoebe in *As You Like It*. Why does Phoebe reject Silvius and why is she attracted to Rosalind/Ganymede? In the many marriages that close the play, are those who marry of the same social status or class? Is marrying a social equal shown as an important indicator of happiness or marital stability?

From *The XXI Idyllion*

NETEHERD:

Eunica scorned me, when her I would have sweetly kiss'd,
And railing at me said: *go with a mischief where thou list.*[1]
Think'st thou, a wretched Neteherd,[2] *me to kiss? I have no will*
After the country guise[3] *to smooch, of city lips I skill.*[4]
My lovely mouth, so much as in thy dream thou shalt not touch.   5
How dost thou look? How dost thou talk? How playest thou the slouch?[5]
How daintily thou speak'st? What courting words thou bringest out?
How soft a beard thou hast? How fair thy locks hang round about?
Thy lips are like a sick man's lips, thy hands, so black they be,
And rankly[6] *thou dost smell, away, lest thou defilest me.*   10
Having thus said, she spatter'd[7] on her bosom twice or thrice,
And still beholding me from top to toe, in scornful wise,
She mutter'd with her lips, and with her eyes she looked aside,
And of her beauty wondrous coy she was, her mouth she wried,[8]
And proudly mock'd me to my face. My blood boil'd in each vein,   15
And red I wox[9] for grief, as doth the rose with dewy rain.
Thus leaving me, away she flung; since when, it vexeth me,
That I should be so scorned, of such a filthy drab[10] as she.
Ye shepherds, tell me true, am I not fair as any swan?[11]
Hath of a sudden any God, made me another man?   20
For well I wot[12] before, a comely grace in me did shine,
Like ivy round about a tree, and deck'd this beard of mine.
My crisped locks, like parsley on my temples wont[13] to spread,

---

[1] *list*: wish.   [2] *Neteherd*: cowherd; shepherd.   [3] *guise*: ways.   [4] *skill*: have knowledge.   [5] In this line and the two following, Eunica is making fun of how the netetherd looks, talks, and acts, ironically implying that he does *not* speak well or have a soft beard or beautiful hair.   [6] *rankly*: strongly.   [7] spatter'd: spit.   [8] wried: twisted.   [9] wox: grew.   [10] drab: disparaging term for a woman.   [11] swan: swain, a country lover.   [12] wot: knew.   [13] wont: accustomed.

And on[14] my eyebrows black, a milk white forehead glistered.
More seemly were mine eyes, than are Minerva's[15] eyes I know.   25
My mouth for sweetness passed[16] cheese, and from my mouth did flow
A voice more sweet than honeycombs. Sweet is my roundelay,[17]
When on the whistle, flute, or pipe, or cornet[18] I do play.
And all the women on our hills, do say that I am fair,
And all do love me well. But these that breathe the city air   30
Did never love me yet. And why? The cause is this I know,
That I a Neteherd am. They hear not, how in vales below
Fair Bacchus[19] kept a herd of beasts; nor can these nice[20] ones tell,
How Venus[21] raving for a Neteherd's love, with him did dwell
Upon the hills of Phrygia,[22] and how she loved again   35
Adonis[23] in the woods, and mourned in woods, when he was slain.
What was Endymion?[24] Was he not a Neteherd? Yet the moon
Did love this Neteherd so, that from the heavens descending soon,
She came to Latmos[25] grove, where with the dainty lad she lay.

[14] on: above.   [15] Minerva's: Roman goddess of wisdom, often described as "gray-eyed."
[16] passed: surpassed.   [17] roundelay: song.   [18] cornet: wind instrument.   [19] Bacchus: mythological god of wine.   [20] nice: ignorant.   [21] Venus: mythological goddess of love.   [22] Phrygia: ancient kingdom in modern-day Turkey.   [23] Adonis: boy whom Venus loved, killed by a boar.
[24] Endymion: in Greek mythology, a shepherd loved by Selene, goddess of the moon.
[25] Latmos: in Asia Minor.

→   VIRGIL

From The First Eclogue   *1589*

Translated by Abraham Fleming

This selection is taken from Abraham Fleming's 1589 translation of Virgil's *Eclogues*. Virgil was a famous Latin poet who lived during the reign of Octavius Caesar in the first century (70–19 B.C.E.). He was probably the most widely imitated poet in early modern England. His twelve-book epic poem *The Aeneid* told of the fall of Troy and the founding of Rome. But he also wrote pastoral and georgic verse. Georgic poetry deals with agricultural practices and the labor involved in rural life. In this first pastoral eclogue, Melibey laments that he is being forced to leave the countryside and enumerates the benefits of country living to Tityrus. Historically, Virgil may be referring to Octavius Caesar's appropriation of land to give to his soldiers after the battle of Philippi, though the poem is careful to praise Octavius, whom Tityrus has seen on a visit to Rome and who has told Tityrus to return to his native country to care for his oxen and

bulls. By contrast, Melibey will be sent out to a strange country and wonders if he will ever see his flocks and his fields again.

Why does country life seem so sweet to Melibey and Tityrus? What pleasures do they enjoy there, and how are these threatened by events in the outside world? How does this compare to Duke Senior's praise of life in the Forest of Arden in *As You Like It*? What contrast does he see between the court and the forest world to which he has fled, especially in his opening speech in act 2 or as articulated in Amiens's song, "Blow, blow, thou winter wind" (2.7.174)? Specifically, what vices do these figures attribute to the world outside the forest, and what virtues do they find within it? Are these the same virtues that old Corin sees in country life when he speaks with Touchstone?

From *The First Eclogue*

FROM THE FIRST ECLOGUE OF VIRGIL, ENTITLED TITYRUS

The Argument:

Melibey a shepherd, and familiar friend of Tityrus (in the person of all the Mantuans), being forced to forsake his lands and possessions in Mantua, took his flight through a piece of ground, where he found Tityrus, and heard him under a beech tree pleasantly piping a song of his sweetheart Amaryllis, and thereupon spoke unto him, saying, O Tityrus, etc. Now you must suppose that Melibey had on a shepherd's coat, which he had privily gotten away to disguise himself in flight, dragging after him a silly goat with his one hand and holding his shepherd's staff in the other, having also upon his neck and shoulders a little fardle or truss, and so drove his flock of goats before him.

The speakers are Melibey and Tityrus: Melibey representing a citizen or townsman of Mantua, and Tityrus the person of Virgil.

[Melibey and Tityrus discuss the bad omens that foretold the destruction of their peaceful life. Then Tityrus tells of his visit to the mighty city of Rome where he met Octavius Caesar who commanded him to return to his rural home to care for his animals. Melibey enviously speaks as follows.]

MELIBEY: O lucky old man therefore thy lambs shall whole remain to thee,
And large enough, albeit that bare stones and fenny floods[1]

[1] fenny floods: swampy areas.

Virgil, *The Bucoliks of Publius Virgilius Maro*, trans. Abraham Fleming (London, 1589), 1–3; STC 24817.

Do overlay the pastures all with muddy rush and sedge.[2]
Unwonted[3] feeding shall not taint thy cattle great with young,
Nor ill disease of neighbors' beasts shall do hurt unto thine.　　　　5
O lucky old man thou oft shall take the fresh and shady cold,
Even here among the rivers known and holy water springs.
On this side shall thy fence or hedge, next by thy neighbor's bounds,
Thy hedge of willow trees whose flowers are eat of Hybla bees,[4]
Shall oft with gentle sound of them persuade thee fall asleep.　　　　10
On the other side the tree-lopper[5] from under mountain high
Shall chant and sing with voice aloud piercing the airy sky,
Yet in the mean time ringdoves[6] hoarse, thy care and great delight,
No turtle dove shall cease to mourn from lofty tree of elm.
TITYRUS:　Therefore the stags, so light of foot, like birds shall feed in the air,　15
The seas shall fail, and fishes leave all bare upon the shore,
The Parthian pilgrim first shall drink of Arax river clear,
Or one of Germany shall drink of Tigris' flowing streams,
The bounds of both gone round about and passed far and near
Before his face and countenance shall slip out of my breast.[7]　　　　20
MELIBEY:　But we will hence depart, some to the thirsty Africans,
Part of us into Scythia[8] by traveling will come,
And to Oaxes rough of Crete, a river passing swift,[9]
And to the Britons parted from the universal world.
Lo, on a day I, beholding of my native country bounds　　　　25
Long time hereafter, seeing too some summers over-passed,
The covering of my cottage poor all made and thatched with turf,
Which cottage was my kingdom, shall I wonder at the same?[10]
Shall wicked soldiers have and hold these fallow fields so trimmed,
And strangers reap this crop of mine? Alack, behold whereto　　　　30
Discord hath brought and drawn by force our woeful citizens,
See now for whom our fields we have with seed in seedtime sown.
O Melibey, now pear trees graft, and vines in order see,

---

[2] sedge: a kind of plant that grows in wet places.　[3] Unwonted: infrequent.　[4] eat of Hybla bees: eaten by honeybees.　[5] tree-lopper: woodsman.　[6] ringdoves: wood pigeons.　[7] The Parthian pilgrim . . . out of my breast: Tityrus suggests, hyperbolically, that he will never forget Caesar, listing highly unlikely things that he says are nevertheless more probable than that possibility: that a person from the eastern Parthian Empire would drink from a northwestern river, or that a person in the north would drink from the famous Tigris in Mesopotamia. The point is that forgetting is as unlikely as these people switching places.　[8] Scythia: the area known in classical antiquity as Scythia included what is now southern Russia, Ukraine, Kazakhstan, Belarus, Poland, and Bulgaria.　[9] Oaxes . . . passing swift: there was a city in Crete called Oxus, but no river named the Oaxes.　[10] beholding . . . same: Melibey asks whether he will one day return and see his country again.

And go my goats, erst happy beasts, to places go unknown,
I being laid along upon a valley fresh and green   35
Hereafter shall not see you hang upon the bushy banks,
I will not sing songs any more, nor you my little goats
Shall never crop the blooming shrub, and bitter willow trees,
I feeding you, or all the while that I provide you food.
TITYRUS: Howbeit here thou mayest thee rest with me this present night,   40
Upon green leaves in grassy ground ripe apples some we have,
Soft chestnuts, and of cream and curds for cheese we have good store,
And now the highest tops of farms far off do cast a smoke,
And greater shadows than before from mountains high do fall.

➔ EDMUND SPENSER

From The Shepheardes Calender   *1579*

Published in 1579, Edmund Spenser's (1552–1599) *The Shepheardes Calender* did much to popularize the pastoral form in Elizabethan England, going through five editions before 1600. The text, with its dense marginal commentary by the wry personality "E. K." (whom many have assumed to be Spenser himself), imitates the apparatus of learned commentary usually reserved for books of great importance, like the Bible or works by classical authors such as Virgil. The presence of this commentary suggests the high value Spenser placed on this work, which signals his intent to proceed from the pastoral toward epic as many of the authors he names in his opening epistle have done. Spenser's language is difficult, and was acknowledged to be so even by his contemporaries. But his archaic word choices and complex syntax were part of a deliberate attempt to make English a language sufficiently complex and weighty to be suitable for creating poetry to rival that produced on the Continent and in Classical Greece and Rome. For those reasons, we have not modernized Spenser's verse but have glossed it liberally so that readers can get a feel for his very particular style.

Spenser's poem is divided into twelve eclogues, one for each month of the year. "Januarye," excerpted on page 137, focuses on the lovesickness of Colin Clout, who has been rejected by his beloved Rosalind who lives in the nearby town. In the woodcut accompanying the "Januarye" eclogue (Figure 4), one can see the disconsolate Colin amid his sheep. At his feet are the broken musical pipes he angrily throws down at the end of his lament, and in the distance one sees the town where Rosalind dwells. In the upper left-hand corner is an image

Edmund Spenser, *The Shepheardes Calender* (London, 1579), 4r, Fol. 1–Fol. 3; STC 23089.

Januarye. *Fol.*1

Ægloga prima.

ARGVMENT.

I N this fyrſt Æglogue Colin cloute *a ſhepheardes boy complaineth him
of his vnfortunate loue, being but newly (as ſemeth) enamoured of a countrie laſſe called* Roſalinde: *with which ſtrong affection being very ſore tra-
ueled, he compareth his carefull caſe to the ſadde ſeaſon of the yeare, to the
froſtie ground, to the froſen trees, and to his owne winterbeaten flocke. And
laſtlye, fynding himſelfe robbed of all former pleaſaunce and delights, hee
breaketh his Pipe in peeces, and caſteth him ſelfe to the ground.*

COLIN Cloute.

Shepeheards boye (no better doe him call)
when Winters waſtful ſpight was almoſt ſpent,
All in a ſunneſhine day, as did befall,
Led forth his flock, that had bene long ypent.
So faynt they woxe, and feeble in the folde,
That now vnnethes their feete could them vphold.

All as the Sheepe, ſuch was the ſhepeheards looke,
For pale and wanne he was, (alas the while,)
May ſeeme he loud, or els ſome care he tooke:
Well couth he tune his pipe, and frame his ſtile.
        A.i.   Tho

FIGURE 4 *A forlorn Colin Clout, forgetting his sheep, stares toward the town where
his unresponsive beloved Rosalind lives. The woodcut "Januarye" from* The Shepheardes Calender *by Edmund Spenser (1579).*

of Aquarius, the water carrier, the zodiac sign for the month of January. Interestingly, even as Colin vainly woos Rosalind, he is in turn wooed by Hobbinol, a country rustic. A note by E. K. that accompanied the poem says, concerning Hobbinol and Colin, that the special friendship between men expresses a love of the soul, not the body, and is in many cases to be preferred to love between man and woman. In what ways does *As You Like It* set up a competition between same-sex and heterosexual love and how does it echo or differ from the Rosalind/Colin/Hobbinol triangle? How does either the poem or the play resolve the tension between these two forms of love?

Much of Spenser's January eclogue concerns the relationship of Colin to the wintry January landscape. How does the landscape mirror his emotions? Is the same thing true in *As You Like It?* Though productions of the play often emphasize the greenness of the landscape, the Duke and his men frequently speak of the winds and rough weather of winter. How would you stage the weather in Arden?

From *The Shepheardes Calender*

From "The General Argument of the Whole Book"

Little I hope, needeth me at large to discourse[1] the first original of eclogues, having already touched the same. But for[2] the word *eclogues* I know is unknown to most, and also mistaken of some the best learned (as they think), I will say somewhat thereof, being not at all impertinent[3] to my present purpose.

They were first of the Greeks the inventors of them called Æglogai . . . that is goatherds' tales,[4] or although in Virgil and others the speakers be more shepherds than goatherds, yet Theocritus in whom is more ground of authority than in Virgil, this specially from that deriving, as from the first head and wellspring the whole invention of his Æglogues, maketh goatherds the person and authors of his tales. . . . These twelve eclogues everywhere answering to the seasons of the twelve months may be well derived into three forms or ranks. For either they be plaintive,[5] as the first, the sixth, the eleventh, and the twelfth, or recreative,[6] such as all those be which conceive matter of love or commendation of special personages, or moral, which for the most part be mixed with some satirical[7] bitterness. . . . [E. K.]

---

[1] **discourse:** explain.   [2] **for:** because.   [3] **impertinent:** irrelevant.   [4] **Æglogai . . . goatherds' tales:** a false etymology current in the Middle Ages and Renaissance defined *eclogue* as "goatherds' speeches," but *eclogue* actually comes from the Greek *eklegein*, to choose.   [5] **plaintive:** lamenting.   [6] **recreative:** recreational.   [7] **satirical:** ridiculing and denouncing vice.

JANUARYE:

ARGUMENT:

In this first Æglogue Colin Cloute a shepheardes boy complaineth him of his unfortunate love, being but newly (as semeth) enamoured of a countrie lasse called Rosalinde: with which strong affection being very sore traveled,[8] he compareth his carefull case to the sadde season of the yeare, to the frostie ground, to the frozen trees, and to his owne winterbeaten flocke. And lastlye, fynding himselfe robbed of all former pleasaunce and delights, hee breaketh his Pipe in peeces, and casteth him selfe to the ground.

COLIN CLOUTE:

A Shepeheards boye (no better doe him call)
When Winters wastful spight was almost spent,
All in a sunneshine day, as did befall,
Led forth his flock, that had bene long ypent.[9]
So faynt they woxe,[10] and feeble in the folde,   5
That now unnethes[11] their feete could them uphold.

All as the Sheepe, such was the shepeheards looke,
For pale and wanne[12] he was, (alas the while,)
May seeme he lovd, or els some care he tooke:
Well couth[13] he tune his pipe, and frame[14] his stile.   10
Tho to a hill his faynting flocke he ledde,
And thus him playnd,[15] the while his shepe there fedde.

Ye Gods of love, that pitie lovers payne,
(If any gods the paine of lovers pitie:)
Looke from above, where you in joyes remaine,   15
And bowe your eares unto my dolefull dittie.
And Pan[16] thou shepheards God, that once didst love,
Pitie the paines, that thou thy selfe didst prove.

Thou barrein ground, whome winters wrath hath wasted,
Art made a myrrhour, to behold my plight: 20
Whilome[17] thy fresh spring flowrd, and after hasted
Thy sommer prowde with Daffadillies dight.
And now is come thy wynters stormy state,
Thy mantle mard, wherein thou maskedst late.

---

[8] **traveled:** travailed, weary.   [9] **ypent:** penned.   [10] **woxe:** grew.   [11] **unnethes:** scarcely.   [12] **wanne:** weak.   [13] **couth:** cleverly could   [14] **frame:** shape.   [15] **playnd:** lamented.   [16] **Pan:** god of nature in Greek mythology.   [17] **Whilome:** once.

Such rage as winters, reigneth in my heart,   25
My life bloud friesing with unkindly cold:
Such stormy stoures[18] do breede my balefull smart,
As if my yeare were wast, and woxen old.
And yet alas, but now my spring begonne,
And yet alas, yt[19] is already donne.   30

You naked trees, whose shady leaves are lost,
Wherein the byrds were wont to build their bowre:[20]
And now are clothd with mosse and hoary frost,
Instede of blosomes, wherwith your buds did flowre:
I see your teares, that from your boughes doe raine,   35
Whose drops in drery ysicles[21] remaine.

All so my lustfull leafe is drye and sere,[22]
My timely buds with wayling all are wasted:
The blossome, which my braunch of youth did beare,
With breathed sighes is blowne away, and blasted,   40
And from mine eyes the drizling teares descend,
As on your boughes the ysicles depend.

Thou feeble flocke, whose fleece is rough and rent,[23]
Whose knees are weake through fast and evill fare:
Mayst witnesse well by thy ill government,   45
Thy maysters mind is overcome with care.
Thou weake, I wanne: thou leane, I quite forlorne:
With mourning pyne I, you with pyning mourne.

A thousand sithes[24] I curse that carefull hower,
Wherein I longd the neighbour towne to see: 50
And eke[25] tenne thousand sithes I blesse the stoure,
Wherein I sawe so fayre a sight, as shee.
Yet all for naught: such sight hath bred my bane.[26]
Ah God, that love should breede both joy and payne.

It is not Hobbinol, wherefore I plaine,   55
Albee[27] my love he seeke with dayly suit:
His clownish gifts and curtsies I disdaine,

---

[18] **stoures:** battles.   [19] **yt:** it.   [20] **bowre:** dwelling place.   [21] **ysicles:** icicles.   [22] **sere:** withered.
[23] **rent:** torn.   [24] **sithes:** times.   [25] **eke:** also.   [26] **bane:** ruin.   [27] **Albee:** although.

His kiddes, his cracknelles,[28] and his early fruit.
Ah foolish Hobbinol, thy gyfts bene[29] vayne:
Colin them gives to Rosalind againe.   60

I love thilke[30] lasse, (alas why doe I love?)
And am forlorne, (alas why am I lorne?)
Shee deignes[31] not my good will, but doth reprove,
And of my rurall musick holdeth scorne.
Shepheards devise[32] she hateth as the snake,   65
And laughes the songes, that Colin Clout doth make.

Wherefore my pype, albee rude Pan thou please,
Yet for thou pleasest not, where most I would:
And thou unlucky Muse,[33] that wontst[34] to ease
My musing mynd, yet canst not, when thou should: 70
Both pype and Muse, shall sore the while abye.[35]
So broke his oaten pype, and downe dyd lye.

By that, the welked[36] Phoebus[37] gan availe[38]
His weary waine,[39] and nowe the frosty Night
Her mantle black through heaven gan overhaile.   75
Which seene, the pensife[40] boy halfe in despight
Arose, and homeward drove his sonned sheepe,
Whose hanging heads did seeme his carefull case to weepe.

[28] cracknelles: crisp biscuits. [29] bene: be in. [30] thilke: this. [31] deignes: condescends.
[32] devise: poems. [33] Muse: one of nine mythological spirits that inspire creativity. [34] wontst:
was accustomed. [35] abye: pay the penalty for. [36] welked: faded. [37] Phoebus: the sun.
[38] availe: give help to. [39] waine: wagon (in mythology, Phoebus the sun god drives a chariot).
[40] pensife: brooding.

→ EDMUND SPENSER

From The Faerie Queene   *1596*

The Faerie Queene is Edmund Spenser's romance epic. It was planned in twelve
books, three of which were published in 1590 and three more in 1596. Each book
follows the adventures of a knight who represents a particular virtue, such as
Holiness or Friendship. All the knights serve Gloriana, an emblem of Queen
Elizabeth I. By the time Spenser was writing *The Faerie Queene*, medieval

Edmund Spenser, *The Faerie Queene* (London, 1596) 477–79; STC 23082.

knighthood was largely a thing of the past, but Spenser used tales of knightly adventure for a contemporary purpose — "to fashion a gentleman or noble person in virtuous and gentle discipline," arguing that readers would be delighted by the stories he recounted and therefore more likely to learn from them than from a more didactic treatise. Book VI, one of the most beautiful of the entire poem, features Calidore, the knight of Courtesy, a virtue frequently celebrated in pastoral literature. Calidore has been sent on a quest to capture the Blatant Beast, a monster that represents Slander and whose bite sickens everyone it catches. In his pursuit of the Blatant Beast, Calidore comes across some shepherds piping and singing, along with the shepherdess Pastorella. Calidore falls in love with her, but she is also loved by a young man named Coridon, whom she scorns. Pausing in his quest, Calidore spends some time in this pastoral world. There he talks with Melibae, the old shepherd who adopted Pastorella when she was a child and who had left a life at court to live a life of simplicity in the countryside. As in much pastoral literature, the burden of Melibae's discourse is the contrast between the corruptions of court life and the virtues of a shepherd's existence.

Throughout Book VI, Calidore's actions exemplify courtesy, a term associated with medieval knighthood, but which influenced the more modern concept of gentility (see Chapter 4). The following stanzas recount his participation in rural sports and his dealings with Coridon and Pastorella. How does his behavior in this passage show his ruling virtue? In *As You Like It*, is there a figure or figures who particularly display the virtue of courtesy? Do any of the characters in *As You Like It* learn courtesy as a result of their experiences in Arden? What evidence would you give to support your views?

It is also instructive to compare Calidore's wrestling match with Coridon to Orlando's match with Charles in act 1 of *As You Like It*. Is the wrestling match in Duke Frederick's court an example of a courteously conducted sport or an act of barbarity? Who is critical of this match? What is different about the wrestling in Spenser's poem?

From *The Faerie Queene*

STANZA 41

One day when as the shepheard swaynes together
Were met, to make their sports and merrie glee,
As they are wont[1] in faire sunshynie weather,
The whiles their flockes in shadowes shrouded bee,
They fell to daunce: then did they all agree,   5

[1]**wont**: accustomed.

That *Colin Clout*[2] should pipe as one most fit;
And *Calidore* should lead the ring, as hee
That most in *Pastorellaes*[3] grace did sit.
Thereat frown'd *Coridon*,[4] and his lip closely bit.

STANZA 42

But *Calidore* of courteous inclination
Tooke *Coridon*, and set him in[5] his place,
That he should lead the daunce, as was his fashion;
For *Coridon* could daunce, and trimly trace.[6]
And when as *Pastorella*, him to grace,[7]   5
Her flowry garlond tooke from her owne head,
And plast on his, he did it soone displace,
And did it put on *Coridons* in stead:
Then *Coridon* woxe frollicke,[8] that earst[9] seemed dead.

STANZA 43

Another time, when as they did dispose[10]
To practise games, and maisteries[11] to try,
They for their Iudge did *Pastorella* chose;
A garland was the meed[12] of victory.
There *Coridon* forth stepping openly,   5
Did challenge *Calidore* to wrestling game:
For he through long and perfect industry,[13]
Therein well practisd was, and in the same
Thought sure t'auenge his grudge, & worke his foe great shame.

STANZA 44

But *Calidore* he greatly did mistake;
For he was strong and mightily stiffe pight,[14]
That with one fall his necke he almost brake,
And had he not vpon him fallen light,

[2] *Colin Clout*: shepherd and poet, one of the personae in Spenser's *The Shepheardes Calender* (1579).   [3] *Pastorellaes*: beloved of Calidore and daughter to Melibae, the shepherd to whom Calidore has been speaking.   [4] *Coridon*: shepherd who loves Pastorella.   [5] set him in: gave him.   [6] trace: move.   [7] grace: show favor unto.   [8] woxe frollicke: began to move animatedly.   [9] earst: before.   [10] dispose: prepare.   [11] maisteries: skills.   [12] meed: reward.   [13] industry: hard work.   [14] stiffe pight: sturdy on his feet.

His dearest ioynt he sure had broken quight.[15]   5
Then was the oaken crowne by *Pastorell*
Giuen to *Calidore*, as his due right;
But he, that did in courtesie excell,
Gaue it to *Coridon*, and said he wonne it well.

STANZA 45

Thus did the gentle knight himselfe abeare[16]
Amongst that rusticke rout[17] in all his deeds,
That euen they, the which his riuals were,
Could not maligne[18] him, but commend him needs:[19]
For courtesie amongst the rudest breeds[20]   5
Good will and fauour. So it surely wrought
With this faire Mayd, and in her mynde the seeds
Of perfect loue did sow, that last forth brought
The fruite of ioy and blisse, though long time dearely bought.

[15] quight: completely.   [16] abeare: conduct.   [17] rout: company.   [18] maligne: speak badly of.
[19] needs: must.   [20] breeds: produces.

→ CHRISTOPHER MARLOWE

The Passionate Shepherd to His Love   *1599*

and

→ SIR WALTER RALEIGH (?)

The Nymph's Reply to the Shepherd   *1600*

An important part of pastoral are the songs of love that shepherds sing to their mistresses, not always with happy results. Christopher Marlowe (1564–1593), a sixteenth-century writer of poems and plays, including *Dr. Faustus*, *Edward II*, and *Tamburlaine*, was the author of one of the most famous of such lyrics from the period, the poem included below in which a shepherd tries to seduce his beloved into living with him amid the fields and pastures. This extremely popular poem circulated widely in manuscript and sparked a number of parodies and responses, one of which was believed to have been written by Sir Walter

England's Helicon (London, 1600), Aa1v–Aa2v; STC 3191.

Raleigh (1554–1618), the dashing early modern courtier, adventurer, and poet. "The Nymph's Reply to the Shepherd" lightly mocks the shepherd, his self-presentation, and his assumptions about pastoral life. Importantly, Marlowe's poem is not a dialogue; it leaves no room for the beloved to speak. This is typical of many pastoral works, in which male speakers pine for or woo a woman who remains silent. When the second poem gives the beloved a voice, what does she object to or question about the shepherd's invitation? With what inconvenient facts does she puncture his vision of their future? How does this pair of poems throw light on the interactions between Orlando and Rosalind in the Forest of Arden, especially after she finds his love poems pinned to trees?

The Passionate Shepherd to His Love

Come live with me, and be my love,
And we will all the pleasures prove,
That valleys, groves, hills and fields,
Woods, or steepy mountain yields.

And we will sit upon the rocks,   5
Seeing the shepherds feed their flocks,
By shallow rivers, to whose falls,
Melodious birds sing madrigals.[1]

And I will make thee beds of roses,
And a thousand fragrant poesies,[2]   10
A cap of flowers, and a kirtle,[3]
Embroidered all with leaves of myrtle.[4]

A gown made of the finest wool,
Which from our pretty lambs we pull,
Fair lined slippers for the cold: 15
With buckles of the purest gold.

A belt of straw and ivy buds,
With coral clasps and amber studs,
And if these pleasures may thee move,
Come live with me, and be my love.   20

---

[1] madrigals: songs with parts for several singers.   [2] poesies: bunches of flowers.   [3] kirtle: gown.
[4] myrtle: type of shrub known for its fragrance.

The shepherd swains shall dance and sing,
For thy delight each May morning,
If these delights thy mind may move,
Then live with me, and be my love.

The Nymph's Reply to the Shepherd

If all the world and love were young,
And truth in every shepherd's tongue,
These pretty pleasures might me move,
To live with thee, and be thy love.

Time drives the flocks from field to fold,   5
When rivers rage, and rocks grow cold,
And Philomel[1] becometh dumb,[2]
The rest complains of cares to come.

The flowers do fade, and wanton[3] fields,
To wayward winter reckoning[4] yields,   10
A honey tongue, a heart of gall,[5]
Is fancy's spring, but sorrow's fall.

Thy gowns, thy shoes, thy beds of roses,
Thy cap, thy kirtle, and thy poesies,
Soon break, soon wither, soon forgotten: 15
In folly ripe, in reason rotten.

Thy belt of straw and ivy buds,
Thy coral clasps and amber studs,
All these in me no means can move,
To come to thee, and be thy love.   20

But could youth last, and love still breed,
Had joys no date, nor age no need,
Then these delights my mind might move,
To live with thee, and be thy love.

---

[1] **Philomel:** the nightingale.   [2] **dumb:** silent.   [3] **wanton:** fickle.   [4] **reckoning:** time of calling to account.   [5] **gall:** bitterness.

➔ **LADY MARY WROTH**

From Pamphilia to Amphilanthus

1623

Women as well as men, of course, wrote pastoral poetry. Lady Mary Wroth (1587–1651/53) was one of those women. The daughter of Robert Sidney and niece of Sir Philip Sidney and Mary Herbert, Countess of Pembroke, she came from a distinguished family of writers and literary patrons. In 1604 she married Sir Robert Wroth, with whom she had one son. Wroth left her a widow encumbered with debt in 1614. She did not remarry, but had two more children, apparently with her cousin William Herbert. A prolific writer, she produced a very long prose romance, *The Countess of Mountgomeries Urania*; a sonnet sequence, "Pamphilia to Amphilanthus," and a tragicomedy, *Love's Victory*. "Pamphilia to Amphilanthus," from which the following pastoral song is taken, exists in two forms, a manuscript written by Wroth that is now in the Folger Library and contains 117 songs and sonnets, and a printed version of 103 of these poems appended to the print version of the 1621 *Urania*. In the sequence, as in the romance, Pamphilia is a faithful lover to the inconstant Amphilanthus, whose name means "lover of two." In the selection included here, Wroth reverses the customary trope of a male shepherd pining for a distant and cold beloved and puts the love complaint in the mouth of a shepherdess. Wroth also employs the familiar trope of a lover whose inner state is at odds with her external environment. In *As You Like It*, Phoebe is, similarly, a love-struck shepherdess who in turn is loved by a shepherd whom she scorns. How does Shakespeare play on the convention of the pining shepherd/shepherdess? What is he doing with these conventional postures, and how are they resolved?

"The Spring now come at last
To trees, fields, to flowers,
And meadows makes to taste
His pride,[1] while sad showers
Which from my eyes do flow   5
Makes known what cruel pains
Cold Winter yet remains
No sign of spring I know.

The sun which to the earth
Gives heat, light, and pleasure,   10
Joys in spring, hateth dearth,

---

[1] **pride:** glory.

Lady Mary Wroth, *Pamphilia to Amphilanthus* (Folger V.a.104), "Song 1."

Plenty makes his treasure —
His heat to me is cold,
His light all darkness is
Since I am barred of bliss[2]   15
I heat nor light behold."

A shepherdess thus said
Who was with grief oppressed
For truest love betrayed
Barred her from quiet rest.   20
And weeping, thus said she:
"My end approacheth near
Now willow must I wear[3]
My fortune so will be.

With branches of this tree   25
I'll dress my hapless head
Which shall my witness be
My hopes in love are dead;
My clothes embroidered all
Shall be with garlands round   30
Some scattered, others bound,
Some tied, some like to fall.

The bark[4] my book shall be
Where daily I will write
This tale of hapless me   35
True slave to fortune's spite;
The root shall be my bed
Where nightly I will lie,
Wailing inconstancy
Since all true love is dead.   40

And these lines I will leave
If some such lover come
Who may them right conceive,
And place them on my tomb:

---

[2] **barred of bliss:** kept from happiness (by the inconstancy of her lover).   [3] **willow . . . wear:** wearing the willow was a token of unrequited love or marked the death of a lover.   [4] **bark:** bark of a tree; in pastoral romances, lovers often carved the names of their beloved on the trees around them or wrote love poems on the bark. See Chapter 2 of this edition.

'She who still constant loved
Now dead with cruel care[5]
Killed with unkind despair,
And change, her end here proved.'"

45

[5] care: sorrow.

Pastoral Critique

As we have seen, pastoral works often involve satiric ridicule and the more serious critique of social ills. *As You Like It* is no exception. The play has at least one character, Jaques, who feels it is his special duty to rail against the evils of the world, though in practice he is often more restrained than he claims he would like to be. One question to consider is the play's attitude toward Jaques. A melancholic man, Jaques paints life in dark colors and wishes for a fool's license to mock everyone (see Chapter 3). Do the other characters, including Duke Senior, take him seriously? Is he a wise man? How does his mode of critique differ from that of Touchstone or Adam?

Whatever one thinks of Jaques, the professional cynic, the play in its entirety does make reference to what were widely perceived as pressing social problems. The texts included in this section provide a glimpse of some of these contemporary concerns that directly or indirectly percolate through Shakespeare's play.

THE DECAY OF HOSPITALITY

When first speaking to Ganymede and Aliena in act 2 about the possibility of his offering them hospitality, old Corin says that:

> . . . I am shepherd to another man
> And do not shear the fleeces that I graze.
> My master is of churlish disposition,
> And little recks to find the way to heaven
> By doing deeds of hospitality.
> Besides, his cote, his flocks, and bounds of feed
> Are now on sale, and at our sheepcote now,
> By reason of his absence, there is nothing
> That you will feed on. (2.4.68–76)

Corin is here referring to several causes for widespread social discontent. One is the decay of rural hospitality. Absentee landlords, such as Corin's master, are not on hand to offer food, drink, and help to strangers such as

Ganymede and Aliena or to their rural neighbors. They are, in effect, stepping back from their role as protectors of those dependent on them and to whom they are bound in webs of mutual obligation. This is not unlike Oliver's cruelty to Adam, the faithful servant of eighty years whom he calls an "old dog" (1.1.60) and is willing to dismiss from his house for aiding Orlando. In both instances, traditional social roles are being overturned.

→ WILLIAM VAUGHAN

From The Golden Grove   *1600*

In 1600 the Welshman William Vaughan (1577–1641) wrote a guide to the proper governance of the self, the household, and the country. In this work he critiqued many of the vices of the time, including the decay of hospitality. In the selections printed below, how does Vaughan define good hospitality, and what, in his view, has caused it to decay? Does anyone in *As You Like It* uphold traditions of hospitality? Does good hospitality require that one be wealthy?

CHAPTER 24

Of Hospitality

Hospitality is the chiefest point of humanity which a householder can show, not only unto his friends but also unto strangers and wayfaring[1] men. For which cause *he that keepth a good house, and entertaineth strangers, is said to receive Christ himself.* Which likewise another holy father confirmeth, saying: *We must tender hospitality without discretion,[2] lest that the person, whom we exclude and shut out of doors, be God himself.* This Abraham knew very well, when he accustomed to sit in his tent door of purpose to call in travelers, and to relieve them. Among whom *he entertained on a time three Angels.* This also was not unknown to *Lot*, when as he used to harbor guests, and *compel Angels being under the shape of pilgrims to come into his house.* We read, that the harlot Rahab, for her hospitality *was saved with all her household from death at the winning of Jericho.* Wherefore, O ye that be rich, see that ye keep good hospitality, and relieve the impotent and distressed. To conclude,

[1]**wayfaring:** wandering.   [2]*discretion:* discrimination (about whom we are hospitable to).

William Vaughan, *The Golden-Groue Moralized in Three Books: a Work Very Necessary for all Such, as Would Know How to Governe Themselves, their Houses, or their Countrey* (1600); STC 24610.

if we consider more narrowly and pierce more deeply with a sharp eye into the benefits of hospitality, though no other cause could persuade us, yet *the monuments of the New Testament* might exhort us thereunto.

CHAPTER 25

Wherein Good Hospitality Consisteth

They are greatly deceived who think that hospitality doth consist in slibber[3] sauces, in spiced meats, or in diversities. For these are not else save[4] fooleries and fond[5] wasting of goods, whereby the flesh is provoked to lechery, and becometh altogether inflamed, massy, and diseased. Further, experience teacheth that none are more subject to sickness than they that gormandize[6] and feed on sundry kinds of dishes. The reason is because . . . those diversities which they eat be repugnant and contrary the one to the other, and breed putrefaction and corrupt humors within their bodies. Whereas contrariwise they that live on one sort of meat and hardly do look fair, lusty, and well-complexioned and most commonly attain unto very old age. Good hospitality therefore consisteth not in gluttonous diversities but rather in one kind of meat, in clothing the naked, and in giving alms unto the poor.

CHAPTER 26

Why Housekeeping Nowadays Is Decayed

The causes why hospitality is nowadays brought to so low . . are five. The first is ambition, which moveth gentlemen that are of large revenues to wear gorgeous attires, to trail a costly port after them, to cavalier[7] it abroad, and giving up housekeeping at home to take a chamber in London where they consume their time in viewing of stage plays, in carousing of healths[8] and, perhaps, in visiting of courtesans. The second is hatred, which pricketh gentlemen to fall out with their neighbors and to enrich the lawyers by commencing of suits and controversies. The third is covetousness,[9] which persuadeth landlords to hoard up substance for the devil, to enhance incomes, to raise rents (for fear lest yeomen keep better hospitality then themselves,) and to convert tillage into pastures.[10] In consideration of which abominable

---

[3]**slibber:** slimy. [4]**nothing else save:** nothing but. [5]**fond:** foolish. [6]**gormandize:** (over) indulge. [7]**cavalier:** play at being gallant. [8]**carousing of healths:** drinking toasts. [9]**covetousness:** greediness. [10]**tillage into pastures:** common areas for grazing into private land. This process was known as "enclosing." It was a continual source of discontent for 150 years as small tenant farmers tried to maintain their traditional right of access to and use of common lands, and landlords tried to convert more and more of those lands into pasturage for sheep.

abuse, it was most prudently enacted in the last Parliament, that all lands, which were converted into sheep pastures, or to the fatting or grazing of cattle (the same having been tillage lands) should be before the first of May in the Year of our Lord 1599 last past, restored to tillage by the possessors thereof, and so should continue forever. It was further enacted in the said Parliament that every person offending against the premises aforesaid should forfeit for every acre not restored the sum of twenty shillings yearly, as long as the offense continued. The fourth reason why hospitality is carried to so low an ebb proceedeth of building, for sooner shall we see a gentleman build a stately house than give alms and cherish the needy. The fifth and last cause of the decay of hospitality is gluttony, which induceth men to prepare artificial cookeries and diverse sorts of meat, whereas one large and wholesome mess of meat could peradventure countervaile, yea, and go beyond all their junkets, and dainty delicacies.

THE EFFECTS OF ENCLOSURES

Toward the end of his description of the decay of hospitality, Vaughan mentions the conversion of commonly owned croplands into pastures for sheep. Beginning in the late medieval period, many of England's large landowners began to fence off or "enclose" once-open farmland to use for grazing the highly profitable sheep on which England's wool industry depended. Raising sheep made money because of the demand for woolen goods and because it was less labor intensive to raise sheep than crops and less dependent on the caprices of the weather. As we will see in some of the following materials, in the late sixteenth century the Midlands, and the borderlands of the Forest of Arden, in particular, were affected by enclosures.[1] One consequence was that many tenants were evicted from land they had customarily rented and farmed. Some became vagrants, wandering the countryside looking for short-term work. Though social historians disagree as to the actual extent of evictions, enclosure was definitely *perceived* as a serious threat to peasant life in England during the sixteenth and seventeenth centuries. Enclosures were one source of outbreaks of peasant unrest, which ranged in intensity from small local disturbances and the symbolic destruction of fences around enclosed property to large-scale insurrections like the Norfolk protests, led by Robert Kett in 1549, which involved as many as 15,000 people. In Shakespeare's play, Corin appears to work for a sheep farmer

---

[1] For a reading of the play that finds traces in it of Midlands' unrest caused by enclosures and tenant evictions, see Richard Wilson, "'Like the Old Robin Hood': *As You Like It* and the Enclosure Riots," *Will Power: Essays on Shakespearean Authority* (Detroit: Wayne State UP, 1993), 63–82.

who is an absentee landlord and may be a beneficiary of the enclosure of lands on the skirts of the forest. Juliet Dusinberre has even speculated that the "old carlot" of whom Corin speaks was a historical person, the notorious encloser and absentee landowner John Quarles.[2] It is the old carlot's sheep and property that Ganymede and Aliena buy.

[2] Juliet Dusinberre, ed., *As You Like It* (London: Arden Shakespeare of Thompson Learning, 2006) 284, note to line 109.

→ SIR THOMAS MORE

From Utopia

1516

Translated by Ralph Robinson

Anti-enclosure sentiment was a constant topic in sermons and political writings of the sixteenth century, the most famous diatribe against the practice occurring in Thomas More's *Utopia*, first written in 1516 in Latin and published in an English translation in 1551. More (1478–1535) was one of the prominent Catholic statesmen of early modern England, most famous, perhaps, for his refusal to sign an oath acknowledging King Henry VIII as head of the Church of England, a refusal for which he paid with his life. More's *Utopia* is one of the great thought experiments of the period. Like most works in the genre of utopian fiction, it is as interested in critiquing contemporary society as in imagining a better one. This is made clear through *Utopia*'s two-part structure. In Book I, Sir Thomas More, a fictional version of the author, recounts his conversations with the traveler, Raphael Hythloday, about what is wrong in English society. Book II, by contrast, describes the practices and customs of the utopian nation Hythloday claims to have visited in the New World. In the section excepted here from Book I, More is quoting Hythloday, who has been recounting a conversation he once had on the topic of English criminal justice with John Morton, Cardinal Archbishop of Canterbury and Lord Chancellor of England, and a dinner guest knowledgeable about English law.

While Shakespeare's play is a comedy and only treats the enclosure issue in passing, Corin's description of the conditions of his work suggests that the Forest of Arden may not be a utopia to those who live there permanently. What social ills outlined in More's text do we see echoed in direct or indirect ways in Shakespeare's play? To what extent are hunger and displacement foregrounded in Arden? Do those who arrive in Arden from the corrupt court of Duke Frederick or the household of Oliver de Boys see Arden differently from those who

Sir Thomas More, *Utopia*, trans. Ralph Robinson (London, 1551), STC 18094.

live there permanently? How do you explain the different perspectives various characters have toward life in Arden? Who sees it as a utopia and why? Who sees it as imperfect?

From *Utopia*

From The First Book of the Communication of Raphael Hythloday, concerning the best state of a commonwealth

". . . But yet this is not only the necessary cause of stealing.[1] There is another, which, as I suppose, is proper and peculiar to you Englishmen alone." "What is that?" quod the Cardinal. "Forsooth my lord," (quod I), "your sheep that were wont[2] to be so meek and tame, and so small eaters, now, as I hear say, have become so great devourers and so wild that they eat up and swallow down the very men themselves. They consume, destroy, and devour whole fields, houses, and cities. For look in what parts of the realm doth grow the finest, and therefore dearest wool: there noble men and gentlemen—yea and certain Abbots,[3] holy men, God wote[4]—not contenting themselves with the yearly revenues and profits that were wont to grow to their forefathers and predecessors of their lands, nor being content that they live in rest and pleasure, nothing profiting, yea much noying[5] the weal public,[6] leave no ground for tillage, they enclose all into pastures, they throw down houses, they pluck down towns, and leave nothing standing, but only the church to make of it a sheephouse.[7] And as though you lost no small quantity of ground by forests, chases, launds,[8] and parks, those good holy men turn all dwelling places and all glebeland[9] into desolation and wilderness. Therefore that one covetous and insatiable cormorant[10] and very plague of his native country may compass about and enclose many thousand acres of ground together within one pale[11] or hedge, the husbandmen be thrust out of their own, or else either by coveyne[12] and fraud, or by violent oppression they be put besides it, or by wrongs and injuries they be so wea-

---

[1] **necessary cause of stealing:** Hythloday has just been arguing that soldiers wounded in the wars and unable to work at their former trades often turn to stealing, as do men who serve as retainers to noblemen who then die and leave them without any means of subsistence. Hythloday is suggesting that people steal when they have no other viable options for survival. [2] **wont:** accustomed. [3] **Abbots:** the heads of monasteries. [4] **God wote:** "God knows," an expression used to emphasize the truth of what has just been or is about to be said. [5] **noying:** irritating or annoying. [6] **weal public:** the best interest or general good of a community, or, alternately, an entity such as the state or the commonwealth. [7] **sheephouse:** a shelter or dwelling for sheep. [8] **launds:** glades, pasture area. [9] **glebeland:** soil. [10] **cormorant:** a large sea bird, used figuratively as a term for a greedy person. [11] **pale:** a fence or boundary. [12] **coveyne:** covin, meaning deceit or treachery.

ried, that they be compelled to sell all: by one means therefore or by other, either by hook or crook they must needs depart away, poor, silly, wretched souls, men, women, husbands, wives, fatherless children, widows, woeful mothers, with their young babes, and their whole household small in substance, and much in number, as husbandry requireth many hands. Away they trudge, I say, out of their known and accustomed houses, finding no place to rest in. All their household stuff, which is very little worth, though it might well abide the sale, yet being suddenly thrust out, they be constrained to sell it for a thing of naught. And when they have wandering about soon spent that, what can they then else do but steal, and then justly, God wot, be hanged, or else go about begging. And yet then also they be cast in prison as vagabonds,[13] because they go about and work not, whom no man will set to work, though they never so willingly proffer themselves thereto. For one shepherd or herdsman is enough to eat up that ground with cattle, to the occupying whereof about husbandry many hands were requisite.[14] And this is also the cause why victuals[15] be now in many places dearer. Yea, besides this the price of wool is so risen, that poor folks, which were wont to work it, and make cloth thereof, be now able to buy none at all. And by this means very many be forced to forsake work, and to give themselves to idleness. For after that so much ground was enclosed for pasture, an infinite multitude of sheep died of the rot, such vengeance God took of their inordinate and insatiable covetousness, sending among the sheep that pestiferous murrain,[16] which much more justly should have fallen on the sheep-masters' own heads. And though the number of sheep increase never so fast, yet the price falleth not one mite, because there be so few sellers. For they be almost all come into a few rich men's hands, whom no need driveth to sell before they lust,[17] and they lust not before they may sell as dear[18] as they lust. Now the same cause bringeth in like dearth[19] of the other kinds of cattle, yea and that so much and more, because that after farms plucked down, and husbandry decayed, there is no man that passeth for the breeding of young store. For these rich men bring not up the young ones of great cattle as they do lambs. But first they buy them abroad very cheap, and afterward when they be fatted in their pastures, they sell them again exceeding dear. And therefore (as I suppose) the whole incommodity[20] hereof is

[13] **cast in prison as vagabonds:** sixteenth-century laws against vagrancy stipulated that able-bodied men without work could be whipped, branded, put to forced labor, or imprisoned. [14] **one shepherd or herdsman . . . many hands were requisite:** the expanded pastureland created by enclosure acts required fewer laborers for grazing livestock than had been necessary under the open field system when the land was used to cultivate crops, thereby putting many people out of work. [15] **victuals:** food. [16] **murrain:** generic name for an infectious disease amongst livestock. [17] **lust:** want. [18] **dear:** expensively, at a high price. [19] **dearth:** scarcity, lack. [20] **incommodity:** disadvantage, injury.

not yet felt. For yet they make dearth only in those places, where they sell. But when they shall fetch them away from thence where they be bred faster than they can be brought up, then shall there also be felt great dearth, when store begineth to fail there, where the ware is bought. Thus the unreasonable covetousness of a few hath turned the thing to the utter undoing of your land, in the which thing the chief felicity of your realm did consist. For this great dearth of victuals causeth men to keep as little houses, and as small hospitality as they possibly may, and to put away their servants: whither, I pray you,[21] but to begging, or else (which these gentle bloods and stout stomachs will sooner set their minds unto) to stealing? Now to amend the matter,[22] to this wretched beggary and miserable poverty is joined greater wantonness, importunate superfluity,[23] and excessive riot. For not only gentlemen's servants, but also handicraft men,[24] yea and almost the ploughmen of the country, with all other sorts of people, use much strange and proud newfangledness in their apparel, and too much prodigal riot,[25] and sumptuous fare[26] at their table. Now bawds, queanes, whores, harlots, strumpets, brothelhouses, stews, and yet other stews,[27] wine taverns, ale houses, and tippling houses, with so many naughty, lewd, and unlawful games as dice, cards, tables,[28] tennis, bowls, quoits,[29] do not all these send the haunters of them straight a stealing, when their money is gone? Cast out these pernicious abominations, make a law that they which plucked down farms and towns of husbandry shall re-edify them, or else yield, and uprender[30] the possession thereof to such as will go to the cost of building them anew. Suffer not these rich men to buy up all, to engross and forestall, and with their monopoly to keep the market alone as please them. Let not so many be brought up in idleness: let husbandry and tillage be restored, let cloth-working be renewed, that there may be honest labors for this idle sort to pass their time in profitably, which hitherto either poverty hath caused to be thieves, or else now be either vagabonds, or idle servingmen, and shortly will be thieves. Doubtless unless you find a remedy for these enormities, you shall in vain advance yourselves of executing justice upon felons."

[21] **I pray you:** I ask you.   [22] **to amend the matter:** to improve the situation, used here sarcastically to suggest the opposite (to make matters worse).   [23] **importunate superfluity:** burdensome and inappropriate waste.   [24] **handicraft men:** artisans, workmen, those who performed skilled handiwork.   [25] **prodigal riot:** wasteful, unrestrained living.   [26] **sumptuous fare:** expensive food.   [27] **bawds . . . stews:** all terms for people and places associated with prostitution. [28] **tables:** chess, backgammon, or other games played on boards.   [29] **quoits:** a game in which the player throws rings at a peg placed in the ground.   [30] **uprender:** render up, give.

→ MICHAEL DRAYTON

From Poly-Olbion
1612

Michael Drayton (1563–1631), a native of Warwickshire where the Forest of Arden was located, specifically blamed enclosures for the decay of the once-great forest and its surroundings. In *Poly-Olbion* (1612), his poetic survey of all the shires of England, Drayton celebrates his ties to the region before having the Forest of Arden speak in her own voice, partly to bewail the enclosures that have encroached on the territory of the forest and the surrounding pastures. Warwickshire was also Shakespeare's birthplace, and Shakespeare himself was peripherally involved in a drawn-out legal battle involving enclosures around Stratford in 1614. He therefore cannot have been unfamiliar with the practice. Interestingly, after the Forest of Arden's complaint, Drayton's poem goes on to describe the deer that populate the forest and then to describe the life of a hermit who has taken refuge there after ten years at court.

In Drayton's poem, what exactly does the forest suggest are the dangers she faces, and, conversely, what does the hermit find of value in Arden and why has he fled there? At the end of *As You Like It*, Duke Frederick, coming to attack Duke Senior, is converted by "an old religious man" (5.4.142) he meets at the edge of the forest. He then resigns his stolen dukedom to pursue a religious life, and Jaques vows to join him. How does Drayton's account of the hermit help to explain why some characters disavow court life and choose another path?

Upon the mid-lands[1] now th'industrious Muse[2] doth fall;
That shire which we the heart of England well may call,
As she herself extends (the midst which is decreed)
Betwixt St. Michael's Mount,[3] and Barwick-bord'ring Tweed,[4]
Brave Warwick;[5] that abroad so long advanc't her bear,[6]   5
By her illustrious Earls renowned everywhere;
Above her neighboring shires which always bore her head.
My native country then, which so brave spirits hast bred,
If there be virtue yet remaining in the earth,
Or any good of thine thou breathd'st into my birth,   10

[1] **the Mid-lands:** area of England whose borders are southern England, northern England, East Anglia, and Wales.   [2] **Muse:** one of the mythological goddesses or spirits that inspire literary and artistic creation.   [3] **St. Michael's Mount:** a tidal island off the coast of Cornwall, in Southern England.   [4] **Barwick-bord'ring Tweed:** the River Tweed forms a border between Scotland and England and flows into the North Sea at Berwick-upon-Tweed.   [5] **Warwick:** Warwickshire.   [6] **her bear:** a bear, represented with a ragged staff, is the traditional emblem of the earls of Warwick.

Michael Drayton, *Poly-Olbion* (London, 1612), 213–14, 215–18; STC 7226.

Accept it as thine own whilst now I sing of thee;
Of all thy later brood th'unworthiest though I be.[7]
Muse, first of Arden tell, whose foot-steps yet are found
In her rough wood-lands more than any other ground
That mighty Arden held even in her height of pride;   15
Her one hand touching Trent, the other, Severn's side.[8]
The very sound of these, the wood-nymphs[9] doth awake:
When thus of her own self the ancient forest spake:
"My many goodly sites when first I came to show,
Here opened I the way to mine own over-throw: 20
For, when the world found out the fitness of my soil,
The gripple[10] wretch began immediately to spoil
My tall and goodly woods, and did my grounds enclose:
By which, in little time my bounds I came to lose.
When Britain first her fields with villages had filled,   25
Her people wexing still, and wanting where to build,
They oft dislodg'd the hart, and set their houses, where
He in the broome and brakes[11] had long time made his lair.
Of all the forests here within this mighty Isle,
If those old Britons then me Sovereign did instile,[12]   30
I needs must be the great'st; for greatness tis alone
That gives our kind the place: else were there many a one
For pleasantness of shade that far doth me excel.
But, of our forests kind the quality to tell,
We equally partake with wood-lands as with plain,   35
Alike with hill and dales and every day maintain
The sundry kinds of beasts upon our copious wastes,
That men for profit breed, as well as those of chase."

. . . .

And near to these our thicks,[13] the wild and frightful herds,
Not hearing other noise but this of chattering birds,
Feed fairly on the lands; both sorts of seasoned deer:
Here walk, the stately red, the freckled fallow[14] there: 90
The bucks and lusty stags amongst the rascalls[15] strew'd,
As sometime gallant spirits amongst the multitude.
Of all the beasts which we for our venerial[16] name,

---

[7] **My native Country . . . th'unworthiest though I be:** Drayton was from Warwickshire. [8] **Arden . . . Severn's side:** the Forest of Arden, bordered by the River Trent on the northeast and the Severn on the southwest. [9] **wood-nymphs:** also called dryads, mythological spirits who dwell in the woods. [10] **gripple:** greedy. [11] **broome and brakes:** shrubbery. [12] **instile:** to call by the name of. [13] **thicks:** the densest part of a forest. [14] **fallow:** a species of deer smaller in size than the stag. [15] **rascalls:** young deer. [16] **venerial:** associated with the chase or hunt.

The hart amongst the rest, the hunter's noblest game:
. . . .
Whereas the hermit leads a sweet retired life,
From villages replete with ragg'd and sweating clowns,   165
And from the loathsome airs of smoky citied towns.
Suppose twixt noon and night, the sun his half-way wrought
(The shadows to be large, by his descending brought)
Who with a fervent eye looks through the twyring[17] glades,
And his dispersed rays commixeth with the shades,   170
Exhaling the milch dew,[18] which there had tarried long,
And on the ranker grass til past the noon-sted[19] hung;
When as the hermit comes out of his homely cell,[20]
Where from all rude resort he happily doth dwell:
Who in the strength of youth, a man at arms hath been;   175
Or one who of this world the vileness having seen,
Retires him from it quite; and with a constant mind
Man's beastliness so loathes, that flying human kind,
The black and darksome nights, the bright and gladsome days
Indifferent are to him, his hope on God that stays.   180
Each little village yields his short and homely fare:
To gather wind-fall'n sticks, his great'st and only care,
Which every aged tree still yieldeth to his fire.
This man, that is alone a king in his desire,
By no proud ignorant lord is basely over-aw'd,   185
Nor his false praise affects, who grossly being claw'd,[21]
Stands like an itchy moyle;[22] nor of a pin he weighs
What fools, abused kings, and humorous ladies raise.
His free and noble thought, ne'er envies at the grace
That oftentimes is given unto a bawd[23] most base,   190
Nor stirs it him to think on the imposter vile,
Who seeming what he's not, doth sensually beguile
The sottish purblind world:[24] but absolutely free,
His happy time he spends the works of God to see,
In those so sundry herbs which there in plenty grow: 195
Whose sundry strange effects he only seeks to know.
. . . .

---

[17] **twyring:** twinkling.   [18] **milch dew:** dew resembling milk.   [19] **noon-sted:** the position of
the sun at noon.   [20] **cell:** a small dwelling place.   [21] **claw'd:** flattered.   [22] **itchy moyle:** mule
afflicted with the itch (the mule's "itch" is only soothed by flattery).   [23] **bawd:** a panderer or
go-between, usually with a sexual connotation.   [24] **sottish purblind world:** foolish and inca-
pable of discernment.

THE ABUSE OF GENTLEMANLY PASTIMES: WRESTLING, DUELING
AND GIVING THE LIE

→ SIR THOMAS ELYOT

From The Book Named the Governor   *1531*

Gentlemen in the early modern period were expected to take care of their bodies as well as their minds and were encouraged to undertake various kinds of
sport and exercise. Wrestling was one of those sports, though it was sometimes
associated with the lower classes and viewed as slightly suspect.[1] In 1636, a book
of celebratory poems by Michael Drayton entitled *Annalia Dubrensia: Upon
the Yearly Celebration of Mr. Robert Dover's Olympic Games upon Cotswold Hills*,
praised Dover for encouraging all the traditional sports connected with
England's rural life. The frontispiece to that work shows scenes of people hunting, jumping, fighting with cudgels, doing acrobatics, and, toward the upper
right-hand corner, wrestling (Figure 5). Those taking part seem to be both
gentlemen and yeomen, and the poems included in the volume celebrate the
social unity promoted by such games, whose revival James I had been particularly eager to encourage. Many conduct books encouraged young men to pursue wrestling, provided that it was undertaken properly, which meant, among
other things, with due regard for the courteous treatment of the opponent. Sir
Thomas Elyot's (1490?–1546) *The Book Named the Governor* (1531) was an influential and popular treatise intended to educate young men for positions of
power. In the excerpts included below Elyot discusses the role of wrestling in
fashioning a gentleman. For Elyot, why should young men practice wrestling?
Under what conditions should it take place? Compare Elyot's recommendations
to the wrestling match we see between Charles and Orlando in act 1 of *As You
Like It*. Is the court wrestling promoted by Duke Frederick a healthful sport?
Is there anything wrong with how the wrestling matches are conducted? Is
Orlando demeaned or elevated by his participation in the wrestling contest?

FROM THE FIRST BOOK

Chapter 16, Of sundry forms of exercise necessary for every gentleman.

Although I have hitherto advanced the commendation of learning, especially in gentlemen, yet it is to be considered that continual study without
some manner of exercise shortly exhausteth the spirits vital, and hindereth

---

[1] For a good treatment of early modern debates about wrestling see Cynthia Marshall, "Wrestling
as Play and Game in *As You Like It*," *Studies in English Literature, 1500–1900* 33.2 (1993): 265–87.

Sir Thomas Elyot, *The Book Named the Governor* (London, 1531), fol. 62–63, 63; STC 7635.

FIGURE 5 *A depiction of the traditional sports of rural England, including two men wrestling (near top right) in the frontispiece from Michael Drayton,* Annalia Dubrensia *(1636).*

natural decoction and digestion, whereby man's body is the sooner corrupted and brought into diverse sicknesses, and finally the life is thereby made shorter. Where contrariwise by exercise, which is a vehement motion (as Galen,[2] prince of physicians, defines), the health of man is preserved, and his strength increased, for as much the members by moving and mutual touching do wax more hard, and natural heat in all the body is thereby augmented. Moreover it maketh the spirits of a man more strong and valiant, so that, by the hardness of the members, all labors be more tolerable; by natural heat the appetite is the more quick, the change of the substance received is the more ready, the nourishing of all parts of the body is the more sufficient and sure.[3] By valiant motion of the spirits[4] all things superfluous be expelled, and the conduits of the body cleansed. Wherefore this part of physic is not to be condemned or neglected in the education of children, and especially from the age of fourteen years upward, in which time strength with courage increaseth. Moreover there be diverse manners of exercises, whereof some only prepareth and helpeth digestion, some augmenteth also strength and hardness of body, other serveth for agility and nimbleness, some for celerity or speediness. There be also which ought to be used for necessity only. All these ought he that is a tutor to a noble man to have in remembrance, and, as opportunity serveth, to put them in experience. . . . And I will now only speak of those exercises, apt to the furniture of a gentleman's personage, adapting his body to hardness, strength, and agility, and to help therewith himself in peril, which may happen in wars or other necessity.

Chapter 17, Exercises whereby should grow both recreation and profit.

Wrestling is a very good exercise in the beginning of youth, so that it be with one that is equal in strength, or somewhat under, and that the place be soft, that in falling their bodies be not bruised.

There be diverse manners of wrestlings, but the best, as well for health of body as for exercise of strength, is when laying mutually their hands one over another's neck, with the other hand they hold fast each other by the arm, and clasping their legs together, they enforce themselves with strength and agility to throw down each other, which is also praised by Galen. And undoubtedly it shall be found profitable in wars, in case that a captain shall

---

[2] **Galen:** (d. early third century C.E.) Roman physician and philosopher whose theories were influential for early modern medical science. [3] **natural heat . . . sufficient and sure:** Galen taught that the amount of heat produced by a body was essential to its degree of perfection. [4] **valiant motion of the spirits:** the animal spirit (responsible for sensation and thought), the vital spirit (the source of life energy), and the natural spirit (responsible for nutrition and growth).

be constrained to cope with his adversary hand to hand, having his weapon broken or lost. Also it hath been seen that the weaker person, by the sleight of wrestling, hath overthrown the stronger, almost, or he could fasten on the other any violent stroke.

→ VINCENTIO SAVIOLO

From Vincentio Saviolo His Practice in Two Books *1595*

In *As You Like It*, the mass movement of noble characters and their retinues from the familiar space of the court to the rural and unfamiliar space of Arden gives characters the freedom to comment on the courtly practices of their old environment. Touchstone, the play's clown, provides some of the most pointed commentary on aristocratic behavior, perhaps especially the practice of dueling and the honor culture that surrounded it. In act 5, Touchstone hilariously recounts to Jaques how he has engaged in quarrels that have included the practice of "giving the lie" (5.4.44–85), a necessary step in precipitating a duel. In theory, dueling was a practice by which one defended oneself against slights to one's honor without the help of the law. Spurred by the publication of Italian manuals that made dueling one of the primary arts of the early modern gentleman, young men took up dueling though it met with monarchical disapproval because it encouraged violence among hotheaded young gentlemen and seemed to put questions of justice outside the legal system. In 1614 King James issued a proclamation forbidding the practice.

Vincentio Saviolo (d. 1598/99) came to London from Padua, Italy, in 1590 and promptly set up a popular fencing school. His popular treatise *Vincentio Saviolo His Practice in Two Books*, written in English, on the use of the rapier and on the rules governing honorable quarrels, was published in 1595. The illustration from the book that appears in this text (Figure 6) suggests the stylized and stylish stances adopted by those who became adept at Italian fencing. In the sections from this treatise given below, how does Saviolo's elaborate description of "giving the lie" compare to Touchstone's story of his management of his quarrels? What is Touchstone satirizing and how does his satire work?

FROM BOOK 2, OF HONOR AND HONORABLE QUARRELS

There be also certain undiscreet men, whose gross fault I cannot overslip without blaming: these men use as they either stand or go in streets, so to stare and look men passing by them in the face, as if they would for some

Vincentio Saviolo, *Vincentio Saviolo His Practice in Two Books* (London, 1595), 322–24, 340–41, 342–43, 346–47, 377–80; STC 21788.

FIGURE 6 *Two well-dressed gentlemen practice their fencing postures in* Vincentio Saviolo His Practice in Two Books *by Vincent Saviolo (1595).*

reason mark them, which breedeth such an offense unto some men so marked that they cannot take it in good part, and therefore it is very dangerous. For it may happen that a man may look so upon one that either is by nature suspicious, or by reason of some secret thing known to himself, may suspect that he is therefore looked upon. Whereupon great quarrels may arise, for the man so looked on may fall a questioning with him that looketh on him, who perhaps answering him overthwartly,[1] may both move him to choler,[2] & be moved himself also, & so bring the matter to some dangerous point. Whereof I have myself seen a notable example, passing through the city of Trieste in the uttermost part of the territories of Friule in Italy, where I saw two brethren, one a most honorable captain, and the other a brave and worthy soldier, who walking together in the streets were very steadfastly eyed of certain young gentlemen of the city, who stared the captain and his brother in the face something unseemly, and (as they took it) discourteously, whereupon they asked the gentlemen in very courteous man-

[1] **overthwartly:** contrarily. [2] **choler:** anger.

ner whether they had seen them in any place before, or whether they knew them. They answered no. Then replied the captain and his brother, why then do you look so much upon us? They answered, because they had eyes. That (said the other) is the crow's fault, in that they have not picked them out. To be short, in the end one word added on the other, and one speech following the other, the matter came from saying to doing, and what the tongue had uttered the hand would maintain, and a hot fight being commenced, it could not be ended before the captain's brother was slain, and two of the gentlemen hurt, whereof one escaped with the rest, but the chiefest cutter of them all was hurt in the leg, and so could not get away, but was taken, imprisoned, and shortly after beheaded. He was very well beloved in the city, but yet could not escape this end, being brought thereto by following his mad-brained conceits, and by being misled by evil company; the rest of his company were banished their country. Now if these gentlemen had more courteously and wisely demeaned themselves, no more hurt had followed that bad beginning. Every man therefore shall do well to have a great regard in this respect, least like disorders be to their danger committed. . . .

A discourse most necessary for all gentlemen that have in regard their honors touching the giving and receiving of the lie, whereupon the duel & the combats in diverse sorts doth ensue, & many other inconveniences, for lack only of the true knowledge of honor, and the contrarie, & the right understanding of words, which here is plainly set down, beginning thus.

A rule and order concerning the challenger and defender:
All injuries are reduced to two kinds, and are either by words or deeds. In the first, he that offereth the injury ought to be the challenger: in the later, he that is injured. Example: Caius sayeth to Seius that he is a traitor, unto which Seius answereth by giving the lie, whereupon ensueth that the charge of the combat falleth on Caius, because he is to maintain what he said, and therefore to challenge Seius. Now when an injury is offered by deed, then do they proceed in this manner: Caius striketh Seius, giveth him a box on the ear or some other way hurteth him by some violent means, wherewith Seius offended, saith unto Caius that he hath used violence towards him, or that he hath dealt injuriously with him, or that he hath abused him, or some such manner of saying. Whereunto Caius answereth, Thou liest, whereby Seius is forced to challenge Caius, and to compel him to fight, to maintain the injury which he had offered him. The sum of all, therefore, is in these cases of honor, that he unto whom the lie is wrongfully given ought to challenge him that offereth that dishonor, and by the sword to prove himself no liar. . . .

What the reason is, that the party unto whom the lie is given ought to become challenger, and of the nature of lies:
Some men marvel why that he unto whom the lie is given ought rather to challenge the combat, than he that is called a traitor or a villain, or by some other injurious name, seeing that it would seem more reasonable that he which is most injured ought to become challenger, and not the other, and that this is a greater injury to say unto a man, Thou art a thief, thou art a villain, & a traitor, than this, Thou lieth. But the laws have no regard of the words, or of the force or efficacy of them, but provide that the burthen of the challenge shall ever fall on him that offereth the injury, for it is thought that every man is honest, just, and honorable until the contrary be proved. And therefore as in common trial by civil judgment and order of law, whosoever is accused of any crime is by simple denying the same delivered from condemnation, unless further proof thereof be brought against him. Even so in this case, whosoever speaketh of another man contrary unto that which is ordinarily presumed of him, it is great reason that the charge of proof should lie upon him, to make that manifest unto the world by force of arms, that such a man is guilty of such and such things as he hath laid to his charge. . . .

Of the manner and diversity of lies:
To the end that the nature of lies may the more easily be known, and when the lie ought to be given and when not, and in what cases, it is requisite I should particularly discourse thereof. For some lies be certain, and some conditional, and both the first and that later, some of them are general and some of them special. Unto which two sorts, I will add a third kind of lies, which may be termed vain-lies.

Of lies certain:
Lies certain are such as are given upon words spoken affirmatively, as if any man should say or write unto another, Thou hast spoken to my discredit, and in prejudice of my honor and reputation, and therefore dost lie. And in this respect is this a lie certain, because I affirm that such a one hath spoken evil of me, yet because I do not particularly mention wherein or how he hath offended me by speech, the lie which I gave him is general, and therefore of no force. For to have the lie given lawfully, it is requisite that the cause whereupon it is given, be particularly specified and declared. Wherefore lies special, and such as are given upon sure and express words, are such as assuredly bind the parties unto whom they be given to prove the same which they have spoken, when as they cannot deny that they have said whereupon the lie was given them. As, for example: *Alexander* thou hast said that I, being

employed by his highness in his service at Pavia,[3] have had secret conference with the enemy, wherefore I say that thou hast lied. This is a sure & a specially [lie], and by consequence lawfully given. . . .

Whether the subject ought to obey his Sovereign, being by him forbidden to combat:
This doubt is often moved by them that write of this matter, concerning which gentlemen are resolved that for their Prince and Sovereign they will gladly hazard their lives even unto greatest dangers, but their honor will they not in any case suffer to be spotted with disgrace or cowardice, whereby they are grown into this custom, that being challenged to the combat, or understanding or perceiving that others mean to challenge them, or else intending and resolved with themselves to challenge others, they will retire into some secret place, where it shall not consist only in their Prince's power to forbid, or stay them from it, and so laying aside all respect either of their Prince's favor or loss of goods or banishment from their country, they take the combat in hand. And whosoever should do otherwise amongst men professing arms should be judged to have greatly impaired his credit and reputation, and dishonored himself in high degree. . . .

. . . Yet will I not deny, but that if a man's country or natural Prince should be interested in the matter, he ought to have a respect both of the one and the other, and especially when a great part of the quarrel should concern either his country or Prince, for that the manner of proceeding therein ought to be plotted by their counsel and advice. But in all other cases, when the matter only concerneth a man's own interest, then ought not any gentleman be backward in challenging, or answering the challenger, and in no case, either upon commandment or upon any penance whatsoever, refuse the combat.

[3] **Pavia:** a town in northern Italy.

PRIMOGENITURE AND THE DILEMMA OF YOUNGER SONS

Shakespeare's play contains two sets of brothers—Oliver, Orlando, and Jaques de Boys and Duke Senior and Duke Frederick. The bad relations between brothers cause much of the trouble that the comedy must resolve. In England, inheritance laws were complex and varied. Popular literature and political writing tended to focus nearly exclusively on the inheritance practices of the gentry; Shakespeare's play is no exception. The dominant mode of inheritance among these families was primogeniture, the custom by which the entire estate and noble titles passed to the eldest son. This practice ensured the replication of the economic and social power of wealthy families, keeping estates together and allowing them to accumulate in a single heir's hands rather than splitting and distributing them among multiple children. This often meant that younger brothers inherited little or no property and depended on the good will of an older sibling for education or resources to make their way in the world. In royal families, elder sons were privileged, and the Crown typically descended from father to oldest male heir. In *As You Like It* Duke Frederick has transgressed social norms by seizing the throne by force from his elder brother, Duke Senior, who has fled to the Forest of Arden as a result. In the de Boys family, Oliver ruthlessly exercises his rights as the eldest son. While he has sent his middle brother to university, he deprives his youngest brother, Orlando, of the education fitting the son of a gentleman and makes no provision for his future well-being.[1] (For more on Orlando's lack of education, see Chapter 4.)

It is notable that both Dukes in *As You Like It* lack male heirs. In such cases, property could pass to a nephew or another male in a branch of the extended family or it could be settled on a daughter and, if she marries, on her husband, since a woman's property became his at marriage. How does the fact that Duke Senior has no male heirs affect Orlando's situation at the end of the play?

It is also notable that Celia imagines a very special fate for her father's wealth. When Rosalind laments her father's banishment, Celia comforts her by saying that when her own father dies "thou shalt be his heir, for what he hath taken away from thy father perforce I will render thee again in affection" (1.2.14–15). In effect, Celia both imagines being her father's heir and then making Rosalind the beneficiary of the wealth she will inherit as if Rosalind were, in effect, Celia's spouse. Once in Arden, the two women set up housekeeping together. What does the ending of the play suggest has happened to this plan for female inheritance?

Of course, not everyone agreed that primogeniture was a good custom or that eldest sons should automatically inherit the throne. The following three texts give some range of opinion on the subject of younger brothers and the custom of primogeniture. The first is a satirical sketch of a younger brother written by John Earle (1601?–1665), a prominent Anglican clergyman and supporter of the Royalist cause in the English Civil Wars. His *Microcosmography*, from which the sketch is taken, is made up of a number

---

[1] For a powerful reading of *As You Like It* in terms of the social difficulties posed by primogeniture, see Louis Montrose, "'The Place of a Brother' in *As You Like It*: Social Process and Comic Form," *Shakespeare Quarterly* 32.1 (1981): 28–54.

of humorous descriptions of early modern characters or social types including an attorney, a cook, a plodding student, and a sordid rich man. In what way does Earle's portrait of a younger son resemble or differ from Shakespeare's portrait of Orlando? Is Orlando in some sense a stereotype or a figure who calls stereotypes in question? What paths does Earle lay out as the future courses open to younger sons? How does Shakespeare rescue Orlando from the sorry fate that Earle's sketch threatens?

The other two texts in this section consider in a more philosophical vein the issue of whether or not primogeniture is a good thing. The first is taken from *Dialogue between Pole and Lupset*, a political treatise written by the humanist Thomas Starkey (1495–1538) in the form of a dialogue between Reginald Pole and Thomas Lupset, historical figures in the reign of Henry VIII. The selection follows from a debate on hereditary kingship. Pole has suggested that the succession of kings according to their birth is a fault against nature and reason and contrary to the ideals of a true commonwealth. Comparing hereditary kingship to the potential dangers of primogeniture, in which the elder son inherits all his father's wealth without regard to his virtue, Pole argues that the free election of a king by a country's citizens is the most conducive to maintaining good order. Yet he agrees with Lupset that the "manners, customs, and nature here of our people" make free election undesirable in England. The English people, he admits, need hereditary kingship and the order it produces and protects. The specter of social disorder raised by the abolition of hereditary kingship haunts the ensuing discussion of primogeniture as well. Again, a practice initially described as unjust and unreasonable is eventually defended, with some qualifications, as necessary to preserve social order.

By contrast, the final pamphlet, the anonymous J. A.'s *An Apology for a Younger Brother*, is ultimately more critical of primogeniture, laying out a number of objections to it and providing examples from history and the Bible of when it has not been observed.

How does Shakespeare handle the issues explored in these two tracts? Is the play critical of primogeniture? Does it call attention to the injustices it can spawn? Does it provide an alternative? How does it resolve the fate of the two younger brothers, Duke Frederick and Orlando? Remember that Orlando, through his marriage to Rosalind, will inherit a dukedom. And his elder brother, Oliver, having fallen in love with Aliena, has said that he will live with her in the pastoral world and "my father's house and all the revenue that was old Sir Rowland's will I estate upon you [Orlando]" (5.2.7–9). Do you think this happens? Is it important that it is said, whether or not it is enacted?

→ JOHN EARLE

From Microcosmography   *1628*

9. YOUNGER BROTHER

His elder brother was the Esau that came out first and left him like Jacob at his heels.[1] His father has done with him, as Pharaoh to the children of Israel, that would have them make brick, and give them no straw,[2] so he tasks him to be a gentleman, and leaves him nothing to maintain it. The pride of his house has undone him, which the elder knighthood must sustain, and his beggary that knighthood. His birth and bringing up will not suffer him to descend to the means to get wealth, but he stands at the mercy of the world, and which is worse, of his brother. He is something better than the servingmen, yet they more saucy with him, than he bold with the master, who beholds him with a countenance of stern awe, and checks[3] him oftener than his liveries.[4] His brother's old suits and he are much alike in request, and cast off now and then one to the other.[5] Nature hath furnished him with a little more wit upon compassion, for it is like to be his best revenue. If his annuity[6] stretch so far he is sent to the university, and with great heart burning takes upon him the ministry as a profession; he is condemned to buy his ill fortune. Others take a more crooked path, yet the King's highway,[7] where at length their vizard is plucked off, and they strike fair for Tyburn,[8] but their brothers' pride, not love, gets them a pardon. His last refuge is the Low countries,[9] where rags and lice are no scandal, where he lives a poor gentleman of a company, and dies without a shirt. The only

---

[1] **Esau . . . Jacob at his heels:** in Genesis 25, Rebekah gives birth to twins, Esau and Jacob. Esau is delivered first, and Jacob is born clutching Esau's heel.   [2] **as Pharaoh to the children of Israel . . . give them no straw:** in Exodus 5, the Pharaoh of Egypt commands the captive children of Israel to start gathering straw to make bricks, drastically increasing their workload and making it nearly impossible for them to fulfill their assigned tasks.   [3] **checks:** strikes or taunts. [4] **liveries:** servants belonging to a family. Liveries can also refer to the clothing or insignia of a noble family, a sense the author draws upon in the following sentence.   [5] **brother's old suits . . . one to the other:** the sentence plays with the dual meaning of "suits" as supplications and as articles of clothing, suggesting that the younger brother receives the hand-me-down clothing of his elder brother and that his petitions for support are likewise rejected.   [6] **annuity:** a yearly allowance.   [7] **King's highway:** figurative expression for becoming a highwayman or robber. [8] **Tyburn:** early modern London's primary location for execution by hanging.   [9] **the Low countries:** today comprising Belgium, the Netherlands, Luxembourg, as well as parts of northern France and western Germany. Site of the Dutch War of Independence from 1568 to 1648. Elizabeth I committed money and soldiers to the anti-Spanish forces there.

John Earle, *Microcosmography, or a Piece of the World Discovered in Essays and Characters* (London, 1628), C4–C5; STC 7441.

thing that may better his fortunes is an art he has to make a gentlewoman, wherewith he baits now and then some rich widow that is hungry after his blood. He is commonly discontented and desperate, and the form of his exclamation is, *that churl*[10] *my brother*. He loves not his country for this unnatural custom, and would have long since revolted to the Spaniard, but for Kent[11] only which he holds in admiration.

[10] *churl*: a villain; also, one who is stingy with his money.   [11] **Kent**: county in southeast England that practiced gavelkind, a system of land tenure in which an owner could dispose of his lands as he pleased in his will.

→ THOMAS STARKEY

From A Dialogue between Pole and Lupset   *c. 1529–1532*

POLE: A like fault unto this,[1] but not so great, is in the succession of private men. You know, by the order of our law the eldest brother succeedeth, excluding all the other from any part of inheritance. In private succession this is a thing as me seemeth[2] far out of order, utterly to exclude the younger brethren out of all parts of the heritage[3] as though they were not the children of that father nor brethren to the heir. Reason and nature also utterly requireth that the children which be as parts of the father and mother should also be admitted to parts of the patrimony,[4] that even like as they have brought them forth into the light, so their goods should maintain and succour[5] them after in their life, wherefore utterly to exclude them from all, as though they had committed some great offence and crime against their parents, is plain against reason and seemeth to minish[6] the natural love betwixt the father and the child, and also increase envy and hate betwixt them which nature hath so bounden together, for betwixt brethren brother and brother, undoubtedly this thing squeaketh[7] much of the brotherly love which nature hath planted and rooted and so this may not be denied to be another misorder in our politic rule and governance.

[1] **this**: hereditary kingship.   [2] **me seemeth**: it seems to me.   [3] **heritage**: inheritance.   [4] **patrimony**: property inherited from the father.   [5] **succour**: help.   [6] **minish**: diminish.   [7] **squeaketh**: diminishes.

Thomas Starkey, *A Dialogue between Pole and Lupset*, ed. T. F. Mayer (London: Royal Historical Society, 1989), 73–76. [Modernized from Mayer's diplomatic transcription of the only surviving ms. of the Dialogue, in the Public Records Office, London, in State Papers of the Reign of Henry VIII (SP 1), vol. 90.]

LUPSET: Sir as touching this I marvel much also what you mean, me seemeth you are about to take utterly away our policy and whole order of this our realm, you note such things to be faults wherein resteth all the honor of our country and which is the ground of all good order and civility. . . . This I think was well-considered of them which first instituted this law of inheritance. They well considered the nature of our people, which by nature be somewhat rude and sturdy[8] of mind, in so much that if they had not in every place some heads and governors to temper[9] their affects[10] rude and unruly there would among them be no order at all, and therefore it was not without cause, as it appeareth, ordained and established that in every great family the eldest should succeed to maintain a head, which by authority, dignity, and power should better contain the rudeness of the people, for this is both certain and sure, that if the lands in every great family were distributed equally betwixt the brethren, in a small process of years, the head families would decay and by little and little utterly vanish away, and so the people should be without rulers and heads, the which then by their rudeness[11] and folly would shortly disturb this quiet life and good policy which by many ages they have laid here in our country. Such should be the dissension and discord one with another, and so me seemeth the maintenance of these heads is the maintenance of all civil order and politic rule here in our nation, wherefore Master Pole if you take this away it appeareth plainly you shall take away the foundation and ground of all our civility, and beside this you shall therewith bring in the ruin of all nobility and ancient stocks,[12] for if you from nobles once take their great possessions, or minister[13] any occasion to the same, you shall in process of years confound[14] the nobles and the commons[15] together after such manner that there shall be no difference betwixt the one and the other. . . .

POLE: Well Master Lupset, notwithstanding[16] your reasons seem to be strong and of great weight, yet if we ever put before our eyes the commonweal before declared, it shall not be hard to make to them answer, howbeit[17] they have also somewhat of the truth mingled withal,[18] for surely after as you say the rudeness of our people requireth heads and governors to contain them in order and quietness and though it be not necessary at all, yet in great families this manner or succession may be suffered right well, howbeit some provision for the second brethren by the order of law also would be had, and not to leave them bare to the only

---

[8] **sturdy:** rebellious.   [9] **temper:** moderate.   [10] **affects:** natural tendencies.   [11] **rudeness:** lack of sophistication and education.   [12] **stocks:** familial lines of descent.   [13] **minister:** serve.   [14] **confound:** mingle.   [15] **commons:** commoners.   [16] **notwithstanding:** in spite of the fact that.   [17] **howbeit:** nevertheless.   [18] **withal:** in addition.

courtesy of their eldest brother, whose love oft times is so cold and weak that he may well suffer his brethren to live in greater poverty than is convenient to their nobility, but if you would suffer this addition and moderation to be joined thereto, your reasons should prove right well, in great houses, and princes, dukes, earls, and baronies, such manner of succession to be allowed as convenient, but now as to the other part to admit the same commonly among all gentlemen of mean[19] sort, whatsoever they be, this is not tolerable, this is, almost as you said, against nature and all good civility, for this bringeth in among the multitude over-great inequality, which is the occasion of dissension and debate. . . .

LUPSET: Sir you say well, for surely you have so in few words declared your mind in this behalf that I cannot deny but that herein lieth a misorder, but at the beginning it appeared a very strange thing, utterly to take away our manner of succession, which so many years hath been allowed and as methought not without great reason. I think also verily that at the first ordinance of our laws even as you say that this manner of succession was only in great families and yet not without some provision for the other brethren, as they have yet in France, Flanders, and in Italy, the second brother hath ever some castle or town appointed to him by the order of their law and custom in every great family, but truly I cannot but confess this manner to be received among all men of mean state and degree to be utterly against all good civility, and without fail riseth of the ground that you well have noted. I have ever thought this manner of entailing of lands commonly not to be allowed by just policy, wherefore me think this is a fault worthy now to be spoken of also, for this entailing specially after such manner only to the eldest son in every base[20] family maketh many reckless heirs, causeth them little to regard neither learning nor virtue, in as much as they are sure to be inheritors to a great portion of entailed land, and so by this assurance they give themselves to all vanity and pleasure without respect, the which I think they would not do, if they were in doubt of such possessions, and the whole inheritance to hand[21] upon their behavior and bearing.

[19] mean: common.   [20] base: of low birth; here, those who are not of the nobility.   [21] hand: depend.

→ J. A.

From An Apology for a Younger Brother   *1641*

CHAPTER 1

The occasion of writing this apology is to prove that fathers may in some cases dispose their worldly estates to which of their sons shall reasonably please, and for so much thereof as they will, and that to be lawful by the law of God, of Nature, and of nations.

. . . All which I doubt not but to make clear to the impartial reader, proving by the law of God and man, that a father's freedom is such that he may lawfully and religiously give his lands and goods, or other his fortunes, to any of his children, for the preservation of his name and comfort of his posterity, without all scruple, as right reason or the better deserts of a son shall persuade him, void of all tenderness or blindness of affection, which oftentimes leads a father's will and corrupts his understanding, so as he be true lord thereof, not tied by consideration of money received, or contract made by marriage of his son, which may alter the case, and make the son lord, and the father to have but the use only during his life,[1] as all our common lawyers[2] well know. . . . Only I mean to argue whether a father possessed in fee tail[3] may in law and equity, upon the former considerations, make any child which he hath his heir, leaving to the rest a competency,[4] and do an act which according to equity[5] and religion may stand good and valuable. . . .

CHAPTER 3

. . . Suppose the law of God did at this present command (which indeed it doth not) that the inheritance should be left to any one particular person, and namely to the elder brother, yet in some cases it would not bind the father to observe it. For as in the former Commandments,[6] upon some con-

---

[1] **during his life:** a man who has "but the use only during his life" is one who cannot dictate what happens to his estate following his death.   [2] **common lawyers:** lawyers who practice common law, or law that developed through court decisions and judicial precedent, rather than legislative statutes.   [3] **fee tail:** a type of inheritance in which the owner of an estate could not sell or otherwise dispose of his estate, which automatically passed to his heir upon his death.   [4] **competency:** a sufficient amount.   [5] **equity:** a set of legal principles (rather than strict laws) in the common law tradition that allowed judges to be flexible in their administration of justice.   [6] **the former Commandments:** the Ten Commandments found in Exodus 20.

J. A., *An Apology for a Younger Brother* (Oxford, 1641), 1, 3–5, 12–13, 45–49; Wing A3592.

siderations the Commandment may be dispensed withal, so in this. For it is not sufficient to be the elder brother, or the nearest in blood, to gain an inheritance in the case which I have now proposed, for other circumstances must concur, which if they be wanting, bare propinquity[7] or ancienty of blood may justly be rejected and he that is second, third, fourth, fifth, or last may lawfully be preferred before the first, and this by all law, divine and human, and by all reason, conscience, and custom of nations Christian.

For if it should happen that the next in blood should be a natural fool,[8] or a madman, or being taken by the Turks or Moors in his infancy and educated in another religion[9] would maintain the same, or if any other such accident ministering cause of just exception should fall out, is it likely that any law would allow that such a man should be admitted to the inheritance? Wherefore how idly should they talk, that would have it to be his birth-right, or that God and Nature had made him heir, since neither God nor Nature doth immediately make heirs, as before is declared. Upon which ground, our common lawyers say that no heirs are born, but men and law make them. . . .

CHAPTER 9

It is not fit perhaps to urge the better acceptance with God of Abel's offering above Cain's the elder brother, but that estate which Abel had in Adam's patrimony.[10] Nor will I reinforce Japhet's share in his father's right to the whole world, though he being the youngest son of three had Europe for his inheritance, which in all arts, and uses of life, far excels Africa, Asia, and all the rest of the earth, whereas, according to the pretences of those customary challenges, Sem should either have had all, or been sovereign lord of all, and Cham and Japhet with their posterity but farmers or free-holders under him.[11]

I will not also (as if there were penury[12] of resemblances) produce again Esau's disinheritance,[13] though that were enough for our present purpose.

---

[7] **bare propinquity:** the simple fact of being a blood relation. [8] **natural fool:** mentally deficient. [9] **another religion:** i.e., Islam. [10] **Abel's offering . . . Adam's patrimony:** in the Old Testament book of Genesis, chapter 4, Adam and Eve's son Cain kills his younger brother Abel because God preferred Abel's offering to his, but the author's point here is that Abel, the younger son, had a share in Adam's estate alongside that of his brother. [11] **Japhet's share . . . free-holders under him:** referring to Noah's three sons, Japhet, Sem, and Cham (also called Japheth, Shem, and Ham). Genesis 10:5 was traditionally interpreted as indicating that Japheth was the father of Europeans. Freeholders were those who held land in fee simple, meaning that they owned the estate completely and could use, sell, or dispose of it as they wished. [12] **penury:** lack. [13] **Esau's disinheritance:** in Genesis 27, Jacob, the younger son of Isaac, disguises himself as his brother Esau and tricks his father into giving him a blessing intended for Esau. Earlier, in Genesis 25, Esau sells Jacob his birthright in exchange for food.

For had it been sin (which neither Scripture, nor Josephus in his *Antiquities*[14] saith), the mother could not have procured it, God would not have prospered it, nor Jacob himself, being a good man, have accepted it, nor Esau (whose anger Jacob feared) have left it unrevenged.[15] Neither is there in Scripture, nor in any written law under heaven, any command to restrain the father's power, but rather the contrary. . . .

[There follows a long list of examples of those who have not followed the practice of primogeniture, including the two following examples.]

. . . But to omit foreign examples (for brevity's sake), wherewith of all times and places books are full, in our country we might allege the fact of Brutus, the proto-parent of our nation,[16] who divided Albion (afterward called Britain) to his three sons, leaving only the best portion to Locrinus, anciently called Loegria, Albania (now Scotland) to Albanact, and Cambria, or Wales, to Camber. . . .

They who know the old fashions of Ireland, either by tradition, or by printed statutes of that nation, can testify of their most ancient tenure, or fundamental custom, which there is called tanistry,[17] by which the land and chiefty of a name, after the predecessor's death, is not awarded to the eldest son, but to the worthiest (if I misremember not), the judgment whereof is left to the people, and such tenants as have interest and right of suffrage[18] (as Alexander the Great, though as it is apparent in the *Maccabees*, very falsely is said to have left his empire).[19] And the custom of equal shares may be in other places also, which never borrowed their equal partitions from gavelkind,[20] a custom, I grant, which some have lately altered in their private families by Parliament.

---

[14]Josephus in his *Antiquities*: Jewish historian and author of the twenty-volume *Antiquities of the Jews* (c. 94).   [15]the mother could not have procured it . . . left it unrevenged: Jacob's mother, Rebekah, helped Jacob trick his father; in Genesis 33 Jacob and Esau make peace with each other.   [16]Brutus, the proto-parent of our nation: medieval historians, most famously Geoffrey of Monmouth, asserted that the founder of Britain was Brutus, a descendant of Aeneas (the survivor of Troy and ancestor of the founders of Rome, whose story is recorded in Virgil's *Aeneid*).   [17]tanistry: a system in which the eldest and worthiest of a deceased's kinsmen was elected to succeed to his estate.   [18]right of suffrage: right to vote.   [19]Alexander the Great . . . left his empire: when Alexander the Great died (323 B.C.E.), there was no obvious heir to his large empire, and some accounts suggested that Alexander had ordered his empire to pass to "the strongest." *Maccabees*, written by a Jewish author around 100 B.C.E., begins with Alexander's death.   [20]gavelkind: a type of land tenure existing primarily in the county of Kent, in which land could be disposed of as a landholder wished, or divided equally among his sons at his death.

Robin Hood and the Greenwood

In the opening scene of *As You Like It*, the wrestler Charles describes Duke Senior's exile, claiming that he and his men "live like the old Robin Hood of England" (1.1.86). The parallels between the Robin Hood legend and the play are notable, including not only the Duke's retreat to the forest with a merry band of men, but also the play's emphasis on hunting, feasting, and fellowship in the greenwood, its critique of the court world left behind, and even its exploration of love.

The Robin Hood legend is an immensely complex and varied body of material popular from at least the thirteenth century. Though historians have long tried to connect Robin Hood with a historical figure, it is not clear that there ever was such an outlaw hero. What is interesting, in any case, are the stories that gradually came to surround this extremely popular character. Most of the extant late-medieval representations are ballads, intended to be sung or read aloud. The legend also circulated widely in festival performances such as May Day games, dances, and quasi-theatrical shows. By the time of Shakespeare the story had also been incorporated into the national histories being written in increasing numbers and had moved into the popular theater. In the 1590s, works such as *George a Greene the Pinner of Wakefield* (Robert Greene[?] 1593[?], pub. 1599) and Anthony Munday's two plays *The Death of Robert, Earle of Huntington* and *The Downfall of Robert, Earl of Huntington* (1601) portrayed distinct aspects of the received material.

In the main, the Robin Hood story is that of a "good outlaw." In early versions of the story he is a yeoman who flees to Sherwood Forest after he helps to rescue a man unjustly detained and threatened with death by officers of a corrupt Sheriff. In later accounts he is a nobleman who wastes his inheritance in prodigal spending and flees to the forest to escape arrest for debt. All agree that once in the forest Robin Hood and his men prey on the rich, especially fat abbots and corrupt churchmen, and help the poor with what they steal. They are always champions of women. There is also a political subtext to many Robin Hood stories. In early ballads he is said to have fled to the forest during the reign of "King Edward," though whether this is Edward I, II, or III is unclear. Together, the three Edwards ruled England from 1271 to 1377. By the sixteenth century, however, Robin Hood becomes associated with the reign of Richard I, also known as Richard the Lionheart, who ruled from 1189 to 1199. Robin is presented as loyal to this distant king, but an enemy of the evil Prince John who rules England while Richard is on crusade. He is thus, paradoxically, both a figure of loyalty and of rebellion, faithful to an absent monarch and trouble for his substitute. Of course, as all lovers of the Robin Hood story know, Robin's most proximate enemy is the Sheriff of Nottingham, whom Robin again and again fools and foils in the sheriff's many attempts to capture him and prevent him from stealing and eating the king's deer. The forest is also a place of games and fellowship. Robin repeatedly challenges those he meets to wrestling matches, swordfights, and archery contests; sometimes he is defeated, but he always invites his hardy opponents to join him in his forest retreat, adding constantly to his band. In late versions of the story, he acquires a love interest, Maid Marian, a figure who in the medieval period was a rather lewd participant in the morris dance, a popular pastime involving choreographed dancing by figures who often wore bells on their shins—and was played by a man. As she gets attached to the Robin Hood story she becomes a chaste love mate for the outlaw hero.

Below are four selections from the many, many texts that recount aspects of the Robin Hood legend. The first two are drawn from histories written in the sixteenth century that include accounts of Robin Hood; the second two are ballads, one early and one late, that give some feel for aspects of the story relevant to Shakespeare's play.

→ JOHN MAJOR

From A History of Greater Britain   *1521*

Translated by Archibald Constable

John Major (1467–1550) took part in the sixteenth-century upsurge of English history writing, a phenomenon that included the production of national histories focused on the reigns of the kings and queens of England such as Raphael Holinshed's *Chronicles of England, Scotland, and Ireland* (1577), and chorographies, county-by-county local histories such as William Camden's *Britannia* (1587). John Major's book was a large chronicle work produced in Latin in 1521, and was the first history to place Robin Hood (whom he called Robert Hood) in the reign of Richard I. Though Major's account had limited circulation, several historians, including Richard Grafton, reprinted and expanded his account, instantiating the idea that Robin Hood was an actual historical personage. The following very brief passage suggests how he characterized the outlaw. What are the attributes of Major's Robin Hood? Is he an admirable figure or a rogue?

John Major, *Historia Majoris Britanniae* (1521), trans. Archibald Constable (Edinburgh, 1892), 156–57.

About this time it was, as I conceive, that there flourished those most famous robbers Robert Hood, an Englishman, and Little John, who lay in wait in the woods, but spoiled of their goods those only that were wealthy. They took the life of no man, unless he either attacked them or offered resistance in defence of his property. Robert supported by his plundering one hundred bowmen, ready fighters every one, with whom four hundred of the strongest would not dare to engage in combat. The feats of this Robert are told in song all over Britain. He would allow no woman to suffer injustice, nor would he spoil the poor, but rather enriched them from the plunder taken from the abbots. The robberies of this man I condemn, but of all robbers he was the humanest and the chief.

→ **RICHARD GRAFTON**

From A Chronicle at Large   *1569*

In 1569, Richard Grafton, a member of the Grocer's Company and the King's Printer under Henry VIII and Edward VI, published a chronicle that essentially copied and greatly expanded John Major's discussion of Robin Hood. How does Grafton's account differ from Major's? Is his view of Robin Hood consistent or contradictory? What now is Robin Hood's class position? In what ways does Duke Senior in Shakespeare's play resemble the Robin Hood of Grafton's account? Does any of the ambiguity in the historical accounts linger in *As You Like It*?

And about this time, as saith John Major in his *Chronicle of Scotland*,[1] there were many robbers and outlaws in England, among the which number he specially noteth Robert Hood, whom we now call Robin Hood, and little John, who were famous thieves. They continued[2] in woods, mountains, and forests, spoiling and robbing, namely such as were rich. Murders commonly they did none, except it were by the provocation of such as resisted them in

---

[1] **John Major in his *Chronicle of Scotland*:** Grafton seems to be conflating two sources of information on Robin Hood: John Major's *Historia Majoris Britanniae* (1521) and Hector Boece's *Scotorum historiae* (1526, trans. 1536 as *The History and Chronicles of Scotland*).   [2] **continued:** carried on, were active.

Richard Grafton, *A Chronicle at Large* (London, 1569), 84–85; STC 12147.

their riflings[3] and spoils. And the said[4] Major saith that the aforesaid Robin Hood had at his rule and commandment[5] a hundred tall yeomen,[6] which were mighty men and exceeding good archers, and they were maintained by such spoils as came to their hands. And he saith moreover that those hundred were such picked[7] men, and of such force,[8] that four hundred men whosever they were, durst[9] never set upon them. And one thing was much commended in him, that he would suffer no woman to be oppressed, violated, or otherwise abused. The poorer sort of people he favored, and would in no way suffer their goods to be touched or spoiled, but relieved and aided them with such goods as he got from the rich, which he spared not, namely the rich priests, fat Abbotts, and the houses of rich Earls. And although this theft and rapine[10] was to be contemned,[11] yet the aforesaid author praiseth him and saith, that among the number of thieves, he was worthy the name of the most gentle thief.

But in an old and ancient pamphlet I find this written of the said Robert Hood. This man (saith he) descended of a noble parentage; or rather being of a base stock and lineage, was for his manhood and chivalry advanced to the noble dignity of an Earl, excelling principally in Archery or shooting, his manly courage agreeing thereunto. But afterwards he so prodigally exceeded in charges and expenses,[12] that he fell into great debt, by reason whereof, so many actions and suits were commenced against him, whereunto he answered not, that by order of law he was outlawed, and then for a lewd shift,[13] as his last refuge, gathered together a company of roisters and cutters,[14] and practiced robberies and spoiling of the kings' subjects, and occupied and frequented the forests or wild countries. The which being certified to the King, and he being greatly offended therewith, caused this proclamation to be made, that whosoever should bring him quick or dead,[15] the king would give him a great sum of money, as by the records in the Exchequer[16] is to be seen. But of this promise, no man enjoyed any benefit, for the said Robert Hood, being afterwards troubled with sickness, came to a certain nunnery in Yorkshire called the Bircklies, where desiring to be let blood,[17] he was betrayed and bled to death. After the whole death the

---

[3] **riflings:** plunderings. [4] **said:** previously mentioned. [5] **rule and commandment:** under his command. [6] **yeomen:** a complex word that could indicate various types of social status and employment during the sixteenth century. In this case, however, it means, roughly, "commoner." [7] **picked:** worthy of selection, fine; something like the modern "hand-picked." [8] **of such force:** of such strength. [9] **durst:** dared. [10] **rapine:** plundering. [11] **contemned:** condemned. [12] **prodigally exceeded in charges and expenses:** got himself into debt. [13] **lewd shift:** a dodgy strategy, but "lewd" also has a social sense of lower class or lowbrow. [14] **roisters and cutters:** swaggering fellows and cutpurses. [15] **quick or dead:** alive or dead. [16] **Exchequer:** the royal treasury. [17] **to be let blood:** to be deliberately bled; this was believed, at the time, to have medical benefits.

Prioress of the same place caused him to be buried by the high way side, where he had used to rob and spoil those that passed that way. And upon his grave the said prioress did lay a very fair stone, wherein the names of Robert Hood, William of Goldenborough, and others were graven.[18] And the cause why she buried him there was for that the common passengers and travelers knowing and seeing him there buried, might more safely and without fear take their journeys that way, which they durst not do in the life of the said outlaws. And at either end of the said Tomb was erected a cross of stone, which is to be seen there at this present.[19]

[18]graven: engraved.   [19]at this present: even now, at the present day.

ROBIN HOOD BALLADS

During much of the medieval and early modern periods, the Robin Hood story circulated in ballad form. These simple songs typically featured a linear narrative that progressed in stanzaic units, each punctuated with a refrain. Ballads borrowed and reinvented material freely, a tendency heightened by their oral dimensions. Because singers could alter a story during a performance, and because the stories of Robin Hood were so widely disseminated, print ballads often captured only one of the many versions of a particular story in circulation at a given time. Printed ballads typically consisted of a single sheet printed with song lyrics, often decorated with woodcuts. No musical notation was included; broadsides instead simply named popular tunes to which the words could be sung.

There were many, many Robin Hood ballads in circulation in early modern England. Some told of Robin's skill at archery, his confrontations with the Sheriff of Nottingham, his rescue of young men condemned to die for killing the king's deer, and the adventures of his great friend Little John. Included here are two ballads with particular relevance to *As You Like It*. The first, "The Ballad of Allin of Dale," shows Robin intervening to help a young man whose beloved has been taken from him by a rich man (see Figure 7). The second, which comes from late in the Robin Hood tradition, depicts Robin's meeting with Maid Marian.

Robin Hood and Allin of Dale,

Or a pleasant Relation how a young Genlteman being in Love with a Young Damsel, which was taken from him to be an Old Knights Bride, and how *Robin Hood* pittying the young mans case, took her from the old Kt. when they were going to be Marryed, and restored her to her own Love again.

Bold Robin Hood *he did the young man right*
And took the Damosel from the Doteing Knight.
To a Pleasant Northern Tune, Or Robin Hood in the Green wood stood.

COme listen to me, you Gallants so free,
All you that loves mirth for to hear,
And I will you tell, of a bold Outlaw,
That lived in Nottingham-shire,
  that lived in Nottingham-shire.
As Robin Hood in the Forrest stood,
All under the Green-wood Tree,
There was he ware of a brave young man
As fine as fine might be,
  as fine, &c.
The youngster was cloathed in Scarlet Red
In Scarlet fine and gay,
And he did frisk it over the Plain
And Chanted a Roundelay,
  and Chanted, &c.
As Robin Hood next morning stood
Amongst the Leaves so gay
There did he espy the same young man
Come drooping along the way,
  came drooping, &c.

The Scarlet he wore the day before,
It was clean cast away,
And every step he fetcht a sigh
A lack and awelladay,
  alack & awelladay.
Then stepped forth brave Little John,
And Nick the Millers Son,
Which made the young man bend his Bow
When as he see them come,
  when as he see them come.
Stand off, stand off, the young man said
What is your will with me,
You must come before our Master straight,
Under yon greenwood Tree,
  under, &c.
And when he came bold Robin before
Robin askt him him courteously
O hast thou any money to spare
For my merry men and me,
  for my, &c.

FIGURE 7 *Robin Hood with his longbow and arrows (left) and presumably Allin of Dale and his beloved at right in the traditional broadside ballad, "Robin Hood and Allin of Dale" (early seventeenth century).*

→ ANONYMOUS

Robin Hood and Allin of Dale   *Date unknown*

The first ballad makes Robin Hood a champion of young love, and it also reveals the irreverence toward the Catholic clergy that one often encounters in the Robin Hood materials. Whose authority is Robin flouting in this ballad? In Shakespeare's play, who are the champions of young love? Does Duke Senior function in that role or do the young take care of themselves? What role do the clergy play in the making of marriages in Shakespeare's work? At the end of the play, what do you make of the fact that it is the god Hymen, rather than a cleric, who presides over the multiple weddings that are promised? Does a tradition of anticlerical satire persist in the play?

Come listen to me, you gallants so free,
    All you that love mirth for to hear,
And I will tell you of a bold outlaw,
    That lived in Nottinghamshire.

As Robin Hood in the forest stood   5
    All under the green wood tree,
There he was aware of a brave young man,
    As fine as fine might be.

The youngster was cloathed in scarlet red,
    In scarlet fine and gay;   10
And he did frisk it over the plain,
    And chanted a round-de-lay.

As Robin Hood next morning stood
    Amongst the leaves so gay,
There did [he] espy the same young man   15
    Come drooping along the way.

The scarlet he wore the day before
    It was clean cast away;
And at every step he fetcht a sigh,
    "Alack and a well a day";   20

Ritson, Joseph ed., *Robin Hood: A Collection of Poems, Songs, and Ballads* (London, 1884), 297–301.

Then stepped forth brave Little John,
    And 'Midge' the miller's son,
Which made the young man bend his bow,
    When as he see them come.

"Stand off, stand off," the young man said,   25
    "What is your will with me?"
"You must come before our master straight,
    Under yon green wood tree."

And when he came bold Robin before,
    Robin askt him courteously,   30
"O, hast thou any money to spare
    For my merry men and me?"

"I have no money," the young man said,
    "But five shillings and a ring;
And that I have kept this seven long years,   35
    To have it at my wedding.

Yesterday I should have married a maid,
    But she from me was tane,[1]
And chosen to be an old knight's delight,
    Whereby my poor heart is slain."   40

"What is thy name?" then said Robin Hood,
    "Come tell me, without any fail."
"By the faith of my body," then said the young man,
    "My name it is Allin a Dale."

"What will you give me," said Robin Hood,   45
    "In ready gold or fee,
To help thee to thy true love again,
    And deliver her unto thee?"

"I have no money," then quoth the young man,
    "No ready gold nor fee,   50
But I will swear upon a book
    Thy true servant for to be."

---

[1] tane: taken.

"How many miles is it to thy true love?
    Come tell me without guile."
"By the faith of my body," then said the young man,   55
    "It is but five little mile."

Then Robin he hasted over the plain,
    He did neither stint nor lin,[2]
Until he came unto the church,
    Where Allin should keep his wedding.   60

"What hast thou here?"The bishop then said,
    "I prithee now tell unto me."
"I am a bold harper," quoth Robin Hood,
    "And the best in the north country."

"O welcome, O welcome," the bishop he said,   65
    "That musick best pleaseth me."
"You shall have no musick," quoth Robin Hood,
    "Till the bride and the bridegroom I see."

With that came in a wealthy knight,
    Which was both grave and old,   70
And after him a finikin[3] lass,
    Did shine like the glistering gold.

"This is not a fit match," quod bold Robin Hood,
    "That you do seem to make here,
For since we are come into the church,   75
    The bride shall chuse her own dear."

Then Robin Hood put his horn to his mouth,
    And blew blasts two or three;
When four and twenty bowmen bold
    Came leaping over the lee.   80

And when they came into the church-yard,
    Marching all on a row,
The first man was Allin a Dale,
    To give bold Robin his bow.

[2] lin: leave off; stop.   [3] finikin: dainty.

"This is thy true love," Robin he said,   85
   "Young Allin, as I hear say,
And you shall be married at this same time,
   Before we depart away."

"That shall not be," the bishop he said,
   "For thy word shall not stand;   90
They shall be three times askt in the church,
   As the law is of our land."[4]

Robin Hood pull'd off the bishops coat,
   And put it upon Little John;
"By the faith of my body," then Robin said,   95
   "This 'cloth' does make thee a man."

When Little John went into the quire,
   The people began to laugh;
He askt them seven times in the church,
   Lest three times should not be enough.   100

"Who gives me this maid?" said Little John.
   Quoth Robin Hood, "that do I;
And he that takes her from Allin a Dale,
   Full dearly he shall her buy."

And thus having ended this merry wedding,   105
   The bride lookt like a queen;
And so they return'd to the merry green-wood,
   Amongst the leaves so green.

[4] **the law of our land:** the Church required those wishing to wed to announce their intent in church on three successive Sundays so that people knowing of any impediment to the marriage could lodge objections.

→ ANONYMOUS

From A Famous Battle between
Robin Hood and Maid Marian   *Date unknown*

The second ballad, though late, shows many of the characteristics of earlier Robin Hood ballads. It involves disguises, a central fight, and then a happy return to the greenwood. However, in this instance, the disguised figure with whom Robin (who is also called Robert, Earl of Huntington in this text) fights is a woman. Compare the function of disguise in the ballad and in Shakespeare's play. What does disguise permit to happen that otherwise would not? What is the difference between a battle of words between Orlando and Rosalind and a swordfight between Robin Hood and Maid Marian? Does Orlando, as well as Duke Senior, evoke associations with Robin Hood?

A bonny fine maid of noble degree,
     With a hey down, down, a down, down.[1]
Maid Marian call'd by name,
Did live in the North, of excellent worth,
     For she was a gallant dame.   5

For favour and face and beauty most rare,
     With a hey &c.
Queen Helen she did excel:[2]
For Marian then was prais'd of all men
     That did in the country dwell.   10

'Twas neither Rosamond nor Jane Shore,[3]
     With a hey, &c.
Whose beauty was clear and bright,
That could surpass this country lass,
     Beloved of lord and knight.   15

[1] *hey down down a down down*: a common refrain in ballads.   [2] **Queen Helen she did excel**: she was more beautiful than Helen of Troy (reputedly the most beautiful woman in the world).   [3] **Rosamond nor Jane Shore**: Rosamund Clifford (d. c. 1176) was the mistress of England's King Henry II, famed for her beauty. Jane Shore (d. c. 1527) was the mistress of King Edward IV of England.

Ritson, Joseph ed., *Robin Hood: A Collection of Poems, Songs, and Ballads* (London, 1884), 389–91.

The Earl of Huntington,[4] nobly born,
　　With a hey, &c.
　That came of noble blood
To Marian went, with a good intent,
　　By the name of Robin Hood.　　　　　　　20

With kisses sweet their red lips meet,
　　With a key, &c.
　For she and the Earl did agree;
In every place,[5] they kindly embrace,
　　With love and sweet unity.　　　　　　　25

But Fortune bearing these lovers a spite,[6]
　　With a hey, &c.
　That soon they were forced to part:
To the merry green wood then went Robin Hood
　　With a sad and sorrowful heart.　　　　　30

And Marian, poor soul, was troubled in mind.
　　With a hey, &c.
　For the absence of her friend;
With finger in eye, she often did cry,
　　And his person did much commend.　　　35

Perplexed and vexed, and troubled in mind
　　With a hey, &c.,
　She drest herself like a page,
And ranged the wood, to find Robin Hood,
　　The bravest of men in that age.　　　　　40

With quiver and bow, sword, buckler, and all,
　　With a hey, &c.
　Thus armed was Marian most bold,
Still wandering about, to find Robin out,
　　Whose person was better than gold.　　　45

---

[4]**The Earl of Huntington:** a popular legend held that Robin Hood was Robert, Earl of Huntingdon.　[5]**did agree, / In every place:** they got along in every possible way. There is also a distinct sexual sense to this assertion.　[6]**Fortune bearing these lovers a spite:** disliking them; having a grudge against them. Fortune was often personified as a spiteful and unreliable female deity.

But Robin Hood, he himself had disguis'd
   With a hey, &c.
And Marian was strangely attir'd
That they prov'd foes, and so fell to blows,
   Whose[7] valor bold Robin admir'd.   50

They drew out their swords, and to cutting they went,
   With a hey, &c.
At least an hour or more,
That the blood ran apace from Robin's face,
   And Marian was wounded sore.[8]   55

"O hold thy hand, hold thy hand," said Robin Hood,
   With a hey, &c.
"And thou shalt be one of my string,[9]
To range in the wood, with bold Robin Hood,
   And hear the sweet nightingale sing."   60

When Marian did hear the voice of her love,
   With a hey, &c.
Her self she did quickly discover[10]
And with kisses sweet she did him greet,
   Like to a most loyal lover.   65

When bold Robin Hood his Marian did see,
   With a hey, &c.
Good Lord, what clipping[11] was there!
With kind embraces, and jobbing[12] of faces,
   Providing of gallant cheer.   70

. . . .

A stately banquet they had full soon,
   With a hey, &c.
All in a shaded bower.
Where venison sweet they had to eat,
   And were merry that present hour.   80

. . . .

---

[7] **whose:** the antecedent here is the disguised Marian.   [8] **wounded sore:** substantially, although not direfully.   [9] **one of my string:** a member of a faction or collection of persons.   [10] **her self she did quickly discover:** she reveals who she actually is, her true identity.   [11] **clipping:** embracing.   [12] **jobbing:** thrusting.

Rural Life

In Sherwood Forest, Robin Hood and his men spend much of their time hunting deer for food, and this is one of the chief reasons they are considered outlaws.[1] Killing deer in royal forests was a major crime, specifically a crime against the monarch who claimed ownership over the beasts who lived in them.

There is no specific indication that the Arden of *As You Like It* is a royal forest, and yet the reference to Duke Senior as a kind of Robin Hood makes it likely that Shakespeare's audience would have assumed that it was. In exile, Duke Senior and his men, like Robin Hood, spend some of their time hunting, and this is part of what makes them both a merry band and also an outlaw band. Act 4, scene 2 begins with Jaques asking: "Which is he that killed the deer?" In production, a dead deer is usually carried on the stage at this point, and a bawdy song ensues that plays on the deer's horns as a traditional symbol of cuckoldry. Men whose wives were unfaithful to them were said to "wear the horns" (see chapter 3).

The five texts that follow provide a more down-to-earth picture of rural activities in and around forests than those afforded either by highly conventional pastoral literature or by the texts we connect to the mythical Robin Hood. They deal, in turn, with laws governing the use of the forest and the deer that live within it, proclamations against unlawful hunting, the lament of a deer being hunted and its account of its useful properties, and finally how one cares for sheep at each stage of the year.

[1] Stuart Daley convincingly argues that the play presents hunting in *As You Like It* as a serious search for food and not as a frivolous pastime. In this regard, the Duke and his men are linked to Robin Hood and other outlaw figures who sought with their longbows to wrest a livelihood from living rough in the forest. See "The Idea of Hunting in *As You Like It*," *Shakespeare Studies* 21 (1993): 72–95.

→ JOHN MANWOOD

From A Treatise and Discourse of the Laws of the Forest

1592

Forests were an extremely important aspect of England's landscape in the early modern period. In 1592, John Manwood (d. 1610) produced his important book

John Manwood, *A Treatise and Discourse of the Laws of the Forest* (London, 1598), 1, 2, 6–8, 8–9, 21–24, 29, 106, 114, 124, 153; STC 17291.

A Treatise and Discourse of the Laws of the Forest, which he put out in an expanded edition in 1598, and which gives a detailed picture of how the period understood what a forest was and who had rights over its resources. Manwood was well suited for this task. A barrister, he had worked as a gamekeeper in one of the king's forests and later acted as a judge for one of the forest courts. Though the word *forest* has a very general meaning to modern readers (something like "wooded area"), the term had a specific legal definition in Shakespeare's time, one that Manwood unpacks at length. How does Manwood define a forest and what is its relationship to royal authority? Then think about what it may mean for Shakespeare to make an exiled ruler a hunter in such a forest. At the beginning of act 2, scene 1, the Duke and his men enter "[*dressed*] *like foresters*" and the Duke says that they are going to "kill us venison" (2.1.21). Given Manwood's account of forest law, would contemporary audiences perceive this act as legal or illegal? Does it matter that the Duke's position has been usurped by his younger brother? How do his hunting activities support a reading of Duke Senior as an outlaw, a good outlaw, or a true king?

The territory delimited as the forest could include pastures and fields as well as densely wooded areas. Those who lived within the bounds of the forest were, as Manwood indicates, strictly forbidden from cutting the king's timber, hunting the many forest animals that counted as "venison," or improving their land. The forest was also, however, surrounded by purlieu, or border areas, where restrictions were less severe. In *As You Like It*, Rosalind and Celia have purchased a cottage on the "skirts of the forest" (3.2.280–81). Are their activities as tenders of sheep presented as legitimate? Have they found a safe refuge from the anger of Duke Frederick?

DEDICATORY EPISTLE:

To the Right Honorable, Charles, Lord Howard, Earl of Nottingham, Baron of Effingham:[1]

... And seeing that so many do daily so contemptuously commit such heinous spoils and trespasses therein, that the greatest part of them are spoiled and decayed: And also that very little, or nothing, as yet is extant concerning the laws of the forest, I thought it very necessary to collect this small treatise, declaring therein the ways and means how to preserve and maintain forests, together with the due punishment of such as shall be found offenders therein, to the intent that thereby men may the better know those laws, wherein they so often offend, and the danger thereof, which being known, they may the better avoid. ...

[1] the Right Honorable, Charles, Lord Howard, Earl of Nottingham, Baron of Effingham: Lord High Admiral from 1585 to 1618, commander in chief of the English fleet that defeated the Spanish Armada in 1588.

CHAPTER I

1. Of the definition of a forest

. . . A forest is a certain territory of woody grounds of fruitful pastures, privileged for wild beasts and fowls of forest, chase,[2] and warren[3] to rest and abide in, in the safe protection of the King, for his princely delight and pleasure, which territory of ground, so privileged, is meered[4] and bounded with unremovable marks, meers, and boundaries, either known by matter of record, or else by prescription: and also replenished with wild beasts of venery or chase, and with great coverts of vert,[5] for the succor of the said wild beasts, to have their abode in. For the preservation and continuance of which said place, together with the vert and venison, there are certain particular laws, privileges and officers belonging to the same, meet for that purpose, that are only proper unto a forest, and not to any other place.

3. An explanation of the aforesaid definition

. . . the killing, hurting, or hunting of any of these beasts or fowls of chase, park, or warren within the territory of the forest is a trespass of the forest, and to be punished by the laws of the forest only, and not by any other law.

CHAPTER 2

1. Of the dignity of the King and his royal prerogative to have forests where he will appoint

The King or sovereign governor of a realm is the most excellent & worthiest part or member of the body of the common weal[6] next unto God. As Bracton[7] saith, *Ipse autem Rex non debet esse sub homine, sed sub Deo & Lege, quia lex facit Regem*, the King ought not to be under man, but under God and the law, because the law doth make him a King, and as he is the head and most excellent part of the body of the common weal, so is he also through his governance the preserver, nourisher, & defender of all the people being the rest of the same body. . . . And therefore in respect of his continual care & labor, for the preservation of the whole realm, being the residue of the same body, the laws do allow unto the King, amongst many other privileges, this prerogative, to have his places of recreation & pastime

---

[2] **chase:** unenclosed land reserved for the hunting of game.   [3] **warren:** enclosed land reserved for the breeding of game.   [4] **meered:** delimited.   [5] **vert:** area of green vegetation.   [6] **common weal:** commonwealth.   [7] **Bracton:** Henry of Bracton (d. 1268), English ecclesiastic, jurist, and author of *De Legibus et Consuetudinibus Angliae* (*On the Laws and Customs of England*).

wheresoever he will appoint: for it is at the liberty and pleasure of the king to reserve the wild beasts & the game to himself for his only delight and pleasure, in such privileged places where he will have a firm peace appointed for them. For the King may by the law make a forest even at his will and pleasure for them to rest and abide in, even as by the law he may enter into the ground of any of his subjects, wheresoever there are any mines of gold or silver to be found, & dig the land at his pleasure for the same mines, and carry them away, for that they are things that do belong unto the king only, in whose freehold[8] or land soever they chance to be found, for gold and silver are things of the most excellency that are upon the earth, and therefore, when they are found in the land of any man, the law doth attribute them, being things of such excellency, to belong to the most excellent person, which is the King. And in like manner wild beasts of venery, and beasts and fowls of chase and warren, being things of great excellency, they are meetest for the dignity of a Prince for his pastime and delight, and therefore they do most properly belong unto the King only. And for that cause, it is not lawful for any man within this land to make any chase, park, or warren, in his own freehold or elsewhere, to keep or preserve any wild beasts or birds of forest, chase, park, or warren in it, without the king's grant or warrant so to do. And if any man do, he is to be punished in a *Quo warranto*,[9] and the franchise to be leased into the King's hands, for such wild beasts do belong unto the king. . . . He also by the common law shall have in his own possession all such things which by the law of nature ought to be common, as wild beasts and fowls that are not tame, which by the law of nature ought to be common, and are made proper by the possession and taking of them, as by fowling, hunting, and such like. And although men may kill such wild beasts in their wildness when they are found wandering, being out of any forest, park, chase, or warren, yet no man hath any property in them, until they have killed them, for during the time of their wildness they are *Nullius in rebus*,[10] and then they must needs be said to be *In manu domini Regis*, in the king's possession. And then the King may privilege them in any place where he will appoint, and to prohibit any man to kill or destroy them.

---

[8] **freehold:** property whose duration of ownership is indeterminate, rather than fixed. [9] *Quo warranto*: medieval Latin for "by what warrant?" referring to the asking of landholders by what warrant they held their lands or exercised their rights; Manwood is reminding his readers that men who might keep a chase, park, or warren without the king's permission do not have that right, and their land can revert to the king. [10] *Nullius in rebus*: Latin, owned by no one.

CHAPTER 18

2. Who may hawk and hunt within the forest, and who may not

The King himself, and all those that have any sufficient warrant or authority from him to hawk or hunt within the forest, they only may hawk & hunt there, & none other, & all such, as have any lawful claim, allowed in eyre[11] by reason of any grant from the king, to hawk or hunt within the forest, they may use that same according to their grant, so they do follow their authority in the same manner that it is granted unto them . . . therefore all knights, squires, gentlemen, and freeholders that do dwell in the forest, they must forbear to hawk or hunt within their own grounds being within the regard of the forest, because it is a trespass & breach of the king's free & firm piece of the forest for any man whatsoever to hawk or hunt within the same, without good warrant from the king.

9. How trespassers and malefactors by hunting in forests shall be punished for the same

. . . Now it shall not be amiss, here in this place to speak some thing, of such as have no color or shadow at all to justify their hunting by, and yet nevertheless do hunt in the forest, and kill and destroy her Majesty's wild beasts there, or at the leastwise in their hunting, if they do not kill any beast of the forest, yet they do vehemently disquiet the wild beasts there, to the breach of their firm peace, which all the kings and princes of this realm have always granted, maintained, and allowed, and that the laws of the forest do yet allow them, and these are generally called trespassers or malefactors in hunting in the King's forest. . . . If any man shall take a wild beast in the forest without warrant, his body shall be arrested, wheresoever he may be found within the bounds of the forest, and when he is so taken and arrested, he shall not be delivered out of prison without a warrant from the king or from the chief justice in eyre of the king's forests. And not withstanding that the words there are, *Si quis ceperit feram*, if any man shall take a wild beast in the forest, yet if any be taken hunting in the forest, although that he have not taken nor killed any wild beast in the forest, yet he is by the law to be punished, as if he had killed and taken a wild beast of the forest.

[11] **allowed in eyre:** accepted by the eyre, the circuit court presided over by magistrates of forest law.

→ JAMES I

From A Proclamation against Unlawful Hunting   *1603*

While Elizabeth I was a hunter, hunting was a special passion of James I (1566–1625), who issued the following proclamation immediately after coming to the throne. Though it postdates the play, the proclamation reveals much about the issues surrounding forest use that would have been familiar to both Shakespeare and the play's early audience. Interestingly, the proclamation acknowledges that the forest laws were often violated.

Forasmuch as his Majesty understandeth, that there be diverse ancient & other good and necessary laws and statutes of this his kingdom of England, which do inflict and impose diverse grievous corporal[1] and pecuniary[2] pains & punishments . . . upon such as unlawfully hunt or enter into any forest, park, chase, or warren, to kill or destroy any deer or game with any dogs, nets, guns, crossbows, stonebows or other instruments, engines, or means whatsoever. . . . And yet his Majesty understandeth withal, that the same good laws and statutes have had (especially of late time) little or no effect . . . by means whereof, such boldness and disobedience hath grown, specially in the vulgar sort,[3] as that of late years, the several games above mentioned, have been more excessively and outrageously spoiled & destroyed, than hath been attempted & practiced in former ages. His Majesty intending a due and speedy reformation of the said abuses and offenses . . . and yet of his Princely clemency[4] and benignity,[5] now in the beginning of his most happy and prosperous reign towards all his loving subjects is graciously pleased, and doth by these presents vouchsafe to publish[6] to all his subjects his intention and determination therein, to the end that none of them, (which his Majesty desireth) might hereafter incur the severity and punishment of the said laws and statutes: but like good and natural subjects for their own safety and good, obey and observe the same. And therefore doth straightly charge and command all and every person and persons, of what estate and degree soever, not to hunt, kill, take, or destroy, by any of the ways or means abovesaid, or by any other unlawful mean, device, or invention whatsoever, any of the games abovesaid, contrary to any of the aforesaid laws or statutes. . . .

---

[1]**corporal:** bodily.   [2]**pecuniary:** monetary.   [3]**the vulgar sort:** the common people.   [4]**clemency:** mercy.   [5]**benignity:** kindness.   [6]**publish:** make publicly known.

James I, Proclamation 7, "A Proclamation against Unlawful Hunting" (May 16, 1603), *Stuart Royal Proclamations, Vol. 1: Royal Proclamations of King James I, 1603–1625*, ed. James F. Larkin and Paul L. Hughes (Oxford: Clarendon Press, 1973), 14–16.

And that if any person or persons shall, after this proclamation made and published, offend in any of the premises, against any of the said laws and statutes, that then he shall not only undergo and suffer the severe sentence and punishment of the same, as well for such offences hereafter to be attempted or done, as for the like offenses formerly committed, but also such pains and penalties as may be inflicted upon such as willingly contemn[7] and disobey his commandment royal.

[7] contemn: disregard.

→ GEORGE GASCOIGNE

From The Noble Art of Venery or Hunting   *1575*

The following excerpt is taken from George Gascoigne's *The Noble Art of Venery or Hunting*, a work that draws heavily on French treatises on the same subject. Gascoigne (c. 1525–1577) was a notable sixteenth-century soldier, poet, and courtier, and his book on hunting was an attempt to attract the attention of an elite audience and even of Elizabeth I, who was known to be fond of hunting. In 1575, Gascoigne had written part of an entertainment for Elizabeth when she visited Kenilworth, the earl of Leicester's country estate. As she returned from hunting, Gascoigne stepped out to speak to her dressed as "a Savage man, all in Ivie." He is said to have frightened her horse. *The Noble Art of Venery or Hunting* is adorned with a number of woodcuts, and the variety of topics in the book bespeaks its appeal to aristocratic audiences for whom hunting was a sign of their class privilege as companions to kings and also to their practical concerns about what to do with various parts of the animal's body.

The sections that follow include the hart's introduction to the book and an extended lament of a weeping deer. That lament recalls both Duke Senior's sorrow that he must kill "the poor dappled fools, / Being native burghers of this desert city" (2.1.22–23) and especially the first lord's account of Jaques's description of the weeping and wounded stag (Figure 8), which he observes as it pauses in its flight from the hunters, as well as his subsequent moralizing on the meaning of the spectacle before him (2.1.26–63). Compare what the hart says to the hunter in Gascoigne's text to what Jaques says *for* the stag in *As You Like It*. How does each use the occasion of the hunt to critique human behavior? What is being satirized or criticized in each account? Is Jaques mainly sorry for the deer, or is he using the deer's plight to vent other concerns? Why, if the Duke pities the deer, does he not stop the hunt? And why does he seem to feel that Jaques, in his "sullen fits" (2.1.67), is worth conversing with? Leaving aside the motives

George Gascoigne, *The Noble Art of Venery or Hunting* (London, 1575), 38–39, 39–40, 136–40; STC 24328.

135 **The booke of Hunting.**

The wofull wordes of the Hart to the Hunter.

SInce I in deepeſt dread, do yelde my ſelfe to Man,
And ſtand full ſtill betwene his legs, which earſt full wildly ran:
Since I to him appeale, when hounds purſue me ſore,
As who ſhould ſay (*Now ſaue me man, for elſe I may no more.*)
Why doſt thou then (ô *Man*) (ô *Hunter*) me purſue,
With cry of hounds, with blaſt of horne, with hallow, and with hue?
Or why doſt thou deuiſe, ſuch nets and inſtruments,
Such toyles & toyes, as hunters vſe, to bring me to their bents?

Since

FIGURE 8 *A weeping stag bewails the cruelty of the hunter in* The Noble Art of Venery or Hunting *by George Gascoigne* (1575).

of the human speakers for a moment, do these depictions of animal pain reframe the debate about forest use? Do they point to an ethics that might operate outside of law or economic need?

From *The Noble Art of Venery or Hunting*

THE PREFACE PRONOUNCED BY THE HART.

I am the hart, by Greeks surnamed so,
Because my head doth with their terms agree,
For stately shape, few such on earth do go,
So that by right they have so termed me.
For King's delight, it seems I was ordained,   5
Whose huntsmen yet pursue me day by day,
In forest, chase, and parks, I am constrained
Before their hounds, to wander many a way.
Wherefore who list to learn the perfect trade
Of venery, and therewithal would know   10
What properties, and virtues nature made
In me (poor hart, oh harmless hart) to grow,
Let him give ear to skillful Tristram's lore,[1]
To Phoebus,[2] Foilloux,[3] and many more.

CHAPTER 43

The woeful words of the hart to the hunter

Since I in deepest dread do yield myself to man,
 And stand full still between his legs, which earst[4] full wildly ran:
Since I to him appeal, when hounds pursue me sore,
 As who should say (*Now save me man, for else I may no more.*)
Why dost thou then (*oh man*) (*oh hunter*) me pursue, 5
 With cry of hounds, with blast of horn, with hallow, and with hue?[5]
Or why dost thou devise, such nets and instruments,
 Such toils & toys, as hunters use, to bring me to their bents?
Since I (as earst was saith) do so with humble cheer

---

[1] **Tristram's lore:** Tristram, also known as Tristan, in Arthurian legend is a Knight of the Round Table and in some medieval accounts noted for his skill with a bow and arrow. [2] **Phoebus:** Apollo, Greek and Roman god of archery. [3] **Foilloux:** Jacques de Fouilloux, French writer whose *La Venerie* (Poitiers, 1562) is the basis for Gascoigne's text. [4] **earst:** in the past. [5] **hallow, and with hue:** loud cries and shouts, often for the purpose of spurring on the hounds.

Hold down my head (as who should say, *lo man I yield me here.*)   10
Why art thou not content, (oh murdering cruel mind)
    Thyself alone to hunt me so, which art my foe by kind,
But that thou must instruct, with words in skillful wit,
    All other men to hunt me eke?[6] O wicked wily wit.
Thou here hast set to shew, within this busy book,   15
A looking glass of lessons lewd, wherein all hunts may look:
    And so whiles world doth last, they may be taught to bring
The harmless hart unto his bane, with many a wily thing.
    Is it because thy mind doth seek thereby some gains?
Canst thou in death take such delight? Breeds pleasure so in pains?   20
    Oh cruel, be content, to take in worth my tears,
Which grow to gum[7] and fall from me: content thee with my hairs,
    Content thee with my horns, which every year I mew,[8]
Since all these three make medicines, some sickness to eschew.
    My tears congealed to gum, by pieces from me fall,   25
And they preserve from pestilence, in pomander or ball.[9]
    Such wholesome tears shed I, when thou pursuest me so,
Thou (not content) dost seek my death, and then thou getst no moe.[10]

. . . .

And yet such horns, such hair, such tears as I have told,
    I mew and cast for man's avail, more worth to him than gold.
But he to quite[11] the same, (O murdering man therewhiles)   55
    Pursues me still and traps me oft, with sundry snares and guiles.
Alas lo now I feel cold fear within my bones,
    Which hangs her wings upon my heels, to hasten for the nones:[12]
My swiftest starting steps, me thinks she bids me bide
    In thickest tufts of coverts close, and so myself to hide.   60
Ah rueful remedy, so shall I (as it were)
    Even tear my life out of the teeth of hounds which make me fear.
And from those cruel curs, and brainsick bawling tikes,[13]
    Which vow foote hote[14] to follow me, both over hedge and dikes.
Me thinks I hear the horn, which rends the restless air,   65
    With shrillest sound of bloody blast, and makes me to despair.
Me thinks I see the toil, the tanglings and the stall,[15]
    Which are prepared and set full sure, to compass me withal:

---

[6] **eke:** in addition.   [7] **gum:** a secretion which hardens when dried but is soluble in water.
[8] **mew:** shed.   [9] **pomander or ball:** a mixture of aromatic substances made into a ball and used
to ward off odors and infection.   [10] **moe:** more.   [11] **quite:** repay.   [12] **for the nones:** indeed, verily.
[13] **tikes:** dogs.   [14] **foote hote:** hastily.   [15] **the toil, the tanglings and the stall:** the trap set up to
ensnare the hart, the ropes to bind him, and the place prepared to hold him.

Me thinks the foster[16] stands full close in bush or tree,
 And takes his level straight and true, me thinks he shoots at me.   70
And hits the harmless hart, of me unhappy hart,
 Which must needs please him by my death, I may it not astart.[17]
Alas and well away, me thinks I see the hunt,
 Which takes the measure of my slots,[18] where I to tread was wont:
Because I shall not miss, at last to please his mind,   75
 Alas I see him where he seeks my latest lair to find.
He takes my fewmers[19] up, and puts them in his horn,
 Alas me thinks he leaps for joy, and laugheth me to scorn.
Hark, hark, alas give ear, *This gear goeth well* (saith he)
 This hart bears dainty venison, in Prince's dish to be.   80
Lo now he blows his horn, even at the kennel door,
 Alas, alas, he blows a seek,[20] alas yet blows he more:
He jeopards and rechates,[21] alas he blows the fall,
 And sounds that deadly doleful note, which I must die withal.

. . . .

[16]**foster:** forester, or officer in charge of the forest, here used to refer to the huntsman.   [17]**astart:** escape.   [18]**slots:** tracks.   [19]**fewmers:** droppings of excrement, which would give the hunter an indication of the hart's size.   [20]**blows a seek:** to sound a series of notes that urge the hounds to the chase.   [21]**jeopards and rechates:** to sound a call that summons the hounds and gathers them together.

→ JOHN FITZHERBERT

From The Booke of Husbandry   *1540*

and

→ LEONARD MASCALL

From The First Book of Cattle   *1591*

The sixteenth century saw a strong interest in the publication of husbandry manuals, books that focused on the arts of farming and estate management. Many of these books were translations or close imitations of classical or Continental texts, and they varied in the degree to which they included new material

John Fitzherbert, *The Booke of Husbandry* (London, 1540), 28, 30; STC 10996.

Leonard Mascall, *The First Book of Cattle* (London, 1591), 202, 215, 227–28, 233, 234; STC 17581.

geared specifically to the English context. How to manage poultry, graft trees, fish, survey, plow, and plant crops—there were manuals that dealt with all these topics and more. Virgil's *Georgics*, which praised a life of agricultural labor, inspired much of this literature, which could be addressed to big landowners bent on improving their rural estates or to smaller farmers interested in the particulars of a specific branch of agricultural work.

John Fitzherbert (1460–1531), member of a prominent Derbyshire family and brother to Sir Anthony Fitzherbert, an important judge and legal writer, wrote one of the first English books of husbandry in 1523; it was frequently reprinted throughout the sixteenth century. Included below are several sections from that manual describing when to wean lambs and how to treat some common diseases of sheep. The second excerpt comes from Leonard Mascall's *The First Book of Cattle*, published in 1591. Mascall (d. 1589) was Clerk of the Kitchen to Matthew Parker, archbishop of Canterbury, and he wrote not only this treatise on the management of cattle or sheep, but also books on planting and grafting trees, the government of poultry, and fishing. The selections from his treatise include a charming poem in praise of all the useful things sheep provide and then some injunctions to shepherds about how to care for sheep and treat their diseases, including directions for when to "piss in the sheep's mouth" as part of a treatment for poison.

In *As You Like It*, concrete discussions of husbandry, especially sheep farming, emerge in the conversation between Touchstone and Corin in act 3, scene 2. How is Corin's account of his labor illuminated by Fitzherbert's and Mascall's descriptions of the care of sheep? More important, what is at stake about the value of different ways of life in the exchange between the rural shepherd and the courtly clown? How does Corin's "philosophy" grow from his labor as a shepherd and how does it challenge the perspective of Touchstone and the other temporary sojourners in Arden? Are there limitations to Corin's philosophy?

From The Booke of Husbandry

WHAT TIME LAMBS SHOULD BE WEANED:

In some places they never sever their lambs from their dams,[1] and that is for two causes: one is, in the best pasture, where the rams go always with their ewes, there it needeth not, for the dams will wax dry, and wean their lambs themselves. Another cause is, he that hath no several and sound pasture, to put his lambs into, when they should be weaned, he must either sell them, or let them suck as long as the dames will suffer them, and it is a common saying, that the lamb shall not rot, as long as it sucketh, except the dam

---

[1] **dams:** mothers, used in reference to animals.

want meat. But he that hath several and sound pasture, it is time to wean his lambs when they be sixteen weeks old, or eighteen at the farthest, and the better shall the ewe take the ram again. And the poor man of the peak country,[2] and such other places where as they use to milk their ewes, they use to wean their lambs at twelve weeks old, and to milk their ewes five or six weeks and etc. But those lambs be never so good as the other that suck long, and have meat enough.

TO GREASE SHEEP:

If any sheep be scabbed, the shepherd may perceive it by the biting, rubbing, or scratching with his horn, and most commonly the wool will rise and be thin or bare in that place. Then take him, and shed the wool with thy fingers, there as the scab is, and with thy finger lay a little tar thereupon, and stroke it a length in the bottom of the wool, that it be not seen above. And so shed the wool by and by, and lay a little tar thereupon, till thou pass the sore, and then it will go no farther.

TO MEDDLE[3] TAR:

Let thy tar be meddled with oil, goose grease, or capon's[4] grease. These three be the best, for these will make the tar to run abroad. Butter and swine's grease, when they be molten, are good, so they be not salty, for tar of himself is too keen, and is a fretter,[5] and no healer, without it be meddled with some of these.

[2] peak country: now the Peak District, a hilly district in Derbyshire and Staffordshire. [3] meddle: mix. [4] capon: a castrated male chicken. [5] fretter: an irritant.

From The First Book of Cattle

A PRAISE OF SHEEP:

These cattle[1] (sheep) among the rest,
Is counted for man one of the best.
No harmful beast nor hurt at all,
His fleece of wool doth clothe us all:
Which keeps us from the extreme cold:
His flesh doth feed both young and old.

[1] cattle: Mascall uses the word to refer to all livestock.

His tallow[2] makes the candles white,
To burn and serve us day and night.
His skin doth pleasure diverse ways,
To write, to wear at all assays.   10
His guts, thereof we make wheel strings,
They use his bones to other things.
His horns some shepherds will not loose,
Because therewith they patch their shoes.
His dung is chief I understand,   15
To help and dung the plowman's land.
Therefore the sheep among the rest,
He is for man a worthy beast.

THE GOVERNMENT OF SHEEP, AND REMEDIES FOR SUCH DISEASES AS DO COME UNTO THEM:

Moreover, the shepherd which doth keep them ought to be wise in govern-ing them with gentleness, as it is commanded to all keepers of cattle what-soever they be, which ought to show themselves conductors and guiders of cattle, and not as masters, and to make them go or to call them, they ought either to cry or whistle, and after to show them the sheep-hook,[3] but to throw nothing at them, for that doth fear them, nor yet to stray far off from them, nor to sit or lie down. If he do not go, he ought to stand, and to sit very seldom. For the office of a shepherd is as a high watchman for his cat-tle, to the end that the slow sheep do not slip from the other. . . .

There comes a scabbiness also among lambs being half a year old, as toward winter, or the next fall of the leafe, ye shall in some places have all your lambs scabby, or the most thereof, which cause is, as shepherds do say, when the rams be scabby that get them, all those lambs will be scabby at the next fall. They do heal it in greasing them with tar mixed with two parts of fresh grease or neat's feet oil,[4] or goose grease if ye can have it, for that is best. There is also another scabbiness which chanceth sometimes on the mousels[5] of sheep and young tegs,[6] and that comes, as shepherds do say, whereas there is great plenty of furze and gorse,[7] that by the eating of the tops and flowers thereof, they prick their lips and mousel, whereby come these sorts of scabs, the which they heal by anointing them with fresh butter. Some

---

[2] tallow: fat.   [3] sheep-hook: a shepherd's crook, which could be fit around the neck of a sheep in order to guide it in a certain direction or keep it from straying.   [4] neat's feet oil: the oil from the heel of a neat, or bovine, animal.   [5] mousels: muzzles.   [6] tegs: sheep in their second year.
[7] furze and gorse: prickly shrubs.

take the juice of plantain[8] and fresh grease boiled together, and therewith anoint them.

If the wool of sheep after a scabbiness do go off, as in some places the wool will go clean off, to make it grow again and fill the aforesaid place, some shepherds do use to grease them with tar mixed with some other thing, as butter, oil, goose-grease, or fresh grease, for tar alone is sharp, a fretter, and whealer,[9] without it be mixed with some of those things aforesaid, to make him run the better. Some use to make the wool come soon again, to mix with tar and oil, the foot of a cauldron's bottom, and so mix with oil and a little tar the powder of a burnt daffodil root, or the powder of the water lily root, or the root of the water-clote,[10] which hath a broad leaf on the water, or garden cress beaten with mustard and laid to, or the herb crowfoot stamped with oil and laid to: these cause both wool and hair to come again in any pilled place. . . .

Sheep oftentimes will be poisoned by eating some evil herb or other things, whereupon they will swell and stagger, in holding commonly their heads down, and within a while after they will foam at the mouth, and then some after, they will fall down and die. The remedy is, shepherds do use as soon as they spy any sheep reel or stagger to take him and open his mouth, and under his tongue at the root, there shall ye see bladders,[11] which they do rub with the powder of loam,[12] or with crumbs of bread, and break them, then they piss in the sheep's mouth, and so wash it down. If ye cannot piss, then ye shall take drink, and pour some into his mouth, and soon after he will do well again, or give him the juice of wormwood,[13] with wine or vinegar. . . .

Also if any lamb be like to die when he is first lambed, ye shall open his mouth and blow therein, and thereby many have recovered soon after, and done well. Wherefore in this time of the year ye must be painful[14] to see your ewes, and to be with them late at night, and early in the morning, and to see and hearken if any ewe do complain or groan, that ye may be ready to help her. . . .

Things good for the easier deliverance of the lambs, to be ministered in time of extremity: nettles boiled in malmsey[15] and given, which will open the neck of the matrix;[16] anise seeds boiled in wine or ale and given; the juice of pennyroyal[17] stamped with ale and given.

---

[8] plantain: a type of low-growing plant popularly used as a remedy for various complaints. [9] a fretter, and whealer: something that irritates and causes wheals or pustules. [10] water-clote: yellow water lily. [11] bladders: boils, blisters, or pustules containing liquid. [12] loam: mud; soil mixed with water. [13] wormwood: a bitter medicinal plant. [14] painful: careful. [15] malmsey: a type of wine from the Mediterranean. [16] matrix: womb. [17] pennyroyal: a mint plant.

CHAPTER 2

Love, Sex, and Marriage

>‹‹

As *You Like It* is not only a pastoral work; it's also a comedy, and comedies typically end in marriage. So does Shakespeare's play. In fact, it concludes with four marriages, and, as a final *coup de théâtre*, Hymen, the god of marriage, arrives on stage to bless the prospective unions. The play, we might say, hyperbolizes the conventional ending of comedy, calling attention to the weight culture places on this institution as the socially acceptable end for the many kinds of love and desire the play puts on display. While the ending is important, most of the play, of course, is spent getting to that ending. The deepest pleasures of *As You Like It* are found in threading the slow, dilatory paths that the play takes toward its destined conclusion. The central structural premise of the play is juxtaposition. The audience watches Rosalind and Orlando spar and emote their way toward the altar as Silvius complains and Phoebe disdains and Touchstone and Audrey ride the wave of their bodily urges. Only for Celia and Oliver is the path smooth. They look, they love, they wed, playing out a highly conventional scenario of love at first sight, which throws into high relief the much more tortuous paths that the other lovers follow.

Marriage, the goal toward which *As You Like It* converges, was one of the most important institutions in early modern culture. It united families and (for the upper classes) the property and wealth each commanded, and it was the vehicle for perpetuating family lineages. However, marriage was not only an institution with economic and lineal ramifications. After the Protestant Reformation, in particular, marriage was also increasingly viewed as the primary site for both emotional and physical intimacy and for the exercise of daily piety. Spiritual exercises, including Bible reading and daily prayers involving all members of the household, were the responsibility of both husband and wife, who were also enjoined to take pleasure in one another's conversation, to embrace the pleasures of the marriage bed, and to cooperate in the running of the household, even though the husband retained his patriarchal role as the official head of the family. A well-run household offered a model of good government, and a marriage of mutual respect lay at the heart of all the other household relationships involving children, servants, and neighbors.[1]

All of this, of course, represented an ideal. In actuality, marriage was as complicated in the early modern period as it is today. For the upper classes, many marriages were arranged by parents who might or might not consult the wishes of the young people whose lives were being joined. There are many accounts of unhappy marriages in the period, cases in which husband and wife proved incompatible; in which they fought over the disposition of property; and in which adultery marred the ideal of married chastity that lay at the heart of Protestant unions. *As You Like It* doesn't show us post-marriage couples. Like most of Shakespeare's early comedies, it shows the run-up to marriage and not the thing itself. Duke Senior and Duke Frederick have daughters but no living spouses, and so we are not given any insight into the texture of the marriages of the prior generation. What we watch, instead, are the vicissitudes of courtship, some of which include anxieties about what marriage might entail. More than anything else, then, *As You Like It* is a courtship play. The pastoral world of Arden affords a place of play, experimentation, and change in which characters feel their way toward the married state. A key question is how the play uses the various couples to compare many ways of being in love and what, if anything, emerges as an ideal. Does a particular kind of courtship prepare one well for the vicissitudes of the married state?

One end of love's spectrum is occupied by Touchstone, who, though he tells Silvius and Rosalind about his alleged earlier wooing of Jane Smile (2.4.40–47), initially functions more as a critic of love's madness than a participant in it. He makes wonderful fun of the love poems Orlando hangs on

---

[1] For an interesting study of the marriages at the heart of the early modern household and their fraught dramatic representations, see Lena Cowen Orlin, *Private Matters and Public Culture in Post-Reformation England* (Ithaca: Cornell UP, 1994).

the trees in the forest, parodying the young man's elevated praise of Rosalind with verses stressing the bawdy and sexual elements of love: the animal urges that link a lover to a deer or a cat; the naturalness of the sexual act in which "love's prick" (3.2.95) finds its resting place in the "sweetest rose" that is Rosalind's vagina (3.2.94). If Orlando makes love a lofty matter, Touchstone's passions are more earthy. Sex, more than lofty passions, drives him, and perhaps for that reason he is fully in touch with the possibility that a wife may bring a man the gift of horns, symbol of cuckoldry (3.3.37–47). Sexual desire can make a woman an adulteress or a man an adulterer as readily as it can entice each to marriage. When Touchstone does decide to wed, he chooses the country wench Audrey, and his path to marriage is strewn with ambivalence. At first he eschews a proper church wedding and for a priest selects the dubious Sir Oliver Mar-text, opining: "he is not like to marry me well; and not being well married, it will be a good excuse for me hereafter to leave my wife" (3.3.68–69). Audrey and Touchstone are an odd couple: he from the court and she from the country, he a wit and she an uneducated goatkeeper. Their differences suggest the many ways that class, background, and unequal natural endowments can make the path of true love rocky. Whatever the eventual stability of their union, it serves as a reminder of the role that sexual passion plays in the making and marring of marriages.

As You Like It employs many early modern rhetorics of love in its varied articulations of passion and desire. The Roman poet Ovid was popular in the Renaissance; his earthy renditions of love in the *Amores (Elegies of Love)* (16 B.C.E.), for example, which was translated into English by Shakespeare's contemporary Christopher Marlowe, gave a warrant for thinking of love as a fully embodied and sexual passion that often paid little heed to the niceties of marriage but followed its own ungovernable path toward physical consummation and pleasure. At some moments Touchstone introduces an Ovidian note into the play. More popular still was the example of Petrarch, Italian poet of the fourteenth century, whose sonnets to Laura were endlessly imitated throughout the early modern period. In Petrarchan discourse, the beloved is extolled by a man who worships her, often from afar. She is his sun, his inspiration for verse, his idea of perfection. Petrarchan poems often describe the beloved by cataloguing her features in a detailed description called a *blazon*: she has teeth like pearls, hair like gold, skin as white as lilies.[2] Typically, however, the woman is unattainable. Petrarchan love is frustrated love, but it stimulates reams of love poetry as sexual passion is sublimated into poetic creativity.

[2] For a classic study of the politics of the blazon see Nancy I. Vickers, "Diana Described: Scattered Woman and Scattered Rhyme," *Critical Inquiry* 58.3 (1976): 374–94.

An important question is the role that Petrarchanism plays in *As You Like It*. The endlessly adoring Silvius — "O Phoebe, Phoebe, Phoebe!" (2.4.37) — may be the play's most obvious Petrarchan lover, but few escape Petrarchanism's idealizing pull, not even Rosalind, and certainly not Orlando. Silvius, moreover, undergoes a startling fate. Rosalind engineers his marriage to Phoebe, a decidedly un-Petrarchan destination for a Petrarchan lover and one of the play's subtle rewritings of its inherited material. Petrarchanism was so prevalent and popular a discourse that it also bred its antithesis, a vivid anti-Petrarchanism that opposed dark-haired and earthy women to the blond, ethereal beloveds of Petrarch's poems and set sex against more rarefied and disembodied forms of devotion. Touches of anti-Petrarchanism can be found in the play, too, especially in Rosalind's deflating accounts of Phoebe's "inky brows," "black silk hair," and "bugle eyeballs" (3.5.46–47) (Figure 9). Each variety of love rhetoric implies a certain understanding of what love is, a particular positioning of lover and beloved. Mixing them up and setting one against another is a key way Shakespeare creates comic effects and also how he makes love and its representation a *problem* in the play and not just a set of clichés or a foregone conclusion. What is it to "be in love"? What does that mean? How does one express love "truly"? Is it a matter of invention or imitation? Can one learn a better or different version of love? Can one be in love in a way that prepares for the daily realities that follow the wedding day? These are some of the big questions that Shakespeare's courtship play poses as it heads toward the socially destined horizon of marriage.

The most complicated courtship of all is, hands down, that of Rosalind and Orlando. At the wrestling match in act 1, they undergo their own version of love at first sight, but their path to marriage is long and giddily complex. In the Forest of Arden, Orlando is a clichéd love melancholic, writing bad love poetry to Rosalind and pinning it on trees. Many readers have felt, however, that through his encounters with Rosalind he comes to display greater maturity or at least more skill in wooing as is expected of a young gentleman (see Chapter 4).[3] One question is whether you agree. Rosalind in her turn spends most of four acts disguised as Ganymede and is not, at least overtly, even recognized by Orlando. The nature of her disguise and the reasons why she stays disguised so long are productive puzzles. They tease thought, inviting us to consider the unpredictable and wayward nature of love and its power, as the Renaissance believed, to transform the self. In his *Metamorphoses*, the Roman poet Ovid told stories of men and gods who were changed by love or fear of its embrace. Pursued by Apollo, Daphne

---

[3] Marjorie Garber, "The Education of Orlando," in A. R. Braunmuller and James C. Bulman, eds., *Comedy from Shakespeare to Sheridan* (Newark: U of Delaware P, 1986), 102–12.

FIGURE 9 *This woodcut literalizes the clichés of the Petrarchan lover's praise of his beloved and in the process renders the woman grotesque. Lilies and roses grow on her cheeks; her breasts are actual globes; arrows dart from her eyes. "The Sonneteers' Beloved," from Charles Sorel,* The Extravagant Shepherd *(1652).*

was transformed into a laurel tree; courting Europa, Jupiter became a bull and carried her away; Iphis, a girl raised as a boy by his mother, fell in love with a woman, Ianthe, and was changed by Hymen, god of marriage, into a man so the wedding could take place. This story forms the basis for John Lyly's play *Gallatea* (published 1592), in which two women fall in love and one is changed into a man by the gods at the moment of marriage. When Rosalind shucks off her male disguise in *As You Like It*'s last scene and reemerges as the about-to-be-married Rosalind, the moment owes much to Lyly, one of Shakespeare's most important predecessors in romantic comedy, as well as to Ovid's many stories of erotic transformation.

The disguise Rosalind assumes in the forest, however, deserves more discussion. Ganymede is not just any name. In classical myth, he was a young man whose beauty bewitched Jupiter, who, taking the form of an eagle, swept Ganymede up to heaven where he became the gods' cupbearer (Figure 10). In many Renaissance texts and images, Ganymede thus symbolized the beauty of homoerotic passion, of love between men. The early modern sex-gender system was somewhat different from our own. In the early modern period, people were not assumed to have "sexual orientations" in the way we have now come to expect; in other words, they were not classified as homosexual or heterosexual, concepts developed only in the nineteenth century.[4] In many circumstances, love between men was highly valued. From classical times onward, the eroticized relationship between a younger and an older man was a particularly prized one, and pastoral was one of the sites of its expression. For example, E. K.'s notes to *The Shepheardes Calender* include a comment praising pederastic love, as such relationships were termed in the period. On the other hand, homoerotic passion could be demonized, especially if it became associated with criminal acts such as treason or atheism. Sodomy was the charge brought to bear in such cases, though it was a term of opprobrium that encompassed not only demonized forms of sex between men, but other crimes such as bestiality or heresy. *Ganymede* could thus be another name for a sodomite, or it could be an entirely positive term of praise, signaling youthful male beauty and positive homoerotic passion. It was also sometimes a term used to describe a boy actor. As you read Shakespeare's play, which of these associations are evoked when Rosalind takes the name Ganymede? However playfully assumed, Rosalind's disguise as Ganymede raises provocative questions

[4] For good work on the early modern sex-gender system, see Mario DiGangi, *Sexual Types: Embodiment, Agency, and Dramatic Character from Shakespeare to Shirley* (Philadelphia: U of Pennsylvania P, 2011); Jonathan Goldberg, *Sodometries: Renaissance Texts, Modern Sexualities* (Stanford: Stanford UP, 1992); Bruce Smith, *Homosexual Desire in Shakespeare's England: A Cultural Poetics* (Chicago: Chicago UP, 1991); and Valerie Traub, *Renaissance Lesbianism in Early Modern England* (Cambridge: Cambridge UP, 2002).

FIGURE 10 *Jove in the form of an eagle sweeps Ganymede up to heaven to serve as his cupbearer.* Jove and Ganymede *by Antonio da Correggio (c. 1531).*

about the protean nature of sexual desire. Rosalind insists that Orlando woo her *as* Rosalind while she is dressed as a young man. While the audience always knows that Ganymede is "really" a girl, what it sees is someone dressed as a man wooing someone else dressed as a man. Ganymede and Orlando even say marriage vows to one another while Rosalind is in her disguise (4.1.92–106). Moreover, Phoebe falls in love with Rosalind when she is playing Ganymede, and much of the final unraveling of the plot depends on Phoebe finally realizing she has been in love with a woman all along, a passion she abandons when Rosalind sheds her disguise and marries Orlando. These playful uses of disguise hint at the multivalent forms that desire can take. Who is to say if Phoebe loves the woman lurking behind Ganymede's male dress, or if she loves the simulacrum of masculinity that Rosalind performs? The same could be said of Orlando. What does he love in the boy/woman he woos? Moreover, the play destabilizes gender itself. Rosalind and Celia talk at court about how Rosalind will perform a masculine part, and she clearly delights in doing so, suggesting that gender postures are not innate and fixed but performative and malleable.

These questions are even more complicated, of course, because of the all-male stage on which Shakespeare's plays were first performed.[5] As far as we know, there were no women actors in early modern public theaters, though foreign actresses sometimes performed in London, and though women had acted in medieval religious drama and still performed in private houses and in court masques.[6] People seeing *As You Like It* performed by Shakespeare's troupe, the Chamberlain's Men, however, would have watched boy actors in their teens in the roles of Rosalind, Celia, Phoebe, and Audrey. When Rosalind becomes Ganymede, Orlando woos a woman character disguised as a youth who is played by a boy actor of the same age. In such circumstances, the trajectories of desire become unstable and delightfully confused. What and whom do the characters love and desire? Do they always know? Do we? Even the affection and friendship felt by Celia for Rosalind—what is its nature? Celia is willing to leave her father's court, accompany Rosalind to Arden, and make her cousin her heir. For much of the play the two figures present themselves as brother and sister in a household that is, in

[5] There is a large literature on the sexual implications of theatrical cross-dressing on the early modern stage. See, for example, Jean E. Howard, "Power and Eros: Crossdressing in Dramatic Representation and Theatrical Practice," in *The Stage and Social Struggle in Early Modern England* (London: Routledge, 1994), 93–128; Stephen Orgel, *Impersonations: The Performance of Gender in Shakespeare's England* (Cambridge: Cambridge UP, 1996); and many of the essays in Susan Zimmerman, ed. *Erotic Politics: Desire on the Renaissance Stage* (New York: Routledge, 1992).
[6] Pamela Allen Brown and Peter Parolin, eds. *Women Players in England 1500–1660: Beyond the All-Male Stage*, (Aldershot: Ashgate, 2005).

reality, overseen by two women, one of whom impersonates a man. Love between women is as much a possibility in Arden as love between men and between men and women. *As You Like It*—the play's very title invites the audience to give itself over to the free play of imagination and desire.

Where there is pleasure there is often, of course, danger. Just as *Ganymede* has "sodomite" as one of its meanings, so the practice of theatrical cross-dressing was often critiqued as an abomination by those who saw the stage as a threat to social order. Wearing clothes of the opposite sex was condemned as confusing distinctions of kind, that is, distinctions of gender, however fun the practice might be and even if it occurred within the special context of theatrical "playing." That Shakespeare so pointedly calls attention to the theater's practices of cross-dressing and puts them at the heart of his play's sexual confusions can hardly have been inadvertent. Using the pleasures of pastoral comedy to cloak his audacity, he nonetheless creates in *As You Like It* a work that takes the part of multivalent desire and gender confusion against those who would limit both.

The four marriages heralded at the end of act 5 might seem to mark the end of free play, to intimate that gender identities have stabilized and the drama's abundant erotic energies have been firmly directed toward the marriage bed. Yet perhaps more than his other pastoral comedies, Shakespeare's *As You Like It* resists the finality of closure and the end of erotic and gender play. After act 5, Rosalind again comes onstage to speak the Epilogue, an act that she herself marks as unusual, since it is typically a male figure who holds this privileged position. She has not dwindled into silence. Moreover, in the Epilogue, Rosalind encourages the audience to exercise choice. She urges the men and women of the audience "to like as much of this play as please you" (Epilogue, lines 9–10). They can embrace the parts of the work that give them pleasure and ignore the rest. Then "Rosalind" again unsettles her own gender with the "if" that reminds the audience she is not only a dramatic female character but also, simultaneously, a boy actor. "If I were a woman I would kiss as many of you as had beards that pleased me" (Epilogue, lines 12–13). "Rosalind" deliberately keeps her gender identity in motion, along with her erotic preferences. If she were a woman, she would kiss men, but since the *if* calls her sex in question, maybe she will kiss women. This ending suggests a deliberate play with closure—delaying, deferring, and complicating it, whether the closure in question refers to the plot of the play or the fixing of gender identities and trajectories of erotic desire.

The texts that follow speak in various ways to the early modern discussions of love and desire in which Shakespeare's play participates. The first documents relate to marriage. They describe its status as a weighty social institution, but also the reasons some fled its embrace and the various ways in which the validity of a marriage could be called in question. The second set of texts deals with early modern love rhetorics, the various languages of desire and passion that formed the matrix from which Shakespeare constructed his play's varied lexicon of love. Last are a series of texts relating to the particularly complex interactions between Rosalind and Orlando, including material on the Renaissance Ganymede, on cross-dressing as theatrical practice, on lovesickness and writing on trees, and on Ovidian metamorphosis. Reading *As You Like It* in relation to this varied body of texts will make clearer the sophistication and daring with which the play took the measure of love and its social forms.

The Celebration of Marriage

The English Reformation—the split between the English Church and the Roman Catholic Church precipitated by Henry VIII—had major consequences for religious practice at all levels. For example, English language preaching replaced the traditional service in Latin. Other measures were adopted that aimed to unify the new Anglican Church, including the mandatory adoption of the Book of Common Prayer, a text containing instructions for the reform of many forms of religious ceremony, and the Book of Homilies, or sermons, read from pulpits at regular intervals throughout the church year. While these texts and the reforms that accompanied them were sometimes unpopular, they articulate the reformed church's basic views about doctrine and practice.

Marriage was one of the religious rites that the church sought to formalize and control. The split with Rome had been triggered in part by disagreement between the king and Rome over his desired divorce from Catherine of Aragon and his subsequent marriage to Anne Boleyn. This, in combination with the influence of Continental reformers, who had denied marriage's status as a sacrament and allowed ministers to marry, ensured that marriage was a key point of Reformation attention. The Anglican Church removed references to marriage as a sacrament in official documents, allowed clergy themselves to marry, and attempted to eliminate the traditional practice of "handfasting," by which a couple could enact a binding union by joining hands before a witness and declaring their intention to marry. The church, attempting to exert control over marriage, wanted all weddings to be performed in church and insisted that the banns, or declaration of intent to marry, be read out on three successive Sundays before a wedding took place in order to give an opportunity for any objections to be aired.

➔ An Homily of the State of Matrimony   *1563*

The Elizabethan Homily of the State of Matrimony is perhaps the closest thing
that we have to an "official" view on marriage from the period, and so its terms
are worth scrutinizing as one thinks of the marriages into which the lovers in *As
You Like It* are headed. According to the excerpts included below, what reasons
are given as to why people should marry? Are they the reasons articulated or
intimated by any of the lovers in Arden? How do you explain the differences
and convergences? What dangers does the homily suggest might imperil marriage? Do the characters in the play recognize those same dangers? What are the
respective positions and duties of husbands and wives as outlined in the homily?
Based on their interactions in courtship, how do you think Orlando and Rosalind would respond to the roles outlined for married couples? How would the
other young couples respond?

The word of Almighty God doth testify and declare whence[1] the original
beginning of matrimony cometh, and why it is ordained. It is instituted of
God, to the intent that man and woman should live lawfully in a perpetual friendly fellowship, to bring forth fruit, and to avoid fornication.[2] . . .
Wherefore,[3] forasmuch as[4] matrimony serveth as well to avoid sin and
offence, as to increase the kingdom of God, you, as all others which enter
that state, must acknowledge this benefit of God with pure and thankful
minds, for that he hath so ruled your hearts, that ye follow not the example
of the wicked world, who set their delight in filthiness of sin, where both of
you stand in the fear of God, and abhor[5] all filthiness. . . . But yet I would
not have you careless, without watching, for the devil will assay[6] to attempt
all things to interrupt and hinder your hearts and godly purpose, if ye will
give him any entry. For he will either labor to break this godly knot once
begun betwixt you, or else at the least, he will labor to encumber[7] it with
diverse griefs and displeasures.

And this is his principal craft, to work dissension of hearts, of the one
from the other, that whereas now there is pleasant and sweet love betwixt
you, he will in the stead[8] thereof, bring in most bitter and unpleasant discord, and surely that same adversary of ours, doth, as it were from above,
assault man's nature and condition. For this folly is ever from our tender age
grown up with us, to have a desire to rule, to think highly by[9] ourself, so that

---

[1] **whence:** from where.   [2] **fornication:** sexual activity outside marriage.   [3] **Wherefore:** because
of which.   [4] **forasmuch as:** seeing that.   [5] **abhor:** loathe.   [6] **assay:** try.   [7] **encumber:** burden.
[8] **stead:** place.   [9] **by:** of.

"An Homily of the State of Matrimony," from *The Second Tome of Homilies* Fol. 255–66 (1563);
STC 13663.3.

none thinketh it meet[10] to give place to another. That wicked vice of stubborn will and self love is more meet to break and to dissever the love of heart, than to preserve concord.[11] Wherefore, married persons must apply their minds in most earnest wise to concord, and must crave continually of God the help of his Holy Spirit, so to rule their hearts, and to knit their minds together, that they be not dissevered by any division of discord. . . . Learn thou therefore, if thou desirest to be void[12] of all these miseries, if thou desirest to live peaceably and comfortably in wedlock, how to make thy earnest prayer to God, that he would govern both your hearts by his Holy Spirit, to restrain the devil's power, whereby your concord may remain perpetually. But to this prayer must be joined a singular diligence, whereof St. Peter giveth his precept,[13] saying: *You husbands deal with your wives according to knowledge, giving honor to the wife, as unto the weaker vessel, and as unto them that are heirs also of the grace of life, that your prayers be not hindered.*[14] This precept doth peculiarly pertain to the husband. For he ought to be the leader and author of love, in cherishing and increasing concord, which then shall take place, if he will use measurableness[15] and not tyranny, and if he yield some things to the woman. For the woman is a weak creature, not endued[16] with like strength and constancy of mind, therefore they be the sooner disquieted, and they be the more prone to all weak affections and dispositions of mind, more than men be, and lighter[17] they be, and more vain in their fantasies and opinions. These things must be considered of the man, that he be not too stiff, so that he ought to wink at some things, and must gently expound[18] all things, and to forbear. . . . Yea he saith more, that the woman ought to have a certain honor attributed to her, that is to say, she must be spared and borne with, the rather for that she is the weaker vessel, of a frail heart, inconstant, and with a word soon stirred to wrath. And therefore considering these her frailties, she is to be the rather spared. By this means, thou shalt not only nourish concord, but shalt have her heart in thy power and will. For honest natures will sooner be retained to do their duty, rather by gentle words, than by stripes. But he which will do all things with extremity and severity, and doth use always rigor in words and stripes: what will that avail[19] in the conclusion? Verily nothing, but that he thereby setteth forward the devil's work, he banisheth away concord, charity, and sweet amity,[20] and bringeth in dissension, hatred, and irksomeness, the greatest griefs that can be in the mutual love and fellowship of man's life. . . . Now as concerning the wife's duty, what shall become[21] her: shall she abuse

[10] **meet**: suitable. [11] **concord**: peace and harmony. [12] **void**: empty. [13] **precept**: command.
[14] **You . . . hindered**: 1 Peter 3:7. [15] **measurableness**: moderation. [16] **endued**: endowed.
[17] **lighter**: more frivolous. [18] **expound**: explain. [19] **avail**: help. [20] **amity**: friendliness.
[21] **become**: suit.

the gentleness and humanity of her husband and at her pleasure turn all things upside down? No, surely, for that is far repugnant[22] against God's commandment. For thus doth St. Peter preach to them: *Ye wives, be ye in subjection to obey your own husband.*[23] To obey is another thing than to control or command, which yet they may do to their children, and to their family. But as for their husbands, them must they obey, and cease from commanding, and perform subjection. For this surely doth nourish concord very much, when the wife is ready at hand at her husband's commandment, when she will apply herself to his will, when she endeavoreth herself to seek his contentation,[24] and to do him pleasure, when she will eschew[25] all things that might offend him. For thus will most truly be verified the saying of the poet: *A good wife by obeying her husband, shall bear the rule,*[26] so that he shall have a delight and a gladness, the sooner at all times to return home to her. But on the contrary part, when the wives be stubborn, froward,[27] and malapert,[28] their husbands are compelled thereby to abhor and flee from their own houses, even as they should have battle with their enemies. Howbeit, it can scantly[29] be, but that some offences shall sometime chance betwixt them, for no man doth live without fault, specially for that the woman is the more frail part. Therefore let them beware that they stand[30] not in their faults and willfulness, but rather let them acknowledge their follies, and say: My husband, so it is, that by my anger I was compelled to do this or that, forgive it me, I hereafter I will take better heed. Thus ought women the more readily to do, the more they be ready to offend. And they shall not do this only to avoid strife and debate, but rather in the respect of the commandment of God, as St. Paul expresseth it in this form of words: *Let women be subject to their husbands as to the Lord, for the husband is the head of the woman, as Christ is the head of the church.*[31] Here you understand, that God hath commanded, that ye should acknowledge the authority of the husband, and refer to him the honor of obedience. . . . This sentence is very meet for women to print in their remembrance. Truth it is, that they must specially feel the griefs and pains of their matrimony, in that they relinquish the liberty of their own rule, in the pain of their travailing,[32] in the bringing up of their children. In which offices they be in great perils, and be grieved with great afflictions, which they might be without, if they lived out of matrimony. But St. Peter saith, that this is the chief ornament of holy matrons,[33] in that they set their hope and trust in God, that is to say, in that they refused not from marriage for the business thereof, for the griefs and perils

---

[22] repugnant: hostile.　[23] ye . . . husband: 1 Peter 3:1.　[24] contentation: contentment.　[25] eschew: avoid.　[26] A . . . rule: probably from the *Sententiae* of Publilius Syrus (fl. first century B.C.E.).　[27] froward: difficult.　[28] malapert: impudent.　[29] scantly: hardly.　[30] stand: remain.　[31] Let . . . church: Ephesians 5:22–23.　[32] travailing: here, childbirth.　[33] matrons: married women.

thereof, but committed all such adventures to God, in most sure trust of help, after that they have called upon his aid. O woman, do thou the like, and so shalt thou be most excellently beautified before God, and all his angels and saints, and thou needest not to seek further for doing any better works. For obey thy husband, take regard of his requests, and give heed unto him to perceive what he requireth of thee, and so shalt thou honor God, and live peaceably in thy house.

➔ EDMUND SPENSER

From Epithalamion

Published 1595

Elizabethan marriages were performed in churches and they were often followed by a wedding feast or other forms of festivity. They were significant events, touching not only those being wed, but also their families and the communities that drew together to celebrate with them. For his own wedding to Elizabeth Boyle in 1594, the poet Edmund Spenser (1552–1599) wrote a twenty-four stanza poem to celebrate the bride and their union. The poem has a strong temporal movement, tracing the wedding day from the rising of the sun and the waking of the bride to the bride and groom's coming to their nuptial bed on the evening after the ceremony. What portrait of the bride do the stanzas included below construct? What are her qualities? How do the women of *As You Like It* resemble Spenser's beloved? Why might there be differences? What gods are mentioned besides Hymen and why? Compare the conclusion of Shakespeare's play with Spenser's poem in terms of the sense of ritual evoked by the poem. How does Spenser's poem shed light on Hymen's presence at the conclusion of *As You Like It?*

STANZA 2

Early before the world's light giving lamp,[1]
His golden beam upon the hills doth spread,
Having disperst the night's uncheerful damp,
Do ye awake and with fresh lustihood[2]
Go to the bower[3] of my beloved love,   5

---

[1] the world's light giving lamp: the sun.   [2] lustihood: vigor.   [3] bower: chamber.

Edmund Spenser, *Epithalamion* from *Amoretti and Epithalamion* (London, 1595), 191–92, 197–98, 201–02, 205, 210; STC 23076.

My truest turtle dove[4]
Bid her awake; for Hymen[5] is awake,
And long since ready forth his mask[6] to move,
With his bright Tead[7] that flames with many a flake,[8]
And many a bachelor to wait on him,   10
In their fresh garments trim.
Bid her awake therefore and soon her dight,[9]
For lo the wished day is come at last,
That shall for all the pains and sorrows past,
Pay to her usury[10] of long delight,   15
And whil'st she doth her dight,
Do ye to her of joy and solace sing,
That all the woods may answer and your echo ring.

STANZA 7

Now is my love all ready forth to come,
Let all the virgins therefore well away,
And ye fresh boys that tend upon her groom
Prepare your selves; for he is coming straight.
Set all your things in seemly good aray[11]   5
Fit for so joyful day,
The joyfulst day that ever sun did see
Faire Sun, shew forth thy favourable ray,
And let thy lifull[12] heat not fervent be
For fear of burning her sunshiney face,   10
Her beauty to disgrace.
O fairest Phoebus,[13] father of the Muse,
If ever I did honour thee aright,
Or sing the thing, that mote[14] thy mind delight,
Do not thy servant's simple boon[15] refuse,   15
But let this day let this one day be mine,
Let all the rest be thine.
Then I thy sovereign[16] praises loud will sing,
That all the woods shall answer and their echo ring.

---

[4] **turtle dove:** symbolic of faithfulness.   [5] **Hymen:** mythological god of the marriage ceremony.
[6] **mask:** masque, a procession of attendants.   [7] **Tead:** pine torch.   [8] **flake:** flame.   [9] **dight:**
dress.   [10] **usury:** a gain.   [11] **aray:** arrangement.   [12] **lifull:** full of life.   [13] **Phoebus:** mythological
sun god.   [14] **mote:** might.   [15] **boon:** request   [16] **sovereign:** supreme.

STANZA 8

Hark how the Minstrels[17] gin to shrill aloud,
Their merry Music that resounds from far,
The pipe, the tabor,[18] and the trembling Crowd,
That well agree withouten breach or jar.
But most of all the Damzels do delight,   5
When they their timbrels[19] smite,
And thereunto do daunce and carrol sweet,
That all the senses they doe ravish[20] quite,
The whiles the boys run up and down the street,
Crying aloud with strong confused noise,   10
As if it were one voice.
Hymen io[21] Hymen, Hymen they do shout,
That even to the heavens their shouting shrill
Doth reach, and all the firmament[22] doth fill,
To which the people standing all about,   15
As in approvance[23] do thereto applaud
And loud advaunce her laud,[24]
And evermore they Hymen Hymen sing,
That all the woods them answer and their echo ring.

STANZA 13

Behold whiles she before the altar stands
Hearing the holy priest that to her speaks
And blesseth her with his two happy hands,
How the red roses[25] flush up in her cheeks,
And the pure snow[26] with goodly vermill[27] stain,   5
Like crimson dyed in grain,
That even th'Angels which continually,
About the sacred Altar do remain,
Forget their service and about her fly,
Oft peeping in her face that seems more fair,   10
The more they on it stare.
But her sad[28] eyes still fastened on the ground,
Are governed with goodly modesty,

---

[17] **Minstrels:** musicians. [18] **tabor:** small drum. [19] **timbrels:** tambourines. [20] **ravish:** fill with delight. [21] **io:** interjection. [22] **firmament:** sky. [23] **approvance:** approval. [24] **laud:** praise. [25] **red roses:** figurative; blush. [26] **pure snow:** figurative; pale skin. [27] **vermill:** vermilion, a shade of red. [28] **sad:** serious.

That suffers not one looke to glaunce awry,[29]
Which may let in a little thought unsound.[30]   15
Why blush ye love to give to me your hand,
The pledge of all our band?
Sing ye sweet Angels Alleluya sing,
That all the woods may answere and your echo ring.

Stanza 14

Now all is done; bring home the bride again,
Bring home the triumph of our victory,
Bring home with you the glory of her gain,
With joyance bring her and with jollity.
Never had man more joyful day then this,   5
Whom heaven would heap with bliss.
Make feast therefore now all this live long day,
This day forever to me holy is,
Pour out the wine without restraint or stay,
Pour not by cups, but by the belly full,   10
Pour out to all that wull,[31]
And sprinkle all the posts and walls with wine,
That they may sweat, and drunken be withal.[32]
Crown ye God Bacchus[33] with a coronall,[34]
And Hymen also crown with wreathes of vine,   15
And let the Graces[35] daunce unto the rest;
For they can do it best:
The whiles the maidens do their carrol sing,
To which the woods shall answer & their echo ring.

Stanza 17

Now cease ye damsels your delights forepast;[36]
Enough is it, that all the day was yours:
Now day is done, and night is nighing[37] fast:
Now bring the Bride into the bridal boures.[38]
Now night is come, now soon her disaray,[39]   5
And in her bed her lay;
Lay her in lilies and in violets,

---

[29]**awry:** to the side.   [30]**unsound:** morally unsafe.   [31]**wull:** will.   [32]**withal:** likewise.   [33]**Bacchus:** mythological god of wine.   [34]**coronall:** circlet for the head.   [35]**Graces:** attendants to Venus, the goddess of love.   [36]**forepast:** over.   [37]**nighing:** approaching.   [38]**boures (bowers):** chambers.   [39]**disaray:** undress.

And silken curtains over her display,
And odourd[40] sheets, and Arras[41] coverlets,
Behold how goodly my fair love does ly   10
In proud humility;
Like unto Maia, when as
Jove her took,
In Tempe,[42] lying on the flowery grass,
Twixt sleep and wake, after she weary was,   15
With bathing in the Acidalian brook[43]
Now it is night, ye damsels may be gone,
And leave my love alone,
And leave likewise your former lay to sing:
The woods no more shall answer, nor your echo ring.   20

Stanza 22

And thou great Juno,[44] which with awful might
The laws of wedlock still dost patronize,[45]
And the religion of the faith first plight[46]
With sacred rites hast taught to solemnize:[47]
And eke[48] for comfort often called art   5
Of women in their smart,[49]
Eternally bind thou this lovely band,
And all thy blessings unto us impart.
And thou glad Genius,[50] in whose gentle hand,
The bridal bowre and genial[51] bed remain,   10
Without blemish or stain,
And the sweet pleasures of their loves delight.
With secret aid doest succour[52] and supply,
Till they bring forth the fruitful progeny,[53]
Send us the timely fruit of this same night.   15
And thou fair Hebe,[54] and thou Hymen free,
Grant that it may so be.
Til which we cease your further praise to sing,
Ne[55] any woods shall answer, nor your Echo ring.

[40] odourd: scented. [41] Arras: embroidered tapestry. [42] Maia . . . Tempe: reference to the mythological story of how Jove, king of the gods, impregnated Maia in the middle of the night. [43] Acidalian brooke: a fountain associated with Venus. [44] Juno: mythological goddess of marriage. [45] patronize: preside over. [46] plight: vowed. [47] solemnize: treat as honorable. [48] eke: also. [49] in their smart: during childbirth. [50] Genius: mythological god of generation. [51] genial: for the purpose of childbearing. [52] succour: assist. [53] progeny: offspring. [54] Hebe: mythological goddess of youth. [55] Ne: nor.

Irregular Marriages

Not all marriages occurred as the church wished. Of particular concern were secret or clandestine marriages that often involved private handfasting ceremonies in which lovers declared their intent to marry in a private ceremony in front of witnesses but without benefit of clergy or a church setting. Clandestine unions also skirted the official publishing of the banns, or declaration of intent to marry, in church on three consecutive Sundays prior to the wedding itself. Sometimes secret weddings were conducted by "hedgepriests," poor, vagabond, or disreputable clerics who for a fee would marry lovers outside the church. Secret unions not only flouted the church's authority, but were opposed by parents who wanted to prevent their children from making economically or socially disadvantageous matches. Clandestine marriages were also thought to protect bigamists, men or women who were betrothed or married to previous partners and who sought a private union to avoid having their behavior exposed.[1]

Below are three texts that bear on secret or "privy" marriages. The first comes from Thomas Beard's *The Theatre of God's Judgments*, an extremely popular religious text from 1597 that collected historical stories of flamboyant sinners and the often-violent divine vengeance they incurred. Beard thunders against secret unions, declaring the progeny that arise from them to be bastards and the fruit of fornication.

The short excerpt from Beard's text is followed by a longer one from John Stockwood's *A Bartholomew Fairing*. Stockwood was a Puritan minister and schoolmaster who at one point had Oliver Cromwell for a pupil. Like many of his Puritan contemporaries, he disliked too much expansion of church power, but he nonetheless disapproved strongly of clandestine marriages. He was particularly incensed that children should undertake to enter into marriage without parental approval.

The final brief text comes from records of the ecclesiastical courts in Nottinghamshire for the 1590s. It recounts many instances of marriages made in some irregular way. The first records a marriage that occurred in church but without the proclaiming of the banns and the punishment meted out to the vicar who performed the ceremony. The second recounts a marriage made in a private house by someone who may or may not have been a clergyman.

These texts together raise several issues of relevance to *As You Like It*. First, how do they shed light on Sir Oliver Mar-text, the figure who was set to marry Touchstone and Audrey in the forest before Jaques interrupted

[1] R. B. Outhwaite, *Clandestine Marriage in England, 1500–1850* (London: Hambledon, 1995).

the ceremony? What is irregular about that proposed ceremony and why might Touchstone and Audrey have attempted it? What does Jaques's objection imply about Mar-text's learning and authority? In what way is Touchstone and Audrey's eventual wedding different from their aborted first one? Second, Stockwood makes much of the importance of receiving parental consent to marriage. With the exception of Duke Senior, parents are not much in evidence in *As You Like It*. How does Rosalind finesse the issue of parental consent? Does she obtain such consent? Does anyone else stand in the place of the parent at the end of the play? Are the marriages properly authorized?

➔ THOMAS BEARD

From The Theatre of God's Judgments   *1597*

From Chapter XXII

Of whoredoms committed under color of marriage

Seeing that oftentimes it falleth out[1] that those which in show seem most honest, think it a thing lawful to converse[2] together as man and wife by some secret and private contract, without making account of the public celebration of marriage as necessary, but for some worldly respects according as their foolish and disordinate[3] affections mispersuadeth them, to dispense[4] therewith: It shall not be impertinent as we go, to give warning how unlawful all such conversation is, and how contrary to good manners, and to the laudable[5] customs of all civil and well-governed people. For it is so far from deserving the name of marriage, that on the other side it can be nothing but plain whoredom and fornication:[6] the which name and title Tertullian[7] giveth to all secret and privy meetings which have not been allowed of, received, and blessed by the church of God. Again besides the evil example which is exhibited, there is this mischief moreover, that the children of such a bed cannot be esteemed legitimate, yea and God himself accurseth such lawless familiarity, as the mischiefs that arise therefrom do declare.

---

[1] falleth out: happens.   [2] converse: live, have sexual intercourse.   [3] disordinate: immoderate. [4] dispense: to forgo.   [5] laudable: praiseworthy.   [6] fornication: sexual activity outside of marriage.   [7] Tertullian: (c. 160–220 C.E.), early Christian author and apologist.

Thomas Beard, *The Theatre of God's Judgments* (London, 1597), 321–22; STC 1659.

→ JOHN STOCKWOOD

From A Bartholomew Fairing   *1589*

Secondly, that these privy[1] contracts, that is to say, such as are made in secret, or in corners, or otherwise in place never so public without the consent of the parents, are not lawful, may this way more plainly appear, if we weigh and consider that children are not at their own liberty and disposition, nor (as they say) their own men, but under the authority and power of their parents, like as servants are at the disposing of their masters. . . .

. . .

The children can say for themselves, we are old enough, and therefore able enough to make our own choice, we see it to be daily practiced by others, yea and peradventure[2] we do know (as having heard our parents sometimes in their merriments[3] to brag of the same) our fathers have matched without the consent of their parents, and have all this notwithstanding done well enough, and lived very well: why therefore should not we also do the like? The question here is not what children in regard either of age or wit are able for to do but what God hath thought meet and expedient,[4] nay, straightly charged and commanded that they should do. For there are many children found sometimes far to exceed their fathers in wit and in wisdom, yea and in all other guises[5] both of mind and body, yet is this no good reason that they should take upon them their fathers' authority. The wife may not therefore be a master, because she hath more knowledge sometimes than her husband, but she must obey, and the husband is to rule, because that God hath willed that it should be so. And albeit[6] that matches made without the consent of parents have often good success, according unto the things which fall out outwardly in this life, yet that is not to be imputed[7] unto this disordered and unnatural course, but unto God his mercy that always doeth better for us than we have deserved. . . . [W]hosoever have in this sort vowed, or promised rashly, let them understand that their vow and promise may a great deal more safely be broken, than performed, except[8] the good will of the parents may be obtained, and yet in this case also, their former rashness is earnestly and with unfeigned[9] and hearty sorrow to be repented, that God through his mercy in Christ do not impute it and lay it unto their charge.[10] And this advice I would have to be understood either of

---

[1] privy: secret. [2] peradventure: as it happens. [3] merriments: fun. [4] meet and expedient: proper. [5] guises: aspects. [6] albeit: even though. [7] imputed: attributed. [8] except: unless. [9] unfeigned: sincere. [10] impute . . . charge: hold them accountable for it.

John Stockwood, *A Bartholomew Fairing* (London, 1589), 18, 82–83, 93–94; STC 23277.

contracts, or of marriage also by such enticing means, though the parents' good will may be afterwards procured. But if after such privy and stolen contracts and marriages, the good liking of the parents cannot be won, what punishment ought to be inflicted and laid upon the offenders, as well in regard of their own default[11] in breach of duty unto their parents, as also that others by their smart[12] may be terrified and feared from running into the like, it is not for me, being no lawmaker, to determine: I leave that unto the wise discretion of the godly magistrate, who I hope hereafter will carry a more heavy hand towards this heinous and notorious crime, and see some discipline also to be ordained for all such disobedient and unruly children, the which by their rash and headstrong attents,[13] have forestalled[14] the right of their godly parents, howsoever afterwards they can get their good will.

[11] default: failure.   [12] smart: punishment.   [13] attents: intentions.   [14] forestalled: prevented.

→ *From* Extracts from the Act Books of the Archdeacons of Nottingham   *1594*

[June 25, 1594: Testimony of George Wolley, vicar of Greasley. The following is a transcription of the account recorded in the Act Books.]

On which day the said George appeared in person and being examined on oath as to the marriage solemnized clandestinely[1] between Launcelot Rollston, gent., and Margaret Ashe of Greasley and upon the other circumstances of the same matter, admitted that he had solemnized a marriage between the said Launcelot and Margaret in the church of Greasley aforesaid on the Wednesday next before Whitsunday[2] last, about four of the morning of the same day, the banns of marriage between them being neither published previously nor dispensed with,[3] in the presence, besides himself and the parties, of Edward Rollston of Annesley and others whose names he did not recall. And then the judge, accepting the confession of the said George, decreed him to be suspended from his office for three years for his contempt and disobedience in solemnizing the said marriage. He was released from his suspension on 19th August following.

[1] clandestinely: secretly.   [2] Whitsunday: the Sunday of Pentecost in the Christian liturgical year, seven weeks after Easter.   [3] dispensed with: officially waived.

R. F. B. Hodgkinson, ed., "Extracts from the Act Books of the Archdeacons of Nottingham," *Transactions of the Thoroton Society of Nottinghamshire* 29 (1929): 19–67 at 24, 31, 32.

[June 21, 1600: Testimony of Richard Hall and Ralph Awcocke. The following is a transcription of the account recorded in the Act Books.]

[Hall and Awcocke admitted] that about a month since upon Monday late in the evening the said Antony[4] was married to his now wife[5] in a house in Elmton in Derbyshire by one who whether he were a minister or not they know not, neither do they know his name and this they do know to be true for they were present at the said marriage.

[4] **Antony:** Antony Hall, of Norton Cuckney [Hodgkinson's note]. [5] **wife:** Agnes Noodill [Hodgkinson's note].

Ambivalence about Marriage

The "Homily on the State of Matrimony" (see p. 213) assumes that marriage is one of society's most essential and central institutions; Edmund Spenser's "Epithalamion" (see p. 216) celebrates the wedding day with solemn praise. But not everyone in early modern culture embraced marriage enthusiastically. In fact, there was a considerable literature debating the relative virtues of the single versus the married life. Before the Reformation, of course, no clergy were married, and there were many religious houses, both for men and women, where people lived lives of celibacy. Even after the Reformation, however, the single life remained attractive to some. An emblem included in Henry Peacham's (c. 1576–1643) *Minerva Britanna*, which was published in 1612, captures the ambivalence that could attend the entry into marriage (Figure 11 with text from below included). The emblem shows Matrimony, described as a "he" in the accompanying poem but also displaying feminine features, standing in a field. He is rendered immobile by having his legs encased in wooden stocks and his shoulders weighed down by the proverbial "yoke" of marriage. In his hand he holds a quince, considered by some to be an aphrodisiac or a sign of marital fruitfulness. What picture of marriage does the emblem present? What are the advantages and disadvantages of marriage as suggested by the image and accompanying poem? In what ways, if any, do characters in *As You Like It* express ambivalence towards marriage?

FIGURE 11 *A severe image of matrimony as a figure immobilized by stocks and weighed down by a huge yoke. The emblem* Matrimonium *from Henry Peacham,* Minerva Britanna *(1612).*

→ HENRY PEACHAM

From Minerva Britanna, an emblem of Matrimonium

1612

Who loveth best, to live in *Hymen's* bands,
And better likes, the careful[1] married state,
May here behold, how *Matrimony* stands,
In wooden stocks, repenting him too late:
The servile yoke his neck and shoulder wears,   5
And in his hand, the fruitful *Quince* he bears.

[1] **careful:** literally, full of care.

Henry Peacham, "E. Matrimonium," *Minerva Britanna* (London, 1612). IIIA; STC 19511.

The stocks do show his want of liberty,
Not as he wont,[2] to wander where he list:
The yoke's an ensign of servility.
The fruitfulness, the *Quince* within his fist,   10
Of wedlock tells, which so Solon did present,
To *Athenian* Brides,[3] the day to Church they went.

[2] **wont:** used to do. [3] *Quince* ... **Brides:** The ancient Greek lawgiver Solon made eating quinces part of weddings, symbolizing fertility and marital union.

→ GEORGE WHETSTONE

From An Heptameron of Civil Discourses   *1582*

In 1582, George Whetstone (c. 1550–1587), an English writer, published *An Heptameron of Civil Discourses*, a collection of Italianate stories and debates all focusing on marriage. On each of seven days a particular theme is considered; for example, the problem of enforced marriages or marriages made between those who are unequal in rank or how to make love last once married. The first excerpt records a debate that takes place on the first day between various courtly figures over which is better, the single or the married life. As in Baldassare Castiglione's famous conduct book *The Courtyer* (see p. 352), a noblewoman, here figured as Queen Aurelia, presides over the debate. What arguments are advanced for and against marriage? What bearing do they have on the conversation between Jaques and Touchstone in act 3, scene 3 of *As You Like It* concerning Touchstone's proposed marriage?

FROM THE FIRST DAY'S EXERCISE

[The assembled group have been entertaining themselves with disputations on the topic of love; Queen Aurelia suggests they pick one particular argument to pursue in detail.]

Madame, (quoth Fabritio), I hold it good, we obey your direction. And for that marriage is the most honorable event of love, and that a single life is the greatest testimony of chastity: a civil contention[1] to prove which is the most worthy of the two would conclude much contentment, for as iron and flint

[1] **contention:** verbal argument or debate.

George Whetstone, *An Heptameron of Civil Discourses* (London, 1582), C2v–C3v, X2r; STC 25337.

beat together have the virtue to smite fire, so men's wits, encountering in doubtful questions, openeth a passage for imprisoned truth.

Queen Aurelia, and the rest of the company, liked very well of the subject, and studying who were the fittest to deal[2] in this controversy, Aurelia (with a glancing eye) beheld that her servant Ismarito witsafed[3] no greater token that he took delight in these actions, than (sometime) the secret bestowing of a modest smile: whereupon she forethought that as floods, when they are most highest, maketh least noise, even so (perchance)[4] his still tongue was governed by a flowing wit, and desirous to sound[5] his sufficiency, she quickened[6] him with this cross surmise.[7]

Servant (quoth she) your sober looks promiseth a hope that you will undertake Diana's[8] quarrel.[9] . . . [T]he little haste you make to marry, witnesseth you honor Hymen[10] with no great devotion, and therefore, I command you to use all your possible proofs[11] in the defense of a single life. . . .

Madame (quoth Ismarito) . . . which vocation[12] of marriage, though I reverently honor, yet I so zealously affect[13] the other, as I hope (where the judges are indifferent) to make the glory thereof to shine as the fair white, above every other color.

Sir, quoth Soranso, though white be a fair color, yet are the choice[14] of all other colors more rich and glorious, so, though virginity (which is the fairest flower of a single life) be precious in the sight of God and in the opinion of men, yet is marriage more precious, in that it is a sacred institution of God, and more honored of men: the married are reverently entertained,[15] when the unmarried are but familiarly saluted.[16] The married in assemblies are honored with the highest places, the unmarried humble themselves unto the lowest. To be short, virginity is the handmaid[17] of marriage. Then, by how much the master is greater than the servant, by so much marriage is more worthy than is single life.

I confess, quoth Ismarito, marriage is an honorable estate, instituted of God, and embraced of men, but whereon had she her beginning? Upon this cause, to keep men from a greater inconvenience:[18] as the law was founded upon this reason, to punish the trespasses of men. But if no offence had been given, the law had not needed.[19] So if man had lived within bounds of

---

[2]**deal:** participate. [3]**witsafed:** granted. [4]**perchance:** perhaps. [5]**sound:** ascertain. [6]**quickened:** animated. [7]**surmise:** allegation. [8]**Diana:** the mythological goddess of virginity. [9]**quarrel:** case. [10]**Hymen:** the mythological god of marriage ceremonies. [11]**proofs:** arguments. [12]**vocation:** calling, mode of life. [13]**affect:** prefer. [14]**choice:** best. [15]**reverently entertained:** given honor and hospitality. [16]**familiarly saluted:** casually paid respect to. [17]**handmaid:** servant. [18]**inconvenience:** injury (in this case, lust). [19]**had not needed:** had not been necessary.

reason (which before any commandment given, was unto him a law), marriage might have been spared, and therefore in the highest degree is but a virtue upon necessity: where chastity is a divine virtue, governed by the motions of the soul, which is immortal, and participating of the same virtue, is always fresh and green. . . .

Therefore (think I) by how much divine things are of greater emprise[20] than earthly, by so much the single life is more worthy than the married.

FROM THE SEVENTH DAY'S EXERCISE

[The argument on chastity versus marriage continues, with Queen Aurelia commanding Segnior Philoxenus to defend marriage.]

Madam (quoth Segnior Philoxenus) so strict is your charge, as I must adventure[21] of this weighty labor, hoping that as by authority you command my opinion, so by the motion of some one of your virtues, you will pardon my errors.

Upon which encouragement, to obey your will, I say, and approve by sacred authority, that this holy institution of marriage was erected by God in the earthly paradise before the transgression of Adam,[22] when he joined him to Eve with these words of blessing, *Increase, multiply, and replenish the earth*.[23] Again, after Adam's fall, and the deluge,[24] to strengthen his first institution,[25] God commanded the good patriarch Noah[26] to increase and multiply the earth anew. Moreover, God would have no more women than men in his ark,[27] to show there should be a sympathy[28] in number, as well as agreement in love, between man and wife: for if the one might lawfully have many wives, and the other many husbands, how should this express commandment of God be unviolated? *You shall be two bodies in one flesh, and no more*.[29]

Compare the joy, honor, and reverence given unto marriage, by[30] the delight that proceedeth from any other cause, and you shall see her gleam like a blazing comet, and the other but twinkle as an ordinary star.

---

[20] emprise: glory. [21] adventure: undertake. [22] transgression of Adam: entrance of sin into the world. [23] *Increase . . . earth*: Genesis 1:28. [24] deluge: the flood Genesis 7 describes as covering the entire earth. [25] first institution: marriage. [26] Noah: survivor of the biblical flood. [27] God . . . ark: in Genesis 7, God tells Noah to build a giant boat and put male-female pairs of animals inside to escape the flood. [28] sympathy: agreement. [29] *You . . . more*: Genesis 2:24. [30] by: to.

➔ SAMUEL ROWLANDS

From The Bride
1617

Not all debates over whether to marry were conducted with the high seriousness assumed by George Whetstone. Samuel Rowlands (1573–1630), a London writer of religious and satirical pamphlets and verse, had an eye for the folly and foibles of Elizabethan and Jacobean society. His lengthy poem "The Bride" stages a debate between a bride, who proudly asserts the superiority of the marriage state, and a number of unmarried maids on the day of the bride's marriage. The woodcut accompanying the poem shows a finely dressed and very large woman surrounded by two much smaller female figures (Figure 12). While many woodcuts were recirculated and used to illustrate different texts, the effect of this particular woodcut attached to this poem is to suggest the preeminence of the bride over other women on her wedding day. The excerpts below present positions on marriage assumed by the bride; by Susan, who favors a life of virginity; and by Grace, who is worried about getting pregnant out of wedlock and so would like to marry, but for less exalted reasons than the bride. The poem ends with the bride moralizing on the duties of a wife. What are the distinctive positions staked out by the various women in the excerpts given below? What mixture of sexual, moral, religious, or social reasons contributes to the decisions about marriage made by the characters in the poem? How do these reasons compare with the reasons that motivate the characters in *As You Like It*? Does Rosalind, in particular, share any of the ambivalence toward marriage articulated by Mistress Susan? How do you know?

THE BRIDE:
 Virgins, and fellow maids (that were of late)
 Take kindly here my wedding day's adieu,[1]
 I entertain degree[2] above your state:
 For marriage life's beyond the single crew,
  Bring me to church as custom says you shall,   5
  And then as wife, farewell my wenches all.

 I go before you unto honor now,
 And Hymen's rites[3] with joy do undertake
 For life, I make the constant nuptial[4] vow,

---

[1] adieu: farewell.   [2] entertain degree: possess a level of social standing.   [3] Hymen's rites: marriage rites (Hymen is the mythological god of marriage).   [4] nuptial: marriage.

Samuel Rowlands, *The Bride* (London, 1617), A3r–A3v, A4v–B1r, D2v–D3v, D4–E3; STC 21365.5.

THE BRIDE

BY S.R.

LONDON
Printed By W. I. for T. P. 1617.

FIGURE 12 *The bride and her attendants. Title page woodcut from Samuel Rowlands,* The Bride *(1617).*

Strive you to follow for your credits'[5] sake,   10
   For greater grace to womankind is none
   Than join with husband, faithful two in one.

God honored thus our great grandmother Eve[6]
And gave thereby the blessing of increase,[7]
For were not marriage we must all believe,   15
The generations of the earth would cease.
   Mankind should be extinguish'd and decreas'd
   And all the world would but consist of beast.

Which caused me to find my maiden folly,
And having found it, to reform the same: 20
Though some of you, thereat[8] seem melancholy[9]
That I forever do renounce your name.
   I not respect what censure[10] you can give,
   Since with a loving man I mean to live.

Whose kindest heart, to me is worth you all,   25
Him to content, my soul in all things seeks,
Say what you please, exclaiming chide and brawl,[11]
I'll turn disgrace unto your blushing cheeks.
   I am your better now by ring and hat,[12]
   No more plain Rose, but Mistress you know what.   30

Marry therefore and yield increase a store,[13]
Else to what purpose were you bred and born:
Those that receive, and nothing give therefore
Are fruitless creatures, of contempt and scorn,
   The excellence of all things doth consist,   35
   In giving, this no reason can resist.

. . . .

MISTRESS SUSAN:
   Good Mistress Bride, now we have heard your speech
   In commendation of your nuptial choice,
   Give me a little favor I beseech,   75
   To speak unto you with a virgin's voice:

---

[5] credits': reputation.   [6] Eve: according to Genesis, the first woman.   [7] increase: reproduction.
[8] thereat: at this.   [9] melancholy: sad.   [10] censure: disapproval.   [11] chide and brawl: scold and
cry.   [12] by ring and hat: wedding apparel.   [13] yield increase a store: reproduce.

Though diverse elder maids in place there be,[14]
Yet I'll begin, trusting they'll second me.

We are your fellows but to church you say,
As custom is that maids should bring the bride,   80
And for no longer than the wedding day,
You hold with us, but turn to the other side:
    Boasting of honor you attend unto,
    And so go forward making much ado.[15]

But this unto you justly I object,   85
In the defense of each beloved maid,
Virginity is life of chaste respect,
No worldly burden thereupon is laid:
    Our single life, all peace and quiet brings,
    And we are free from careful earthly things.   90

We may do what we please, go where we list,
Without pray "husband will you give me leave,"
Our resolutions no man can resist,
Our own's our own, to give or to receive,
    We live not under this same word obey: 95
    "Till death depart us," at our dying day.

We may delight in fashion, wear the same,
And choose the stuff of last devised[16] sale:
Take tailor's counsel[17] in it free from blame,
And cast it off as soon as it grows stale: 100
    Go out, come in, and at self-pleasure live,
    And kindly take, what kind young men do give.

We have no checking churlish[18] taunts to fear us,
We have no grumbling at our purse expense:
We seek no miser's favor to forbear us,   105
We use no household wranglings[19] and offence:
    We have no cock to overcrow our comb.[20]

      . . . .

---

[14] diverse . . . there be: though there are older virgins present.   [15] much ado: a fuss.   [16] last
devised: latest.   [17] Take tailor's counsel: consult a professional clothing maker.   [18] churlish:
rude.   [19] wranglings: arguments.   [20] no cock . . . our comb: no one to overpower our will.

GRACE:

This is a story that seems very strange,[21]
And for my part, it doth me full persuade,
My maidenhead[22] with some man to exchange,   525
I will not live in danger of a maid:
    The world, the flesh, the devil tempts us still,
    I'll have a husband, I protest I will.

If I were sure none of you here would blab,
I would even tell you of a dream most true,   530
And if I lie, count me the veriest[23] drab,[24]
That ever any of you saw or knew:
    When a friend speaks in kindness do not wrong her:
    For I can keep it (for my life) no longer.

One night (I have the day of month set down)   535
Because I will make serious matters sure,
Me thought I went a journey out of town,
And with a proper man I was made sure:[25]
    As sure as death, me thought we were assured,
    And all things for the business were procured.   540

We did agree, and faith and troth did plight,[26]
And he gave me, and I gave him a ring,
To do as Mistress Bride will do[27] at night,
And I protest me thought he did the thing:
    The thing we stand so much upon[28] he took,   545
    And I upon the matter big did look.

Forsooth[29] (in sadness), I was big with child,
And had a belly, (marry God forbid),
Then fell a' weeping, but he laughed and smil'd,
And boldly said, we'll stand to[30] what we did: 550

---

[21]**story . . . strange:** referring to the story just related by the Bride of Adhan, the mother of Merlin, who refused all husbands and was mysteriously made pregnant by an unknown "stranger" who somehow got into her locked chamber. The implication is that the father is not a fully human creature. From this, Adhan deduces that she should not have refused an earthly husband when one was offered, and she urges all the maids to marry.   [22]**maidenhead:** virginity.   [23]**veriest:** most.   [24]**drab:** a dirty or untidy woman.   [25]**made sure:** engaged.   [26]**faith . . . plight:** made a promise to marry.   [27]**do as Mistress Bride will do:** to have sexual intercourse.   [28]**thing we stand so much upon:** virginity.   [29]**Forsooth:** for truly.   [30]**we'll stand to:** take responsibility for.

Fie, fie,[31] (quoth I), whoever stands I fall,
Farewell my credit, maidenhead and all.

Thus as I cried and wept and wrung my hands,
And said dear maids and maidenhead adieu,
Before my face methought my mother stands,   555
And question'd with me how this matter grew:
    With that I start awake as we are now,
    Yet feared my dream had been no dream I vow.

I could not (for my life) tell how to take it,
For I was stricken in a mighty maze,   560
Therefore if marriage come I'll not forsake it,
'Tis danger to live virgin diverse ways,
    I would not in such fear again be found,
    Without a husband, for a thousand pound.[32]
. . . .

BRIDE:
I pray you here this contention end,
(We being all of selfsame womankind),
And each the other, with advice befriend,
Because I see some of you well inclin'd: 580
    To take good ways, and so become good wives,
    I'll teach you certain rules to lead your lives.

You that intend the honorable life,[33]
And would with joy live happy in the same,
Must note eight duties do concern a wife,   585
To which with all endeavor she must frame:
    And so in peace possess her husband's love,
    And all distaste from both their hearts remove.

The first is that she have domestic cares,[34]
Of private business for the house within,   590
Leaving her husband unto his affairs,
Of things abroad that out of doors have been;
    By him performed as his charge to do,
    Not busybody-like inclin'd thereto.

---

[31] **Fie, fie:** an exclamation of disdain.   [32] **thousand pound:** at the time, a very large amount of money.   [33] **the honorable life:** i.e., the married life.   [34] **have domestic cares:** take care of domestic matters.

Nor intermeddling as a number will,   595
Of foolish gossips,[35] such as do neglect
The things which do concern them, and too ill
Presume in matters unto no effect:
 Beyond their element, when they should look,
 To what is done in kitchen by the cook.   600

Or unto children's virtuous education,
Or to their maids that they good huswives be,
And carefully contain a decent fashion,
That nothing pass the limits of degree:[36]
 Knowing her husband's business from her own, 605
 And diligent do that, let his alone.

The second duty of the wife is this,
(Which she in mind ought very careful bear)
To entertain in house such friends of his,
As she doth know have husband's welcome there: 610
 Not her acquaintance without his consent,
 For that way jealousy breeds discontent.

An honest woman will the scandal shun,
Of that report is made of wantonness,[37]
And fear her credit will to ruin run,   615
When evil speakers do her shame express:
 And therefore from this rule a practice draws,
 That the effect may cease, remove the cause.

Third duty is, that of no proud pretence,
She move her husband to consume his means,   620
With urging him to needless vain expense,
Which toward the Counter, or to Ludgate[38] leans:
 For many idle huswives (London knows)
 Have by their pride been husbands' overthrows.

A modest woman will in compass keep,   625
And decently unto her calling go,

---

[35] **gossips:** women who delight in idle talk. [36] **That . . . degree:** dress no better than their rank allows. [37] **wantonness:** sexual misconduct. [38] **Counter . . . Ludgate:** names of London prisons where debtors were incarcerated.

Not diving in the frugal purse too deep,
By making to the world a peacock show:
    Though they seem fools, so yield unto their wives,
    Some poor men do it to have quiet lives.[39]   630

Fourth duty is, to love her own house best,
And be no gadding gossip up and down,
To hear and carry tales amongst the rest,
That are the news reporters of the town:
    A modest woman's home is her delight,   635
    Of business there, to have the oversight.

At public plays she never will be known,
And to be tavern guest she ever hates,
She scorns to be a street-wife (idle one),
Or field wife[40] ranging with her walking mates: 640
    She knows how wise men censure of such dames:
    And how with blots they blemish their good names.

And therefore with the dove[41] she'll rather choose,
To make abode where she hath dwelling place,
Or like the snail that shelly house doth use,   645
For shelter still, such is good huswives' case:
    Respecting residence where she doth love,
    As those good householders, the snail and dove.

    ·

[The remaining four duties of a wife include obeying the husband, bearing with his anger, conforming to his will, and being faithful to him even in adversity.]

And thus fair virgins, to you all farewell,   715
What I have spoken do proceed from love,
The joys of marriage I want art to tell,
And therefore no more talk, but try and prove:[42]
    With wedding rings, be wives of credit known
    God send good husbands to you every one.   720

---

[39] **wives . . . quiet lives:** some poor men, though they seem fools, yield to their wives (in the matter of money) to keep a quiet house.   [40] **field wife:** woman who spends her time walking in the fields.   [41] **dove:** bird symbolizing innocence and known for faithful guarding of her nest.
[42] **try and prove:** undertake (marriage) and test its joys by experience.

Languages of Love

PETRARCHANISM AND ANTI-PETRARCHANISM

Poets in the early modern period who wrote about love often followed the example of Petrarch (1304–1374), Italian writer and humanist, who wrote a number of poems to a real or fictional woman named Laura. The woman in Petrarch's poems is always unattainable, but dazzling in her beauty. Again and again the speaker of the Laura poems catalogs her features and her coldness toward him. The woman almost never speaks, and attention focuses on the distracted suffering of the male lover and on the woman's beauty. Below are three sonnets, the first by the early modern courtier and poet Sir Thomas Wyatt (1503–1543). Wyatt is credited with bringing the sonnet form to England through his many translations of Petrarch and his own compositions. Sonnets are fourteen-line lyrics, often treating of love. Unlike the Petrarchan sonnet, which consists of an eight-line octave and a six-line sestet rhyming *abbaabba, cdecde*, the English sonnet typically consists of three four-line quatrains and a couplet rhyming *abba, cddc, effe, gg*. In the Wyatt sonnet printed below, the speaker records the effect on him of the light that blazes from his beloved's eyes and of the "nay" that signals her rejection of him.

While most Petrarchan sonnets are written by men and focus on the man's experience of love, women could also manipulate Petrarchan conventions. The second sonnet is written by Mary Wroth (1587–1651/53) of the famous Sidney family. Her sonnet sequence *Pamphilia to Amphilanthus* details the suffering of a faithful woman, Pamphilia, at the hands of a distant and faithless lover, Amphilanthus. In this particular sonnet, the speaker shares the Petrarchan fixation with the beauty of the beloved's features, explaining how she was plunged into pain when struck by Cupid's arrow and the sight of her beloved's eyes and lips. William Shakespeare (1564–1616), whose sonnets were published in 1609, wrote the final poem. In this particular sonnet the speaker makes fun of Petrarchan conventions by praising a "dark lady" whose features are catalogued in a surprisingly ambivalent way, indicating the speaker's interest in a more earthy love than the unrequited passions of Petrarchan lovers.

From these poems, what do you take the stance of the Petrarchan lover to be? Which, if any, of the men in *As You Like It* resemble this figure? How? Which, if any of the women? Does the play sympathize with or make fun of such lovers? How does Rosalind respond to Petrarchan lovers? What role do women play in the Petrarchan scenario? What do you think is the point of Shakespeare's anti-Petrarchan poem? What anti-Petrarchanists, if any, are there in Arden?

→ SIR THOMAS WYATT

The Lover Describeth His Being Stricken
with Sight of His Love   *Date unknown*

XXV

The lively sparks that issue from those eyes
Against the which there vaileth[1] no defence
Have perst[2] my heart and done it none offence
With quaking pleasure more than once or twice.
Was never man could anything devise   5
Sunbeams to turn with so great vehemence
To daze man's sight, as by their bright presence
Dazed am I, much like unto the guise
Of one stricken[3] with dint of lightning,
Blind with the stroke, erring[4] here and there,   10
So call I for help, I not[5] when nor where,
The pain of my fall patiently bearing.
For straight after the blaze, as is no wonder,
Of deadly noise[6] hear I the fearful thunder.

[1] vaileth: avails. [2] perst: pierced [3] stricken: struck. [4] erring: wandering. [5] not: know not.
[6] In some later versions of the poem "noise" is changed to "nay," indicating explicitly that it is
the lady's refusal that has thunderstruck him.

Sir Thomas Wyatt, from *Songs and Sonnets Written by the Right Honorable Lord Henry Howard
Late Earl of Surrey, and Others* (London, 1557); STC 13861.

→ LADY MARY WROTH

From Pamphilia to Amphilanthus   *c. 1615–1620*

Oft did I wonder why the sweets of love
Were counted pains, sharp wounds, and cruel smarts,
Till one blow sent from heavenly face proved darts[1]
Enough to make those deemed sweets bitter prove.

[1] one blow . . . darts: the speaker is referring to the eye beams that supposedly pieced the heart
of the beloved like an arrow.

Lady Mary Wroth, *Pamphilia to Amphilanthus* (Folger V.a.104), F113.

One shaft[2] did force my best strength to remove,   5
And armies brought of thoughts, which thought imparts,
One shaft so spent may conquer courts of hearts,
One shot but doubly sent my spirit did move.

Two sparking eyes were gainers of my loss,[3]
While love-begetting lips their gain did cross,[4]   10
And challenged half of my heart-mastered prize,[5]

It[6] humbly did confess they won the field,
Yet equal was their force, so did it yield
Equally still to serve those lips, and eyes.

---

[2] **shaft:** arrow (from Cupid's bow).   [3] **Two . . . loss:** the beloved's eyes won the heart the speaker had lost.   [4] **While . . . cross:** the beloved's lips fought with his eyes to claim the speaker's lost heart.   [5] **heart-mastered prize:** the prize, which was the mastered heart of the speaker.
[6] **It:** the mastered heart.

➜ **WILLIAM SHAKESPEARE**

Sonnet 130   *1609*

My mistress' eyes are nothing like the sun,
Coral is far more red, than her lips red,
If snow be white, why then her breasts are dun:[1]
If hairs be wires, black wires grow on her head:
I have seen roses damask'd,[2] red and white,   5
But no such roses see I in her cheeks,
And in some perfumes is there more delight,
Than in the breath that from my mistress reeks.
I love to hear her speak, yet well I know,
That music hath a far more pleasing sound: 10
I grant I never saw a goddess go,
My mistress when she walks treads on the ground,
        And yet by heaven I think my love as rare,
        As any she belied[3] with false compare.[4]

---

[1] **dun:** dingy brown or grayish color.   [2] **damask'd:** pinkish-red.   [3] **belied:** described untruthfully.   [4] **compare:** comparisons.

William Shakespeare, *Shake-speares Sonnets* (London, 1609), H1r, H4r; STC 22353.

OVIDIANISM

The Petrarchan was not the only love rhetoric available to Elizabethan poets and writers. Ovid's earthy love elegies, the *Amores*, were a model for another kind of writing about love. The Elizabethan dramatist and poet Christopher Marlowe (1564–1593) translated the *Amores* into English and himself wrote poems much influenced by the Roman poet's freedom of expression and acceptance of bodily desire. Below is his translation of Ovid's "In Bed with Corinna." How does the speaker's relationship to Corinna compare to the Petrarchan lover's relationship to his beloved? How do their descriptions of their lovers' bodies differ? What are the Ovidian elements in *As You Like It*? Does the frank expression of physical desire play any part in the courtships it represents?

→ OVID

In Bed with Corinna
1603

Translated by Christopher Marlowe

CORINNAE CONCUBITUS[1]

In summer's heat and mid-time of the day,
To rest my limbs upon a bed I lay.
One window shut, the other open stood,
Which gave such light, as twinkles in a wood.
Like twilight glimpse at setting of the Sun,   5
Or night being past, and yet not day begun.
Such light to shamefast[2] maidens must be shown,
Where they may sport, and seem to be unknown.
Then came Corinna in a long loose gown,
Her white neck hid with tresses hanging down.   10
Resembling fair Semiramis[3] going to bed,
Or Lais[4] of a thousand wooers sped.
I snacht her gown being thin, the harm was small,
Yet striv'd she to be covered there withall.

---

[1] Corinnae Concubitus: "In Bed with Corinna." [2] shamefast: shamefaced. [3] Semiramis: legendary Assyrian queen. [4] Lais: legendary courtesan.

Ovid, *Amores (Elegies of Love)*, trans. Christopher Marlowe (London, 1603), A5R; STC 18931.

And striving thus as one that would be cast,   15
Betray'd her self, and yielded at the last.
Stark naked as she stood before mine eye,
Not one wen[5] in her body could I spy.
What arms and shoulders did I touch and see,
How apt her breasts were to be prest by me.   20
How smooth a belly under her wast saw I?
How large a leg, and what a lusty thigh?
To leave the rest all lik'd me passing well,
I cling'd her naked body, down she fell,
Judge you the rest, being tired she bid me kiss,   25
Jove send me more such after-noons as this.

[5] wen: flaw.

THE NATIVE BALLAD TRADITION

Writing about love did not always mean drawing on Continental authors for precedent. There were also a number of songs and ballads that made use of the popular ballad form to talk about love, marriage, and desire. Just as there were numerous Robin Hood ballads printed on large single sheets of paper called broadsides, so there were a number of high-spirited accounts of love printed in this form and sold for a penny each. Some ballads let women speak and appealed to them as customers and performers. Many ballads were sold to women, who sang them alone and with others. Rather than simply being described by a male wooer, women in these ballads express their own views on love. Below are two ballads in which a man discusses with a woman whether or not she will love him. How does the dialogue form of the ballads construct the relationship between the man and the woman? Who has the upper hand? How would you describe the language of these poems? Where can you see traces of these popular ballads in the love exchanges in Arden? Several of these ballads are given on the following pages, including one illustrated with the woodcut you see here (Figure 13).

FIGURE 13 *A male wooer and his strong-willed beloved in "A Merry New Jig," a broadside ballad by Valentine Hamdultun (1630).*

→ VALENTINE HAMDULTUN

A Merry New Jig; or, the Pleasant Wooing
betwixt Kit and Peg   *1630*

To the Tune of Strawberry Leaves Make Maidens Fair

M: Well met, fair maid, my chiefest joy!
W: Alas, blind fool, deceiv'd art thou.
M: I prithee,[1] sweet Peg, be not so coy.
W: I scorn to fancy such a cow.

M: Thy beauty, sweet Peg, hath won my heart.   5
W: For shame! leave off thy flattery.
M: From thee I never mean to part.
W: Good lack, how thou canst cog[2] and lie!

M: For Peggie's love poor Kit will die.
W: In faith what color then shall it be?   10
M: In time my constant heart will try.
W: Then pluck it out that I may see.

M: My life I will spend to do thee good.
W: Alas! good sir, thou shalt not need.
M: For thee I will not spare my blood.   15
W: God send your goslings[3] well to speed.

M: Yet fain[4] would I be thy wedded mate.
W: Alas! good sir, I am already sped.[5]
M: What luck had I to come so late?
W: Because thou broughtest a calf[6] from bed.   20

M: O pity me, sweet Peg, I thee pray.
W: So I have done long time, God wot.[7]
M: Why dost thou then my love deny?
W: Because I see thou art a sot.[8]

[1] **prithee:** pray thee. [2] **cog:** cheat. [3] **goslings:** young geese; here, young and foolish persons.
[4] **fain:** gladly. [5] **sped:** spoken for. [6] **calf:** fool. [7] **wot:** knows. [8] **sot:** fool.

Valentine Hamdultun, "A Merry New Jig; or, the Pleasant Wooing betwixt Kit and Peg" (London, 1630); STC 12725.

➜ VALENTINE HAMDULTUN

A Pleasant New Song between Two Young Lovers
That Lasted Not Long; or, the Second Part   *1630*

To the Same Tune [As in the prior ballad]

M: Why, Ich[1] have wealth and treasure store.
W: And wit as small as small may be.
M: A chain of gold I might have wore.
W: A cocks-comb[2] fitter had been for thee.

M: Thou lov'st the Miller of the Glen.   5
W: What if I do, what is that to thee?
M: I will bang the miller's love from him,
And therefore wend[3] and gang[4] with me.

W: Great boast! Small roast[5] such brags will make;
But if Tom Miller he were nigh,[6]   10
He would bang thee well for Peggie's sake,
And like a puppy make thee cry.

M: Yet kiss me now for my good will,
And if my life thou meanest to save.
W: To give a kiss I think it best,   15
To rid me from a prating[7] knave.

Be packing hence, you rustic clown.[8]
M: No haste but good I hope there be.
W: Adieu,[9] kind Kit, with all my heart,
I am glad I am rid of thy company.   20

M: All you young men, take heed by me,
That unto women set your mind;
See that your lovers constant be,
Lest you be served in like kind.[10]

[1] Ich: I.   [2] cocks-comb: a cap worn by a professional fool.   [3] wend: turn.   [4] gang: walk.
[5] Small roast: talk lacking in substance.   [6] nigh: near.   [7] prating: chattering.   [8] clown: an
uncultured person.   [9] Adieu: farewell.   [10] kind: manner.

Valentine Hamdultun, "A Pleasant New Song between Two Young Lovers That Lasted Not
Long; or, the Second Part" (London, 1630); STC 12725.

Lovers Who Write On Trees

In the early modern period, love revealed itself by excessive literary production. Lovers obsessively wrote love poems, and sometimes they carved those poems onto the bark of trees or settled for the less laborious task of simply engraving the name of their beloved on those tree trunks. Orlando does both. He hangs sheets of love verse on trees throughout the Forest of Arden, but he also says that "These trees shall be my books, / And in their barks my thoughts I'll character"; "Run, run, Orlando, carve on every tree / The fair, the chaste, and unexpressive she" (3.2.5–6, 9–10).

There is a long literary tradition of lovers carving their names into the bark of trees.[1] An influential example is the tree-carving episode in Ludovico Ariosto's (1474–1533) Italian romance epic *Orlando Furioso*. Ariosto's poem, first published in Italy in 1516, was translated into English by John Harington in 1591, just a few years before *As You Like It* was written. Shakespeare might also have known of it through *The History of Orlando Furioso*, Robert Greene's 1592 adaptation of the story for the stage, which appeared immediately after Harington's translation. The poem chronicles the madness of the valiant Christian knight Orlando, who is tempted away from his military duties when he falls in love with and pursues the pagan princess Angelica. Hot on her trail, he discovers that she has fallen in love with another knight, Medoro, when he sees their names carved on a tree trunk. Driven mad with jealousy, Orlando rampages across Europe burning towns and killing many. By the end of the poem, however, Orlando is cured both of his jealousy and his original love for Angelica, which the poem portrays as a species of madness. The moment when Medoro carves his and Angelica's names on the tree became a popular theme for Renaissance visual artists, including Giorgio Ghisi (see Figure 14), in which Cupid in one corner holds aloft the flaming torch of love, while Medoro uses a knife to carve Angelica's and his own name in the bark of the tree.

There are marked connections between *Orlando Furioso* and *As You Like It*. Both were published in England within the same decade; both have male protagonists named Orlando who are overcome by love. Below are the stanzas from Harington's translation of *Orlando Furioso* in which Orlando comes across the names *Angelica* and *Medoro* carved on a tree. Compare how Ariosto and Shakespeare use the motif of writing on trees. Who does the writing and to what end? Who finds the writing and how do they react? What is the play's attitude toward this convention? What does the writing on trees say about love madness?

---

[1] Rensselaer W. Lee, *Names on Trees: Ariosto into Art* (Princeton: Princeton UP, 1977).

FIGURE 14 *The Saracen knight Medoro carves his name and that of his beloved, Angelica, on a tree in an episode from Lodovico Ariosto's* Orlando Furioso. *Engraving entitled* Angelica and Medoro *by Giorgio Ghisi (c. 1570).*

→ LUDOVICO ARIOSTO

From Orlando Furioso

1591

Translated by John Harington

BOOK 19, STANZAS 25–28

[Angelica has helped to heal Medoro after he has been wounded in battle. They have taken refuge in a poor shepherd's cottage where she declares her love for him.]

25

> She suffers poor *Medoro* take the flower,[1]
> Which many sought, but none had yet obtained,
> That fragrant rose that to that present hour
> Ungathered was, behold *Medoro* gained.
> And over her to give him perfect power   5
> With sacred rites a marriage was ordained,
> And with the veil of this so sacred order,
> She covers this her folly and disorder.

26

> After the solemn marriage was done,
> Of which god *Cupid* ask the banes (I trow[2]),
> She going forward as she hath begun,
> Continued there with him a month and more,
> From rising to the setting of the sun,   5
> With him she doth sit, talk, lye, stand and go,
> Forgetting so all maidenly sobriety
> That she of him could never have satiety.

27

> If in the house she stayed, then would she crave
> *Medoro* in the house with her to stay.
> If in the field she walked, then must she have
> *Medoro* lead or guide her in the way.
> And by a river in a shady cave,   5
> They oft did use to spend the heat of day,

[1] **flower:** i.e., her virginity   [2] **I trow:** I believe.

Ludovico Ariosto, *Orlando Furioso in English Heroical Verse*, trans. John Harington (London, 1591); STC 746.

Like to a cave where (shunning stormy weather)
The Trojan duke and *Dido* met together.[3]

28

Amid these joys (as great as joys might be)
Their manner was on every wall within,
Without on every stone or shady tree,
To grave their names with bodkin, knife, or pin,
Angelica and *Medoro* you plain might see,   5
(So great a glory had they both therein),
Angelica and *Medoro* in every place,
With sundry knots and wreaths they interlace.

BOOK 23, STANZAS 78–80 AND 86–87

[Orlando seeking relief from the heat of the day, comes upon a shady grove where he discovers the traces of Angelica and Medoro's love.]

78

For looking all about the grove, behold,
In sundry places fair engraven he sees
Her name, whose love he more esteems than gold,
By her own hand in barks of diverse trees.
This was the place where before I told,   5
Medoro used to pay his surgeon's fees,[4]
Where she, to boast of that that was her shame,
Used oft to write hers and *Medoro's* name.

79

And then with true love knots and pretty posies[5]
(To show how she to him by love was knit)
Her inward thoughts by outward words discloses,
In her much love to show her little wit.
Orlando knew the hand and yet supposes   5
It was not she that had such posies writ,
And to beguile himself—"tush, tush" (quoth he)
"There may be more *Angelicas* than she."

---

[3]**Trojan . . . together:** referring to an episode from Virgil's *Aeneid* in which Aeneas, who has landed in Carthage on his way to Italy, makes love to Dido, queen of Carthage, in a cave.
[4]**pay . . . fees:** i.e., repay Angelica for nursing him to health.   [5]**posies:** love poems.

80

Yes, but I know too well that pretty hand;
Oft hath she sent me letters of her writing.
Then he bethinks how she might understand[6]
His name and love under that new inditing.[7]
And how it might be done long time he scanned   5
With this fond thought, fondly himself delighting.
Thus with small hope, much fear, all malcontent,
In these and such conceits the time he spent.

[In a nearby shady grove Orlando then finds a poem in which Medoro details his and Angelica's love.]

86

Twice, thrice, yea five times he doth read the rhyme,
And though he saw and knew the meaning plain,
Yet that his love was guilty of such crime
He will not let it sink into his brain.
Oft he perused it, and every time   5
It doth increase his sharp tormenting pain,
And ay the more he on the matter mused,
The more his wits and senses were confused.

87

Even then was he of wit well nigh bestraught,[8]
So quite he was given over unto grief
(And sure if we believe as proof hath taught
This torture is of all the rest the chief)
His spirit was dead, his courage quailed with thought.   5
He doth despair and look for no relief.
And sorrow did his sense so surprise
That words his tongue and tears forsook his eyes.

BOOK 23, STANZAS 102–108

[Orlando comes upon the shepherd who served as host to Medoro and Anglica and from him learns the whole story of their love and marriage. Orlando falls into despair and then into a dangerous rage.]

---

[6] **understand:** signify.   [7] **inditing:** writing.   [8] **bestraught:** bereft.

102

I am not I, the man that erst[9] I was.
Orlando, he is buried and dead.
His most ungrateful love (ah foolish lass)
Hath killed *Orlando* and cut off his head.
I am his ghost that up and down must pass,   5
In this tormenting hell forever led
To be a fearful sample[10] and a just,
To all such fools as put in love their trust.

103

Thus wandering still in ways that have no way,
He hapt again to light upon the cave
Where (in remembrance of their pleasant play)
Medoro did that epigram engrave.
To see the stones again his woes display   5
And her ill name and his ill hap[11] deprave[12]
Did on the sudden all his sense enrage,
With hate, with fury, with revenge and rage.

104

Straightways he draweth forth his fatal blade
And hews the stones; to heaven the shivers flee.
Accursed was that fountain, cave, and shade,
The arbor, and the flowers and every tree.
Orlando of all places havoc made   5
Where he those names together joined may see;
Yea to the spring he did perpetual hurt,
By filling it with leaves, boughs, stones, and dirt.

105

And having done this foolish frantic feat,
He lays him down all weary on the ground,
Distempered in his body with much heat,
In mind with pains that no tongue can expound.
Three days he does not sleep nor drink nor eat,   5
But lay with open eyes as in a sound.[13]
Then forth with rage and not with reason waked,
He rents his cloths and runs about stark naked.

[9] erst: formerly.   [10] sample: example.   [11] hap: luck.   [12] deprave: slander.   [13] sound: fainting fit.

106

His helmet here he flings, his poulderns[14] there;
He casts away his curats[15] and his shield;
His sword he throws away, he cares not where;
He scatters all his armor in the field.
No rag about his body he doth bear   5
As might from cold or might from shame him shield.
And save[16] he left behind his fatal blade,
No doubt he had therewith great havoc made.

107

But his surpassing force did so exceed
All common men that neither sword nor bill
Nor any other weapon he did need;
Mere strength sufficed him to do what he will.
He roots up trees as one would root a weed;   5
And even as birders laying nets with skill
Pare slender thorns away with easy strokes,
So did he play with ashs, elms, and oaks.

108

The herdmen and the shepherds that did hear
The hideous noise and unacquainted sound
With fear and wonder great approached near
To see and know what was hereof the ground.
But now I must cut off this treatise here,   5
Lest this my book do grow beyond his bound.
And if you take some pleasure in this text,
I will go forward with it in my next.

[14] **poulderns:** pouldrons; armor for the shoulders.   [15] **curats:** cuirasses; armor for the breast and back.   [16] **save:** except.

→ LADY MARY WROTH

From The Countess of Mountgomeries Urania   *1621*

As we saw with Angelica, women as well as men carved on trees and were affected by seeing their name and that of their beloved entwined together on tree bark. Lady Mary Wroth (1587–1651/53), Sir Philip Sidney's niece, played on this convention in her *The Countess of Mountgomeries Urania* (1621), the first romance to be written by an Englishwoman. In this notoriously dense text there are hundreds of characters in dozens of sprawling subplots. The main thrust of the work, however, narrates the unwavering love of the Lady Pamphilia for her inconstant lover Amphilanthus. In the episode described below, Pamphilia, like Shakespeare's Orlando, expresses her frustrated desires on the bark of a nearby tree. What are her motives for choosing trees as an engraving surface? Are they the same as Orlando's? Both Ludovico Ariosto's Orlando (see p. 248) and Wroth's Pamphilia despair of enjoying their beloved. How does each respond to that despair? In what ways do the tree-carving episodes in *As You Like It* seem similar to or different from those in Ariosto's and Wroth's romances? What is the significance of the fact that Rosalind does *not* carve Orlando's name on a tree?

[Pamphilia has taken herself to a dark and solitary part of the woods to think about Amphilanthus with whom she is deeply in love, but who does not yet recognize her passion for him.]

Oft would she blame his cruelty, but that again she would salve with his being ignorant of her pain; then justly accuse herself, who in so long time and many years could not make him discern her affections (though not by words plainly spoken), but soon was that thought recalled and blamed with the greatest condemnation, acknowledging her loss in this kind to proceed from virtue.[1] Then she considered he loved another. This put her beyond all patience, wishing her sudden end, cursing her days, fortune, and affection, which cast her upon this rock of mischief. Oft would she wish her dead, or her beauty marred, but that she recalled again; loving so much as yet in pity she would not wish what might trouble him, but rather continued according to her own wish, complaining, fearing, and loving, the most distressed, secret, and constant Lover that ever *Venus* or her blind Son[2] bestowed a wound or dart upon.

---

[1] **virtue:** namely, the virtue of modesty that would not let her directly express her passion.
[2] **Son:** Cupid.

Lady Mary Wroth, *The Countess of Mountgomeries Urania* (London, 1621), Part I, Book I, 74–76 (L1v–L2v); STC 26051.

In this estate she stayed a while in the wood, gathering sometimes flowers which there grew, the name of which began with the letters of his name, and so placing them about her.[3] "Well, *Pamphilia*," said she, "for all these disorderly passions, keep still thy soul from thought of change, and if thou blame anything, let it be absence, since his presence will give thee again thy fill of delight. And yet what torment will that prove, when I shall with him see his hopes, his joys, and content come from another? O Love, O froward fortune, which of you two should I most curse? You are both cruel to me, but both alas are blind, and therefore let me rather hate myself for this unquietness, and yet unjustly shall I do too in that, since how can I condemn my heart for having virtuously and worthily chosen? Which very choice shall satisfy me with as much comfort as I felt despair. And now poor grass," said she, "thou shalt suffer for my pain, my love-smarting body thus pressing thee."

Then laid she her excelling self upon that (then most blessed ground), "and in compassion give me some rest," said she, "on you which well you may do being honored with the weight of the loyalist, but most afflicted Princess that ever this Kingdom knew. Joy in this and flourish still, in hope to bear this virtuous affliction. O *Morea*, a place accounted full of Love, why is Love in thee thus terribly oppressed, and cruelly rewarded? Am I the first unfortunate Woman that bashfulness hath undone? If so, I suffer for a virtue, yet gentle pity were a sweeter lot. Sweet Land, and though more sweet Love, pardon me, hear me, and commiserate my woe." Then hastily rising from her low green bed, "Nay," said she, "since I find no redress, I will make other in part taste my pain and make them dumb partakers of my grief." Then taking a knife, she finished a Sonnet, which at other times she had begun to engrave in the bark of one of those fair and straight Ashes, causing that sap to accompany her tears for love, that for unkindness.

> Bear part with me most straight and pleasant Tree,
>   And imitate the Torments of my smart,
>   Which cruel Love doth send into my heart.
>   Keep in thy skin this testament of me,
> Which Love engraven hath with misery,
>   Cursing with grief the unresisting part,
>   Which would with pleasure soon have learned love's art,
>   But wounds still cureless must my rulers be.
>
> Thy sap doth weepingly bewray[4] thy pain,
> My heart-blood drops with storms it doth sustain.
>   Love senseless neither good nor mercy knows

---

[3] **placing . . . her:** i.e., laying out the flowers so that they form a cypher or code for her beloved's name.   [4] **bewray:** reveal.

> Pitiless I do wound thee, while that I
> Unpitied, and unthought on, wounded cry.
> Then out-live me, and testify my woes.

And on the roots, whereon she had laid her head, serving (though hard) for a pillow at that time to uphold the richest World of wisdom in her sex, she writ this.

> My thoughts thou hast supported without rest,
> My tired body here hath lain oppressed
> With love and fear; yet be thou ever blest;
> Spring, prosper, last. I am alone unblest.

Having ended it, again laying her sad perfections on the grass, to see if then some rest would have favored her, and have thought travel had enough disturbed her,[5] she presently found passion had not yet allowed time for her quiet. Wherefore rising and giving as kind a farewell look to the tree as one would do to a trusty friend, she went to the brook, upon the bank whereof were some fine shady trees and choice thorn bushes, which might as they were mixed, obtain the name of a pretty Grove. Whereinto she went, and sitting down under a Willow, there anew began her complaints, pulling off those branches, sometimes putting them on her head. But remembering herself, she quickly threw them off, vowing however her chance was, not to carry the token of her loss openly on her brows, but rather wear them privately in her heart.

[5] and have . . . her: and although she thought her labors had enough unsettled her (so that she could sleep).

The Renaissance Ganymede

While Rosalind does not write on trees, she does go in disguise in *As You Like It*. This disguise has been the cause of much critical comment, both because it involves cross-dressing as a man and because the man she impersonates is named Ganymede. Below are three selections that throw light on the complexities of this name. The first is a moralizing image from Henry Peacham's (c. 1576–1643) famous emblem book of 1612 (Figure 15). His view of Ganymede is utterly condemnatory. He associates Ganymede with every sort of crime, from sorcery, poison, murder, witchcraft, and counterfeiting to sodomy. Sodomy, in fact, was a catchall term in the period for the worst or most heinous crimes. It did not refer simply to a particular sex act, but to the unspeakable. Compare Peacham's image of Ganymede perched on a cock to the sensuous image of Ganymede carried to heaven by Jupiter (see

Figure 10, p. 209) to begin to get a feel for the range of associations this name could conjure.

By contrast, Christopher Marlowe's (1564–1593) play *The Tragedie of Dido, Queene of Carthage* (published 1594) opens with a scene of Jupiter on Mount Olympus engaged in amorous love play with a highly eroticized Ganymede. The darling of Jupiter's eye, this Ganymede seems to compete with Juno, Jupiter's wife, for Jupiter's attention, and, according to Venus, distracts Jupiter from the serious business of rescuing Aeneas, the leader of the Trojans, from drowning at sea. What kind of erotic figure is Marlowe's Ganymede? In what particular ways, if any, does Rosalind resemble him?

The final selection consists of some beautiful and witty poems written by Richard Barnfield (1574–1620), an English poet best known for erotic verse. In 1594 his *Affectionate Shepherd, Containing the Complaint of Daphnis for the Love of Ganymede* portrayed with some explicitness the love of a man for a "fair boy," Ganymede, even imitating Christopher Marlowe's famous poem "The Passionate Shepherd to His Love" (see p. 143). Barnfield obviously received some pushback, for at the beginning of his next collection, *Cynthia*, in 1595, he took pains to declare that he was only following the pastoral model laid down in Virgil's *Eclogues* and that the love between the two men was entirely proper. Whatever censure Barnfield received, it did not prevent him from including some sonnets to Ganymede in his second collection. How does Barnfield adapt the conventions of Renaissance love lyric to the figure of Ganymede as the beloved? To what extent does Barnfield paint himself as a frustrated Petrarchan lover and Ganymede as his aloof beloved? How does his use of Ganymede compare to Shakespeare's use of this persona in his depiction of Rosalind in disguise? Is Shakespeare's Ganymede wooed by a lover whom she appears to scorn? Collectively, how do these contemporary depictions of Ganymede affect our understanding of what was at stake in having Rosalind assume this disguise?

→ HENRY PEACHAM

From Minerva Britanna, an emblem of Ganymede   *1612*

Upon a cock, here Ganymede doth sit,
Who erst[1] rode mounted on Jove's eagle's back,
One hand holds Circe's[2] wand, and joined with it,

---

[1] erst: once.   [2] Circe: mythological sorceress.

Henry Peacham, *Minerva Britanna* (London, 1612), 48; STC 19511.

FIGURE 15 *Condemnatory image of Ganymede on the back of a cock and holding emblems of his wickedness, including a cup of poison. From Henry Peacham,* Minerva Britanna *(1612).*

A cup top-fil'd with poison, deadly black:
 The other medals,[3] of base metals wrought,
 With sundry[4] monies, counterfeit and nought.[5]   5

These be those crimes, abhorr'd[6] of God and man,
Which Justice should correct, with laws severe,
In Ganymede, the foul Sodomitan:[7]
Within the cock, vile incest doth appear: 10
 Witchcraft, and murder, by that cup and wand,
 And by the rest, false coin[8] you understand.

---

[3] **medals:** other metallic objects he holds. [4] **sundry:** different. [5] **nought:** wicked. [6] **abhorr'd:** hated. [7] **Sodomitan:** one who commits sodomy. [8] **false coin:** counterfeiting

➜ CHRISTOPHER MARLOWE

From The Tragedie of Dido

1594

Here the Curtains draw. There is discovered Jupiter *dandling* Ganymede *upon his knee, and* Mercury *lying asleep.*

JUPITER: Come, gentle *Ganymede*, and play with me,
I love thee well, say *Juno*[1] what she will.
GANYMEDE: I am much better for your worthless love,
That will not shield me from her shrewish blows.
Today when as I filled into your cups   5
And held the cloth of pleasance[2] whiles you drank,
She reached me such a rap for that[3] I spilled,
As made the blood run down about mine ears.
JUPITER: What? Dares she strike the darling of my thoughts?
By *Saturn's*[4] soul and this earth-threatening hair,   10
That shaken thrice, makes Nature's buildings quake,
I vow, if she but once frown on thee more,
To hang her, meteor-like, twixt heaven and earth,
And bind her hand and foot with golden cords,
As once I did for harming *Hercules*.[5]   15
GANYMEDE: Might I but see that pretty sport afoot,
O how would I with *Helen's* brother[6] laugh,
And bring the Gods to wonder at the game.
Sweet *Jupiter*, if ere I pleased thine eye,
Or seemed fair, walled in with Eagle's wings,   20
Grace my immortal beauty with this boon,
And I will spend my time in thy bright arms.
JUPITER: What is't, sweet wag,[7] I should deny thy youth,
Whose face reflects such pleasure to mine eyes,
As I, exhaled with thy fire-darting beams,[8]   25
Have oft driven back the horses of the night,[9]

---

[1] *Juno*: wife of Jupiter.   [2] **cloth of pleasance**: a napkin with which to wipe the drinking cup. [3] **that**: that which.   [4] **Saturn**: father of Jupiter.   [5] *Hercules*: son of Jupiter, famous for his strength.   [6] *Helen's* **brother**: Castor or Pollux, the two brothers of Helen of Troy.   [7] **wag**: mischievous boy.   [8] **exhaled . . . beams**: left breathless from your fiery glances.   [9] **horses of the night**: figurative; Jupiter has made the night last longer than it normally would.

Christopher Marlowe, *The Tragedie of Dido, Queene of Carthage* (London, 1594), A2–A2v; STC 62481.

Whenas they would have haled[10] thee from my sight.
Sit on my knee, and call for thy content;[11]
Control proud Fate, and cut the thread of time.
Why, are not all the Gods at thy command   30
And heaven and earth the bounds of thy delight?
Vulcan[12] shall dance to make thee laughing sport,
And my nine Daughters[13] sing when thou art sad.
From *Juno's* bird[14] I'll pluck her spotted pride
To make thee fans wherewith to cool thy face,   35
And *Venus's*[15] swans shall shed their silver down
To sweeten out the slumbers of thy bed.
Hermes[16] no more shall show the world his wings,
If that thy fancy in his feathers dwell,
But as this one I'll tear them all from him.   40

[*Jupiter plucks a feather from Hermes' wing.*]

Do you but say "their color pleaseth me."
Hold here, my little love. These linked gems[17]
My *Juno* wore upon her marriage day
Put thou about thy neck, my own sweet heart,
And trick thy arms and shoulders with my theft.   45
GANYMEDE: I would have a jewel for mine ear,
And a fine brooch to put into my hat,
And then I'll hug with you an hundred times.
JUPITER: And shall have, *Ganymede*, if thou wilt be my love.

Enter Venus

VENUS: Ay, this is it. You can sit toying there   50
And playing with that female wanton boy,
Whiles my *Aeneas*[18] wanders on the Seas
And rests a prey to every billow's pride.

---

[10] **haled:** pulled.   [11] **call . . . content:** ask for what you desire.   [12] *Vulcan:* god of fire, who is crippled. His dancing would therefore be awkward and amusing.   [13] **nine Daughters:** the Muses.   [14] *Juno's* **bird:** the peacock.   [15] *Venus:* goddess of love.   [16] *Hermes:* messenger of the gods, with feathered wings.   [17] **linked gems:** a necklace.   [18] *Aeneas:* Venus's son, leader of the survivors of Troy.

➜ RICHARD BARNFIELD

From The Affectionate Shepherd   *1594*

Scarce had the morning star hid from the light
Heaven's crimson canopy with stars bespangled,[1]
But I began to rue[2] th'unhappy sight
Of that fair boy that had my heart entangled;
 Cursing the time, the place, the sense, the sin;   5
 I came, I saw, I view'd, I slipped in.

If it be sin to love a sweet-fac'd boy,
(Whose amber locks truss'd[3] up in golden trammels[4]
Dangle adown his lovely cheeks with joy,
When pearl and flowers his fair hair enamels[5])   10
 If it be sin to love a lovely lad;
 Oh then sin I, for whom my soul is sad.

His ivory-white and alabaster[6] skin
Is stain'd throughout with rare vermilion[7] red,
Whose twinkling starry lights do never blin[8]   15
To shine on lovely Venus[9] (beauty's bed):
 But as the lily and the blushing rose,
 So white and red on him in order grows.

 . . . .

O would to God he would but pity me,
That love him more than any mortal wight;[10]
Then he and I with love would soon agree,
That now cannot abide his suitor's sight.
 O would to God (so I might have my fee[11])   95
 My lips were honey, and thy mouth a bee.

Then shouldst thou suck my sweet and my fair flower
That now is ripe, and full of honey-berries:

---

[1] **bespangled:** adorned. [2] **rue:** regret. [3] **truss'd:** trussed, tied up. [4] **trammels:** braids. [5] **enamels:** covers. [6] **alabaster:** smooth and white. [7] **vermilion:** bright red. [8] **blin:** cease. [9] **Venus:** mythological goddess of love. [10] **wight:** creature. [11] **fee:** reward.

Richard Barnfield, *The Affectionate Shepherd, Containing the Complaint of Daphnis for the Love of Ganymede* (London, 1594), lines 1–18, 91–114, 223–35; STC 1480.

Then would I lead thee to my pleasant bower[12]
Fill'd full of grapes, of mulberries, and cherries;   100
    Then shouldst thou be my wasp or else my bee,
    I would thy hive, and thou my honey be.

I would put amber bracelets on thy wrests,[13]
Crownets[14] of pearl about thy naked arms:
And when thou sitt'st at swilling[15] Bacchus[16] feasts   105
My lips with charms should save thee from all harms:
    And when in sleep thou took'st thy chiefest pleasure,
    Mine eyes should gaze upon thine eyelids' treasure.

And every morn by dawning of the day,
When Phoebus[17] riseth with a blushing face,   110
Silvanus[18] chapel-clerks[19] shall chant a lay,[20]
And play thee hunts-up[21] in thy resting place:
    My cote[22] thy chamber, my bosom thy bed;
    Shall be appointed for thy sleepy head.

   . . . .

When will my May come, that I may embrace thee?
When will the hour be of my soul's joying?
Why dost thou seek in mirth still to disgrace me?   225
Whose mirth's my health, whose grief's my heart's annoying.
    Thy bane[23] my bale,[24] thy bliss my blessedness,
    Thy ill my hell, thy weal[25] my welfare is.

Thus do I honor thee that love thee so,
And love thee so, that so do honor thee,   230
Much more than any mortal man doth know,
Or can discern by love or jealousy:
    But if that thou disdain'st my loving ever;
    Oh happy I, if I had loved never.

---

[12]**bower:** chamber. [13]**wrests:** wrists. [14]**crownets:** circlets. [15]**swilling:** heavily drinking. [16]**Bacchus:** mythological god of wine and feasting. [17]**Phoebus:** mythological sun god. [18]**Silvanus:** mythological spirit of woods and fields. [19]**chapel-clerks:** assistants to a priest who sings the mass. [20]**lay:** song. [21]**hunts-up:** an old song used to wake huntsmen from sleep. [22]**cote:** cottage. [23]**bane:** ruinous thing. [24]**bale:** misery. [25]**weal:** well-being.

→ RICHARD BARNFIELD

From Cynthia

1595

FROM "TO THE COURTEOUS GENTLEMEN READERS":

Some there were, that did interpret *The Affectionate Shepherd* otherwise than (in truth) I meant, touching the subject thereof, to wit, the love of a shepherd to a boy; a fault, the which I will not excuse, because I never made. Only this, I will unshadow[1] my conceit:[2] being nothing else, but an imitation of Virgil,[3] in the second Eclogue of Alexis.[4] . . .

SONNET VIII:

Sometimes I wish that I his pillow were,
    So might I steal a kiss, and yet not seen,
    So might I gaze upon his sleeping eyen,[5]
Although I did it with a panting fear:
But when I consider how vain my wish is,   5
    Ah foolish bees (think I) that do not suck
    His lips for honey, but poor flowers do pluck
Which have no sweet in them: when his sole kisses,
Are able to revive a dying soul.
    Kiss him, but sting him not, for if you do,   10
    His angry voice your flying will pursue:
But when they hear his tongue, what can control,
    Their back return? For then they plain may see,
    How honeycombs from his lips dropping be.

SONNET XV:

A fairest Ganymede,[6] disdain me not,
    Though silly shepherd I, presume to love thee,
    Though my harsh songs and sonnets cannot move thee,
Yet to thy beauty is my love no blot.

[1] **unshadow:** reveal. [2] **conceit:** meaning. [3] **Virgil:** (70–19 B.C.E.) Roman poet. [4] **second Eclogue of Alexis:** the second of Virgil's *Eclogues* (c. 44–38 B.C.E.) is on the love of the shepherd Coridon for the boy Alexis. [5] **eyen:** eye. [6] **Ganymede:** beautiful Trojan boy stolen by Jove.

Richard Barnfield, *Cynthia* (London, 1595), A3r, C1v, C3r, D1r; STC 1484.

Apollo,[7] Jove,[8] and many gods beside   5
    S'daind[9] not the name of country shepherds swains,[10]
    Nor want we pleasure, though we take some pains,
We live contentedly: a thing call'd pride,
Which so corrupts the Court and every place,
    (Each place I mean where learning is neglected,   10
    And yet of late, even learning's self's infected)
I know not what it means, in any case:
    We only (when Molorchus[11] gins to peep)
    Learn for to fold, and to unfold our sheep.

[7]**Apollo:** mythological god of poetry and healing.   [8]**Jove:** mythological king of the gods.
[9]**S'daind:** disdained.   [10]**swains:** farm laborers.   [11]**Molorchus:** poor man with whom the
mythological hero Hercules stayed.

Cross-Dressing and Female Homoeroticism

To play Ganymede, Rosalind engages in cross-dressing, putting on the clothes of the opposite sex. Female characters on the Renaissance stage were always already cross-dressed boys because women were forbidden to perform in the public theaters, but many contemporary plays added an additional layer of complexity by having female characters dress as boys. Despite its theatrical popularity, the practice of cross-dressing on the street was condemned by those who connected it to prostitution or painted it as fashion madness when, for example, wealthy woman vied with one another in showing off "mannish" fashions such as doublets and little spurs. The theatrical practice also came under fire, even as the public theater flourished and gained royal patronage in the closing years of the sixteenth century. This intellectual culture of antitheatricality had deep roots in classical authors such as Plato and Tertullian, but it assumed a new and virulent form in the spectacularly vicious and polemical pamphlets produced by radical Puritan authors. In these accounts, the theater was a wellspring of innumerable and often interchangeable vices, providing a space in which various threats to social order could be located, such as the threat of sexual licentiousness. Antitheatrical writers were unanimous in seizing on the theatrical practice of cross-dressing as a special threat to stable and traditional ideas of gender and sexual order. Below are two passages from antitheatrical tracts that condemn the theater as a space of amoral confusion.

The first excerpt, from *Th'Overthrow of Stage-Plays*, is taken from a published exchange of argumentative letters between the prominent scholar and minister John Rainolds and his fellow academic William Gager, written about a series of academic plays performed in Oxford in the early 1590s. Academic drama, which frequently received a free pass from antitheatrical-ists because of its purported "educational purpose" and because it occurred in a more private venue than the big London theaters, was not spared by Rainolds, who treats it as part of a larger problem of theatricality. What arguments does Rainolds advance against the theater? What kind of power is implicitly ascribed to drama through these objections? Does it explain the appeal some audiences might have found in a play as filled with cross-dressing as *As You Like It*?

→ JOHN RAINOLDS

From Th'Overthrow of Stage-Plays   *1592–1593*

Th'Overthrow of Stage-Plays, composed of six letters written by or to the Puri-tan scholar and clergyman John Rainolds (1549–1607) in 1592–1593, showcases Rainolds's contribution to an ongoing contemporary debate about staged theat-rical performances. The letters, which circulated in manuscript around Oxford for several years before they were printed, were first published in the Neth-erlands by a printer known to publish radical Puritan books. In this selection from a letter to the dramatist William Gager (1555–1622), Rainolds reiterates and defends his objections to plays against what he believed was Gager's mockery of those views in his adaptation of Seneca's *Hippolytus* (staged at Christ Church, Oxford, in 1592). In particular, Rainolds, like many other antitheatricalists, criti-cizes the practice of boys playing women's parts, suggesting that this kind of role-playing is likely to inspire lust in both the actors imitating female "wanton-ness" and in the audience watching those actions. He argues that it is shameful for males to dress and act as women, in no small part because such performances are also delightful and moving. Moreover, the passions inspired by the practice seem to incite men to desire both for the woman being impersonated and for the boy performing the role, thus confusing the end of erotic desire.

Yet the third reason, wherein plays are charged, not for making young men come forth in whores' attire, like the lewd woman in the Proverbs;[1] but for teaching them to counterfeit her actions, her wanton[2] kiss, her impudent face, her wicked speeches and enticements; should have been allowed even

---

[1] **lewd woman in the Proverbs:** Proverbs 7:10 describes an adulteress dressed as a prostitute.
[2] **wanton:** lustful.

John Rainolds, *Th'Overthrow of Stage-Plays* (Middelburg, 1599), 17–18; STC 20616.

by your own gloss and exposition[3] of the text: sith[4] you say upon it, that different behaviour becometh different sexes, and, it beseemeth not men to follow women's manners. . . . How much less seemly then is it for young men to dance like women, though like those, who praised God with dances:[5] and much less seemly yet to dance like unhonest women, like Herodias?[6] whereby what a flame of lust may be kindled in the hearts of men, as ready for the most part to conceive this fire, as flax is the other, Christian writers shew in part by Herod's example: but a heathen poet more fully by his own experience; affirming that he was not ravished so much with his mistress's face, though marvellous fair and beautiful, nor with her hair hanging down loose after the fashion about her smooth neck; nor with her radiant eyes, like stars; nor with her silks, & outlandish bravery; as he was with her gallant dancing.[7] And greater reason is it you should condemn all stage-plays, wherein young men are trained to play such women's parts. . . . When Critobulus kissed the son of Alcibiades, a beautiful boy, Socrates said he had done amiss and very dangerously:[8] because, as certain spiders, if they do but touch men only with their mouth, they put them to wonderful pain and make them mad: so beautiful boys by kissing do sting and pour secretly in a kind of poison, the poison of incontinency,[9] as Clemens Alexandrinus speaking of unholy and amatory[10] kisses, saith: Amatory embracing goeth in the same line with amatory kissing, if not a line beyond it.[11] Amatory dancing is, in Homer's wantons,[12] as oil unto the fire: and the commendation that Tully giveth it in banquets,[13] S. Ambrose giveth it in stage-plays.[14] Herewithall if amatory pangs be expressed in most effectual sort: can wise men be persuaded that there is no wantonness in the players' parts, when experience sheweth (as wise men have observed) that men are made adulterers and enemies of all chastity by coming to such plays? that senses are

---

[3] **gloss and exposition:** interpretation.   [4] **sith:** since.   [5] **those, who praised God with dances:** the Israelite women of Exodus 15:20.   [6] **Herodias:** in Mark 6, Salome, the daughter of Herodias, pleases him so much with her dancing that he promises to grant any request. She asks for the head of John the Baptist.   [7] **heathen poet . . . gallant dancing:** a reference to Book II, Elegy 3 of the Latin poet Propertius (c. 50–c. 15 B.C.E.).   [8] **Critobulus . . . dangerously:** the Greek historian Xenophon (c. 430–354 B.C.E.), a student of the philosopher Socrates (c. 469–399 B.C.E.), recounts this anecdote in his *Memorabilia*, a collection of Socratic dialogues.   [9] **incontinency:** lack of self-restraint.   [10] **amatory:** pertaining to sexual love.   [11] **Clemens Alexandrinus . . . beyond it:** the Christian theologian Clement of Alexandria (c. 150–c. 215 C.E.) makes this assertion in his *Paedagogus.*   [12] **Homer's wantons:** in the *Odyssey* (c. eighth century B.C.E.), an ancient Greek epic poem attributed to Homer, Odysseus's female servants behave inappropriately with Penelope's suitors.   [13] **Tully giveth it in banquets:** in *Against Piso*, the Roman orator and statesman Marcus Tullius Cicero (106–43 B.C.E.) criticizes the drunken dancing, feasting, and debauchery of certain public figures.   [14] **S. Ambrose giveth it in stage-plays:** in his Epistle 58, the famous theologian Saint Ambrose (c. 337–397 C.E.) notes the unseemliness of men dancing like women or imitating "players."

moved, affections are delighted, hearts though strong and constant are van-quished by such players? that an effeminate stage-player, while he feigneth[15] love, imprinteth wounds of love?

[15] **feigneth:** pretends.

→ WILLIAM PRYNNE

From Histrio-Mastix   *1633*

The second excerpt is taken from William Prynne's massive antitheatrical tract *Histrio-Mastix (The Player Whipped)*. Prynne (1600–1699) was a prolific pam-phleteer and religious controversialist, and his gargantuan volume, which ran to more than 1,000 folio pages, launched an extreme Puritan assault on a broad spectrum of "theatrical" practices ranging from public theater to court masques to country holiday traditions such as dancing around the Maypole. He was particularly incensed by theatrical practices that promoted "unnatural" sexual behavior, as in the passage given below, which inveighs against boy actors play-ing female roles. Compare Prynne's more extreme objections to those leveled by John Rainolds in the previous selection. What does Rainolds think the theater has power to do to its spectators, and how does Prynne extend this argument? Think about the moments in *As You Like It* that dramatize characters reacting to the sight of cross-dressed characters. How do these moments confirm or refute Rainolds's and Prynne's view of the erotic power of crossdressing?

FROM ACT 5, SCENE 6

Now a man's attiring himself in woman's array . . . perverts one principal use of garments, to difference men from women; by confounding, inter-changing, transforming these two sexes for the present, as long as the play or part doth last. . . .

Lastly, this putting on of woman's array (especially to act a lascivious, amorous, whorish, love-sick play upon the stage), must needs be sinful, yea abominable; because it not only excites many adulterous filthy lusts, both in the actors and spectators; and draws them on both to contemplative and actual lewdness, (as the marginal authors[1] testify) which is evil; but likewise

[1] **marginal authors:** theologians who wrote interpretive commentary on the Bible.

William Prynne, *Histrio-Mastix* (London, 1633), 207–11; STC 20464.

instigates them to self-pollution, (a sin for which Onan was destroyed)[2] and to that unnatural sodomitical sin of uncleanness,[3] to which the reprobate Gentiles[4] were given over; (a sin not once to be named,[5] much less than practiced among Christians), which is worse: this the detestable examples of Heliogabalus,[6] Sardanapalus,[7] Nero & Sporus,[8] the male-priests of Venus with the passive beastly sodomites in Florida, Gayra, and Peru,[9] evidence; who went clad in women's apparel, the better to elicit, countenance, act, and color their unnatural execrable uncleanness, which I abhor to think of. This the usual practice of other ancient Incubi,[10] who clothed their Galli,[11] Succubi,[12] Ganymedes[13] and Cynadi[14] in women's attire, whose virilities[15] they did oft-times dissect,[16] to make them more effeminate, transforming them as near as might be into women, both in apparel, gesture, speech, behavior. And more especially in long unshorn womanish, frizzled, lust-provoking hair and love-locks, (grown now too much in fashion with comely pages, youths, and lewd effeminate ruffianly[17] persons; as they were with these unnatural pagans, I dare not write, to amorous beastly purposes, to which they are strong allectives,[18] of which they were ancient symptoms, as sundry profane and Christian writers testify: which should cause all chaste ingenious Christians for ever to detest them, the better to avoid the snares, the badges, the suspicions of incontinency,[19] and this most filthy sin), the more to extenuate[20] this their unnatural wickedness, or rather the more freely to embolden, to allure and provoke them to the undaunted, unlamented practice of it, by reducing it as near to natural lewdness[21] as they could

[2] **self-pollution . . . Onan was destroyed:** masturbation; in Genesis 38 Onan is put to death for spilling his semen on the ground instead of impregnating his sister-in-law.   [3] **unnatural sodomitical sin of uncleanness:** in Romans 1:27 Paul refers to men engaging in sexual acts with other men.   [4] **reprobate Gentiles:** unrepentant non-Jews about whom Paul was speaking.   [5] **a sin not once to be named:** in Ephesians 5:3 Paul writes that there should not even be a hint of sexual immorality among Christians.   [6] **Heliogabalus:** (c. 203–222 C.E.), Roman emperor also known as Elagabalus or Marcus Aurelius Antoninus who, according to classical historians, liked to dress as a woman and have sexual relations with men.   [7] **Sardanapalus:** legendary king of Assyria whose effeminate clothing and behavior were claimed to have contributed to the downfall of the Assyrian kingdom.   [8] **Nero & Sporus:** Sporus was a slave of the Roman emperor Nero (37–68 C.E.) whom Nero was said to have castrated, dressed as a woman, and publicly married.   [9] **male-priests of Venus . . . Peru:** in *Purchas His Pilgrimage*, Samuel Purchas (c. 1575–1626), an English travel writer, suggested that in the so-called New World male prostitutes dressed as women to attract their customers.   [10] **other ancient Incubi:** legendary demons in male form who had sex with sleeping women.   [11] **Galli:** castrated priests of the goddess Cybele in ancient Roman religion.   [12] **Succubi:** legendary demons in female form who seduced men while they slept.   [13] **Ganymedes:** in Greek mythology, Ganymede was the beautiful Trojan boy whom Zeus kidnapped.   [14] **Cynadi:** *cinaedi*, or men who dress as women and engage in sexual acts with other men.   [15] **virilities:** testicles.   [16] **dissect:** cut off.   [17] **ruffianly:** rough, dangerous.   [18] **allectives:** things which have the power to allure.   [19] **incontinency:** lack of self-restraint.   [20] **extenuate:** diminish.   [21] **natural lewdness:** unchaste sexual activity between men and women.

devise: since few of them were so prodigiously impudent,[22] so unmeasurably outrageous at the first, as desperately to rush upon this unnatural filthiness in its superlative[23] native vileness, without some extenuating varnishes[24] cast into it, to charm their consciences, and inflame their lusts. Yea this the execrable precedents of ancient, of modern play-poets and players witness, who have been deeply plunged in this abominable wickedness, which my ink is not black enough to decipher.

[22] **prodigiously impudent:** greatly lacking in shame and modesty. [23] **superlative:** the highest degree of something. [24] **extenuating varnishes:** outward embellishments that make something appear less unattractive.

→ JOHN LYLY

From Gallatea   *Published 1592*

Despite the outcry from some quarters about theatrical cross-dressing, the theaters not only flourished but staged a number of plays in which cross-dressing featured as a plot element. Shakespeare, for example, employed cross-dressing in *The Merchant of Venice*, *Twelfth Night*, and *Cymbeline*, as well as in *As You Like It*. He was not alone. One predecessor, John Lyly (c. 1554–1606), a court dramatist whose plays were frequently performed before Elizabeth I, wrote a play in the mid-1580s, *Gallatea* (published 1592), that bears some resemblances to *As You Like It*. Based on the Ovidian story of Iphis and Ianthe, it involves two fathers who separately worry that their daughters will be selected to be fed to the sea monster Agar, who yearly demands a sacrifice of their nation's most beautiful virgin. To avoid this, they dress the daughters, named Phillida and Gallatea, as boys and send them into the forest. The two women meet in the woods and fall in love, each believing the other to be a boy. At the play's end, when their true sex is revealed and marriage declared impossible, all problems are solved by Venus's intervention and her promise to transform one of them into a boy. For most of the play, the audience watches two women dressed as men fall in love. The eventual revelation of the biological sex of the two women does nothing to dim their passion, and the transformation of one of them into a boy seems merely a sop to convention. Their ardor is primarily homoerotic.

As You Like It shares with *Gallatea* a setting in the forests and fields, an interest in cross-dressing, and the potential to create humorous and titillating situations of sexual ambiguity. Below are excerpts from two scenes of Lyly's play. In the first, the disguised girls woo and verbally spar in the forest, trying to determine each other's gender; in the second, Venus descends to adjudicate the wed-

John Lyly, *Gallatea* (London, 1585); STC 17080.

ding at the play's end. Both scenes engage with themes central to Shakespeare's comedy and his portrayal of Rosalind as a cross-dressed figure who inspires passion in another woman, Phoebe. In the first scene, what confusion does cross-dressing cause for the two women, who are dressed as men? What makes the scene funny and/or moving? Does it stretch the boundaries of erotic possibility? What light does it shed on Phoebe's attraction to Ganymede in *As You Like It*? By what plot devices are social conventions around marriage accommodated in each play? Does either play put an end to the possibility of female homoeroticism?

Act 3, Scene 2

[*Enter*] PHILLIDA and GALLATEA. [*disguised as boys*]

PHILLIDA: It is pity that Nature framed you not a woman, having a face so fair, so lovely a countenance, so modest a behavior.

GALLATEA: There is a tree in Tylos,[1] whose nuts have shells like fire, and being cracked, the kernel is but water.

PHILLIDA: What a toy is it to tell me of that tree, being nothing to the   5
purpose? I say it is pity you are not a woman.

GALLATEA: I would not wish to be a woman, unless it were because thou art a man.

PHILLIDA: Nay, do not wish to be a woman, for then I should not love thee, for I have sworn never to love a woman.   10

GALLATEA: A strange humor in so pretty a youth, and according to mine, for myself will never love a woman.

PHILLIDA: It were a shame, if a maiden should be a suitor, (a thing hated in that sex), that thou shouldst deny to be her servant.

GALLATEA: If it be a shame in me, it can be no commendation in you, for   15
yourself is of that mind.

PHILLIDA: Suppose I were a virgin (I blush in supposing myself one), and that under the habit of a boy were the person of a maid: if I should utter my affection with sighs, manifest my sweet love by my salt tears, and prove my loyalty unspotted, and my griefs intolerable, would not then   20
that fair face pity this true heart?

GALLATEA: Admit that I were as you would have me suppose that you are, and that I should with entreaties, prayers, oaths, bribes, and whatever can be invented in love, desire your favor, would you not yield?

PHILLIDA: Tush, you come in with "admit."   25

GALLATEA: And you with "suppose."

---

[1] **Tylos**: island in the Persian Gulf.

PHILLIDA: [*Aside*] What doubtful speeches be these? I fear me he is as I
am, a maiden.

GALLATEA: [*Aside*] What dread riseth in my mind! I fear the boy to be as I
am, a maiden.   30

PHILLIDA: [*Aside*] Tush, it cannot be. His voice shows the contrary.

GALLATEA: [*Aside*] Yet I do not think it, for he would then have blushed.

PHILLIDA: Have you ever a sister?

GALLATEA: If I had but one, my brother must needs have two. But I pray,
have you ever a one?   35

PHILLIDA: My father had but one daughter, and therefore I could have no
sister.

GALLATEA: [*Aside*] Ay me, he is as I am, for his speeches be as mine are.

PHILLIDA: [*Aside*] What shall I do? Either he is subtle or my sex simple.²

GALLATEA: [*Aside*] I have known divers³ of Diana's nymphs⁴ enamored of   40
him, yet hath he rejected all, either as too proud to disdain, or too childish not to understand, or for that he knoweth himself to be a virgin.

PHILLIDA: [*Aside*] I am in a quandary. Diana's nymphs have followed him,
and he despised them, either knowing too well the beauty of his own
face, or that himself is of the same mould.⁵ I will once again try him.   45
[Aloud] You promised me in the woods that you would love me before all
Diana's nymphs.

GALLATEA: Ay, so you would love me before all Diana's nymphs.

PHILLIDA: Can you prefer a fond boy as I am, before so fair ladies as they
are?   50

GALLATEA: Why should not I as well as you?

PHILLIDA: Come, let us into the grove, and make much one of another,
that cannot tell what to think one of another.

Exeunt.

From Act 5, Scene 3

DIANA: Now things falling out⁶ as they do, you must leave these fond-   135
found⁷ affections. Nature will have it so, necessity must.

GALLATEA: I will never love any but Phillida. Her love is engraven in my
heart, with her eyes.

---

²subtle . . . simple: either he is cunning or I am slow to understand.   ³**divers**: many.
⁴**Diana's nymphs**: chaste young women who are followers of Diana.   ⁵**mould**: form.   ⁶**falling
out**: turning out.   ⁷**fond-found**: found to be foolish.

PHILLIDA: Nor I any but Gallatea, whose faith is imprinted in my thoughts
  by her words.   140
NEPTUNE: An idle choice, strange, and foolish, for one virgin to dote on
  another, and to imagine a constant faith where there can be no cause of
  affection. How like you this, Venus?
VENUS: I like well and allow it. They shall both be possessed of their
  wishes, for never shall it be said that Nature or Fortune shall overthrow   145
  love and faith. Is your loves unspotted, begun with truth, continued with
  constancy, and not to be altered till death?
GALLATEA: Die, Gallatea, if thy love be not so.
PHILLIDA: Accursed be thou, Phillida, if thy love be not so.
DIANA: Suppose all this, Venus. What then?   150
VENUS: Then shall it be seen that I can turn one of them to be a man, and
  that I will.
DIANA: Is it possible?
VENUS: What is to love or the mistress of love unpossible? Was it not
  Venus that did the like to Iphis and Ianthes?[8] How say ye, are ye agreed,   155
  one to be a boy presently?
PHILLIDA: I am content, so I may embrace Gallatea.
GALLATEA: I wish it, so I may enjoy Phillida.
MELIBEUS: Soft, daughter, you must know whether I will have you a son.
TITYRUS: Take me with you, Gallatea. I will keep you as I begat you, a   160
  daughter.
MELIBEUS: Tityrus, let yours be a boy and if you will, mine shall not.
TITYRUS: Nay, mine shall not, for by that means my young son shall lose
  his inheritance.
MELIBEUS: Why then get him to be made a maiden, and then there is   165
  nothing lost.
TITYRUS: If there be such changing, I would Venus could make my wife
  a man.
MELIBEUS: Why?
TITYRUS: Because she loves always to play with men.   170
VENUS: Well you are both fond.[9] Therefore agree to this changing, or suf-
  fer your daughters to endure hard chance.
MELIBEUS: How say you, Tityrus? Shall we refer it to Venus?
TITYRUS: I am content, because she is a goddess.
VENUS: Neptune, you will not dislike it?   175
NEPTUNE: Not I.

---

[8] **Iphis and Ianthes:** in Book X of Ovid's *Metamorphoses* (8 c.e.), Venus turns the female Iphis
into a male so she can marry Ianthe.   [9] **fond:** foolish.

VENUS: Nor you, Diana?
DIANA: Not I.
VENUS: Cupid shall not?
CUPID: I will not.   180
VENUS: Then let us depart. Neither of them shall know whose lot it shall
          be till they come to the church door. One shall be. Doth it suffice?
PHILLIDA: And satisfy us both, doth it not, Gallatea?
GALLATEA: Yes, Phillida.

➜ CONSTANTIA FOWLER

Letter to Herbert Aston   *1636*

John Lyly's *Gallatea* plays with the possibility of love between women, a love
that, in order to be consecrated by marriage, required that one of the two be
transformed into a man. Historically, we have evidence that love between
women existed in the early modern period, though it was usually written about
in terms of friendship. There are traces of many intense friendships between
women in the period, sometimes between women who were married and whose
love for their own sex was compatible with their duties within marriage. At least
one poet, Katherine Phillips, wrote love poems to a fictional beloved, Lucrasia,
that employ all the tropes of passionate love made popular by poets such as John
Donne. It is never clear, of course, when platonic friendship merges into something more explicitly erotic, and it is perhaps a mistake to try to make such distinctions perfectly clear. Included below, however, is part of a letter written in
1636 by Constantia Fowler (d. 1664), married to Walter Fowler, to her brother,
Herbert Aston. The letter concerns her new friend Katherine Thimelby, who
later was to become her brother's wife. The lengthy letter urges her brother to
marry Katherine because Constantia's own happiness depends on continued
intimacy with her brother's fiancée. What does the language of this letter suggest about Constantia's feelings for Katherine? What kind of rhetoric does she
employ in describing her relationship to her, and how might it throw light on
the many varieties of erotic attraction coursing through *As You Like It*? How
does it compare with the bond "dearer than the natural bond of sisters" between
Rosalind and Celia (1.2.219), expressed in Celia's declaration that "thou and I
am one" (1.3.86)?

Constantia Fowler, *Tixall Letters, or the Correspondence of the Aston Family and Their Friends,
During the Seventeenth Century*, 2 vols., ed. Arthur Clifford (London: Longman, Hurst, Rees,
Orme and Brown, 1815), 1:100.

[Constantia Fowler tells her brother she loves Katherine Thimelby, and urges him to marry her.]

For I believe I am blest with the most perfectest and constant lover as ever woman was blest with. Oh, if you would know the story of our affection, you must come hither and read volumes of it, afore you can be able to understand half the dearness of our love. I keep them apurpose for your sight, and no creature breathing but myself ever saw them or knows of them else. You will say, I am certain, when you puruse them that there was never any more passionate affectionate lovers than she and I, and that you never knew two creatures more truly and deadly in love with one another than we are. . . . For after I had made known to her by letters how infinitely I honoured her, and how I had done so since I first saw her here, she writ me the sweetest answers, that from that very hour I confess I have been most deadly in love with her as ever lover was. . . .

. . . Do what you can to compass that happiness for yourself which I so thirst after, that my dearest friend and you being united in one, your hearts may likewise become one, and so I may keep them with more ease in my breast than now I can, they being divided.

CHAPTER 3

Calling Fools into a Circle

Fools and Folly: Types and Paradoxes

Arden is overrun by fools, although only Touchstone wears the traditional garb. When Jaques claims he is "ambitious for a motley coat" and makes up nonsense "to call fools into a circle" (2.7.43, 2.5.51) he names an impulse basic to the play. Folly encircles and defines *As You Like It*, with its madcap princesses, zany jesters, fumbling lovers, inept priests, and witless goat-girls, not to mention pretentious satirists who want to be fools. Jaques's impulse extends beyond the play into the real world, in which queens, kings, and dukes did call fools to their sides for amusement, and in which audiences crowded around stages to see actors play the fool. In Shakespeare's theater, fools like Touchstone were played by stage clowns—comic actors who specialized in laugh-getting and whose skills often made them the most powerful members of their companies. To an unusual degree, *As You Like It* depends on witplay and clowning by the entire ensemble, but especially by the boy actor who (in Shakespeare's time) played Rosalind, a girl who pretends to be a boy who plays at being a girl. The role is difficult in its length as well as its gender complexity: Rosalind is the longest female part in Shakespeare and one of the most challenging roles in the canon.

The most familiar kind of fool is still the medieval jester with his cap and bells. In wealthy households, a "liveried fool" was a special servant who provided pleasure-seekers with laughter and an escape from the ordinary, and he or she generally wore distinctive patched or checked costumes called motley. Some fools did not wear motley but a rich suit of clothes. Onstage, Touchstone can be played either way—as a liveried servant who might pass for a gentleman or as a jester in motley. Shakespeare pairs Touchstone with his mistress Celia and her cousin Rosalind, and they steal away from the palace in disguise, forming a comic trio that would have struck audiences as excitingly wayward and prone to folly. Rosalind conceives the plan to take him along; as she tells Jaques, "I had rather have a fool to make me merry than experience to make me sad" (4.1.19–20). Both male and female aristocrats kept fools and like monarchs in France, Italy, and Spain, Elizabeth I had both fools and witty jesters and natural fools in her household, and might call one to her side to enjoy a temporary lessening of constraint and formality.

There were as many kinds of professed fools as there are comedians today, but the English divided all fools into two major groups according to their sanity or lack of it. Those with little or no control over their minds and actions were called "natural fools" and all others were called "witty" or "artificial" fools. *Natural* fools were insane or imbecilic and did not act the fool deliberately. Today they would be called people with mental disabilities. Naturals depended utterly on masters and keepers for their care, though they were often treated cruelly. *Artificial* fools, in contrast, lived by their wits and might exercise some degree of choice and control over their fates. They amused with a variety of tricks and jests, verbal and physical. Some fools were highly verbal and cerebral, and others were obscene and violent.

Alternately applauded and mocked, despised and protected, fools tended to foster paradox and contradiction. For example, Jaques says he envies Touchstone. What is contradictory or ironic about that claim? Is Touchstone a witty fool or a natural, and what is your evidence? Who are the naturals in the play and how do they fare alongside the witty fools?

Fool and *clown* are related concepts, yet each has different connotations and each word has changed in meaning from the sixteenth century. The term *fool* can signify a fictional figure or a living person. The English stage clown, on the other hand, was a professional actor who specialized in comic roles in plays. He little resembled the circus clown of today. To make the situation more confusing, the word *clown* was applied loosely to country folk and peasants. In the mouths of city folk the word was an insult, like "yokel" or "oaf," implying coarseness and ignorance. When Touchstone hails the rustic Corin rudely ("Holla: you, clown!") Rosalind berates him: "Peace, fool, he's not thy kinsman" (2.4.56–57). Rosalind plays on the fact that the actor who played Touchstone actually *was* a stage clown, either Will Kemp, famous for dancing jigs, singing, and extemporizing, or Kemp's successor Robert Armin (Figure 16), known for his small size, his singing, and his ability to play the natural or the witty fool. Armin also wrote plays and jest books about fools, including *A Nest of Ninnies* (p. 291).

In this play Shakespeare casts a wide net for fools. Those who point out other's flaws are as vulnerable to folly as the witless and the innocent. Since *folly* is an umbrella concept that is highly relative, the word provides a handy index of the worldview and mind-set of the person using it. Seemingly sane actions such as falling in love, practicing one's faith, or traveling abroad might be put down as folly, depending on the outlook of the speaker. The word was variously applied to madness, rage, love, lust, violence, obsession, childishness, gullibility, rudeness, and even to crimes such as heresy. Satirists who railed at folly drew fire for their own excesses. Jaques seems wise in his famous "Ages of Man" speech, calling men and women mere players and prone to acting foolish at any age, but the metaphor of the theater-as-world was a well-worn commonplace not original to Shakespeare (in Miguel de Cervantes's *Don Quixote* [1605], Sancho Panza calls it a cliché he has heard too many times). Jaques is given to striking attitudes, weeping over a dying deer, and crowing with laughter over a fool's jokes. Even the rightful head of state, the exiled Duke Senior, is likened to Robin Hood. Given the expansiveness of the term, does anyone in the play escape being a fool at least once? When is their folly evil, and when is it deliberately mischievous and playful, as opposed to merely ignorant? When are the most serious also foolish? What characters other than Jaques point out folly in others, and what norms do they seek to enforce? Is their satire effective? Is their own folly equal to or greater than the folly they denounce?

Folly had serious uses in the moralizing literature of the day. Examples of folly drove home many a lesson, while offering a bit of humor to enliven a sermon. Priests and teachers alike used the negative example of the fool to warn young and old, the illiterate and the learned, men and women, against following bad habits, and to point the way to a godly and moderate life. Emblem books illustrated old adages, such as "Accident is the master of fools," and their symbols and moralizing were recycled in plays such as *As You Like It*. Defenders of theater claimed that comedies full of fools and knaves taught playgoers to avoid the folly on display. Churchgoers heard stories of the wise man and the fool from the Bible, especially in the Psalms, Proverbs, and Ecclesiastes. Churchgoing was required by law, and many people learned entire sections of the Bible by heart from hearing them read

THE
Hiſtory of the two Maids of More-clacke,

VVith the life and ſimple maner of IOHN
in the Hoſpitall.

Played by the Children of the Kings
Maieſties Reuels.

VVritten by ROBERT ARMIN, ſeruant to the Kings
moſt excellent Maieſtie.

LONDON,
Printed by *N.O.* for *Thomas Archer*, and is to be ſold at his
ſhop in Popes-head Pallace, 1 6 o 9.

FIGURE 16 *Actor-author Robert Armin playing a natural fool dressed in childish long coats, from Robert Armin,* The History of the Two Maids of More-clacke with the Life and Simple Manner of John in the Hospital *(1609).*

aloud so often. Most people could quote most of the well-known sayings, such as *answer a fool according to his folly*. Mortal sins such as atheism were also laid at the feet of folly: *The fool hath said in his heart, There is no God*.[1] Religious opponents found the figure of the fool useful in the struggle to claim the position of the wise and correct interpreters of scripture or doctrine. Popular satire and polemic (highly charged writings attacking an opponent) detected folly in their rivals, and vied with them to show that their enemies were foolish, ignorant, and ridiculous. Folly's opposites are wit and wisdom, but those two qualities are not always paired in the same person. It's fairly easy to point out the clowns, fools, and wits in *As You Like It*, but who are the truly wise? Does anyone give good counsel about what wise and virtuous behavior would be?

Certainly wit is not distributed evenly in Arden, where two young women, Rosalind and Celia, dominate the action and much of the comedy. The presence of abundant wit in women was a challenge to the prevailing theory governing gender and intellect in the period. The term *wit* extended to one's strength of mind, language skills, reason, and capacity to make wise choices. Wit was a wedge that could separate health and sanity from madness, social power from weakness, and intelligence from idiocy. Supposedly, it also divided male from female, since women were supposed to be born with a weaker mental capacity than men. Today the word has dwindled in meaning to something like cleverness. To be witty is a compliment that distinguishes more verbal or clever humor from cruder forms, and we use it when we consider whether someone or something is amusing, and in what way. Yet even today we speak of having our wits about us or losing our wits, showing that our own definition still retains a trace of the more expansive meaning of the distant past, which extended it to the realms of medicine and psychology.

The now-outmoded humoral model, derived from the teaching of the ancient Greek physician Galen, held that every person's temperament and intellect, and even gender identity, was governed by four humors: black bile, yellow bile, blood, and phlegm. Medical treatises explained that melancholy temperaments were produced by a predominance of black bile; volatile and choleric (easily angered) ones by yellow bile, also called choler; sanguine or sunny ones by blood; and slow, stolid, phlegmatic ones by phlegm. While science retired this system long ago, these terms are still used today to describe people's moods and personalities. In Shakespeare's time, males were supposedly dominated by the "hot" humors of blood and choler, enhancing wit and intelligence, and females by the "cold" humors of black bile and phlegm, limiting the same qualities. Women's humoral imbalance,

[1] Proverbs 26:5; Psalms 14:1.

aggravated by their menstrual cycles and so-called "wandering" wombs, supposedly made them volatile, unstable, talkative, and prone to folly and lust—"reason being but weak in them, and their judgment feeble, and minds not well order'd."[2] This medical discourse went hand in hand with antifeminist doctrine: religion, law, and philosophy held that women should not wield political power and authority because they were inferior spiritually, physically, and intellectually to men. Wooing, sex, and marriage were necessary evils, in the views of some male writers who warned men to avoid falling in love as complete folly, because it placed fate and honor in female hands. In the long-standing "controversy over women" or *querelle des femmes*, attacks on women were countered by defenses, but many of the same arguments were recycled endlessly.

More than one character in the play calls women fickle, untrustworthy, and treacherous, in conversations that seem to be quite light-hearted. What males deploy this "humorous" misogyny and to what effect? Why does Rosalind/Ganymede herself promote this way of thinking, as when she says all men are destined to be cuckolds (4.1.43–44)? Rosalind draws fire from Celia for abusing women in her "love prate" (4.1.155), and even Touchstone dares to say she should be "carted" or publically punished (3.2.91). What norms has she violated in their eyes, and how does she react to their chiding? When do the other women of the play (Celia, Phoebe, Audrey) act in ways that are stereotypically, negatively female in early modern eyes? Are these attitudes criticized, or, perhaps, modified by irony?

Under the prevailing assumptions about gender in the period, bold, outspoken women like Rosalind and Celia might be criticized as exceptional, insubordinate, and mannish, while slower-witted women were held up as proof that the female was "the weaker sex." But the widely held belief by many readers today that women in Shakespeare's time were silent and powerless victims of monolithic patriarchy is a simplistic projection from our own time. Early modern men and women would not have thought in those terms. Most women's lives were restricted in many ways and oppression was real: ordinary women had no official voice in politics and most were denied the advanced schooling provided to boys and young men, so they were far less literate as a group. Women and girls could be beaten legally by fathers and husbands, within certain limits, and many had harsh lives dominated by work, poverty, and frequent childbearing. No Englishwomen acted on the professional stage, and few were writers or artists, so male actors and writers created images of women with varying degrees of distortion and bias.

---

[2] Levinus Lemnius (1658), qtd. in Russ McDonald, *The Bedford Companion to Shakespeare*, 2nd ed. (New York: Palgrave, 2001), 255.

But the scope of female autonomy was far wider than these facts suggest. People's actual experiences in the home and marketplace constantly tested the ideology of women's inferiority and necessary subjection. No one could deny that a learned queen sat on the throne and ruled England and her courtiers, or that noblewomen governed large estates, while less wealthy widows ran businesses and kept male apprentices, and women of all sorts worked, managed finances and property, litigated, and made wills. Many women had some leisure and enough cash to spend on playgoing and on chapbooks and ballads; a few even wrote books, poems, and songs themselves. In short, women could and did hone their wits and exercise a measure of control over their lives and those of others; how much depended on many factors, including status, family, education, work, religion, and wealth. With Elizabeth as queen and the presence of witty and resourceful women in daily life, people were faced with a conflict between image and reality that produced ruptures and ripples in gender norms. These contradictions affected the way writers and actors wrote and staged comedy and conceived of folly, reason, and wit.

Consider how gender and class affect the horizons of social power in *As You Like It,* and in particular how social rank operates to mute the so-called "natural superiority" of men. How is male and female wit distributed—who has most and least, and what governs these distinctions? Is lack of wit more risky for women than for men, and why or why not? Is it possible to be both witty and foolish at the same time, and what characters qualify?

Early modern thinkers often used the classical emblem of the horse and rider to signify the relationship of desire to reason. Celia alludes to this trope when she says, "all's brave that youth mounts and folly guides" (3.4.35–36). In this case, bravery does not mean courage, but rather, willful bravado. A wise rider controls and directs his or her will and desires, but a weak one will be carried hither and yon directly into the realm of folly, or thrown off entirely. Youth and love were both thought to weaken reason and spur the erotic will, even to the point of disease and madness. By taking us into the world of pastoral leisure, where desires and thoughts can be pursued out of the reach of sober reason, stern parents, or frowning officials, *As You Like It* shows us what amusing and even productive follies result if people loosen the harsh bridle of self-control. Self-control was the first principle of manners, civility, and knowing one's place in a highly hierarchical universe, as will be explored in Chapter 4.

Chapter 3, however, will focus on the many faces and masks of folly, and show why folly was such an indispensable part of both pastoral pleasure and the genre of comedy. Folly entices viewers into the theater, provides the prime materials for comedy, and lures all kinds of lovers to its domain. But as the sections on biblical interpretation show, the wide cultural conversation about fools and folly did far more in the period. Sometimes stories about folly warned readers and listeners about the dangerous pleasures of untrammeled, self-centered will (especially female will); and at others they generated paradoxes useful for teaching about Christian charity and faith, and how these contradict common sense. Finally, folly in its traditional holiday guises was a political bone of contention, as many godly types tried to attack the ritual forms of holiday that traded on various forms of merry-making, from parades of giants and tales of Robin Hood to Maypoles and morris dances. License to speak and satirize could also bring down harsh punishment, and such speech was damned as malicious folly. Folly was never wholly carefree, yet it remained a vital force that could not be fully controlled—a horse that might be ridden, but never wholly tamed.

A GALLERY OF FOOLS, CLOWNS, AND WITS

→ SEBASTIAN BRANT

From Stultifera Navis . . . The Ship of Fools   *1570*

Translated by Alexander Barclay

The Ship of Fools, first published in German in 1494, attacked folly with such comic flair that it was closer to an illustrated jest book than a moral tract. Crammed with images of fools from every walk of life, the book offers long verses castigating terrible vices and minor peccadilloes, from ingratitude, neglectful parenting, violence against kin, and hypocrisy, to wanderlust and thinking too much—a list reminiscent of the foibles in *As You Like It*. As in the old saw, fools are everywhere. In one famous woodcut, sots board ships eager to sail to Fool-land, a fabulous place where folly reigns supreme and every sort of absurdity is practiced. Singing songs of jubilation, dozens of fools crowd on board; some lose their footing and fall in the sea (Figure 17). The urge to classify and label this infinitude derives in part from medieval "estates satire," which methodically targeted the three estates (nobles, clergy, and commoners). Brant's blend of crude jest and earnest moralizing is also part of a long-lived sermon tradition in which priests used jokes and funny proverbs to explain religious doctrine to a largely illiterate audience.

Brant wrote the book in German, but it was quickly translated and read in other countries. In his translation of the Latin version of Brant's work, Alexander Barclay relocates the fools' voyage off the coast of England and calls himself

Sebastian Brant, *Stultifera Navis. . . . The Ship of Fools*, trans. Alexander Barclay (London, 1570), iii–vi, ix–x; STC 3546.

FIGURE 17 *A clueless but joyous crew sets sail for the land of folly from Sebastian Brant,* The Shyppe of Fooles *(1517), translated by Henry Watson.*

captain of the "fool-ship," warning away rivals for that title. Who would you say acts as captain of the fools in *As You Like It*? Love folly obviously pervades the play; what other types of folly named by Barclay resemble those of Shakespeare? Does the play ever align qualities of a more positive cast, such as book knowledge, love of travel, and ambition, with folly? Do the temporary residents of Arden leave any wiser, and if so, what works this change? If the play suggests any guidelines for avoiding folly, what are they? Who articulates or provides models for them?

From *The Ship of Fools*

THE CLAMOUR[1] TO THE FOOLS.

To Ship, gallants! The sea is at the full.
The wind calls us, our sails are displayed.
Where may we best put to shore? At Lynn or at Hull?
To us may no haven in England be denied.
Why do we tarry? The anchors are upweighed.   5
If any cord or cable hinder us, let it go.
Let the end slip overboard, or else cut it asunder.

Turn your eyes, look over to the shore.
There is a great number that would fain be aboard.
They get no room, our Ship can hold no more   10
. . . .
God guide us from rocks, quicksand, tempest, and ford,
If any man of war, weather, or wind appear
Myself shall try the wind and keep the steer.

But I pray you readers, do not disdain me,   15
Though Barclay has presumed out of audacity
To rule this Ship as chief master and Captain.
Though some think themselves much worthier than he.
It were great marvel, in truth, since he has been
A scholar so long: and that in diverse schools;   20
But he might well be Captain of a Ship of Fools
. . . .
[I]f I had a hundred tongues, and wit to feel
All things natural and supernatural,

---

[1] **clamour:** the cry of "all-aboard!"

A thousand mouths, and a voice as hard as steel,   30
And seen all the seven sciences liberal,[2]
Yet could I never touch the vices all,
And sin of the world, nor their branches comprehend,
Not though I lived unto the world's end.

But if these vices which mankind doth encumber   35
Were clean expelled, and virtue [set] in their place,
I could not have gathered of fools so great a number
Whose folly chases from them God's grace.
But every man that knows him in that case
To this rude Book let him gladly attend.   40
And learn the way his lewdness to amend.

FROM THE PROEME

All is disordered; virtue hath no reward.
Alas, compassion and mercy both are slain.
Alas, the stony hearts of people are so hard
That nought can constrain their follies to refrain
But still they proceed, and each other maintain.[3]   5
So wander these fools, increasing without number.
That all the world they utterly encumber.[4]

Blasphemers of Christ, hostlers and taverners,[5]
Crackers[6] and boasters, with courtiers adventurous,[7]
Bawds[8] and pollers[9] with common extortioners   10
Are taken[10] nowadays in the world most glorious.
But the gifts of grace and always gracious
We have excluded. Thus live we carnally:
Utterly subdued to all lewdness[11] and Folly.

Thus is of Fools a sort almost innumerable.   15
Defiling the world with sin and villainy,
Some thinking themselves most wise and commendable,
Though all their days they live unthriftily.

[2] **seven sciences liberal:** also called the liberal arts, the seven liberal sciences are grammar, rhetoric, dialectic, arithmetic, geometry, astronomy, and music.   [3] **maintain:** encourage.   [4] **encumber:** crowd and weigh down.   [5] **hostlers and taverners:** grooms and drunkards.   [6] **Crackers:** braggarts.   [7] **courtiers adventurous:** roistering gallants.   [8] **Bawds:** procuresses or whores.   [9] **pollers:** robbers.   [10] **Are taken:** are judged.   [11] **lewdness:** sinfulness.

No goodness they perceive, nor to no good apply.
But if he have a great womb[12] and his coffers full   20
Than is none held wiser between London and Hull.[13]

But to assemble these fools in one band
And their demerits worthily to note
Fain shall I ships of every manner land.
None shall be left: bark, galley, ship, nor boat.[14]   25
One vessel cannot bring them all afloat
For if all these fools were brought into one barge
The boat should sink, so sore should be the charge.[15]

The sails are hawsed,[16] a pleasant cool doth blow.
The fools assembleth as fast as they may drive.   30
Some swimmeth after, others as thick doth row
In their small boats, as bees about a hive.
The number is great, and each one doth strive
For to be chief as purser[17] and captain,
Quartermaster,[18] lodesman,[19] or else boatswain.[20]   35
. . . .
We are full laden and yet forsooth I think
A thousand are behind, whom we may not receive
For if we do, our navy clean[21] shall sink!   45
He oft all loses who covets all to have.
From London rocks almighty God us save,
For if we there anchor, other boat or barge
There be so many that they us will overcharge.[22]

Ye London gallants, arear,[23] you shall not enter!   50
We keep the stream, and touch not the shore
In city nor in court we dare not well adventure[24]
Lest, perchance, we should displeasure have therefore.
But if ye will needs, some shall have an oar,
And all the remnant shall stand afar at large   55
And read their faults painted about our barge.

---

[12]**great womb:** a glutton's big belly. [13]**Hull:** city in Northern England. [14]**bark . . . boat:** various vessels, from rowboats to ships. [15]**sore . . . charge:** the cargo would be so heavy. [16]**hawsed:** hoisted. [17]**purser:** officer in charge of provisions. [18]**Quartermaster:** officer who runs ship's day-to-day operations. [19]**lodesman:** navigator. [20]**boatswain:** in charge of rigging, sails, and masts. [21]**clean:** here, certainly. [22]**overcharge:** weigh us down too much. [23]**arear:** stay back. [24]**adventure:** go.

STAGE CLOWNING AND WITPLAY

Comedy does not thrive on fools alone. Witty playwrights and satirists contributed their own more cerebral jests to the formulas of romance and the "jigging veins of rhyming mother-wits," as Christopher Marlowe called stage clowns such as Richard Tarlton and Will Kemp. Marlowe's scorn cleared the way for his new style of tragedy, but he could not unseat the stage clown as the acknowledged master of laugh-getting and extemporal witplay in any genre in which he appeared. The presence of the professional clown in a play did not preclude other characters from being witty and recruiting admiring laughter, of course. Touchstone is the official clown in *As You Like It*, but he is not the only laugh-getter. Rosalind, Jaques, Celia, and Phoebe are also very funny, and their comic performances depend on a blend of foolery and wit unleashed by the unusual liberty of Arden.

Early modern stage clowning depended on give and take with other characters onstage and with the audience, sometimes at the same time. Characters who pride themselves on their wit show the ability to trade quips with a range of challengers. In breeches or out, Rosalind is full of bold retorts and quick answers, and at times she resembles Touchstone in her style of joking. When she amuses Orlando by talking about the relative speed of time (3.2.260–78), she hits on the same topic that Jaques hears Touchstone musing on (2.7.20–28). How does her handling of topics resemble Touchstone's oration on dueling near the end of the play (5.4)? Does her wooing of Orlando resemble in any way the encounters of Touchstone and Audrey? Locate the scenes in which Touchstone and Rosalind interact. Is there a subtle competition going on for the audience's laughter? Who emerges on top at any given moment?

Rosalind also forms a comic duo with her best friend Celia, who is also clever and quick at the tennis game of banter. Note how they "devise sports" together (1.2.18) and how Celia teases Rosalind before she reveals she has seen Orlando (3.2.143–87). Rosalind breeds laughter because she knows how to sting with a satiric mock (as she does with Phoebe in act 3, scene 5) and how to slip nimbly from topic to topic with comic flair (as she does in joking with Orlando about snails, horns, playacting, kissing, and dying for love, all in act 4, scene 1). She also knows how and when to aim her ironies and laugh lines at the audience (Orlando: "But will my Rosalind do so?" Rosalind: "By my life, she will do as I do" 4.1.119–20). She shows wit in extremity when her passion breaks through her boyish mask ("Alas the day, what shall I do with my doublet and hose?" (3.2.188) and inventiveness when she develops a single topic (as when she lectures Orlando on the standard signs of being in love in 3.2.309–15). What are other examples of comic skill and wit on the part of characters other than Touchstone?

To possess wit was a form of social power, as manuals on rhetoric and manners declared. To be witty in daily life, one had to have a gift for words and a sharply honed sense of timing and occasion, seizing the moment to speak just as an actor would onstage, appealing to an audience. Wit is a social performance sparked by the presence of auditors and a fleeting moment. "Readiness is all," says Hamlet (5.7.196), and this is especially true of wit. The best wits were always ready to grab an opportunity that presented itself. Works as refined as Baldassare Castiglione's *The Courtier* and as popular as the jest book *Tales and Quick Answers* lavished praise on those who could instantly reply to an insult with a comic comeback, or who could amuse others with a well-delivered funny tale.

This was not a game for the fainthearted, as suggested by this lampoon of a "mere empty wit" who tries too hard:

> He speaks best on the present apprehension, for meditation stupefies him, and the more he is in travail, the less he brings forth. His things come off then, as in a nauseating stomach, where there is nothing to cast up strains, and convulsions, and some astonishing bombast which men only, till they understand, are scared with. A verse or some such work he may sometimes get up to, but seldom above the stature of an epigram, and that with some relief out of Martial,[1] which is the ordinary companion of his pocket, and he reads him as he were inspired. . . . [A]ll their words go for jests, and all their jests for nothing. They are reasonable in the fancy of some ridiculous thing, and reasonable good in the expression. Nothing stops a jest when it's coming, neither friends, nor danger, but it must howsoever, though their blood come out after, and then they emphatically rail, and are emphatically beaten.[2]

Modern comedians say that to fail before an audience is to die. All comedians live with the risk of failing, because no one can ensure the success of any given joke or wield complete power over laughter. Tarlton and Kemp were especially acclaimed for their extemporal jests, but the outcome of a wit battle was never predictable: even a rank amateur or a socially less powerful figure (a woman, a child) could sometimes best the adult professional, gaining a victory that even the greatest clown had to accept with grace. In some of the jokes from *Tarlton's Jests* shown below, the famous actor spars with women several times, and he does not always emerge on top.

[1] **Martial:** Roman satirist and poet. [2] John Earle, *Microcosmography* (London, 1628), sig C2v; STC 7441.

➔ RICHARD TARLTON

From Tarlton's Jests
1638

Just before Shakespeare began his career, the most famous and beloved stage clown in England was Richard Tarlton (d. 1588). Born in the country, he created the persona of the wisecracking country clown, forging a tie to the thousands of people who had just arrived in the city themselves. In his rustic motley and buttoned cap, he was able to rouse peals of laughter just by sticking his droll face through a stage curtain. One of the first major stars of the English stage, Tarlton became a household name, and his face and form were so instantly recognizable that tradespeople used his image on signs. Tarlton juggled two demanding careers: he was called the queen's jester and often performed for her, though he did not live permanently at court; and he was a full-blown stage star with enough clout to be able to improvise far more often than other actors could or would dare to. He was also an accomplished and pugnacious swordsman. Spectators flocked to theaters to see Tarlton no matter what play he was in, and they mourned his death in 1588. He never appeared in a play by Shakespeare but he deeply influenced all those in the business of getting laughs and creating comic characters, from playwrights such as Shakespeare and Ben Jonson to clowns such as Will Kemp and Robert Armin.

Tarlton excelled at bold banter with his fans, in rapid-fire exchanges that could bring down the house. In the first excerpt below, Elizabeth herself enters the fray by joking with him. The exchange is included in a famous jest book called *Tarlton's Jests*. Although the book was published long after the clown's death, the publisher offered readers a compilation purporting to be his best bits. Most of the jokes (like many in *As You Like It*) are contests in which each "player" strives to show whose tongue is sharper, making the other the butt of laughter. Elizabeth tries to annoy him by refusing his demand for more drink. Turning the tables, Tarlton puts her down as a cheating alewife whose ale is weak. Is it likely he was punished for this audacity? What does Elizabeth get out of this kind of jesting? Does Touchstone take similar risks in *As You Like It*?

Improvisation was the heart of Tarlton's technique, and a contemporary applauded his "wondrous plentiful pleasant extemporal wit."[1] Tarlton sometimes made up rhymes and songs on the spot, generally to confound and mock hecklers. In "Tarlton's jest of a gridiron," a roaring boy calls out "it is a thing unfit / To see a gridiron turn the spit." Tarlton's comeback is quick: "Me thinks it is a thing unfit, / To see an ass have any wit," which causes the "theme-giver" to exit with his tail between his legs.[2] (When Touchstone rattles off bawdy couplets in 3.2.79–97 that parody Orlando's verses, he is showing off in the man-

---

[1] From an insert in Stow's *Annals*, qtd in *English Professional Theatre 1530–1660*, ed. Glynne Wickham, Hebert Berry, and William Ingram (Cambridge: Cambridge UP, 2000), 208.
[2] *Tarlton's Jests* (1613), C3v–C4v.

Richard Tarlton, *Tarlton's Jests* (London, 1638), sigs. A2, A3, C4, Ev–E2, E3r–v; STC 23684.

ner of Tarlton.) Once in a while, however, a clown's challenger got the last word. In the following jests, Tarlton trades barbs and quips with gentlewomen, the hostess at an inn, and a country wench. Why does the jest book include moments when Tarlton is put down, not just when he comes out on top?

Consider the language and subject matter of these jests. How do these back-and-forth jests differ from each other, depending on the woman's social status? What moments show "extemporal" or improvisatory skill, and by whom? What scenes in *As You Like It* show moments in which a character instantly invents a trick or a story, or has to think fast to improvise a comeback or a cover-up? How does Touchstone handle comic encounters with women? How does Tarlton's extemporal wit compare with Touchstone's? How does it compare with Rosalind's?

*H*ow Tarlton played the drunkard before the Queen.

The queen being discontented, which Tarlton perceiving, took upon him to delight her with some quaint jest. Whereupon he counterfeited[1] a drunkard and called for beer, which was brought immediately. Her Majesty, noting his humor, commanded that he should have no more, "For," quoth she, "he will play the beast, and so shame himself." "Fear you not," quoth Tarlton, "for your beer is small[2] enough." Whereat her Majesty laughed heartily, and commanded that he should have enough.

How a Maid drove Tarlton to a Non-Plus.[3]

Tarlton meeting with a wily country wench, who gave him quip for quip: "Sweetheart," says he, "I would my flesh were in thine." "So would I, sir," says she: "I would your nose were in my I-know-where."[4] Tarlton, angered at this, said no more, but goes forward.

How Tarlton and his Hostess of Waltham met.

Tarlton, riding with diverse citizens his friends to make merry at Waltham, by the way he met with his hostess riding toward London, whom he (told of his old acquaintance) saluted. She demands whither they went? Tarlton told her, to make merry at Waltham. "Sir," says she, "then let me request your company at my house at the Christopher,[5] and (for old familiarity) spend your money there." "Not unless you go back," says Tarlton, "we will else go to the Hound."[6] But she, loath to lose her customer, sent to London by her man,[7] and goes back with them, who by the way had much mirth, for she

---

[1] counterfeited: pretended to be, impersonated. [2] small: weak and watery. [3] Non-Plus: a state of speechlessness. [4] I-know-where: euphemism, implying "my ass." [5] the Christopher: an inn. [6] the Hound: another inn. [7] her man: her servant, i.e., she sent him to do her business in London.

was an exceeding merry honest woman, yet would take any thing;[8] which Tarlton hearing, as wise[9] as he was (thinking her of his mind) he was deceived. . . . He asked her if the biggest bed in the house were able to hold two of their bigness (meaning himself and her). "Yes," says she, "and tumble up and down at pleasure." "Yea, one upon another?" says Tarlton. "And under too," says she. Well, to have their custom, she agreed to everything, like a subtle hostess,[10] and it fell so out that Tarlton, having her in a room at her house, asked her which of those two beds were big enough for them two. "This," said she, "therefore go to bed, sweetheart. I'll come to thee."

"Mass!"[11] says Tarlton, "Were my boots off, I would indeed." "I'll help you, sir," says she, "if you please." "Yea," thought Tarlton, "is the wind in that door?"[12] [Saying to her,] "Come on then." And she very diligently begins to pull, until one boot was half off. "Now," says she, "this being hard to do, let me try my cunning on the other, and so get both off." But having both half off his legs, she left him alone in the shoemaker's sticks,[13] and got her to London. Here Tarlton was three hours, and had no help. But being eased of his pain, he made this rhyme . . . singing it all the way to London:

> Women are wanton, and hold it no sin,
> By tricks and devices to pull a man in.

How Tarlton answered a wanton gentlewoman.
A gentlewoman, merrily disported, being crossed[14] by Tarlton, and half angry, said, "Sirrah, a little thing would make me requite you with a cuff."[15] "With a cuff, Lady?" says Tarlton. "So would you spell my sorrow forward: but spell my sorrow backward,[16] then cuff me and spare not." When the gentlemen by considered of the word, they laughing, made at the simple-meaning gentlewoman blush for shame.

Tarlton's Jest of a Horse and a Man.
In the city of Norwich, Tarlton was on a time invited to a hunting. Here, there was a godly gentlewoman who, bravely mounted on a black horse, rode exceeding well, to the wonder of all the beholders, and neither hedge nor ditch stood in her way, but Pegasus her horse (for so we may term him for swiftness) flew over all, and she sat him well.[17] When every one returns

---

[8] **would take any thing:** although she was honest, she enjoyed bawdy talk and jesting.   [9] **wise:** clever.   [10] **custom . . . hostess:** to get their business she agreed, like the shrewd hostess she was.   [11] **Mass!:** a mild oath, like "Great God!"   [12] **is the wind in that door?:** aha, is that what she's up to?   [13] **shoemaker's sticks:** long shoehorns that required help to use.   [14] **crossed:** irritated.   [15] **cuff:** strike or blow.   [16] **backward:** cuff (spoken backward) is an obscene word.   [17] **sat him well:** rode him well.

home, some at dinner commended his hound, others his own hawk, and she above all, her horse. And said she: "I love no living creature so well (at this instant) than my gallant horse."

"Yes, lady, a man better," says Tarlton.

"Indeed no," said she, "not now. For since my late husband died, I hate them most, unless you can give me medicines to make me love them." Tarlton made this jest instantly:

> Why, a Horse mingeth whey, Madam, a Man mingeth amber[18]
> A Horse is for your way, Madam, but a man for your chamber.

"God have mercy, Tarlton!" said the men. Which, the gentlewoman noting, seeing they took exception at her words, to make all well, answered thus:

> That a Horse is my chief opinion[19] now, I deny not,
> And when a man doth me more good in my chamber,
> Him I defy not.

"But till then give me leave to love something," [said she]. "Then something will please you," said Tarlton, "I am glad of that, therefore I pray God lend you a good thing,[20] or none at all."

[18] *A horse mingeth . . . amber*: a horse pisses cloudy urine, a man pisses yellow.   [19] *chief opinion*: favorite thing.   [20] **thing**: bawdy quibble for penis.

→ ROBERT ARMIN

From A Nest of Ninnies
1608

The clown Robert Armin (1563–1615) proudly claimed to inherit the mantle of Richard Tarlton, who reportedly chose him to be his successor after he heard him improvise some jests. Armin (who may have played Touchstone) was known for being short, for singing well, and for being able to impersonate both the childlike natural fool and the urbanely witty artificial fool. Far more literary than most clowns, he was a writer and playwright who became an authority on jesters and fools, writing jest books that chronicled the lives and feats of famous fools he had actually met or heard about who lived at court or in the great houses of England.

A Nest of Ninnies begins and ends with a mocking skirmish between two witty fools, Lady World and Sotto, a cynical satirist who claims to be a philosopher-magus. Each tries to prove the other is the greater fool. Armin's World is the

---

Robert Armin, *A Nest of Ninnies* (London, 1608); STC 772.7, A3r–v, E2–E4, G4r–v.

FIGURE 18 *Lady World ringed by clownish vices in* De dans om de wereld (The Dance Around the World), *after Pieter Baltens (c. 1600).*

goddess of worldly pleasures, the personification of folly, and a close relative of emblems such as Vanity, Pride, and Luxury (Figure 18). Armin paints her as a woman-about-town who is seeking distractions to cure her hangover. At the beginning of the book she visits Sotto to tease him and to hear him rail at her as is his habit. (The cynical Jaques resembles him when he invites Orlando to "rail against our mistress the world" [3.2.236–37].)

Sotto tries to shame Lady World by showing her all her "children," a series of natural fools, in a magic glass. One of them is a natural named Jack Miller. Armin's portrait involves a group of traveling players, a cross-dressed boy player (nicknamed Gentlewoman Boy), and Jack, who is mistreated and mocked for his singed face and severe stutter. Who is the biggest fool in the group, and what leads you to this opinion? How do you define folly in this instance? What kind of laughter does the natural fool provoke? Does the mocking relationship between World and Sotto resemble that of Rosalind and Jaques in act 4, scene 1 of *As You Like It*? What traits distinguish Touchstone from Jack Miller? Does Rosalind share any traits with World or with the boy who plays the Lady? At the conclusion of the book, the pair clash in a battle of insults. Why does World win, and what makes her the sharper satirist?

From *A Nest of Ninnies*

The World wanton sick[1] . . . is now leaning on her elbow, devising what Doctor may deliver her, what Physic may free her, and what antidotes may anticipate so dangerous a Dilemma. She now begins to grow buxom as a lightning before death, and gad she will: riches, her chamberlain, could not keep her in, beauty, her bed-fellow, was bold to persuade her. . . .

Out she would, tucks up her trinkets like a Dutch Tannikin[2] sliding to market on the ice and away she flings, and whither think you? Not to the Law,[3] that was too loud, not to the Church, that was too proud, not to the Court, that was too stately, nor to the City, she was there lately, nor to the Camp, that was too keen, no nor to the Country where seldom seen . . . but of all into a Philosopher's cell, who because he was always poking at Fortune with his forefinger, the wise wittily named him *Sotto*,[4] as one besotted. A grumbling sir, one that was wise enough, and fond enough, and sold all for a glass prospective,[5] because he would wisely see into all men but himself, a fault general in most, but such was his, who thus busied was took napping by the weal public,[6] who smiles upon him with a wapper[7] eye, a jealous countenance, and bids him all hail.

Mistress (says *Sotto*) I will not say welcome, because you come ill to him that would be alone, but since you are come, look for such entertainment as my folly fits you with, that is, sharp sauce with bitter diet, no sweetness at all. . . . The bauble I play with is men's estates, which I so tumble from hand to hand, that weary with it I see (gluttingly and grievedly, yet mingled with smiles too) in my glass prospective, what shall become of it.

The World curling her locks with her fingers, and anon scratching her brain with her itching pin, as one little regarding, answers, What then?

(*Sotto*) I'll show thee. See, World, in whose bosom ever hath abundance been powered, what thy imps of impiety be, for as they (ay) all for the most part, as these which I will present to thee in my glass prospective, mark them well, and see what thou breedest in thy wantonness, six Children like thee. . . . but mark me and my glass, see into some (and in them thyself) whom I have decried, or described, these six parts of folly in thee, thou shalt see them as clear as day.

---

[1] **wanton sick:** from a hangover.   [2] **Tannikin:** generic term for a Dutch woman or girl.   [3] **Law:** law courts or possibly the Inns of Court.   [4] *Sotto*: a pun combining "sot" (fool) and Italian *sotto* ("under," "beneath"). Armin probably intends an echo of Scoto, a famous Italian mountebank who played before Elizabeth.   [5] **glass prospective:** a magic glass or telescope for seeing distant or future events.   [6] **weal public:** the commonweal, i.e., world.   [7] **wapper:** blinking.

[Sotto and World look in his magic mirror and see six fools. One is Jack Miller, a natural fool, who lives in a house that is visited by traveling players.]

But look who is here. . . . One that was more beloved among Ladies than thought can hatch, or opinion produce. His name is *Jack Miller,* he lives yet & hath been in this city within few days, and give me leave to describe him thus. . . . In a Gentleman's house where *Jack Miller* resorted as he was welcome to all: it chanced so there was a play, the players dressed them in the gentleman's kitchen, and so entered through the entry into the hall. It was after dinner when pies stood in the oven to cool for supper: *Jack* had not dined, and seeing the oven stand open, and so many pies there untold (he thought because they seemed numberless) O says *Jack,* for one of them p. p. pyes, for so he stammered in speaking.

The Players' Boy being by (and in his Lady's Gown) could have found in his heart to creep in clothes and all: but he persuaded *Jack* to do so, to which he was willing, and very nimbly thrusts in his head into the hot Oven, which being but newly opened, on the sudden he was singed both of head and face, and almost not a hair left on his eyebrows, or beard: *Jack* cries, O I burn, and had not the wit to come back, but lay still: the Gentlewoman Boy[8] took him by the heels & pulled him out, but how he looked I pray you judge that can discern favors, *Jack* was in a bad taking with his face poor soul, and looked so ugly and so strangely, that the Lady of the Play[9] being ready to enter before the Gentles[10] to play her part, no sooner began but remembering *Jack,* laughed out, and could go no further: the Gentleman mused at what he laughed, but such a Jest, being easily seen, was told the Gentleman, who sent in for *Jack Miller,* who came like bald Time,[11] to tell them time was past of his hair: but he so strangely looked, as his countenance was better then the Play. . . .

Jack Miller welcomed to all places, & hard of none,[12] came to a Gentleman, who being at dinner, requested him for mirth, to make him a play, which he did, and to sing Derry's faire, which was in this manner. First it is to be noted, he stuttered hugely. . . . One standing by noting his humour that b. and p. plagued him, bade him say this after him, which *Jack* said he would do.

"Buy any flan, pasties, pudding pies, plum pottage, or peascods."[13] O it was death to *Jack* to do it: but like a willing Fool he fell to it*: Buy any, buy any fla flan: p p p pasties, and p p p pudding p p p pies, p p p, &c.* And ever as he hit on the word, he would pat with his finger on his other hand, that more and more it would make a man burst with laughing. . . .

---

[8] **Gentlewoman Boy:** the cross-dressed boy actor.   [9] **Lady of the Play:** the same boy player.
[10] **Gentles:** gentlemen and gentlewomen.   [11] **bald Time:** the personification of Time was old and bald.   [12] **hard of none:** unwelcome at none.   [13] **peascods:** peas; the phrase is a street seller's cry.

[After Sotto tells World about more fools, he starts to attack her for breeding knaves who do real harm.]

(Sotto.) But let me tell ye this by the way World, there are knaves in thy seams, that must be ripped out. Ay, says the World and such I fear was your father. O no says the Critic, he was the silly Gentleman that stayed while the fool brought home his boots, & so forfeited his bond, that his good conditions lay at gage for it. Marry yes, says the World, and was after cancelled at the gallows, for such as he lies in wait to cousin simplicity,[14] and for a groat buy that, which well got deserves a portague.[15] . . . At this the Cynic fretted, and here they begin to challenged the combat . . . . Well the World so buffeted the Cynic at his own weapon, that he plays with her as weak fencers, that carries flesh up and down for others to dress.[16] Such was the Cynic, unskillful in quips and worldly flaunts, rather to play with short rods and give venies[17] till all smart again, not in the brains, as the World did, but in the buttocks as such do, having their hoses displayed, making them expert till they cry it up in the top of question.

Our sullen Cynic sets by his glass in malice, knits a beetle-brow till the room grew dark again, which the wanton World seeing, flings out of his cell like a girl at barley break, leaving the last couple in hell, [18] away she gads and never looks behind her. A whirlwind, says the Cynic, go after, is this all my thanks? The old payment still, doth the World still reward mortality thus, is virtue thus bedridden, can she not help herself? and looks up to heaven as he should say, some power assist. But there he sat fretting in his own grease, and for ought I know nobody came to help him.

[14] Ay. . . . simplicity: (World) Your father was a knave. (Sotto) No, he was a good simple man but too trusting, and he went into debt because of it. (World) Yes, he was hanged to cancel his debt, which he deserved, because he cheated so many simple folks out of their money. [15] portague: Portuguese gold coin. [16] that carries . . . dress: who provide targets for better fencers. [17] venies: weak parries. [18] barley . . . hell: country game in which teams try to capture each other, with losers left in "hell."

BIBLICAL AND PROVERBIAL FOLLY

Folly was an extraordinarily flexible and adaptable concept: no one could entirely escape the epithet, no matter his or her rank, age, class, or gender. The common denominator of fallible humanity, folly makes comedy possible and inspires humility in the wiser sort. It's no surprise to find fools in jest books and comedies, but they also inhabit the sober pages of the Bible. Most biblical fools are shallow, shortsighted, selfish, garrulous, and lacking in understanding. Citations about folly warn against pride and ignorance, as in Thomas Trevelyon's "Fooles, or foolishnesse," a compilation of harsh

Fooles. or foolishnes

Speake, in the eares of afoole: for he will despise the wisedome of thy wordes: The way of afoole is right in his owne eyes: but hee that heareth counsell, is wise: A foole in a day shall-be knowen by his anger: but he that couereth sham is wise: A fooles lips come with strife, and his mouth calleth for stripes: A fooles mouth is his owne destruction. and his lips are asnare for his soule: Prouer: 18: 6. 7: As snowe in the sommer, and as the raine in the haruest are not meete. so is honour Vnseemly for afoole: Vnto the horse belongeth awhippe. to the asse abridle, and arodde to the fooles backe: Prouer: 26: 1: 3: Take no counsell at afoole for he cannot keepe athing close: Ecclesiast: 8: 17: A foole will reproch churlishly, and agift of the enuious puffeth out the eyes: Ecclesiasticus: 18: 17: Doctrine vnto fooles is as fettres on the feete. and like manicles vpon the right hand: A foole lefteth vp his voyce with laughter, but awise man doth scarse smile secretly; A foolish mans foot is soone in his nighbours house but aman of experience is ashamed to looke in: A foole will peepe in at the doore into the house: but he that is well nourtured, will stand without: It is the poynt of afoolish man to harken at the doore: for he that is wise, will be greued with such dishonour: The heart of afoole is in their mouth: but the mouth of the wise is in their heart: Ecclesiast: 21: 19: to: 27

FIGURE 19 *A gentleman encounters a fool, from Thomas Trevelyon's* Miscellany, *an illustrated manuscript book (1608).*

biblical quotations he illustrated with this oddly merry scene of a gentleman and a dog with a smiling fool (Figure 19). Some of the sayings inscribed by Trevelyon, a skilled scribe and pattern-maker (b. ca. 1548), still circulate today in sermons and popular culture. All folly is obviously negative here, and following in the path of the fool will lead the soul ever downward, to destruction, but some types of biblical foolishness are clearly more vicious than other. What are the sins of these biblical fools that the writers want to punish with whipping and the rod? Are these fools jesters, like Touchstone and this childish fool in the drawing? As you read through these questions, do you find biblical overtones in any of the fool mockery in the play? Folly is sometimes a mortal sin, and sometimes resembles lightheartedness and curiosity. What aspects of folly sound more appealing than biblical wisdom? Which kinds of folly, whether severe or minor, correspond to characters and actions of *As You Like It*?

→ THOMAS TREVELYON

From Fooles, or Foolishnesse

Speake not in the eares of a foole: for he will despise the wisdom of thy words. The way of a foole is right in his own eyes: but he that heareth counsell, is wise: A fool in a day shall be known by his anger, but he that covereth sham[e] is wise: A fooles lips come with strife, and his mouth calleth for stripes:[1] *A foole's mouth is his own destruction and his lips are a snare for his soul. Prover[bs] 18:6:7. As the snowe in the sommer and as is the raine in the harvest are not meete, so is honour unseemly for a foole. Unto the horse belongeth a whip, to the ass a bridle, and a rodde to the foole's back. Prover. 26:1:3: Take no counsell at a foole, for he cannot keep a thing close. Ecclesiast. 8:17: A foole will reproch churlishly and a gift of the envious putteth out the eyes. Ecclesiasticus 18:17: Doctrine unto fooles is as fetters on the feet and like manacles upon the right hand: A fool lifteth up his voyce with laughter, but a wise man doth scarse smile secretly: A foolish mans foot is soone in his nighbours house, but a man of experience is ashamed to look in: A fool will peepe in at the door in to the house: but he that is well nourtured, will stand without. It is the poynt of a foolish man to harken at the doore: for he that is wise will be grieved with such dishonour: The heart of a foole is in their mouth but the mouth of the wise is in their heart: Ecclesiast: 21:19 to 27.*

---

[1] **stripes:** marks left by whipping

Thomas Trevelyon, "Fooles, or foolishnesse." Folger MS V.b.232, 210v. Folger Shakespeare Library, Washington, DC.

→ DESIDERIUS ERASMUS

From Praise of Folly   *1668*

Translated by John Wilson

The most radical departure from the "fool-as-sinner" convention is in the teachings of Saint Paul. In letters to the Corinthians and Romans Paul calls himself a "fool for Christ" and argues it is better to realize one's own ignorance before the workings of God than to believe oneself wise. In other words, in the matter of true Christian faith, the humble fool is wiser than the wisest theologian or philosopher, because he does not pretend to know all. In other passages Paul uses *fool* and *folly* in a positive sense, while explaining the limits of reason before the divine. Paul's provocative words led to centuries of interpretation by biblical explicators.

The Dutch humanist Desiderius Erasmus (1466?–1566) took the high road to folly in *Moriae encomium* (*Praise of Folly*, first published in Latin in 1511). Erasmus wrote the work in England while visiting Sir Thomas More, loading it with playful humor meant to amuse his friend. Even the title is a pun on More's name, which means "fool" in Latin, and the phrasing makes the book both a praise *of* and *by* Folly (Figure 20). A female incarnation of folly, Stultitia ("Stupidity" or "Ignorance") is the speaker. Dressed in cap and bells, she mounts the lectern to deliver an oration lauding fools for their gaiety and gifts of joy to the melancholy and studious, and then grows more serious as she applauds fools for following Christ's example in their total rejection of all worldly wisdom. Erasmus exploits to the fullest Paul's first letter to the Corinthians: "For the wisdom of this world is foolishness in God's sight, As it is written: 'He catches the wise in their craftiness'" (1 Corinthians 3:19). Erasmus plays on the common expectation that fools may speak the truth when they criticize and tease their superiors, even at the risk of offending the powerful. Stultitia celebrates her own galloping tongue and invites listeners to imitate her.

At the end, however, instead of delivering an epilogue, she instructs her spectators to forget everything she said, since she is just a woman and foolish by nature. In one of Hans Holbein's famous sketches in the margins of Erasmus's work, he shows Stultitia delighting the crowd with her witty-foolish oration. Erasmus made his orator a woman to signal the lowly simplicity and lack of reason of the faithful, but any male who learned from such a speaker might be dubbed a fool, as well. In casting his orator, Erasmus was using a long tradition rooted in festive culture and farce. A female folly might speechify like Stultitia or flirt and dally with clowns, and during special holidays she might even be

Desiderius Erasmus, *Praise of Folly*, trans. John Wilson (1668), n. pag. Web. 2 July 2012 <http://www.gutenberg.org/cache/epub/9371/pg9371.txt>.

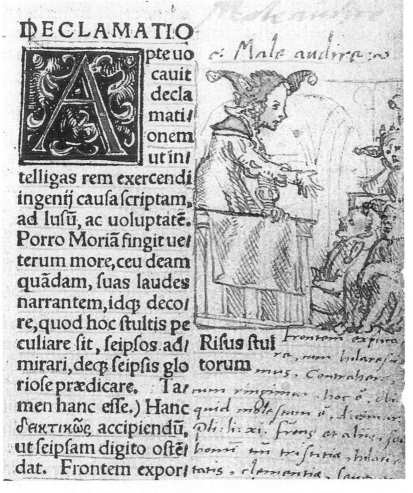

FIGURE 20 *Folly praises herself, in a marginal drawing by Hans Holbein in a copy of Desiderius Erasmus,* Moriae encomium *(1515).*

crowned as a queen. Many of her incarnations suited the principle of reversal allowed to operate only in holiday, when the world can turn topsy turvy, temporarily raising the less powerful over those in command, and the female over the male. Festivals run by fools' societies in France, for example, paid homage to the legendary *Mère Folle* (Mother Folly), who typically wore a jester's dress and carried bellows to pump up her followers with laughter and to fan the fires of excess.[1]

Stultitia breeds laughter because she ignores rules of propriety and permits her listeners to relax and be foolish. During holidays and in comedies, Folly can seem harmless and gay, like Stultitia joking from the podium in place of a dignified professor or a priest. Does that make her message less significant? Both Rosalind and Stultitia end their performances by joking with the audience. In what ways does Rosalind/Ganymede's epilogue resemble Stultitia's final words? What are examples of gender and class reversal or other kinds of topsy turvy in the play? Does any character, male or female, possess wisdom that goes beyond wit? How is wisdom different from simply being funny or causing laughter, and when does it resemble civility and kindness?

From *Praise of Folly*

PRAISE OF FOLLY. AN ORATION, OF FEIGNED MATTER,[2] SPOKEN BY FOLLY IN HER OWN PERSON

At what rate soever the world talks of me (for I am not ignorant what an ill report Folly has got, even among the most foolish), yet that I am that she, that only she, whose deity recreates both gods and men, even this is a sufficient argument, that I no sooner stepped up to speak to this full assembly than all your faces put on a kind of new and unwonted pleasantness. So suddenly have you cleared your brows, and with so frolic and hearty a laughter given me your applause, that in truth as many of you as I behold on every side of me seem to me no less than Homer's gods drunk with nectar and nepenthe;[3] whereas before, you sat as lumpish and pensive as if you had come from consulting an oracle. And as it usually happens when the sun begins to show his beams, or when after a sharp winter the spring breathes afresh on the earth, all things immediately get a new face, new color, and recover as it were a certain kind of youth again: in like manner, by but beholding me you have in an instant gotten another kind of countenance; and so what the otherwise great rhetoricians with their tedious and long-studied orations can hardly effect, to wit, to remove the trouble of the mind, I have done it at once with my single look. But if you ask me why I appear before you in this strange dress,[4] be pleased to lend me your ears, and I'll tell you; not those ears, I mean, you carry to church, but abroad with you, such

---

[1] Donald Gwynn Watson, "Erasmus' *Praise of Folly* and the Spirit of Carnival," *Renaissance Quarterly* 32.3 (1979): 333–53.   [2] **feigned matter:** made-up topics.   [3] **nepenthe:** magic drink that made sorrows vanish.   [4] **strange dress:** jester's garb.

as you are wont to prick up to jugglers, fools, and buffoons, and such as our friend Midas once gave to Pan.[5] For I am disposed awhile to play the sophist[6] with you. . . .

Their business was to celebrate the praises of the gods and valiant men. And the like encomium shall you hear from me, but neither of Hercules nor Solon,[7] but my own dear self, that is to say, Folly. Nor do I esteem a rush that[8] call it a foolish and insolent thing to praise one's self. Be it as foolish as they would make it, so they confess it proper: and what can be more than that Folly be her own trumpet?

[Folly enlists Saint Paul to show that Christianity is the best kind of folly, and Christ himself chose to become human, therefore a kind of fool.]

I would only desire you to consider this, that if so great doctors may be allowed this liberty, you may the more reasonably pardon even me also, a raw, effeminate divine, if I quote not everything so exactly as I should. And so at last I return to Paul. "Ye willingly," says he, "suffer my foolishness,"[9] and again, "Take me as a fool,"[10] and further, "I speak it not after the Lord, but as it were foolishly,"[11] and in another place, "We are fools for Christ's sake."[12] . . . Nor can I give you any reason why it should seem so strange when Saint Paul imputes a kind of folly even to God himself. "The foolishness of God," says he, "is wiser than men."[13] . . . And again, when Christ gives Him thanks that He had concealed the mystery of salvation from the wise, but revealed it to babes and sucklings, that is to say, fools. For the Greek word for babes is fools, which he opposes to the word wise men. To this appertains that throughout the Gospel you find him ever accusing the Scribes and Pharisees and doctors of the law . . . but seems chiefly delighted in little children, women, and fishers. Besides, among brute beasts he is best pleased with those that have least in them of the foxes' subtlety. And therefore he chose rather to ride upon an ass when, if he had pleased, he might have bestrode the lion without danger. . . . Add to this that in Scripture there is frequent mention of harts, hinds, and lambs; and such as are destined to eternal life are called sheep, than which creature there is not anything more foolish. . . . And yet Christ professes to be the shepherd of this flock and is himself delighted with the name of a lamb; according to Saint John, "Behold the Lamb of God!" Of which also there is much mention in

---

[5] ears . . . Pan: ass's ears (Folly has it backward, as befits a fool). [6] sophist: subtle rhetorician-teacher. [7] Solon: famous Greek judge and lawgiver. [8] esteem . . . that: don't care about those who. [9] Ye . . . foolishness: misquoting 2 Corinthians 11:19 ("ye suffer fools gladly"). [10] Take me as a fool: Folly inverts the original "Let no one take me as a fool" (2 Corinthians 11:16). [11] I . . . foolishly: 2 Corinthians 11:17. [12] We . . . sake: 1 Corinthians 4:10. [13] The foolishness . . . men: 1 Corinthians 1:25.

the Revelation. And what does all this drive at, but that all mankind are fools — nay, even the very best?

And Christ himself, that he might the better relieve this folly, being the wisdom of the Father, yet in some manner became a fool when taking upon him the nature of man, he was found in shape as a man; as in like manner he was made sin that he might heal sinners. Nor did he work this cure any other way than by the foolishness of the cross and a company of fat apostles, not much better, to whom also he carefully recommended folly but gave them a caution against wisdom and drew them together by the example of little children, lilies, mustard-seed, and sparrows, things senseless and inconsiderable, living only by the dictates of nature and without either craft or care. . . . And to the same purpose is it that that great Architect of the World, God, gave man an injunction against his eating of the Tree of Knowledge, as if knowledge were the bane of happiness.

[Folly concludes her oration and bids her followers good-bye.]

But I forget myself and run beyond my bounds. Though yet, if I shall seem to have spoken anything more boldly or impertinently than I ought, be pleased to consider that not only Folly but a woman said it; remembering in the meantime that Greek proverb, "Sometimes a fool may speak a word in season," unless perhaps you expect an epilogue, but give me leave to tell you you are mistaken if you think I remember anything of what I have said, having foolishly bolted out such a hodgepodge of words. 'Tis an old proverb, "I hate one that remembers what's done over the cup." This is a new one of my own making: I hate a man that remembers what he hears.

Wherefore farewell, clap your hands, live and drink lustily, my most excellent disciples of Folly!

HOLIDAY HUMORS

Folly invents its own seasons. Rosalind sets the pace, urging Orlando on when she feels her spirits rise: "Come, woo me, woo me, for now I am in a holiday humor, and like enough to consent" (4.1.50–51). Holiday humor is a valuable commodity: it manages to transform a plot full of fratricidal hatred, tyranny, violence, and exile into leisurely comedy. *As You Like It* does not specify a particular holiday, but it begins in chilly winter and looks forward to spring, both seasons earmarked for folly's pleasures and departures from everyday duty and constraint. Extended periods of holiday unleashed the powers of folly, generating extreme appetites and utopian fantasies. Folly was given a freer rein during the six-week Christmas season from Decem-

FIGURE 21 Peasant Couple Dancing, *by Albrecht Dürer (1514).*

ber to mid-January, and during early May and midsummer, when people indulged in plays, masking, feasting, flirting, sex, and dancing (Figure 21). Comedies are often set during holiday time, or they constitute a break from ordinary time in other ways, trading on festive license, comic confusion, and shifting identities.

Folly also stimulates comically outsized desires. Rosalind says her passion "hath an unknown bottom, like the Bay of Portugal" (4.1.160), and when she showers Celia with questions about Orlando, Celia retorts she would need "Gargantua's mouth" to answer (3.2.193), a response befitting a French princess in a play about having it as you like it. Gargantua is a French giant who was born yelling *drink, drink!* His appetite mirrors Rosalind's own huge thirst for news of her lover and for artful wooing. To Shakespeare's audience, any mention of a giant would also summon traditional English merrymaking, since in many towns male and female giants were paraded through streets during summer holidays, along with shows of Robin Hood and Saint George slaying the dragon. Why does Shakespeare pack his play so full of folktales and larger-than-life mythic figures, from Robin Hood and Gargantua to Hymen? What other passions, desires, and emotions are magnified and outsized in *As You Like It*? Where and when does the play focus on literal and metaphoric hunger and its satisfaction?

The pursuit of pleasure affects everyone's sense of time. Rosalind and Celia escape the Duke's fatal deadline in a place where clocks don't exist, noblemen "fleet the time carelessly" imitating Robin Hood and his men, shepherds and shepherdesses perform pageants of true love and proud disdain, and boy singers keep time with "hey ding a ding, ding" (1.1.87–88, 3.5.42–45, 5.3.17). Clowns and tricksters muse on time's passing, but only in jest. Touchstone philosophizes about hours ripening and rotting, and Rosalind jokes about "who Time gallops withal, and who he stands still withal" (3.2.261–62). Mounting the horse of folly, she hides her identity from her father, and later improvises a rushed mock wedding in which her galloping desire "runs before her actions" (4.1.106)

Holiday folly comes to a head in the final scene with a great gathering of lovers who enter like pairs of beasts coming to the Ark or fools crowding onto the Ship of Fools. The forest has served as a magnet for vagrants and exiles, with hidden groves conducive to stolen kisses and sudden marriage contracts. The Edenic side of Arden ensures that the world will be set to rights after being set on its ear. All perilous encounters transform there into loving bonds, and if it takes a pagan god to "bar confusion" (5.4.107) he will be produced, like a rabbit out of a hat. (That sense of the utopian neverland is echoed in the passage from François Rabelais, describing the Abbey of Thélème [p. 311], in which gentlemen and gentlewomen live happily together at leisure, with mutual love but no jealousy, and obey the Abbey's one rule: "Do As Thou Wilt.")

Part of the allure of turning the world upside down in the real world was the unruly ambiguity that resulted, which could be adapted as a political strategy or as a theatrical spectacle to draw a crowd. Protests and performances of all sorts featured the festive specter of "woman on top" and fools gone wild. Bold women took active part in riots and rebellions against enclosures or unfair market practices, often during the turbulence of holiday. Small boys might play May Kings or Queens, and adult men might cross-dress or blacken their faces in uprisings that challenged property owners or other authorities, using disguise for self-protection. Young women went manhunting during Hocktide, a holiday in October in which women caught male passersby and tied them up, demanding money to free them, thus gathering funds for church coffers; on the next day young men took their turn at the "hunt." When identities became unfixed in this way, whether in jest or in earnest, new ideas and possibilities could come into view, especially for women, and these brief moments of gender reversal could provide women with useful models and a productive fantasy for the future, as Natalie Zemon Davis has argued.[1] How is the world upside down (or at least askew) in *As You Like It*? How do cross-class and cross-gender disguises contribute to this effect? Are moments of "women on top" only temporary or do they have long-term effects? How do these differ from moments of "fools on top"?

Not everyone wanted the world turned upside down, or even shaken up. Holiday revels in real communities could anger and provoke local residents, and local authorities charged with maintaining order often showed a deep suspicion of crowds of merrymakers. Celia's cry "to liberty, and not to banishment" (1.3.127) might well have alarming overtones to certain auditors who firmly believed in hierarchy, godliness, and order, and feared what might disrupt them. "Liberty" summoned specters of uncontrolled sexuality, unruly and unsettled subjects, and unorthodox beliefs. In addition, a *liberty* was a political-geographical term defining an urban area adjacent to the city in which the city's laws did not fully apply. In London the liberties harbored theaters and brothels as well as bearbaiting rings and cockpits. The spectacle of two unmarried young gentlewomen roaming at will, and in disguise, far beyond the walls (and wills) of their fathers, in a play staged in the liberties, might well seem insubordinate, lusty, and "libertine" rather than chaste and prudent.

The play's many allusions to traditional holiday pastimes raised specters of unorthodox beliefs, since almost all predated the Reformation. Zealous Protestants tirelessly campaigned to stamp out the rites of May and even Christmas, festive periods laden with plays and communal rituals denounced as pagan vestiges of Catholicism. This campaign coincided with the decline

---

[1] Natalie Zemon Davis, "Women on Top," *Society and Culture in Early Modern France* (Stanford: Stanford UP, 1975), 143.

of public feasts hosted by the wealthy, who had once fed the poor but were increasingly withdrawing from the country for the city (for more on the decay of hospitality, see p. 147). As the godly were fond of pointing out, young people often made hasty matches during holidays, and some maids became pregnant out of wedlock, bearing bastards who became public charges. Even more dangerous in their view, unfettered merrymaking and mockery might call into question the subjugation of all beings to God and threaten or disrupt rigid gender, family, and class hierarchies on which they believed society depended. Mocking a local priest for lechery or ignorance, for example, might be read as a broader attack on orthodox doctrine or the established church, rather than criticism of a mere individual. Some took a hard line against almost any recreation after required attendance at Sunday services, even though it was the only day free from work. Vehement reformers denounced plays, songs, and stories about popular heroes such as Robin Hood and the knight-adventurer Amadis de Gaul, calling them sinful and lewd pursuits that turned people away from thoughts of God. They also wished to stamp out such "idle pastimes" as hunting, wrestling, and singing, especially on the Sabbath, while the moderate majority of the clergy defended them as traditional and beneficial. Traditional pastimes also had royal defenders who believed they fostered stability over time, provided needed recreation, and most important, cemented the loyalty of subjects to the state and crown. Both Elizabeth and James defended many festivities and sports as long as they did not interfere with religious services, and James issued a proclamation defending sports, which his son Charles I later reissued. In the world of professional theater, playwrights launched a series of counterattacks against the Puritans who reviled plays and called for stages to be pulled down.[2]

Consider the various sports and games of Orlando, Rosalind, Jaques, and Duke Senior and his men in the context of this tug-of-war. Does the play present popular recreations and entertainments (hunting, playacting, wrestling, singing, country weddings, festive cross-dressing) in a positive or negative light? If any objections are voiced, what are they, and who voices them?

---

[2] For more on the controversy and James's *Book of Sports* see Leah Marcus, *The Politics of Mirth: Jonson, Herrick, Milton, Marvell and the Defense of Old Holiday Pastimes* (Chicago: U of Chicago P, 1989).

→ "Disordered Assemblies":
Court Records from Chester   *1620*

The document below from a court case in Chester shows people full of "holiday humor," having fun in many of the ways we see in Arden—men and women performing playlets and acting out roles; singing, dancing, and feasting; and cross-dressing (both in the sense of dressing oneself and dressing someone else). Costumed revelers ritually present food to the appointed "lady of the game," in ways similar to the Duke's men ritually presenting the slain deer to the Duke in act 4, scene 2 of *As You Like It*. Defendants stand accused of making too much noise and jamming the streets with people on the Sabbath, but the greater sin appears to be the hilarious topsy-turvy atmosphere led by "women on top" (especially Elizabeth Symme) suspected of sexual license, and the presence of men or boys dressed as women. The complaint refers to "the gross misdemeanors of some ungodly perso[ns]" who drew "great multitudes of rude and disordered [people] on the sabbath day and at other times; [con]trary to the express warrant of his Majesti[es] Justices of Assise."[1] The term *ungodly* alerts us that the transgression is rooted in political and religious differences, since the "godly" were the pious Protestants who were denounced as Puritans by people like these revelers. The Chester records refer to the leaders as "chief authors." In what way is organizing such activities like composing or writing? Which elements in the play echo those in Chester and who are the "authors" of these pastimes, skits, and games? What counterforces are ranged against them? What events in the play might a godly observer judge to be ungodly, rude, and disordered?

T he first disordered assembly was occasioned by Richard Coddingtoun who was put in a woman's apparel on the Sabbath day in July last, by Elizabeth Symme and others, at her father's house (a disordered alehouse) which Elizabeth Symme together with David Wilkinson (two persons notoriously suspected of adultery) were thought to be the chief authors both of attiring the aforesaid Coddingtoun in woman's apparel, and using him as a messenger with a great train of rude people tumultuously gadding[2] after him from thence to the church hill to bring a present of cherries to the said Elizabeth, where she sat as lady of the game[3] ready to receive them. . . .

The second tumultuous assembly was July 25, occasioned by Thomas Brooke & Thomas Manninge in women's apparel dancing like women after one Peacocke, a fiddler. And by William Arrowsmith and Richard Stubbs

---

[1]**Justices of Assise:** royal legal officials.   [2]**gadding:** gaily following.   [3]**lady of the game:** queen of the feast.

Chester Court Records, PRO CHES 24/115/4 (July–August 1620), *English Parish Drama*, ed. Alexandra Johnston and Wim Husken (Amsterdam: Rodopi, 1996), 36–37.

both of them in disguised apparel with naked swords in their hands dancing with those that were in women's apparel, a great multitude of disordered and rude people gadding along after them. . . .

The third disordered & riotous assembly was August 5. Thomas Symme and Margaret Bettely the elder [were] chief authors of the same, gathering together a greater multitude, by carrying about a great & large garland decked with flours, ribbons, tinsel & scarfs for the making whereof money was gathered: & Richard Vernon a piper hired, & so rioting from one township to another, men and women so promiscuously & lasciviously danced about Thomas Symme (as about a maypole) bearing up the garland.

→ **FRANÇOIS RABELAIS**

From Gargantua and Pantagruel   *1532*

Translated by Thomas Urquhart and Peter Antony Motteux

The French told stories about the comic giant Gargantua long before François Rabelais (1494–1553) made him a literary giant. Rabelais was a writer, monk, and physician best known for his broad, scatological humor, his humanist ideals of religious toleration, and for his satire of the empty argumentation of university scholasticism. A figure of constant controversy during the religious wars of the first half of the sixteenth century, Rabelais was often rebuked by clerical and secular authorities, and his writings were banned in 1544. *Pantagruel* appeared in 1532, *Gargantua* soon after, and copies circulated in England in the last decades of the century. The infant Gargantua was born wailing for something to drink; Celia alludes to his legend by joking about his huge mouth (3.2.193). Shakespeare may have heard of Gargantua from a story or chapbook, but he may also have seen a copy of Rabelais's famous book; in any case, he depended on his audiences to get the joke when Celia says she'd need "Gargantua's mouth" to answer all of Rosalind's frantic questions about Orlando.

BOOK I, CHAPTER 7

After what manner Gargantua had his name given him, and how he tippled, bibbed, and curried the can.[1]

[1] **tippled . . . can:** sipped, guzzled, and caressed the bottle.

François Rabelais, *The Works of Rabelais Faithfully Translated from the French*, trans. Thomas Urquhart and Peter Antony Motteux (Darby: Moray Press, 1894), n. pag. Web. 2 July 2012 <http://www.gutenberg.org/files/8166/8166-h/8166-h.htm#2HCH0001>.

The good man Grangousier, drinking and making merry with the rest, heard the horrible noise which his son had made as he entered into the light of this world, when he cried out "Some drink, some drink, some drink"; whereupon [Grandgousier] said in French "Que grand tu as et souple le gousier!"; that is to say, "How great and nimble a throat thou hast!" Which the company hearing, said that verily the child ought to be called Gargantua, because it was the first word that after his birth his father had spoke, in imitation and at the example of the ancient Hebrews; whereunto he condescended, and his mother was very well pleased therewith. In the meanwhile, to quiet the child, they gave him [so much] to drink his throat was like to crack with it; then was he carried to the font, and there baptized, according to the manner of good Christians.

Immediately thereafter were appointed for him seventeen thousand, nine hundred, and thirteen cows of the towns of Pautille and Brehemond to furnish him with milk, . . . for it was impossible to find a nurse sufficient for him in all the country, considering the great quantity of milk that was requisite for his nourishment, although there were not wanting[2] some doctors of the opinion of Scotus,[3] who affirmed that his own mother gave him suck, and that she could draw out of her breasts one thousand, four hundred, two pipes, and nine pails of milk at every time.

Which indeed is not probable, and this point hath been found duggishly[4] scandalous and offensive to tender ears, for that it savored a little of heresy. Thus was he handled for one year and ten months; after which time, by the advice of physicians, they began to carry him, and then was made for him a fine little cart drawn with oxen . . . wherein they led him hither and thither with great joy; and he was worth the seeing, for he was a fine boy, had a burly physiognomy, and almost ten chins. He cried very little, but beshit himself every hour: for, to speak truly of him, he was wonderfully phlegmatic[5] in his posteriors, both by reason of his natural complexion and the accidental disposition which had befallen him by his too much quaffing of the Septembral juice.[6] Yet without a cause did not he sup one drop; for if he happened to be vexed, angry, displeased, or sorry, if he did fret, if he did weep, if he did cry, and what grievous quarter[7] soever he kept, in bringing him some drink, he would be instantly pacified, reseated in his own temper, in a good humor again, and as still and quiet as ever. One of his governesses told me (swearing by her fig[8]), how he was so accustomed to this . . . that . . . at the sound of pints and flagons, he would on a sudden fall into an ecstasy,

<hr>

[2]**wanting:** lacking.   [3]**Scotus:** Duns Scotus, medieval philosopher.   [4]**duggishly:** nonsense word: "breastily" (dug is slang for breast).   [5]**phlegmatic:** loose in his bowels.   [6]**Septembral juice:** wine.   [7]**what grievous quarter:** in whatever way he was upset.   [8]**fig:** slang for female genitals.

as if he had then tasted of the joys of paradise; so that they, upon consideration of this, his divine complexion, would every morning, to cheer him up, play with a knife upon the glasses, on the bottles with their stopples,[9] and on the pots with their lids and covers, at the sound whereof he became gay, did leap for joy, would loll and rock himself in the cradle, then nod with his head, monochordizing with his fingers, and barytonizing[10] with his tail.

[9] **stopples:** bottle stoppers.   [10] **monochordizing . . . barytonizing:** clicking his fingers and farting in harmony.

From *Gargantua and Pantagruel*

The next excerpt describes one of Gargantua's inventions: the fabulous Abbey of Thélème, which he founded for young pleasure-loving gentlemen and gentlewomen, and from which all pious and ascetic monks and nuns are forever banned. Behind these walls no one prays or works, love and kindness reign, and the device above its door is FAIT CE QUE VOUDRAS — "do what thou wilt" or "do as you'd like." Sexual desire is no sin, and when a gentleman wishes to marry, he chooses a lady and they leave in order to marry, so that no one fears being made a cuckold. In this optimistic (and to many of his readers, bizarre) view of human nature, men and women live in equality and harmony, and have total liberty to choose and act as they please. This freedom causes virtue rather than vice to triumph. Unorthodox ideas like these brought Rabelais many enemies and admirers, and the book was banned in his lifetime. Rabelais's account is full of irony, since such perfection is limited to an educated elite and only men may choose spouses, and in any case, such total harmony of interests and desires does not seem humanly possible.

Shakespeare's engaging title, *As You Like It*, resembles Thélème's motto, though it is less direct. Like Thélème, Arden offers an escape from ordinary duties and rules in the workaday world, and allows young lovers to govern their own lovemaking as they like; but the social scope and setting are in marked contrast, as is the presence of violence and hunger. How does the invitation in their titles function differently in Rabelais and Shakespeare? Who is being addressed in each instance? In what important ways do the Thélèmites differ from the denizens of Arden? Which retreat, Gargantua's or Shakespeare's, offers a greater scope for erotic pleasures of all kinds? Which view of human nature "at liberty" is more satiric and cynical? Whose creation is more egalitarian? More utopian?

The Abbey of Thélème

Book 1, Chapter 57

How the Thélèmites were governed, and of their manner of living.
All their life was spent not in laws, statutes, or rules, but according to their own free will and pleasure. They rose out of their beds when they thought good; they did eat, drink, labour, sleep, when they had a mind to it and were disposed for it. None did awake them, none did offer to constrain them to eat, drink, nor to do any other thing; for so had Gargantua established it. In all their rule and strictest tie of their order there was but this one clause to be observed,

DO WHAT THOU WILT;

because men that are free, well born, well-bred, and conversant in honest companies, have naturally an instinct and spur that prompteth them unto virtuous actions, and withdraws them from vice, which is called honour. Those same men, when by base subjection and constraint they are brought under and kept down, turn aside from that noble disposition by which they formerly were inclined to virtue, to shake off and break that bond of servitude wherein they are so tyrannously enslaved; for it is agreeable with the nature of man to long after things forbidden and to desire what is denied us.

By this liberty they entered into a very laudable emulation[1] to do all of them what they saw did please one. If any of the gallants or ladies should say, Let us drink, they would all drink. If any one of them said, Let us play, they all played. If one said, Let us go a-walking into the fields they went all. If it were to go a-hawking or a-hunting, the ladies mounted upon dainty well-paced nags, seated in a stately palfrey saddle, carried on their lovely fists, miniardly[2] begloved every one of them, either a sparrowhawk or a laneret or a marlin,[3] and the young gallants carried the other kinds of hawks. So nobly were they taught, that there was neither he nor she amongst them but could read, write, sing, play upon several musical instruments, speak five or six several languages, and compose in them all very quaintly, both in verse and prose. Never were seen so valiant knights, so noble and worthy, so dexterous and skilful both on foot and a-horse-back, more brisk and lively, more nimble and quick, or better handling all manner of weapons than were there. Never were seen ladies so proper and handsome, so miniard and

---

[1] **emulation:** envy; here, desire to imitate.   [2] **miniardly:** delicately.   [3] **a sparrowhawk or a laneret or a marlin:** birds of prey used to hunt other birds.

dainty, less froward,[4] or more ready with their hand and with their needle in every honest and free action belonging to that sex, than were there. For this reason, when the time came that any man of the said abbey, either at the request of his parents, or for some other cause, had a mind to go out of it, he carried along with him one of the ladies, namely, her whom he had before that chosen for his mistress, and they were married together. And if they had formerly in Thélème lived in good devotion and amity, they did continue therein and increase it to a greater height in their state of matrimony; and did entertain that mutual love till the very last day of their life, in no less vigor and fervency than at the very day of their wedding.

[4] froward: stubborn or shrewish.

Strange Capers: Love Folly and Its Cure

We that are true lovers run into strange capers; but as all is mortal in nature, so is all nature in love mortal in folly. (Touchstone, 2.4.45–47).

In François Rabelais's Thélème, all love is peaceful and reciprocal, all lovers equal in nature and fortune. That is why it is an impossible fantasy. In other early modern writing love is compared more often to a battlefield, a sickroom, or a madhouse than a pleasure resort. Lovers were thought to be especially prone to foolish excesses of agony and ecstasy, and especially vulnerable because their passions could bring on the disease of melancholy and even insanity. Poets from Ovid onward approached love-madness as a convention and wrung changes on it to generate great poetry and comedy. The first selection by Ovid accepts responsibility for making his readers fall in love, then provides highly ironic and amusing advice on the antidote — but he finally concedes most of it entails lying to oneself.

Delighted to find Orlando smitten with her, Rosalind/Ganymede promptly offers to play doctor and cure him of his pain, just as Ovid does. Her seemingly daft idea of performing a theatrical cure of Orlando through role-playing might have sounded reasonable, however, to Robert Burton, the leading authority on melancholy (from the Greek for "black bile"), the humoral imbalance that caused depression, lovesickness, and suicidal despair (see p. 317). In the second passage below, Burton defines melancholy and lovesickness, and then in a later chapter of his work provides guidelines instructing readers how to use theatrical tricks to cure obsessions.

→ OVID

From Ovidius Naso His Remedie of Love   *1600*

Rosalind declares that a fool for love "deserves as well a dark house and a whip as madmen do" (3.2.328–29). Although many insane people were indeed treated this way, her harsh words are immediately undercut, because she adds that "the whippers are in love too" (3.2.330–31). She proposes a less sadistic treatment, namely to wean Orlando away from folly by pretending to be his Rosalind, and making him allergic to love.

The poet Ovid advised the lovelorn in Augustan Rome to do much the same thing in his *Remedie of Love*, a sequel to his famous *Art of Love* (for more on Ovid see Chapter 2). Rosalind's sometimes bawdy love talk and joy in amorous folly are thoroughly Ovidian, especially when she promises to fill Orlando's ears with a long litany of female vices, thus showing him how vain, shallow, childish, and irritating women can be. Rosalind claims to have learned this technique from an imaginary uncle, but then she warns Orlando such a list will be boring since these alleged sins are "all like one another as halfpence are" (3.2.294–95). Her airy dismissal of the list of flaws casts doubt on the misogynist writers who repeated centuries-old slanders on women and warned men to shun marriage and women's love. When Rosalind does follow up by listing women's faults, what is ironic about comparing them with those of boys? Why does Celia accuse her of betraying her sex in the mock wedding scene? In another echo of Ovid, Rosalind mocks poetic clichés about dying for love: "Men have died from time to time, and worms have eaten them, but not for love" (4.1.78–79). She catalogues the typical signs of being in love — messy clothes, sunken eyes, pale cheeks, and so on. Why does she take such delight in teasing Orlando for showing none of them?

[Ovid offers to cure those in love, after admitting that his *Art of Love* caused their woes.]

Come then sick youth unto my sacred skill,
Whose love hath fallen cross[1] unto your mind:
Learn how to remedy that pleasing ill,
Of him that taught you your own harms to find.
For in that selfsame hand your help is found,   5
Whence first ye did receive your careful[2] wound.

---

[1] **fallen cross**: displeased, upset.   [2] **careful**: worrisome, painful.

Ovid, *Ovidius Naso His Remedie of Love* (London, 1600), sigs. A4–B, D–D2v; STC 18974.

So the earth which yields us herbs of sovereign grace[3]
Doth nourish weeds, of virtue pestilent;[4]
The burning nettle[5] chooseth oft her place,
Next to the rose, that yields so sweet a scent.   10
Achilles' spear,[6] that wounded his stern foe,
Restored him health, and cured the grievous blow.

Now what prescriptions we do give to men,
Maids think them spoken unto you likewise.
To both parts we give weapons, use them then   15
With secret art, and with discretion wise

. . . .

And profitable is our argument,
To quench that secret and consuming flame   20
To free thy mind from sin and ill intent
To loose those bands that drew thee into shame.
Phyllis[7] had lived had I her tutor been,
That three times thrice walkt path she oft had seen.

Nor Dido[8] dying from her stately tower,   25
Should have beheld the Trojans thence to fly

. . . .

Give me Pasiphae,[9] she shall cease to love
The filthy shape of that strange monstrous beast,
Bring Phaedra[10] forth, and I will soon remove
Her deep incestuous lust, that never ceased.
Lived Paris,[11] Helen he should not desire,   35
Nor should the Greeks waste Pergamus[12] with fire.

Had wicked Scylla read our argument,
Nisus should not have lost his fatal hair;[13]

---

[3] **sovereign grace:** great power. [4] **virtue pestilent:** harmful quality. [5] **burning nettle:** small plant with stinging hairs. [6] **Achilles' spear:** magic weapon that wounded King Telephus and later cured him. [7] **Phyllis:** Tragic maid who killed herself after Demophon seemed to abandon her; he returned, but too late. [8] **Dido:** queen of Carthage who killed herself after Aeneas left her to found Rome. [9] **Pasiphae:** semi-divine woman who, enchanted by Poseidon, lusted after a bull and conceived the Minotaur. [10] **Phaedra:** figure from Greek legend who fell in love with her stepson Hippolytus. [11] **Lived Paris:** if Paris had lived. [12] **Pergamus:** Troy, which the Greeks destroyed to retake Helen from Paris. [13] **Nisus . . . hair:** Greek king with a magical lock of purple hair; his daughter Scylla, who was in love with his enemy, betrayed him by cutting it off.

I'll teach you to assuage the greedy bent
Of burning lust, and make the weather fair: 40
I'll steer your ship aright in seas of love,
And from each rock I will you safely move.

Ovid was to be read with studious care,
When first your love began with fruit to grow
Ovid is to be read, in your ill fare,[14]   45
When first your love with deep disdain shall flow.
I do profess to gain your liberty,
Then follow me, revenge your misery.

[Ovid recounts suffering for love, and his attempts to cure himself.]

Lately I set my fancy on a maid,
That fully answered not[15] to my desire,
And therefore strived my fancy to have stayed,[16]
A poor physician to so great a fire.
Yet the remembrance of her viler parts,   430
Released the fury of tormenting smarts.

How ill and excellent unshaped her thigh,[17]
Yet to confess the truth, it was not so;
How foul[18] her arms, thus would I say and sigh,
Yet if they were not thus, I well did know: 435
How short of stature, yet her stature tall;
Thus envy, loathsomeness to me did call.

Good things do neighbor bad, and sit them by,
Oft virtue thus of vice doth bear that blame,
Feign to thy self, and tell thyself a lie,   440
And clothe her virtues with foul vice's shame.
Thus shalt thou change thy mind with subtle art,
And wear away thy still encumbering smart.

If she be fat, that she is swollen say;
If brown, then tawny like the African moor: 445
If slender, lean, meager, and worn away;
If courtly, wanton, worst of worst before;

[14] ill fare: when things start to go badly.   [15] answered not: who did not fully return my love.
[16] stayed: stopped.   [17] ill ... thigh: how badly shaped her thigh was.   [18] foul: ugly.

If modest, strange, as fitteth woman-head;[19]
Say she is rustic, clownish,[20] and ill bred.

Yea, whatsoever gift (for none hath all)   450
Thy mistress, entreat her still to use.[21]
If that her voice be ill, or cunning small,[22]
Importune her to sing, never let her choose;
If that she cannot move her feet in measure,
To see her dance . . . let it be thy pleasure.   455

Is she of small discourse and slender wit?
Converse with her, that she may wound thine ear,
To instruments hath she not learned to fit
Her fingers? Then desire a lute to hear.
Hath she an ill, uncomely and strange gait?   460
Cause her to walk both early forth and late.

Hath she a swelling, and downe hanging breast?
Desire thou still to see her fair white skin.
Are her teeth black, or wants she of the best?
Relate some merry jest that she may grin: 465
Is she compassionate? Tell then some woeful case,
So shall she show thee antics in her face.

. . . .

So shalt thou disappoint her in her guile,   480
See her defects, and cool thy burning love;
Yet trust not to this rule, which other while[23]
Fallacious and dangerous doth prove:
For careless behavior that doth banish art,
Hath mighty force, to hold a wounded heart.   485

Yet while with curious skill she paints her face,
Be not asham'd, but presse thou to her sight:
Then shalt thou find her boxes[24] in the place,
Wherein her beauty lies, and borrowed light.
Then shalt thou see her body all begreas'd   490
With ointments that hath thee so greatly pleas'd.

---

[19] strange, as fitteth woman-head: coy and affected, as fits all womankind. [20] clownish: vulgar and stupid. [21] entreat her still to use: trick her into revealing her bad points. [22] cunning small: low intelligence. [23] other while: at other times, in other situations. [24] boxes: makeup boxes.

Of savor worse than Phineus'[25] tables were,
Whose filthinesse a plague to him was sent,
With these my stomach could not often bear,
But evermore to ease itself was bent;   495
But now even what we use in midst of love,
I will thee teach that passion to remove.

For by all means we must this fire expel;
But I do shame even needful things to show:
Yet thou by those which I to thee shall tell,   500
May well conceive the rest, and easy know.
For some dispraise my rhymes to envy bent,
And say my muse is shameless[26] impudent.

[25] **Phineus:** a seer in Greek myth tormented by having his food defiled by harpies.   [26] **shameless:** shamelessly.

→ **ROBERT BURTON**

From The Anatomy of Melancholy   *1638*

The most famous treatise on melancholy was written by Robert Burton (1577–1640), a brilliantly eccentric Oxford scholar whose vast *Anatomy of Melancholy* was first published in 1621. The treatise is divided into three parts or partitions. The first deals with the causes and symptoms of various kinds of melancholy; the second concerns cures; and the third part focuses particularly upon love melancholy and religious melancholy. It is in this third part that Burton presents his most extensive description of the odd and obsessive behavior of those who suffer from love melancholy. Burton kept adding to the book throughout his lifetime, with the sixth and longest version being published after his death in 1651.

The remarkable frontispiece attached to later editions of the *Anatomy*, reproduced on page 318, gives some idea of melancholy's reach (Figure 22). Surrounding the title are a number of images illustrating various kinds of melancholy including the ravings of madmen, the melancholy caused by solitude, jealousy, religious superstition, and love. At the top of the page is Democritus, the ancient Greek philosopher who was also known as the laughing philosopher, or the mocking philosopher, because of his wry attitude toward human folly. Directly below the title appears Democritus Junior, the speaker of *The Anatomy of Melancholy*, who models himself on the ancient Greek philosopher and

Robert Burton, *The Anatomy of Melancholy* (London, 1638), 504, 512, 515, 533; STC 4163.

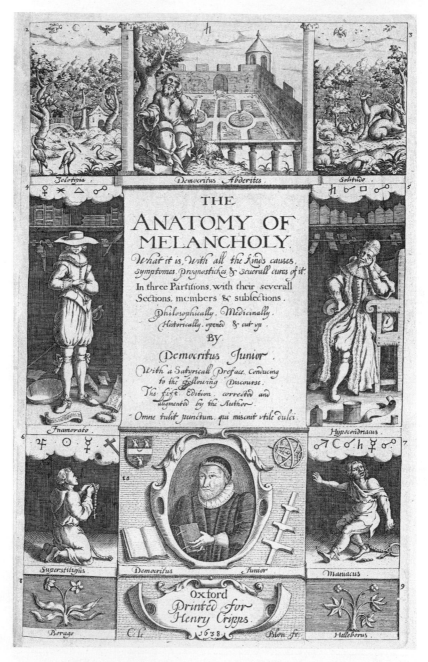

FIGURE 22 *Multifaceted melancholy, dissected on the frontispiece from Robert Burton*, The Anatomy of Melancholy *(1638).*

represents Burton himself, looking very much like an Oxford don. The inamorato, or male lover, is pictured with a broad hat pulled down over his eyes and with a lute and writing implements at his feet, since a lover was given to writing poems and love songs. In editions published after 1632, the lover is described in the "Argument of the Frontispiece."

A Renaissance doctor would seek out a cure for the wan inamorato. After reading about the signs of love melancholy that appear below, who would you say suffers from this ubiquitous disease in *As You Like It*? Is it limited to one sex or the other? How, within the play, is love melancholy cured? Why does Rosalind take on the role of a physician, if she is afflicted too? In the end, does she help herself and others, such as Orlando, Silvius, and Phoebe? To consider these questions, read the final excerpt from Burton on curing lovesickness. He recommends that doctors or friends should devise dramatic inventions amounting to psychological trickery to shock or sway those suffering depressional delusions, including those arising from love. Does Rosalind's "psychodrama" treatment plan for Orlando resemble those Burton describes? Is her aim to cure Orlando of love, or to tease and woo him? Why does the treatment proceed if Orlando says he is unwilling to be cured (3.2.345)? Does her witty device use fair means or foul means to heal him? Does her medicine relieve his symptoms, or is Orlando merely contracting a new kind of folly? What final theatrical act does Rosalind stage that has the most power to cure him?

Among the other introductory matter to this very long treatise is included a poem, "The Author's Abstract of Melancholy," that captures the paradox that melancholy can be experienced both as an enjoyable condition and as a painful one. Is the paradoxical nature of melancholy apparent in *As You Like It*?

From *The Anatomy of Melancholy*

FROM "THE ARGUMENT OF THE FRONTISPIECE"

Ith' under Columne[1] there doth stand,
Inamorato with folded hand.
Downe hanges his head, terse[2] and polite,
Some dittie sure he doth indite.
His lute and books about him lye,   5
As symptoms of his vanity.
If this doe not enough disclose,
To paint him, take thy self by th' nose.[3]

---

[1] *Ith' under Columne*: in the lower part.   [2] *terse*: refined.   [3] *take . . . nose*: take yourself for a fool (i.e., as the model for the love melancholic).

FROM "THE AUTHOR'S ABSTRACT OF MELANCHOLY"

When to myself I act and smile,
With pleasing thoughts the time beguile,
By a brook side or wood so green,
Unheard, unsought for, or unseen,
A thousand pleasures do me bless,   5
And crown my soul with happiness.
   All my joys besides are folly,
   None so sweet as melancholy.
When I lie, sit, or walk alone,
I sigh, I grieve, making great moan,   10
In a dark grove, or irksome den,
With discontents and Furies then,
A thousand miseries at once,
Mine heavy heart and soul ensconce.
   All my griefs to this are jolly,   15
   None so sour as melancholy.

PARTITION 3, SECTION 2, MEMBER 3, SUBJECT 1

Symptoms or Signs of Love Melancholy

She is ill at ease and sick till she see him again, peevish in the meantime, discontent, heavy, sad, and why comes he not? Where is he? Why breaks he promise? Why tarries he so long? Sure he is not well; sure he hath some mischance; sure he forgets himself and me, with infinite such. And then confident again, up she gets, out she looks, listens and inquires, harkens, kenns.[4] Every man a far off is sure he, every stirring in the street, now he is there, that's he. *Male aurorae, male soli dicit, dejeratque, etc.*[5] The longest day that ever was, so she raves, restless and impatient, but *Amor non patitur moras:* Love brooks no delays.[6] . . .

   So that to say truth, as *Castilio* describes it, *The beginning, middle, end of Love is naught else but sorrow, vexation, torment, irksomeness, wearisomeness, so that to be squalid, ugly, miserable, solitary, discontent, dejected, to wish for death, to complain, rave, and to be peevish, are the certain signs, and ordinary actions of a lovesick person.* This continual pain and torture makes them forget themselves, if they be far gone with it, in doubt, despair of obtaining or eagerly bent, to neglect all ordinary business. . . .

[4] **kenns:** looks around. [5] *Male . . . etc.:* she speaks badly of the dawn and the sun, she curses, etc. [6] *Amor non patitur moras:* quotation from Seneca's *Hercules Furens.*

And tis the humor of them all to be careless of their persons and their estates, as the shepherd in *Theocritus, Et hac barba inculta est, squalidia, capilli.*[7] Their beards flag, and they have not more care of pranking[8] themselves or of any business, they care not as they say, which end goes forward. . . .

Every Lover admires his mistress, though she be very deformed of herself, ill-favored, wrinkled, pimpled, pale, red, yellow, tanned, tallow-faced, have a swollen Juggler's platter face,[9] or a thin, lean, chitty face,[10] have clouds in her face, be crooked, dry, bald, goggle-eyed, blear-eyed, or with staring eyes, she looks like a squished cat, hold her head still awry, heavy, dull, hollow-eyed, black or yellow about the eyes, or squint-eyed, sparrow mouthed . . . have filthy long unpared nails, scabbed hands or wrists, a tanned skin, a rotten carcass, crooked back, lame, splay-footed, *as slender in her middle as a cow in the waist* . . . if he love her once, he admires her for all this; he takes no notice of any such errors or imperfections of body or mind.

But above all the other Symptoms of Lovers, this is not lightly to be overpassed, that likely of what condition soever, if once they be in love, they turn, to their ability, Rymers, Ballad-makers, and Poets. For as *Plutarch* sayeth, *They will be witnesses and trumpeters of their Paramours' good parts, bedecking them with verses and commendatory songs, as we do statues with gold, that they may be remembered and admired of all.* Ancient men will dote in this kind sometimes as well as the rest; the heat of love will thaw their frozen affections, dissolve the ice of age, and so far enable them, though they be 60 years of age above the girdle,[11] to be scarce 30 beneath.

PARTITION 6, SECTION 2

Help from friends by counsel, comfort, fair and foul means, witty devices, satisfaction, alteration of his course of life, removing objects, &c.

When the patient of himself is not able to resist, or overcome these heart-eating passions, his friend or physician must be ready to supply that which is wanting. . . . If his weakness be such, that he cannot discern what is amiss, correct or satisfy, it behooves them by counsel, comfort or persuasion, by faire or foul means to alienate his mind by some artificial invention, or by some contrary passion, to remove all objects, causes, companies, occasions, as may any ways molest him, to humor him, please him, divert him, and if it be possible, by altering his course of life, to give him satisfaction. If he

---

[7] *Et . . . capilli:* 'And their beards are uncut, dirty, unkempt.'   [8] **pranking:** dressing up.   [9] **platter face:** a broad, round face.   [10] **chitty face:** thin, pinched face.   [11] **above the girdle:** from the waist up.

conceal his grievances . . . they must observe by his look, gestures, motions, fantasy, what it is that offends him, and then to apply remedies unto him: many are instantly cured, when their minds are satisfied. . . . First, they must especially beware, a melancholy discontented person (be it in what kind of melancholy soever) never be left alone or idle. . . . [S]et him about some business, exercise or recreation, which may divert his thoughts, and still keep him otherwise intent; for his fantasy is so restless, operative and quick, that if it be not in perpetual action, ever employed, it will work upon itself, melancholise,[12] and be carried away instantly, with some fear, jealousy, discontent, suspicion, some vain conceit or other. . . . If he have sustained any great loss, suffered a repulse, disgrace, &c., if it be possible, relieve him. If he desire aught, let him be satisfied; if in suspense, fear, suspicion, let him be secured: and if it may conveniently be, give him his heart's content; for the body cannot be cured till the mind be satisfied. Socrates, in Plato, would prescribe no physic for Charmides' headache, till first he had eased his troubled mind; body and soul must be cured together, as head and eyes.

> Oculum non curabis sine toto capite,
> Nec caput sine toto corpora,
> Nec totum corpus sine anima.[13]

If that may not be hoped or expected, yet ease him with comfort, cheerful speeches, fair promises, and good words, persuade him, advise him. Many, saith Galen,[14] have been cured by good counsel and persuasion alone. . . . Assuredly a wise and well-spoken man may do what he will in such a case; a good orator alone, as Tully[15] holds, can alter affections by power of his eloquence, comfort such as are afflicted, erect[16] such as are depressed, expel and mitigate fear, lust, anger, &c. And how powerful is the charm of a discreet and dear friend? . . .

Sometimes again by some feigned lie, strange news, witty device, artificial invention, it is not amiss to deceive them. . . . If they say they have swallowed frogs or a snake, by all means grant it, and tell them you can easily cure it; 'tis an ordinary thing. Philodotus,[17] the physician, cured a melancholy king, that thought his head was off, by putting a leaden cap thereon; the weight made him perceive it, and freed him of his fond imagination. A woman, in the said Alexander, swallowed a serpent as she thought; he gave

---

[12] melancholise: make itself melancholy. [13] Oculum . . . anima: "It is not possible to cure the eye without the whole head, / Nor is it possible to cure the head without the whole body / Nor the whole body without the spirit." [14] Galen: Greek physician and philosopher who codified humoral theory. [15] Tully: Marcus Tullius Cicero (106–43 B.C.E.), better known as Cicero, the most famous Roman orator-philosopher. [16] erect: raise up, cheer up [17] Philodotus: classical medical authority, like Laurentius and Forestus.

her a vomit, and conveyed a serpent, such as she conceived, into the basin; upon the sight of it she was amended. The pleasantest dotage[18] that ever I read, saith Laurentius,[19] was of a gentleman at Senes in Italy, who was afraid to piss, lest all the town should be drowned; the physicians caused the bells to be rung backward, and told him the town was on fire, whereupon he made water, and was immediately cured. Another supposed his nose so big that he should dash it against the wall if he stirred; his physician took a great piece of flesh, and holding it in his hand, pinched him by the nose, making him believe that flesh was cut from it. Forestus . . . had a melancholy patient, who thought he was dead, he put a fellow in a chest, like a dead man, by his bedside, and made him rear himself a little, and eat: the melancholy man asked the counterfeit, whether dead men use to eat meat? He told him yea; whereupon he did eat likewise and was cured. [Among] the rest[20] I find one most memorable, registered in the French chronicles of an advocate of Paris before mentioned, who believed verily he was dead, &c. I read a multitude of examples of melancholy men cured by such artificial inventions.

[18] **pleasantest dotage**: most amusing obsession.   [19] **Laurentius**: Like Forestus, a learned doctor
[20] **the rest**: other medical scholarship.

Writing and Righting Love Folly in Letters

Love letters and poems could stoke passion or cure love folly. A message from a lover could tickle, woo, and even win over a beloved, but it could also put a reader off and make her scorn the writer. Billets-doux (love letters) were sometimes merely amusing love tokens, but sometimes they could be used as legal evidence to sue for broken contracts of marriage.[1] Achieving the right tone was important. Because falling in love was treated as a kind of frenzy of the soul, a lover who did not lose his or her head or claim to be despondent might be accused of coldness by those who wanted a show of emotion. Writing fervent poems, as Orlando does, was one way to display the requisite passion. Some lovers, like Phoebe, could dash off tailor-made love letters in verse in which they threatened to kill themselves if rejected, but others copied their love letters out of books of model letters.

Many women and men consulted letter-writing manuals such as *Cupid's Messenger* to persuade their lovers that they were sincere and their situations were desperate, using models like the one below from the early seventeenth century. Note that the lady's words were in all likelihood created by a male author, but might indeed find their way into a letter sent by a woman as her

[1] Alan Stewart, *Shakespeare's Letters* (Oxford: Oxford UP, 2008), 238.

own. Or a reader might simply smile at the letter's melodramatic allusions and ripe hyperboles, which echo the artifices of Phoebe's letter. Why does the fictional author below choose to mention the scandalously incestuous Myrrha and Biblis, given the context? She also says she is in danger of dying for love if rejected. Are these warnings to be taken seriously by the recipient, and how do you judge this? Has love folly been tamed by literary convention?

→ *From* Cupid's Messenger   *1629*

A LETTER OF A GENTLEWOMAN TO A GENTLEMAN
WITH WHOM SHE FELL IN LOVE.

If ever I could wish my self unborn (most worthy sir) or my well being taken from me, I call truth and my sometimes modesty to witness, [that] it is now — not that I have found you, but that I am forced thus to seek you. Call to mind (fair, and I hope virtuous, sir) some horrid and violent women, taken with the love of their own fathers, as was Myrrha,[1] or incestuously pursuing their nearest brother, as was Byblis,[2] so my affection will appear more modest, and my suit more pardonable. I dearly love you, (and in saying methinks the gods blush to hear me,) who in the secret laws of desire are most worthy to be loved, whose virtues might inflame a nun, and excellentest qualities take the most retired:[3] If I have (as I know too well I have) contrary to the nature and custom of virgins, overshot myself in my violent passions, pardon her that had rather die than make it known, yet chooseth rather to make it known, then not enjoy you so desired, and far more worthie to be desired. If you were acquainted what afflictions I suffer in my discovery, yet fearing all well not serve, you will, I hope, rather incline to pity than disdain: little will the death of a silly maiden avail the triumph of your beauty, and the overthrow of my credit[4] less benefit your virtue. Raise me from the one by your love, & assure me from the other by your secrecy: whilst I will ever remained a most constant votaress[5] to all your perfections, blessing the parents that left behind such an issue.

Never less her own,
R. D.

[1]**Myrrha:** Greek maiden who seduced her father; she changed into a tree when he tried to kill her.   [2]**Byblis:** Greek maiden who fell in love with her brother Caunus.   [3]**retired:** sedate.   [4]**credit:** (sexual) reputation.   [5]**votaress:** female worshipper at a sacred shrine.

Cupid's Messenger: or, A Trusty Friend Stored with Sundry Sorts of Serious, Wittie, Pleasant, Amorous, and Delightful Letters (London: 1629), 33–34; STC 6122.

→ DOROTHY OSBORNE

Letter to Sir William Temple

c. 1652

The form letter in *Cupid's Messenger* might not have the intended result, of course. Wooing is a great breeder of comedy and forms the basic plot of many a play; but for real women, misery and even tragedy could well result if the husband proved to be a bad bargain. More practical considerations about property, compatibility, and temperament were uppermost in many women's minds as they prepared to marry, and their friends and family took an active and sometimes obstructionist role in the decision. Collections of letters are an important source of information about negotiations over marriage among the gentry. One of the best known collections is Dorothy Osborne's letters to Sir William Temple, which tell a tale of love delayed. Born to a Royalist gentry family in Bedforshire, Osborne (1627–1695) shows a distinctive charm and candor in her letters, which also contain a wealth of detail useful to historians. Her family long opposed her choice of Temple because they sought a richer and more powerful match; but the pair did finally succeed in marrying after seven years of courtship.

In the letter below, Osborne tries to persuade her lover to shake off his melancholy. She cheers him by telling him what she wants in a husband and making it plain that he is her ideal, without resorting to melodrama and hyperbole. Appealing and humorous, with a touch of irony, she deftly sketches comic types in order to mock them and organize her critique, in the mode fashionable on stage and in popular satire. Is her authorial voice similar to Rosalind's, and if so, in what way? How does it differ from Phoebe's? What kinds of men would she refuse, and why? When is she serious, when playful, and how well does she argue? What qualities of character does she show that would make it difficult for her family to bend her to their will, and what does her literacy and literary skill contribute to that character?

Sir,

Why are you so sullen, and why am I the cause? Can you believe that I do willingly defer my journey? I know you do not. Why, then, should my absence now be less supportable to you than heretofore? Nay, it shall not be long (if I can help it), and I shall break through all inconveniences rather than deny you anything that lies in my power to grant. But by your own rules, then, may I not expect the same from you? Is it possible that all I have said cannot oblige you to a care of yourself?[1] What a pleasant distinction

---

[1] **oblige you to a care of yourself:** persuade you to take care of yourself.

Dorothy Osborne, *The Love Letters of Dorothy Osborne to Sir William Temple, 1652–54,* ed. Edward Abbott Parry, 3rd ed. (London and Sydney, 1888), letter 36, n. pag. Web. 2 July 2012 <http://www.gutenberg.org/files/12544/12544-h/12544-h.htm>.

you make when you say that 'tis not melancholy makes you do these things, but a careless forgetfulness. Did ever anybody forget themselves to that degree that[2] was not melancholy in extremity? Good God! how you are altered; and what is it that has done it? I have known you when of all the things in the world you would not have been taken for a discontent;[3] you were, as I thought, perfectly pleased with life at Chicksands.[4] Your condition—what has made it so much worse since [then]? I know nothing you have lost, and am sure you have gained a friend that is capable of the highest degree of friendship you can propound, that has already given an entire heart for that which she received, and 'tis no more in her will than in her power ever to recall it or divide it; if this be not enough to satisfy you, tell me what I can do more? There are a great many ingredients [that] must go to the making me happy in a husband. First, as my cousin Franklin says, our humours[5] must agree; and to do that he must have that kind of breeding that I have had, and used that kind of company.[6] That is, he must not be so much a country gentleman as to understand nothing but hawks and dogs, and be fonder of either than his wife; nor of the next sort of them whose aim reaches no further than to be Justice of the Peace, and once in his life High Sheriff, who reads no book but statutes, and studies nothing but how to make a speech interlarded with Latin that may amaze his disagreeing poor neighbors,[7] and fright them rather than persuade them into quietness. He must not be a thing that began the world in a free school, was sent from thence to the university, and is at his furthest when he reaches the Inns of Court, has no acquaintance but those of his form in these places, speaks the French he has picked out of old laws, and admires nothing but the stories he has heard of the revels that were kept there before his time.[8] He must not be a town gallant[9] neither, that lives in a tavern and an ordinary,[10] that cannot imagine how an hour should be spent without company unless it be in sleeping, that makes court to all the women he sees, thinks they believe him, and laughs and is laughed at equally. Nor a traveled Monsieur[11] whose head is all feather inside and outside, that can talk of nothing but dances and duets, and has courage enough to wear slashes[12] when everyone else dies with cold to see him. He must not be a fool of no sort, nor peevish, nor

---

[2] **that:** who.   [3] **discontent:** a discontented person.   [4] **Chicksands:** the Osborne family home in Bedfordshire.   [5] **humours:** temperaments.   [6] **he must have . . . that kind of company:** i.e., her husband must have a background like hers and socialize with the same kinds of people.   [7] **disagreeing poor neighbors:** neighbors fighting over a minor matter.   [8] **he must . . . his time:** he must not be a boring drudge from a minor family who reached his social zenith at the Inns of Court.   [9] **gallant:** man about town.   [10] **ordinary:** an inn, particularly a cheap inn where meals are provided at a regular (or ordinary) price.   [11] **Monsieur:** probably an affected man who apes foreign manners.   [12] **slashes:** cuts in a garment revealing another garment of a different color; impractical, fashionable, and costly.

ill-natured, nor proud, nor covetous; and to all this must be added, that he must love me and I him as much as we are capable of loving. Without all this, his fortune, though never so great, would not satisfy me; and with it, a very moderate one would keep me from ever repenting my disposal.[13] I have been as large and as particular in my descriptions as my cousin Molle is in his of Moor Park, but that you know the place so well I would send it you, nothing can come near his patience in writing it, but my reading on't. Would you had sent me your father's letter, it would not have been less welcome to me than to you; and you may safely believe that I am equally concerned with you in anything.

[13] **disposal:** choice (of a husband).

Dangerous Games: Railing Satire and Censorship

Lovers burn with passion in *As You Like It*, but more literal burning haunts the play, which shows how dangerous words can be. Verbal liberty leads to attempted arson and fratricide and forced exile. After Orlando erupts in fury at his brother, Oliver plots to have him killed and then burns down his house. When Duke Frederick calls Rosalind treacherous, she defends herself with words he denounces as devious and banishes her on pain of death. Such crises would not have sounded far-fetched in early modern England, where the reigning queen had spent her youth in dread of being executed as a traitor, where powerful families were torn apart by internal feuds over money and land, and where courtiers risked being accused as traitors or heretics by speaking too freely or by defending the honor of fathers who had died as traitors. Writers who rankled the crown could be censored or they could undergo more drastic punishments, like Puritan John Stubbs, who lost his right hand for daring to criticize the queen's plan to marry the duke of Anjou, a Frenchman and a Catholic, or like Ben Jonson, whose satiric play *Isle of Dogs* (1597) landed him in jail.

Satire is the art of detraction that aims to correct and reform institutions and people. Satiric speech is critique with an edge of ridicule, so it is inherently dangerous. The self-appointed satirist in Arden is Jaques, who promises he will "through and through / Cleanse the foul body of th'infected world" if only he can have the fool's "liberty" to "blow on whom I please, for so fools have" (2.7.59–60, 47, 49). The Duke upbraids him for being as bad or worse as those he would criticize; and although Jaques threatens to "rail" against the world, he never erupts with the volcanic anger of the harshly insulting ("railing") satirist. The fool's license he longs for is illusory anyway: Shakespeare makes it obvious that Touchstone too must keep his tongue within bounds. When Touchstone tells a joke about a foolish knight, Celia cuts him off because he mentions her father: "Speak no more of him; you'll be whipped for taxation one of these days." Touchstone answers back, but at a risk: "The more pity that fools may not speak wisely what wise men do foolishly" (1.2.61–64). In other words, a witty fool had to fear being punished for his mocking insults ("taxation") because fools were indeed whipped when they ventured too close to the bone. Celia, surprisingly, replies that he has a point: "By my troth, thou sayest true; for since the little wit that fools have was silenced, the little foolery that wise men have makes a great show" (1.2.65–66).

Celia's pointed lines about silencing sound strikingly topical to many readers. Shakespeare may be referring to the general censorship of plays by the Master of Revels (the official who oversaw the content of plays), but a more likely context is the church's violent attempt to gag satirists, writers who vigorously "taxed" vices and follies of people and institutions. Writers of satire traditionally justified themselves by asserting they sought to purge society of its "diseases" and to defend both its ethical norms and its legitimate rulers, but at this moment some satirists were mocking every aspect of human life as fallen, decadent, and diseased, without offering cures or virtuous models.[1] The official response was severe: in 1599 a handful of writers in the satiric mode were subjected to an unprecedented act of censorship. Their books were recalled and then burned on the order of church officials. The offensive generated controversy among more moderate satirists who felt that the railing satirists deserved what they got; the following pair of documents forms a kind of "snarling" dialogue between John Marston, a key target of the censors, and one of his many detractors.

A CLASH OF SATIRISTS

In his notorious *Scourge of Villainy*, playwright-poet John Marston created the persona of a "railing" satirist full of bitterly acid denunciations, modeled on the "savage indignation" of Roman satirist Juvenal. Satirists increasingly painted themselves as snapping dogs, cruel doctors, and furious masters, ready to punish folly (Figure 23). Writers who took the more moderate Horace as their ideal condemned Marston and others for their insubordinate excesses. Even these moderates may have felt a touch of fear, however,

[1] William R. Jones, "The Bishops' Ban of 1599 and the Ideology of English Satire," *Literature Compass* 7.5 (May 2010): 332–46. Web. <http://onlinelibrary.wiley.com/doi/10.1111/j.1741-4113 .2010.00701.x/abstract>.

FIGURE 23 *A railing Wit punishes a foolish writer with the help of Time, from I. D.,* A Scourge for Paper-Persecutors, Or Papers Complaint, Compil'd in Ruthfull Rimes, against the Paper-Spoylers of These Times *(1625).*

in June 1599, when the Bishops' Ban was issued. The document regulated the censorship of histories and plays and banned satire outright (whether in the form of book-length verses or short witty epigrams), ruling "That no *Satires or Epigrams* be printed hereafter." On June 4, the wardens of Stationers' Hall made a bonfire of John Marston's *Pygmalion* and *The Scourge of Villainy,* Edward Guilpin's *Skialethia,* T. M.'s *Snarling Satires,* John Davies'

Epigrams, and the scathing antifeminist satires *Of Marriage and Wiving* and *The Fifteen Joys of Marriage,* among other works.

Satire could not be so easily put down, and quickly migrated to other genres, including drama.[2] Written in this period, *As You Like It* shows a sustained interest in the conflict between liberty of thought and speech that taught and upheld morality, and malicious license to spew rancorous and lewd catalogues of vice into the public ear. Pastoral leisure created the space for satire in the dialogues about court corruption in particular (see Chapter 1), but satire is politically risky because it tends to criticize not only individual fools, but also corrupt institutions. Satirists of every stripe defended themselves from charges of seditious overreaching by saying, just as Jaques does, that they are like physicians who must hurt to heal, lancing the boils of vice in order to "Cleanse the foul body of th'infected world" (2.7.60). Duke Senior appears to echo the general backlash when he accuses Jaques of being a hypocrite and venting "all th'embossèd sores and headed evils" into society and infecting it anew (2.7.67).

In the London literary world, some writers rushed to differentiate themselves from the Juvenalian-Marstonian railers. The poet, epigrammatist, and antiquary John Weever (1576–1632) blasted them in *The Whipping of the Satyre* (1601), arguing that railers usurped the authority rightfully belonging to the throne to diagnose and correct wrongs and vices. More pamphlets followed, and Weever himself was satirized in plays by Marston, Jonson, and Dekker. The following pair of excerpts show Marston baiting the lightweights and dilettantes who attack the lofty and superior "Satyrist" (whose name refers to the shaggy half-goat, half-man that some writers wrongly identified as the originator of satire). Marston eggs on his foes, saying their scorn will only make him more famous. Weever sneers back at him, calling his verses libelous and Marston worthy of hanging. (Obviously, while Weever takes on the scourger for violating "the law of all civility," he was not above wielding the whip himself.) How do these satirists throw light on the style of Jaques? Who and what are his targets and does he violate civility with violent abuse? Is his railing like that of Marston, or does he respect authority with moderation, as endorsed by Weever? How does the Duke berate him for present speech or past deeds (2.7.62), and is he deadly serious or partly joking?

---

[2] Lynda E. Boose, "The 1599 Bishops' Ban, Elizabethan Pornography, and the Sexualization of the Jacobean Stage," *Enclosure Acts: Sexuality, Property, and Culture in Early Modern England,* ed. Richard Burt and John Michael Archer (Ithaca: Cornell UP, 1994), 185–200.

→ JOHN MARSTON

From The Scourge of Villainy   *1598*

Fie Satyr[1] fie, shall each mechanic slave,
Each dunghill peasant, free perusal have
Of thy-well labored lines? Shall each satin suit,
Each quaint fashion-monger, whose sole repute
Rests in his trim gay clothes, lie slavering[2]   5
Tainting thy lines with his lewd censuring?
Shall each odd puisny of the Lawyers' Inn,[3]
Each barmy-froth,[4] that last day did begin
To read his little, or his *nere a whit*,[5]
Or shall some greater ancient, of less wit,   10

. . . .

Lie gnawing on thy vacant time's expense?
Tearing thy rhymes, quite altering the sense?
Or shall perfum'd *Castilio*[6] censure thee?   15
Shall he oerview thy sharp-fang'd poesy?
(Who nere read farther than his Mistress' lips)
Nere practic'd ought, but some spruce capering skips
Nere in his life did other language use,
But, *Sweete Lady, faire Mistress, kind hart, dear coz*,[7]   20
Shall this *Fantasma*, this *Colosse*[8] peruse
And blast with stinking breath, thy budding Muse?
Fie, wilt thou make thy wit a Curtezan[9]
For every broking hand-crafts artizan?
Shall brainles Cytern heads, each jubernole,[10]   25
Pocket the very Genius of thy soul?
Aye Phylo,[11] aye, I'le keep an open hall,
A common, and a sumptuous festival,
Welcome all eyes, all eares, all tongues to me,
Gnaw peasants on my scraps of poesy.   30

---

[1] **Satyr**: satirist (Marston); also the genre personified.   [2] **slavering**: drooling like a dog.   [3] **puisny of the Lawyers' Inn**: novice at the Inns of Court.   [4] **barmy-froth**: know-nothing.   [5] *nere a whit*: formulaic legal phrases.   [6] *Castilio*: a typical fop.   [7] *coz*: cousin, used as term of endearment.   [8] *Fantasma*, this *Colosse*: illusion, monster.   [9] **make thy wit a Curtezan?**: shall I sell my wit like a whore?   [10] **Cytern heads, each jubernole**: witless slackers and idiots.   [11] **Phylo**: friend of the satirist.

John Marston, *The Scourge of Villainy. Three Books of Satires* (London, 1598), sigs. B–B3v; STC 17485.

Castilios, Cyprians, court-boys, Spanish blocks,
Ribanded ears, granado-netherstocks,[12]
Fiddlers, Scriveners, peddlers, tinkering knaves,
Base blue-coats, tapsters, broadcloth-minded slaves,
Welcome i'faith, but may you nere depart,   35
Till I have made your galled hides to smart.
Your galled hides? Avaunt, base muddy scum.
Think you a Satire's dreadful sounding drum
Will brace[13] it selfe? and deign to terrify,
Such abject peasants' basest roguery?   40
No, no, pass on ye vain fantastic troupe
Of puffy youths; Know I do scorn to stoop
To rip your lives. Then hence lewd nags, away,
Go read each post, view what is played to day.
Then to Priapus gardens.[14] You Castilio,   45
I pray thee let my lines in freedom go,
Let me alone, the Madams call for thee
Longing to laugh at thy wit's poverty.
Sirrah, livery cloak,[15] you lazy slipper slave,
Thou fawning drudge, what would'st thou Satyres have?   50
Base mind away, thy master calls, begone,
Sweet Gnato[16] let my poesy alone.
Goe buy some ballad of the Fairy King,
And of the beggar wench,[17] some roguey thing
Which thou mayst chant unto the chamber-maid   55
To some vile tune, when that thy Master's laid.[18]
But will you needs stay? am I forc'd to bear,
the blasting breath of each lewd Censurer?
Must naught but clothes, and images of men
But sprightless trunks,[19] be Judges of my pen?   60
Nay then come all, I prostitute my Muse,
For all the swarm of Idiots to abuse.
Read all, view all, even with my full consent,
So you will know that which I never meant;
So you will nere conceive, and yet dispraise,   65
That which you nere conceiv'd, & laughter raise:
Where I but strive in honest seriousness,

[12] Castilios . . . granado-netherstocks: fops, lechers, ganymedes, fashionistas.   [13] brace: mute.
[14] Priapus gardens: Priapus was a phallic god, so, a brothel district.   [15] livery cloak: a servant,
perhaps a gentleman.   [16] Gnato: court-flatterer, from character in Terence's *Eunuch*.   [17] Fairy
King . . . wench: typical penny ballad.   [18] laid: asleep.   [19] sprightless trunks: headless zombies.

To scourge some soul-polluting beastliness.
So you will rail, and find huge errors lurk
In every corner of my Cynic work.   70
Profess, read on, for your extrem'st dislikes
Will add a pinion,[20] to my praises' flights.
O, how I bristle up my plumes of pride,
O, how I think my Satires dignifi'd,
When I once heare some quaint Castilio,   75
Some supple mouth'd slave, some lewd Tubrio,
Some spruce pedant, or some span-new come fry
Of Inns a-court,[21] striving to vilify
My dark reproofs. Then do but rail at me,
No greater honor craves my poesy.   80

[20] **add a pinion:** add a feather, i.e., your scorn will make me famous.   [21] **Inns a-court:** Inns of Court.

→ JOHN WEEVER

From The Whipping of the Satyre   *1601*

The Satyrist now, like a masty[1] dog,
Chained in his kennel for to make him curst,
Lay grinning long, at last he broke his clog;[2]
But with his collar almost choked first,
And with full mouth, or rather foul-mouthed speech   5
He roared at all, or else he worried each.

What though the world was surfeited[3] with sin,
And with the surfeit dangerously sick,
And with the sickness had miscarried been
Must it of force his filthy physic[4] lick,   10
Who little knowing what it ought to have
For purging pills, a pilled purgation[5] give?

[1] **masty:** burly.   [2] **clog:** physical restraint.   [3] **surfeited:** filled to overflowing.   [4] **filthy physic:** disgusting medicine.   [5] **pilled purgation:** a defective emetic or enema.

John Weever, *The Whipping of the Satyre* (London, 1601), sigs. B7v–Cv, C6v, Er–v; STC 14071.

And seeming wondrously carefully inclined
Did Lopez-like[6] pretend arch-villainy,[7]
Mixing the poison of malicious mind,   15
Instead of a present sovereign remedy:
For that we may think there's poison foisted in,
Because the world swells bigger sin with sin.

O wonder great! Is it not villainy,
That one should live by reckoning up of vice,   20
And be a sin-monger[8] professedly,
Involuming offenses[9] for a price?
Yet by the same doth purchase but the shame,
And blaming others, merits others' blame.

O, is it not a work of wickedness,   25
To pick up sins, and pack up villainies,
To flesh one's pen with fat of filthiness,
And heap together men's iniquities?
Fearing belike (but fearing it to show)
That some dear year of sin[10] would soon ensue.   30

. . . .

Thus you supposed the people's hearts to win
By Machiavellian damned policy:[11]
For seeing men inclined to such sin,
You feasted them with all variety,
And lest you should this vile pretense reveal,   40
Did hypocrite it with a show of zeal.[12]

. . . .

Was one not hanged of late for libelling?
Yes questionless. And you deserve the same   50
For you before whole volumes forth did bring,
And whom you pleased, did liberally defame.
For shall we his by right a Libel call,
That touched but some? not yours, that aimed at all?

. . . .

---

[6] **Lopez-like:** like Rodrigo Lopez, Queen Elizabeth's physician, executed in 1594 (possibly wrongly) for plotting to poison the queen.   [7] **pretend arch-villainy:** performed evil deeds.
[8] **sin-monger:** dealer in sins.   [9] **Involuming offenses:** stocking up on sins.   [10] **dear year of sin:** storing up sins against some future dearth (like a dealer in commodities).   [11] **Machiavellian damned policy:** devious evil supposedly promoted by Niccolò Machiavelli (1469–1527).   [12] **hypocrite . . . zeal:** played the hypocrite in pretending to be pious.

Our noble princess[13] (Lord preserve her Grace)
Made godly laws to guide this commonweal   80
And hath appointed officers in place,
By those her laws with each offence to deal:
Well look those rolls,[14] no office over-skip,
And see if you can find the satyr-ship.[15]

If not, dare you usurp an office then   85
Without the license of her Majesty,
To punish all her subjects with the pen,
Against the law of all civility?
I have him up,'tis petty treason all
And therefore fear to break his neck this fall.[16]   90

Aye, but he sees the laws are broken still,
And cannot bridle[17] men's licentious lives.
Well, if he cannot, yet his worship will,[18]
And in these satyr-ship above it strives,
Thinking (O heavens) his vile injurious speech   95
Will princes' laws, law's justice over-reach.

[13] **Princess:** Queen Elizabeth. [14] **rolls:** records. [15] **satyr-ship:** (joking) "chief satirist." [16] **"I have him up . . . this fall":** I've thrown him (as in wrestling or bearbaiting) but can't kill him because his crime is only petty treason. [17] **bridle:** discipline, control. [18] **if he . . . worship will:** i.e., he will keep trying.

HORNING, SLANDER, AND WAYWARD WIT

As the burning of satires indicates, attacking others with harsh mockery and satiric speech could be risky. *As You Like It* shows various wits playing with fire despite this fact. Sure of herself in her doublet and hose, Rosalind indulges in witplay that spurs Celia to chide her as a traitor to her sex. Prime among these are jokes about cuckoldry, or female infidelity, that gave husbands imaginary sets of horns. Ganymede/Rosalind teases Orlando that as a married man he will constantly worry about his wife's sexual fidelity to him. The paradox is that she seems to be slandering herself as lustful. She crows about her ability to save her own skin, even if he catches her in another man's bed, saying that the most headstrong women have the sharpest wits ("The wiser, the waywarder" 4.1.122–23).

Such barbed joking springs out of the tradition of women's horn humor with roots in Italian tales called novellas; a tale in which a wife caught red-handed saves her own life with a witty answer appears in the second text below by Giovanni Boccaccio. In popular culture, the fear of the horn bred many jokes, stories, and plays in which women got the laugh. Some jokes were casual and offhand, just like the misogynist jests men leveled at women. How do Touchstone, Rosalind, and Jaques all play in different ways on horn humor (3.3, 4.1, 4.2)? Such jesting was a double-edged sword, painting wives as whorishly prone to sin, but also revealing women's power over men, including the power to shame them. During the raucous fall holiday called Horn Fair, women openly reveled in displaying and blowing horns, and sang songs mocking men for their real or imagined horns. Women could use the threat of "horning" to control their abusive husbands or they could attack enemies using horns to damage their reputations or those of other women. Some women and men used horning to enliven festivals and mock their neighbors at the same time, as the following documents of a famous libel case in Wells demonstrate.

☞ From *Hole* v. *White*: A Lawsuit for Libel in Wells *1607–08*

Because being called cuckold was so feared by men, women and men could use horning to target political opponents. A notorious example took place in the English town of Wells in 1607–08, when a group of people organized elaborate spectacles to shame and mock a godly constable named John Hole using symbols of cuckoldry. Their goal was revenge: Hole and his supporters had tried to suppress the popular midsummer shows, annual revels that generated funds for the parish church and drew huge crowds of spectators. Hole's faction angered a large number of townsfolk (including the mayor and the dean of Wells Cathedral), and they and most of the town rallied against Hole's group and in support of the shows. For weeks on end the streets were filled with drummers, parades, cross-dressed boys and men, effigies of giants and characters from Robin Hood legends, morris dancing, music, and sports of many kinds.

During the festivities Hole and his friends were subjected to various forms of mocking street theater by his neighbors, who branded them adulterers and cuckolds. He filed a complaint alleging he had been slandered, naming Edmund and Thomasine White as principal actors and defendants, along with several others. The following excerpt specifies one of his key charges. He claims that the defendants planned and carried out actions defaming him as an adulterer and his friend John Yard as a cuckold, since Hole was depicted as sleeping with

---

Hole v. *White* (1607–08), PRO: STAC 8/161/1 sheet 2 19* (19 April), sheet 220* (10–15 May), sheets 5v–6 (15 May). In James Stokes, ed., *Records of Early English Drama: Somerset* (Toronto: U of Toronto P, 1996). Web. 9 July 2012 <http://archive.org/stream/somersetREED01stokuoft/ somersetREED01stokuoft_djvu.txt>.

Yard's wife and a mocking rhyme repeated this claim. At one point a man on horseback rode through town holding up a board punched with holes for balls below pictures of Hole, Yard, and Yard's wife, signifying they were playing "the holing game" of adultery. The whole town was soon repeating the mocking rhyme that went with the game, and it was even reprinted in London. Hole's complaint is followed by the answer of defendant Thomasine White, who (like Jaques) denied she singled out anyone in particular for satire; she also denied dressing boys up as women, or having "hooped and hallowed" outside Hole's door as he claimed. Nonetheless, Hole was successful in his suit, which resulted in heavy fines for Edmund White and the public shaming of his fellow mockers in the pillory, showing the dangerous power of cuckoldry jesting and popular satire.

The documents in *Hole* v. *White* are unusual for the length, intensity, and variety of the popular satire they record, but all of the elements were familiar parts of popular culture. Horns and horn jokes were in constant use in all sorts of mocking acts and texts by women and men, few instances of which reached the law courts. Why does Rosalind, as Ganymede, tease Orlando by predicting he will wear horns when he is a married man? Is she deliberately abusing her own sex, as Celia says later (4.1.155)? In reading the legal document below, note the use of cross-dressing as part of revelry and popular satire. Does Rosalind's male mask make her more bold and reckless? If her "wayward" female wit leads her to make horn jokes, how does she cover herself with more joking?

[John Hole's complaint of libel.]

Edmund White . . . and the rest of the said confederators, still practicing to disgrace the good name of your said subject and of the said John Yard, Humphrey Palmer, and Hugh Mead, did . . . devise, make, and put into writing, publish, and divulge . . . one false, slanderous, infamous & wicked libel in rhyme or verse against your said subject, thereby maliciously and slanderously defaming & disgracing your said subject and the said John Yard, Hugh Mead, and Humphrey Palmer, and thereby setting forth and expressing the said disordered sports, shows and representations, which infamous libel or rhyme followeth in these words (videlicet):

> My loving friend that love to play
> Use not my Holing game by day,
> For in the night I take it best
> When all the birds are in their nest,
> Then I do live in quiet rest
> and think my Holing game the best. . . .

Which libel doth scandalize and defame your said subject John Hole in the words . . . "the Holing game" throughout the said libel, alluding to your said subject John Hole his name. . . . The which infamous libel as well the said Edmund White & Thomasine his wife as also all the rest of the said confederate & ill-disposed persons did oftentimes in and since the said month of July read, sing, and publish, and caused to be read, sung, or published, and scattered divers copies thereof in Wells aforesaid and in divers and sundry other places, towns & parishes both within your said county of Somerset and elsewhere. . . .

[Interrogatories for Thomasine White, Defendant]

Item: Upon the third day of May . . . did [you] who were chosen and named lords and ladies . . . dance hand-in-hand . . . till you . . . danced near to the complainant's house and there hooped and hallowed[1] and beat up drums? And did you . . . dance there hence, till you came to a tavern in the said town, and did you and your company thence continue dancing the long dance till you did meet the complainant and compass in[2] the complainant and beat or strike up one or two drums round about or near the plaintiff. . . .

Item: Did you, or any other by your abetment[3] or procurement[4] upon Ascension Day in the said fifth year of the king's . . . reign apparel[5] diverse boys and maids in women's apparel? [If you did so, did] those boys and maids, both before and after service that day, [go thusly] appareled . . . about the streets of the said town with other company of Morris dancers, drums, muskets, and other shows, whereby[6] there were two thousand persons or thereabouts [who were] there assembled from diverse places, [to attend] churches and divine service, [who instead beheld] the said shows, [and were] the said boys and maids were not kept in an inn or garden and elsewhere with diverse other[s] at prayer time that day?

[Response of Thomasine White]

To the fifth interrogatory this defendant said that . . . she this defendant and sundry other women of the said town, [with] their husbands in their company, did in sport and merriment dance together hand-in-hand in [a] civil manner along the streets in Wells and so they did pass . . . near the said complainant's house as they did by other men's houses in the said town at which time they had only musicians in their company and not any drum. Nor doth [she] remember that any person did hoop and hallow when they

---

[1] **hooped and hallowed:** hooted and hollered.   [2] **compass in:** surround.   [3] **by your abetment:** with your encouragement.   [4] **procurement:** assistance.   [5] **apparel:** as a verb, to dress.   [6] **whereby:** here, as a result of which.

came near . . . the said complainant as they were so dancing, but as she this defendant and others of the then company were then standing still hand-in-hand at or near the door of this defendant's house the now complainant came amongst them and would have thrust this defendant from her door without any occasion[7] given him by the defendant. Whereupon this defendant used words to the said complainant, viz: "Master Constable I am at my own door and here I will stand." But neither this defendant nor any other by her means did then thrust or jostle the said complainant and compass in the said complainant and beat or strike up any drum about or near him. . . .

To the ninth [interrogatory] she said that neither she this defendant nor any other by her abetment or procurement did upon Ascension Day in the fifth year of his Majesty's reign apparel any boys or maids. . . . [I]n women's apparel, either before morning or evening prayer that day. But after evening prayer that day . . . this defendant did apparel and dress a little girl that day to go and make a show with diverse other little children in the said town in such honest and civil manner as hath been heretofore [customary], and behold such May sport as were then made in the said town. At which time diverse persons were in the streets of the said town to behold the said May sports. But no persons to her knowledge did absent themselves from divine service for that purpose.

[7] occasion: reason.

→ GIOVANNI BOCCACCIO

From The Decameron   *1620*

Laughter is an unpredictable force. Women who participate in jesting, especially with men, might easily find themselves the targets of misogynist attacks equating female jesting with whorishness. Even in a comedy in which a princess indulges in love games and bawdy jokes, the specter of violent shaming cannot be banished. When Touchstone parodies Orlando's poems, he tosses out a loaded line: "Then to cart with Rosalind" (3.2.91). This image summons up the noisy street where prostitutes were "carted," that is, tied to a cart and paraded through town, sometimes stripped to the waist and whipped. Rosalind's instant desire for Orlando, her joyful flight away from male surveillance, and his "publication" of his infatuation (hanging her name on every tree) make her vulnerable to the poison barbs of the fool who paints her as wanton. She is also an exile on

Giovanni Boccaccio, *The Decameron Containing an Hundred Pleasant Novels* (London, 1620), sigs. D3–D4v; STC 3172.

the lam, and might fear being hunted by Duke Frederick because she has fled with his daughter. But she seems not to fear such dangers, and continues on with her pleasures until she is ready to end the game. The one person with the standing to object to her willfulness, Duke Senior, does not—a sure sign that the invitation expressed in the play title extends to women as well as to men.

In her jesting with Orlando, Rosalind edges even closer to danger but then dispels it through laughter. How does Rosalind plan to talk her way out of being found in her neighbor's bed (4.1.131–34)? Is such wit "wise" or "wayward," and is such wit an unstoppable force (4.1.122–27)? In what other ways do women in the play risk ruining their reputations, and by what means does the play ensure that the ending is happy, at least for the moment?

The woman who can talk her way out of anything and get the best of her husband is a prominent feature of the Italian novella tradition given literary form by Giovanni Boccaccio (1313–1375) in the fourteenth century and imitated and adapted by many writers. *The Decameron* is a series of stories told by three gentlemen and seven gentlewomen who have fled from the plague in Florence together. They spend their days in a beautiful villa and to try to forget the terrible scenes they have left behind, they trade stories on given themes. English playwriting was deeply affected by tales of this kind, and Shakespeare based many of his plots on Italian novellas. In some of these Italian stories, when women pursue sexual and romantic wills, the quest leads not to erotic bliss or marriage but to tragedy and death. In others, women who face such a crisis manage to pull off a dangerous gamble with their reputations and lives.

In the following story from the *Decameron*, a woman caught in adultery by her husband faces a sentence of death, but she comes up with an answer that convulses the court in laughter and saves her own life. Her wit also moves the court to change its laws concerning adultery. Does *As You Like It* place any "laws" or rules governing gender roles, love, sex, and marriage in question? What part do wise and wayward women play in this questioning?

From *The Decameron*

[Sixth Day, Seventh Novella]

Wherein is declared, of what worth it is to confesse a truth, with a facetious and witty excuse.

Madam Philippa, being accused by her Husband Rinaldo de Pugliese because he took[1] her in adultery with a young gentleman named Lazarino de Guazzagliotri: caused her to be cited before the Judge. From whom she delivered herself[2] by a

---

[1] *took*: caught   [2] *delivered herself*: saved herself

sudden, witty, and pleasant answer, and moderated a severe strict statute formerly made against women.

After that Madame Fiammetta had given over speaking, . . . the queen enjoined Philostratus to proceed on next with his novel,[3] which caused him to begin thus.

"Believe me Ladies, it is an excellent and most commendable thing to speak well and to all purposes: But I hold it a matter of much greater worth, to know how to do it, and when necessity doth most require it. Which a Gentlewoman (of whom I am now to speak) was so well instructed in, as not only it yielded the hearers mirthful contentment, but likewise delivered her from the danger of death, as (in few words) you shall hear related.

"In the city of Prato, there was an edict or statute, no less blameworthy (to speak uprightly) then most severe and cruel, which (without making any distinction) gave strict command that every woman should be burned with fire, whose husband found her in the act of adultery with any secret or familiar friend, as one deserving to be thus abandoned, like such as prostituted their bodies to public sale or hire. During the continuance[4] of this sharp edict, it fortuned that a gentlewoman who was named Phillippa was found in her chamber one night in the arms of a young gentleman of the same city, named Lazarino de Guazzagliotri . . . by her own husband, called Rinaldo de Pugliese, she loving the young gallant as her own life, because he was most complete in all perfections, and every way as dearly addicted to[5] her.

"This sight was so irksome to Rinaldo that, being overcome with extreme rage, he could hardly contain from[6] running on them, with a violent intent to kill them both. But fear of his own life caused his forbearance, meaning to be revenged by some better way. Such was the heat of his spleen[7] and fury, as, setting aside all respect of his own shame, he would needs prosecute the rigor of the deadly edict, which he held lawful for him to do, although it extended to the death of his wife.[8] Hereupon, having witnesses sufficient to prove the guiltiness of her offence, a day being appointed, without desiring any other counsel, he went in person to accuse her, and required justice against her.

"The gentlewoman—who was of a high and undauntable spirit, as all such are who have fixed their affection resolvedly and love upon a grounded deliberation—concluded, quite against the counsel and opinion of her

---

[3] novel: story. [4] continuance: the period the law was in force. [5] addicted to: devoted to. [6] contain from: stop himself from. [7] spleen: anger and vengefulness. [8] setting aside . . . wife: ignoring the shame it would bring him, he insisted on seeking the full punishment allowed by law, even though it would cause his wife's death.

parents, kindred, and friends, to appear in the court, as desiring rather to die by confessing the truth with a manly courage, than by denying it and her love unto so worthy a person as he was, in whose arms she chanced to be taken. . . . So, before the potestate[9] she made her appearance, worthily accompanied both with men and women, all advising her to deny the act. But she, not minding them or their persuasions, looking on the judge with a constant countenance and a voice of settled resolve, craved to know of him what he demanded of her?

"The potestate well noting her brave carriage, her singular beauty and praiseworthy parts, her words apparently witnessing[10] the height of her mind, began to take compassion on her and doubted, lest she would confess some such matter as should enforce him to pronounce the sentence of death against her. But she, boldly scorning all delays or any further protraction of time, demanded again, what was her accusation?

"'Madame,' answered the potestate, 'I am sorry to tell you what needs I must: your husband (whom you see present here) is the complainant against you, avouching[11] that he took you in the act of adultery with another man; and therefore he requires that, according to the rigor of the statute here in force with us, I should pronounce sentence against you, and consequently the infliction of death.[12] Which I cannot do, if you confess not the fact, and therefore be well advised, how you answer me, and tell me the truth, if it be as your husband accuseth you, or no.'

"The lady, without any dismay or dread at all, pleasantly thus replied: 'My Lord, true it is, that Rinaldo is my husband and that he found me, on the night named, between the arms of Lazarino, where many times heretofore he hath embraced me according to the mutual love re-plighted together,[13] which I deny not, nor ever will. But you know well enough, and I am certain of it, that the laws enacted in any country ought to be common and made with consent of them whom they concern, which in this edict of yours is quite contrary.[14] For it is rigorous against none, but poor women only, who are able to yield much better content and satisfaction generally than remaineth in the power of men to do. And moreover, when this law was made, there was not any woman that gave consent to it, neither were they called to like or allow thereof,[15] in which respect it may deservedly be termed, an unjust law. And if you will, in prejudice of[16] my body, and of

---

[9] potestate: magistrate. [10] witnessing: demonstrating. [11] avouching: claiming, or, possibly, swearing. [12] infliction of death: execution. [13] re-plighted together: the mutual love they professed to one another. [14] which . . . contrary: your edict runs against this general principle. [15] neither . . . thereof: nor were they asked whether they liked or would allow the law. [16] in prejudice of: to the injury of.

your own soul, be the executioner of so unlawful an edict it consisteth in your power to do as you please.

'But before you proceed to pronounce any sentence, may it please you to favour me with one small request: namely, that you would demand of my husband, if at all times, and whensoever he took delight in my company, I ever made any curiosity,[17] or came to him unwillingly.' Whereto Rinaldo, without tarrying[18] for the potestate to move[19] the question, suddenly answered that (undoubtedly) his wife at all times, and oftener then he could request it, was never sparing of her kindness, or put him off with any denial. Then the lady, continuing on her former speeches, thus replied: 'Let me then demand of you my Lord, being our potestate and judge, if it be so, by my husband's own free confession, that he hath always had his pleasure of me, without the least refusal in me, or contradiction; what should I do with the over-plus remaining in mine own power,[20] and whereof he had no need? Would you have me cast it away to the dogs? Was it not more fitting for me, to pleasure therewith a worthy gentleman, who was even at death's door for my love, than (my husband surfeiting,[21] and having no need of me) to let him lie languishing and die?'[22]

Never was heard such an examination before, and to come from a woman of such worth, the most part of the honourable Pratosians (both lords and ladies) being there present, who hearing her urge[23] such a necessary question, cried out all aloud together with one voice (after they had laughed their fill) that the lady had said well, and no more than she might. So that, before they departed thence, by comfortable advice proceeding from the potestate, the edict (being reputed over-cruel) was modified, and interpreted to concern them only, who offered injury to their husbands for money.[24] By which means Rinaldo, standing as one confounded, for such a foolish and unadvised enterprise, departed from the auditory—and the lady, not a little joyful to be thus freed and delivered from the fire, returned home with victory to her own house.

---

[17] made any curiosity: acted peculiarly. [18] tarrying: waiting. [19] move: ask. [20] over-plus . . . power: her surplus desire after marital sex. [21] surfeiting: satisfied. [22] at death's door . . . die: i.e., wasn't it better to help my lover who was suffering from extreme desire? [23] urge: ask. [24] interpreted . . . for money: i.e., the law was changed to punish only wives who took money for sex.

CHAPTER 4

The Civilizing Process

><

No one is born civilized. A child slowly acquires this trait through myriad encounters with codes of acceptable behavior. Today we tend to see civilization as a place, and being civil as basic politeness. These usages would sound odd to the early modern English, who saw civility as much more — including "refinement," "orderly behavior," and "citizenship."[1] In Jaques's speech about the Ages of Man (2.7.138–65) a child grows out of untamed infancy and wild youth into a more civil and settled adulthood. Yet each age is vulnerable to some excess, whether it is erotic passion, ambition, or finally senility. Civility placed a curb on extremes, but the quality was more than good manners, confirming one's political integrity and sociability. Whether one was judged to be civil was deeply affected by status, religion, gender, wealth, education, and access to leisure.

A high level of civility was commonly associated with the *gentry*, the well-to-do elites. Displaying civility demonstrated one's upbringing and might create the impression of gentry status. For these reasons civility was an indispensable quality to cultivate for those seeking to rise in the world and achieve gentle status. Closely associated with civility was the ambiguous term *gentle*, which sometimes connoted gentry status, but was often applied

---

[1] "Civility," *Oxford English Dictionary*.

to anyone who was considered especially charitable, educated, well-spoken, or dignified. Such qualities had to be nurtured by parents and teachers or acquired though will and discipline. In short, the production of a civil self was a complex process. The title of this chapter is taken from a book by Norbert Elias that demonstrates that civilization is an ongoing process of an entire society over the centuries, and that it involves the increasing surveillance and control of the body to make it more governable by the state.[2] In this section, however, we adopt the term somewhat playfully, to signify the transformation that a few people can go through in the course of a holiday in the greenwood.

Birth, Gentility, and Grace

Civility and gentleness suggested one might be a member of the gentry, then, but did not confirm it. Could true gentility be found among ordinary people? What entitled one to be called a gentleman or gentlewoman? Could one learn to seem gentle even if not born to the gentry? Some commentators held that birth and wealth were crucial to achieving gentle status, while others singled out the absence of labor: to be gentle meant one could afford to live without working. Still others insisted that virtue, good manners, and grace were more important, and that a rich but rude and vicious son of a gentleman (Oliver comes to mind) was not a true gentleman. Some who were not born gentle rose to the gentry by amassing property and paying for titles, to the sneers of writers such as Henry Peacham, who denounced those who rose through wealth "raked up by Mechanick and base means." Many readers who sought to appear more gentle and civil studied self-help books like Peacham's; he also attracted readers by arguing against inherited privilege, saying that only grand and noble actions make a gentleman, not his "race or Lineage."[3]

There were other ways to learn about gentle manners. Many people flocked to theaters where they could see actors impersonating courtiers and aristocrats, thus gaining lessons in conduct at second hand. These lessons were not always straightforward. *As You Like It*, for example, suggests that high birth alone can teach or confer gentility, since it opens with a violent clash between brothers who are gentle only in the most limited senses of the word. Since their father's death, Sir Oliver de Boys has inherited his title

[2] Norbert Elias, *The Civilizing Process: The History of Manners*, trans. Edmund Jephcott (Oxford, UK and Cambridge, MA: Blackwell, 1982).
[3] Henry Peacham, *The Compleat Gentleman* (London, 1622), 2–4; STC 19502.

and lands and rules the family as a tyrant, invested by primogeniture with all the powers of a living father. Orlando bitterly resents his brother for giving him no training in the qualities he has a right to by birth. He demands that Oliver "breed" him as befits "the gentle condition" of his blood, giving him "such exercises as may become a gentleman" (1.1.3, 33, 53). Orlando sees these exercises as more precious than money or property, and his own behavior shows the damage done to him by the lack of proper education in the fullest sense of the word. But all is not lost. To his own great good fortune, he has been blessed with a quality given to only a few people, and one that can make up for almost any lack: his own "graces" (2.3.11), which are so great they arouse envy.

This quality of *grazia* or grace (which also might be translated as charm) is at the heart of the most important work in the Renaissance on the art of acting the gentleman: Baldassare Castiglione's *Il libro del Cortegiano* which appeared in the English translation, *The Courtyer*, by Sir Thomas Hoby in 1561. A renowned courtier himself, Castiglione (1478–1529) treats gentility as a demanding social performance of great complexity. In his book noblemen and noblewomen debate whether the ideal courtier must possess noble blood above all, or instead show the more rare quality of *grazia* in all he does. This leads them to a related question: can the quality of grace be acquired, and if so, what is the best way to do so? The discussion naturally turns to education and imitation, two concepts that were firmly associated in the period. Who could serve as the best teachers and models for the aspiring courtier, and what are the best regimens for instruction?

SCHOOLING VS. TRAINING

Education did not turn a boy or girl into a gentleman or a lady, but it could help create the impression of gentility. One could gain an education by being tutored at home (a possibility for both girls and boys) or by spending years at the grammar school, open to boys only. There they were taught Latin and other subjects from age six or so, lasting seven or eight years. Only a few students sought higher learning after that. Orlando envies his brother Jacques for being sent to university, where "report speaks goldenly of his profit" (1.1.4–5). University was not a requirement for becoming a member of the gentry, however. Traditionally, English nobles and the gentry did not consider a period at university necessary or even desirable for their sons, largely because of the stigma of labor attached to scholarship. By the 1590s more scions of privilege were going to university or the Inns of Court than ever before, but the total numbers were still not large.

Orlando's weighty grievance clearly extends beyond being kept from school or university. He has been denied any training in the complex art of gentility, which connotes a high degree of literacy and culture, religious piety, wise judgment and self-control, and conformity to decorums that fix him within the social hierarchy, especially deference and service to his superiors. A gentleman had to know how to manage his own estate and how to ride and hunt. He had to be reverent, pious, and modest at certain times, canny and politic at others. He had to be generous and affable as both host and guest. He was groomed to maintain family honor and political interests, to marry, and to father heirs, and he had to know how to court a lady gracefully. All this was expected of any gentleman, but special training in music, dancing, fencing, languages, and poetry added cosmopolitan polish.

Orlando complains he has been taught none of this. To drive the point home he castigates Oliver for taking better care of his prize horses, who "are taught their manage, and to that end riders dearly hired" (1.1.9). His complaint echoes that of Elizabeth's tutor Roger Ascham, who fumed that

> more care is had, yea and that among very wise men, to find out rather a cunning man for their horse than a cunning man for their children . . . for the one they will gladly give a stipend of 200 crowns a year and loath to offer the other two hundred shillings. God that sitteth in Heaven laugheth their choice to scorn and rewardeth their liberality as it should be he suffereth them to have a tame and well-ordered horse but wild and unfortunate children.[4]

Oliver has been even stingier than these fathers, since he has given Orlando nothing but the care granted the lowliest farmworker on his estate. This neglect is cruel and unloving, but Orlando sees it as even worse: a violent act that unnaturally pits brother against brother in civil war. He paints Oliver as an enemy who digs under his feet, seeking to destroy his native gentility by educating him so badly: "He lets me feed with his hinds, bars me the place of a brother, and as much as in him lies, mines my gentility with my education" (1.1.13–15). Just as Ascham predicts, Oliver's neglect of Orlando produces a "wild and unfortunate" youth prone to violence, an outcome deplored in moralizing texts both high and low (Figure 24).

Both Ascham and Orlando refer to horse training, an analogy that reveals much about the early modern mind-set about both parenting and schooling. Writers on education often compared small boys to animals whose natural

---

[4] Kenneth Charlton, *Education in Renaissance England* (London and New York: Routledge, 2007), 213–14.

FIGURE 24 *Bad nurture: brothers fight in front of a father-fool, from Sebastian Brant,* Stultifera Navis . . . The Ship of Fools, *trans. Alexander Barclay (1570).*

wildness had to be curbed by strong discipline. Orlando's wildness stems from never having been "tamed" correctly by a careful father, not from lack of ability. He shows so much natural talent that even Oliver marvels at it: "Yet he's gentle, never schooled and yet learned, full of noble device, of all sorts enchantingly beloved" (1.1.120–22). The play's action bears out his observation—to a degree. Orlando introduces himself to admiring ladies with elaborate self-deprecation, wrestles skillfully, and shows kindness and paternal care toward his old servant Adam. When Duke Senior finds out who

Orlando's father is, he invites Orlando to join his court in exile, conferring on him a higher status than he ever had at home. Now at leisure in the forest, Orlando composes verses and dallies with a pretty "ganymede," just as a worldly courtier might (for more on the meanings of *ganymede*, see Chapter 2). Yet Orlando has flaws of rudeness, and he knows it. What in his actions toward his brother and Duke Senior shows that he cannot manage "the show / Of smooth civility" (2.7.95–96)? When does he show lack of training in sociable conversation, especially in speaking to gentlewomen? When he tries to act the role of a gentle lover, why are his poems laughed at?

Rosalind and Celia outclass Orlando and Oliver de Boys in almost every way. Sir Roland was a knight of some fame, but that title is lowly compared to a duke's. In contrast, Rosalind and Celia are princesses. As daughters of dukes, their status is second only to that of their fathers, and they have been raised and educated together at court, probably by tutors. Celia is the sole heir of a duke with a vast estate, much larger than that of Oliver de Boys, and she prudently brings gold with her to make her escape. Rosalind is also sole heir of the rightful duke, Duke Senior, who is restored to power (along with his property, presumably). Despite the gentlewomen's holiday humor, they never speak or act with the rougher wildness that both of the men display, and they quickly settle into a leisured life in the forest. Unlike Orlando and Touchstone, Celia and Rosalind address most strangers politely. Their language is witty and casually literary, packed with wordplay and allusions as they joke about Hercules, Gargantua, Pythagoras, and Caesar. They are used to teasing each other and mocking courtiers and fools, but they switch instantly into formal language when necessary. How does their diction (choice of words) and tone change when addressing the angry Duke Frederick?

Orlando has no such reservoir of training in speaking well, but his awkwardness stems from lack of experience with the highborn, not just from lack of schooling or "exercises." To serve in the household of a prominent person was a golden opportunity for gentlemen's sons to acquire social graces. Many scions were sent for periods to the houses of well-off family friends or relatives, where they acted as pages and servants, absorbing culture, manners, and conversation from watching their elders. This training was in some ways more important than a university education, and many leading Elizabethan courtiers had, in their youth, waited on great men in their households. Loving bonds and friendship between gentle servants and the master and his family could easily develop because a gentleman-servant was of the same, or nearly the same, social status as those he served. The character Amiens, for example, is not a mere servant-entertainer who must sing when bidden, but a gentleman and courtier who happens to sing well, and that is why Jaques must cajole him into singing.

Orlando has taken all his meals with farm laborers; therefore he is unlikely to know or practice manners appropriate to his status. When Orlando tells Rosalind/Ganymede he must leave for two hours to "attend the Duke at dinner" (4.1.137), he probably serves him at table, thus acquiring a taste of gentle manners. Even though Orlando has started off on the wrong foot, mistaking the Duke for someone "savage" and threatening him, the Duke forgives him and accepts him quickly into his inner circle. Part of the comedy is that Orlando has a special charisma that glosses over his flaws. As Adam puts it, "Why are you virtuous? Why do people love you? / And wherefore are you so gentle, strong, and valiant?" (2.3.5–6). He's so charming that no one objects to the idea that a penniless younger brother with no education will attract and marry the Duke's brilliant daughter and acquire her fortune. That scenario would be unlikely in the real world, but it was a fantasy of social mobility that was popular in many plays and tales, and it would probably appeal to the workers and apprentices in Shakespeare's audience who had never seen the inside of a grammar school, either.

CONDUCT LITERATURE

For those who were literate in English as well as ambitious, like Orlando, but lacked gentle skills, there was the printed word. In the late sixteenth century, more books in English were being published than ever before, and many publishers found a lucrative niche in "courtesy books" and "conduct literature," or guides to virtuous living, good manners, courtiership, and conversation, as well as sports and pastimes such as hawking, hunting, and dancing. More than a thousand such books were printed in the sixteenth century (Figure 25).[5] English writers found they could profit from providing manuals for the expanding and ambitious middle classes, though many guides were translations of Italian or French works, such as Castiglione's *The Courtyer* and Vincentio Saviolo's book on dueling (see p. 161 in this volume), which Touchstone parodies near the end of the play: "Oh, sir, we quarrel in print, by the book; as you have books for good manners" (5.4.76–77).

Training in civil conversation and manners was best begun early in life, but those who struggled to play catch-up might well consult Desiderius Erasmus's international best seller *A Little Book of Good Manners for Children*

---

[5] Ruth Kelso, *The Doctrine of the English Gentleman in the Sixteenth Century* (Gloucester: P. Smith, 1964), appendix.

FIGURE 25 *Male and female models of gentility, from Richard Brathwaite,* The English Gentleman and English Gentlewoman *(1641).*

(p. 366) or pore through Giovanni della Casa's *Galateo* (p. 401) to improve their table talk. Readers who hoped to rise socially via a good match could consult manuals on composing poetry (such as John Brinsley's *Ludus Literarius*, p. 380) and writing persuasive love letters (see *Cupid's Messenger*, p. 324). Conduct writers drew fine distinctions between civil and rude behaviors, no matter how minor. Activities meant to be relaxing, such as sports and games, and simple actions of daily life, such as walking, eating, talking, and joking, received detailed scrutiny. Books aimed at women were far more concerned with sexual reputation than those for men, as the excerpt below from *The English Gentlewoman* will show. One of the paradoxes of such manuals is that they urge the reader to seem natural and unaffected, yet they hammer home the point that society will judge the would-be gentleman and gentlewoman on how they perform gentility, especially that hard-to-fake quality known as "grace," discussed by the aristocrats at the court of Urbino, the setting for Castiglione's hugely influential book.

→ BALDASSARE CASTIGLIONE

From The Courtyer   1561

Translated by Thomas Hoby

Diplomat, courtier, and writer Baldassare Castiglione (1478–1529) was one of the foremost thinkers in the Renaissance, primarily known for *Il libro del Cortegiano*, his book about the ideal courtier, which he wrote and rewrote from 1513 to 1528. Read widely in England, the work takes the form of a dialogue, presenting a fictional series of conversations and debates by noblemen and women gathered in the palace of Urbino, where Castiglione served Duke Guidobaldo da Montefeltro for many years, often traveling abroad to foreign courts, including the English court of Henry VII. The speakers in *The Courtyer* are historical figures personally known to Castiglione, including cardinals, counts, duchesses, and other prominent members of his circle. The debates on *cortigianeria* (courtiership) are lively and often dramatic, even comic at times, with many contrasting points of view by distinctive personalities.

Castiglione's book became an international phenomenon, read in the original and in translation in Italy, Spain, France, England, northern Europe, and

Baldassare Castiglione, *The Courtyer of Baldessar Castilio, Divided into Four Books, Very Necessary and Profitable for Young Gentlemen and Gentlewomen Abiding in Court, Palace, or Place*, trans. Thomas Hoby (London, 1561), bk. I, sigs. C1–C3v, E1–E3, bk. III, sigs. BbIII, Cc1, Cc2; STC 4778.

even farther afield. The work offered guidance for those in power at court and, for the multitudes of readers who were not, a window into the refined mores of a cultural elite as well as instruction in acquiring gentle manners, paving the way for the ambitious and the clever to rise in status. While in Paris, Sir Thomas Hoby, a diplomat and translator, produced an English version that was published in 1561. Castiglione's example influenced later English writing on conduct and education, including Sir Thomas Elyot's *The Book Named the Governor* (1531; see p. 158) and Roger Ascham's *The Schoolemaster* (1570), as well as books debating love and marriage, such as George Whetstone's *An Heptameron of Civil Discourses* (1582; see p. 227) and John Lyly's fashionable novel *Euphues, the Anatomy of Wit* (1578).

The Courtyer is divided into four books, and each stresses grace, elegance, naturalness, and skill in conversation, both as topics for discussion and by example, since the group is full of brilliant talkers and wits. The main debates are between men, but the noblewomen play a crucial role as moderators and questioners, often joking with and teasing the debaters. The Duchess of Urbino, Elizabetta Gonzaga, presides over the meetings of the group, and her companion Lady Emilia Pia takes an active role in some exchanges. Castiglione covers a wide variety of matters, including techniques and rules about jesting, how a courtier may best serve and advise a prince, the qualities a lady must have to be a suitable match for an ideal courtier, and the limits and potential of love for the aging courtier.

In the excerpts below, two noble courtiers hold forth on what constitutes gentility. Count Ludovico da Canossa[1] takes the conservative line that blue blood must come first and foremost, but Gasparo Pallavicino[2] forcefully argues the opposite view. How would Gasparo judge the degree of gentility shown by Oliver as opposed to Orlando, or Duke Frederick as opposed to his brother, Duke Senior? What distinctions would Canossa draw between these pairs of brothers, if any? Who are the most gracious and graceful characters in the play and how are they distinguished from those who do not possess this quality? Canossa speaks of "nurture," and so does Orlando (2.7.96–97), which signifies how one is raised, but how does each link the quality of that nurture to gentle parentage? Gasparo argues that true grace does not depend on high birth. Note that Oliver envies Orlando his inborn virtues, and that Duke Frederick tells Celia that her cousin Rosalind's virtues outshine hers, and that she should shun her. What about pressure to become the ideal courtier might foster not just gracious manners, but envy and rivalry within families and at court? How does personal charm and beauty figure into this debate? How does the playful debate over the gifts of Fortune and Nature in act 1, scene 2 echo the topics raised by Castiglione?

---

[1] **Canossa:** Veronese nobleman, bishop, and ambassador of Pope Leo X to England and France; friend and kinsman of Castiglione.　[2] **Gasparo Pallavicino:** close friend of Castiglione; nobleman from Cortemaggiore; takes misogynist position in later debates.

From *The Courtyer*

[Duchess Elizabetta Gonzaga[3] directs her guests to devise a pastime or game for the company. Of the ideas offered, one game pleases her best: they will "shape in words a good Courtier, specifying all such conditions and particular qualities, as of necessity must be in him that deserveth this name." Count Canossa is chosen to begin the debate, and he maintains that the ideal courtier must be noble by birth.]

[Count Canossa.] I will have this our Courtier therefore to be a gentleman born and of a good house. For it is a great deal less dispraise for him that is not born a gentleman to fail in the acts of virtue than for a gentleman. If he swerve from the steps of his ancestors, he staineth the name of his family, and doeth not only not get, but loseth that is already gotten. For nobleness of birth is (as it were) a clear lamp that showeth forth and bringeth into light, works both good and bad, and enflameth and provoketh unto virtue, as well with the fear of slander, as also with the hope of praise. . . . Therefore it chanceth always (in a manner) both in arms and in all other virtuous acts, that the most famous men are gentlemen. Because nature in every thing hath deeply sowed that privy seed, which giveth a certain force and property of her beginning, unto whatsoever springeth of it, and maketh it like unto her self. As we see by example not only in the race of horses and other beasts, but also in trees, whose slips and grafts always for the most part are like unto the stock of the tree they came from: and if at any time they grow out of kind, the fault is in the husbandman. And the like is in men, if they be trained up in good nurture, most commonly they resemble them from whom they come and often times pass them, but if they have not one that can well train them up, they grow (as it were) wild, and never come to their ripeness. Truth it is, whether it be through the favour of the stars or of nature, some there are borne endowed with such graces, that they seem not to have been born, but rather fashioned with the very hand of some God, and abound in all goodness both of body and mind. As again we see some so unapt and dull, that a man will not believe, but nature hath brought them into the world for a spite and mockery. And like as these with continual diligence and good bringing up for the most part can bring small fruit: even so the other with little attendance climb to the full perfection of all excellency. . . . The Courtier therefore, beside nobleness of birth, I will have him to be fortunate in this behalf, and by nature to have not only a witty, and a comely shape of person and countenance, but also a certain grace, and (as

[3] **Duchess Elizabetta Gonzaga:** wife of Guidobaldo da Montefeltro, Duke of Urbino, and a close friend of Castiglione.

they say) a hue,[4] that shall make him at the first sight acceptable and loving unto who so beholdeth him. And let this be an ornament to frame and accompany all his acts, and to assure men in his look, such a one to be worthy the company and favor of every great man.

[Gasparo Pallavicino disagrees: the ideal courtier is distinguished not by high birth but by his virtuous charm and grace.]

I say . . . that this nobleness of birth is not so necessary for the Courtier. And if I wist[5] that any of you thought it strange or a new matter, I would allege unto you sundry,[6] who for all they were born of most noble blood, yet have they been heaped full of vices: and contrariwise, many unnoble that have made famous their posterity.[7] And if it be true that you said before, that the privy force of the first seed is in every thing, we should all be in one manner condition,[8] for that we had all one self beginning, and one should not be more noble then another. But beside the diversities and degrees in us of high and low, I believe there be many other matters, wherein I judge fortune to be the chief, because we see her bear a stroke[9] in all worldly things, and (as it were) take a pastime to exalt[10] many time whom pleaseth her without any desert at all, and bury in the bottomless depth the most worthy to be exalted. I confirm your saying as touching the happiness of them that are born abounding in all goodness both of mind and body: but this is seen as well in the unnoble, as in the noble of birth, for nature hath not these so subtle distinctions: yea (as I have said) we see many times in persons of most base degree, most high gifts of nature. Therefore seeing this nobleness[11] is gotten neither with force, nor art, but is rather a praise of our ancestors than our own, me think it a strange opinion that the parents of our Courtier being unnoble, his good qualities should be defaced, and these our good conditions which you have named should not be sufficient to bring him to the top of all perfection: that is to say, wit, beauty of physiognomy, disposition of person,[12] and that grace which at the first sight shall make him most acceptable unto all men.

COURTLY GRACE AND *SPREZZATURA*

The next section explores the indispensable quality of grace that makes a courtier admired and loved; a few are blessed with it, but others may try to

---

[4] hue: "air" or attitude. [5] wist: believe. [6] sundry: various people. [7] posterity: descendents. [8] one manner condition: all the same status. [9] bear a stroke: have a hand. [10] take a pastime to exalt: have fun raising up. [11] this nobleness: this so-called nobleness. [12] beauty . . . person: loveliness in face and graceful bearing.

acquire it by seeking out and imitating "the most cunning men." Finally, the Count discusses a trait that gives the impression of grace, called *sprezzatura*, which literally means "setting a lower price on" something. The best courtiers will not display his talents in a way to show off how much effort it took to acquire them; instead, he will toss them off lightly as not being very important or difficult. In this way the courtier appears to achieve something effortlessly, rather than with labor and study. Indeed, he must use "art to hide art"—he must be clever in concealing his own effort in order to seem naturally blessed with grace.

Does any noncourtly character have grace, and if not, is this a certain marker of gentle status in the play? When Touchstone invents verses mocking Orlando, is he displaying grace and *sprezzatura*, or their opposite? What actions and speeches show that Orlando might possess grace but not *sprezzatura*? When and how does Rosalind act with *sprezzatura*? If she also possesses grace, is it inborn or acquired, and in what scenes does Shakespeare show evidence of this?

[Count Canossa is asked how one may acquire *grazia*, or grace.]

[Cesare Gonzaga.[1]] If I do well bear in mind . . . the Courtier ought to accompany all his doings, gestures, demeanors, finally all his motions with a grace, and this, me thinks, you put for a sauce to every thing, without the which all his other properties and good conditions were little worth. And I believe verily that every man would soon be persuaded therein, for by the virtue of the word a man may say, that whoso hath grace is gracious. But because you have said sundry times that it is the gift of nature and of the heavens, and again where it is not so perfect, that it may with study and diligence be made much more, . . . I would fain know what art, with that learning, and by what mean they shall compass this grace, as well in the exercises of the body (wherein ye think it so necessary a matter) as in all other things that they do or speak. Therefore as you have in praising this quality to us engendered (I believe) in all a fervent thirst to come by it, by the charge ye received of the Lady Emilia, so with teaching it us, ye are bound to quench it.

[Count Canossa:] Bound I am not (quoth the Count) to teach you to have a good grace, nor anything else, saving only to show you what a perfect Courtier ought to be. . . . Notwithstanding to fulfill your request in what I am able, although it be (in manner) in a proverb that grace is not to be learned, I say unto you, whoso mindeth to be gracious or to have a good grace in the exercises of the body, (presupposing first that he be not of

[1] **Cesare Gonzaga:** member of the ruling family of Mantua, friend and cousin of Castiglione.

nature unapt) ought to begin betimes, and to learn his principles of cunning men.[2] . . . And of men whom we know nowadays, mark how well and with what a good grace Sir Galeazzo Sanseverino, master of the horse to the French king, doth all exercises of the body: and that because, beside the natural disposition of person that is in him, he hath applied all his study to learn of cunning men, and to have continually excellent men about him. . . . And even as the bee in the green meadows flieth always about the grass choosing out flowers: so shall our Courtier steal this grace from them that to his seeming have it,[3] and from each one that parcel that shall be most worthy praise. . . .

[Count Canossa discusses the vital quality of nonchalance (*sprezzatura*).]

But I, imagining within myself oftentimes how this grace cometh, leaving a part such as have it from above, find one rule that is most general which in this part (methinks) taketh place in all things belonging to man in word or deed above all other. And that is to eschew as much as a man may, and as a sharp and dangerous rock, *Affectation* or curiosity and (to speak a new word) to use in everything a certain *Recklessness*[4] [*sprezzatura*], to cover art withal, and seem whatsoever he doth and sayeth to do it without pain, and (as it were) not minding it. And of this do I believe grace is much derived, for in rare matters and well brought to pass every man knoweth the hardness of them, so that a readiness therein maketh great wonder. And contrarywise to use force, and (as they say) to hale by the hair, giveth a great disgrace, and maketh everything how great so ever it be, to be little esteemed. Therefore that may be said to be a very art that appeareth not to be art, neither ought a man to put more diligence in any thing then in covering it: for in case it be open, it loseth credit clean, and maketh a man little set by.[5] And I remember that I have read in my days, that there were some excellent orators, which among other their cares, enforced themselves to make every man believe that they had no sight[6] in letters, and dissembling their cunning, made semblant[7] their orations to be made very simply, and rather as nature and truth led them, than study and art, the which if it had been openly known, would have put a doubt in the people's minds for fear lest he beguiled them. You may see then how to show art and such bent[8] study taketh away the grace of every thing.

---

[2] **cunning men:** wise and skillful men.   [3] **so shall . . . have it:** he will imitate those who possess grace.   [4] *Recklessness:* Hoby's translation is too negative; "nonchalance" is closer to the mark.   [5] **Therefore . . . set by:** i.e., you should strive to conceal your own artfulness, because if it's too obvious, it won't impress anyone.   [6] **no sight:** no understanding.   [7] **made semblant:** made it seem.   [8] **bent:** labored.

FEMALE COURTIERSHIP

Many scenes in *As You Like It* show repartee between courtly ladies and their objects of desire, or lightly mocking byplay between pastoral lovers (see Chapter 1). The omnipresent parallel was to Elizabeth's court, with a glance at French and Italian courts across the sea, where queens, duchesses, and their ladies set a high standard for wit and conversation and performed in or watched many pastoral plays and entertainments. Elizabeth was Italianate in her tastes, and her court was highly attuned to the manners cultivated on the Continent, gaining knowledge through foreign travel and through travelers' accounts, courtesy books, stage plays, language manuals, collections of Italian poetry and novellas, and romance epics by Tasso and Ariosto, as well as contacts with Italians in London and exposure to commedia dell'arte players who performed pastorals and comedies occasionally at court.[1]

Castiglione's book was a prime resource in this quest, and literate Englishwomen who aspired to serve or participate at court, or simply wished to refine their conversation and comportment, mined its pages avidly. They were sure to turn to Book 3, in which the question of what constitutes the ideal Court Lady is considered. Most of her sought-after qualities, such as "noble courage," mirror those of the male Courtier, but a special importance is given to beauty and to discretion—the ability to safeguard her sexual reputation through prudence, moderation, and excellence in judgment when conversing with men. The company agrees that in addition to being wise, courageous, and virtuous, the ideal Court Lady is expected to display her skill in verbal repartee and badinage; "a ready liveliness of wit, whereby she may declare herself far wide from all dullness" (see p. 359).

Do the four women of *As You Like It* display the attributes of Castiglione's ideal Court Lady, and if so, who exemplifies which traits? What positive qualities do they share with Castiglione's ideal male Courtier? Does Shakespeare show a contrast between the two gentlewomen reared at court, Celia and Rosalind, on any of these points? Note that neither the court of Duke Frederick nor Duke Senior's court-in-exile features men interacting graciously with women; would Cesare Gonzaga maintain that neither shows true courtiership because they are basically all-male? Is Shakespeare implying that the byplay of gentle couples in the forest is more civil and courteous?

---

[1] See Michael Wyatt, *The Italian Encounter with Tudor England: A Cultural Politics of Translation* (Cambridge: Cambridge UP, 2005).

BOOK 3

[The Duchess directs Giuliano de'Medici[2] to discuss the ideal Gentlewoman. When one nobleman objects that it is irrelevant when they should be discussing the Courtier, Cesare Gonzaga rebuts him soundly:]

You are in a great error, answered Lord Cesar Gonzaga . . . no court, how great ever it be, can have any sightliness, or brightness in it, or mirth without women, nor any Courtier can be gracious, pleasant or hardy, nor at any time undertake any gallant enterprise of chivalry unless he be stirred with the conversation and with the love & contentacion[3] of women, even so in like case the Courtier's talk is most unperfect ever more, if the intercourse of women give them not a part of the grace wherewithal they make perfect and deck out their playing the Courtier.

[Giuliano de' Medici considers first what qualities distinguish the Court Lady from the Courtier, and what qualities she shares with him.]

For many virtues of the mind I reckon be as necessary for a woman, as for a man. Likewise nobleness of birth, avoiding *Affectation* or curiosity, to have a good grace of nature in all her doings, to be of good condition, wit, foreseeing, not haughty, not envious, not ill-tongued, not light, not contentious, not untowardly, to have the knowledge to win and keep the good will of her Lady and of all others, to do well and with a good grace those exercises comely for women. Methink well beauty is more necessary in her than in the Courtier, for (to say the truth) there is a great lack in the woman that wanteth[4] beauty. She ought also to be more circumspect and to take better heed that she give no occasion to be ill reported of, and so to behave herself, that she be not only not spotted with any fault, but not so much as with suspicion. Because a woman hath not so many ways to defend herself from slanderous reports, as hath a man. . . . I say that for her that liveth in Court, methinks there belongeth unto her above all other things, a certain sweetness in language that may delight, whereby she may gently entertain all kinds of men with talk worth the hearing. . . . Accompanying with sober and quiet manners and with the honesty that must always be a stay to all her deeds, a ready liveliness of wit, whereby she may declare herself far wide from all dullness: but with such a kind of goodness, that she may be

---

[2] **Giuliano de'Medici:** youngest son of Lorenzo de'Medici and brother of Pope Leo X; called Lord Julian in Hoby's text. [3] **contentacion:** pleasingness, charm. [4] **wanteth:** lacks.

360 | THE CIVILIZING PROCESS

esteemed no less chaste, wise and courteous, than pleasant, feat, conceited[5]
& sober: & therefore must she keep a certain mean very hard . . . and come
just to certain limits, but not pass them.[6] This woman ought not therefore
(to make herself good and honest) be so squeamish and make wise to abhor
both the company and the talk (though somewhat [of] wantonness)[7] if she
be present, to get her thence by and by, for a man may lightly guess that she
feigned to be so coy to hide that in herself, which she doubted others might
come to the knowledge of: & such nice fashions[8] are always hateful. Neither
ought she again (to show herself free and pleasant) speake words of dishon-
esty, nor use a certain familiarity without measure & bridle . . . but being
present at such kind of talk, she ought to give the hearing with a little blushing & shamefastness. . . .

[How the Gentlewoman should speak to a Gentleman.]

Let her beware of praising her self indiscreetly, or being too tedious that she
make him not weary. Let her not go mingle with pleasant and laughing talk,
matters of gravity: nor yet with grave, jests and feat conceits. Let her not
foolishly take upon her to know that she knoweth not, but soberly seek to be
esteemed for that she knoweth, avoiding (as is said) *curiosity*[9] all things. In
this manner . . . her talk shall be plenteous and full of wisdom, honesty, and
pleasantness: and so shall she be not only beloved but reverenced of all men,
and perhaps worthy to be compared to this great Courtier, as well for the
qualities of the mind as of the body.
   I will that this woman have a sight[10] in letters, in music, in drawing or
painting, and skilful in dancing, and in devising sports and pastimes, accompanying with that discreet sober mode and with the giving a good opinion
of herself, the other principles also that have been taught the Courtier. And
thus in conversation, in laughing, in sporting, in jesting, finally in everything she shall be had in very great price, and shall entertain accordingly
both with jests & feat conceits meet for her, every person that cometh in her
company. And albeit staidness, nobleness of courage, temperance, strength
of the mind, wisdom and the other virtues a man would think belonged not
to entertain, yet will I have her endowed with them all, not so much to
entertain (although notwithstanding they may serve thereto also) as to be
virtuous: and these virtues to make her such a one, that she may deserve to
be esteemed, and all her doings framed by them.

[5] **feat, conceited**: neat, witty.   [6] **keep . . . them**: she should find a middle ground and not go to
extremes.   [7] **This . . . wontonness**: she should not, to show off her virtue, criticize people and
run away when bawdy talk is going on.   [8] **such nice fashions**: affectedly prudish behavior.
[9] *curiosity*: affectation, pretension.   [10] **have a sight**: have some knowledge of.

→ **RICHARD BRATHWAITE**

From The English Gentlewoman   *1631*

Written a century after Baldassare Castiglione's *The Courtyer*, Richard Brathwaite's courtesy book is far more moralistic, concerned with female propriety
and appearances rather than with wisdom or sophisticated wit. Brathwaite
(1587/8–1673) was a barrister's son who attended Oxford, Cambridge, and Gray's
Inn and inherited a sufficient estate to live as a gentleman. His first conduct
book, *The English Gentleman*, was published in 1630, followed quickly by *The
English Gentlewoman*, dedicated to the Countess of Pembroke, Lady Anne
Clifford. In the chapter on "Behavior" excerpted below, Brathwaite advises
readers that the road to gentility is full of pitfalls for women, who are expected
to guard their sexual reputations vigilantly. He continually harps on the dangers
for women of having liberty when young, and too much company or social con-
tact. He gives special attention to encounters with potential lovers, warning
women not to become overconfident so that they can guard against falling in
love. Some women grow so bold in mocking suitors and love itself that they
"make a very *whirligig* of love" (see p. 362). Which women in *As You Like It*
treat suitors or love this way, and do they succumb to love as Brathwaite predicts? What might be the reaction of the women in the play to the proverb he
quotes: *they should be seen and not heard*, or to other passages telling gentlewomen to dress modestly, not to flirt or joke, and to shun society? How does
Castiglione's ideal gentlewoman differ from Brathwaite's, for example, in how
she deals with men's bawdy talk? Which of the two ideal types does Rosalind
resemble, the Italian or the English? What would Brathwaite say to Celia's
excitement over escaping to enjoy liberty in the forest? Are the play's attitudes
toward female liberty and outspokenness as critical as Brathwaite's, and how can
you tell?

Now, *Gentlewomen*, you are to put on your veils, and go into *company*.
Which (I am persuaded) you cannot enter without a maiden blush, a modest tincture. Herein you are to be most cautelous,[1] seeing no place can be
more mortally dangerous. . . . Would you preserve those precious odors of
your good names? Consort with such whose names were never branded,
converse with such, whose tongues for immodesty were never taxed. As by
good words evil manners are corrected, so by evil words are good ones corrupted. Make no reside there, where the least occasion of lightness is ministered; avert your ear when you hear it, but your heart especially, lest you

---

[1] **cautelous:** cautious.

Richard Brathwaite, *The English Gentlewoman* (London, 1631), 41–43, 158, 183, 187; STC 3565.

harbor it. To enter into much discourse or familiarity with strangers, argues lightness or indiscretion: what is spoken of maids, may be properly applied by a useful consequence to all women: *They should be seen, and not heard.* A traveler sets himself best out by discourse, whereas their best setting out is silence. You shall have many trifling questions asked, as much to purpose as if they said nothing: but a frivolous question deserves to be resolved by silence. For your *carriage*, it should neither be too precise, nor too loose. . . . You may possibly be wooed to interchange favors: rings or ribands are but trifles; yet trust me, they are no trifles that are aimed at in those exchanges. Let nothing pass from you, that may any way impeach you, or give others advantage over you. . . . It is dangerous to enter parley with a beleaguering[2] enemy: it implies want or weakness in the besieged. Chastity is an *enclosed garden*, it should not be so much as assaulted, lest the report of her spotless beauty become soiled. . . . How subject poor *Women* be to lapses. . . . I have known divers[3] so resolute in their undertakings, so presuming of their womanish strength, so constantly devoted to a single life, as in public consorts they held it their choicest merriment to give love the affront, to discourse of affection with an imperious contempt, jeer their amorous suitors out of countenance, and make a very *whirligig*[4] of love. But mark the conclusion of these insulting spirits: they sport so long with love, till they fall to love in earnest. A moment makes them of sovereigns, captives,[5] by enslaving them to that deservedly, which at first they entertained so disdainfully. The way then to prevent this malady, is to wean you from consorting with folly. What an excellent impregnable fortress were *woman*, did not her *windows*[6] betray her to her enemy? But principally, when she leaves her chamber to walk on the public theater; when she throws off her veil, and gives attention to a merry tale; when she consorts with youthful blood, and either enters parley, or admits of an interview with love. It is most true what the sententious moral sometimes observed: We may be in *security*, so long as we are sequestered from *society*.

---

[2]**beleaguering:** besieging, attacking. [3]**divers:** several women [4]*whirligig:* spinning toy or top. [5]**A moment . . . captives:** in an instant they change from being like queens to slaves. [6]*windows:* eyes.

➜ **WILLIAM HARRISON**

From The Description and Chronicles of England   *1577*

By one estimate, the gentry made up only 5 percent of the population of Elizabethan England. What separated this tiny elite from ordinary people? Was it possible to become a gentleman by growing wealthy and buying land? Was it possible to work and be called a gentleman? Such questions preoccupied the status-obsessed society of the day, where sons of craftsmen and small landowners were amassing property and breaking into the ranks of the gentry for the first time, just as Shakespeare did. (His father was a glovemaker, but his son acquired so much property that he managed to obtain a coat of arms and the name of a gentleman in 1596, despite working in the socially "low" professional theater.) Another way one could become gentle overnight was by fighting in a war under the earl of Essex, who knighted one hundred and fifty of his soldiers after victories in Spain and Ireland in the late 1590s.[1] These upstarts generated a great deal of negative press.

In the passage below William Harrison (1535–1593), a scholar and cleric educated at the Westminster School and Oxford University, defines the four "sorts" or degrees of status in England and takes up the question of birth versus worth. Instead of providing a definitive answer, he leaves it in suspension: "Gentlemen be those whom their race and blood, or at the least their virtues, do make noble and known" (see p. 364). His style seems curt after the elegancies of Castiglione, but his directness and sarcasm do evoke the social turmoil going on in post-Reformation England, where it was possible for a gentleman to "be made so good cheap" (see p. 364). Those who have neither high birth nor outstanding virtues draw his scorn, and he levels barbs at the self-made men who were buying their way into the gentry. Harrison spends far less time on the merchants, farmers, servants, and workers of many kinds who make up 95 percent of the country, and women are not mentioned at all.

Using his definitions of the four sorts, where do you place the major and minor characters in the play? Does anyone inhabit the borderline between gentle and nongentle status? Does anyone go downward or upward in status by the end, and by what means? Which characters are to rule, and which "to be ruled and not to rule other" (see p. 365)? Is the social hierarchy in the play more, or less, stable than the real world outside the theater at this time?

[1]Maurice A. Hunt, *Shakespeare's* As You Like It: *Late Elizabethan Culture and Literary Representation* (New York: Palgrave, 2008), 177n15.

William Harrison, "The Description and Chronicles of England," in Raphael Holinshed, ed., *The First Volume of the Chronicles of England, Scotland, and Ireland*, vol. 1 (London, 1577), 103–05; STC 135686.

From *The Description and Chronicles of England*

OF DEGREES OF PEOPLE IN THE COMMONWEALTH OF ENGLAND.

We in England divide our people commonly into four sorts, as gentlemen, citizens or burgesses, yeomen, and artificers[2] or labourers. Of gentlemen the first and chief (next the king) be the prince, dukes, marquesses, earls, viscounts, and barons; and these are called gentlemen of the greater sort, or (as our common usage of speech is) lords and noblemen: and next unto them be knights, esquires, and, last of all, they that are simply called gentlemen. So that in effect our gentlemen are divided into their conditions, whereof in this chapter I will make particular rehearsal.

[Harrison defines what sets a gentleman apart from citizens, yeomen, and artificers.]

Gentlemen be those whom their race and blood, or at the least their virtues, do make noble and known. The Latins call them *nobiles et generosos*, as the French do *nobles* or *gentlehommes*. . . . Whosoever studieth the laws of the realm, whoso abideth in the university giving his mind to his book, or professeth physic and the liberal sciences, or beside his service in the room of a captain in the wars, or good counsel given at home, whereby his commonwealth is benefited, can live without manual labour, and thereto is able and will bear the port,[3] charge, and countenance of a gentleman, he shall for money have a coat and arms bestowed upon him by heralds (who in the charter of the same do of custom pretend antiquity and service, and many gay things[4]) and thereunto being made so good cheap, be called master (which is the title that men give to esquires and gentlemen), and reputed for a gentleman ever after. Which is so much less to be disallowed of, for that the prince doth lose nothing by it, the gentleman being so much subject to taxes and public payments as is the yeoman or husbandman, which he likewise doth bear the gladlier[5] for the saving of his reputation. Being called also to the wars (for with the government of the commonwealth he meddleth little[6]), whatsoever it cost him, he will both array and arm himself accordingly, and show the more manly courage, and all the tokens of the person which he representeth. No man hath hurt by it but himself who peradven-

---

[2] **burgesses, yeomen, and artificers:** burgesses are well-off local officeholders; yeomen are small landholders; artificers are crafts workers. [3] **port:** the outward bearing and habit. [4] **of custom . . . gay things:** who generally pretend their families are longtime gentry (ironic). [5] **gladlier:** more gladly. [6] **meddleth little:** doesn't get involved.

ture will go in wider buskins than his legs will bear, or, as our proverb saith, "now and then bear a bigger sail than his boat is able to sustain."[7] . . .

Citizens and burgesses have next place to gentlemen, who be those that are free within the cities and are of some likely substance to bear office in the same. But these citizens and burgesses are to serve the commonwealth in their cities and boroughs, or in corporate towns where they dwell. . . .

Yeomen are those which by our law are called *Legales homines*, free men born English, and may dispend of their own free land in yearly revenue to the sum of forty shillings sterling, or six pounds as money goeth in our times. . . . This sort of people have a certain pre-eminence, and more estimation that labourers and the common sort of artificers, and these commonly live wealthily, keep good houses, and travel to get riches. They are also for the most part farmers to gentlemen . . . and with grazing, frequenting of markets, and keeping of servants (not idle servants, as the gentlemen do, but such as get both their own and part of their masters' living), do come to great wealth, insomuch that many of them are able and do buy the lands of unthrifty gentlemen, and often setting their sons to the schools, to the universities, and to the Inns of the Court, or, otherwise leaving them sufficient lands whereupon they may live without labour, do make them by those means to become gentlemen. These were they that in times past made all France afraid. And albeit they be not called "Master," as gentlemen are, or "Sir," as to knights appertaineth, but only "John" and "Thomas," etc., yet have they been found to have done very good service. . . .

The fourth and last sort of people in England are day-labourers, poor husbandmen,[8] and some retailers (which have no free land), copyholders,[9] and all artificers, as tailors, shoemakers, carpenters, brickmakers, masons, etc. [These] have neither voice nor authority in the commonwealth, but are to be ruled and not to rule other.

[7]**buskins . . . sustain:** i.e., overreaches and overspends.   [8]**husbandmen:** farmers.   [9]**copyholders:** tenants.

Rude and Civil Manners

Books on conduct associated rudeness with the country and the civil with the city. Those who lived in or near city and court had greater access to high culture, sophisticated conversation, and worldly knowledge, compared to the supposedly simple manners and crude mind-set and speech of country folk. The association of civility with cities is ancient, rooted in the concept that only city-dwellers can be truly cultured and mature citizens, unlike the childish peasants who were said to labor like beasts on the land. Before the sixteenth century, urbanity was one of the knightly virtues cultivated by the medieval courtier (namely fortitude, measure, moderation, decorousness, elegance, affability, wit, magnanimity, gracefulness, and naturalness) and these virtues, collectively known as *courtesy*, were absorbed into the courtly ideal described by Castiglione and others.

Shakespeare complicates and questions this traditional bias in favor of city and court. Country folk in Arden are far from urbane, but they are certainly affable and generous to the exiles from court who ask them for help. Corin kindly offers information and advice to Rosalind and Celia, serves as a middleman to help them buy land and shelter, and then works as their "friendly feeder" or servant; Silvius confides in the gentlewomen and shares his feelings freely with them. Phoebe gives her heart to Ganymede, and Audrey the goatkeeper is so taken with Touchstone that she marries him. If the country folk were more urbane and less childlike and trusting, they would perhaps be more wary of the strangers in their midst. Rosalind mocks Phoebe and tricks her into folly, for example. Touchstone intends to seduce and abandon Audrey after the wedding; and he lords it over Corin, peppering him with insults and paradoxes: "Thou worms' meat, in respect of a good piece of flesh indeed! Learn of the wise, and perpend" (3.2.53–54). Finally Corin has had enough, saying mildly, "You have too courtly a wit for me. I'll rest" (3.2.56). In these scenes who can most justly be called affable, natural, magnanimous, or measured, to cite some of the virtues associated with civility? In the scenes involving Adam, Orlando, and Oliver; and Silvius, Phoebe, and Rosalind, what characters show they possess gentility in the fullest sense of the word? Which of them seems to have absorbed the underlying lessons of humility and concern for others that Desiderius Erasmus and Giovanni della Casa teach in the works that follow?

→ DESIDERIUS ERASMUS

From A Little Book of Good Manners for Children *1532*

Translated by Robert Whittinton

"No man can choose to himself father and mother or his country; but condition, wit, and manners any man may counterfeit."[1] This invitation by the great scholar Erasmus (1466?–1566) struck a nerve with hundreds of thousands of readers

[1] sig. D3r.

Desiderius Erasmus, *A Little Book of Good Manners for Children*, trans. Robert Whittinton (London, 1532), sigs. B5v, C3, C4, D3; STC 10467.

eager to find out how. His "little book" on table manners was quickly translated and published all over the Continent, reaching England in 1532. Erasmus dedicated the book to a young prince, but he did not set up aristocrats and their outmoded ideal of chivalric courtesy as the model for mannerly behavior for people of all classes. While many of his rules (such as the classic "Don't talk with your mouth full") were centuries old, Erasmus offered something new by ignoring the courtly nobility as his prime model. He often uses dark humor and irony to teach boys the need for self-restraint to avoid the omnipresent danger of shaming oneself, and how to achieve that goal by cultivating the ability to read other people's reactions and anticipate their desires. In homely and direct language he spells out how to handle pressing bodily needs, such as blowing noses and relieving oneself, and how to converse and behave so as not to depress, annoy, or disgust other people.

The Erasmian civil body is both sociable and obedient. "Of Manners at Table" quells rebellion in that body, training it to show its subjection to authority. Erasmus shames the child from self-centered behavior by comparing bad manners to the deeds of criminals, madmen, animals, and lowly workers. The underlying message of this regime is that a child must learn to control voice, body, and emotions to ensure a respectable place in civil society. He must regulate his hunger and thirst especially at table, showing patience and piety as he says grace, gives way to elders, and takes his turn. Which Erasmian rules does Orlando break when he invades the Duke's feast? Does he learn to change this behavior, and how? Extrapolating from these principles, what codes of civil behavior are violated by other characters in the play, whether in the forest or at court? Does a person's social degree express his or her degree of civility, or do gentle characters err as much as, or more than, nongentle ones?

OF MANNERS AT TABLE

At table or at meat, let mirth be with thee, let ribaldry be exiled. Sit not down until thou have washed, but let thy nails be pared before that. [Let] no filth stick in them lest thou be called a sloven and a great niggard:[2] remember the common saying & and before make water and if need require ease thy belly, and if thou be girded too straight, to unloose thy girdle is wisdom,[3] which to do at the table is shame. When thou wipest thy hands, put forth of thy mind all grief, for at table it becometh not to be sad or to make others sad.

Commanded to say grace, apply thy countenance and thy hands to devout manner, beholding either the master of the feast or the image of Christ or of our lady: at this name Jesu or his mother Mary virgin make

---

[2] **niggard:** lazy person.   [3] **girdle . . . wisdom:** if your belt is too tight, loosen it before eating.

curtsey with both knees. If this office of saying grace be put to another both take diligent heed and make answer with like devout manner. Give place[4] with good will to another of the highest place, and if thou be bid to sit in a higher place generally refuse it, but if a man in authority bid thee often and earnestly, obey him mannerly lest though shouldest seem shamefast for lack of manners. . . . [A] child ought not come uncalled, nor let him not tarry there . . . but after he hath repasted himself sufficiently, take up his trencher, make curtsey and salute them at the table, especially the greatest person at the table.

See that thou put not thy hand first in the dish, not only because it showeth thee to be greedy, but because it is sometime joined with peril; as when [a child] taketh anything scalding into his mouth either he must spit it out again or if he swallow it down it will scald his throat: on both sides he shall be laughed at and taken as a fool. A child must somewhat tarry to accustom himself to forbear his appetite. . . . If a child sit at table with his betters, let him sit lowest,[5] nor let him not put his hand to the dish but he be bid. To thrust his fingers into his dish of pottage is the manner of carters:[6] but let him take up the meat with his knife or else his fork; nor let him not choose out this or that sweet morsel out of the whole dish, which is the property of a lickerish[7] person, but that which chanceth [to] lie toward him. . . . And if that or this morsel be very dainty, leave it to another and take of that which is next. And like as it is the manner of a glutton to thrust his hand into every part of the dish, so it is unmannerly to turn the dish up. . . . To swallow thy meat whole down is the manner of storks and devouring gluttons.

If anything be cut by another it is against manners to put forth thy hand or thy trencher before [he] offer it to thee, lest thou shouldest seem to catch that which was appointed for another. . . . To gnaw bones is the property of dogs; to pick it with thy knife is good manners. . . . Some rather devour than eat their meat, none otherwise than such as be led in to prison. This ravening and devouring is appropriate to thieves. . . .

To drink or speak with bridled or full mouth is neither honesty nor surety. . . .

Some without pause still eat and drink, not because they be hungry and thirsty but because they can no otherwise order or behave themselves. But if they scratch their head or pick their teeth or show lewd gestures with their hands or their knife or cough, hem, or spit, this manner comes all of the cart,[8] and hath in a manner a resemblance of madness.

---

[4] **Give place:** give up your seat. [5] **lowest:** farthest from the head of the table. [6] **carters:** like haulers and porters, connoting vulgarity. [7] **lickerish:** gluttonous. [8] **of the cart:** vulgar.

LEAVING THE TABLE POLITELY. SERVING AT TABLE.

[I]f thou must rise from long supper, take up thy trencher with fragments and salute him that seemeth the greatest man at the table and other likewise, and so depart: but by and by return lest thou be noted to depart because of play or of other light cause.

Returning, wait [to see] if anything lacks, or honestly attend at the table and look if any man command anything. If thou set down anything or take up, take heed thou shed nothing upon other men's clothes. . . .

Commanded to say grace, order well thy behavior, showing thyself ready unto the company, keeping silent [until] time comes to [speak]. In the mean time, let thy countenance be stable with reverence regarding the greatest man at the table.

→ BALDASSARE CASTIGLIONE

From The Courtyer   1561
A Noble Lady Shames an Uncivil Man

Translated by Thomas Hoby

Courtiership and gentility were never all-male affairs. Indeed, as Baldassare Castiglione pointed out, male gentility was confirmed in their social interactions with women, especially gentlewomen of their own rank. A famous anecdote soon after the opening of *The Courtyer* makes this point concisely. At a ball, a gentlewoman receives rude treatment from a military man who brags of his prowess, but she fashions a quick put-down that causes him to endure laughter and ridicule. Count Canossa provides a moral to the story: a courtier must never brag or boast, because a true courtier must be modest or at least clever in tooting his own horn, or risk such a social disaster. Its deeper message is that women are social players and that their participation and judgment are crucial regulating forces that tend to promote civility. The military man has violated the new codes of mixed-gender conversation and sociability at the heart of Renaissance courtly culture, which was no longer wholly dominated by male elites: women were coming into their own as performers on the stage of court life.[1]

---

[1] Fabio Finotti, "Women Writers in Renaissance Italy: Courtly Origins of New Literary Canons," *Strong Voices, Weak History: Early Women Writers & Canons in England, France, & Italy*, ed. Pamela J. Benson and Victoria Kirkham (Ann Arbor: U of Michigan P, 2005).

Baldassare Castiglione, *The Courtyer of Baldassar Castilio, Divided into Four Books, Very Necessary and Profitable for Young Gentlemen and Gentlewomen Abiding in Court, Palace, or Place*, trans. Thomas Hoby (London, 1561), bk. 1, sig. Dɪɪ-v; STC 4778.

Consider this story in relation to the moment of Orlando's gaffe at the wrestling match, when he cannot answer Rosalind. Despite all their obvious differences, how are these moments similar? When does Rosalind, or any other female character, show a similar laughing disdain toward a male, and for what reasons? What do the play's courtly gentlewomen, Rosalind and Celia, require in terms of male gentility and civility, for example, in relation to Orlando, Oliver, and Duke Frederick? How do the men reciprocate and react? What are the signs in Oliver's conversation with Celia and Rosalind that he has become more civil and gentle after being saved by Orlando? What is "ungentle" about the speech and manners of the man of action, Charles the wrestler?

From *The Courtyer*

A Noble Lady Shames an Uncivil Man

[Count Lodovico Canossa.] But to come to some particularity, I judge the principal and true profession of a Courtier ought to be in feats of arms, the which above all I will have him to practice lively, and to be known among other for his hardiness, for his achieving of enterprises, and for his fidelity toward him whom he serveth. And he shall purchase himself a name with these good conditions, in doing the deeds in every time and place: for it is not for him to feint at any time in this behalf without a wondrous reproach. . . .

Yet will we not have him for all that so lusty to make bravery in words, and to brag that he hath wedded his harness for his wife, and to threaten with such grim looks, as we have seen Berto[2] do oftentimes. For unto such may well be said that a worthy gentlewoman in a noble assembly spoke pleasantly unto one, that shall be nameless for this time, whom she to show him a good countenance, desired to dance with her, and he refusing both that, and to hear music and many other entertainments offered him, always affirming such trifles not to be his profession, at last the gentlewoman demanding him, "What is then your profession?" He answered with a frowning look: "To fight."

Then said the gentlewoman: "Seeing you are not now at the war nor in place to fight, I would think it best for you to be well besmeared[3] and set up in an armory with other implements of war till time were that you should be occupied, least you wax more rustier then you are." Thus with much laughing of the bystanders she left him with a mock in his foolish presumption.

[The Courtier] therefore that we seek for, where the enemies are, shall show himself most fierce, bitter, and evermore with the first. In every place

---

[2] **Berto:** a fool in the papal court. [3] **besmeared:** oiled, greased.

beside, lowly, sober, and circumspect, fleeing above all things bragging and unshameful praising himself, for therewith a man always purchaseth himself the hatred and ill will of the hearers.

→ NICHOLAS BRETON

From The Court and Country   *1618*

Touchstone takes courtly bias against the country to its comic extreme, telling Corin that anyone who has not been to court to see good manners is therefore wicked, and therefore damned. The old shepherd comes back with the solid pleasures and virtues of country life (3.2.28–69). Debates over whether the virtuous life was best lived in country or city and its courts were features of pastoral literature and popular texts, including the following dialogue by Nicholas Breton (1554/5–c. 1626).

The Court and Country paints an England highly conscious of its own traditional allegiance to solid country virtues and the allures and risks of the court. Breton's background made him familiar with the utter fragility of titles and courtly pretensions (Figure 26). He was descended from an old noble family from Essex, but lost his claim to the family fortune to his stepfather when his mother remarried. He became a highly regarded poet, subsisting on patronage from Mary Herbert, the sister of Sir Philip Sidney. In his book Breton expands on some of the same topics raised in *As You Like It* by Corin, Touchstone, and Duke Senior.

The debate between the foppish Courtier and his merry cousin, the Countryman, resolves nothing, but it does show a certain bias in characterization: the Courtier's manner is haughty and hyperbolic in contrast to the Countryman, who is cheerful and garrulous, but also more pious. Which of his country pleasures sound most like Corin's? Why does Shakespeare make a jester, Touchstone, the defender of courtly life? Which courtiers in the play most enjoy the country, and how are their reasons different from those of the Countryman? Who are the snobs in the comedy, and are their attitudes depicted satirically or favorably? Does any non-Courtier show true gentility in the mode described by the Countryman? If the Duke and his men enjoy the forest life, why do they return to court? Why are Audrey and William caricatured, and why is Corin depicted more favorably? What qualities mark Audrey as lacking gentility, and what cues us that she is a clown, twice over—a simple countrywoman, played by a stage comedian?

Nicholas Breton, *The Court and Country, or A Briefe Discourse Dialogue-wise Set Down between a Courtier and a Country-man Containing the Manner and Condition of their Lives* (London, 1618), sigs. A4–Dv; STC 3641.

FIGURE 26 *A farmer debates a fop, from Nicholas Breton,* The Court and Country, or A Briefe Discourse Dialogue-wise Set Down betweene a Courtier and a Country-man Containing the Manner and Condition of Their Lives *(1618).*

From *The Court and Country*

COURTIER: Cousin, well met. I see you are still for the country. Your habit,[1] your countenance, your footing, and your carriage do all plainly show you are no changeling,[2] but every day alike, one, and the same.

COUNTRYMAN: I am so indeed, and wish that you were so too; for then should you not be so great an eyesore[3] to your friends, nor such an enemy to yourself: for, I fear the place you live in is more costly than profitable. . . .

COURTIER: Oh Cousin, you cannot but confess that blind men can judge no colors, and you that live plodding to purchase a pudding,[4] cannot but distaste[5] any meat that may compare with it. . . . Oh, the gallant life of the court, where so many are the choices of contentment, as if on earth it were the paradise of the world, the majesty of the sovereign, the wisdom of the council, the honor of the lords, the beauty of the ladies, the care of the officers, the courtesy of the gentlemen, the divine service in the morning and evening, the witty, learned, noble, and pleasant discourses all day, the variety of wits, with the depth of judgments, the dainty fare, sweetly dressed and neatly served, the delicate wines and rare fruits, with excellent music and admirable voices, masks and plays and dancing and riding . . . and in the course of love such carriage of content, as so lulls the spirit in the lap of pleasure, that if I should talk of the praise of it all day, I should be short of the worth of it at night.

COUNTRYMAN: [Y]ou are like a musician that only plays upon one string. . . . But since you speak so scornfully of the country life, if you were or could be so happy as to apprehend the true content in the course of it, you would shake the head, and sigh from the heart to be so long from the knowledge of it, and never be at rest till you were gotten to it. . . .

Now for your ladies, we have pretty wenches, that, though they be not proud, yet they think their penny good silver,[6] and if they be fair it is natural.[7] . . . And for your gentlemen, we have good yeomen[8] that use more courtesy, or at least kindness, than curiosity; more friendship than compliments, and more truth than eloquence: and perhaps I may tell you, I think we have more ancient and true gentlemen that hold the plough in the field, than you have in great places that wait with a trencher at a table;[9] and I have heard my father say, that I believe to be true,

---

[1] habit: clothes.   [2] changeling: a fairy or shape-shifter.   [3] eyesore: because he's overdressed.   [4] plodding . . . pudding: working hard for plain food.   [5] distaste: dislike.   [6] they . . . silver: they know their own worth.   [7] fair . . . natural: they don't use cosmetics like court ladies.   [8] yeomen: owner of a small landed estate, usually a farm.   [9] that wait with a trencher at table: who serve as servants (many gentlemen's sons spent their youth serving in great houses).

that a true gentleman will be better known by his inside than his outside, for (as he said) a true gentleman will be . . . sober, but not proud; liberal[10] and yet thrifty; wise, but not full of words; and better seen in the law than be too busy with the laws;[11] one that fears god, will be true to his king, and well knows how to live in the world, and whatsoever god sends, hath the grace to be content with it, loves his wife and his children, is careful for his family, is a friend to his neighbor, and no enemy to himself. And this (said my father) is indeed the true gentleman. . . .

[The Countryman denounces court parasites, panders, and hypocrites, then praises country pleasures.]

COUNTRYMAN: For pleasures, believe it, we will put you down a world of steps.[12] For, first of all we rise with the lark and go to bed with the lamb, so that we have the break of the day and the brightness of the sun to cheer our spirits in our going to our labors, which many of you bar your-selves by making day of the night and night of the day. . . . We have again in our woods, the birds singing; in the pastures the cow lowing, the ewe bleating, and the fowl neighing, which with profit and pleasure makes us better music than an idle note and a worse ditty. . . .

Furthermore, at our meetings on the holidays between our lads and the wenches, such true mirth at honest meetings, such dancing on the green, in the market house, or about the maypole, where the young folks smiling kiss at every turning, and the old folks checking with laughing at their children. . . . After casting of sheep's eyes,[13] and faith and troth for a bargain, clapping of hands are seals to the truth of hearts, when a pair of gloves and a handkerchief, are as good as the best obligation[14] . . . having all this, if we serve God withal, what in god's name can we desire to have more? . . .

COURTIER: Oh Cousin, I am sorry to see your simplicity, what a deal of ado you have made about nothing? But I see the proverb holds true in you, *He that lives always at home sees nothing but the same,* and your edu-cation being but according to your disposition, somewhat of the mean-est manner of good fashion. . . . Oh Cousin, we have[15] learning in such reverence, wisdom in such admiration, virtue in such honor, valor in such esteem, truth in such love, and love in so rare account, that there doth almost nothing pass in perfection . . . furthermore, for knowledge, we

---

[10] liberal: generous.   [11] in the law . . . laws: living peacefully rather than litigating.   [12] we will put . . . steps: (idiom) we'll leave you in the dust.   [13] After casting of sheep's eyes: after looking lovingly at each other.   [14] clapping . . . obligation: by taking hands, the lovers are betrothed and exchange gifts as pledges.   [15] have: hold.

have . . . the deciphering of characters, enditing[16] of letters, hearing of orations, delivering of messages, congratulating of princes, and the form of ambassages,[17] all which are such delights of the spirit. . . .

Believe me, Cousin, there is no comparison. . . . Alas, let the cow low after her calf, and the ewe bleat after her lamb, the ass bray, the owl sing, and the dog bark; what music is in this medley? . . . To see lads lift up leaden heels, and wenches leer after their lubbers,[18] to see old folks play the fools to laugh at the birds of their own breed, and the young colts wighie[19] at their parting with their fillies, when Madge must home to milking, and Simon must go serve the beasts. What conceit is in all these courses—but to trouble a good spirit with spending time in idleness? . . .

COUNTRYMAN: Now to answer your proverbs, and as I can remember, most points of your discourses. First, let me tell you, that I hold it better to see something of mine own at home, then travel so far that I see nothing of mine own abroad, for I have heard that rolling stones gather no moss. And for my education, if it hath been simple, and my disposition not subtle, if I be not fashioned according to the world, I shall be the fitter for heaven. . . .

Now for wisdom, I heard our parson in our church read it in the holy Book of God, "*That the wisdom of the world is but foolishness before God.*"[20] And why then should a man seek to befool himself before God, with more wit then is necessary for the knowledge of the world . . . I have read in the Book of the best wisdom, "*that the fear of God is the beginning of wisdom,*"[21] and surely, he that begins his lesson there may continue his learning the better, and come to be a good scholar at last. . . . [We] content ourselves with that wisdom which is most necessary for us, to love God above all, and our neighbors as ourselves, to rise with the day rays and go to bed with a candle, to eat when we are hungry, drink when we are thirsty, travel when we are lusty, and rest when we are weary: fear God, be true to the crown, keep the laws, pay scot and lot,[22] breed no quarrels, do no wrongs, and labor all we may to have peace, both with God and man.

. . . Truly Cousin, I think every thing is best in his own nature, as one is bred so let him be: for as a Courtier cannot hold the plough, but he will be soon seen to be no workman, so a countryman cannot court it, but he will show in somewhat from whence he comes.

---

[16] **enditing:** writing.   [17] **ambassages:** embassies.   [18] **lubbers:** crude louts (with a pun on lovers).
[19] **wighie:** whinny.   [20] *That the wisdom . . . God:* 1 Corinthians 3:19.   [21] *that the fear . . . wisdom:* Proverbs 9:10.   [22] **pay scot and lot:** pay one's taxes.

Formal Schooling: Boys to Men

Education is a key motif in *As You Like It* because schooling was an indelible mark of distinction. Gentlemen were expected to be able to read and write in English and Latin by the time they reached their teens, but most of their sisters were taught only reading, sewing, writing, and elementary math. Formal schooling was neither mandatory nor free, so possessing learning served as a status marker. Many children from nongentry families spent very little time getting educated, learning their letters and numbers from mothers or servants, while others attended "petty" or "dame" schools, elementary schools often run by women who taught the basics for a small fee. As a result reading ability was far more widespread than knowing how to write, because writing instruction came at a higher price and was taught separately, placing it out of reach of many. Many more boys than girls acquired facility in writing. In 1558 at Elizabeth's accession, by one estimate, less than 5 percent of women and 20 percent of men could sign their names. A much higher number of both genders had some reading ability, perhaps as much as 50 percent of the adult population.[1]

At the age of six or seven, boys whose families could absorb the cost of losing their labor embarked on the long and painful road to Latin literacy, which lasted for seven or eight years, from sunup to sundown. No wonder students crept "unwillingly to school" (2.7.146). Gentlemen's sons might learn their Latin and other subjects from tutors at home, but more children of the gentry and middling sort took advantage of the free grammar schools that existed in many towns, such as the King's School in Stratford-upon-Avon, which Shakespeare, the son of an artisan, probably attended. After learning the rules of Latin grammar, schoolboys would proceed through a curriculum of reading and translating classical Roman works of history, philosophy, letters, orations, and poetry, a program influenced by Continental humanism. Their classical training would exceed that provided in many universities today. Plutarch, Ovid, Virgil, Cicero, and Quintilian were heavy favorites, influencing playwrights and poets who studied in such schools, including Christopher Marlowe, Ben Jonson, and Shakespeare.

Much of the teaching involved memorizing vast lists of words and rules, but some teachers stressed the use of enticing literature to gain the interest of students and lure them on to better efforts. Schoolboys were supposed to gain fluency in speaking Latin, not just reading ability. Some teachers had students act out comedies by Terence and Plautus in order to make them bold, audacious, and graceful in speaking. Losing one's fear of performing

[1] Adam Fox, *Oral and Literate Culture in England, 1500–1700* (Oxford: Oxford UP, 2000), 18–19.

FIGURE 27 *An Elizabethan schoolroom, featuring Latin, music, writing, and whipping, from "A Birching."*

must have been difficult since teaching frequently involved shouted threats of violence, and the most common teaching aid in the schoolroom was the birch rod. Some educators and thinkers, such as Erasmus, Roger Ascham, and John Brinsley, argued against beatings and promoted a more friendly and encouraging environment, but they were in the minority. Woodcuts of the schoolrooms frequently show a boy with his breeches down being beaten by a master, as if to prove this is indeed a schoolroom, a place defined by scenes of punishment and pain (Figure 27).[2]

When he left grammar school behind, the youth of sixteen or seventeen might go on to university, which meant either Cambridge or Oxford, where the typical coursework consisted of lectures in Latin, generally a reading of an authority such as Aristotle followed by commentary. Some chose not to go at all: university was meant for those who were preparing to preach or to

[2] Lynn Enterline, *Shakespeare's Schoolroom: Rhetoric, Discipline, Emotion* (Philadelphia: U of Pennsylvania P, 2011).

teach, and many wealthy sons had no intention of doing either, contented for the most part to pursue lives of sport and leisure, hunting and hawking, interrupted with a stint in Parliament or at court for the more ambitious and energetic. The situation changed only slowly under Elizabeth, with a slight upturn in the number of rich men's sons who spent time at university. For those young gentlemen who did not go to university, but wanted to be surrounded by learning and wit, the third choice was the Inns of Court in London. These resembled exclusive social clubs, since no fellowships were offered. A few future lawyers and judges studied for a life in the law, but they were outnumbered by gentlemen seeking polish, pleasure, and friendship among gallants and wits. At both the Inns of Court and in the colleges of the universities, young men formed relationships and tastes that would last for years and affect their careers as politicians and courtiers. This period of socialization would also provide what Orlando longs for: "exercises as may become a gentleman" (1.1.53).

→ RICHARD MULCASTER

From Positions   *1581*

One of the foremost educational reformers and teachers of Latin and Greek in his time, Richard Mulcaster (1531/2–1611) was headmaster at the famous Merchant Taylor's School, and then of St. Paul's School, both in London. Some of his students achieved great renown, including Edmund Spenser. Mulcaster argued that poor and middling students, not just rich ones, deserved access to schooling based on merit, but he did not support access for all. More controversially, he advocated education for girls as well as boys, though he maintained girls needed less rigorous schooling on fewer topics and he opposed admitting women to university. He strongly advocated physical education as part of the curriculum, and was known for encouraging acting and for supervising plays; his students performed for Queen Elizabeth and her court several times.

In the following excerpt Mulcaster maintains that failing to provide schooling to children who already have "stirring wits" (quick intellects) will lead to an unstable state because without a suitable outlet for their energies, they will soon grow disorderly and seditious. Do the opening scenes between Orlando and Oliver bear out his warning? When Orlando is driven out of his home and says he must either beg or steal for his living, what would Mulcaster have seen as the cause? When he calls girls less worthy and politically important than boys, is it a

---

Richard Mulcaster, *Positions* (London, 1581), sigs. R3v–S3; STC 18253.

truism all his readers would accept at that time; for example, would women like Rosalind and Celia accept it? He also argues that education is necessary for boys but an optional "accessory" for girls. How does the accessory known as female education play a crucial role in the development of the play? Is it possible that even Rosalind and Celia are disobedient and unruly because they are not matched to public roles equal to their intellects?

CHAPTER 36

That both young boys, and young maidens are to be put to learn. Whether all boys [should] be set to school. That too many learned be too burdenous, too few too bare: wits well sorted civil, miss-sorted, seditious.[1]

[W]e are next to consider of those persons, which are to be instructed . . . which I take to be children of both sorts, *male* and *female*, young *boys* and young *maidens*, which though I admit here generally, without difference of sex, yet I restrain particularly upon difference in cause, as hereafter shall appear. But young *maidens* must give me leave to speak of *boys* first: because naturally the *male* is more worthy, and politically he is more employed. . . . Touching the first question, whether all children [should] be set to school or no, without repressing the infinity of multitude, it is a matter of great weight, and not only in knowledge to be resolved upon, but also in deed so to be executed. . . . For the body of a commonweal[2] in proportion is like . . . a natural body. In a natural body, if any one part be too great or too small, besides the eyesore, it is mother to some evil by the very mis-forming whereupon great distemper must needs follow in time, and disquiet the whole body. And in a body politic, if the like proportion be not kept in all parts, the like disturbance will creep throughout all parts. . . . Whereof I say thus: that too many learned be too burdenous, that too few be too bare, that wits well sorted be most civil, that the same misplaced be most unquiet and seditious.

Too many [learned] burdens any state too far, for want of provision. For the rooms which are to be supplied by learning being within number, if they that are to supply them, grow on beyond number, how can it be but too great a burden for any state to bear? To have so many gaping for preferment[3] . . . and to let them roam helpless, whom nothing else can help, how can it be but that such shifters must needs shake the very strongest pillar in that state where they live, and loiter without living?

---

[1] *wits . . . seditious*: well-managed wits are civil, badly managed wits are seditious. [2] **commonweal**: commonwealth; the nation. [3] **preferment**: jobs, positions in the government.

Wits well sorted be most civil. . . . The chief signs of *civility* be *quietness, concord, agreement, fellowship* and *friendship*—which *likeness* doth link, *unlikeness* undoeth; *fitness* make fast, *unfitness* doth loose: *propriety* bears up, *impropriety* pulleth down: *right matching* makes, *mismatching* mars. How then can civil society be preserved, where wits of unfit humors for service are in places of service. . . . If fire be to inflame and cause things burn where water should cool . . . is the place not in danger? If that wit falls to preach, who were fitter for the plough, and he to climb a pulpit, which is made to scale a wall . . . ? And so is it in all kinds of life, in all trades of living, where fitness and right placing of wits doth work agreement and ease, unfitness and misplacing have the contrary companions: disagreement and disease.

Again wits misplaced [are] most unquiet and seditious, as anything else strained against nature. Light things press upward, and will ye force *fire* down? Heavy things bear downward, and will ye have *lead* to leap up? An imperial wit, for want of education and ability, being placed in a mean calling[4] will trouble the whole company if he have not his will, as wind[5] in the stomach. And if he have his will, then shall ye see what his nature did shoot at. He that beareth a tankard[6] by meanness of degree, and was born for a cockhorse[7] by sharpness of wit will . . . be master of his company. Such a stirring thing it is to have wits misplaced, and their degrees mis-allotted by the inequity of *Fortune*, which the equity of *nature* did seem to mean unto them.

[4] **mean calling:** lowly job.   [5] **wind:** gas.   [6] **beareth a tankard:** works serving ale.   [7] **cockhorse:** position of ascendancy.

→ JOHN BRINSLEY

From Ludus Literarius, or the Grammar School   *1612*

How did the young William Shakespeare and Edmund Spenser learn the basics of writing poetry? Mostly through arduous memorization and translation, assisted by the taste of the master's whip. The basic goal was close imitation of classical poets, above all Virgil and Ovid. In this excerpt, educator John Brinsley (c. 1566–1624) offers readers an easier way to this prized skill. Brinsley had been a "sizar" or scholarship student at Christ College, Cambridge. After working as a curate and schoolmaster in Leicestershire, his severe personality and strict Puritan views lost him his job in 1617. He moved to London, where he was reli-

John Brinsley, *Ludus Literarius, or the Grammar School* (London, 1612), 190–95; STC 3768.

censed to preach and teach. Despite his personal severity, Brinsley wrote *Ludus Literarius*, a book aimed at teachers, on making education more enjoyable and effective; he also stresses the importance of studying and writing English as well as Latin. Brinsley argues against the continual whipping and humiliation that prevailed in schools, and urges teachers to rely less on rote memorization and more on exercises, games, and acting in plays. Boys learn literature with less pain and acquire the civilizing arts of quick thinking and good delivery at the same time, learning to manage their voices and bodies through role-playing.

The book takes the form of a dialogue between two schoolmasters, the less experienced Spoudeus and the wise Philoponus, who gives pointers on teaching boys to write verses "with delight and certainty" (see below). The master should encourage scholars by setting up an engaging gamelike competition between them, rather than threaten with the rod. Exercises turning prose into verse are intended to increase fluency and confidence. The most important is the exercise known as "double translation," in which a student translates Latin verse into English and back into Latin, and then sees how close he came to the original. By practicing many variations on this method, a student would develop the ability to write his own verses that could pass for Virgil's—quite a trick for a schoolboy.

Orlando has had no lessons in Latin or verse-making to guide him, but he dashes off many poems praising his beloved, as a gentle lover in the throes of passion was expected to do. Fortunately for Orlando, he does not hear the mocking laughter of Rosalind, Celia, and Touchstone as they read his verses. Clearly they know how to recognize poetic "bodging," or bungling. Why do they compare his verses to a "tedious" sermon (3.2.136), and to a lame body with too many feet (3.2.144–48)? In what way does their improvised punning and wordplay contrast with Orlando's writings? What aspect of Orlando's rhymes spurs Touchstone to rattle off his parodies? If Orlando was never schooled, how might he have learned to read and to write poetry?

CHAP. XIIII.

How to enter to make[1] verses with delight and certainty, without bodging;[2] and to train up scholars to imitate and express Ovid or Virgil, both their phrase & stile.

PHILOPONUS: Though Poetry be rather for ornament then for any necessary use; and the main matter to be regarded in it, is the purity of phrase and of style: yet because there is very commendable use of it, sometimes in occasions of triumph and rejoicing, more ordinarily at the funerals of

---

[1] **enter to make:** begin to compose.   [2] **bodging:** botching or bungling.

some worthy personages, and sometimes for some other purposes; it is not amiss to train up scholars even in this kind also. And the rather because it serveth very much for the sharpening of the wit, and is a matter of high commendation, when a scholar is able to write a smooth and pure verse, and to comprehend a great deal of choice matter in a very little room.

SPOUDEUS: Surely sir though it is, as you say, but an ornament, yet it is such a one, as doth highly grace those who have attained it, in any such measure as you speak of; and two such verses are worth two thousand, of such flash and bodge[3] stuff as are ordinarily in some schools. But this I have found also to be full of difficulty, both in the entering, the progress, and also in the end; that my scholars have had more fear in this, than in all the former, and my self also driven to more severity: which I have been enforced unto, or else I should have done no good at all with the greatest part.

And yet when I have done my uttermost, I have not had any to come to such perfection as you mention, to write so pithily or purely. . . . Therefore I entreat you to guide me, how I may redress this evil, and prevent these inconveniences.[4]

PHILOPONUS: Though I be no Poet, yet I find this course to be found most easy and plain to direct my scholars:

1. To look that they be able in manner to write true Latin, and a good phrase in prose, before they begin to meddle with making a verse.

2. That they have read some poetry first; as at least these books or the like, or some part of them: *viz.* Ovid *de Tristibus*, or *de Ponto*, some piece of his *Metamorphosis*,[5] or of Virgil, and be well acquainted with their poetical phrases.

3. I find this a most easy & pleasant way to enter them,[6] that for all the first books of poetry which they learn in the beginning, they use to read them daily out of . . . translations: first resolving every verse into the grammatical order . . . after into the poetical, turning it into verse. . . . For this practice of reading their poetry, out of the translations into verse, a little trial will soon shew you, that very children will do it as fast almost as into prose: and by the use of it, continually turning prose into verse, they will be in a good way towards the making a verse, before they have learned any rules therof.

---

[3] **flash and bodge:** shallow and botched. [4] **inconveniences:** impediments, annoyances. [5] **Ovid . . . Metamorphosis:** i.e., works by the Roman poet Ovid: *Tristia*, *Epistulae ex Ponto*, and *Metamorphoses*. [6] **enter them:** start them off; also compose.

4. Then when you would have them to go in hand with making a verse, [train them so] that they be made very cunning in the rules of versifying, so as to be able to give you readily each rule, and the meaning therof.

5. That they be expert in scanning a verse, and in proving every quantity,[7] according to their rules, and so use to practice in their lectures daily.

6. To keep them that they shall never bodge ... but to enter with ease, certainty and delight; this you shall finde to be a most speedy way:

Take *Flores Poetarum*[8] and ... make choice of Ovid's verses, or if you find any other which be pleasant and easy; and making sure that your scholars know not the verses beforehand, use to dictate unto them as you did in prose. Cause also so many as you would have to learn together, to set down the English as you dictate.

Secondly to give you, and to write down all the words in Latin *verbatim*, or grammatically.[9]

Thirdly, having just the same words, let them try which of them can soonest turn them into the order of a verse: which they will presently do, being trained up in the use of the translations, which is the same in effect.

And then lastly, read them over the verse of Ovid, that they may see that themselves have made the very same; or wherein they missed: this shall much encourage and assure them.

[He describes an advanced exercise: "contracting" or condensing Virgilian verses into shorter passages retaining the sense and style.]

Thus they may proceed if you will, from the lowest kind of verse in the *Eclogues*, to something a loftier in the *Georgics*, and so to the stateliest kinds in the *Aeneid*,[10] wherein they may be tasked to go thorough some book of the *Aeneid*, every day contracting a certain number, as some five or six a day, for some of their exercises, striving who can express their Author most lively. By which daily contention you shall find, that those who take a delight in Poetry, and have sharpness & dexterity accordingly, will in a short time attain to that ripeness, as that they who know not the places which they imitate, shall hardly discern in many verses, whether the verse be Virgil's verse, or the scholar's.

---

[7] **proving every quality:** determining the metrical pattern.   [8] *Flores Poetarum*: anthology of extracts from Latin classical poets, probably *Illustrium Poetarum Flores* by Octavian Mirandula. [9] **Secondly ... grammatically:** next tell them to turn the English into Latin word for word, in normal word order.   10 *Eclogues ... Georgics ... Aeneid*: Virgil's major works in pastoral and epic.

Debating Female Education

When Rosalind and Celia find bad love poems on the trees in Arden, they treat them with scorn because their education and upbringing have made them critics as well as readers. Shakespeare makes it evident that these dukes' daughters have ample experience of courtly manners and an unusually broad access to literature, probably gained under the eye of tutors or governesses. Celia says she and Rosalind were schooled together:

> We still have slept together,
> Rose at an instant, learned, played, eat together,
> And wheresoe'er we went, like Juno's swans
> Still we went coupled and inseparable. (1.3.62–65)

Phoebe is also a rarity, but her literacy is a convention that befits the standard nymph of pastoral (see Chapter 1). Her passionate letter in verse to Rosalind/Ganymede shows she possesses skill in writing and versifying: few real-life shepherdesses could read, much less write.

Female learning was not taken for granted by Shakespeare's audiences. In fact, it was perceived as a luxury that made these women different from most women in his audience. Girls did not attend grammar school where Latin was acquired, along with the knowledge of literature. Only a handful of Englishwomen were fortunate enough to be born to humanist fathers who promoted female learning, like Sir Thomas More, Sir Anthony Cooke, and Sir Robert Wroth, whose renowned daughters were tutored in writing Latin and languages as well as history and philosophy, learning alongside their university-trained brothers and fathers. As unusually *literary* aristocrats, Rosalind and Celia may be imagined to have received educations comparable to that enjoyed by these female paragons, or perhaps like that enjoyed by female aristocrats in France and Italy, where learned women and female authors were achieving great renown. All such women were so extraordinary that Jaques could scarcely generalize about their lives as he does about men in his speech (2.7.138–65) on the "Ages of Man" (Figure 28).

The intellectual and political lives of most women were far more restricted than those of men. If Jaques had spoken on "The Ages of Woman" he would have stressed her family identity and sexual and reproductive status, rather than her roles in the outside world. The earliest years of boys and girls were more alike than they are today: until the age of six, both genders were dressed alike, and like their sisters, boys wore skirts or long coats, as you see in Figure 28, in which a boy in dress appears. At six or so, a boy would be "breeched," or allowed to wear pants for the first time, signaling his transition to the masculine world and his readiness for school. Suddenly,

FIGURE 28 *A man goes from cradle to grave in this variant on "The Ages of Man."*
This image would look quite different if it showed "The Ages of Woman" instead.
From As in a Map Here Man May Well Perceive, How Tyme Creeps on til
Death His Life Bereaue *(late seventeenth century).*

the paths of boys and girls diverged. Many boys would enter a largely male
world of schooling, and girls would not. Every morning many boys from
families who could afford it would trudge to school to read and write in
Latin, while girls stayed at home, doing housework and learning to sew,

read (in English, not Latin), and do simple math. In the next stage that Jaques describes, the boy has become a melancholy lover, busily composing a Petrarchan sonnet to his mistress's eyebrow. It would be rare to find a young woman who could woo someone with her own poetic inventions. Most young girls in their teens would not be able to devise their own amorous verses as Phoebe does in the play, because most girls received little training in literature, even if they were taught to write. Without Latin training they could not properly translate and imitate classical poetry, considered the first step to becoming a poet (see John Brinsley, p. 380). Nonetheless, more than a few women gained high literacy on their own or with tutors, and some became translators and writers in the period, and a few even published their work (see works by Lady Mary Wroth, in Chapters 1 and 2).

Education helped bridge the domestic and the public for women, helping them gain both knowledge and a purchase on political power, but many male educators were opposed to schooling for girls that went beyond the most elementary practical training. Those who advocated more for the talented or the titled followed the famous precepts set down in midcentury by the Spanish humanist Juan Luis Vives, the tutor for Mary I (Elizabeth's stepsister and predecessor). His widely circulated book *The Instruction of a Christian Woman* (1529) refuted the idea that teaching was wasted on women because they were intellectually inferior and had no use for it. Vives argued neglecting women's education led them to idleness and vice, and he outlined a curriculum for girls and women stressing piety, domestic work, and reading of the church fathers and the Bible; Latin was strictly reserved for the exceptional woman or girl.[1] Vives set the terms for much of the debate on women's education throughout the sixteenth century.

In the following tracts, two scholars debate whether to allow real learning to girls and women or to limit them to the most rudimentary forms of training. Richard Mulcaster (1531/2–1611) is most concerned with men fulfilling their Christian duty to develop the natural abilities of girls, thus training good wives and mothers, but Giovanni Bruto stresses the need for the female sex to remain completely sheltered from corrupting influences, including book learning. For Bruto, the supreme virtues of female innocence and chastity conflict with and outweigh the need for girls and women to grow intellectually.

---

[1] Juan Luis Vives, *A Verie Fruitfull and Pleasant Booke, Called the Instruction of a Christian Woman*, trans. Richard Hyrde (London, 1529), STC 24856.5.

→ RICHARD MULCASTER

From Positions

1581

CHAPTER 38

When I did appoint the persons which were to receive the benefit of education I did not exclude young *maidens*, and therefore seeing I made them one branch of my division I must of force say somewhat more of them. . . . And to prove that they are to be trained I find four special reasons, whereof any one, much more all, may persuade any. . . .

For the first: If I should seem to enforce any novelty, I might seem ridiculous, and never see that thing take place, which I tender so much: but. . . . I set not young *maidens* to public grammar schools, a thing not used[1] in my country, I send them not to the universities, having no precedent thereof in my country, I allow them learning with distinction in degrees, with difference of their calling, with respect to their ends, wherefore they learn, wherein my country confirmeth my opinion. We see young *maidens* be taught to read and write, and can do both with praise; we hear them sing and play, and both passing well; we know that they learn the best and finest of our learned languages, to the admiration of all men. . . . These things our country doth stand to.[2] . . .

For the second point: The duty which we owe them doth straightly[3] command us to see them well brought up. For what be young *maidens* in respect of our sex? Are they not the seminary of our succession?[4] The natural fry from whence we are to choose our natural, next, and most necessary friends?[5] . . .

Their *natural towardness*,[6] which was my third reason, doth most manifestly call upon us to see them well brought up. If nature have given them abilities to prove excellent in their kind, and yet thereby in no point to let their most laudable duties in marriage and match, but rather to beautify them with most singular ornaments, are not we to be condemned of extreme unnaturalness if we guide not that by discipline, which is given them by *nature*? . . .

---

[1] **used:** customarily done.   [2] **stand to:** believe in.   [3] **straightly:** clearly.   [4] **seminary of our succession:** mothers of our children.   [5] **fry . . . friends:** the young creatures from which we are to choose wives.   [6] **towardness:** talent and ability.

Richard Mulcaster, *Positions* (London, 1581), sigs. X4–Z4; STC 18253.

That young *maidens* can learn nature doth give them, and that they have learned our experience doth teach us; with what care to themselves, [they] themselves can best witness; with what comfort to us, what foreign example can more assure the world than our diamond at home? Our most dear sovereign lady and princess,[7] by nature a woman, by virtue a worthy, not one of the nine[8] but the tenth above the nine . . . she is known to contain all perfections in nature, all degrees in valor, and to become a precedent to those nine worthy men as *Apollo* is accounted to the nine famous women.[9] . . . If no story did tell it, if no state did allow it, if no example did confirme it that young *maidens* deserve the training this our own mirror,[10] the majesty of her sex, doth prove it in her own person and commends it to our reason. We have besides her highness as undershining stars many singular ladies and gentlewomen so skillfull in all cunning, of the most laudable and loveworthy qualities of learning, as they may well be alleged for a precedent to praise, not for a pattern to prove like by. . . .

[On which subjects should be taught to girls and women.]

Reading if for nothing else it were, as for many things else it is, is very needful for religion, to read that which they must know, and ought to perform, if they have not whom to hear, in that matter which they read; or if their memory be not steadfast by reading to revive it. If they hear first and after read of the selfsame argument, reading confirms their memory. Here I may not omit many and great contentments, many and sound comforts, many and manifold delights, which those women that have skill and time to read, without hindering their housewifery, do continually receive by reading of some comfortable and wise discourses, penned either in form of history, or for direction to live by.

As for *writing*, . . . Many good occasions are oftentimes offered where it were better for them to have the use of their pen, for the good that comes by it, than to wish they had it when the default is felt; and for fear of evil, which cannot be avoided in some, to avert that good, which may be commodious to many.

---

[7] **sovereign lady and princess:** Queen Elizabeth.   [8] **nine:** the nine worthies, a collection of great men widely recognized in the Renaissance as embodying human excellence.   [9] **nine famous women:** the Muses.   [10] **mirror:** Queen Elizabeth.

→ GIOVANNI BRUTO

From The Necessary, Fit, and Convenient Education of a Young Gentlewoman *1598*

Rosalind and Celia's education did not teach them total obedience to fathers. They seek their own liberty in the woods, and they choose husbands without consulting anyone. Clearly neither Duke Frederick nor Duke Senior seems to have followed the precepts of the humanist author Giovanni Michele Bruto (1517–1592). A translator and historian from a patrician family, Bruto lived in Venice until he was suspected of heresy and exiled in the 1540s. He tried to establish himself in Florence but had to flee Italy to escape the Inquisition, and after a period under various patrons in eastern Europe, he died while en route to Germany.

Despite Bruto's heterodox beliefs and unruly life he was keen to ferret out the disorder he saw lurking in the idea of allowing women to read books and become educated. His book *La Institutione di una Fanciulla Nata Nobilmente* (*The Upbringing of a Nobly Born Girl*, 1555) attacks women's learning as destructive of female virtue and as inspiring lustful will and rebellion against patriarchal authority; only devotional reading might be permissible for women. Its narrow-minded assault on female education attracted interest in England and was translated twice, first by Thomas Salter who published it in 1579 under his own name, as *The Mirror of Modestie*, and again by "W. P." in 1598, with Bruto's name on the title page.[1]

In his epistle to "The Wise and Vertuous Gentlewoman Mistresse Catanea," Bruto condescendingly explains that he will address her father, a Genoese shipping magnate who was the author's client. A father should provide a model governess who will train his daughter in virtue and chastity, and keep her away from the lewd chatter of maids. A daughter should be taught to read but not to become learned or to write poems, tales, or songs herself, because it might foster pride, wantonness, and rebellion. The study of science and philosophy should be forbidden, as should the light tales of Ovid and Boccaccio. Women must not show themselves "audacious in public" or at "theaters and common spectacles." Instead, from infancy onward she should be fed on catalogues of virtuous ladies and tales of saints. Bruto also criticizes as poor models "Matinea, Assiothea, Lasthemia" who "changing their feminine habits, entered in men's apparel into Plato's school: & among the amorous and effeminate young men, openly disputed of the motions, principles and causes of love."

How might Rosalind or Celia respond to the opinions of Mulcaster and Bruto? Do you think most women in Shakespeare's audiences would have shared

---

[1] Janet Butler Holm, "Thomas Salter's *The Mirrhor of Modestie*: A Translation of Bruto's *La Institutione Di Una Fanciulla Nata Nobilmente*," *The Library* s6–5.1 (1983): 53–57.

Giovanni Bruto, *The Necessary, Fit, and Convenient Education of a Young Gentlewoman*, trans. W. P. (London, 1598), sigs. E5v F7; STC 3947.

Bruto's strong views against educating girls? Could Bruto point to Rosalind's literary witplay or to Phoebe's letter writing as evidence that women should be kept ignorant of book learning? What might be Mulcaster's answer to Bruto? Does *As You Like It* portray girls' natural abilities as positive (as Mulcaster does) or negative (as Bruto does)? Does the play imply this capacity should be nurtured by education or suppressed?

From *The Necessary, Fit, and Convenient Education of a Young Gentlewoman*

I know some that are of the opinion that young gentlewomen should be taught learning and sciences,[2] which for my part I think not convenient. . . . I mean sufficiently to prove, that in a young gentlewoman of good birth . . . the dangers which therein are featured being much heavier than the good that thereby is hoped may be profitable, if she be brought up in learning. They will [say] that the learning propounded unto her should be full of chastity and purity, whereunto nevertheless she cannot attain, but by convenient means, and having gotten it, no man can let[3] her, but she will read . . . books of love composed by Ovid, Catullus, Propertius, Tibullus,[4] and Virgil, of Aeneas and Dido,[5] and among the Greek poets, the foolish love of the gods themselves, and in Homer their adulteries and fornications. Likewise (seeing we are so ambitious, to cause our daughters to dispute in philosophers' schools) she will be no less able when it pleaseth her as well to defend the opinions of Epicurus[6] . . . and because it is their desire that she should learn the philosophy and wisdom of Plato. I will not altogether deny that a strange gentlewoman, unknown to me (yet you must not understand that I would permit the same unto my daughter) may read Plato's discourse, the impudent actions, loves, and dalliances of Alcibiades.[7] They appoint her a master who is learned, grave, diligent, and of honest behavior, let it be so, yet may he corrupt nature and show himself a man (as the wise man well and learnedly declareth) and the provocations of lust, which are always prompt and ready, by acquaintance and familiarity with that sex, and at such age, may be sufficient matter to give him occasion to attempt such

---

[2] **sciences:** here, science can mean any academic field.   [3] **let:** prevent.   [4] **Ovid, Catullus, Propertius, Tibullus:** Roman poets.   [5] **Virgil, of Aeneas and Dido:** Virgil was Rome's great epic poet; in his *Aeneid*, the Trojan hero Aeneas loves and then abandons Queen Dido, who kills herself.   [6] **Epicurus:** Greek philosopher, advocated the pursuit of pleasure.   [7] **Alcibiades:** man about town who flirts with Socrates and others; see Plato's *Symposium*.

things. . . . Dama that taught the world the doctrine of Pythagoras her father, and Aspasia, Diotima, and Thargelia⁸ that beautified the studies of philosophy, have not more deserved the praise of excellent and learned matrons, then an opinion of [being] light and uncivil⁹ women, and I think there is not any man of good judgment that had not rather have his daughter unlearned and shamefast¹⁰ than suspected of her honesty and excellent in the study of philosophy and of great renown among the learned. . . . I am not therefore of opinion, in any sort whatsoever, that a young gentlewoman should be instructed in learning and humane arts, in whom we account honesty and true virtue to be more comely and a better ornament, than the report and light renown of great science and knowledge by her attained unto. For that seeing in the study of learning are two principal points: the one recreation, the other profit that cannot be hoped for in a women, who as by nature she is given us for a companion in our labors, so she ought to be active and attentive to govern our houses, nor this matter of study which procureth delight may not be granted unto her, without great danger to offend the beauty and glory of her mind.

⁸ **Dama . . . Aspasia, Diotima, and Thargelia:** famous learned women in classical Greece.
⁹ **light and uncivil:** unchaste and coarse.   ¹⁰ **shamefast:** shy, modest, prudish.

Informal Schooling: Travel and Observation

Rosalind puts down Jaques as "Monsieur Traveler" (4.1.24) but he is proud of his travels and what they have taught him. Despite all the mockery directed at him, Jaques is not easy to dismiss. He is the most versatile and learned courtier on display: his witty melancholy amuses the Duke, and he easily invents songs and dances, "moralizes" spectacles, teaches with wise saws, and even serves as the arbiter of proper marriage. At the end of the play he blesses the four couples with comic gravity, like a worldly wise philosopher, then departs to pursue more knowledge, seeking out the reformed Duke Frederick as tutor ("Out of these convertites / There is much matter to be heard and learned" 5.4.166–67). Clearly he has been given most forms of training "as may become a gentleman" (1.1.53), as Orlando puts it, namely formal and informal schooling, foreign travel, exposure to courtly manners, and service at the tables of the great. The Duke and his men have acquired their cultured gentility through similar training. These are the exercises that Orlando refers to when he demands that his brother give him an education fitting his gentle status.

The chance to travel for education or pleasure was granted to very few. But even if the travel was enforced, as Orlando's is, the experience might be valuable and instructive. As a runaway Orlando endures some hardship, but the irony is that he is exposed to more fascinating people and experiences than he would have been back home. In the excerpt below by the famous French essayist Michel de Montaigne, the author urges his patroness to allow her sons to travel at an early age, arguing it widens a youth's horizons and makes him more knowledgeable and resourceful. That attitude was not prevalent among the insular English, who had a reputation for disliking foreigners and believing firmly in their own superiority. Many shared a strong ambivalence about travel, especially to Catholic Europe, which pious Protestants regarded as the seedbed of papistry and sedition. Nonetheless, some of the wealthier families did choose to send their sons abroad to study and to gain exposure to foreign political systems, intellectuals, and languages. English students attended universities in cities such as Paris, Padua, and Bologna, and studied for periods ranging from a few months to years. Others visited famous scholars while studying the government, geography, and history of the region with the help of tutors. Some educators of a strong Protestant bent warned young men against going abroad lest they take on foreign habits and fashions, which might alter or contaminate their Englishness. They deplored in particular the siren call of Italy, where the vices of overrefinement, heresy, effeminacy, sodomy, luxury, and double-dealing were thought to lie in wait for the unwary.

While some English travelers crossed the Channel to seek knowledge and pleasure, far more fled to avoid being persecuted for their religious beliefs, most often Catholicism. Englishmen and women also left for periods in order to study at Catholic seminaries and convents, and some risked their lives to go back. These associations led to a marked trend in satiric writings and plays attacking the traveler as pretentious at the best, and corrupt and treasonous at the worst. Antitravel bias shapes the Italianate character of Jaques, who prides himself on his intellect and his philosophical nature. Yet he is often rude, moody, misanthropic, insulting, and self-centered. Shakespeare's portrait of Jaques is complicated by his positive qualities, making him an ambiguous figure. In what ways does Jaques differ from Montaigne's ideal traveler? In what speeches does he support the ultimate goals of educational travel set out by Montaigne? When Duke Senior comments on the value of living in the forest and learning from each object, do you agree? Why does Shakespeare have only the fool express a longing to go home?

→ MICHEL DE MONTAIGNE

From Essays Written in French by Michael Lord of Montaigne
1613

Translated by John Florio

Michel de Montaigne (1533–1592) has been credited with inventing the personal essay, taking himself as his prime topic. He became a writer, traveler, and philosopher after a career as a magistrate and mayor of Bordeaux, and as a mediator at the French court between France's contentious religious factions. His influential *Essais* (1587), translated into English in 1603 by John Florio, promotes toleration and gentleness and a degree of skepticism toward received ideas. Montaigne received a unique education in Latin and the classics at home. His father believed in a humane and encouraging teaching environment, in contrast to the beatings administered in the conventional schools of the day. Montaigne was raised speaking Latin as his first language, and did not speak French until he was six. In this passage, Montaigne condemns rote learning and memorization, and argues that travel and study should be undertaken early in life for the purpose of gaining a greater understanding of the world.

What speakers in Arden articulate ideas that resemble those of Montaigne? Do the courtly travelers learn anything from living there for a period; that is, do they carry away valuable ideas and feelings from the forest when they return to the court? Do the country people change, and if so, how? Does the play suggest that spectators might take away something other than pure comic entertainment, and that they too might read the "books in the running brooks, / Sermons in stones" (2.1.16–17)? Montaigne writes that even the most seemingly trivial stories might help a wise traveler gain knowledge of a foreign culture and him or herself. In what way is the comic pastoral world of Arden like a foreign land we briefly visit? Does Shakespeare offer something seemingly trivial that can be deciphered by the wise and made significant? Does he offer either characters or audiences a wider canvas than their own lives and societies, which helps put their self-centered views into perspective?

CHAPTER 25. "OF THE INSTITUTION AND EDUCATION OF CHILDREN."

[The world and society are the best books.]

There is a marvelous clearness or, as I may term it, an enlightening of man's judgment drawn from the commerce of men, and by frequenting abroad in

Michel Eyquem de Montaigne, *Essays Written in French by Michael Lord of Montaigne*, trans. John Florio (London, 1613), 69–72; STC 18042.

the world: we are all so contrived and compact in ourselves that our sight is made shorter by the length of our nose. When *Socrates* was demanded whence he was,[1] he answered not of *Athens* but of the world; for he, who had his imagination more full, and farther stretching, embraced all the world for his native city, and extended his acquaintance, his society, and affections to all mankind—not as we do, who look no further than our feet. If the frost chance to nip the vines about my village, my priest doth presently argue that the wrath of God hangs over our head and threateneth all mankind, and judgeth that the pip is already fallen upon the cannibals.[2]

In viewing these intestine and civil broils[3] of ours, who doth not exclaim that this world's vast frame is near unto a dissolution and that "the day of judgment is ready to fall on us," never remembering that many worse revolutions have been seen, and that whilst we are plunged in grief and overwhelmed in sorrow a thousand other parts of the world besides are blessed with all happiness and wallow in pleasures and never think on us? Whereas, when I behold our lives, our license, and impunity, I wonder to see them so mild and easy. He on whose head it haileth thinks all the hemisphere besides to be in a storm and tempest . . . we are all insensible of this kind of error, an error of great consequence and prejudice. But whosoever shall present unto his inward eyes, as it were in a table, the idea of the great image of our universal mother nature, attired in her richest robes, sitting in the throne of her majesty, and in her visage shall read, so general, and so constant a variety; he that therein shall view himself, not himself alone, but a whole kingdom, to be in respect of a great circle but the smallest point that can be imagined, he only can value things according to their essential greatness and proportion. This great universe (which some multiply as *species* under one *genus*) is the true looking glass wherein we must look if we will know whether we be of a good stamp or in the right bias. To conclude, I would have this world's frame to be my scholar's choice-book:[4] so many strange humors, sundry sects, varying judgments, diverse opinions, different laws, and fantastical customs teach us to judge rightly of ours, and instruct our judgment to acknowledge its imperfections and natural weakness, which is no easy an apprenticeship. So many innovations of estates, so many falls of princes, and changes of public fortune, may, and ought, to teach us not to make so great account of ours. So many names, so many victories, and so many conquests buried in dark oblivion makes the hope to perpetuate our names but ridiculous. . . . The pride and fierceness of so many strange

---

[1] **whence he was:** where he was from.　[2] **pip . . . cannibals:** i.e., the New World has already been hit by the frost.　[3] **intestine and civil broils:** the French civil wars of the sixteenth century.
[4] **to be my scholar's choice-book:** to be the book that the pupil studies most intensely.

and gorgeous shows; the pride-puffed majesty of so many courts and of their greatness ought to confirm and assure our sight, undauntedly, to bear the affronts and thunder-claps of ours without sealing our eyes. So many thousands of men, low-laid in their graves afore us, may encourage us, not to fear, or be dismayed to go meet so good company in the other world; and so of all things else.

[Understanding is the purpose of study and travel.]

The good that comes of study (or at least should come) is to prove better, wiser, and honester. It is the understanding power (said *Epicharmus*[5]) that seeth and heareth; it is it that profiteth all and disposeth all; that moveth, swayeth, and ruleth all — all things else are but blind, senseless, and without spirit. And truly in barring him of liberty to do anything of himself, we make him thereby more servile and more coward. . . . To know by rote is no perfect knowledge, but to keep what one hath committed to his memory's charge is commendable: what a man directly knoweth, that will he dispose of, without turning still to his book, or looking to his pattern. A mere bookish sufficiency is unpleasant. All I expect of it is an embellishing of my actions and not a foundation of them, according to *Plato's* mind, who saith constancy, faith, and sincerity are true philosophy. As for other sciences, and tending elsewhere, they are but garish[6] paintings. I would fain have *Paluel* or *Pompey*,[7] those two excellent dancers of our time, with all their nimbleness, teach any man to do their lofty tricks, and high capers, only with seeing them done, and without stirring out of his place, as some pedantical fellows would instruct our minds without moving or putting it in practice. And glad would I be to find one that would teach us how to manage a horse, to toss a pike, to shoot off a piece,[8] to play upon the lute or to warble with the voice, without any exercise, as these kind of men would teach us to judge, and how to speak well, without any exercise of speaking or judging.[9] In which kind of life, or as I may term it, apprenticeship, what action or object soever presents itself unto our eyes may serve us instead of a sufficient book. A pretty prank of a boy, a knavish trick of a page, a foolish part of a lackey, an idle tale or any discourse else, spoken either in jest or earnest, at the table or in company, are even as new subjects for us to work upon — for furtherance [of] commerce or common society among men, visiting of foreign countries, and observing of strange fashions are very necessary . . .

---

[5] *Epicharmus*: Greek philosopher.   [6] **garish**: ornate.   [7] *Paluel* or *Pompey*: famous dancers, now unknown.   [8] **piece**: weapon.   [9] **And glad . . . judging**: meant ironically, since such "learning" is impossible.

that they may the better know how to correct and prepare their wits by those of others. I would therefore have him begin even from his infancy to travel abroad; and first, that at one shot he may hit two marks, he should see neighbor-countries, namely where languages are most different from ours; for unless a man's tongue be fashioned unto them in his youth he shall never attain to the true pronunciation of them if he once grow in years.

→ SIR WILLIAM CORNWALLIS

From Essays
1600–01

One of the first writers to imitate Michel de Montaigne's essays was Sir William Cornwallis the younger (1579–1614), a courtier-writer who was the son of a diplomat. He was knighted in 1599 after serving in Ireland under the earl of Essex, and he twice served as a member of Parliament. Under James I he became a member of the king's privy chamber and in 1605 he served as a royal courier to his father, then ambassador to Spain. Cornwallis mirrors Montaigne in asserting that philosophy and instruction can spring from any human encounter or natural object, even with popular works in cheap print that end up as his toilet paper. What encounters in *As You Like It* resemble that of the author and the husbandman in this selection by Cornwallis? How does his process of observation and reflection on common people and things echo what the courtiers in Arden make of their surroundings? What does the play imply is more important to acquiring gentility and knowledge: travel, meeting new people, and observation; or book learning and a university education?

ESSAY 15: OF THE OBSERVATION AND USE OF THINGS

I come now from discoursing with a husbandman,[1] an excellent stiff slave, without observation,[2] respect, or civility, but not without a great deal of wit, if it were refined, and separated from the dirt that hangs about it. I have sold him an hour of my time, and . . . this time hath not been lost, for his experience, his learning of tradition, and his natural wit hath informed me of many things, I have picked out of him good philosophy, and astronomy, and other observations of time and of the world: all which, though he employs about dirt,[3] . . . hinder not me from making a more worthy use of them.

[1] **husbandman:** farmer. [2] **stiff . . . without observation:** stubborn and not inclined toward gestures of deference. [3] **employs about dirt:** applies to farming.

Sir William Cornwallis, *Essays* (London, 1600–01), sigs. I7–K3v; STC 5775.

There is not that thing upon the earth, that well examined, yields not something worthy of knowledge. That divine artisan that made them, never fashioned anything unprofitably, nor ever set forth any of his workmanship[4] without some inward virtue. I do first prescribe[5] [to] them that desire to prove excellent in distilling these simples, to lay in good store of the fuel of learning: whatsoever he hath of his own natural wit is not sufficient, it makes not the fire hot enough: for there is a great deal of tough vile stuff to be drawn out, before what is pure can be gotten: but then (I tell Ignorance a miracle now) he shall not see, nor touch that thing, that will not add to his wisdom: for things are akin to one another, they come all out of one fountain, and the knowing one, brings you acquainted with another, and so to others. All kind of books are profitable, except printed bawdiness; they abuse youth. But pamphlets, and lying stories, and news, and twopenny poets I would know them, but beware of being familiar with them. My custom is to read these, and presently to make use of them, for they lie in my privy,[6] and when I come thither, and have occasion to employ it, I read them, half a side at once is my ordinary,[7] which when I have read, I use in that kind that waste paper is most subject to,[8] but to a cleanlier profit. I see in them the difference of wits, and dispositions, the alterations of arguments pleasing the world, and the change of style. . . . I have not been ashamed to adventure mine ears with a ballad-singer, and they have come home loaden to my liking, doubly satisfied, with profit, and with recreation. The profit, to see earthlings[9] satisfied with such course stuff, to hear vice rebuked, and to see the power of virtue that pierces the head of such a base historian and vile auditory.[10] . . . There is not anything retained in my memory from the first that profits me not: sometimes I renew my nurse's stories, and being now strong, and able to digest them, I find them not without nourishment. My afterlife[11] . . . is not without profit. I was bound then to *Arthur of Brittany*,[12] and things of that price, for my knowledge was not able to traffic with anything more rich, Stow's *Chronicle*[13] was the highest, yet I have found good use of them, they have added to my experience. [In] my exercises, and recreation, or rather (as I then used them) occupations I find worth somewhat. I would not lose my knowledge of hawks, and running horses for anything; they are not without use; I meet often with people that understand no other language, and then they make me sociable and not displeasing to the company. If out of these dregs there be good juice to be got, what is there

---

[4] **his workmanship**: his works. [5] **prescribe**: recommend, advise [6] **privy**: toilet stall or bath room. [7] **my ordinary**: my typical habit. [8] **I use . . . subject to**: i.e., I use it as toilet paper. [9] **earthlings**: plowmen. [10] **base historian and vile auditory**: vulgar ballad seller and audience. [11] **afterlife**: adulthood. [12] *Arthur of Brittany*: popular Arthurian romance (1560). [13] **Stow's** *Chronicle*: popular English history by John Stow (1565).

out of more noble observations? Truly an incredible knowledge: he that can make use of them, may leave reading, and profit no less by these. If out of these blotters of paper many things may be extracted not unworthy of note, what may we expect from Homer, Virgil, and such poets?

Civil Tongues and the Art of Conversation

Words are palpable forces in *As You Like It*. Written on paper, they sprout from trees; set to music and sung, they make the forest and theater vibrate with song; spoken, they force people into exile and create bonds of marriage. To a greater degree than in Shakespeare's other comedies, the play concentrates its energies on exploring how humans manage or mismanage the almost unlimited social and artistic power inherent in words. One popular proverb held that *wit is a witch*, meaning a great talker has an uncanny power to persuade and seduce others. Words give some the power to make others fall in love, to persuade them to change, to order them to bend, to make them laugh, to make the impossible seem plausible, and to delight an audience with poetic fictions. The function of a writer is not just to manipulate or to entertain, but to civilize — at least according to Orlando. As soon as he is taken into the Duke's rustic court, he takes on the task of transforming the forest from a bare "desert" to a schoolroom: "Tongues I'll hang on every tree, / That shall civil sayings show" (3.2.108–09). Even touched with love mania, his aim is to civilize through wise sayings and poetry.

People in the play don't just chat: they converse in ways that seem casual, but deliberately showcase the civilized art of words — spoken, written, printed, or sung. The court and forest resound with voices turning over topics, debating, joking, and singing together, philosophizing for each other, and reading out loud. When they aren't riffing on a topic, joking around, or flirting madly, people talk about talking. They also listen: courtiers and lovers eavesdrop on one another and quote one another. They mull over what others say and wonder at their meaning. Lovers drink up the words of those they love. It is not looks alone that makes Phoebe swoon over Ganymede:

> Think not I love him, though I ask for him.
> 'Tis but a peevish boy — yet he talks well —
> But what care I for words? Yet words do well
> When he that speaks them pleases those that hear. (3.5.108–11)

"Yet he talks well": talking well was of prime importance in the period, and part of that skill was knowing how to project civility, that irreplaceable quality of polite amiability, delivered with a degree of poise and good humor. Speaking correctly and urbanely was the goal of those who strove for respectability and social advancement. This emphasis has shifted today. Although speech is of course still important, it is possible to become powerful indeed without speaking very well, or being especially sociable or convivial. In Shakespeare's times, a person's identity and social horizons were closely bound up with how he or she spoke. "Speak that I may see thee," wrote Ben Jonson, a great stylist in prose and poetry, in his celebrated essay on what a person's verbal style reveals about personality, opinions, and upbringing.

> *Language* most shows a man: speak that I may see thee. It springs out of the most retired, and inmost parts of us, and is the Image of the Parent of it, the mind. No glass renders a man's form, or likeness, so true as his speech. Nay, it is likened to a man; and as we consider feature, and composition in a man; so words in Language: in the greatness, aptness, sound, structure, and harmony of it.[1]

Hordes of less talented writers busily churned out a vast number of self-help books on manners and especially conversation, but this need also led to any number of less somber jestbooks and jesting dialogues. Forums on love between men and women in the mode of Giovanni Boccaccio and Marguerite de Navarre show them conversing with elegant civility, but without dangerous bawdiness or tiresome efforts at flirtation. In George Whetstone's *An Heptameron of Civil Discourses* (see p. 227), Lady Aurelia sets the rules for the games they will play for three days. She matches each gentleman with a gentlewoman, and instructs each man not to "talk love" incessantly, but to entertain his lady with civil speeches or forfeit the game: "For he was accounted base mannered, or very gross-witted, that could not pleasantly entertain time with a civil discourse."[2]

To be adept at civil discourse one had to be familiar with the *topoi*, or common topics, discussed in polite company and in literary and didactic works. Rosalind and Celia amuse themselves discussing the gifts of Nature and Fortune, a frequent topic in romance and allegory; Orlando and Jaques touch on "the woman question" (in this case, whether women are worthy of men's love), the subject of countless religious and polemical tracts; Duke Senior and his court consider how to endure adversity, a topic that Plato, Seneca, and Boethius had all meditated on before them. Language spoken so that it "pleases those that hear" (3.5.111) was also commercially valuable,

---

[1] Ben Jonson, *Discoveries Made Upon Men and Some Matter* (1641), n. pag. Web. <http://www.gutenberg.org/dirs/etext04/dscvi0.txt>.
[2] George Whetstone, *An Heptameron of Civil Discourses* (London, 1582), sig. B4v; STC 25337.

spurring the rapid growth of the theater business. Audiences made play-going an entrenched habit, because plays were geared to the pleasures of the ear as well as eye. Playgoers made stars of actors who could deliver courtly, heroic, and poetic language well, and they laughed when the clown misused and mistook words on purpose, or delivered mock orations. Watching plays such as *As You Like It*, they could listen to "conceited" banter between lovers and enjoy set pieces on the follies of love or the *theatrum mundi* (the world as stage). Whether they had any schooling or not, they could absorb Ovidian erotic wit and Petrarchist poetry, and hear the superb Englishing of Italian-style pastoral, in a romantic comedy filled with echoes of Torquato Tasso, Christopher Marlowe, Sir Philip Sidney, Edmund Spenser, and Michel de Montaigne. They could revel in the wayward wit of sexy female aristocrats or saucy boys, or both at the same time. They carried home scraps of this feast in their memories or jotted them down in notebooks, using them to embellish their own conversation.

To talk well also meant, in some circles, to talk in the accents of the "inland" culture of the major towns and cities and especially the court, *not* in the accents of "outlandish" or remote places such as the wastes and woods of northern and western England.[3] Orlando quickly notices that Ganymede is not a simple country boy, and puts Rosalind on the spot because she sounds far more genteel than she seems to be. She gets out of this tight spot with a quick answer:

ORLANDO: Your accent is something finer than you could purchase in so removed a dwelling.

ROSALIND: I have been told so of many. But indeed an old religious uncle of mine taught me to speak, who was in his youth an inland man, one that knew courtship too well, for there he fell in love. (3.2.334–39)

Orlando, on the other hand, merely asserts his "inland" status without needing to invent an uncle. He uses the term during his tense confrontation with Duke Senior. Realizing he is coming across like a starving vagrant from the hinterlands, Orlando assures the Duke he is capable of "smooth civility" since he is actually "inland bred / And know some nurture" — an interesting statement, since he has loudly griped that Oliver has given him no nurture at all (2.7.96–97). If he has been raised among servants, he should sound like Adam; but no one questions his accent at any time. Therefore, he probably sounds like a knight's son, just like his brother Oliver. The automatic superiority conferred by his "inland" accent may derive from the same fairy-tale force that makes him "never schooled and yet learned" (1.1.121). What is cer-

---

[3] Madeline Doran, "Yet am I inland bred," *Shakespeare Quarterly* 15.2 (1964): 100.

tain is that Orlando succeeds because he realizes his shortcomings and endures training and criticism. Because he subjects himself to the civilizing process in word and deed (embodied in his teachers, Rosalind and Duke Senior), he ends up with all the prizes: Rosalind (and her property), a contrite brother (and his property), and, potentially, even a dukedom.

The documents in this section address the very wide playing field of words that the characters use in the play, emphasizing the civilized pursuits of lovemaking (a term signifying courtship and flirtation) and the creation of a well-ordered, intelligent, and genteel subject, all through speaking and writing (or even singing) in the right way. The jests in the last section dwell on mistakings and manipulations in the difficult game of courtship, a notorious breeder of faux pas and comedy. In these jokes, as in the play, women are the chief critics of the male suitors' advances.

→ GIOVANNI DELLA CASA

From Galateo

1576

Translated by Robert Peterson

The conduct book *Galateo* was the most famous work of Giovanni della Casa (1503–1556), Florentine churchman, poet, diplomat, archbishop of Benevento, and papal nuncio to Venice. One of the premier arbiters of taste and manners of his day, della Casa was an important figure in the world of letters and of Counter-Reformation politics. When he was given the difficult task of suppressing Protestant tendencies in Venice, he helped launch the Venetian Inquisition and the *Index Prohibitum*—the list of books banned by the Church—but he failed to achieve his lifelong ambition to become a cardinal.

Like many courtesy books, *Galateo* is a dialogue, but in this case the lead speaker is an old, wise, but illiterate gentleman who is giving pointers to a young student on good manners in speaking and behaving in company. (Della Casa made him illiterate to play up the idea that his wisdom comes from experience rather than book learning.) His theme is that the goal of each person in a civil society is to be part of a larger group, and to be liked and accepted. From that affection flows their power and influence, more than through deeds or virtues. The old man recommends a golden mean in behavior: he warns against being silent, antisocial, and withdrawn (see Figure 29), but he also frowns at the person given to talking too much and too fast. The melancholy guest is not truly

---

Giovanni della Casa, *Galateo*, trans. Robert Peterson (London, 1576), 1–5, 26, 27, 86, 88–89, 91–92, 94; STC 4738.

FIGURE 29 *The emblem of Melancholy as a silent, sullen misanthrope, from Henry* Peacham, Minerva Britanna *(1612).*

civil, and should try to hide his sadness by being amiable and pleasant to others. Jaques inflicts his moods on everyone he meets, but when Celia gently berates Rosalind for being so gloomy, Rosalind brightens up for her friend's sake, and "devise[s] sports" or witgames to distract them both (1.2.18), showing her self-control and civility.

Rosalind doesn't always follow della Casa's precepts, however. When Celia berates Rosalind for throwing her "out" (making her lose the thread of her speech), for example, what principle is her friend ignoring? What other moments show people straying from della Casa's rules? Which denizens of Arden are the most courteous, by della's Casa's definition? Does politeness always gain characters praise or affection? Does anyone become sought after, loved, or admired despite, or because of, his or her seeming rudeness?

Note that della Casa deals with bodily functions and advises his listener not to annoy others with the sight, smell, or even the thought of them. Comedy does not spring from polite and normal behavior, trading instead on verbal or physical recklessness and excess. If so, why do we enjoy it instead of getting

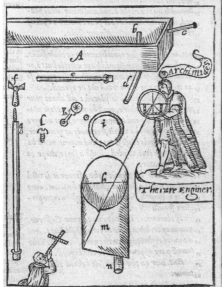

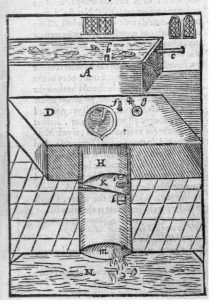

FIGURE 30 *A new kind of "jakes," or toilet, designed by Sir John Harington. Conduct books warned readers not to speak, joke about, or remind others of lower body functions. Harington, the godson of Queen Elizabeth, ignored the rules of civil speech in writing this comic pamphlet about his whimsical invention, the flush toilet, and for this transgression he was roundly mocked. The odd name "Jaques" may allude to Harington and his new-fangled jakes. Centuries would pass before flush toilets became accepted and widespread in England. Diagram from John Harington,* An Anatomie of the Metamorpho-sed Ajax *(1596).*

angry or offended? Some of the banter in the play is scatalogical, dwelling on excrement and other bodily functions. In fact, *As You Like It* brings in "toilet" humor every time Jaques's name is mentioned, because the word sounds so like "jakes," which means an outhouse or privy (Touchstone uses a euphemism for "jakes" when he addresses him as "Master What-ye-call-'t"). Modern flush toilets were unknown, and even the idea was treated as a bawdy joke (Figure 30). Touchstone brings up the "uncleanly flux" or discharge of a civet cat and "the copulation of cattle" (3.2.55, 65–66) and later Rosalind talks about spitting before kissing. Are they well within the realm of civil conversation, or are they exceeding its limits, justified only by the verbal liberties granted to wits and clowns?

From *Galateo*

I will begin to discourse of such things as many men will deem, perchance, but trifles: I mean what manner of countenance and grace behooveth[1] a man to use, that he may be able, in communication and familiar acquaintance with men, to show himself pleasant, courteous, and gentle. . . . it behooves thee to frame and order thy manners and doings, not according to thy own mind and fashion, but to please those with whom thou livest, and after that sort direct thy doings. . . .

We say then, that every act that offendeth any [of] the common senses, or overthwarteth[2] a man's will and desire, or else presenteth to the imagination and conceit matters unpleasant . . . which the mind doth abhor, such things I say be naught, and must not be used: *for we must not only refrain from such things as be foul, filthy, loathsome and nasty: but we must not so much as name them. And it is not only a fault to do such things, but against good manners, by any act or sign to put a man in mind of them.* And therefore, it is an ill-favored fashion, that some men use, openly to thrust their hands in what part of their body they list. Likewise, I like it as ill to see a gentleman settle himself, to do the needs of nature, in presence of men: and after he hath done, to truss himself again before them. . . .

[Controlling the voice; against interrupting or being silent in company.]

The voice would be neither hoarse nor shrill. And, *when you laugh and sport in any sort, you must not cry out and criche*[3] *like the pulley of a well: nor yet speak in your yawning.* I know well it is not in us, to give ourselves a ready tongue or perfect voice at our own will and pleasure. He that doth stutter, or is hoarse: let him not always babble and gab, and keep a court alone:[4] let him rather a mend the defect of his tongue with silence, and hearing:[5] and withal (if he can) with study diminish the fault of nature. *It is an ill noise to hear a man raise his voice high, like to a common crier.*[6] . . .

I would not for all this, that you should use so base a speech, as the scum, as it were, and the froth of the meanest and vilest sort of people, launderers and hucksters:[7] but such as gentlemen should speak and talk. . . . And if you have skill to choose amongst the words of your own country speech, the

---

[1]**behooveth:** suits. [2]**overthwarteth:** thwarts. [3]**criche:** creak or shriek. [4]**keep a court alone:** stay by himself. [5]**hearing:** listening. [6]*crier:* town crier or street seller. [7]**hucksters:** street sellers.

purest and most proper, such as have the best sound, and best sense, touching nor remembering, in no case, no matter that is foul, vile and base: and if you can, place your words in good order . . . pronounce your words and your syllables with a certain grace and sweetness, not as a *Schoolmaster* that teacheth young children to read and to spell. Neither must you mumble them nor sup them up, as if they were glued and pasted together one to another. If you remember these and such other rules and precepts, your talk will be liked, and heard with pleasure enough: and you shall well maintain the state and countenance that well beseemeth a gentleman well taught and honest.

Besides these, there be some that never hold their tongue. . . . And there be other so full of babble, that they will not suffer another to speak. . . . And sure, such manner of people induce men to quarrel and fight with them for it. For, if you do mark it well: *Nothing moves a man sooner to anger: then when he is suddenly cut short of his will and his pleasure, be it of never so little and small importance.* . . . And, when a man tells his tale, you must give good ear unto him: that you may not say otherwhile, *O what?* Or, *how?* which is many a man's fashion to do. And this is as much trouble and pain to him that speaketh, as to shuffle against the stones, to him that goeth. All these fashions, and generally, that which may stop, and that which may traverse the course of another man's talk, must be shunned. . . .

But, as over-much babble makes a man weary: so doth over-much *Silence* procure as great disliking. For, *To use silence in place where other men talk to and fro: is in manner, as much a fault, as not to pay your share and scot[8] as other men do.* And as speech is a means to show men your mind, to whom you speak: so, doth *Silence* again make men ween[9] you seek to be unknown. So that, as those people which use to drink much at feasts, and make themselves drunk, are wont to thrust them out of their company, that will not take their drink as they do; so be these kind of mute and still fellows coldly welcome to pleasant and merry company, that meet to pass the time away in pleasure and talk. So that *It is good manner for a man to speake, and likewise to hold his peace, as it comes to his turn, and occasion requires.*

[8] *share and scot*: your part of the bill or your ante.   [9] **ween**: guess or think.

→ GEORGE PUTTENHAM

From The Art of English Poesie 1588

This selection from George Puttenham's *The Art of English Poesie* sketches the development of early modern English out of a multitude of local and regional dialects and languages. George Puttenham (1529–1590/91), a poet and writer, was the second son of a Hampshire gentleman; his upbringing and education were "gentle," though his life was full of family conflict, sometimes violent. He spent his younger adult years in litigation over control of his property and embroiled in a rancorous divorce. His relations with his stepson were almost as violent as those of Orlando and Oliver: he was stabbed and kidnapped by his stepson and jailed in the 1570s and 1580s, and his case reached the highest courts. It was politic, therefore, for Puttenham to dedicate *The Art of English Poesie* to Lord Burghley, Queen Elizabeth's chief advisor.

The book became famous for providing the first comprehensive overview of English poetry, and for advising writers how to compose and adorn their verses. Puttenham also addresses what has been called "the question of language": out of many forms and dialects of the non-Latin vernacular or "mother tongue," which was the most genteel type of English for speaking and writing? Puttenham's decree that writers should use the accent and diction of London and environs reflects the extraordinary growth of the city and its suburbs in the sixteenth century and the protonationalist drive to consolidate the disparate peoples of the island under the banner of "pure" English. Languages spoken and written in places far from London by people like Corin and Audrey were thus rendered marginal and, at the same time, demoted in status and political power. We may not hear the contrasting accents of court and country today in every performance (especially in American productions), but we can be sure Shakespeare's actors performed their roles with them in mind. What is the difference in manner of speaking (word choice, rhythm, sentence length and structure) between Corin and Touchstone, and between Audrey and Rosalind? What in Phoebe's speech and writing shows she is not a country laborer like Audrey? What about Ganymede's style and manner alert Orlando that the boy is not entirely rustic? What kind of speech is associated with "uplandish" or remote areas, and what kind is therefore "inland," a word both Orlando and Rosalind use about their own upbringing?

George Puttenham, *The Art of English Poesie, English Reprints*, ed. Edward Arber (Birmingham, 1869), 164–66.

From *The Art of English Poesie*

FROM BOOK 3, CHAPTER 4

Of Language

[A]fter a speech is fully fashioned to the common understanding, and accepted by consent of a whole country and nation, it is called a language, and receiveth none allowed alteration, but by extraordinary occasions by little and little, as it were insensibly bringing in of many corruptions[1] that creep along with the time, of all which matters we have more largely spoken in our books of the originals and pedigree of the English tongue. Then, when I say language, I mean the speech wherein the poet or maker[2] writeth, be it Greek or Latin or as our case is the vulgar English, and when it is peculiar unto a country it is called the mother speech of that people — the Greeks term it *idioma*, so is ours at this day the Norman English. Before the Conquest of the Normans it was the Anglo-Saxon, and before that the British, which as some will, is at this day the Welsh or as others affirm the Cornish.[3] . . . This part in our maker or poet must be heedily[4] looked unto, that it be natural, pure, and the most usual of all his country, and for the same purpose rather that which is spoken in the king's court, or in the good towns and cities within the land, than in the marches[5] and frontiers, or in port towns, where strangers haunt for traffic's sake, or yet in universities where scholars use much peevish affectation of words out of the primitive[6] languages, or finally, in any uplandish[7] village or corner of a realm, where is no resort but of poor rustical or uncivil people. Neither shall he follow the speech of a craftsman or carter[8] or other of the inferior sort, though he be inhabitant or bred in the best town and city in this realm, for such persons do abuse good speeches by strange accents or ill-shapen sounds, and false orthography.[9] But he shall follow generally the better brought up sort, such as the Greeks call *charientes*, men civil and graciously behaviored and bred. Our maker therefore at these days shall not follow *Piers Plowman* nor *Gower* nor *Lydgate* nor yet *Chaucer*,[10] for their language is now out of use with us. Neither shall he take the terms of Northern-men, such as they use in daily

---

[1] **corruptions:** changes in words; also foreign words. [2] **maker:** author. [3] **Conquest . . . Cornish:** Anglo-Saxon England was invaded and conquered by the Normans under William in 1066. Ancient Britons spoke a language related to Welsh and Cornish. [4] **heedily:** carefully. [5] **marches:** borderlands. [6] **primitive:** ancient; referring to Greek and Latin. [7] **uplandish:** remote. [8] **carter:** cart driver. [9] **orthography:** spelling. [10] *Piers Plowman . . . Chaucer*: William Langland's *Piers Plowman* was a fourteenth-century poem written in Middle English, like works by John Gower, John Lydgate, and Geoffrey Chaucer.

talk, whether they be noble men or gentlemen, or of their best clerks all is a matter; nor in effect any speech used beyond the River of Trent,[11] though no man can deny but that theirs is the purer English Saxon at this day, yet it is not so courtly nor so current as our southern English is; no more is the far Western-man's speech: Ye shall, therefore, take the usual speech of the court and that of London and the shires lying about London within 60 miles and not much above. I say not this but that in every shire of England there be gentlemen and others that speak but specially write as good southern as we of Middlesex or Surrey do, but not the common people of every shire, to whom the gentlemen, and also their learned clerks, do for the most part condescend, but herein we are already ruled by the English dictionaries and other books written by learned men, and therefore it needeth none other direction in that behalf. Albeit peradventure[12] some small admonition be not impertinent, for we find in our English writers many words and speeches amendable, and ye shall see in some many inkhorn terms[13] so ill-affected brought in by men of learning as preachers and schoolmasters, and many strange terms of other languages by secretaries and merchants and travelers, and many dark words and not usual nor well-sounding, though they be daily spoken in court. Wherefore great heed must be taken by our maker in this point that his choice be good.

[11] **River of Trent:** traditionally marked the boundary between northern and southern England.
[12] **peradventure:** perhaps.   [13] **inkhorn terms:** obscure and pedantic words.

→ DESIDERIUS ERASMUS

From On Copia of Words and Ideas   *1512*

Translated by Donald B. King

To possess *copia*, or an abundance of verbal material ready for any occasion, was a much sought after talent. As Giovanni della Casa reminds us, it can be just as rude not to speak, as to speak rudely. At a feast or a meeting, a person's silence can easily offend and puzzle others who expect engagement. The fear of speaking silenced many a passionate lover, because so much stress was placed on the ability to invent and sustain witty or amorous conversation during the long courtships common in early modern society. In business or political matters, verbal fluency was highly prized and considered a mark of gentility and educa-

Desiderius Erasmus, *On Copia of Words and Ideas,* trans. Donald B. King, Medieval Philosophical Texts in Translation 12 (Milwaukee: Marquette U P, 1963).

tion. A man or woman who could not speak fully and inventively was at a distinct disadvantage.

Orlando feels this inability keenly after his defeat of Charles the wrestler. When Rosalind tries to engage him in conversation and gives him her necklace, he says nothing, but stands there frozen and tongue-tied. He cries out in frustration after she leaves, comparing himself to a crude wooden dummy and blaming passion for muting his natural gentility: "Can I not say, 'I thank you'? My better parts / Are all thrown down, and that which here stands up / Is but a quintain, a mere lifeless block" (1.2.191–93).

As some of his spectators could have told him, Orlando needs the facility set out in Desiderius Erasmus's *De Utraque Verborum ac Rerum Copia* (*On Copia*), which advised readers how to store their minds with phrases and methods to extend the variety of spoken thought, and to ensure they will never be "graveled for lack of matter," as Rosalind puts it later (4.1.54). Erasmus (1466?–1566) provides one exercise that has become justly famous: almost casually and without great effort, he spins out hundreds of variations on one statement: "I thank you for your letter, which has delighted me very much." What would Erasmus have said in the same situation that confronted Orlando? How many ways might he have found to respond to Rosalind's initiative?

CHAPTER VIII. FOR WHAT THINGS THIS TRAINING IS USEFUL

Now in order that this studious youth may apply itself to this study with an eager disposition we shall make clear in a few words for what things it is of use. First of all then, this training in varying speech will be useful in every way for attaining good style, which is a matter of no little moment. In particular, however, it will be useful in avoiding tautology, that is, repetition of the same word or expression, a vice not only unseemly but also offensive. It not infrequently happens that we have to say the same thing several times, in which case, if destitute of *copia*[1] we will either be at a loss, or, like the cuckoo, croak out the same words repeatedly, and be unable to give different shape or form to the thought. And thus betraying our want of eloquence we will appear ridiculous ourselves and utterly exhaust our wretched audience with weariness. . . . Moreover, who is so patient a listener that he would even for a short time put up with a speech unvarying throughout? Variety everywhere has such force that nothing at all is so polished as not to seem lacking its excellence. Nature itself especially rejoices in variety; in such great throng of things she has left nothing anywhere not painted with some wonderful artifice of variety. And just as the eye is held more by a varying

---

[1] *copia*: copiousness, or fullness and variation in speech and writing.

scene, in the same way the mind always eagerly examines whatever it sees as new. And if all things continually present themselves to the mind without variation, it will at once turn away in disgust. Thus the whole profit of a speech is lost. This great fault he will shun easily who is prepared to turn the same thought into many forms, as the famous Proteus[2] is said to have changed his form. And in truth this training will contribute greatly to skill in extemporaneous speaking or writing, it will assure that we will not frequently hesitate in bewilderment or keep shamefully silent. . . .

CHAPTER XXXIII. PRACTICE

Now, to make the matter clearer, let us set forth an expression as an experiment and try how far it is possible to have it turn like Proteus into several forms; not that every method of varying is suitable in any one instance, but as many as are, we shall use. Let us take the following sentence for an example: *Your letter has delighted me very much.* . . .

Now then let us make trial: Your letter has delighted me very much. In a wonderful way your letter has delighted me; in an unusually wonderful way your letter has delighted me. (Up to this point nothing has been varied except the word order.) By your letter I have been greatly delighted. I have been delighted in an unusually wonderful way by your letter. (Here only the voice of the verb has been changed.) Your epistle has cheered me exceedingly. In truth by your epistle I have been exceedingly cheered. Your note has refreshed my spirit in no indifferent manner. By the writing of your humanity I have been refreshed in spirit in no indifferent manner. From your most pleasing letter I have received incredible joy. Your paper has been the occasion of an unusual pleasure for me. From your paper I have received a wondrous pleasure. . . .

Anyone may easily compose others for himself. . . . When I received your letter an incredible joy seized my spirit. Your epistle caressed me with extraordinary pleasure. What you wrote to me was most delightful. That you sent a letter to me was exceedingly pleasant. Nothing could have given me more pleasure than that you deemed me worthy of your letter. Your dear letter has made me rejoice exceedingly.

[Dozens of examples follow, becoming increasingly hyperbolic.]

Immortal God! what great joy came to us from your letter? O wonderful, what great cause of joy your letter supplied? Good gods, what a great num-

[2] **Proteus:** shape-shifting Greek god.

ber of joys did your letter afford me? Your letter brought me greater joy than I can express. . . . I would die if anything more pleasing than your letter ever happened. I would perish if anything in life occurred more pleasurable than your letter. I call the muses to witness that nothing has ever before brought me more joy than your letter. Do not believe that Fortune can offer anything more pleasing than your letter. The delight your letter gives me is equaled only by the love I bear you. Oh wonderful! How much joy your letter aroused in me. What laughter, what applause, what exultant dancing your letter caused in me. Reading your most elegant letter I was touched with a strange joy. . . . What wine is to man thirsting for it, your letter is to me. What clover is to bees, what willow boughs are to goats, what honey is to the bear, your letter is to me. The letter of your sublimity was sweeter to me than any honey. When I received your so eagerly awaited letter, you would have said that Erasmus was certainly drunk with joy. . . .

If any of these appear to be of such a sort as would scarcely be considered suitable in prose, remember that this exercise is adapted to the composition of verse also.

"Wit, Whither Wilt?" Jest Books and Quick Answers

With four couples pairing up, *As You Like It* is rife with flirting and banter, but as in tennis, one needs a skillful partner in order to show one's skill and play the game well. Touchstone bemoans the fact that his best quips go for nothing, because Audrey cannot even understand simple terms like "poetical," but the other pairs of lovers show themselves much more accomplished players — though Orlando is still feeling his way toward fluency.

Comedy was just one popular genre that dwelled on witty and witless wooing. Playwrights and clowns drew on cheaply printed, widely circulating comic ballads and jestbooks, which treated courtship as an endless source of humor (see the ballads in Chapter 2). Jests poked fun at the gentleman who failed at serenading his lady, or the inept rube and the plainspoken country bride; others told of the tricks and escapades dreamt up by young lovers to make love or to marry in secret. Many jests figure women as laugh-getters as they put down a suitor in his straits. A successful flirtation is rare, though many a suitor tries to seduce a woman through artful talk that may make her "laugh and lie down," as one rude proverb put it.

The following excerpts from three jest books provide a tiny sample of these jests. Are any reminiscent of the exchanges between Phoebe and Silvius? Rosalind and Orlando? How does Rosalind's wordplay with her father (3.4.28–30) resemble the daughter's trick in *Banquet of Jests*? Consider the last two jests in the selection. Do they perhaps put the women's mockery of Orlando's poems in a different light? Are all of these gentlemen's artistic efforts gauche and awkward, or is it simply amusing for women to trade quips at the expense of ardent suitors? In Copley's first jest, in which a gentleman suitor has the last word, is his answer to being spat on a clown's punch line to laugh at, or a speech to admire? What in its tone and literary style show he is truly gentle, and may yet win the day?

A SELECTION OF WOOING JESTS

→ *From* A Banquet of Jests   *1657*

[A Father and His Daughter]

A country man suspicious of his Daughter, and no way affecting a certain young fellow that was suitor to her, took his daughter to schooling,[1] making her vow, never more to come into his company without asking leave. A little after her father sitting by the fire and she having notice given her that her friend was at the door, she feigned to reach something behind her father, and as she stooped, said, Father by your leave: Marry good leave have you, Daughter, saith he. Which was no sooner spoken, but out she went to her sweetheart; and saw her father no more, til she came home a married wife.

[1] schooling: took her to task; insisted.

A Banquet of Jests New and Old (London, 1657), Wing A3705, 167.

→ *From* An Anonymous Commonplace Book   *c. 1635*

[Wooing and Horsetrading]

A young gallant of fair state being a suitor to a proper young gentlewoman . . . fell into special liking of an eased-paced Mare that was the old gentleman's, and desired to buy her. But the old gentleman told him she was only for his own saddle, and desired to be excused, but all the horses he had besides were at his service. The young gentleman grew so peremptory to have her that [he told him] if he would not sell him his Mare he would not marry his Daughter; the old man growing choleric, they parted.

Commonplace Book (c. 1635), 70r. HM 1338. Huntington Library, San Marino, California.

After a fortnight upon remembrance of his mistress's beauty he could not but repair to her father's house, but it was the young gentlewoman [who] chanced to meet him at the door, and it was he asking how she did? She made as if she knows of him not,[1] and thereupon he told her who he was. "I cry you mercy," [said she,] "for that now I well remember you; you are he that came a-wooing to my father's Mare."

[1] made as if she knows of him not: she pretended she didn't know him.

→ ANTHONY COPLEY

From Wits, Fits and Fancies   *1614*

[Wit at a Window]

A Gentleman passing along under his Mistress's window, she chanced (spitting out thereat) to spit upon him, and forthwith perceiving her amiss,[1] craved pardon of him therefore; who answered: "Forsooth (Lady) a Fisherman wets and dabbles himself all day long, and perchance catcheth but shrimps in the end: and I to catch so fair a trout as you, do you think I can loath so light a dew? Faith, no."

A Gentleman made music at his Mistress's window, and sung her a song which began thus: "My secret passions," &c. Another gentlewoman being then in place, and hearing him begin so, said, "Belike your servant is sick of the piles."[2]

A Gentleman that played well upon the balidore,[3] and had but a bad voice, played and sung in an evening under his Mistress's window, and when he had done, asked how she liked his music? She answered, "You have played very well, and you have sung too."

[1] amiss: mistake.   [2] piles: hemorrhoids.   [3] balidore: small stringed instrument.

Anthony Copley, *Wits, Fits and Fancies* (London, 1614), 51, 73, 74; STC 5741.

Bibliography

><

Primary Sources

A Banquet of Jests New and Old. London, 1657. Wing A3705.

"An Homily of the State of Matrimony." *The Second Tome of Homilies*. London, 1563. STC 13663.3.

Ariosto, Ludovico. *Orlando Furioso in English Heroical Verse*. Trans. John Harington. London, 1591. STC 746.

Armin, Robert. *The History of the Two Maids of More-clacke with the Life and Simple Manner of John in the Hospital*. London, 1609. STC 773.

———. *A Nest of Ninnies*. London, 1608. STC 772.7.

Ascham, Roger. *The Schoolemaster*. London, 1570. STC 832.

Barnfield, Richard. *The Affectionate Shepherd, Containing the Complaint of Daphnis for the Love of Ganymede*. London, 1594. STC 1480.

———. *Cynthia*. London, 1595. STC 1484.

Beard, Thomas. *The Theatre of God's Judgments*. London, 1597. STC 1659.

Boccaccio, Giovanni. *The Decameron Containing an Hundred Pleasant Novels*. London, 1620. STC 3172.

Brant, Sebastian. *The Shyppe of Fooles*. Trans. Henry Watson. London, 1517. STC 3547a.

———. *Stultifera Navis. . . . The Ship of Fools*. Trans. Alexander Barclay. London, 1570. STC 3546.

415

Brathwaite, Richard. *The English Gentleman, and the English Gentlewoman.* London, 1641. Wing B4262.

———. *The English Gentlewoman.* London, 1631. STC 3565.

Breton, Nicholas. *The Court and Country, or A Briefe Discourse Dialogue-wise Set Down between a Courtier and a Country-man Containing the Manner and Condition of Their Lives.* London, 1618. STC 3641.

Brinsley, John. *Ludus Literarius, or the Grammar School.* London, 1612. STC 3768.

Bruto, Giovanni. *The Necessary, Fit, and Convenient Education of a Young Gentlewoman.* Trans. W. P. London, 1598. STC 3947.

Burton, Robert. *The Anatomy of Melancholy What It Is. With all the Kindes, Causes, Symptoms, Prognostickes, and Seuerall Cures of It.* 1621. STC 4159.

———. *The Anatomy of Melancholy.* London, 1638. STC 4163.

Camden, William. *Britannia.* London, 1587. STC 4504.

Castiglione, Baldassare. *Il libro del Cortegiano.* Venice, 1528.

———. *The Courtyer of Baldessar Castilio, Divided into Four Books, Very Necessary and Profitable for Young Gentlemen and Gentlewomen Abiding in Court, Palace, or Place.* Trans. Thomas Hoby. London, 1561. STC 4778.

Cervantes, Miguel de. [Don Quixote.] *El ingenioso don Quijote de la Mancha.* Madrid, 1605, 1615.

Commonplace Book. ca. 1635. HM 1338. The Huntington Library, San Marino, CA.

Copley, Anthony. *Wits, Fits and Fancies.* London, 1614. STC 5741.

Cornwallis, William. *Essays.* London, 1600–01. STC 5775.

Cupid's Messenger: or, A Trusty Friend Stored with Sundry Sorts of Serious, Wittie, Pleasant, Amorous, and Delightful Letters. London, 1629. STC 6122.

della Casa, Giovanni. *Galateo.* Trans. Robert Peterson. London, 1576. STC 4738.

Drayton, Michael. *Annalia Dubrensia: Upon the Yearly Celebration of Mr. Robert Dover's Olympic Games upon Cotswold Hills.* London, 1636. STC 24954.

———. *Poly-Olbion.* London, 1612. STC 7226.

Earle, John. *Microcosmography, or a Piece of the World Discovered in Essays and Characters.* London, 1628. STC 7441.

Elyot, Thomas. *The Book Named the Governor.* London, 1531. STC 7635.

Erasmus, Desiderius. *A Little Book of Good Manners for Children.* Trans. Robert Whittinton. London, 1532. STC 10467.

———. *Moriae Encomium.* Basel, 1515.

———. *On Copia of Words and Ideas.* Trans. Donald B. King. Mediaeval Philosophical Texts in Translation 12. Milwaukee: Marquette UP, 1963.

———. *Praise of Folly.* Trans. John Wilson. London, 1668. n. pag. Web. 2 July 2012. <http://www.gutenberg.org/cache/epub/9371/pg9371.txt>.

Fitzherbert, John. *The Booke of Husbandry.* London, 1540. STC 10996.

Fowler, Constantia. "Letter to Herbert Aston." *Tixall Letters, or the Correspondence of the Aston Family and Their Friends, During the Seventeenth Century.* Ed. Arthur Clifford. Vol. 1. London: Longman, Hurst, Rees, Orme and Brown, 1815.

Gascoigne, George. *The Noble Art of Venery or Hunting.* London, 1575. STC 24328.

Grafton, Richard. *A Chronicle at Large.* London, 1569. STC 12147.

Greene, Robert (?). *George a Greene, the Pinner off Wakefield.* London, 1599. STC 12212.

Hamdultun, Valentine. "A Merry New Jig; or, the Pleasant Wooing betwixt Kit and Peg." London, 1630. STC 12725.

———. "A Pleasant New Song between Two Young Lovers That Lasted Not Long; or, the Second Part." London, 1630. STC 12725.

Harington, Sir John. *An Anatomie of the Metamorpho-sed Ajax.* London, 1596. STC 12772.

Harrison, William. "The Description and Chronicles of England." In *The First Volume of the Chronicles of England, Scotland, and Ireland.* Raphael Holinshed. Vol. 1. London, 1577. STC 135686.

Hodgkinson, R. F. B., ed. "Extracts from the Act Books of the Archdeacons of Nottingham." *Transactions of the Thoroton Society of Nottinghamshire* 29 (1929): 19–67.

Holinshed, Raphael. *The First Volume of the Chronicles of England, Scotland, and Ireland.* London, 1577. STC 135686.

I. D. [John Davies]. *A Scourge for Paper-Persecutors, Or Papers Complaint, Compil'd in Ruthfull Rimes, against the Paper-Spoylers of these Times.* London, 1625. STC 6340.

J. A. *An Apology for a Younger Brother.* Oxford, 1641. Wing A3592.

James I of England. "A Proclamation against Unlawful Hunting." May 16, 1603. *Stuart Royal Proclamations, Vol. 1: Royal Proclamations of King James I, 1603–1625.* Ed. James F. Larkin and Paul L. Hughes. Oxford: Clarendon, 1973. 14–16.

Jonson, Ben. *Discoveries Made Upon Men and Some Matter.* 1641. Web. 9 July 2012. <http://www.gutenberg.org/dirs/etext04/dscv10.txt>.

Lodge, Thomas, *Rosalynde. Euphues Golden Legacie.* London, 1590. STC 16664.

———. *Rosalynde. Euphues Golden Legacie.* London, 1592. STC 16665.

Lyly, John. *Euphues and His England.* London, 1580. STC 17069.

———. *Euphues. The Anatomy of Wit.* London, 1578. STC 17051.

———. *Gallatea.* London, 1592. STC 17080.

Major, John. *Historia Majoris Britanniae.* 1521. Trans. Archibald Constable. Edinburgh, 1892.

Manwood, John. *A Treatise and Discourse of the Laws of the Forest.* London, 1598. STC 17291.

Marlowe, Christopher. "The Passionate Shepherd to His Love." *England's Helicon.* London, 1600. STC 3191.

———. *The Tragedie of Dido, Queene of Carthage.* London, 1594. STC 62481.

Marston, John. *The Scourge of Villainy. Three Books of Satires.* London, 1598. STC 17485.

Mascall, Leonard. *The First Book of Cattle.* London, 1591. STC 17581.

Montaigne, Michel de. *Essays Written in French by Michael Lord of Montaigne.* Trans. John Florio. London, 1613. STC 18042.

More, Sir Thomas. *Utopia.* Trans. Ralph Robinson. London, 1551. STC 18094.

Mulcaster, Richard. *Positions.* London, 1581. STC 18253.

Munday, Anthony. *The Downfall of Robert, Earle of Huntington.* London, 1601. STC 18271.

———. *The Death of Robert, Earle of Huntington.* London, 1601. STC 18269.

Osborne, Dorothy. "Letter to Sir William Temple." *The Love Letters of Dorothy Osborne to Sir William Temple, 1652–54.* Ed. Edward Abbott Parry. 3rd ed. London and Sydney, 1888.

Ovid. *Elegies.* Trans. Christopher Marlowe. London, 1603. STC 18931.

———. *The XV Books of P. Ovidius Naso entitled Metamorphosis.* Trans. Arthur Golding. London, 1584. STC 18958.

———. *Ovidius Naso His Remedie of Love.* Trans. F. L. London, 1600. STC 18974.

Peacham, Henry. *The Compleat Gentleman.* London, 1622. STC 19502.

———. *Minerva Britanna.* London, 1612. STC 19511.

Prynne, William. *Histrio-Mastix.* London, 1633. STC 20464.

Puttenham, George. *The Art of English Poesie, English Reprints.* Ed. Edward Arber. Birmingham, 1869.

Rabelais, François. *The Works of Rabelais Faithfully Translated from the French.* Trans. Thomas Urquhart and Peter Antony Motteux. Darby: Moray Press, 1894.

Rainolds, John. *Th'Overthrow of Stage-Playes.* Middelburg, 1599. STC 20616.

Raleigh, Walter (?). "The Nymph's Reply to the Shepherd." *England's Helicon.* London, 1600. STC 3191.

Ritson, Joseph, ed. *Robin Hood: A Collection of Poems, Songs, and Ballads.* London: George Routledge and Sons, 1884.

Rowlands, Samuel. *The Bride.* London, 1617. STC 21365.5.

Saviolo, Vincentio. *Vincentio Saviolo His Practice In Two Books.* London, 1595. STC 21788.

Shakespeare, William. *As You Like It.* Ed. Juliet Dusinberre. Arden Shakespeare. London: Thomson Learning, 2006.

———. *The Complete Works of Shakespeare,* Sixth Edition. Ed. David Bevington. Upper Saddle River: Pearson, 2009.

———. *Mr. William Shakespeare's Comedies, Histories, and Tragedies.* London, 1623. STC 22273.

———. *Shake-speares Sonnets.* London, 1609. STC 22353.

Sidney, Philip. *Astrophil and Stella.* London, 1591. STC 22537.

———. *The Countess of Pembroke's Arcadia.* London, 1593. STC 22540.

Sorel, Charles. *The Extravagant Shepherd.* London, 1652. Wing S4704.

Spenser, Edmund. *Amoretti and Epithalamion.* London, 1595. STC 23076.

———. *The Faerie Queene.* London, 1596. STC 23082.

———. *The Shepheardes Calender.* London, 1579. STC 23089.

Starkey, Thomas. *A Dialogue between Pole and Lupset.* Ed. T. F. Mayer. London: Royal Historical Society, 1989.

Stockwood, John. *A Bartholomew Fairing*. London, 1589. STC 23277.

Stokes, James, ed. *Records of Early English Drama: Somerset*. Toronto: U of Toronto P, 1996.

Tarlton, Richard (?). *Tarlton's Jests*. London, 1638. STC 23684.

Taylor, John. *Taylor's Pastoral*. London, 1624. STC 23801.

Theocritus. *Six Idyllia, That Is, Six Small, or Petty Poems, or Eglogues, Chosen out of the Right Famous Sicilian Poet Theocritus, and Translated into English Verse*. Oxford, 1588. STC 23937.

Trevelyon, Thomas. "Fooles, or foolishnesse." *Thomas Trevelyon's Miscellany*, 1608. Folger MS V.b.323. Folger Shakespeare Library, Washington, DC.

Vaughan, William. *The Golden-groue Moralized in Three Books: A Work Very Necessary for All Such, as Would Know How to Governe Themselves, Their Houses, or Their Country*. London, 1600. STC 24610.

Virgil. *The Bucoliks of Publius Virgilius Maro*. Trans. Abraham Fleming. London, 1589. STC 24817.

Vives, Juan Luis. *A Verie Fruitfull and Pleasant Booke, Called the Instruction of a Christian Woman*. Trans. Richard Hyrde. London, 1529. STC 24856.5.

Weever, John. *The Whipping of the Satyre*. London, 1601. STC 14071.

Whetstone, George. *An Heptameron of Civil Discourses*. London, 1582. STC 25337.

Wroth, Lady Mary. *The Countess of Mountgomeries Urania*. London, 1621. STC 26051.

———. *Pamphilia to Amphilanthus*. Folger V.a.104, F113. Folger Shakespeare Library, Washington, D.C.

Wyatt, Sir Thomas. "The Lover Describeth His Being Stricken with Sight of His Love." *Songs and Sonnets Written by the Right Honorable Lord Henry Howard Late Earl of Surrey, and Others*. London, 1557. STC 13861.

Secondary Sources

Alpers, Paul. *What Is Pastoral?* Chicago: U of Chicago P, 1996.

Alulis, Joseph. "Fathers and Children: Matter, Mirth, and Melancholy in *As You Like It*." *Shakespeare's Political Pageant*. Ed. Joseph Alulis and Vickie Sullivan. Lanham: Rowman and Littlefield, 1996. 37–60.

Arditi, Jorge. *A Genealogy of Manners: Transformations of Social Relations in France and England from the Fourteenth to the Eighteenth Century*. Chicago: U of Chicago P, 1998.

Barnaby, Andrew. "The Political Conscious of Shakespeare's *As You Like It*." *SEL: Studies in English Literature, 1500–1900* 36.2 (1996): 373–95.

Barton, Anne. "*As You Like It* and *Twelfth Night*: Shakespeare's Sense of an Ending." *Shakespearean Comedy*. Ed. Malcolm Bradbury and David Palmer. New York: Crane, Russnak, 1972. 168–80.

Baumgartel, Stephan. "Body Politics between Sublimation and Subversion: Critical Perspectives on Twentieth-Century All-Male Performances of Shakespeare's *As You Like It*." *The Shakespeare International Yearbook*. Ed.

Graham Bradshaw, Tom Bishop, and Laurence Wright. Aldershot: Ashgate, 2009. 247–68.

Beckman, Margaret Boerner. "The Figure of Rosalind in *As You Like It*." *Shakespeare Quarterly* 29.1 (1978): 44–51.

Bennett, Robert B. "The Reform of a Malcontent: Jacques and the Meaning of *As You Like It*." *Shakespeare Studies* 9 (1976): 183–204.

Billington, Sandra. *The Social History of the Fool*. Sussex: Harvester, 1984.

Black, Joseph. "'Handling Religion in the Style of the Stage': Performing the Marprelate Controversy." *Religion and Drama in Early Modern England: The Performance of Religion on the Renaissance Stage*. Ed. Jane Degenhardt and Elizabeth Williamson. Aldershot: Ashgate, 2011. 153–72.

———. *The Martin Marprelate Tracts: A Modernized and Annotated Edition*. Cambridge: Cambridge UP, 2008.

Bloom, Harold. *William Shakespeare's* As You Like It: *Modern Critical Interpretations*. New York: Chelsea, 1988.

Bono, Barbara, J. "Mixed Gender, Mixed Genre in Shakespeare's *As You Like It*." *Renaissance Genres: Essays on Theory, History, and Interpretation*. Ed. Barbara Kiefer Lewalski. Cambridge: Harvard UP, 1986. 189–212.

Boose, Lynda E. "The 1599 Bishops' Ban, Elizabethan Pornography, and the Sexualization of the Jacobean Stage." *Enclosure Acts: Sexuality, Property, and Culture in Early Modern England*. Ed. Richard Burt and John Michael Archer. Ithaca: Cornell UP, 1994. 185–200.

Bracher, Mark. "Contrary Notions of Identity in *As You Like It*." *SEL: Studies in English Literature, 1500–1900* 24.2 (1984): 225–40.

Bristol, Michael D. "Shamelessness in Arden: Early Modern Theater and the Obsolescence of Popular Theatricality." *Print, Manuscript, Performance: The Changing Relations of the Media in Early Modern England*. Ed. Arthur F. Marotti and Michael D. Bristol. Columbus: Ohio State UP, 2000. 279–306.

Brown, Pamela Allen. *Better a Shrew Than a Sheep: Women, Drama and the Culture of Jest in Early Modern England*. Ithaca: Cornell UP, 2003.

———. "'Cattle of this colour': Boying the Diva in *As You Like It*." *Early Theatre* (January 2012): 145–66.

Brown, Pamela Allen, and Peter Parolin, eds. *Women Players in England 1500–1660: Beyond the All-Male Stage*. Aldershot: Ashgate, 2005.

Bryson, Anna. *From Courtesy to Civility: Changing Codes of Conduct in Early Modern England*. Oxford: Clarendon, 1998.

Burke, Peter. *The Art of Conversation*. Ithaca: Cornell UP, 1993.

———. *The Fortunes of the Courtier: The European Reception of Castiglione's Courtier*. University Park: Penn State UP, 1995.

Burnett, Mark Thornton. *Masters and Servants in Early Modern Drama and Culture: Authority and Obedience*. New York: St. Martin's, 1997.

Burt, Richard, and John Archer, eds. *Enclosure Acts: Sexuality, Property, and Culture in Early Modern England*. Ithaca: Cornell UP, 1994.

Bushnell, Rebecca. *A Culture of Teaching: Early Modern Humanism in Theory and Practice*. Ithaca: Cornell UP, 1996.

Campbell, Julie D. "'Merry, nimble, stirring spirit[s]': Academic, Salon and Commedia dell'arte Influence on the *Innamorate* of *Love's Labour's Lost.*" *Women Players in England, 1500–1600: Beyond the All-Male Stage.* Ed. Pamela Allen Brown and Peter Parolin. Aldershot, UK: Ashgate, 2005. 145–70.

Carlson, Susan. "Women in *As You Like It*: Community, Change, and Choice." *Essays in Literature* 14.2 (1987): 151–69.

Chambers, E. K. *The Elizabethan Stage.* 4 vols. Oxford: Clarendon, 1923.

Charlton, Kenneth. *Education in Renaissance England.* London and New York: Routledge, 2007.

Cirillo, Albert R. "*As You Like It*: Pastoralism Gone Awry." *ELH* 38.1 (1971): 19–39.

Cole, Howard C. "The Moral Vision of *As You Like It.*" *College Literature* 3.1 (1976): 17–32.

Colie, Rosalie. "Perspectives on Pastoral: Romance, Comic, and Tragic." *Shakespeare's Living Art.* Princeton: Princeton UP, 1974. 243–83.

Costa de Beauregard, Raphaëlle. "Laughter Chastened or Arden Language: A Study of Comic Languages in *As You Like It.*" *For Laughs: Puzzling Laughter in the Plays of the Tudor Age.* Bern: Peter Lang, 2002. 211–29.

Crawford, Julie. "The Homoerotics of Shakespeare's Elizabethan Comedies." *A Companion to Shakespeare's Works: The Comedies.* Ed. Richard Dutton and Jean E. Howard. Oxford: Blackwell, 2003. 137–58.

Daley, A. Stuart. "The Idea of Hunting in *As You Like It.*" *Shakespeare Studies* 21 (1993): 72–95.

———. "The Tyrant Duke of *As You Like It*: Envious Malice Confronts Honor, Pity, Friendship." *Cahiers Elisabéthains: Late Medieval and Renaissance Studies* 34 (1988): 39–51.

Davis, Natalie Zemon. "Women on Top." *Society and Culture in Early Modern France.* Stanford: Stanford UP, 1975. 124–51.

DiGangi, Mario. *The Homoerotics of Early Modern Drama.* Cambridge: Cambridge UP, 1999.

———. *Sexual Types: Embodiment, Agency, and Dramatic Character from Shakespeare to Shirley.* Philadelphia: U of Pennsylvania P, 2011.

Dillon, Janette. *Shakespeare and the Solitary Man.* Totowa: Rowman and Littlefield, 1981.

Doran, Madeline. "Yet am I inland bred." *Shakespeare Quarterly* 15.2 (1964): 99–114.

Dusinberre, Juliet. "*As You Like It.*" *A Companion to Shakespeare's Works: The Comedies.* Ed. Richard Dutton and Jean E. Howard. Malden: Blackwell, 2006. 411–28.

———. "Introduction." *As You Like It.* By William Shakespeare. London: Arden Shakespeare of Thomson Learning, 2006. 1–142.

———. "Pancakes and a Date for *As You Like It.*" *Shakespeare Quarterly* 54.4 (2003): 371–405.

———. "Topical Forest: Kemp and Mar-text in Arden." *In Arden: Editing Shakespeare. Essays in Honour of Richard Proudfoot.* Ed. Ann Thompson and Gordon McMullan. London: Thomson Learning, 2003. 239–51.

Elam, Keir. "'As They Did in a Golden World': Romantic Rupture and Semantic Rupture in *As You Like It*." *Canadian Review of Comparative Literature* 18 (1991): 217–32.

Elias, Norbert. *The Civilizing Process: The History of Manners*. Trans. Edmund Jephcott. Oxford, UK and Cambridge, MA: Blackwell, 1994.

Enos, Carol. "Catholic Exiles in Flanders and *As You Like It*; Or, what if you don't like it at all?" *Theater and Religion: Lancastrian Shakespeare*. Ed. Richard Dutton, Alison Findlay, and Richard Wilson. Manchester: Manchester UP, 2003. 130–42.

Enterline, Lynn. *Shakespeare's Schoolroom: Rhetoric, Discipline, Emotion*. Philadelphia: U of Pennsylvania P, 2011.

Erickson, Peter B. "Sexual Politics and the Social Structure in *As You Like It*." *Massachusetts Review: A Quarterly of Literature, the Arts and Public Affairs* 23.1 (1982): 65–83.

Evett, David. *Discourses of Service in Shakespeare's England*. New York: Macmillan, 2005.

Fendt, Gene. "Resolution, Catharsis, Culture: *As You Like It*." *Philosophy and Literature* 19.2 (1995): 248–60.

Fink, Z. S. "Jaques and the Malcontent Traveler." *Philological Quarterly* 14 (1935): 237–52.

Finotti, Fabio. "Women Writers in Renaissance Italy: Courtly Origins of New Literary Canons." *Strong Voices, Weak History: Early Women Writers & Canons in England, France, & Italy*. Ed. Pamela Joseph Benson and Victoria Kirkham. Ann Arbor: U of Michigan P, 2005. 121–45.

Fisher, Will. "Home Alone: The Place of Women's Homoerotic Desire in Shakespeare's *As You Like It*." *Feminisms and Early Modern Texts: Essays for Phyllis Rackin*. Ed. Rebecca Ann Bach and Gwynne Kennedy. Selinsgrove: Susquehanna UP, 2010. 99–118.

Fitter, Christopher. "'Betrayed to Every Modern Censure': *As You Like It* and Vestry Values." *Radical Shakespeare: Politics and Stagecraft in the Early Career*. New York: Routledge, 2012. 191–228.

———. "Reading Orlando Historically: Vagrancy, Forest, and Vestry Values in Shakespeare's *As You Like It*." *Medieval and Renaissance Drama in England* 23 (2010): 114–41.

Fortin, Rene E. "'Tongues in Trees': Symbolic Patterns in *As You Like It*." *Texas Studies in Literature and Language: A Journal of the Humanities* 14 (1973): 569–82.

Fox, Adam. *Oral and Literate Culture in England, 1500–1700*. Oxford: Oxford UP, 2000.

Fuchs, Barbara. *Romance*. New York: Routledge, 2004.

Garber, Marjorie. "The Education of Orlando." *Comedy from Shakespeare to Sheridan*. Ed. A. R. Braunmuller and James C. Bulman. Newark: U of Delaware P, 1986. 102–12.

Gay, Penny. *As You Like It*. London: Northcote House/British Council, 1999.

Gibbons, Brian. "Amorous Fictions in *As You Like It*." *Shakespeare and Multiplicity*. Cambridge: Cambridge UP, 1993. 153–81.

Goldberg, Jonathan. *Sodometries: Renaissance Texts, Modern Sexualities*. Stanford: Stanford UP, 1992.

Grafton, Anthony, and Lisa Jardine. *From Humanism to the Humanities*. London: Duckworth, 1986.

Halio, Jay L., et al. *As You Like It: An Annotated Bibliography, 1940–1980*. New York: Garland, 1985.

Harley, Marta Powell. "Rosalind, the Hare, and the Hyena in Shakespeare's *As You Like It*." *Shakespeare Quarterly* 36.3 (1985): 335–37.

Hayles, Nancy K. "Sexual Disguise in *As You Like It* and *Twelfth Night*." *Shakespeare Survey* 32 (1979): 63–72.

Heal, Felicity. *Hospitality in Early Modern England*. Oxford: Clarendon, 1990.

Hedrick, Donald K. "Merry and Weary Conversation: Textual Uncertainty in *As You Like It*, II.iv." *ELH* 46.1 (1979): 21–34.

Henke, Robert. "Back to the Future: A Review of Twentieth-Century Commedia-Shakespeare Studies." *Early Theatre* 11.2 (2008): 227–40.

Hennessy, Michael. "'Had I Kingdoms to Give': Place in *As You Like It*." *Essays in Literature* 4 (1977): 143–51.

Hieatt, Charles W. "The Quality of Pastoral in *As You Like It*." *Genre* 7 (1974): 164–82.

Holm, Janet Butler. "Thomas Salter's *The Mirrhor of Modestie*: A Translation of Bruto's *La Institutione Di Una Fanciulla Nata Nobilmente*." *The Library* s6–5.1 (1983): 53–57.

Howard, Jean E. *The Stage and Social Struggle in Early Modern England*. London: Routledge, 1994.

Hunt, Maurice. "Kairos and the Ripeness of Time in *As You Like It*." *Modern Language Quarterly: A Journal of Literary History* 52.2 (1991): 113–35.

———. *Shakespeare's* As You Like It: *Late Elizabethan Culture and Literary Representation*. New York: Palgrave Macmillan, 2008.

——— "Words and Deeds In *As You Like It*." *The Shakespeare Yearbook* 2 (1991): 23–48.

Hutton, Ronald. *The Rise and Fall of Merry England: The Ritual Year, 1400–1700*. Oxford: Oxford UP, 1994.

Johnston, Alexandra, and Wim Husken, eds. *English Parish Drama*. Amsterdam: Rodopi, 1996.

Jones, William R. "The Bishops' Ban of 1599 and the Ideology of English Satire." *Literature Compass* 7.5 (May 2010): 332–46. Web. <http://onlinelibrary.wiley.com/doi/10.1111/j.1741-4113.2010.00701.x/abstract>.

Kaiser, Walter. *Praisers of Folly*. Cambridge: Harvard UP, 1963.

Keevak, Michael. "The Playing of Sodomy in *As You Like It*." *Studies in Language and Literature* 9 (2000): 37–60.

Kelso, Ruth. *The Doctrine of the English Gentleman in the Sixteenth Century*. Gloucester: P. Smith, 1964.

Kerrigan, William. "Female Friends and Fraternal Enemies in *As You Like It.*" *Desire in the Renaissance: Psychoanalysis and Literature.* Ed. Valeria Finucci and Regina Schwartz. Princeton: Princeton UP, 1984. 184–207.

Kinney, Clare R. "Feigning Female Faining: Spenser, Lodge, Shakespeare, and Rosalind." *Modern Philology* 95.3 (1998): 291–315.

Kronenfeld, Judy Z. "Social Rank and the Pastoral Ideals of *As You Like It.*" *Shakespeare Quarterly* 29.3 (1978): 333–48.

Lecercle, Ann. "Dissonance in *As You Like It.*" *As You Like It: Essais Critiques.* Ed. Jean-Paul Débax and Yves Peyré. Toulouse: Presses Universitaires du Mirail, 1998.

Lee, Rensselaer W. *Names on Trees: Ariosto into Art.* Princeton: Princeton UP, 1977.

Leinwand, Theodore. "Conservative Fools in James's Court and Shakespeare's Plays." *Shakespeare Studies* 19 (1987): 219–37.

Lennox, Patricia. "A Girl's Got to Eat: Christine Edzard's Film of *As You Like It.*" *Transforming Shakespeare: Contemporary Women's Re-visions in Literature and Performance.* Ed. Marianne Novy. New York: Palgrave, 1999.

Lewis, Cynthia. "Horns, the Dream-Work, and Female Potency in *As You Like It.*" *South Atlantic Review* 66.4 (2001): 45–69.

Lin, Ya-Huei. "The Women Who Disappear on the Shakespearean Stage: *As You Like It*, *The Taming of the Shrew*, and the Misogynic Poetics of Deduction." *Misogynism in Literature: Any Place, Any Time.* Ed. Britta Zangen. Frankfurt: Peter Lang, 2004. 59–70.

Mann, David. *Shakespeare's Women: Performance and Conception.* Cambridge: Cambridge UP, 2008.

Marcus, Leah. *The Politics of Mirth: Jonson, Herrick, Milton, Marvell and the Defense of Old Holiday Pastimes.* Chicago: U of Chicago P, 1989.

Marriette, Amelia. "Urban Dystopias: Reapproaching Christine Edzard's *As You Like It.*" *Shakespeare, Film, Fin de Siècle.* Ed. Mark Thornton Burnett, Ramona Wray, and Peter Holland. Basingstoke and New York: Palgrave Macmillan, 2000.

Marshall, Cynthia. "The Doubled Jaques and Constructions of Negation in *As You Like It.*" *Shakespeare Quarterly* 49.4 (1998): 375–92.

———. "Wrestling as Play and Game in *As You Like It.*" *SEL: Studies in English Literature, 1500–1900* 33.2 (1993): 265–87.

Masten, Jeffrey. "Textual Deviance: Ganymede's Hand in *As You Like It.*" *Field Work: Sites in Literary and Cultural Studies.* Ed. Marjorie Garber, Paul B. Franklin, and Rebecca L. Walkowitz. New York: Routledge, 1996. 153–63.

Maurer, Margaret. "Facing the Music in Arden: ''Twas I, but 'Tis Not I.'" *As You Like It from 1600 to the Present.* Ed. Edward Tomarken. New York: Garland, 1997. 475–509.

McCabe, Richard A. "Elizabethan Satire and the Bishops' Ban of 1599." *The Yearbook of English Studies* 11 (1981): 188–93.

McDonald, Russ. *The Bedford Companion to Shakespeare.* 2nd ed. New York: Palgrave Macmillan, 2001.

McLuskie, Kathleen. "'Nay, faith, let me not play a woman, I have a beard coming': Women in Shakespeare's Plays." *Critical Survey* 4.2 (1992): 114–23.

Montrose, Louis. "Gentlemen and Shepherds: The Politics of Elizabethan Pastoral Form." *English Literary History* 50 (1983): 415–59.

———. "'The Place of a Brother' in *As You Like It*: Social Process and Comic Form." *Shakespeare Quarterly* 32.1 (1981): 28–54.

Morris, Harry. "*As You Like It*: Et in Arcadia Ego." *Shakespeare Quarterly* 26.3 (1975): 269–75.

Morse, Ruth. "*As You Like It*: Fools, Madness, and Melancholy." *As You Like It: Essais Critiques*. Eds. Jean-Paul Débax and Yves Peyré. Toulouse: Presses Universitaires du Mirail, 1998.

O'Day, Daniel. "Reconciliation in *As You Like It*: World Enough and Time?" *Reconciliation in Selected Shakespearean Dramas*. Ed. Beatrice Batson. Newcastle upon Tyne: Cambridge Scholars, 2008. 135–56.

Orgel, Stephen. *Impersonations: The Performance of Gender in Early Modern England*. Cambridge: Cambridge UP, 1996.

Orlin, Lena Cowen. *Private Matters and Public Culture in Post-Reformation England*. Ithaca: Cornell UP, 1994.

Orme, Nicholas. *Education and Society in Medieval and Renaissance England*. London: Hambledon, 1989.

Ormerod, David A. "Love's Labour's Lost and Won: The Case for *As You Like It*." *Cahiers Elisabéthains: Late Medieval and Renaissance Studies* 44 (1993): 9–21.

Otto, Beatrice L. *Fools Are Everywhere: The Court Jester Around the World*. Chicago: U of Chicago P, 2001.

Outhwaite, R. B. *Clandestine Marriage in England, 1500–1850*. London: Hambledon, 1995.

Owens, Anne. "*As You Like It*: Or, the Anatomy of Melancholy." *QWERTY: Arts, Littératures & Civilisations du Monde Anglophone* 7 (1997): 15–26.

Palmer, D. J. "Art and Nature in *As You Like It*." *Philological Quarterly* 49 (1970): 30–40.

———. "*As You Like It* and the Idea of Play." *Critical Quarterly* 13 (1971): 234–45.

Parker, Patricia. *Inescapable Romance: Studies in the Poetics of a Mode*. Princeton: Princeton UP, 1979.

Pierce, Robert B. "The Moral Languages of Rosalynde and *As You Like It*." *Studies in Philology* 68 (1971): 167–76.

Poggiolo, Renato. *The Oaten Flute*. Cambridge: Harvard UP, 1975.

Priest, Dale G. "Oratio and Negotium: Manipulative Modes in *As You Like It*." *SEL: Studies in English Literature, 1500–1900* 28.2 (1988): 273–86.

Rackin, Phyllis. "Androgyny, Mimesis and the Marriage of the Boy Heroine on the English Renaissance Stage." *PMLA* 102 (1987): 29–41.

Richards, Jennifer. *Rhetoric and Courtliness in Early Modern Literature*. Cambridge: Cambridge UP, 2003.

Rickman, Alan. "Jaques in *As You Like It*." *Players of Shakespeare*. Ed. Russell Jackson and Robert Smallwood. New York: Cambridge UP, 1988.

Robinson Marsha, S. "The Earthly City Redeemed: The Reconciliation of Cain and Abel in *As You Like It*." *Reconciliation in Selected Shakespearean Dramas*. Ed. Beatrice Batson. Newcastle upon Tyne: Cambridge Scholars, 2008. 157–74.

Rohy, Valerie. "*As You Like It*: Fortune's Turn." *Shakesqueer: A Queer Companion to the Complete Works of Shakespeare*. Ed. Madhavi Menon. Durham: Duke UP, 2011.

Ronk, Martha. "Locating the Visual in *As You Like It*." *Shakespeare Quarterly* 52.2 (2001): 255–76.

Sanders, Eve Rachele. *Gender and Literacy on Stage in Early Modern England*. Cambridge: Cambridge UP, 1998.

Schalkwyk, David. *Shakespeare, Love, and Service*. Cambridge: Cambridge UP, 2008.

Schleiner, Louise. "Voice, Ideology, and Gendered Subjects: The Case of *As You Like It* and *Two Gentlemen*." *Shakespeare Quarterly* 50.3 (1999): 285–309.

Scott, William O. "'A Woman's Thought Runs before Her Actions': Vows as Speech Acts in *As You Like It*." *Philosophy and Literature* 30.2 (2006): 528–39.

Scoufos, Alice-Lyle. "The Paradiso Terrestre and the Testing of Love in *As You Like It*." *Shakespeare Studies* 14 (1981): 215–27.

Segal, Janna. "'and Browner than Her Brother': 'Misprized' Celia's Racial Identity and Transversality in *As You Like It*." *Shakespeare* 4.1 (2008): 1–23.

Shaw, Fiona, and Juliet Stevenson. "Celia and Rosalind in *As You Like It*." *Players of Shakespeare II: Further Essays in Shakespearean Performance*. Ed. Russell Jackson and Robert Smallwood. New York: Cambridge UP, 1988. 55–71.

Singman, Jeffrey. *Robin Hood: The Shaping of the Legend*. Westport: Greenwood, 1998.

Smallwood, Robert. "'to Seek My Uncle in the Forest of Arden': Plot Manipulation and the Happy Ending of *As You Like It*." *As You Like It: Essais Critiques*. Ed. Jean-Paul Débax and Yves Peyré. Toulouse: Presses Universitaires du Mirail, 1998. 27–43.

Smith, Bruce. *Homosexual Desire in Shakespeare's England: A Cultural Poetics*. Chicago: U of Chicago P, 1991.

Southworth, John. *Fools and Jesters at the English Court*. Stroud: Sutton, 1998.

Stallybrass, Peter. "'Drunk with the cup of liberty': Robin Hood, the Carnivalesque, and the Rhetoric of Violence in Early Modern England." *Semiotica* 54 (1985): 113–45.

Stanton, Kay. "Shakespeare's Use of Marlowe in *As You Like It*." *'A Poet and a Filthy Playmaker': New Essays on Christopher Marlowe*. Ed. Kenneth Friedenreich, Roma Gill, and Constance B. Kuriyama. New York: AMS, 1988. 23–35.

Stewart, Alan. *Shakespeare's Letters*. Oxford: Oxford UP, 2008.

Stirm, Jan. "'for Solace a Twinne-Like Sister': Teaching Themes of Sisterhood in *As You Like It* and Beyond." *Shakespeare Quarterly* 47.4 (1996): 374–86.

Stokes, James, ed. *Records of Early English Drama: Somerset.* Toronto: U of Toronto P, 1996. Web. 9 July 2012. <http://archive.org/stream/somersetREED01stokuoft/somersetREEDo1stokuoft_djvu.txt>.

Strout, Nathaniel. "*As You Like It*, Rosalynde, and Mutuality." *SEL: Studies in English Literature, 1500–1900* 41.2 (2001): 277–95.

Taylor, Donn Ervin. "'Try in Time in Despite of a Fall': Time and Occasion in *As You Like It*." *Texas Studies in Literature and Language* 24.2 (1982): 121–36.

Tennant, David. "Touchstone in *As You Like It*." *Players of Shakespeare II: Further Essays in Shakespearean Performance.* Ed. Russell Jackson and Robert Smallwood. New York: Cambridge UP, 1988. 30–44.

Thirsk, Joan. *Tudor Enclosures.* London: Routledge and Paul, 1959.

Thompson, Sophie. "Rosalind (and Celia) in *As You Like It*." *Players of Shakespeare.* Ed. Russell Jackson and Robert Smallwood. New York: Cambridge UP, 1988. 77–86.

Tiffany, Grace. "'that Reason Wonder may Diminish': *As You Like It*, Androgyny, and the Theater Wars." *Huntington Library Quarterly: A Journal for the History and Interpretation of English and American Civilization* 57.3 (1994): 213–39.

Totaro, Rebecca C. "Shakespeare's Fortunate Travellers: *As You Like it* and Nashe's *Unfortunate Traveller*." *Q/W/E/R/T/Y: Arts, Littératures & Civilisations du Monde Anglophone* 7 (1997): 27–31.

Traub, Valerie. *Renaissance Lesbianism in Early Modern England.* Cambridge: Cambridge UP, 2002.

Tvordi, Jessica. "Female Alliance and the Construction of Homoeroticism in *As You Like It*." *Maids and Mistresses, Cousins and Queens: Women's Alliances in Early Modern England.* Ed. Susan Frye and Karen Robertson. New York: Oxford UP, 1999. 114–30.

Uhlig, Claus. "'the Sobbing Deer': *As You Like It*, II.i.21–66, and the Historical Context." *Renaissance Drama* n.s. 3 (1970): 79–109.

Vickers, Nancy J. "Diana Described: Scattered Woman and Scattered Rhyme." *Critical Inquiry* 58.3 (1976): 374–94.

Waddington, Raymond B. "Moralizing the Spectacle: Dramatic Emblems in *As You Like It*." *Shakespeare Quarterly* 33.2 (1982): 155–63.

Walen, Denise. *Constructions of Female Homoeroticism in Early Modern Drama.* Basingstoke: Palgrave Macmillan, 2005.

Watson, Donald Gwynn. "Erasmus' *Praise of Folly* and the Spirit of Carnival." *Renaissance Quarterly* 32.3 (1979): 333–53.

Welsford, Enid. *The Fool: His Social & Literary History.* London: Faber & Faber, 1935.

Whigham, Frank. *Ambition and Privilege: The Social Tropes of Elizabethan Courtesy Theory.* Berkeley: U of California P, 1984.

Wiles, David. *Shakespeare's Clown: Actor and Text in the Elizabethan Playhouse.* Cambridge: Cambridge UP, 1987.

Whitworth, Charles. "Wooing and Winning in Arden: Rosalynde and *As You Like It.*" *Etudes Anglaises* 50 (1997): 387–99.

Williamson, Marilyn L., and Richard L. Nochimson, eds. *As You Like it, Much Ado about Nothing, and Twelfth Night, Or what You Will: An Anotated Bibliography of Shakespeare Studies, 1673–2001.* Fairview: Pegasus, 2003.

Willis, Paul J. "'Tongues in Trees': The Book of Nature in *As You Like It.*" *Modern Language Studies* 18.3 (1988): 65–74.

Wilson, Rawdon. "The Way to Arden: Attitudes Toward Time in *As You Like It.*" *Shakespeare Quarterly* 26.1 (1975): 16–24.

Wilson, Richard. "'Like the Old Robin Hood': *As You Like It* and the Enclosure Riots." *Will Power: Essays on Shakespearean Authority.* Detroit: Wayne State UP, 1993. 63–82.

Wolk, Anthony. "The Extra Jaques in *As You Like It.*" *Shakespeare Quarterly* 23.1 (1972): 101–05.

Woodbridge, Linda. "Country Matters: *As You Like It* and the Pastoral-Bashing Impulse." *Re-Visions of Shakespeare: Essays in Honor of Robert Ornstein.* Ed. Evelyn Gajowski. Newark: U of Delaware P, 2004. 189–214.

Wyatt, Michael. *The Italian Encounter with Tudor England: A Cultural Politics of Translation* Cambridge: Cambridge UP, 2005.

Zimmerman, Susan, ed., *Erotic Politics: Desire on the Renaissance Stage.* New York: Routledge, 1992.

Acknowledgments (continued from p. iv)

Figure 1. "Hymenaeus and Cupido," by Wenceslas Hollar (b. 1607–d. 1677). Courtesy of the Thomas Fisher Rare Book Library, University of Toronto. *As You Like It* from *The Complete Works of Shakespeare*, Sixth Edition, © 2009. Ed. David Bevington. Reprinted by permission of Pearson Education, Inc. Upper Saddle River, New Jersey.

CHAPTER 1
Figure 2. Map of Warwickshire, from *Poly-Olbion*, by Michael Drayton (1612). This item is reproduced by permission of The Huntington Library, San Marino, California.
Figure 3. "June," from *A booke of diverse and sorts of pictures with the alphabets of letters . . .*, a manuscript book by Thomas Fella (c. 1585–1622). By permission of the Folger Shakespeare Library, Washington, DC.
Figure 4. "Januarye" from *The Shepheardes Calender* by Edmund Spenser (1579). This item is reproduced by permission of The Huntington Library, San Marino, California.
Figure 5. Cotswold Games, from Michael Drayton, *Annalia Dubrensia* (1636). This item is reproduced by permission of The Huntington Library, San Marino, California.
Figure 6. Fencers from *Vincent Saviolo His Practice* by Vincent Saviolo (1595). This item is reproduced by permission of The Huntington Library, San Marino, California.
Figure 7. "Robin Hood and Allin of Dale," broadside ballad (early seventeenth century). By permission of the University of Glasgow Library, Special Collections.
Figure 8. From *The Noble Art of Venery or Hunting*, by George Gascoigne (1575). This item is reproduced by permission of The Huntington Library, San Marino, California.

CHAPTER 2
Figure 9. "The Sonneteers' Beloved," from Charles Sorel, *The Extravagant Shepherd* (1652), call number FC6.So683.Eg653da. By permission of Houghton Library, Harvard College Library.
Figure 10. *Jove and Ganymede*, Antonio da Correggio (c. 1531). By permission of Kunsthistorisches Museum, Vienna.
Figure 11. *Matrimonium*, emblem from Henry Peacham, *Minerva Britanna* (1612). This item is reproduced by permission of The Huntington Library, San Marino, California.
Figure 12. Frontispiece woodcut, from Samuel Rowlands, *The Bride* (1617). This item is reproduced by permission of The Huntington Library, San Marino, California.
Figure 13 "A Merry New Jig; or, the Pleasant Wooing betweixt Kit and Peg" broadside ballad by Valentine Hamdultan (seventeenth century). © The British Library Board.
Figure 14. *Angelica and Medoro*, c. 1570, by Giorgio Ghisi (Italian, 1520/24–1582) after Teodoro Ghisi (Italian, died 1601), engraving, printed in black, on paper, 299 × 209 mm (plate), Gift of Bernard F. Rogers, Sr. Collection, 1935.119, The Art Institute of Chicago, Photography © The Art Institute of Chicago.
Figure 15. "Crimes Most Grave," from Henry Peacham, *Minerva Britanna* (1612). This item is reproduced by permission of The Huntington Library, San Marino, California.

CHAPTER 3

Figure 16. From Robert Armin, *The History of the Two Maids of More-clacke with the Life and Simple Manner of John in the Hospitall* (1609). This item is reproduced by permission of The Huntington Library, San Marino, California.

Figure 17. From Sebastian Brant, *The Shyppe of Fooles* (1517), translated by Henry Watson. © The British Library Board.

Figure 18. *De dans om de wereld* (*The Dance Around the World*), after Pieter Baltens (c. 1600). By permission of Rijksmuseum Amsterdam.

Figure 19. "Fooles, or foolishnesse," from *Thomas Trevelyon's Miscellany*, an illustrated manuscript book (1608). By permission of the Folger Shakespeare Library, Washington, DC.

Figure 20. Marginal drawing by Hans Holbein in Desiderius Erasmus, *Moriae encomium* (1515). Kunstmuseum Basel, Kupferstichkabinett. Photo: Kunstmuseum Basel, Martin P. Bühler.

Figure 21. *Peasant Couple Dancing* (1514), by Albrecht Dürer (German, 1471–1528), engraving on white laid paper, 118 x 75 mm (image/sheet), Bequest of Mrs. Potter Palmer, Jr., 1956.949, The Art Institute of Chicago Photography © The Art Institute of Chicago.

Figure 22. Frontispiece from Robert Burton, *The Anatomy of Melancholy* (1638). This item is reproduced by permission of The Huntington Library, San Marino, California.

Figure 23. Title page from I. D., *A Scourge for Paper-Persecutors, Or Papers Complaint, Compil'd in Ruthfull Rimes, against the Paper-Spoylers of These Times* (1625). © The British Library Board.

CHAPTER 4

On Copia of Words and Ideas. Desiderius Erasmus of Rotterdam. Donald B. King and H. David Rix, Translators. ISBN 0-87462-212-3/978-0-87462-212-6. (Mediaeval Philosophical Texts in Translation No. 12) Copyright © 1963 by Marquette University Press, Milwaukee, Wisconsin, USA. Used by permission of the publisher. All rights reserved. www.marquette.edu/mupress/

Figure 24. Brothers fighting from *Stultifera Navis . . . The Ship of Fools*, trans. Alexander Barclay (1570). © The British Library Board.

Figure 25. Frontispiece from Richard Brathwaite, *The English Gentleman, and English Gentlewoman* (1641). Reproduced by kind permission of the Syndics of Cambridge University Library.

Figure 26. From Nicholas Breton, *The Court and Country, or A Briefe Discourse Dialogue-wise Set Down between a Courtier and a Country-man Containing the Manner and Condition of Their Lives* (1618). By permission of the Folger Shakespeare Library, Washington, DC.

Figure 27. From "A Birching." By permission of the Hulton Archive/Getty Images.

Figure 28. From *As in a Map Here Man May Well Perceiue, How Tyme Creeps on til Death His Life Bereaue* (late seventeenth century). By permission of the Folger Shakespeare Library, Washington, DC.

Figure 29. Emblem from Henry Peacham, *Minerva Britanna* (1612). This item is reproduced by permission of The Huntington Library, San Marino, California.

Figure 30. Diagram from John Harington, *An Anatomie of the Metamorpho-sed Ajax* (1596). This item is reproduced by permission of The Huntington Library, San Marino, California.

Index

434 | INDEX

conversation, in *As You Like It*, 398–401, 408–09

Cooke, Sir Anthony, 384

Copia of Words and Ideas, On, excerpt (Erasmus)
  background to, 408–09
  text of, 409–11

Copley, Anthony
  Wits, Fits and Fancies, excerpt, 413

Corin (character, *As You Like It*), 3, 147–48, 150–51, 275–76, 366, 371, 406

Cornwallis, Sir William, 396
  Essays, excerpt, 396–98

Correggio, Antonio da
  "Jove and Ganymede," 209 (fig.)

costumes. *See also* cross-dressing; fools
  "liveried fool," motley and long coats, 275, 277 (fig.), 282 (fig.), 299 (fig.)

Countess of Mountgomeries Urania, The, excerpt (Wroth)
  background to, 253
  text of, 253–55

Court and Country, The, excerpt (Breton)
  background to, 371
  text of, 373–75
  title page, 372 (fig.)

Court Lady, 358–62

courtesy books. *See* conduct literature

courtiership. *See also* civility; education; manners
  and *As You Like It*, 6
  cortigianeria, 352
  early training and service, 349–50
  grazia ("grace"), 356
  ideal Court Lady, 358–62
  noble birth versus merit, 353–55
  sprezzatura ("nonchalance"), 357
  urbanity and, 365–66, 371–75

courtship. *See also* love; marriage
  and comedy, 411–13
  couples, diverse, in *As You Like It*, 3, 203
  Phoebe and Rosalind/Ganymede, 210
  prescribed behavior of women in, 361–62
  Rosalind/Ganymede and Orlando, 203, 206, 208, 210
  same-sex desire, 126, 206–215, 272–73
  Silvius and Phoebe, 206

Touchstone and Audrey, 3, 7, 203, 366, 411
  vicissitudes of, 204–05, 366
  women's jests mocking suitors, 411–414

Courtyer, The, excerpts (Castiglione). *See also* courtiership
  backgrounds to, 352–53, 355–56, 358
  texts of, 354–55, 356–57, 359–60, 370–71

Courtyer, The (A Noble Lady Shames an Uncivil Man), excerpt (Castiglione),
  background to, 369–70
  text of, 370–71

Cromwell, Oliver, 221

cross-dressing. *See also* boy actor; homoeroticism
  central to plot of *As You Like It*, 211
  as disguise during rebellions, 305
  during festivals, 307–08
  Gallatea (Lyly), 6, 268–72
  Maid Marian, 186–87
  Nest of Ninnies (Armin), 293
  Puritan attitudes toward, 4, 266–68
  in relation to Epilogue, 211
  on the Renaissance stage, 263
  in Shakespeare's plays, 268
  by women students of Plato, 389

cuckoldry
  Boccaccian novella and, 339–43
  Horn Fair, 336
  horning jokes, 335–43
  libel lawsuit *Hole v. White* and, 336–39
  stag, horned, as symbol of, 127, 188
  women's witty excuses for adultery, 340–43

Cupid's Messenger, excerpt, 323–24
  background to, 323–24
  text of, 324

Cynthia, excerpt (Barnfield)
  background to, 256
  text of, 262–63

da Canossa, Count Ludovico, 353
da Montefeltro, Duke Guidobaldo, 352
dancing
  morris, 176
  part of education of young men, 347, 350
  "Peasant couple dancing" (Dürer), 303 (fig.)
  Puritan attitudes toward, 266